6net

IPv6

AF884983

Deployment Guide

Javvin Technologies Inc. Distribution

6net

An IPv6 Deployment Guide

Editor: Martin Dunmore

Javvin Technologies Inc. Distribution

http://www.javvin.com
http://www.networkdictionary.com

Table of Contents

List of Figures

List of Tables

PART I

IPv6 Fundamentals

Chapter 1

Introduction

Internet Protocol version 6 (IPv6) is the new generation of the basic protocol of the Internet. IP is the common language of the Internet, every device connected to the Internet must support it. The current version of IP (IP version 4) has several shortcomings which complicate, and in some cases present a barrier to, the further development of the Internet. The coming IPv6 revolution should remove these barriers and provide a feature-rich environment for the future of global networking.

1.1 The History of IPv6

The IPv6 story began in the early nineties when it was discovered that the address space available in IPv4 was vanishing quite rapidly. Contemporary studies indicated that it may be depleted within the next ten years – around 2005! These findings challenged the Internet community to start looking for a solution. Two possible approaches were at hand:

1. Minimal: Keep the protocol intact, just increase the address length. This was the easier way promising less pain in the deployment phase.
2. Maximal: Develop an entirely new version of the protocol. Taking this approach would enable incorporating new features and enhancements in IP.

Because there was no urgent need for a quick solution, the development of a new protocol was chosen. Its original name IP Next Generation (IPng) was soon replaced by IP version 6 which is now the definitive name. The main architects of this new protocol were Steven Deering and Robert Hinden.

The first set of RFCs specifying the IPv6 were released at the end of 1995, namely, RFC 1883: Internet Protocol, Version 6 (IPv6) Specification [RFC1883] and its relatives. Once the definition was available, implementations were eagerly awaited. But they did not come.

The second half of the nineties was a period of significant Internet boom. Companies on the market had to solve a tricky business problem: while an investment in IPv6 can bring some benefits in the future, an investment in the blossoming IPv4 Internet earns money now. For a vast majority of them it was essentially a no-brainer: they decided to prefer the rapid and easy return of investments and developed IPv4-based products.

Another factor complicating IPv6 deployment was the change of rules in the IPv4 domain. Methods to conserve the address space were developed and put into operation. The most important of these was Classless Inter-Domain Routing (CIDR). The old address classes were removed and address assignment rules hardened. As a consequence, newly connected sites obtained significantly less addresses than in previous years.

The use of CIDR may well have delayed the need for IPv6 in the eyes of many people, but not in all. Somewhat perversely, the use of CIDR accelerated the perception of a lack of address space in the eyes of those who were relatively new to the Internet. Since the Internet was booming, requests for new address blocks were increasing, yet the size of assigned address blocks were being reduced. Thus, new or expanding sites had to develop methods to spare this scarce resource. One of these approaches is network address translation (NAT) which allows a network to use an arbitrary number of non-public addresses, which are translated to public ones when the packets leave the site (and vice versa). Thus, NATs provided a mechanism for hosts to share public addresses. Furthermore, mechanisms such as PPP and DHCP provide a means for hosts to lease addresses for some period of time.

The widespread deployment of NAT solutions weakened the main IPv6 driving force. While IPv6 still has additional features to IPv4 (like security and mobility support), these were not strong enough to attract a significant amount of companies to develop IPv6 implementations and applications. Consequently, the deployment of IPv6 essentially stalled during this period.

Fortunately, the development of the protocol continued. Several experimental implementations were created and some practical experience gained through to operation of the 6bone network. This led to the revisited set of specifications published in the end of 1998 (RFC 2460 and others).

An important player in the IPv6 field has always been the academic networks, being generally keen on new technologies and not that much interested in immediate profit. Many of them deployed the new protocol and provided it to their users for experimentation. This brought a lot of experience and also manpower for further development.

Probably the most important period for IPv6 so far has been the first years of the 21st century, when IPv6 finally gained some momentum. The increasing number of implementations forced remaining hardware/software vendors to react and to enhance their products with IPv6 capabilities.

The new protocol also appeared in a number of real-world production networks. Network providers in Asia seemed to be especially interested in IPv6 deployment. The reason for this is clear – the Internet revolution started later in these countries, so they obtained less IPv4 addresses and the lack of address space is thus considerably more painful here. In short, the rapid growth of Internet connectivity in Asia cannot be served by the relatively miniscule IPv4 address space assigned to the region. This even led to some governments declaring their official support for IPv6.

The deployment of IPv6 in Europe has been boosted by the Framework Programmes of European Commission. Funding was granted for projects like 6NET and Euro6IX that focused on gaining practical experience with the protocol. Also, the largest European networking project - the academic backbone GÉANT – would include IPv6 support once sufficient confidence and experience had been gained from the 6NET project.

The main focus of the GÉANT project was to interconnect national research and education networks in European countries. As these networks were interested in IPv6, its support in the backbone was one of the natural consequences. After a period of experiments, IPv6 has been officially provided by GÉANT since January 2004.

Euro6IX focused on building a pan-European non-commercial IPv6 exchange network. It interconnected seven regional neutral exchange points and provided support for some transition mechanisms. Other objectives were to research and test IPv6-based applications over the infrastructure and disseminate the experience.

Between 2000 and 2004, the vast majority of operating system and router vendors implemented IPv6. These days it is hard to find a platform without at least some IPv6 support. Although the implementations are not perfect yet (advanced features like security or mobility are missing in many of them), they provide a solid ground for basic usage. Moreover, in most cases one can see dramatic improvements from one release to the next.

All in all, after some years of hesitation IPv6 finally leaves the status of a high-tech extravagance and starts to be a usable tool.

1.2 The 6NET Project

6NET was a three-year European IST project to demonstrate that continued growth of the Internet can be met using new IPv6 technology. The project built and operated a pan-European native IPv6 network connecting sixteen countries in order to gain experience of IPv6 deployment and the migration from existing IPv4-based networks. The network was used to extensively test a variety of new IPv6 services and applications, as well as interoperability with legacy applications. This allowed practical operational experience to be gained, and provided the possibility to test migration strategies, which are important considering that IPv4 and IPv6 technologies will need to coexist for several years.

6NET involved thirty-five partners from the commercial, research and academic sectors and represented a total investment of €18 million; €7 million of which came from the project partners themselves, and €11 million from the Information Society Technologies Programme of the European Commission. The project commenced on 1st January 2002 and was due to finish on 31 December 2004. However, the success of the project meant that it was granted a further 6 months, primarily for dissemination of the project's findings and recommendations. The network itself was decommissioned in January 2005, handing over the reigns of pan-European native IPv6 connectivity to GÉANT.

The principal objectives of the project were:

- Install and operate an international pilot IPv6 network with both static and mobile components in order to gain a better understanding of IPv6 deployment issues.
- Test the migration strategies for integrating IPv6 networks with existing IPv4 infrastructure.
- Introduce and test new IPv6 services and applications, as well as legacy services and applications on IPv6 infrastructure.
- Evaluate address allocation, routing and DNS operation for IPv6 networks.
- Collaborate with other IPv6 activities and standardisation bodies.
- Promote IPv6 technology.

The project had important collaborations with other IPv6 activities such as the Euro6IX project and the IPv6 Cluster, and contributed to standardisation bodies such as the IETF (Internet Engineering Task Force) and GGF (Global Grid Forum). 6NET also played an important role in promoting IPv6 technology at both the national and international level.

6NET has demonstrated that IPv6 is deployable in a production environment. Not only does it solve the shortage of addresses, but it also promises a number of enhanced features which are not an integral part of IPv4. The success of the testbed spurred the existing GÉANT and NORDUnet networks to move to dual-stack operation earlier than anticipated, and in turn, encouraged many NRENs (National Research and Education Networks) to offer production IPv6 services as well. Having served its purpose, and with 6NET partners now having native IPv6 access via GÉANT, the 6NET testbed was decommissioned in January 2004. During its lifetime, the 6NET network was used to provide IPv6 connectivity to a number of worldwide events, including IST 2002 (November 2002), IETF 57 (July 2003), IST 2003 (November 2003) and the Global IPv6 Service Launch (January 2004), showing that it is ready for full deployment.

The experience gained during the project has been turned into a number of 'cookbooks' (project deliverables) aimed at network administrators, IT managers, network researchers and anyone else interested in deploying IPv6. All project documentation: deliverables, papers, presentations, newsletters etc., are freely available on the 6NET website:

http://www.6net.org/

The information contained in this book is taken from the project's deployment cookbooks and other deliverables. Since each cookbook/deliverable generally concentrates only on specific IPv6 features or deployment scenarios (e.g. site transition, multicast, mobility, DHCP, routing etc.), we believe that providing all the important information in a single reference book is much more preferable to the reader than negotiating our multitude of project deliverables.

We hope you find this reference book informative and that it helps smooth your IPv6 deployment process. Please bear in mind that this book is a 'snapshot in time' and by the very nature of IPv6 protocols and their implementations it is easy for the information in these chapter to become out of date. Nevertheless, through the 6DISS project many ex-6NET partners will endeavour to keep the information up to date and you can freely download the latest electronic version from the 6NET website:

http://www.6net.org/book/

The 6NET project was co-ordinated by Cisco Systems and comprised:

ACOnet (Austria)
CESNET (Czech Republic)
DANTE
DFN (Germany)
ETRI (South Korea)
FCCN (Portugal)
GRNET (Greece)
HUNGARNET (Hungary)
IBM
GARR (Italy)
Lancaster University (UK)
NORDUnet
NTT (Japan)
PSNC (Poland)
RENATER (France)
SURFnet (Netherlands)
SWITCH (Switzerland)
Telematica Instituut (Netherlands)
TERENA
UKERNA (UK)
ULB (Belgium)
UCL (UK)
University of Southampton (UK)
CSC (Finland)
CTI (Greece)
DTU (Denmark)
Fraunhofer FOKUS (Germany)
INRIA (France)
Invenia (Norway)
Oulu Polytechnic (Finland)
ULP (France)
Uninett (Norway)
University of Oulu (Finland)
WWU-JOIN (Germany).

Chapter 2

IPv6 Basics

Inside this chapter we cover the protocol basics: the datagram format, the headers and related mechanisms. You will see that these aspects have been simplified significantly in comparison to IPv4 to achieve higher performance of datagram forwarding.

2.1 Datagram Header

The core of the protocol is naturally the datagram format defined in RFC 2460 [RFC2460]. The datagram design focused mainly on simplicity - to keep the datagram as simple as possible and to keep the size of the headers fixed. The main reason for this decision was to maximise processing performance - simple constant size headers can be processed quickly, at or very close to wire-speed.

The IPv4 header format contains a lot of fields including some unpredictable optional ones leading to fluctuating header sizes. IPv6 shows a different approach: the basic header is minimised and a constant size. Only essential fields (like addresses or datagram length) are contained. Everything else has been shifted aside into so called extension headers, which are attached on demand - for example a mobile node adds mobility related extension headers to its outgoing traffic.

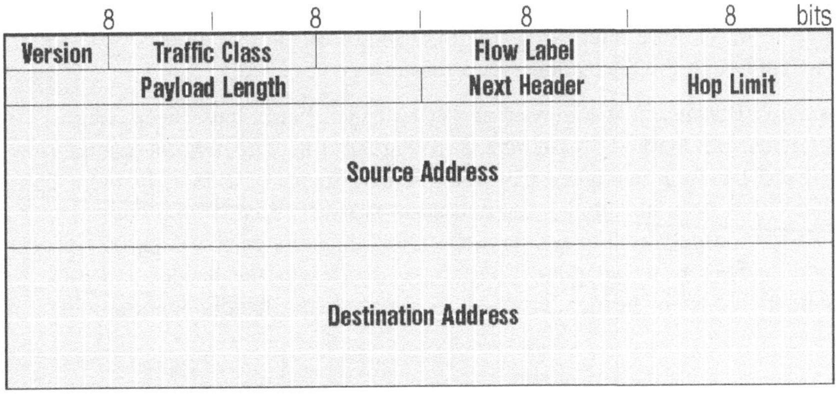

Figure 2-1 Basic IPv6 Datagram Header

The basic datagram header format is showed in Figure 2-1. The contents of individual fields are following:

Version

Protocol version identification. It contains value 6 to identify IPv6.

Traffic Class

Intended for the Quality of Service (QoS). It may distinguish various classes or priorities of traffic (in combination with other header fields, e.g. source/destination addresses).

Flow Label

Identifies a flow which is a "group of related datagrams".

Payload Length

Length of the datagram payload, i.e. all the contents following the basic header (including extension headers). It is in Bytes, so the maximum possible payload size is 64 KB.

Next Header

The protocol header which follows. It identifies the type of following data - it may be some extension header or upper layer protocol (TCP, UDP) data.

Hop Limit

Datagram lifetime restriction. The sending node assigns some value to this field defining the reach of given datagram. Every forwarding node decreases the value by 1. If decremented to zero, the datagram is dropped and an ICMP message is sent to the sender. It protects the IPv6 transport system against routing loops - in the case of such loop the datagram circulates around the loop for a limited time only.

Source Address

Sender identification. It contains the IPv6 address of the node who sent this datagram. Addressing is described in more detail in the next chapter.

Destination Address

Receiver identification. This is the target - the datagram should be delivered to this IPv6 address.

Before we dive deeper into some header specialties let us compare the IPv4 and IPv6 headers (see Figure 2-2). The result is quite interesting: the total length of the datagram header doubled (from 20 bytes to 40 bytes) although the IPv6 addresses are four times as long.

How is it possible? Because just a subset of IPv4 header fields have been adopted by IPv6 - the corresponding fields are marked by numbers in Figure 2-2. The whole second line of the IPv4 datagram, designed for fragmentation, has been moved to an extension header. The CRC (cyclic redundancy check) has been abandoned for two good reasons: First, frame consistency is checked in lower layers, so it is largely redundant. Second, CRC decelerates the datagram processing - every forwarding node decreases the datagram lifetime, so it changes the header and must recalculate the CRC. Thanks to the constant header length the corresponding header length field is not necessary anymore.

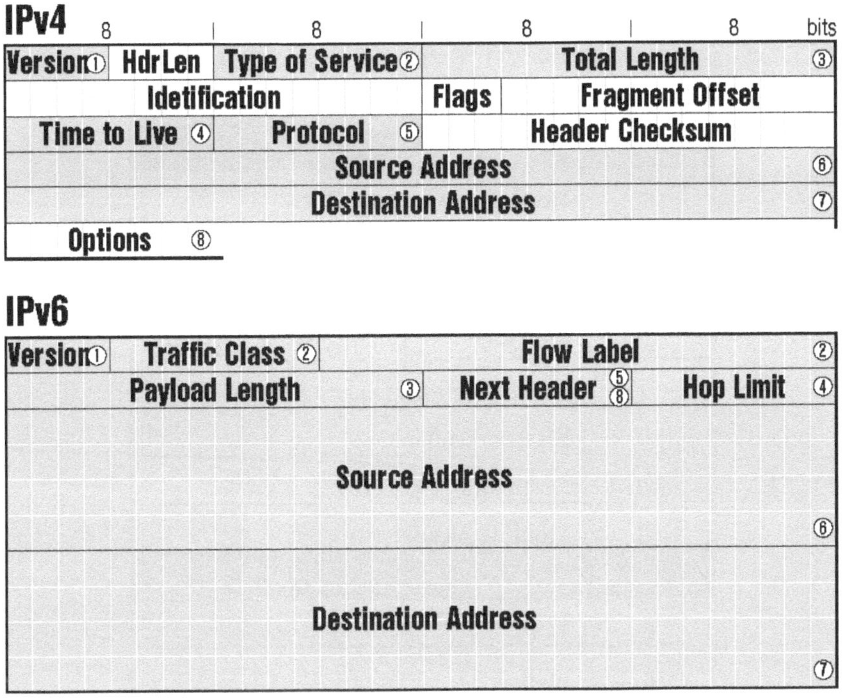

Figure 2-2 IPv4 and IPv6 Header Comparison

2.2 *Header Chaining*

Instead of placing optional fields to the end of datagram header IPv6 designers chose a different approach - extension headers. They are added only if needed, i.e. if it is necessary to fragment the datagram the fragmentation header is put into it.

Extension headers are appended after the basic datagram header. Their number may vary, so some flexible mechanism to identify them is necessary. This mechanism is called header chaining. It is implemented using the Next Header field. The meaning of this field in short is to identify "what follows".

Actually, the Next Header field has two duties: it determines the following extension header or identifies the upper-layer protocol to which the datagram content should be passed. Because many datagrams are plain - they do not need any extension header at all. In this case the Next Header simulates the Protocol field form IPv4 and contains value identifying the protocol (e.g., TCP or UDP) which ordered the data transport.

If there is an extension header present then the Next Header field determines its type. Every extension header also contains its own Next Header field identifying the following data. Any number of extension headers may be chained in this way - each header simply announces who will be the next header, the last header identifies the upper-layer protocol to which the datagram content belongs.

Table 2-1 Extension Headers

Value (decimal)	*Extension Header*
0	Hop-by-hop option
43	Routing
44	Fragment
50	Encapsulating Security Payload (ESP)
51	Authentication Header (AH)
59	No next header
60	Destination Option
62	Mobility Header
	Protocols
6	TCP
8	EGP
9	IGP
17	UDP
46	RSVP
47	GRE
58	ICMP

There is one complication hidden in the header chaining mechanism: the processing of complete headers may require a walk through quite a long chain of extension headers which hinders the processing performance. To minimise this, IPv6 specifies a particular order of extension headers. Generally speaking, headers important for all forwarding nodes must be placed first, headers important just for the addressee are located on the end of the chain. The advantage of this sequence is that the processing node may stop header investigation early - as soon as it sees some extension header dedicated to the destination it can be sure that no more important headers follow. This improves the processing performance significantly, because in many cases the investigation of fixed basic header will be sufficient to forward the datagram.

Figure 2-3 illustrates some examples of header chaining. The first datagram is plain IPv6 and TCP, the second one contains a single extension header (Routing) and the chain in third datagram includes two extension headers (Routing and Fragment).

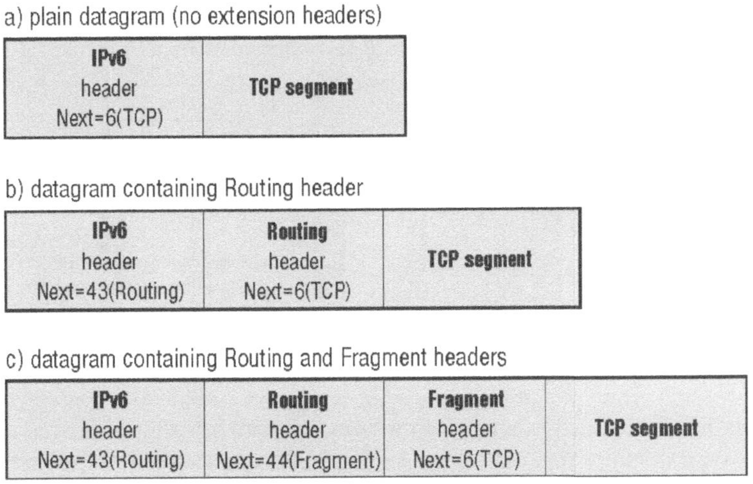

Figure 2-3 Header Chaining Examples

In the rest of this chapter we cover the most important general extension headers - options, routing and fragment. Headers related to particular mechanisms (e.g., mobility header) will be explained in their corresponding chapter.

2.3 Routing Header

The Routing header influences the route of the datagram. It allows you to define some sequence of "checkpoints" (IPv6 addresses) which the datagram must pass through.

Two types of Routing header (identified by a field inside the extension header) have been defined: Type 0 is a general version allowing an arbitrary checkpoint sequence and type 2 is a simplified version used for mobility purposes. The definition is extensible, so more types can be added later.

Let's describe the general one first. In this case the Routing header contains two pieces of information:

1. sequence of checkpoint addresses
2. counter (named Segments Left) identifying how many of them remain to pass through

The datagram sender wanting to use this feature adds the Routing header to the datagram. It places the address of first checkpoint into the Destination address field inside the basic header. It also adds the Routing header containing the sequence of remaining checkpoints. The final datagram destination (its real target) is the last member of this sequence. Segments Left contains the number of elements in the sequence. Than the datagram is sent as usual.

When delivered to the Destination Address (actually the first checkpoint) the router finds the Routing header and realises that it is just an intermediate station. So it swaps the address in the Destination Address and the Nth address from behind of the Routing header sequence (where N is the current value of Segments Left). Segments Left is than decreased by 1 and datagram is sent to the new destination (which is the next checkpoint).

This procedure is executed on every checkpoint. As you can see the Segments Left header actually separates the addresses already passed and addresses to be visited in the checkpoint sequence. When the addressee sees that Segments Left contains zero, it knows that this is the final datagram destination and the datagram will be processed and passed to the upper layer protocol. The whole mechanism is illustrated in Figure 2-4.

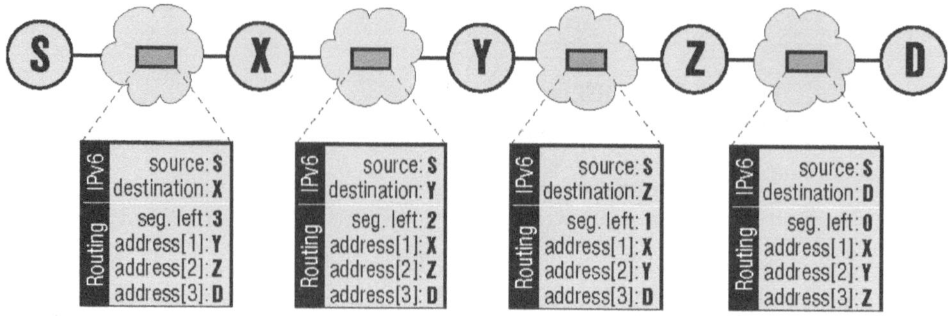

Figure 2-4 Changes in the Routing Header During Datagram Transport

The type 2 Routing header defined as a part of mobility support is a simplified version of the general type described above. It contains just one address instead of sequence of checkpoints. The general idea is following: some mobile node having a permanent address (so called home address) is travelling at present. It is connected to some strange network and obtained a temporary (care-of) address. The goal is to deliver datagrams to the care-of address, but to hide its existence from the upper layers.

So when a datagram is sent to the mobile node, the care-of address is used as the destination in basic IPv6 header. However, a routing header Type 2 is attached containing the home (permanent) address of the mobile node. When the datagram arrives at the target, the addresses are swapped and the home address is presented as the destination to upper layers.

2.4 Fragmentation

Every lower-layer technology used to transport IPv6 datagrams has some limitation regarding the packet size. It is called MTU (Maximum Transmission Unit). If the IPv6 datagram is longer than the MTU, its data must be divided up and inserted into set of smaller IPv6 datagrams, called fragments. These fragments are than transported individually and assembled by the receiver to create the original datagram. This is fragmentation.

Every fragment is an IPv6 datagram carrying part of the original data. It is equipped by a Fragment extension header containing three important data fields:

- *Identification* is unique for every original datagram. It is used to detect fragments of the same datagram (they are holding identical identification values).
- *Offset* is the position of data carried by current fragment in the original datagram.
- *More fragments* flag announces if this fragment is the last one or if another fragment follows.

The receiving node collects the fragments and uses Identification values to group the corresponding fragments. Thanks to the Offsets it is able to put them in the correct order. When it sees that the data part is complete and there are no more fragments left (it receives the fragment identifying that no more fragments follow), it is able to reconstruct the original datagram.

The main benefit of fragmentation is that it allows the transportation of datagrams which are larger than the what the lower-layer technology can transport. The main drawback is the performance penalty. The datagram assembly at the receiver's side is a complicated procedure requiring some buffers to collect the fragments, some timers (to limit the reassembly time and free buffers from obsolete fragments) and so on. It lowers the reliability of the datagram connection because if one single fragment is lost, whole original datagram is doomed.

Because of this, fragmentation is often seen as an undesirable entity. By contrast to IPv4 (which is quite willing to fragment) IPv6 tries to minimise it by means of some restrictions and requirements:

- Minimum allowed MTU on IPv6 supporting links is 1280 Bytes (1500 Bytes is recommended). It decreases the need for fragmentation.
- Only the sender is allowed to fragment a datagram. If some intermediate node needs to forward it through a line with insufficient MTU, it must drop the datagram and send an ICMP message to the sender announcing the datagram drop and the MTU which inflicted it.
- Every node has to watch the path MTU for all its addressees to keep the communication as efficient as possible.

Path MTU is the minimal MTU along the route between the sender and destination of the datagram. This is the largest datagram size deliverable along the given route. Datagrams of this size should be sent if possible, because they are the most efficient (lowest overhead/data ratio).

Path MTU is based on ICMP messages announcing datagram drops due to the insufficient MTU size. The algorithm to calculate it is simple: the MTU of outgoing link is used as the first estimation. The sender tries to send a datagram of this size and if it obtains an ICMP message reporting smaller MTU, is decreases the value and tries again until the destination address is reached.

From a theoretical point of view the path MTU is flawed because the routing is dynamic, so the paths are changing and every next datagram can be delivered through a different route. In practice however, the routing changes are not so frequent. If the path MTU drops due to a routing change, the sender is informed immediately by obtaining ICMP error message and so it lowers the path MTU value.

2.5 Options

Headers containing options may provide some additional information related to the datagram or its processing. They are separated into two groups: options dedicated to every node forwarding the datagram (hop-by-hop options), and options intended for the destination host only (destination options). Table 2-2, "Hop-by-hop options" and Table 2-3, "Destination options" contain the list of defined options.

Hop-by-hop options (if present) are placed at the start of extension headers chain, because they are important for every node forwarding the datagram. The location of destination options is a bit more complicated. Actually there are two kinds of destination options: options dedicated to the final target (they are located on the end of extension headers chain) and options assigned to the next host specified by Routing header (located just before the Routing header).

Table 2-2 Hop-by-hop Options

Value	*Meaning*
0	Pad1
1	PadN
5	Router alert
194	Jumbo payload

Table 2-3 Destination Options

Value	*Meaning*
0	Pad1
1	PadN
201	Home Address

The meaning of the individual options is as follows:

Pad1, PadN

Padding. They do not carry any content, they just align the following content to the appropriate position.

Router alert

Advice to the router on content which may be important. For example RSVP sends control messages dedicated to all routers along the path, so they are equipped with a Router alert option announcing that an RSVP message is carried by the datagram.

Jumbo payload

Allows the transportation of datagrams which exceed the 64 KB maximum. The hop-by-hop option asks for special handling which is necessary to process these jumbograms.

Home Address

It is a part of the mobility support. It contains the home (stable) address of the travelling mobile node.

Chapter 3

Addressing

Rapid depletion of the available IPv4 address space was the main initiator of IPv6. In consequence, the demand to never again have to develop a new protocol due to the lack of addresses was one of the principal requirements to the new address space design. Let's look how it was fulfilled.

The basic rules of IPv6 addressing are laid down by RFC 3513 [RFC3513]. Some accompanying RFCs define the specialties and rules for specific address types.

3.1 Addressing Essentials

The address length has been increased significantly to expand the available address space. The IPv6 address is 128 bits (or 16 bytes) long, which is four times as long as its predecessor. Because every single bit of added address length doubles the number of addresses available, the size of the IPv6 address space is really huge. It contains 2^{128} which is about 340 billion billion billion billion different addresses which definitely should suffice for a very long time.

Addresses are written using 32 hexadecimal digits. The digits are arranged into 8 groups of four to improve the readability. Groups are separated by colons. So the written form of IPv6 address looks like this:

2001:0718:1c01:0016:020d:56ff:fe77:52a3

As you can imagine DNS plays an important role in the IPv6 world, because the manual typing of IPv6 addresses is not an easy thing. Some abbreviations are allowed to lighten this task at least a little. Namely: leading zeroes in every group can be omitted. So the example address can be shortened to

2001:718:1c01:16:20d:56ff:fe77:52a3

Secondly, a sequence of all-zero groups can be replaced by pair of colons. Only one such abbreviation may occur in any address, otherwise the address would be ambiguous. This is especially handy for special-purpose addresses or address prefixes containing long sequences of zeroes. For example the loopback address

0:0:0:0:0:0:0:1

may be written as

::1

which is not only much shorter but also more evident. Address prefixes are usually written in the form:

prefix::/length

Where prefix defines the value of bits in the address beginning and length contains the number of important bits from the start. Because the rest of the prefix is not important, zeroes are used in this part of the address, and the "::" abbreviation is deployed. So for example prefix dedicated to the 6to4 transition mechanism is

2002::/16

which means that the starting 16 bits (two bytes, corresponding to one group in the written address) have to contain value 2002 (hexadecimal), the rest is unimportant.

Not all addresses are handled equally. IPv6 supports three different address types for which the delivery process varies:

Unicast (individual) address

identifies one single network interface (typically a computer or similar device). The packet is delivered to this individual interface.

Multicast (group) address

identifies group of interfaces. Data must be delivered to all group members.

Anycast (selective) address

also identifies a group of network interfaces. But this time the packet is delivered just to one single member of the group (to the nearest one).

Broadcast as an address category is missing in IPv6, because broadcast is just a special kind of multicast. Instead of including a separate address category, IPv6 defines some standard multicast addresses corresponding to the commonly used IPv4 broadcast addresses. For example ff02::1 is the multicast address for all nodes connected to given link.

Let's look at the features of different address types in more detail.

3.2 Unicast Addresses

This is the most important address type because unicast addresses are the "normal" addresses identifying the common computers, printers and other devices connected to the network.

Let's look at the most important subtype of unicast addresses first - at the global unicast addresses defined by RFC 3587 [RFC3587]. The internal unicast address structure defined by this RFC is quite simple. It contains just three parts as depicted in Figure 3-1: global routing prefix, subnet ID, and interface ID.

Figure 3-1 Structure of the Global Unicast Address

Global routing prefix

is the network address in IPv4 parlance. This address prefix identifies uniquely the network connected to the Internet.

Subnet ID

is the identifier of a subnet. The end-network may be partitioned into to subnets (for example every building of some institution may hold separate subnet). This part of the address serves to identify individual subnets.

Interface ID

holds the identifier of single network interface. Interface identifiers are unique inside the same subnet only, there may be devices holding the same interface ID in different subnets. Internet standards request the modified EUI-64 (described below) to play the role of interface ID.

In reality the address structure is even more simple, because all used addressing schemes have the common length of the global prefix (48 bits) and subnet identifier (16 bits). In consequence the typical unicast address has the structure showed in Figure 3-2.

Figure 3-2 Real-world Structure of the Global Unicast Address

Not all unicast addresses are global. Some of them are limited just to a single physical (layer 2) network. These link-local addresses are distinguished by prefix fe80::/10. They can be used for intra-link communication only – both the sender and recipient of the datagram must be connected to the same local network. A router must not forward any datagram having such a destination address.

Theses addresses are used in some mechanisms, such as the autoconfiguration of network parameters. RFC 3513 actually defines two scoping levels: link-local (prefix fe80::/10) and site-local (fec0::/10) addresses. But due to a long-term lack of consensus on the definition of "site" RFC 3879 [RFC3879] deprecated the usage of site-local addresses and prohibits new IPv6 implementations to handle the fec0::/10 prefix. RFC 3879 states that the given prefix is reserved for potential future usage.

Note:

Although, in theory, site-local addresses have been deprecated by RFC 3879, many IPv6 implementations and IPv6 applications still use site-local prefixes and this will probably remain true for some time. Indeed, some of the configuration examples in this book contain site-local addresses.

Consequently, unicast addresses have just two scope levels: link-local (starting with fe80::/10) or global (all the others).

3.3 *Interface Identifier – Modified EUI-64*

Providing 64 bits to identify the interface in the scope of a single subnet seems to be a huge extravagance. For example 48 bits are sufficient for Ethernet addresses which are world-wide unique. Subnets for which 16 bits would not suffice to identify all the nodes are hard to imagine. On the other hand this 64-bit long interface identifier simplifies significantly some autoconfiguration mechanisms.

RFC 3513 specifies the use of modified EUI-64 identifiers in this part of the IPv6 address. EUI-64 is a network interface identifier defined by the IEEE. The modification deployed in IPv6 is related to 7th bit of the 64-bit identifier. This bit distinguishes global identifiers (world-wide unique) from the local ones (unique only in the scope of single link). The value of this bit is inverted in IPv6 addresses. Hence the value 0 of this bit means a local identifier, while a value of 1 indicates a global ID.

How do we determine the value of this final part of the IPv6 address? The answer depends on the lower-layer address which the corresponding interface has. Basic rules are following:

Interface has an EUI-64 identifier

This is the simplest case. The 7th bit of the existing EUI-64 identifier is inverted and the resulting value is used.

Interface has a MAC (Ethernet) address

There is a simple algorithm converting the MAC address into a modified EUI-64: the global flag (7th bit) of the MAC address is inverted and the value fffe is inserted between the 3rd and 4th byte of the MAC address. For example the MAC address 00:8c:a0:c2:71:35 is converted to interface ID 028c:a0ff:fec2:7135 (the conversion is illustrated in Figure 3.3).

Otherwise

In other cases the network manager simply assigns some identifier to the interface. Typically some simple identifiers (like 0:0:0:1 and 0:0:0:2) are used. Such artificial identifiers are used for example for serial lines, which do not provide any values usable as a ground for the identification.

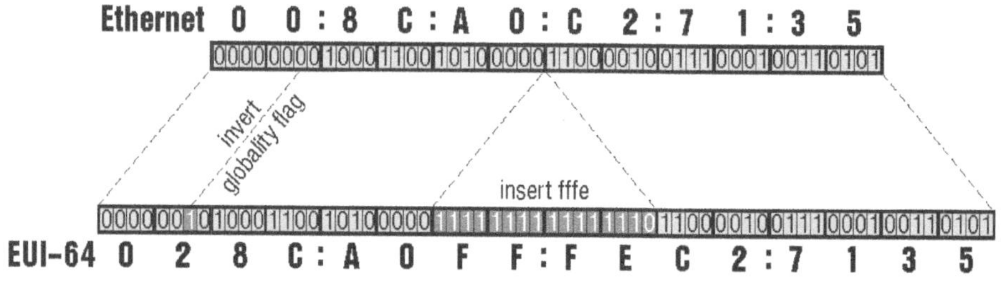

Figure 3-3 Conversion of MAC Address to Interface Identifier

From a technical point of view this is a perfect working mechanism. But there is a hidden drawback - a threat to privacy. Since a common computer is equipped by some MAC-addressed network card, the second rule is used for the vast majority of computers. But this means that even if the user is travelling and changing the networks used to connect to the Internet, the interface identifier of his/her computer remains constant. In other words the computer can be tracked.

RFC 3041 [RFC3041] solves this problem. It recommends the interface to have several identifiers. One of them is a fixed, EUI-64 based identifier. This is used in the "official" (DNS registered) address and is used mainly for incoming connections. The additional identifiers are randomly generated and their lifetime can be limited to a few hours or days. These identifiers are used for outgoing connections, initiated by the computer itself. Thanks to these short-lived identifiers the systematic long-term tracking of computer activities is much more difficult.

3.4 *Anycast Addresses*

The essential idea behind anycast is that there is a group of IPv6 nodes providing the same service. If you use an anycast address to identify this group, the request will be delivered to its nearest member using standard network mechanisms.

An anycast address is hard to distinguish. There is no separate part of the address space dedicated for these addresses, they are living in the unicast space. The local configuration is responsible for identification of anycast addresses.

Common routing methods should be used to maintain the information about the nearest anycast group member. It means that routers inside the network part containing the whole group should have a dedicated entry for this anycast address in their routing tables. This is a serious drawback for large-scale anycast deployment, where the anycast group members are spread around the global Internet. Every such anycast address involves a separate entry in global routing tables. It contradicts one of the essential IPv6 addressing design principles: hold the global routing tables as small as possible.

But this is not the sole problem of anycast addresses. Another problem is found in the heart of the anycasting mechanism. Selection of a particular receiver of an anycast-addressed datagram is left to IP, which means it is stateless. In consequence the receiver can change during running communication which can be truly confusing for the transport and application layers.

Yet another problem is related to security. How do we protect anycast groups from intruders falsely declaring themselves to be holders of given anycast addresses and stealing the data or sending false responses. It is extremely inadvisable to use IPSec to secure anycast addressed traffic (it would require all group members to use the same security parameters).

There is a research focused on solving the anycast problem. Until it succeeds, there are serious limitations to the anycast usage. Especially:

- Anycast addresses must not be used as a sender address in the IP datagram.
- Anycast addresses may be assigned to routers only. Anycast-addressed hosts are prohibited.

In summary: anycast addresses represent an experimental area where many aspects are still researched. They are already deployed in limited scope - for example anycast address is used when a mobile node looks for home agent. The scope of this address is limited to its home network only, which makes anycast perfectly usable for such application. RFC 2526 [RFC2526] defines reserved IPv6 anycast addresses with the group span restricted to single subnet.

3.5 Multicast Addresses

Compared to anycast, multicast is a well-known entity. It is used in the contemporary IPv4 Internet, mainly to transport video/audio data in real time (e.g., videoconferencing, TV/radio broadcast). Multicast in IPv6 is just an evolution of the mechanisms already in use.

There is a separate part of the IPv6 address space dedicated to multicast. It is identified by the prefix ff00::/8. So every multicast address starts with "ff" which makes them easy to distinguish. The internal structure of the remaining 120 bits is shown in Figure 3-4.

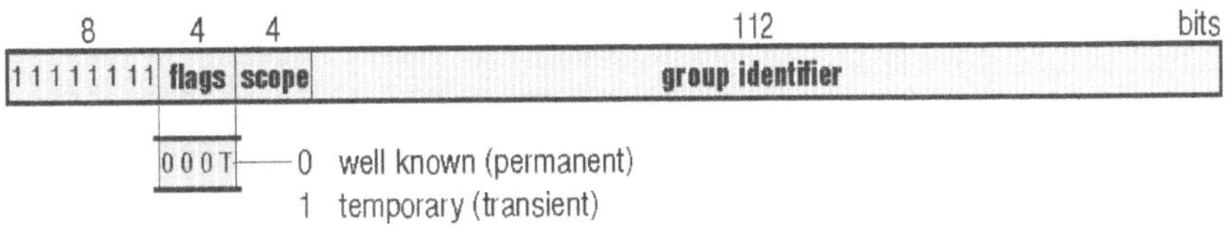

Figure 3-4 Structure of the IPv6 Multicast Address

IPv6 multicast and multicast Addressing is discussed in more detail in Chapter 8.

3.6 Required Addresses and Address Selection

There is a serious difference between IPv4 and IPv6. Every interface has just a single address in IPv4. If you want to assign more addresses to the same interface, you have to use various hacks (i.e., virtual sub-interfaces) or vendor specific implementations that do not adhere to open standards such as DHCP.

IPv6 is different. Not only does it allow you to assign more addresses to the same interface, it even urges you to do so because multiple addresses are needed for the full complement of IPv6 functionality. Required addresses for a common host (computer, printer or any other device which does not forward the datagrams) are as follows:

- link-local address for every interface
- assigned (configured) unicast and multicast addresses for the interfaces
- loopback address (::1)
- all-nodes multicast addresses (ff01::1, ff02::1)
- solicited node multicast address
- assigned multicast addresses (identifying groups to which the node belongs)

For example a PC equipped with a single Ethernet network card having a MAC address of 00:2a:0f:32:5e:d1 sitting in two subnets (2001:a:b:c::/64 and 2001:a:b:1::/64) and participating in the group ff15::1:2:3 must receive data on all these addresses:

- fe80::22a:fff:fe32:5ed1 (link-local)
- 2001:a:b:c:22a:fff:fe32:5ed1 (configured unicast)
- 2001:a:b:1:22a:fff:fe32:5ed1 (another configured unicast)
- ::1 (loopback)
- ff01::1 (all nodes on the interface)
- ff02::1 (all nodes on the link)
- ff02::1:ff32:5ed1 (solicited node multicast)
- ff15::1:2:3 (configured multicast)

A router has even more required addresses. It must support all the addresses obligatory for a node plus:

- anycast address for all routers in the subnet for every interface on which it acts as a router
- all assigned anycast addresses
- all-routers multicast (ff01::2, ff02::2, ff05::2)

Suppose that the aforementioned node is a router. It operates as a home agent (see Chapter 10 about mobility for the description of this) in both subnets, so it should listen to the corresponding all-home-agents anycast addresses. In this case it must in addition to addresses already stated support:

- 2001:a:b:c:: (routers in first subnet)
- 2001:a:b:1:: (routers in second subnet)
- 2001:a:b:c::fdff:ffff:ffff:fffe (home agents in first subnet)
- 2001:a:b:1::fdff:ffff:ffff:fffe (home agents in second subnet)
- ff01::2 (all routers on the interface)
- ff02::2 (all routers on the link)
- ff05::2 (all routers in the site)

Having more addresses on the same interface brings a new problem: Which one should be used? Suppose for example that you typed www.somewehere.com into your WWW browser and the request to DNS returns four different IP addresses. The selection of particular address influences datagram routing and the behaviour of the network in general. So it is quite important.

RFC 3484 [RFC3484] brings the rules for this situation. It defines an imperative algorithm to select the sender and receiver addresses for an IP datagram. The general idea behind the address selection is following. The application willing to communicate will call some system service (typically the getaddrinfo() function) to obtain a list of available addresses for given target host. It takes the first of these addresses, selects some appropriate source address and tries to establish the communication. In the case of failure the next potential destination address from the list is used.

We do not cover the exact rules to judge between addresses here because they are important for the implementers of IPv6, not for its users. But one aspect of these rules should be mentioned here – the policy table.

It is a dedicated data structure used to express relationships (affinity) between addresses. Every entry of the policy table contains: address prefix, precedence and label. When evaluating some address, the entry containing longest matching prefix is used to assign the precedence and label to the address. Generally speaking: two addresses (source and destination) having the same label are related which increases their chance to be selected.

Using the policy table you may influence the address selection algorithm by assigning labels to particular prefixes. Of course it is not obligatory, there is a default policy table defined by RFC 3484 which will be used in such case.

3.7 *Real-world Addresses*

Leaving aside the addressing 'theory', in reality the IPv6 address space has been partitioned into a few areas which have a fixed meaning. You can see the allocation in Table 3-1.

Table 3-1 IPv6 Address Allocation

::0/128	Unspecified address
::1/128	Loopback address
ff00::/8	Multicast addresses
fe80::/10	Link-local addresses
fec0::/10	Deprecated (former site-local addresses)
other	Global unicast addresses

The vast majority of the address space is occupied by global unicast addresses. But just a tiny part of this allocation is really used – no more than three /16 prefixes (see Table 3-2, "Global unicast prefixes in real use").

Table 3-2 Global Unicast Address Prefixes in Use

2001::/16	Regular IPv6 addresses
2002::/16	6to4 addresses
3ffe::/16	6Bone addresses (to be deprecated 6 June 2006)

The 2002::/16 prefix is dedicated to 6to4 mechanism allowing automatic tunnelling of IPv6 datagrams over common IPv4 Internet (described later in this book). The 3ffe::/16 prefix was used in the 6bone network – an experimental overlay network intended to gain practical experience with IPv6 operation. Allocations from this address space have been stopped. The support (routing) of these addresses will be deprecated at the end of June 2006 (RFC 3701 describes the 6bone phase-out schedule). In consequence the usage of 3ffe::/16 prefix drops and many 6bone addresses have already been abandoned.

The most important address prefix is the 2001::/16 from which all the regular global unicast addresses in the contemporary Internet originate. Allocation of addresses from this prefix is managed by Regional Internet Registries (RIRs) – the same organisations which also manage the IPv4 address space.

Every RIR has obtained some part of the 2001::/16 prefix from which it allocates smaller parts. Regions covered by a single RIR are quite large (e.g. a continent), so the allocation is not made directly. It is made in collaboration with Local Internet Registries (LIRs), which are typically the Internet providers. The mechanism is similar – every LIR obtains some part of the address space from which it allocates prefixes to its customers.

All the RIRs have agreed on common allocation rules and the address structure displayed in Figure 3-5. This clear and well-arranged structure is the result of a few years of evolution. One of the really nice features of this contemporary addressing structure is that the borders between different authorities are situated at the colons in the address written form.

The first four hexadecimal digits are fixed, they are 2001. The next four are assigned by the RIRs. It means that if some LIR asks for an address space to manage it obtains a 32-bit prefix from which 48-bit prefixes are allocated to its customers (end-sites). So the specification of the third quadruple is up to the LIR. Finally, the last foursome of hexadecimal digits in the first half of the address contains the subnet ID. This is assigned by the local network manager.

16	16	16	16 bits
2001	**Assigned by RIR**	**Assigned by LIR**	**Subnet ID**

Figure 3-5 Structure of the Real-world Global Unicast Address Prefix

Let's look at an example: CESNET is the operator of Czech National Research and Education Network and also the LIR serving organisations connected to this network. CESNET obtained from RIPE NCC (RIR responsible for Europe) the prefix 2001:718::/32. /48 prefixes from this space are assigned to institutions connected to the CESNET network – for example the Czech technical University in Prague obtained the prefix 2001:718:2::/48. Its subnet number 1 has the prefix 2001:718:2:1::/64.

It is possible for the address holder to define some hierarchy of addressing scheme in the address part for which it is responsible. For example the end-site can specify the rules to assign subnet IDs. Say that the network is spread around few buildings. Natural hierarchy in this case could be to use the first part of subnet ID to identify the building and the rest to distinguish particular LANs inside the same buildings.

If you decide to deploy such a hierarchy, it is tempting to say "First N bits is the building identifier, the remaining 16–N bits identify the subnets inside building." RFC 3531 recommends not to do so, because later you may decide that your estimation about future network development was bad and some part of the hierarchy does not suffice for the network growth.

It is better to assign upper-layer identifiers from the left side of the selected address part and growing bitwise to the right. So in our example the first building will be identified by 1000...0 bitwise (or 8000 hexadecimal), the second by 0100...0 (4000), the third by 1100...0 (c000), etc. The lower-layer identifier is then growing conventionally from right to left. So first LAN inside every building is

0...0001 (0001), the second is 0...0010 (0002), the third 0...0011 (0003), etc. When combined for example 4003 means third LAN in second building. This opposite growth ensures the postponement of part-border assignment up to the moment when the growing lengths of both parts meet. You may then find that instead of the planned division of bit 8:8 for building and LAN identifiers, the real need is to use 6:10.

Similarly the LIR can define some system in the third quadruple to assign /48 prefixes to customers. For example the first part may identify the node (point of presence), the second one distinguishes customers connected to the same node. The IPv6 addressing structure provides freedom for such decisions. The hierarchy inside individual parts marked in Figure 3-5 is not strictly defined by the RFCs, nor prohibited. It is up to the manager of the corresponding part to develop the rules. In most cases these rules are just internal, they are not communicated to the customers.

And finally we should answer the Big Principal Question: "How to get IPv6 addresses for my network?"

The answer is that it depends on your position in the addressing "food chain". If you are an end-customer, simply ask your IPv6 connectivity provider. The correct answer would be to ask the corresponding LIR, but the provider and LIR are usually the same body. You should get a 48-bit prefix. If the provider tries to assign you some longer prefix (smaller address space), argue and fight for /48, because RFC 3177 clearly states that /48 should be the standard network prefix length for almost all networks.

If you are a LIR and would like to provide IPv6 addresses to your customers, your situation is more complicated. You must ask your RIR to assign you some part of the address space. It is done the usual way – by filling in an application form. But there are some requirements which you have to meet to qualify for getting some address space. In the time of writing this text the requirements are:

- You have to be a LIR.
- You must not be an end site.
- You must develop a plan to provide IPv6 connectivity to connected sites. You have to assign /48 prefixes to these sites and aggregate all these prefixes to a single routing table entry used to advertise your network to the rest of world.
- You have to have a plan for assign at least 200 prefixes to other organisations within two years.

If you meet these criteria and ask for it, you should obtain a /32 prefix to manage and use for your assignments. There are running discussions about the fourth criterion, which is a little difficult to regulate. Having a plan does not mean that you really connect 200 organisations. Connecting 10 big companies means a lot more computers than connecting 300 home networks, etc. It may be the case that the fourth criterion will be abandoned someday but it is still valid for the present.

Chapter 4

Essential Functions and Services

This chapter looks at what we consider to be 'essential' functions and services of IPv6. In other words, without these functions and services we would not be able to achieve satisfactory IPv6 operation (or even no connectivity at all). First, we briefly describe Neighbour Discovery and look at several router configurations. Next we detail how DNS works in IPv6 and describe how this worked in the 6NET network. Finally, we describe DHCPv6 along with several available implementations.

4.1 Neighbour Discovery

Neighbour discovery is a protocol that allows different nodes on the same link to advertise their existence to their neighbours, and to learn about the existence of their neighbors. It is a basic functionality all implementations of IPv6 on any platform must include.

Neighbor discovery for IPv6 replaces the following IPv4 protocols: router discovery (RDISC), Address Resolution Protocol (ARP) and ICMPv4 redirect.

Neighbor discovery is defined in the following documents:

- RFC 2461, Neighbor Discovery for IP Version 6 [RFC2461]
- RFC 2462, IPv6 Stateless Address Autoconfiguration [RFC2462]
- RFC 2463, Internet Control Message Protocol (ICMPv6) for the Internet Protocol Version 6 Specification. [RFC2463]

RFC 2461 and 2462 are currently in the process of being revised by the IPv6 working group of the IETF. These drafts [RFC2461bis], [RFC2462bis] will eventually replace the older RFCs.

The combination of these protocols allow IPv6 hosts to automatically detect the presence of other hosts on the link including, of course, the presence of on-link routers. From the messages sent by routers, IPv6 hosts can automatically configure themselves with appropriate addresses and other state necessary for operation. Neighbour Discovery mandates duplicate address detection so that a host cannot try to use an IPv6 address already in use by another host on the link and also allows a host to detect when another host on the link becomes unreachable.

Neighbor discovery uses the following Internet Control Message Protocol Version 6 (ICMPv6) messages:

- router solicitation (RS)
- router advertisement (RA)
- neighbor solicitation (NS)

- neighbor advertisement (NA)
- redirect.

4.1.1 Router Discovery

Router Discovery is achieved through the receipt of a router advertisement sent from an on-link router. This will either be in the form of a router advertisement sent periodically to the all nodes multicast address, or in response to a router solicitation sent by the IPv6 host.

Router advertisements can contain a list of prefixes. These prefixes are used for stateless address autoconfiguration of hosts on the link and to maintain a database of on-link prefixes as well as for duplicate address detection. For routers the list of prefixes, which are on-link is used for forwarding decisions. If the destination address in an IP packet belongs to an on-link prefix, the router forwards the packets to that node. If the node is not on-link, the packets are sent to the next router for consideration. For IPv6 router advertisements, each prefix in the prefix list can contain a prefix length, valid lifetime for the prefix, preferred lifetime for the prefix, an on-link flag and an autoconfiguration flag. This information enables address autoconfiguration and the setting of link parameters such as maximum transmission unit (MTU) size and hop limit.

To summarise, router advertisement messages typically include the following information:

- One or more on-link IPv6 prefixes that nodes on the local link can use to automatically configure their IPv6 addresses;
- Lifetime information for each prefix included in the advertisement;
- Sets of flags that indicate the type of autoconfiguration (stateless or statefull) that can be completed;
- Default router information (whether the router sending the advertisement should be used as a default router and, if so, the amount of time (in seconds) the router should be used as a default router);
- Additional information for hosts, such as the hop limit and MTU a host should use in packets that it originates.

4.1.2 Automatic Address Configuration

An IPv6 host can configure itself with an IPv6 address to be used on the network. Address configuration can be performed in a stateful or a stateless manner. An IPv6 host may use both stateless and stateful address configuration completely independently from one another. The precise method to be used can be signalled with the setting of various flags in router advertisement messages.

Of course, a host may also be configured by manual means. However, most sane network operators would not allow or even wish for its users to manually configure addresses. However, it is possible that state other than IPv6 addresses may be left to the user to configure manually.

4.1.2.1 Stateless Address Configuration

There are two ways in which an IPv6 node can configure its address in a stateless fashion:

1. Using automatic address configuration with prefix discovery
2. Using stateless DHCPv6

Automatic address configuration utilising prefix discovery is specified in [RFC2462]. If the 'autonomous' flag of a Prefix Information Option contained in a router advertisement is set, the IPv6 host may automatically generate its global IPv6 address by appending its 64-bit interface identifier to the prefix contained in the router advertisement. There are different ways in which the host may choose how to generate its interface identifier (e.g. based on MAC address, random or cryptographically generated).

Stateless DHCPv6 is not mentioned as an option given in router advertisements [RFC2461]. However, recent discussions in the IPv6 w.g. have suggested signalling the usage of stateless DHCPv6 via the 'O' flag in router advertisements. At the time of writing the exact way of signalling that hosts should use stateless DHCPv6 is not clear. However, since there are few available implementations, this is not a major concern.

4.1.2.2 Stateful Address Configuration

As far as the IPv6 host is concerned, using stateful DHCPv6 is little different to using stateless DHCPv6 as the observed request/response times should be the same in most cases. However, it is possible that the extra overhead of reading and writing state to memory inside the DHCPv6 server may lead to a small increase in latency when compared to its stateless equivalent. This may be important for the configuration time of mobile nodes, which must perform address configuration when moving into a new network.

It is worth noting that most network operators (certainly those in 6NET) seem to favour the use of stateful DHCPv6 over stateless address configuration due to the extra control and documenting of address assignments that it provides.

4.1.3 Duplicate Address Detection

Once an IPv6 host has configured its addresses, it must perform DAD (Duplicate Address Detection) to ensure that its configured addresses are unique on the link. This holds true regardless of whether the an address has been obtained by stateless, stateful or manual means.

In IPv6, the DAD procedure is defined in RFC 2462 [RFC2462], and uses the neighbour discovery procedures defined in RFC 2461 [RFC2461]. A host cannot begin to use a configured address until the DAD procedure has been successfully executed. Until DAD has succeeded, the address is seen as tentative, in that it can only be used for neighbour discovery purposes (of which the DAD procedure is part of). If a host was to use an address before successful DAD and another node was using the same address on the link, the host would erroneously process packets intended for the other node.

To perform DAD, the host sends out a neighbour solicitation message with its own address as the target address of the solicitation message. The destination address in the IPv6 header of the neighbour solicitation is set to the solicited-node multicast address of the target address with the source address being the unspecified address. If there is another node on the link that is using the same address as the hosts's address, one of two things will happen:

1. The duplicate node will receive the host's neighbour solicitation message and reply with a neighbour advertisement (sent to the all-nodes multicast address) thus exposing the duplicated address to the host.
2. The host will receive a neighbour solicitation with its address as the target address from a duplicate node that is also in the process of performing DAD.

Thus, the DAD procedure will give an explicit indication to the host should there be another node on the network that is using its address. However, (and to the detriment of any node wishing to perform autoconfiguration at haste) the DAD procedure provides no explicit indication that a host's address is *not* being used by another node on the network. Indeed, the point at which DAD can be considered to have succeeded is quite vague. According to RFC 2462, a node performing DAD can consider its tentative address unique if no indications of a duplicate address is observed within RETRANS_TIMER milliseconds after sending DUP_ADDR_DETECT_TRANSMITS number of neighbour solicitations. Both the values of RETRANS_TIMER and DUP_ADDR_DETECT_TRANSMITS are configurable parameters and by default are set to 1,000 and 1 respectively. Therefore, under default conditions DAD will take a minimum of 1,000 milliseconds (1 second) plus additional delay for link transmissions and logic computation.

Note that RFC 2462 states that a node should delay sending its neighbour solicitation for DAD by a random time interval between 0 and MAX_RTR_SOLICITATION_DELAY seconds if it is the first packet sent from the interface after (re)initialisation . In RFC 2461, MAX_RTR_SOLICITATION_DELAY is defined as being 1 second in duration. Therefore, unless the host has previously sent a router solicitation, it will incur further delay during its autoconfiguration process. In the average case (assuming a pure random function) this will be an extra 500ms, and up to 1000ms (1 second) in the worst case.

Note that in order to speed up the autoconfiguration process, a host may choose to initiate DAD in parallel to router discovery. Since the value of the node's link-layer identifier is known in advance, the host can perform DAD on its link local address before receiving a router advertisement. If the router advertisement instructs the host to use stateless address configuration, the host need not perform DAD on its resultant global unicast address if it has already verified the uniqueness of its link-local address.

As a router may delay responding to a router solicitation by a few seconds, a host that performs DAD only after receiving a valid router advertisement may experience significantly longer autoconfiguration latency than performing the steps in parallel when stateless addressing is used.

4.1.4 Neighbour Unreachability Detection

Neighbour Unreachability Detection works in the following manner. When an IPv6 host has a packet to send, it checks the Neighbour Cache to determine the link layer address of the next hop node (either an on-link neighbour or a router). The Neighbour cache also has an associated state with each neighbour entry. A neighbour state of REACHABLE indicates that the neighbour is considered reachable.

In IPv6 a host considers a neighbour reachable if it has recently received confirmation that packets sent to the neighbour have been received. This is achieved in two ways: the receipt of a neighbour advertisement from the neighbour in response to a neighbour solicitation sent by the host or a hint from upper layer protocols. The IPv6 stack utilises the acknowledgements of upper layer protocols to register the fact that a packet has recently been received from a given destination address and so is considered reachable.

The IPv6 host will send a neighbour solicitation in the event that the neighbour cache entry not being set as REACHABLE when there is a packet to send.

4.1.5 Router Configurations for Neighbour Discovery

In the context of router configuration Neighbour Discovery along as Router Discovery has a few special implications. A router periodically sends a router advertisement from each of its multicast interfaces, announcing its availability. Hosts listen for these advertisements for address autoconfiguration and discovery of link-local addresses of the neighboring routers. When a host starts, it multicasts a router solicitation to ask for immediate advertisements.

The router discovery messages do not constitute a routing protocol. They enable hosts to discover the existence of neighboring routers, but are not used to determine which router is best to reach a particular destination. If more than one router advertises its presence on the link, it depends on the IPv6 implementation of the host how it decides which router to use as its preferred default route.

4.1.5.1 Cisco IOS

Cisco IOS allows the configuration of the following router parameters in router advertisements:

- The time interval between periodic router advertisement messages;
- The "router lifetime" value, which indicates the usefulness of a router as the default router (for use by all nodes on a given link);
- The network prefixes in use on a given link;
- The time interval between neighbor solicitation message retransmissions (on a given link);
- The amount of time a node considers a neighbor reachable (for use by all nodes on a given link).

Enabling Router Advertisement Messages

The configured parameters are specific to an interface. The sending of router advertisement messages (with default values) is automatically enabled on Ethernet and FDDI interfaces when the ipv6 unicast-routing global configuration command is configured. This means that a router will automatically send out router advertisements for the prefix corresponding to the (global) addresses configured on an interface belonging to the particular link. That is, if there is a statement of the form:

```
Router (config-if)# ipv6 address address/prefix-length
```

Within the interface configuration context the router will automatically send router advertisements for the prefix this address was built from. However, for stateless autoconfiguration to work properly, the advertised prefix length in router advertisement messages must always be 64 bits.

For other interface types, the sending of router advertisement messages must be manually configured by using the `no ipv6 nd suppress-ra global` configuration command. The sending of router advertisement messages can be disabled on individual interfaces by using the `ipv6 nd suppress-ra` interface configuration command.

Example

If an interface is configured in the following way, the router will automatically send out router advertisements for the prefix 2001:638:500:101::/64 on the link this interface is attached to.

```
interface Ethernet0/0
        ipv6 address 2001:638:500:101::/64 eui-64
```

If the interface was additionally configured as follows, the prefix list in router advertisements on this link would include prefix 2001:638:102::/64.

```
ipv6 address 2001:638:500:102:aaaa:bbbb:cccc:dddd/64
```

Customizing Prefix Information in Router Advertisement Messages

Aside from the prefixes to be advertised on a link Cisco IOS allows the configuration of the following router parameters in router advertisements:

- If more than one address is configured on an interface the network prefixes to be advertised on a given link. It is also possible to advertise prefixes not configured on the interface itself .

- The time interval between periodic router advertisement messages. This parameter is set for the interface in general. That means all prefixes to be advertised on the interface will be advertised at the same time albeit possibly with different lifetimes.
  The "router lifetime" value, which indicates the usefulness of a router as the default router (for use by all nodes on a given link). This means that routers can theoretically advertise prefixes for use with stateless address autoconfiguration while not acting as default router for hosts on.
- The time interval between neighbor solicitation message retransmissions (on a given link).
- The amount of time a node considers a neighbour reachable (for use by all nodes on a given link).

Command Syntax:

```
Router (config-if)# ipv6 nd prefix ipv6-prefix/prefix-length \\
        | default [[valid-lifetime preferred-lifetime] \\
        | [at valid-date preferred-date] | infinite \\
        | no-advertise | off-link | no-autoconfig]]
```

This command allows control over the individual parameters per prefix, including whether or not the prefix should be advertised at all.

As mentioned above, prefixes configured as addresses on an interface using the `ipv6 address` command are advertised in router advertisements by default. However, if you configure prefixes for advertisement using the `ipv6 nd prefix` command, then only these prefixes are advertised.

The `default` keyword can be used to set default parameters for all prefixes.

With the at `valid-date preferred-date` option a date can be set to specify the expiration of a prefix. The `valid` and `preferred lifetimes` are counted down in real time. When the expiration date is reached, the prefix will no longer be advertised.

If not otherwise specified all prefixes configured on interfaces that originate IPv6 router advertisements are advertised with a valid lifetime of 2592000 seconds (30 days) and a preferred lifetime of 604800 seconds (7 days).

When `onlink` is "on" (by default), the specified prefix is assigned to the link. Nodes sending traffic to such addresses that contain the specified prefix consider the destination to be locally reachable on the link.

When `autoconfig` is "on" (by default), it indicates to hosts on the local link that the specified prefix can be used for IPv6 autoconfiguration.

Timing Router Advertisements and Lifetimes

To configure the interval between IPv6 router advertisement transmissions on an interface, use the `ipv6 nd ra-interval` command in interface configuration mode.

```
Router (config-if)# ipv6 nd ra-interval seconds
```

The interval between transmissions defaults to 200 seconds. It should be less than or equal to the IPv6 router advertisement lifetime if the router is configured as a default router by using the `ipv6 nd ra-lifetime` command. To prevent synchronization with other IPv6 nodes, randomly adjust the actual value used to within 20 percent of the specified value.

To configure the "router lifetime" value in IPv6 router advertisements on an interface, use the `ipv6 nd ra-lifetime` command in interface configuration mode.

```
Router (config-if)# ipv6 nd ra-lifetime seconds
```

The "router lifetime" value defaults to 1800 seconds and is included in all IPv6 router advertisements sent out the interface. The value indicates the usefulness of the router as a default router on this interface. Setting the value to 0 indicates that the router should not be perceived a default router on this interface. The "router lifetime" value can be set to a non zero value to indicate that it should be considered a default router on this interface. The non zero value for the "router lifetime" value should not be less than the router advertisement interval.

To configure the amount of time that a remote IPv6 node is considered reachable, after some reachability confirmation event has occurred, use the `ipv6 nd reachable-time` command in interface configuration mode.

```
Router (config-if)# ipv6 nd reachable-time milliseconds
```

As a default 0 milliseconds (unspecified) is advertised in router advertisements and the value 30000 (30 seconds) is used for the neighbour discovery activity of the router itself.

The configured time enables the router to detect unavailable neighbors. Shorter configured times enable the router to detect unavailable neighbors more quickly; however, shorter times consume more IPv6 network bandwidth and processing resources in all IPv6 network devices. Very short configured times are not recommended in normal IPv6 operation.

The configured time is included in all router advertisements sent out of an interface so that nodes on the same link use the same time value. A value of 0 means indicates that the configured time is unspecified by this router.

Examples

a) The following example includes the IPv6 prefix 2001:0DB8::/64 in router advertisements sent out Ethernet interface 0/0 with a valid lifetime of 1000 seconds, a preferred lifetime of 900 seconds, and both the "onlink" and "autoconfig" flags set:

```
Router(config)# interface ethernet 0/0
Router(config-if)# ipv6 nd prefix 2001:0DB8::/64 1000 \\
900 onlink autoconfig
```

b) The following example configures an IPv6 router advertisement interval of 201 seconds for Ethernet interface 0/0:

```
Router(config)# interface ethernet 0/0
Router(config-if)# ipv6 nd ra-interval 201
```

c) The following example configures an IPv6 router advertisement lifetime of 1801 seconds for Ethernet interface 0/0:

```
Router(config)# interface ethernet 0/0
Router(config-if)# ipv6 nd ra-lifetime 1801
```

d) The following example configures an IPv6 reachable time of 1,700,000 milliseconds for Ethernet interface 0/0:

```
Router(config)# interface ethernet 0/0
Router(config-if)# ipv6 nd reachable-time 1700000
```

4.1.5.2 Juniper JunOS

To configure neighbour discovery on a JunOS platform, you include the following statements. Router advertisement are configured on a per-interface basis.

```
protocols {
    router-advertisement {
        interface interface-name {
            current-hop-limit number;
            default-lifetime seconds;
            (managed-configuration | no-managed-configuration);
            max-advertisement-interval seconds;
            min-advertisement-interval seconds;
            (other-stateful-configuration | no-other-stateful-configuration);
            prefix prefix {
                (autonomous | no-autonomous);
                (on-link | no-on-link);
                preferred-lifetime seconds;
                valid-lifetime seconds;
            }
            reachable-time milliseconds;
            retransmit-timer milliseconds;
            traceoptions {
                file name <replace> <size size> <files number> <no-stamp>
                    <(world-readable | no-world-readable)>;
                flag flag <detail> <disable>;
            }
        }
    }
}
```

Configuring Prefix Information in Router Advertisements

You can set two fields in the router advertisement message to enable stateful autoconfiguration on a host: the `managed-configuration` field and the `other-stateful-configuration` field. Setting the managed configuration field enables the host to use a stateful autoconfiguration protocol for address autoconfiguration, along with any stateless autoconfiguration already configured. Setting the other stateful configuration field enables autoconfiguration of other non address-related information.

By default, stateful autoconfiguration is disabled.

On-Link / Not On-Link

Router advertisement messages carry prefixes and information about them. A prefix is on-link when it is assigned to an interface on a specified link. The prefixes specify whether they are on-link or not on-link. A node considers a prefix to be on-link if it is represented by one of the link's prefixes, a neighboring router specifies the address as the target of a redirect message, a neighbor advertisement message is received for the (target) address, or any neighbor discovery message is received from the address. These prefixes are also used for address autoconfiguration. The information about the prefixes specifies the lifetime of the prefixes, whether the prefix is autonomous, and whether the prefix is on-link.

You can specify prefixes in the router advertisement messages as on-link. When set as on-link, the prefixes are used for on-link determination. By default, prefixes are on-link.

To explicitly set prefixes as on-link or not on-link, include the `on-link` or `no-on-link` statement:

```
[edit protocols router-advertisement interface interface-name prefix prefix]
on-link | no-on-link;
```

Autonomous / Not Autonomous

You can specify prefixes in the router advertisement messages as autonomous. When set as autonomous, the prefixes are used for stateless address autoconfiguration. By default, prefixes are autonomous.

To explicitly specify prefixes as autonomous, include the autonomous or no-autonomous statement:

```
[edit protocols router-advertisement interface interface-name prefix prefix]
autonomous | no-autonomous;
```

Preferred Lifetime

The preferred lifetime for the prefixes in the router advertisement messages specifies how long the prefix generated by stateless autoconfiguration remains preferred. By default, the preferred lifetime is set to 604,800 seconds.

To configure the preferred lifetime, include the preferred-lifetime statement:

```
[edit protocols router-advertisement interface interface-name prefix prefix]
preferred-lifetime seconds;
```

If you set the preferred lifetime to 0xffffffff, the lifetime is infinite.

The preferred lifetime value must never exceed the valid lifetime value.

Valid Lifetime

The valid lifetime for the prefixes in the router advertisement messages specifies how long the prefix remains valid for on-link determination. By default, the valid lifetime is set to 2,592,000 seconds.

To configure the valid lifetime, include the valid-lifetime statement:

```
[edit protocols router-advertisement interface interface-name prefix prefix]
valid-lifetime seconds;
```

If you set the valid lifetime to 0xffffffff, the lifetime is infinite.

The valid lifetime value must never be smaller than the preferred lifetime value.

Trace Options

To trace router advertisement traffic, you can specify options in the global `traceoptions` statement at the `[edit routing-options]` hierarchy level, and you can specify router advertisement options by including the `traceoptions` statement:

```
[edit protocols router-advertisement]
traceoptions {
    file name <replace> <size size> <files number> <no-stamp>
        <(world-readable | no-world-readable)>;
    flag flag <flag-modifier> <disable>;
}
```

Note: Use the trace option `flag` detail with caution. These flags may cause the CPU to become very busy.

Timing and Configuring Router Advertisements

Default Lifetime

The default lifetime in router advertisement messages indicates the lifetime associated with the default router. To modify the default lifetime timer, include the `default-lifetime` statement:

```
[edit protocols router-advertisement interface interface-name]
default-lifetime seconds;
```

By default, the default router lifetime is three times the maximum advertisement interval.

Min/Max Advertisement Interval

The router sends router advertisements on each interface configured to transmit messages. The advertisements include route information and indicate to network hosts that the router is operational. The router sends these messages periodically, with a time range defined by minimum and maximum values.

To modify the router advertisement interval, include the `min-advertisement-interval` and `max-advertisement-interval` statements:

```
[edit protocols router-advertisement interface interface-name]
min-advertisement-interval seconds;
max-advertisement-interval seconds;
```

By default, the maximum advertisement interval is 600 seconds and the minimum advertisement interval is one-third the maximum interval, or 200 seconds.

Reachable Time

After receiving a reachability confirmation from a neighbor, a node considers that neighbor reachable for a certain amount of time without receiving another confirmation. This mechanism is used for neighbor unreachability detection, a mechanism for finding link failures to a target node.

To modify the reachable time limit, include the reachable-time statement:

```
[edit protocols router-advertisement interface interface-name]
reachable-time milliseconds;
```

By default, the reachable time period is 0 milliseconds.

Current Hop Limit

The `current-hop-limit` field in the router advertisement messages indicates the default value placed in the hop count field of the IP header for outgoing packets. To configure the hop limit, include the `current-hop-limit` statement:

```
[edit protocols router-advertisement interface interface-name]
current-hop-limit number;
```

The default hop limit is 64.

4.1.5.3 Quagga

Quagga is an advanced routing software package that provides TCP/IP based routing protocols. Information on Quagga in this book is based on the Quagga Manual for version 0.96. Quagga is started as a fork of GNU Zebra and incorporates the Zebra protocol today as part of the suite.

Currently Quagga supports GNU/Linux, BSD and Solaris. Below is a list of OS versions on which Quagga runs. Porting Quagga to other platforms is not so difficult. Platform dependent codes exist only in the ZEBRA daemon. Protocol daemons are platform independent.

- GNU/Linux 2.0.37
- GNU/Linux 2.2.x and higher
- FreeBSD 2.2.8
- FreeBSD 3.x
- FreeBSD 4.x
- NetBSD 1.4
- OpenBSD 2.5
- Solaris 2.6
- Solaris 7

Some IPv6 stacks are in development. Quagga supports the following IPv6 stacks. For BSD, we recommend KAME IPv6 stack. Solaris IPv6 stack is not yet supported.

- Linux IPv6 stack for GNU/Linux 2.2.x and higher.
- KAME IPv6 stack for BSD.

- INRIA IPv6 stack for BSD.

Since Quagga supports IPv6 in many ways, is easy and cheap to deploy, it is an ideal solution for IPv6 integration into networks where hardware routing devices are not yet IPv6 enabled or should not yet be involved in IPv6 routing for fear of corrupting IPv4 service. It is therefore expected that it might be used by network administrators who don't have any experience with it yet. For this reason we will include rather a little more basic installation and configuration information about Quagga than we do for any other routing platform.

Installation

Quagga is installed like any other UNIX software by "configure", "make" and "make install". If no special options are specified with the configure script, all deamons as well as IPv6 support will be compiled into the binaries.

Quagga daemons have their own terminal interface or VTY. After installation, you have to setup each daemon's port number to connect to them. Please add the following entries to `/etc/services`.

```
zebrasrv      2600/tcp         # zebra service
zebra         2601/tcp         # zebra vty
ripd          2602/tcp         # RIPd vty
ripngd        2603/tcp         # RIPngd vty
ospfd         2604/tcp         # OSPFd vty
bgpd          2605/tcp         # BGPd vty
ospf6d        2606/tcp         # OSPF6d vty
ospfapi       2607/tcp         # ospfapi
isisd         2608/tcp         # ISISd vty
```

Basic Configuration

Each of the daemons has its own config file, which are usually located in `/usr/local/etc`. They are called `*.conf`, so for example the zebra configuration file is `zebra.conf`. However, you can specify any config file using the `-f` or `--config-file` options when starting the daemon.

Quagga can either be configured by editing the individual configuration files manually or via a command line interface very similar to that of Cisco IOS. The commands/directives are the same.

```
!
! Zebra configuration file
!
hostname Router
password zebra
enable password zebra
!
log stdout
!
!
```

'!' and '#' are comment characters. If the first character of the word is one of the comment characters then from the rest of the line forward will be ignored as a comment.

If a comment character is not the first character of the word, it's a normal character. So in the following example '!' will not be regarded as a comment and the password is set to 'zebra!password'.

```
password zebra!password
```

To configure Quagga/Zebra via the command line you can connect to the daemon using the telnet protocol.

To enable a VTY interface, you have to setup a VTY password. If there is no VTY password, one cannot connect to the VTY interface at all.

```
% telnet localhost 2601
Trying 127.0.0.1...
Connected to localhost.
Escape character is '^]'.

Hello, this is zebra (version 0.96)
Copyright 1997-2000 Kunihiro Ishiguro


User Access Verification


Password: XXXXX
Router> ?
  enable              Turn on privileged commands
  exit                Exit current mode and down to previous mode
  help                Description of the interactive help system
  list                Print command list
  show                Show running system information
  who                 Display who is on a vty
Router> enable
Password: XXXXX
Router# configure terminal
Router(config)# interface eth0
Router(config-if)# ip address 10.0.0.1/8
```

Basic Configuration Commands

```
Router(config)# hostname <hostname> {}
```

Set hostname of the router.

```
Router(config)# password <password> {}
```

Set password for VTY interface. If there is no password, a VTY won't accept connections.

```
Router(config)# enable password <password> {}
```

Set enable password.

```
Router(config)# (no) log stdout {}
```

Set/Unset logging output to stdout.

```
Router(config)# log file <filename> {}
```

If you want to log into a file please specify filename as follows:

```
        Router(config)# log file /usr/local/etc/bgpd.log
```

```
Router(config)# (no) log syslog {}
```

Set/Unset logging output to syslog.

```
Router# write terminal {}
```

Displays the current configuration to the VTY interface.

```
Router(config)#  write file {}
```

Write current configuration to configuration file.

```
Router# configure terminal {}
```

Change to configuration mode. This command is the first step to configuration.

```
Router# terminal length <0-512> {}
```

Set terminal display length to <0-512>. If length is 0, no display control is performed.

```
Router#  who {}
Router# list {}
```

List commands.

```
Router(config)# service password-encryption {}
```

Encrypt password.

```
Router(config)# service advanced-vty {}
```

Enable advanced mode VTY.

```
Router(config)# service terminal-length <0-512> {}
```

Set system wide line configuration. This configuration command applies to all VTY interfaces.

`Router# show version {}`

Show the current version of the Quagga and its build host information.

`Router(config)# line vty {}`

Enter VTY configuration mode.

`Router(config)# (no) banner motd default {}`

Set default motd string. To delete a set banner string use the no keyword without any string specification.

```
exec-timeout <minute> {}
exec-timeout <minute> <second> {}
```

Set VTY connection timeout value. When only one argument is specified it is used for timeout value in minutes. Optional second argument is used for timeout value in seconds. Default timeout value is 10 minutes. When timeout value is 0, it means no timeout.

`no exec-timeout {}`

Do not perform timeout at all. This command is as same as exec-timeout 0 0.

```
access-class <access-list> {}
Restrict VTY connections with an access list.
```

Running Quagga/Zebra

The Quagga daemons can be started from `/etc/init.d/<daemon>` with several different options, which are the same for all daemons.

- `-d` or `--daemon`: Runs in daemon mode.
- `-f file` or `--config_file=file`: Set configuration file name.
- `-h` or `--help`: Display help.
- `-i` file or `--pid_file=file`: Upon startup the process identifier of the daemon is written to a file, typically in `/var/run`. This file can be used by the init system to implement commands such as `.../init.d/zebra status`, `.../init.d/zebra restart` or `.../init.d/zebra stop`. The file name is a runtime option rather than a configure-time option so that multiple routing daemons can be run simultaneously. This is useful when using Quagga to implement a routing looking glass. One machine can be used to collect differing routing views from different points in the network.
- `-A address` or `--vty_addr=address`: Set the VTY local address to bind to. If set, the VTY socket will only be bound to this address.
- `-P port` or `--vty_port=port`: Set the VTY TCP port number. If set to 0 then the TCP VTY sockets will not be opened.
- `-u user` or `--vty_addr=user`: Set the user and group to run as.
- `-v` or `--version`: Print program version.

Besides the common invocation options, the Zebra itself has some specific options:

- `-b` or `--batch`: Runs in batch mode. Zebra parses configuration file and terminates immediately.
- `-k` or `--keep_kernel`: When Zebra starts up, don't delete old self inserted routes.
- `-l` or `--log_mode`: Set verbose logging on.
- `-r` or `--retain`: When program terminates, retain routes added by Zebra.

Configuring Router Advertisements and Neighbor Discovery

Router Advertisements are configured per interface, so the following commands have to be entered in the context of an interface:

Command Syntax:

```
Router(config-if)# (no) ipv6 nd suppress-ra {}
```

Either switches off or on (no keyword) sending router advertisements on that interface.

Command Syntax:

```
Router(config-if)# (no) ipv6 nd prefix <ipv6prefix> [valid-lifetime] \\
[preferred-lifetime] [off-link] [no-autconfig] {}
```

This command configures the IPv6 prefix to include in router advertisements. Several prefix specific optional parameters and flags may follow:

- `valid-lifetime`: The length of time in seconds during which the prefix is valid for the purpose of on-link determination. Value infinite represents infinity (i.e. a value of all one bits (0xffffffff)). Range: <0-4294967295> Default: 2592000
- `preferred-lifetime`: The length of time in seconds during what addresses generated from the prefix remain preferred. Value infinite represents infinity. Range: <0-4294967295> Default: 604800
- `off-link`: Indicates that advertisements makes no statement about on-link or off-link properties of the prefix. Default: not set, i.e. this prefix can be used for on-link determination.
- `no-autoconfig`: Indicates to hosts on the local link that the specified prefix cannot be used for IPv6 autoconfiguration. Default: not set, i.e. prefix can be used for autoconfiguration.

Command Syntax:

```
Router(config-if)# (no) ipv6 nd ra-interval <seconds> {}
```

The maximum time allowed between sending unsolicited multicast router advertisements from the interface, in seconds. Must be no less than 3 seconds. The default is 600. Omit <seconds> to delete the statement with the no keyword.

Command Syntax:

```
Router(config-if)# (no) ipv6 nd ra-lifetime <seconds> {}
```

This command sets the value to be placed in the Router Lifetime field of router advertisements sent from the interface, in seconds. It indicates the usefulness of the router as a default router on this interface. Setting the value to zero indicates that the router should not be considered a default router on the connected link. The value must be either zero or between the value specified with `ipv6 nd ra-interval` (or default) and 9000 seconds. The default is 1800 seconds. Omit `<seconds>` to delete the statement with the no keyword.

Command Syntax:

```
Router(config-if)# (no) ipv6 nd reachable-time <milliseconds> {}
```

Use this command to set the value to be placed in the Reachable Time field in the router advertisements messages sent by the router, in milliseconds. The configured time enables the router to detect unavailable neighbors. If set to zero it means this time is unspecified (by this router). The value set must be no greater than 3,600,000 milliseconds (1 hour). The default is 0. Omit `<milliseconds>` to delete the statement with the no keyword.

Command Syntax:

```
Router(config-if)# (no) ipv6 nd managed-config-flag {}
```

This statement sets/unsets the flag in IPv6 router advertisements, which indicates to hosts that they should use managed (stateful) protocol for addresses autoconfiguration in addition to any addresses autoconfigured using stateless address autoconfiguration. As a default this flag is not set.

Command Syntax:

```
Router(config-if)# (no) ipv6 nd other-config-flag {}
```

This statement sets/unsets the flag in IPv6 router advertisements which indicates to hosts that they should use administered (stateful) protocol to obtain autoconfiguration information other than addresses. As a default this flag is not set.

A sample IPv6 interface may be configured as follows:

```
interface eth0
 no ipv6 nd supress-ra
 ipv6 nd prefix 2001:0DB8:5009::/64
```

This interface will send out router advertisements for the prefix 2001:0DB8:5009::/64 every 600 seconds.

4.1.5.4 Linux and Radvd

"Radvd" stands for "Router Advertisement Daemon". It can be installed on any Linux system, which acts as a default IPv6 gateway router.

Radvd is configured in a configuration file that is typically located at `/etc` and called `radvd.conf`. It includes information about the prefix(es) to be advertised, lifetimes and (optionally) the frequency of router advertisements.

Following is a typical Radvd configuration file:

```
interface eth0 {
        AdvSendAdvert on;
        MinRtrAdvInterval 3;
        MaxRtrAdvInterval 10;
        Prefix 2001:638:500:101::/64 {
                AdvOnLink on;
                AdvAutonomous on;
                AdvRouterAddr on;
        };
};
```

For more information about configuration options and runtime parameters please refer to the manpage radvd(8).

4.2 The Domain Name System

4.2.1 Overview of the DNS

DNS, the Domain Name System for the Internet, is a pretty complex set of functions and services which can provide a reliable translation service from names (FQDNs) to addresses (IPv4 and IPv6) and from addresses to names, as well as for particular support functions for specific applications (like MX for routing of electronic mail, supporting ISATAP, NAT-PT).

Implementation of DNS services for a particular (set of) domain(s) requires the operation of Name Servers (master and slave servers: those machines which manage, maintain and hold the relevant parts of the distributed nameservice database) and a method for communicating with the clients. On the client side the functional entity is a resolver or a resolver library, which accepts the query requests from an application program and then talks to the name servers on behalf of the application. In general the query requests made by applications will be for either forward or reverse domain name lookups.

4.2.1.1 Forward DNS:

The forward DNS service provides name-based identification and access to the various components accessible on an internet, by supplying a destination IP address.

These components to be addressed are individual hosts, particular interfaces on a network, services accessible for end users and the like.

4.2.1.2 Reverse DNS:

This service provides the translation of numeric IP addresses (IPv4 or IPv6) back to meaningful names for "human consumption", as well as for debugging tools and some (weak) security facilities.

Reverse DNS is some sort of "inverse" function to the forward DNS service, although the information returned upon a particular reverse DNS lookup is not necessary consistent with the content of the corresponding forward name.

Depending on the point of view, this can be seen as a flaw or as a necessary degree of freedom in managing an internet.

4.2.1.3 Implementation:

DNS is implemented as a distributed database with "weak" replication mechanisms. The term "weak" refers to the fact that the replicas are updated across the network, according to predefined schedules and/or trigger and notification mechanisms. This approach can result in some delay in the update process which can (sometimes) become noticeable for the end users.

The master copy of DNS data for a particular domain is stored and maintained in a zone file at the Primary Name Server to which a domain has been delegated. Note that a particular host (a name server) can support many different domains at the same time, both as a master and as a slave name server for distinct domains.

In order to maintain consistency, the terms "Master Server" (or simply "master") and "Slave Server" (or "slave") are used. For most aspects the term "Master Server" is equivalent to the (traditional) notion of a "Primary Name Server", and the term "Slave Server" is equivalent to "Secondary Name Server". Explaining the subtle implementation differences that were introduced in BIND for version 9, which led to the change in terminology is beyond the scope of this book.

4.2.1.4 DNS and IPv6

In order to ensure proper operation of the whole system, the types of data stored in the database (RRs: resource records) and the flow of information between the servers and the clients (resolvers) need careful attention. One of the most important aspects here is that there is no "fixed" relationship between the types of records stored in the database (e.g. type A for an IPv4 address, type AAAA for an IPv6 address) and the transport protocol used to send data back and forth between name servers and between name servers and a resolver (IPv4 or IPv6).

Indeed, it is perfectly normal these days to already store IPv6-related data in some zones (in the distributed database), but to still use IPv4 to submit queries, perform recursion (also known as "tree-walk") and return the results. Also, most of the zone transfers between slave servers and a master server actually use IPv4 (TCP) for the data transfer.

These considerations apply equally to communication with the root name servers and the TLD name servers.

Using this approach has the big advantage that the software in the existing system of nameservers (root, TLD, second level domains) requires very little change. In order to preserve the stability of the DNS for the Internet, the community is reasonably reluctant to embark on big or hurried upgrade projects.

The big disadvantage of this approach is the fact that end systems (usually hosts) typically still need an IPv4 protocol stack to talk to the DNS, even if the applications would already be able to use IPv6 exclusively. If this dual-stack method is not appropriate, then a more complex system of resolvers and (forwarding or translating) name servers needs to be deployed. This can take care of the continued IPv4 address space consumption but adds complexity, and sometimes single points of failure, to the whole systems.

4.2.2 DNS Service for 6NET

Given the background described above, it was obvious that 6NET needed to use IPv6 as the transport protocol as widely as possible during the life-cycle of the project. (See Appendix A2 for a snap-shot of systems used to provide name services for 6NET). The overall aim of 6NET was to "go native" as early as possible. The network layer itself needed to be as stable as reasonably possible. This meant that routine operations, management, fault identification and repair needed be straight-forward. This required alignment and integration of the DNS service for 6NET with the existing IPv4-based Internet. This meant operation of DNS services on the top of IPv4 protocol stack, and completing the IPv6-based communication provisions.

In order to understand some of the decisions taken, it should be noted that DNS is *both* an application (in fact a distributed and replicated database which uses the basic network transport services IPv4 TCP/UDP and IPv6 TCP/UDP) and an essential support service for the operation and management of an IP-based internet.

Most of the partners in 6NET (NRENs, companies) either have a working DNS environment already at their disposal or can use the services of their "upstream" service providers (e.g. individual university partners can make use of the services of their NREN). Therefore the initial goal for a DNS service for 6NET was to take care of the operational requirements of the 6NET backbone.

4.2.2.1 Requirements

Those requirements were:

- Forward DNS service to provide name-based access to the various components of the network, to support the day-to-day operational and management tasks, as well as fault isolation and repair.
- Reverse DNS as a support function for routine management tasks. It is an essential support service for the network engineers, required to perform fault isolation and repair and configuration change management.

Reverse DNS is already essential for troubleshooting in the IPv4-based Internet that uses 32bit wide addresses. By convention those addresses are presented as a set of 4 decimal numbers, separated by dots (i.e. 131.130.1.11). It is even more essential in an IPv6-based Internet that uses 128bit wide addresses. By convention those addresses are written as a set of 4-digit hexadecimal character groups, separated by colons (i.e. 2001:628:402:0:8000::5).

4.2.2.2 Non-Goals

Given the fact that most of the project partners already do manage their own name space (e.g. domains like UniVie.ac.at or ACO.net, cisco.com, DANTE.org.uk,...) and address space (IPv4 and IPv6), no attempt is made to devise a new naming structure or DNS service to replace the existing structures. Rather the DNS service for 6NET is meant to complement the existing services and to extend the services where appropriate.

These boundary conditions limit the functionality of the DNS service for 6NET to the functionality which is actually needed during the implementation and acceptance phase, the early operational phase and the fault isolation and repair scenarios for the 6NET backbone. This includes access links to the partners and equipment connected directly to the backbone.

4.2.2.3 Implementation considerations

From an operational point of view, 6NET should "look and feel similar" to and be compatible with the logistics developed for GÉANT, because a considerably big number of persons and entities have to deal with both environments at the same time.

From an implementation point of view, the DNS service for 6NET was available when the new IPv6-based network were installed, configured and accepted. To achieve this goal, the environment which already exists in the NRENs and in GÉANT/DANTE was used to implement the DNS service for 6NET.

From a "corporate identity" point of view for the project (WebSite, mailing lists, etc.), activities had to be started even before the formal commencement date of 6NET.

4.2.3 DNS Service Implementation

4.2.3.1 Forward DNS Service for 6NET

Early activities and basic functionality

Towards the end of 2001 SURFNET went ahead and obtained the delegation of a domain name for the project, on behalf of the emerging 6NET Consortium

Actually two names were registered: sixnet.org and 6net.org and the basic DNS service for those domains were implemented by SURFNET.

Note that 6net.net had already been delegated to a different entity and is in no way related to 6NET.

While SURFNET has a professional environment in place to provide name services, maintaining both the master and the slave name server within the same operational environment is not the optimal solution.

Several other NRENS joined in to provide secondary name service (see Appendix A2). Those name servers have to be accessible with IPv4 transport (for compatibility reasons) and IPv6 transport.

In due course GRNET requested participation in this effort. While it was not necessary, or even useful, to have as many slave nameservers as NRENs involved, GRNET seemed to be a special case since GRNET's connection to the 6NET core was implemented as a tunnelled link. Thus it was proposed, at least for the initial phase, to add a machine in GRNET as an additional slave server.

The basic (prototype) service for the domains 6net.org and sixnet.org supported the consortium's website, mailing lists, and - in due course - other infrastructure functions.

The initial configuration for 6net.org and sixnet.org is as follows:

```
$ dig 6net.org. soa
        [ ... ]
;; ANSWER SECTION:
6net.org.                86400  IN SOA  zesbot.ipv6.surfnet.nl. ipv6.surfnet.nl.

;; AUTHORITY SECTION:
6net.org.                86400  IN      NS      zesbot.ipv6.surfnet.nl.
6net.org.                86400  IN      NS      ns.ipv6.uni-muenster.de.
6net.org.                86400  IN      NS      foo.grnet.gr.
6net.org.                86400  IN      NS      ns3.surfnet.nl.
6net.org.                86400  IN      NS      scsnms.switch.ch.

;; ADDITIONAL SECTION:
foo.grnet.gr.            3035   IN   A    194.177.210.211
foo.grnet.gr.            3035   IN   AAAA 2001:648:0:1000:194:177:210:211
ns3.surfnet.nl.          85835  IN   A    195.169.124.71
ns3.surfnet.nl.          85835  IN   AAAA 2001:610:1:800b:a00:20ff:fe9a:16eb
scsnms.switch.ch.        85835  IN   A    130.59.1.30
scsnms.switch.ch.        85835  IN   A    130.59.10.30
scsnms.switch.ch.        254    IN   AAAA 2001:620::1
zesbot.ipv6.surfnet.nl.  85835  IN   A    192.87.110.60
zesbot.ipv6.surfnet.nl.  85835  IN   AAAA 2001:610:508:110:2a0:c9ff:fedd:67e7
```

```
$ dig sixnet.org. soa
        [ ... ]
;; ANSWER SECTION:
sixnet.org.              86400  IN SOA  zesbot.ipv6.surfnet.nl. ipv6.surfnet.nl.

;; AUTHORITY SECTION:
sixnet.org.              86400  IN      NS      zesbot.ipv6.surfnet.nl.
sixnet.org.              86400  IN      NS      ns.ipv6.uni-muenster.de.
```

```
sixnet.org.                 86400   IN      NS      foo.grnet.gr.
sixnet.org.                 86400   IN      NS      ns3.surfnet.nl.
sixnet.org.                 86400   IN      NS      scsnms.switch.ch.

;; ADDITIONAL SECTION:
ns3.surfnet.nl.             81287   IN  A       195.169.124.71
ns3.surfnet.nl.             81287   IN  AAAA    2001:610:1:800b:a00:20ff:fe9a:16eb
zesbot.ipv6.surfnet.nl. 86400   IN  A       192.87.110.60
zesbot.ipv6.surfnet.nl. 86400   IN  AAAA    2001:610:508:110:2a0:c9ff:fedd:67e7
```

Support functions for network operations

Based on the experience gained in TEN-34, TEN-155 and GÉANT, DANTE has developed a formal naming scheme which encodes certain pieces of operational and management information into the FQDNs which are used to refer to individual systems and/or to individual interfaces on a particular system (router).

In particular, individual components of this naming system encode the country of a particular PoP location, a particular router in a PoP, a particular interface and the link information to connect to a PoP in a different country. As this system has proven to be very useful for such an environment (see the output of a traceroute command in GÉANT), it has been adopted to also label the components used to implement 6NET.

```
$ traceroute www.dante.org.uk
traceroute to www.dante.org.uk (193.63.211.4), 30 hops max, 38 byte packets
 1  Wien1.ACO.net (192.153.174.1)                 0.747 ms   0.203 ms   0.217 ms
 2  aconet.at1.at.geant.net (62.40.103.1)         0.393 ms   0.419 ms   0.377 ms
 3  at.ch1.ch.geant.net (62.40.96.2)             17.373 ms  17.341 ms  17.336 ms
 4  ch.fr1.fr.geant.net (62.40.96.30)            26.064 ms  26.041 ms  26.039 ms
 5  fr.uk1.uk.geant.net (62.40.96.90)            33.282 ms  33.303 ms  33.947 ms
 6  janet-gw.uk1.uk.geant.net (62.40.103.150) 33.369 ms  33.238 ms  33.219 ms
    [ ... ]
 12  zeta.dante.org.uk (193.63.211.4)             43.012 ms  40.986 ms  41.417 ms
```

This system requires the creation (and delegation) of subdomains in 6net.org to support the proposed naming structure. The well-defined (and well-known) ISO3166 2-letter country-codes are used to denote individual PoP locations.

Many of those subdomains in 6net.org have already been delegated to DANTE to support the development of the naming scheme for 6NET and the planning for the roll-out of the network. This approach allows pre-configuration of entries for those components for which the technical details (and the PoP location) have already been specified (by the end of March 2002).

Here is an example of such an initial delegation:

```
> dig uk.6net.org soa
[...]
```

```
;; QUESTION SECTION:
;uk.6net.org.                  IN      SOA

;; ANSWER SECTION:
uk.6net.org.              0            IN          SOA        dns.dante.org.uk.
hostmaster.dante.org.uk. 2003070202 86400 14400 172800 86400

;; AUTHORITY SECTION:
uk.6net.org.           86400   IN     NS      sixpack.ipv6.ja.net.
uk.6net.org.           86400   IN     NS      dns.dante.org.uk.
uk.6net.org.           86400   IN     NS      scsnms.switch.ch.

;; ADDITIONAL SECTION:
dns.dante.org.uk.      350175  IN     A       193.63.211.16
scsnms.switch.ch.      17830   IN     A       130.59.10.30
scsnms.switch.ch.      17830   IN     A       130.59.1.30
```

For a complete list of these domains (which might become delegated and populated in due course) refer to Appendix A1: "List of per PoP-Location Support Domains".

Again, much like for the basic DNS service, other NRENS provide secondary name service for those domains and to make them accessible by IPv6-based transport as soon as possible.

In addition to the "default" secondary name service provision by those partners, all NREN partners are urged to eventually implement secondary name service for their respective xx.6net.org domain (e.g. JANET for uk.6net.org., GARR for it.6net.org. and so on). The reason for this approach is to supply name service in close proximity, and to encourage the deployment of the technology and the dissemination of knowledge.

DNS root name server in 2004

By 2004 several root name severs were accessible in IPv6.

There were:

- B at 2001:478:65::53
- F at 2001:500::1035
- H at 2001:500:1::803f:235
- M at 2001:dc3::35

You can consult http://www.root-servers.org/ for updated information.

And we can hope to have IPv6 glue in the root file zone in 2004. Thus a DNS IPv6 only service is possible in the near future.

4.2.3.2 Reverse DNS Service for 6NET

Early experience with managing IPv6-based networks in the framework of 6Bone has proven that reverse DNS in an IPv6-based environment is, in principle, at least as essential and useful as it is for the traditional IPv4-based Internet.

From a software technology perspective, no changes to the name server software in itself are required in order to support the translation of literal IPv6 addresses into name strings. For both protocol families the same basic mechanisms and the same RR type are used: the PTR record. But the rules to convert a literal address to a lookup string are different!

IPv4 uses the decimal encoded external representation of an IPv4 address to build the lookup string, e.g.

Working with

```
131.130.1.11
```

Leads to an attempt to find a PTR record for

```
11.1.130.131.in-addr.arpa.
```

But IPv6 uses a nibble-based hexadecimal digit encoding which generates a much longer lookup string:

`2001:610:508:110:2a0:c9ff:fedd:67e7` becomes

```
7.e.7.6.d.d.e.f.f.f.9.c.0.a.2.0.0.1.1.0.8.0.5.0.0.1.6.0.1.0.0.2.ip6.arpa.
```

However, much like in the forward DNS environment, the same issues apply for the transport protocol(s). For legacy reasons IPv4 has still to be supported as the transport mechanism initially, being extended to allow IPv6 as the transport mechanism as soon as possible.

In reality, obtaining a delegation, properly configuring the name service and using the services for the IPv6 address to name translation is quite a bit more complicated:

- The strings that have to be maintained in the zone files are much longer than those for the IPv4 world (see the previous example);
- As the sTLA allocations made by the RIRs under the "bootstrap procedures" are not aligned on a nibble boundary , classless delegation mechanisms must be used to properly delegate the reverse zones;
- Initially the sub tree ipv6.int. in the DNS namespace was used to refer to the "reverse DNS for IPv6". Alas, the "int." TLD is reserved for organisations established under an international treaty or multi-national agreement - which is not really appropriate for reverse DNS in the IPv6 based Internet.

Efforts have already been started to move that support function back to the "arpa." TLD - into the ip6.arpa. subtree. This migration has already begun, but it is a complex and lengthy process because the "knowledge" about the subtree in the namespace (required for the generation of the lookup label) is hardcoded into the resolver libraries.

In 2004, the migration should be finished, thus we only consider the ip6.arpa subtree.

```
$ dig ip6.arpa soa
[ … ]
;; ANSWER SECTION:
ip6.arpa.                  0          IN          SOA          dns1.icann.org.
hostmaster.icann.org. 2003080400 3600 1800 604800 10800


;; AUTHORITY SECTION:
ip6.arpa.               172800  IN      NS      ns.ripe.net.
ip6.arpa.               172800  IN      NS      ns.apnic.net.
ip6.arpa.               172800  IN      NS      ns.icann.org.
```

```
ip6.arpa.               172800  IN      NS      tinnie.arin.net.

;; ADDITIONAL SECTION:
ns.ripe.net.            101778  IN      A       193.0.0.193
ns.icann.org.           65365   IN      A       192.0.34.126
tinnie.arin.net.        2331    IN      A       63.146.182.189
ns.ripe.net.            110559  IN      AAAA    2001:610:240:0:53::193
```

By the end of March 2002, none of the name servers for ip6.arpa. were accessible with IPv6 as the transport protocol, but at least 3 of the name servers for ip6.int. seem to be IPv6-enabled.

In 2004, there is now one name server of ip6.arpa accessible in IPv6.

For a while implementing both reverse subtrees should be considered. How this is to be done can be deducted from the following example which refers to the RIPE NCC's address aggregate:

```
$ dig 7.0.1.0.0.2.ip6.arpa. soa
        [ ... ]
;; QUESTION SECTION:
;7.0.1.0.0.2.ip6.arpa.          IN      SOA

;; ANSWER SECTION:
7.0.1.0.0.2.ip6.arpa.   0       IN      SOA     ns.ripe.net. ops.ripe.net.
2004020901 43200 7200 1209600 7200

;; AUTHORITY SECTION:
7.0.1.0.0.2.ip6.arpa.   431653  IN      NS      ns.ripe.net.
7.0.1.0.0.2.ip6.arpa.   431653  IN      NS      ns3.nic.fr.
7.0.1.0.0.2.ip6.arpa.   431653  IN      NS      sec1.apnic.net.
7.0.1.0.0.2.ip6.arpa.   431653  IN      NS      sec3.apnic.net.
7.0.1.0.0.2.ip6.arpa.   431653  IN      NS      sunic.sunet.se.
7.0.1.0.0.2.ip6.arpa.   431653  IN      NS      auth03.ns.uu.net.
7.0.1.0.0.2.ip6.arpa.   431653  IN      NS      tinnie.arin.net.
7.0.1.0.0.2.ip6.arpa.   431653  IN      NS      munnari.oz.au.

;; ADDITIONAL SECTION:
ns.ripe.net.            98853   IN      A       193.0.0.193
ns3.nic.fr.             82089   IN      A       192.134.0.49
sec1.apnic.net.         135878  IN      A       202.12.29.59
sec3.apnic.net.         411     IN      A       202.12.28.140
sunic.sunet.se.         82899   IN      A       192.36.125.2
auth03.ns.uu.net.       51944   IN      A       198.6.1.83
tinnie.arin.net.        10217   IN      A       63.146.182.189
munnari.oz.au.          109009  IN      A       128.250.22.2
munnari.oz.au.          109009  IN      A       128.250.1.21
ns.ripe.net.            107633  IN      AAAA    2001:610:240:0:53::193
```

```
ns3.nic.fr.                269321   IN        AAAA     2001:660:3006:1::1:1
```

The goal for the early operations phase of 6NET is to strongly encourage all the participants in the 6NET project to get the proper reverse delegations for their sTLAs in place - both in ip6.int. (for supporting older client versions) and in ip6.arpa. (to comply with the more stable solution).

4.2.3.3 DNSSEC

DNSSEC is a protocol extension of DNS based on cryptographic tools (keys and signatures). DNSSEC protect the DNS data and transactions. DNSSEC takes full advantage of the hierarchical structure of the DNS: the zones are secured locally, but they can also become a part of a more global scheme, where chains of trust are built to allow a zone to authenticate the keys of its children zones, as well as to allow a zone to be authenticated by its parent zone.

Delay of this activity

Originally, we anticipated the implementation of DNSSEC in the 6NET DNS infrastructure by the end of year 1. At the time when this schedule was made, the DNSSEC specification was considered to be nearly finished and expected to move through the IETF standardisation process quickly. Later, the DNSEXT working group of the IETF started a major revision of the specification to address a number of scalability and management issues. As a consequence, it was decided to postpone the DNSSEC related activity of WP3 to the end of March 2004.

Deployment Plan

This focuses on the planned action for testing DNSSEC when the updated software versions become available, during 2004.

DNSSEC will be deployed in 6NET. As a minimum, DNSSEC will be applied to the inverse address mapping of the 6NET address space 2001:0798::/40 in the manner describer bellow. If time permits, this will be extended to the 6net.org zone, which is more interesting as it contains more non-trivial delegations (i.e., delegations to different organizations).

- All authoritative name servers for the zones 8.9.7.0.1.0.0.2.ip6.arpa. and 8.9.7.0.1.0.0.2.ip6.int. and their sub-zones run a DNSSEC-capable name server.
- The administrators of the top-level zones of these DNS subtrees generate at least one key per zone ("zone-signing keys") and sign the zone contents with it. When they are transmitted to all participants in a secure manner, the public parts of these keys establish a "secure entry point" to those particular sub-trees. This step is necessary as long as DNSSEC is not deployed all the way down from the root of the DNS.
- The organizations that want to be able to verify the signatures on the resource records of these zones must install DNSSEC-capable caching servers and establish secure communications between the caches and the stub-resolvers. They must obtain and install authenticated copies of the public keys described above to establish the secure entry points.
- Each sub-zone must maintain its own set of zone-signing keys and communicate them to their parent zone through an authenticated channel to establish a secure delegation.

The procedures for key management in the DNSSEC framework have not yet been fully established. This area of work is considered to be out of scope for 6NET. Therefore, only a minimal set of key management procedures will be established in 6NET, consisting of :

- proper generation of keying material (e.g. use of a decent random number generator)
- transmission of public keys over authenticated channels only (e.g. by using the PGP web-of-trust that has already been established among 6NET participants)

- manual key roll-overs

More sophisticated key management functions may be implemented if the DNSSEC-specific guidelines become available in time.

Note : there are two types of DNSSEC Key : zone-signing-key (ZSK) that signed all RR of the zone and key-signing key (KSK) that signed only the KEY RR. Only the KSK is transmitted to the parent zone. This permit to do an easier key rollover: you can change the ZSK without change the KSK.

In special case when there is only one Key: it's a ZSK and this Key is transmitted to the parent zone.

4.2.3.4 Internationalizing Domain Names in Applications (IDNA)

IDNA is described in the RFC 3490 [RFC3490] and contains a mechanism called Internationalizing Domain Names in Applications (IDNA). With IDNA, applications can use certain ASCII name labels to represents non-ASCII name. IDNA doesn't have impact on 6NET DNS structure. From RFC3490 : "*In particular, IDNA does not depend on any changes to DNS servers, resolvers, or protocol elements, because the ASCII name service provided by the existing DNS is entirely sufficient for IDNA.*"

Thus IDNA is transparent for the DNS transport.

4.3 DHCPv6

Despite the existence of stateless autoconfiguration for IPv6 (RFC 2462), there is still a need for DHCP in IPv6. DHCP can be a complement to the stateless autoconfiguration where it can supply hosts with DNS, NTP and other configuration data. DHCP can also take care of address allocations, and replace stateless autoconfiguration completely.

Using the same address allocation system as DHCPv4 for IPv6 would mean that 2^{64} addresses are available per link. Thus a stripped down "lightweight" version of DHCPv6 (stateless DHCPv6) was also developed but this is in fact a different protocol to DHCPv6. However, it is based on DHCPv6 in order to save design and implementation time.

4.3.1 Using DHCP Together With Stateless Autoconfiguration

A typical host will need to configure at least IP addresses and a recursive DNS server address in order to be used. The major problem of the current stateless autoconfiguration, is that it does not supply a DNS server address. The DNS server address might be a bit more stable, but it's still a problem to find and configure the correct address. People have suggested various techniques for configuring this, DHCP being but one of them (the others included multicasting and anycasting).

DHCP was assessed as a good solution, since a client might also need other configuration data like domain search path, NTP servers etc. Some have claimed that DHCP is too complex, but a DHCP server in an environment with stateless autoconfiguration does not need to support IP address delegations, and does not need any per-client state. There are also other features that could be omitted in a DHCP server if necessary. Also note that even if the client has an address from stateless autoconfiguration, it might wish to request additional addresses from DHCP, some possible reasons are described in the next section.

4.3.2 Using DHCP Instead of Stateless Autoconfiguration

In this case we not only wish to configure DNS etc. as described in previous section, but also IP addresses. There are several reasons one might want to do this. Stateless autoconfiguration as described in RFC 2462 creates addresses based on interface identifiers that are typically EUI-64 identifiers. On e.g. Ethernet this will be created from the MAC address on the hosts Ethernet interface. This means that the IPv6 address will depend on the physical Ethernet interface. One might wish for a host to have a stable address independent of which Ethernet interface is used though, and there are also some privacy concerns. It can also be a pain to have meaningful PTR records in the DNS for reverse lookups. DHCP can help to fulfill all of these requirements.

4.3.3 Overview of the Standardisation of DHCPv6

Several years ago, the IETF took on the initiative to develop a version of DHCP for IPv6 (DHCPv6). The specification became a Dynamic Host Configuration working group (DHC WG) work item and has been under development in that working group since the initiative was started.

There are a couple of reasons for the long development and approval process for DHCPv6. While DHCPv6 is similar to DHCPv4 [RFC2131], [RFC2132] in its goals and scope, all of the details of the protocol operation are different. For example, because the configuration of an interface with multiple IPv6 addresses is a fundamental feature of IPv6, DHCPv6 can manage the assignment of multiple addresses, potentially assigned over a period of time. In contrast, DHCPv4 can only assign a single address to an interface. Dhcpv6 also addresses several deficiencies in the DHCPv4 protocol, including the operation of relay agents and security.

Another reason for the long development period for DHCPv6 is that there has been some debate in the IETF about the utility and role for DHCPv6, so the specification has been tracking a moving target.

There have been many significant changes to the DHCPv6 specification in the revisions of the DHCPv6 Internet-Draft. Implementations of earlier drafts will not interoperate with the final specification as documented in RFC 3315 [RFC3315].

One question about the use of DHCPv6 is the specification of stateless address autoconfiguration. For IPv4, the primary use of DHCP is the assignment of IP addresses to hosts. In IPv6, a host can use stateless address autoconfiguration to obtain its IPv6 addresses independent of any server-based address assignment mechanism. However, a host that has used stateless address autoconfiguration may still require additional configuration information, such as a list of addresses for DNS servers. Thus, "Stateless DHCPv6", specified in RFC 3736 [RFC3736], is used to provide these additional configuration parameters.

4.3.3.1 DHCPv6 Options

DHCPv6 uses "options" in the variable format section of a DHCPv6message. Several options, necessary for the operation of the protocol, are defined in section 22 of the DHCPv6 specification (RFC 3315). Several other options have been in development and are described in the remainder of this section.

IPv6 Prefix Options for DHCPv6

The "Prefix Option" is used for prefix delegation in DHCPv6. An ISP uses prefix delegation to configure a CPE device (typically a router) with one or more prefixes to use in the customer's network. This option is specified in RFC 3633 [RFC3633].

DSTM Options for DHCPv6

There are three dual-stack transition mechanism (DSTM) [Bou05], options for DHCPv6. The first two options are used to assign IPv4 addresses to a host using DSTM and to give the address of a DSTM tunnel endpoint. These options are documented in [RB05]

DSTM Ports Option for DHCPv6

The third option DSTM DHCPv6 specifies the ports to be used by a host for IPv4-mapped IPv6 addresses, and is documented in [Shi05]. The progress of all three DSTM options will be synchronized with the progress of the DSTM specification through the IETF.

DNS Configuration options for DHCPv6

There are two DNS configuration options documented in RFC 3646 [RFC3646]. The first passes the IP addresses of a list of DNS servers to a host. The second option passes a list of domains to be used as a domain search list by the host.

NIS/NIS+ Configuration Options for DHCPv6

There are four DHCPv6 options for NIS and NIS+ configuration, which are documented in [RFC3898]. Two of the options provide a list of NIS servers and an NIS domain to a host, and two options provide a list of NIS+ servers and an NIS+ domain.

Time Configuration Options for DHCPv6

There are two DHCPv6 options for time configuration. One option provides a list of NTP servers to the host and is described in RFC 4075 [RFC4075]. The other option provides time zone information to the host and is currently specified by the Internet Draft draft-ietf-dhc-dhcpv6-opt-tz-00 [Kal03].

Client Preferred Prefix option for DHCPv6

The client preferred prefix option allows a client to indicate the prefixes form which it would prefer to have its addresses assigned. This option is documented in [Vij03], and is still under discussion by the DHC WG.

Load Balancing for DHCPv6

DHCPv6 provides for the operation of multiple servers. Under normal circumstances, all servers respond to each request for service and the requesting client picks a server for service. The Internet Draft "Load Balancing for DHCPv6" [Vol02] describes a mechanism through which multiple cooperating DHCPv6 servers can determine which server should respond to a specific client. The DHCPv6 load balancing mechanism was submitted to the IESG for approval as a Proposed Standard in January 2003.

4.3.3.2 Guide About the Stateless DHCPv6 server

The DHCPv6 service of providing configuration information without address assignment is called "stateless DHCPv6", because the DHCPv6 server need not maintain any dynamic state about individual clients while providing the service. Stateless DHCPv6 requires only a subset of the DHCPv6 protocol and is significantly easier to implement and deploy. It is anticipated that stateless DHCPv6 will be the primary way in which DHCPv6 is used in IPv6 networks.

Stateless DHCPv6 may be provided through centralized DHCPv6 servers, similar to the deployment of DHCPv4 service. Because stateless DHCPv6 is a relatively simple protocol, it may be provided by a CPE router, using, for example, DNS configuration information configured by the CPE administrator or obtained through DHCPv6 from the ISP. Stateless DHCPv6 service may also be provided by DNS servers, which would respond directly to hosts with DNS configuration information.

The requirements for implementing stateless DHCPv6 are documented in draft-droms-dhcpv6-stateless-guide [Dro02]. This Internet Draft lists the messages and services that must be implemented in servers and hosts to provide stateless DHCPv6 service.

4.3.4 Overview of the DHCPv6 Specifications

The architecture and message exchanges in DHCPv6 are similar to DHCPv4. A DHCPv6 client initiates a DHCPv6 transaction by first locating a DHCPv6 server, and then making a request for configuration information from that server. As in DHCPv4, an IPv6 address is assigned to a host with a lease, and the host can initiate a transaction with the DHCPv6 server to extend the lease on an address.

A DHCPv6 client uses a link-local address when exchanging messages with a DHCPv6 server. To avoid the requirement that a DHCPv6 server be attached to every link, DHCPv6 relay agents forward DHCPv6 messages between hosts and off-link servers. The mechanism through which relay agents forward DHCPv6 messages allows for the use of multiple relay agents between a host and a server. Relay agent options, through which a relay agent can provide additional information to the DHCPv6 server, are included as a design feature in the base DHCPv6 specification.

The address assignment mechanism in DHCPv6 allows for the assignment of multiple addresses to an interface, and allows for the dynamic assignment of additional addresses over time. Addresses are assigned to a host with a lease, a preferred lifetime and a valid lifetime. The mechanism can support renumbering through the assignment of new addresses whose lifetimes overlap existing addresses to allow for graceful transition. Addresses are grouped together for management into an "identity association", which the host and server exchange for address assignment. DHCPv6 can also be used for assignment of temporary addresses [RFC3041].

Each DHCPv6 host has a "DHCP Unique Identifier" (DUID), which remains unchanged throughout the lifetime of the host. Servers use this DUID to identify hosts reliably even if the host roam between links.

Security is included in the DHCPv6 base specification. The security mechanism uses a framework similar to the security mechanism for DHCPv4 defined in RFC 3118 [RFC3118]. In addition, security for messages exchanged between relay agents and servers is provided by the use of IPSec.

A DHCPv6 server can trigger a message exchange with a host through the Reconfigure message. Security is included for the Reconfigure message to prevent intruder attacks against DHCPv6 clients.

Stateless DHCPv6 uses a two-message exchange between a client and a server. To obtain configuration information without address assignment through stateless DHCPv6, the host sends an Information-request message. The DHCPv6 server responds with the requested configuration information. The DHCPv6 server can be configured with host-specific configuration, to allow for customized configuration of different classes of hosts. Stateless DHCPv6 service requires only a subset of the mechanism and messages of the full DHCPv6 protocol, and is easier to implement and deploy.

An ISP wishing to delegate a prefix or prefixes to a customer can use the prefix delegation option. To use prefix delegation, the CPE initiates a DHCPv6 transaction with the ISP edge router. The ISP router selects the prefix or prefixes to be assigned to the customer, through the ISP's policy or customer provisioning process, and returns those prefixes to the CPE. The prefixes are then available for use in the customer's network. For example, the customer may be assigned a /48 prefix, which is delegated to the CPE through DHCPv6 prefix delegation. The CPE can then assign /64 prefixes from the delegated /48 prefix to links in the customer's network.

4.3.4.1 Differences between DHCP for IPv4 and IPv6

There are many differences, since DHCP IPv6 is a completely new protocol. We only list some of the more obvious differences here.

- Hosts always have a link local address that can be used in requests (in IPv4 0.0.0.0 is used as source address)
- Uses special multicast addresses for relay agents and servers
- No compatibility with BOOTP, since no BOOTP support on IPv6.
- Simplified two-message exchange for simple configuration cases
- A client can request multiple IPv6 addresses
- Client can send multiple unrelated requests to the same or different servers
- There is a reconfigure message where servers can tell clients to reconfigure. This feature is optional.

4.3.5 DHCPv6 Implementations Overview

We found in general, that because of significant changes throughout the lifetime of the DHCPv6 specification, only the most recent implementations will likely be close to compatible with the final specification.

After some investigation we found the implementations listed below. We only make a brief description of each implementation. A test report of the DHCP implementations used in 6NET is available in Deliverable 3.2.3 [D3.2.3].

1. http://www.hycomat.co.uk/dhcp/dhcpv62809.tar.bz2
2. http://www.hycomat.co.uk/dhcp/kamedhcpv6linport.tar.gz
3. http://www.hycomat.co.uk/dhcp/dhcpv6.tgz
4. http://www.cs.ipv6.lancs.ac.uk/ftp-archive/Code/Alpha/DHCPv6/
5. ftp://ftp.kame.net/pub/kame/snap/
6. HP-UX implementation
7. Motorola experimental implementation
8. Cisco DHCPv6 in the IOS

1. dhcp62809.tar.bz2

The dhcp62809 is based on the ISC DHCP3 release candidate 10. The work is located under dhcp6/work.linux-2.2. Only one README file. The development seems to have ceased since September 2001.

2. kamedhcpv6linport.tar.gz

This program is based on the KAME proof-of-concept DHCPv6 server/client. The server can distribute only the DNS (server address and domain name) and Time-zone information. However The implemented client can receive these information, but does not install them in the system configuration files. This implementation is based on a subset of draft 15.

3. dhcpv6.tgz

This program is written by Dhawal Kumar in 1999/2000 for the INRIA IPv6 stack to test the DHCPv6 concept. It is based on draft 15.

4. dhcpv6-1.0.tar.gz

This program was written by Yunzhou Li in 1996 (Very old). It was supported by Digital Equipment Corp. (DEC), University of New Hampshire (UNH) and National University of Singapore (NUS). This is also a test program as it is stated in the description: "*The purpose of this implementation is to verify the feasibility of DHCPv6 and Extensions for DHCPv6 protocols. Hopefully, the code can be useful for the further development of these two protocols and other research on IPv6.*" The program is based on the draft 8 therefore it is extremely outdated.

5. KAME

The current KAME dhcp implementation is substantially different the earlier proof-of-concept dhcpv6 implementation. Earlier the goal was to test the best DNS configuration for IPv6. One candidate was the DHCPv6. For testing this concept earlier a very lightweight DHCPv6 was developed and eventually dropped. The current KAME implementation is based on the draft version 26 ofDHCPv6, but does not implement the full DHCPv6 draft. According the authors: "*dhcp6c is incomplete and violates DHCPv6 protocol spec, in several aspects. In particular, it does not handle address allocation via DHCPv6. This is, however, rather intentional; the authors believe stateless address autoconfiguration is enough for IPv6 and will not implement the stateful method in the future.*". It implements only prefix distribution, DNS options, rapid commit and site identifier. It is using the All_DHCP_Relay_Agents_and_Servers or the DHCP_Anycast address.

6. HPUX implementation

Available at:

http://www.software.hp.com/cgi-bin/swdepot_parser.cgi/cgi/displayProductInfo.pl?productNumber=DHCPv6

HPUX DHCPv6 supports the following features:

- IPv6 address allocation
- Multiple IP addresses for an interface
- Reconfiguration messages
- Relay mechanism
- Request for configuration parameters from different servers within the same domain
- DNS server address
- DNS suffix
- NTP server address
- NIS domain name
- NIS server address
- NIS+ client domain name
- NIS+ server address
- SLP DA address and its scope
- SLP service scope
- Timezone
- IPv6 address allocation
- New message types
- Multiple IP addresses for an interface
- Reconfiguration messages
- Relay mechanism
- Request for configuration parameters from different servers within the same domain

It seems to be the most complete implementation at the time of writing.

7. Motorola implementation

This implementation is targeted to Linux to test address delegation of DHCPv6.

8. Cisco DHCPv6 in the IOS

The Cisco DHCPv6 implementation is part of IOS, and runs in Cisco routers. It is based on the -28 revision of the DHCPv6 specification (which has been accepted by the IESG as a Proposed Standard), the prefix delegation RFC 3633 [RFC3633] and the DNS configuration options RFC 3646 [RFC3646].

The Cisco DHCPv6 client and server are specifically intended as a prefix delegation solution and do not implement the entire DHCPv6 protocol. At present, Cisco's DHCPv6 implements prefix delegation, the rapid-commit mechanism, stateless DHCPv6 ("DHCPv6-lite") and the following options:

- Client Identifier option
- Server Identifier option
- Option Request option
- Preference option

- Status Code Option
- Rapid Commit option
- Identity Association for Prefix Delegation option (IA_PD option)
- IA_PD Prefix option
- Domain Name Server option
- Domain Search List option

Each interface can be independently configured to run a DHCPv6 server or client. For example, a CPE router can be configured to use a DHCPv6 client on its interface to the link from an ISP for prefix delegation, and configured to provide DHCPv6 service on its interfaces to other links. Prefixes can be delegated to a client through either a manually configured binding for the client or dynamically from a pool of available prefixes.

A prefix delegated to a client may be used as a pool of prefixes for assignment to other interfaces. For example, if a CPE is delegated 2001:DB8:0:1::/48, the client can assign 2001:DB8:0:1:0::/64, 2001:DB8:0:1:1::/64, etc., to interfaces on links inside the customer premises.

Chapter 5

Integration and Transition

In this chapter we look at the problem of IPv6 integration and transition with existing IPv6 networks. Expanding IPv6 functionality from a small infrastructure to a large site network can be a complex and difficult venture. But if it is planned effectively, the deployment can be done in a phased and controlled manner that maximises the chances of a smooth service introduction. For a large site there are a lot of different requirements, and different conditions which make it necessary to employ various transition mechanisms according to the peculiarities of, for example, a given subnet, wireless or mobile environment or dial-in technology. In this chapter we explain which potential options and techniques exist to integrate IPv6 into a site network, which solution is appropriate for any special kind of network infrastructure and of course how exactly one has to set up and configure these techniques. Where possible, we also point to existing (current) problems and interoperability issues, for example in running IPv4 and IPv6 in parallel or having IPv6-only hosts which still need to be able to communicate with IPv4-only hosts on occasion. Numerous transitioning mechanisms and procedures are described including tunnelling methods such as IPv6-in-IPv4 tunnelling, Tunnel Brokers, ISATAP, 6to4, Teredo and translation methods such as NAT-PT, SIIT, SOCKS, ALGs and Bump-in-the-Stack/API.

An overview of security issues in transition is available as an Internet Draft that was originally produced as a result of 6NET experience [DKS05]. The security issues of individual transition mechanisms are discussed in Chapter 9.

5.1 Problem Statement

With an IPv6 host or local network configured, getting connectivity to the global IPv6 Internet is vital if you wish to communicate with other IPv6 systems. Today, this is usually accomplished either natively or, more commonly, with an IPv6-in-IPv4 tunnelling technique using either manual or automatic tunnel configuration methods.

The academic participants of the 6NET project are mostly fortunate enough to have native connectivity to their National Research and Education Networks (NRENs) and from there to a globally connected native IPv6 network (spanning GÉANT, and links to Abilene in the US and WIDE in Japan). Other sites may not be so lucky; for them a tunnelling mechanism is the only realistic option for IPv6 connectivity.

IPv6-only deployments are rare, especially in Europe, but are an interesting exercise with a view to the end game of IPv6 deployment. However, the practical reality is that sites deploying IPv6 will not transition to IPv6-only, but transition to a state where they support both IPv4 and IPv6 (dual-stack). The dual-stack environment then allows IPv6-only devices to be introduced, as a site slowly phases out IPv4. For this reason, translation mechanisms between IPv4 and IPv6 systems are less frequently required; however we discuss transition mechanisms, from viewpoints of the network, transport and application layers at which translation may be applied.

IPv6 can be introduced to a site in three basic ways, categorized into how connectivity of each system to the IPv6 Internet is achieved and how the network and hosts themselves have to be enhanced to make IPv6 possible. We call these categories "dual stack", "additional IPv6 infrastructure" (which generally involves IPv6-in-IPv4 tunnelling) and "IPv6-only networking". In a large-scale network one will never only use one technique or another. It is much more likely that the best way for getting systems connected within a site has to be decided for each subnet or even each host anew, which leads to the deployment of many different techniques according to the different demands and peculiarities of a certain part of the network. This chapter focuses on the theoretical description of each of the three general transition scenarios "dual stack", "additional IPv6 infrastructure" and "IPv6-only networks". Descriptions of special transition mechanisms as they come into place within those scenarios are included in the next chapter.

Once the internal networking is determined, the next step is to arrange external connectivity for the whole site, which involves external routing issues and is really only possible either natively or via some tunnelling mechanism. With IPv6, the choice of an external connectivity method will determine the IPv6 addressing prefix within the site. A site prefix is usually (as recommended by the RIRs) a /48 prefix, which allows 16 bits of subnet address space for the /64 subnets.

5.1.1 Dual Stack

One of the conceptually easiest ways of introducing IPv6 to a network is called the "dual stack mechanism", as described in [NG05], which is an update of RFC 2893 [RFC2893]. Using this method a host or a router is equipped with both IPv4 and IPv6 protocol stacks in the operating system (though this may typically be implemented in a hybrid way). Each such node, called an "IPv4/IPv6 node", is configured with both IPv4 and IPv6 addresses. It can therefore both send and receive datagrams belonging to both protocols and thus communicate with every node in the IPv4 and IPv6 network. This is the simplest and most desirable way for IPv4 and IPv6 to coexist and is most likely to be the next step in a network's evolution in general, before a wider transition to an IPv6-only Internet can be achieved worldwide (in the long term future).

There are no real transition mechanisms to use within the dual stack scenario, as "Dual Stack" is a method to integrate IPv6 itself.

One challenge in deploying an IPv6/IPv4 Dual Stack network lies in configuring both internal and external routing for both protocols. If one has for example used OSPFv2 for intra site routing before adding IPv6 to the Layer 3 network one will either have to transition to a protocol, which is both IPv4 and IPv6-capable like IS-IS or be forced run one IS-IS or OSPFv3 in addition to OSPFv2. Since configuring IPv6 routing in a dual stack network is usually completely independent from the configuration of IPv4 routing the reader can refer to Chapter 6 for most of the issues concerning basic routing setup.

Another challenge lies in the interaction of the two protocols, and how this interaction is managed, given that a dual-stack network will (in an early stage of worldwide IPv6 deployment) generally be interacting with IPv4 external networks. An example is the deployment of email servers for SMTP, and how the MX servers are provisioned for both protocols by offering IPv4 or IPv6 reachability, and how failover is handled between the protocols.

5.1.2 Additional IPv6 Infrastructure (Tunnels)

By additional IPv6 infrastructure we mainly mean tunnelling techniques that one can use on top of the present IPv4 infrastructure without having to make any changes to the IPv4 routing or the routers. This method is often used where the complete infrastructure, or parts of it, is not yet capable of offering native IPv6 functionality. Therefore IPv6 traffic has to cross the existing IPv4 network, which is possible with several different tunnelling techniques described in the following sections. These techniques are often chosen as a first step to test the new protocol and to start integration of IPv6.

Tunnelling is also called encapsulation. It is a process by which information from one protocol is encapsulated inside the packet of another protocol, thus enabling the original data to be carried over the second protocol. This mechanism can be used when two nodes or networks that use the same protocol want to communicate over a network that uses another network protocol. The tunnelling process involves three steps: encapsulation, decapsulation, and tunnel management. It requires two tunnel endpoints, which in the general case are dual-stack IPv4/IPv6 nodes (usually routers), to handle the encapsulation and decapsulation. There will be performance issues associated with tunnelling, both for the latency in (en/de)capsulation and the additional bandwidth used, though the latter is usually marginal.

A tunnel can be configured in four different ways:

1. Router to router, which spans one segment of the end-to-end path between two hosts. This is probably the most common method
2. Host to router, which spans the first segment of the end-to-end path between two hosts, as may be found in the tunnel broker model (described later).
3. Host to host, which spans the entire end-to-end path between two hosts.
4. Router to host, which spans the last segment of the end-to-end path between two hosts.

Depending on what kind of setup is used, a tunnel might be "configured" (both sides need to be configured accordingly), "semi-configured" (only one side has to be configured, the other side acts as a gateway) or "automatic", where nearly nothing needs to be done for the two hosts to communicate via a tunnel.

5.1.3 IPv6-only Networks (Translation)

In IPv6-only networks communication between nodes is just that: IPv6-only. Communication between a node on the IPv6-only network and a remote node reachable only over IPv4 is not possible, because the hosts can only communicate using IPv6 at the network layer. This is where translation techniques come into place, which can operate at many different layers. We categorize translation techniques by the layer they may appear in, that is the network layer, the transport layer or the application layer.

In the network layer the header of a datagram is translated from IPv6 to IPv4 (or vice versa), which happens in the operating system of the originating host. In the transport layer the general mechanism is the use of a relay, which the data has to pass through. This relay is commonly a dual stack device that will translate and pass on datagrams between the different networks. In the application layer an "application layer gateway" (ALG) is used, e.g. a web proxy. While in the network and transport layer translating and relaying IPv4/IPv6 datagrams is mostly application independent, application layer gateways have to be set up for each and every application or service one wants to offer.

5.2 *Tunnelling Methods*

In this section we describe methods for carrying IPv6 over existing IPv4 networks, which invariably means using some kind of tunnelling mechanism, either manually or automatically configured.

5.2.1 Configured Tunnels

Configured tunnelling is defined in the update to RFC 2893 [NG05] as IPv6-over-IPv4 tunnelling where the IPv4 tunnel's endpoint address is determined by configuration information on the encapsulating node. Therefore the encapsulating node must keep information about all the tunnel endpoint addresses. These kinds of tunnels are point-to-point and need to be configured manually. For control of the tunnel paths, and to reduce the potential for tunnel relay denial-of-service attacks, manually configured tunnels can be advantageous over automatically configured tunnels.

Configured tunnels are best employed when providing external IPv6 connectivity to a whole network. There are not yet many providers who offer IPv6 in any way but if one has the possibility to get initial IPv6 connectivity from an already IPv6-connected site, one of the easiest, most stable and secure ways to get the IPv6 traffic routed to the (as yet) unconnected site is via an IPv6-in-IPv4 tunnel. One can even set up a BGP peering on that link, although if the tunnel is the only off-site link, BGP is not required unless the connecting site is interested in seeing the BGP routing information of its upstream provider. Usually static routes meet the requirements.

Within a site, configured IPv6-in-IPv4 tunnels can also be used if there is a part of the network that cannot (for whatever reason) be natively connected to the rest of the IPv6 topology. Since these kinds of tunnels have to be configured by hand this only makes sense if there is a requirement for just a few of those tunnels. There is no point in connecting a lot of different isolated hosts or subnets by a manually configured tunnel. There are other tunnelling methods specifically designed for this purpose, such as tunnel brokers, 6to4, Teredo or ISATAP (see below for more details on those). In sites that support IEEE 802.1q VLAN Layer 2 mechanisms, the VLANs can be used to carry IPv6 traffic between disparate subnets in the site, as described in [Cho04b].

Note that IPv6-in-IPv4 tunnels may be used for OSPFv3 routing but not with IS-IS as IS-IS is based on Layer 2 while IPv6-in-IPv4 tunnels are completely Layer 3. For IS-IS to work over a tunnelled link generic encapsulation (GRE tunnels [RFC2784]) can be used.

5.2.2 Tunnel Broker

Instead of manually configuring each tunnel endpoint it is possible to use executable scripts instead. This "automatic" alternative is called a "tunnel broker" and is presented in RFC 3053 [RFC3053].

Like manually configured tunnels, the tunnel broker is useful where a user has a dual-stack host in an IPv4-only network, and wishes to gain IPv6 connectivity. The basic philosophy of a tunnel broker is that it allows a user to connect to a web server, (optionally) enter some authentication details, and receive back a short script to run and establish an IPv6-in-IPv4 tunnel to the tunnel broker server.

The operation of a typical tunnel broker service is illustrated in Figure 5-1. The provider of a tunnel broker service needs to provide a web server available over IPv4 and a dual stack router capable of accepting automated setup commands to create new tunnels to client endpoints. It is possible that both functions can be served from one machine.

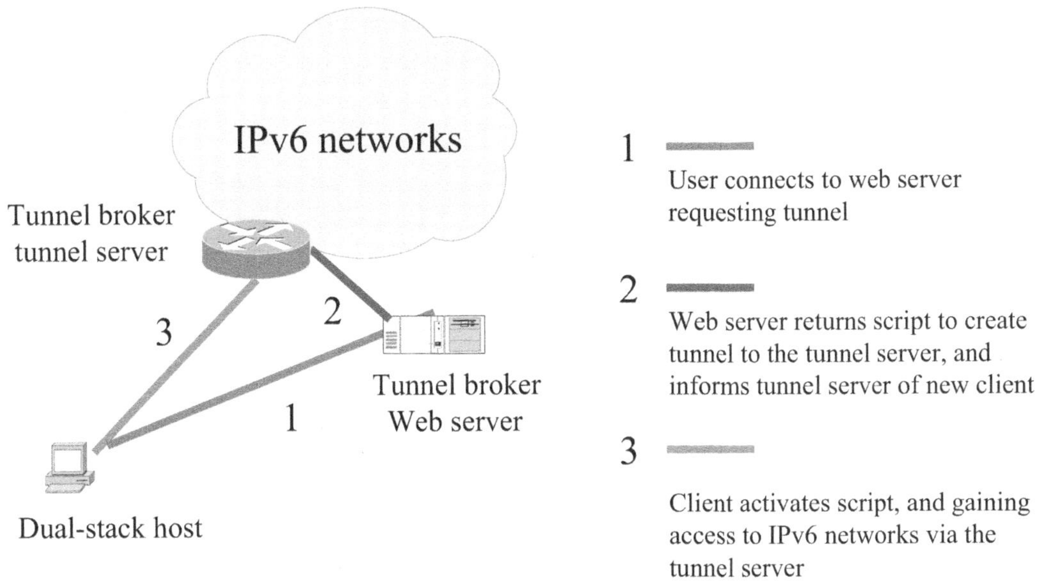

Figure 5-1 Tunnel broker components and setup procedure

A tunnel broker can be implemented in many ways and is not constrained to IPv6-in-IPv4 tunnels. Layer 2 or GRE tunnels may be used as well. The requirement for the service is that it needs to keep track of the tunnels created and whom they belong to. Ideally it should have some authentication to grant access to the service, but in practice early implementations have not required this. The Freenet6 service (http://www.freenet6.net) is perhaps best known, but being based in Canada is not ideal for use in European networks (the first hop to any destination would be thousands of miles away). SixXS (http://www.sixxs.com) is another example more suitable and available in Europe; ideally any ISP should offer local tunnel broker facilities for its users, if no native IPv6 service is present.

Tunnel brokers can serve subnet tunnels, as well as single host tunnels. In the former case the host obtaining the tunnel is in reality a router, and the mechanism for obtaining the tunnel can be more generic (using for example TSP, the tunnel setup protocol [BP05]), and may need specific functions to activate or deactivate the tunnel.

The tunnel broker service is generally easy to use for the client, but there are some concerns about the deployment of server systems, e.g. in security of access, and in reallocation of tunnels where clients use dynamic IPv4 addresses (as is typical behind commodity dialup). If using standard IPv6-in-IPv4 tunnelling, any intervening firewall must pass Protocol 41 to/from the tunnel server. Doing so, and without further control of the tunnelled traffic, a site administrator may be blissfully unaware of users on their site who use tunnel brokers, thus not creating any site demand for "proper" IPv6 deployment and possibly creating security holes which the administrator does not know about and therefore does not guard against.

Some tunnel broker implementations will handle clients with dynamically changing IPv4 addresses or that are behind IPv4 NATs. Such features are often highly desirable. Heartbeat features are often used for the former problem, while [BP05] offers a solution for the latter, negotiating a UDP-based encapsulation method that can work through a NAT. Use of TSP will need the client to run a special client however.

A tunnel broker is an important transition aid; it enables easy-to-use IPv6 network access, and we see a number of supported brokers used in the 6NET environment during the project. The tunnel brokers may be deployed by sites (universities) or by NRENs (as not every university will wish to run its own broker). If no broker is available to a national participant, remote brokers may be used, but doing so will naturally reduce the efficiency of the tunnelling, since the first IPv6 hop for the client will be in the (distant) remote network, even if the target is relatively local.

5.2.3 Automatic Tunnels

This type of tunnel mechanism has been one of the first to be developed and has since then mostly been replaced by more sophisticated mechanisms. It uses IPv4-compatible IPv6 addresses on the tunnel endpoints. The address of the recipient node is specified by the packet that is being encapsulated. This method can only be used on router-to-host and host-to-host communication since these are the only schemes where one tunnel endpoint is also the recipient. Due to the use of particular addresses it only works on IPv6 over IPv4 tunnelling and not vice versa.

Such automatic tunnelling has now been deprecated, and has been written out of the [NG05] update. One reason for that lies in the ad-hoc nature of connectivity that results, lacking structure in the IPv6 domain; solutions such as ISATAP or 6to4 (see below) are generally considered preferable. The authors of this book strongly advise not to use this technique anymore, even where implementations still exist.

5.2.4 6to4

The transition mechanism known as 6to4 [RFC3056] is a form of automatic router-to-router tunnelling that uses the IANA-assigned IPv6 prefix 2002::/16 to designate a site that participates in 6to4. It allows isolated IPv6 domains to communicate with other IPv6 domains with minimal configuration. An isolated IPv6 site will assign itself a prefix of 2002:V4ADDR::/48, where V4ADDR is the globally unique IPv4 address configured on the appropriate interface of the domain's egress router (see Figure 5-2). This prefix has exactly the same format as normal /48 prefixes and thus allows an IPv6 domain to use it like any other valid /48 prefix. In the scenario where 6to4 domains wish to communicate with other 6to4 domains, no tunnel configuration is needed. Tunnel endpoints are determined by the value of the global routing prefix of the IPv6 destination address contained in the IPv6 packet being transmitted, which includes the IPv4 address. In this scenario, an arbitrary number of 6to4 domains may communicate without the need for any tunnel configuration. Furthermore, the 6to4 routers do not need to run any exterior IPv6 routing protocol as IPv4 exterior routing performs the task instead.

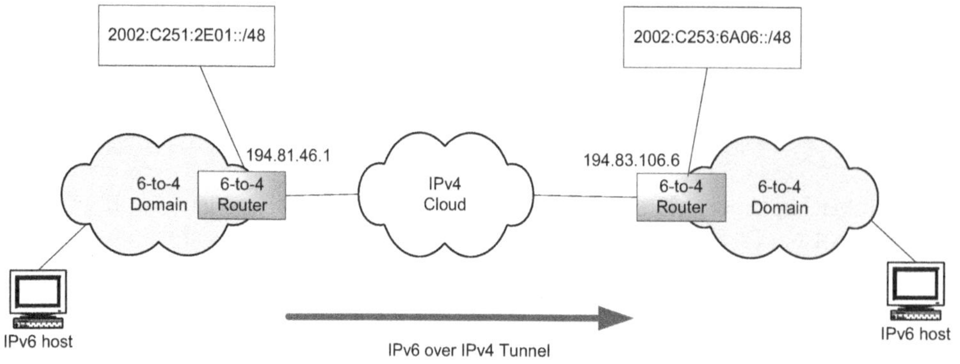

Figure 5-2 6to4 Service Overview

When 6to4 domains wish to communicate with non-6to4 IPv6 domains however, the situation is a little more complex. In this case, connectivity between the domains is achieved via a relay router, which is essentially a router that has at least one logical 6to4 interface and at least one native IPv6 interface. Unlike with the previous scenario, IPv6 exterior routing must be used. The relay router advertises the 6to4 2002::/16 prefix into the native IPv6 routing domain. In addition the relay router may advertise native IPv6 routes into its 6to4 connection. The relay router can be discovered using IPv4 anycast, as described in RFC 3068 [RFC3068].

Most ISPs/NRENs only advertise their 6to4 relay within their own network. There are very few "public" relays, in part due to the security concerns described below. Despite such concerns, and concerns over provision of multicast over 6to4, the protocol does offer a very convenient, automatic way for an IPv4 site to gain IPv6 connectivity.

The general use of 6to4 is as a mechanism for an IPv6 site border router with only IPv4 external connectivity to establish automatic connectivity to the IPv6 public Internet. Other methods (e.g. ISATAP or native IPv6 networking if available) can then be used inside the site. It can also be used on a host, but such usage is (we expect) rather less common and not originally intended.

5.2.5 6over4

6over4 is defined in RFC 2529 [RFC2529]. It interconnects isolated IPv6 hosts in a site through IPv6-in-IPv4 encapsulation without explicit tunnels. It uses IPv4 addresses as interface identifiers and creates a virtual link using an IPv4 multicast group with organization-local scope. IPv6 multicast addresses are mapped to IPv4 multicast addresses to allow neighbour discovery. The 6over4 method has fallen out of favour due to a number of reasons, including the general lack of IPv4 multicast support in site/ISP networks.

There have been a small number of implementations, including those by 3Com and Cisco, but practically no adoption. We thus do not consider 6over in any detail, as the method seems (in effect) deprecated. We would thus not recommend its use.

5.2.6 ISATAP

An alternative to 6over4 is ISATAP (Intra-Site Automatic Tunnel Addressing Protocol) [TGTT05]. ISATAP also uses the site's IPv4 infrastructure as a virtual link, but it does not use IPv4 multicast, so the link is NBMA (Non-Broadcast Multiple Access).

ISATAP, like 6over4, creates an interface identifier based on the interface's IPv4 address. ISATAP supports both autoconfiguration and manual configuration of addresses, but the IPv4 address of the interface will be embedded as the last 32 bits of the IPv6 addresses. As with 6over4, the IPv4-address needs only be unique in the network the service is deployed in.

Usually multicast is used for neighbour discovery operations like address resolution and router solicitations or advertisements. Since the IPv4 address is always embedded in the IPv6 address, address resolution is trivial. For router solicitations to work, the host must somehow have learned of IPv4 addresses of possible ISATAP routers (through DHCP, DNS, TEP, manual configuration etc.), and will then send solicitations as unicast. The router always sends advertisements as unicast and only as a reply to a host's solicitation. Each ISATAP host will regularly send solicitations to the ISATAP routers it knows of.

ISATAP has been implemented on some platforms, e.g. Windows XP and IOS, although it has been removed from USAGI Linux now. The authors feel that while it has applicability in some sites, where a phased, managed introduction of IPv6 is desired, an approach like [Cho04b] is preferable. In either case, the solution is an interim step until dual-stack network elements are available for the site.

5.2.7 Teredo

The Teredo transitioning mechanism [Hui05], is a form of automatic tunnelling intended to provide IPv6 connectivity to IPv4 hosts that are located behind a NAT [RFC1613] and therefore do not possess permanent, global-scope IPv4 addresses. It is a host-to-host automatic tunnelling mechanism that provides IPv6 connectivity, when dual-stack hosts are located behind one ore multiple NATs by encapsulating IPv6 packets in IPv4-based User Datagram Protocol (UDP) messages.

As illustrated in Figure 5-3, the Teredo service employs two entities, a Teredo server and a Teredo relay, in order to provide IPv6 connectivity to Teredo clients located behind a NAT. Unlike other tunnelling mechanisms, Teredo encapsulates IPv6 packets in UDP (instead of directly over IPv4). A well-known UDP port (3544) is used by the Teredo server to listen for requests from the Teredo clients. Teredo addresses have the following structure:

Table 5-1 The Teredo Address Structure

32 bits	32 bits	16 bits	16 bits	32 bits
Teredo Prefix	IPv4 Address of Teredo Server	Flags	Mapped Client UDP Port	Mapped Client IPv4 Address

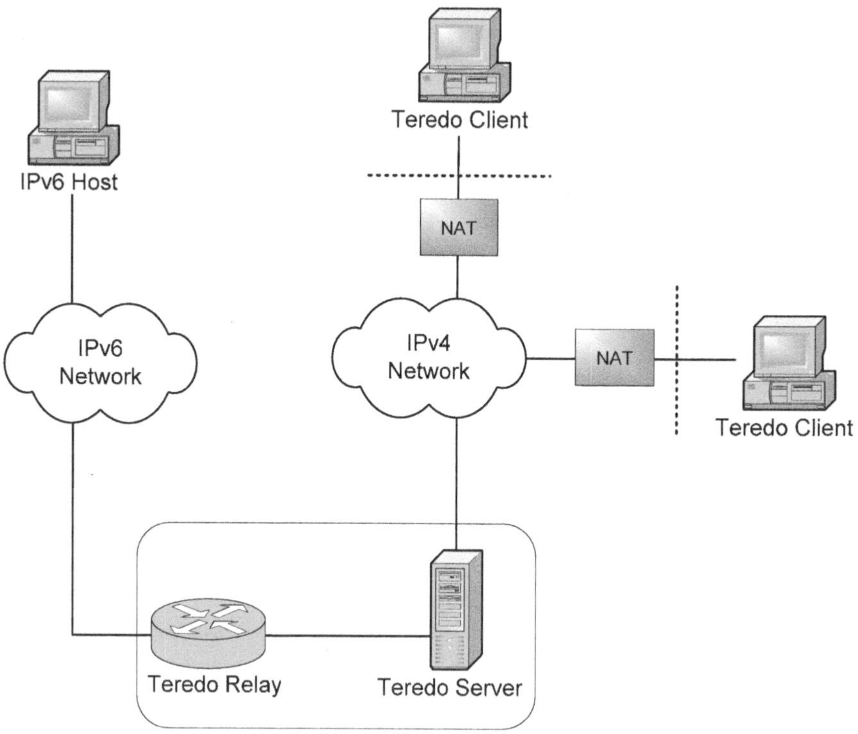

Figure 5-3 Teredo Infrastructure and Components

Both the "mapped client UDP port" and the "mapped client IPv4 address" are obfuscated; each bit in the address and port number is reversed. Note that IPv6 addressing rules specify that for all unicast addresses, Interface IDs are required to be 64 bits *except* those that begin with binary value 000. Hence the flags field has to be encoded to conform to this requirement (see [Hui05] for more details).

The Teredo server listens for requests from Teredo clients, responding with an IPv6 address for them to use. The Teredo server forwards the IPv4-encapsulated IPv6 packets sent from Teredo clients to the Teredo relay. The server also forwards IPv6 packets received from the Teredo relay, that are destined for a Teredo client, to the appropriate IPv4 address and UDP port of the client. The Teredo relay thus acts as an IPv6 router and forwards IPv6 packets destined for Teredo clients to the Teredo server from the IPv6 Internet and forwards IPv6 packets received from the Teredo server to the IPv6 Internet. The Teredo relay also advertises the reachability of the Teredo service into the IPv6 Internet. It is likely that the Teredo server and relay entities would be co-located as shown in Figure 5-3.

Analysing the Teredo IPv6 address format it becomes evident that the Teredo specification makes rather inefficient use of the IPv6 address space with respect to the injection of routing prefixes. This is because the Teredo relay must advertise the reachability of the Teredo service to the rest of the IPv6 Internet. The 32-bit Teredo prefix is common to all Teredo servers, so the relay must advertise IPv6 prefixes consisting of at least the Teredo prefix plus the IPv4 address of the Teredo server. This means that routing prefixes for every distinct Teredo server must be injected into the IPv6 Internet. In theory, this could mean injecting a routing prefixe into the IPv6 Internet for every IPv4 site that employs NAT.

As such, the Teredo service should only be used as a 'last resort' where direct IPv6 connectivity or co-locating a 6to4 router with the NAT is not possible. Furthermore, the Teredo method is complex, and cannot be guaranteed to work across all NATs due in part to variations in NAT implementations.

5.2.8 Tunnel Setup Protocol

The Tunnel Setup Protocol (TSP) [BP05] is a general method designed to simplify the setup of (authenticated) IPv6 tunnels over IPv4 networks. The TSP method was initially applied to tunnel brokers, but the scope of the TSP applicability is much wider. As the name implies TSP is less of a transition mechanism itself than a protocol to describe the proper (automatic) setup of any kind of tunnel to transport IPv6 via a part of the network, where IPv6 is not available.

TSP offers advantages for tunnel brokers, including better support for IPv4 NAT traversal and support for authentication of the tunnel setup.

5.2.9 Dual Stack Transition Mechanism (DSTM)

DSTM (Dual Stack Transition Mechanism) [Bou05] is a tunnelling solution for IPv6-only networks, where IPv4 applications are still needed on dual-stack hosts within an IPv6-only infrastructure. IPv4 traffic is tunnelled over the IPv6-only domain until it reaches an IPv6/IPv4 gateway, which is in charge of packet encapsulation/decapsulation and forwarding between the IPv6-only and IPv4-only domains. The solution proposed by DSTM is transparent to any type of IPv4 application and allows the use of layer 3 security.

Usually with a tunnelling scheme, one IPv4 address is required for every host wishing to connect to the IPv4 Internet. DSTM reduces this constraint by dynamically allocating addresses only for the duration of the communication making it possible for several hosts to share the same address on a large time scale.

DSTM can be implemented if a network infrastructure only supports IPv6, but some of the nodes on the network have dual-stack capability (and make use of IPv4-only applications). DSTM consists of three components:

1. a DSTM server,
2. a DSTM gateway or TEP (Tunnel End Point) and
3. a dual-stack host (called a "DSTM client") wishing to communicate using IPv4.

For the sake of simplicity, we have decided to present the server and the gateway as different equipment, but in actual deployments, these two functionalities are co-located on the same equipment. Figure 5-4 presents the interaction between these three elements.

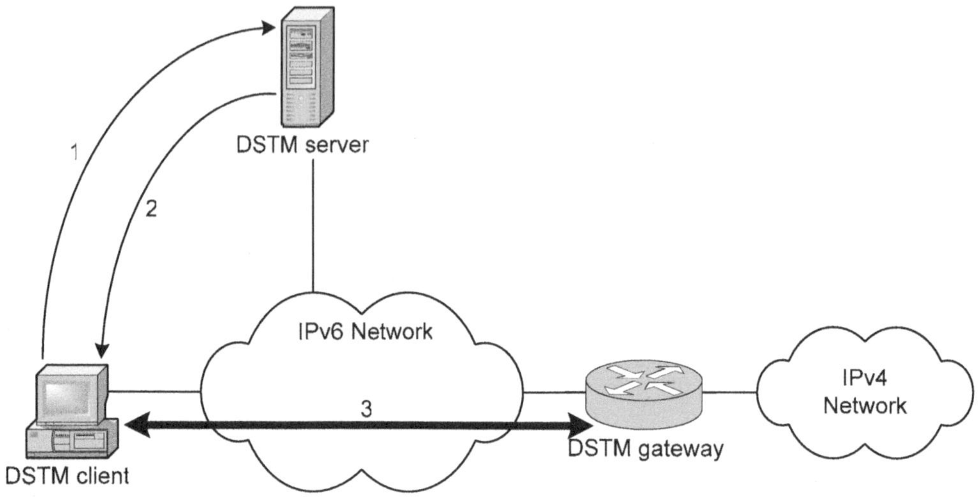

Figure 5-4 DSTM Architecture

As long as communications can take place in native IPv6, none of the capacities of DSTM are required. This applies to protocols like HTTP or SMTP, where the use of ALGs (Application Level Gateways) is to be preferred. When a DSTM node detects the need of an IPv4 address by a query to the DNS resulting in an IPv4 destination address or an application opening an IPv4 socket, the DSTM process is launched.

When the first IPv4 packet needs to be sent, the DSTM client asks the server for an address (step 1 in Figure 5-4). A number of protocols (DHCPv6 [RFC3315], TSP [BP02], RPC) have already been proposed to perform this task. Native IPv6 transport is the only restriction in this matter. DSTM developers are currently discussing whether a single method can be agreed for all DSTM implementations.

Following an address request, the server asks the DSTM gateway to add a Tunnel End Point (TEP) for the requesting DSTM client. It is the server who controls the IPv4/IPv6 address mapping performed at the DSTM gateway. Initial versions of DSTM considered that the gateway would build its IPv6/IPv4 mapping table dynamically by observing packet headers, but this approach is now obsolete due to security concerns.

If the end point for the new tunnel is successfully created, following the answering message from the gateway, the DSTM server (who manages an IPv4 address pool) replies to the host with the following information (step 2):

- The allocated IPv4 address,
- The period over which the address has been allocated

- IPv4 and IPv6 addresses of the TEP.

This information is used by the client to configure an IPv4-over-IPv6 tunnel towards the DSTM gateway (step 3). At this point, the DSTM client has IPv4 connectivity and, if it obtained a global IPv4 address, it will be able to connect to any external IPv4 host.

In DSTM, the period of allocation can be configured based on address availability. Clients are required to ask for allocation renewal before allocation time expires. Depending on local policy and client behaviour, the DSTM server may accept or deny extending the allocation. In normal operation, requests for allocation renewal are periodically sent until the address is no longer needed by the client. As long as the address allocation is extended, the DSTM server is not required to update the IPv4/IPv6 mapping table at the gateway. However, when the allocation expires, the gateway must be informed in order to update its tables and to allow other clients to reuse the TEP for the freed IPv4 address.

The DSTM gateway is in charge of packet forwarding between the IPv6-only domain and IPv4 networks. It performs packet encapsulation/decapsulation using an IPv4/IPv6 mapping table. For successful bi-directional communication, it is very important to allow IPv4 forwarding at the gateway and to make sure that, for any IPv4 packet coming from the outside, the route to the DSTM client points to the TEP.

DSTM should be used in a network domain where IPv6 routing is enabled and ALL nodes within that domain are able to communicate using IPv6. In this case, IPv4 support can be turned off. Thus the burden of maintaining an IPv4 addressing plan and supporting IPv4 routing is removed. However, given the huge number of IPv4-only hosts and applications in the Internet, a number of hosts inside IPv6-only domains will still require IPv4 connectivity.

DSTM can be deployed where no other solutions, such as ALGs, can be implemented. DSTM allows dual-stack nodes to obtain an IPv4 address and offers a default route (through an IPv4-in-IPv6 tunnel) to an IPv4 gateway. Any IPv4-only application can run over an IPv6-only network if such a scheme is used and, if DSTM is configured to allocate Global IPv4 addresses, hosts inside that domain will be able to communicate with any other host on the Internet.

DSTM may be deployed in several phases. As a first step, IPv4 connectivity may be assured by manually configuring tunnels from dual-stack nodes to a Tunnel End Point (TEP). In a second phase, when address allocation or tunnel set up protocols become available (DHCPv6, TSP), it would be possible to dynamically assign an IPv4 address to nodes which need one. In this phase, the address may be allocated for the whole lifetime of the requesting node, reducing the complexity of address management. Finally, when IPv4 address availability becomes a problem, DSTM may be configured to allocate addresses only for small periods of time, based on the real needs of requesting hosts.

Since the address allocation process in DSTM is triggered only when IPv4 connectivity is strictly necessary, the size of the IPv4 address pool required by the mechanism should decrease with time (as more hosts and applications become IPv6 aware). However, if the lack of IPv4 address space continues, DSTM may be extended to include the 'ports option' [Shi05], allowing simultaneous use of the same address by several hosts, but increasing complexity.

5.2.9.1 The VPN Scenario

An alternative use of DSTM concerns what has been called "the VPN scenario" [RMT02]. It concentrates on the situation where a DSTM node is outside its home domain. Supposing that the node can easily obtain an IPv6 address on the visited network but no IPv4 configuration is possible, the DSTM node can negotiate with its home DSTM server and TEP for IPv4 connectivity. If authentication succeeds and the nomad node obtains an address, the node's IPv4 traffic will be sent to the TEP at its home network using an IPv4-in-IPv6 tunnel. Even if the path is not optimal, the node obtains access to private IPv4 resources in its home domain and may obtain global IPv4 connectivity.

5.2.10 The Open VPN based Tunnelling Solution

This method is based on the OpenVPN project (http://openvpn.sourceforge.net/).

OpenVPN is basically a Layer 3 tunnel over UDP/IPv4 or TCP/IPv4, so it is used to set up a router that uses the tunnel interface to route IPv6. It is capable of traversing NATs and can, if needed, use strong encryption over SSL.

This method is a solution for those calling for a more robust way to offer IPv6 connectivity in a NAT environment.

5.2.10.1 Definition of the term "Tunnel Broker"

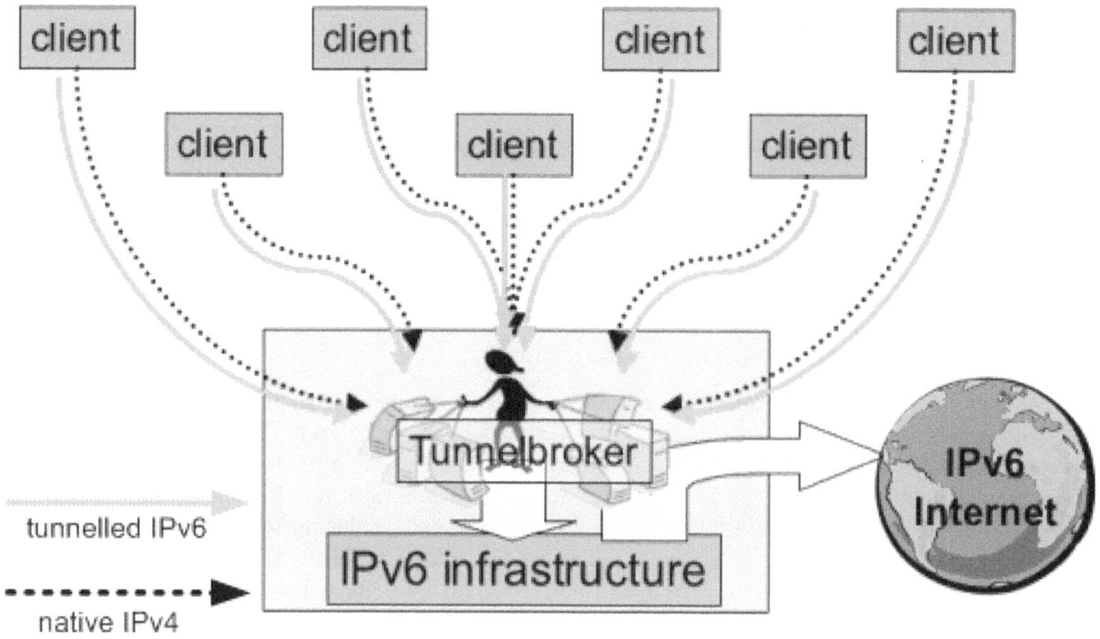

Figure 5-5 Tunnel Broker Scenario

There are many different definitions of the term "tunnel broker". To clarify what this term means in the context of this paragraph, it is necessary to summarise the tasks that the OpenVPN-based tunnel broker should fulfil:

- provide IPv6 connectivity to a subscribed client
- manage a set of X.509 certificates and keys and a certification authority (CA)
- check authorisation of a client
- assign a fixed IPv6 prefix to each client (either /64 or /128 for a single address)
- adjust routing according to prefix/address assignment
- on subscription of a new client, create client configuration for server and as archive file for client

- handle subscription information

To handle all of the above tasks, the tunnel broker needs to consist at least of the following components:

- OpenVPN server(s)
- OpenSSL certification authority (CA)
- client database
- dedicated router for clients (is identical to OpenVPN server)
- IPv6 infrastructure to route IPv6 traffic to and from clients

To visualise the interaction of these components, take a look at the following figure.

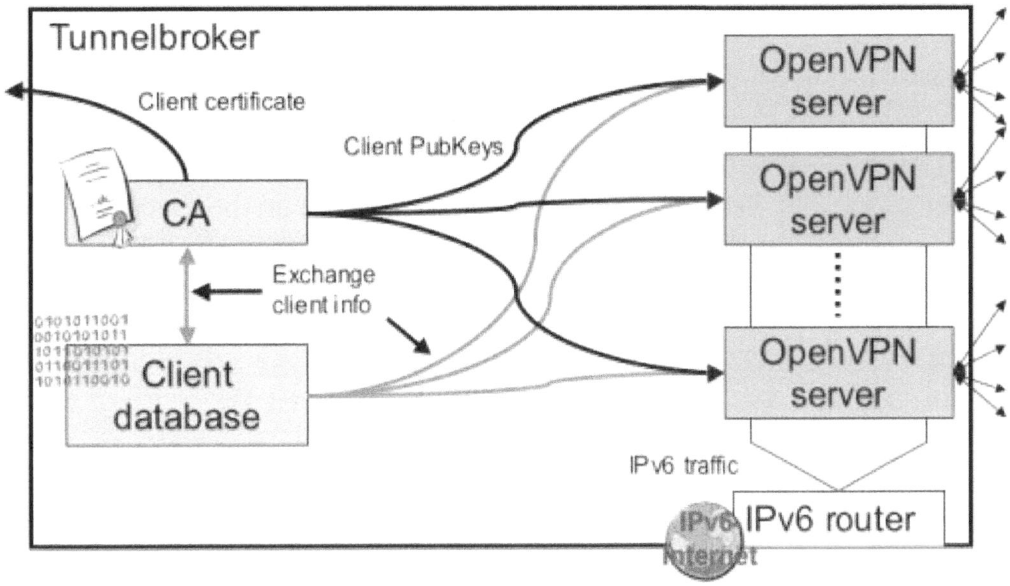

Figure 5-6 Interaction of tunnel broker components

The components in detail may look like this:

- OpenVPN server: powerful Linux or *BSD PC with latest OpenVPN software (at the time of writing, this is a version that is more recent than 1.6_rc2)
- OpenSSL CA: may be any kind of machine with an OpenSSL installation which provides the openssl-binary to create X.509 keys and certificates
- Client database: almost any form of database for holding information about clients ranging from simple text file to dedicated database systems
- Dedicated IPv6 router: normally the same Linux or *BSD machine that runs the OpenVPN server; routes need to be adjusted on that particular machine
- IPv6 infrastructure: your institution's IPv6 backbone

The above components form what we call a "tunnel broker" for the remainder of this section. It is clear that for the sake of scalability, many of the services (e.g. the OpenVPN server) may be spread across numerous different servers. This is not difficult to achieve and can easily be implemented.

5.2.10.2 Tunnel Broker Clients

Another part of the tunnel broker is obviously the tunnel broker client. To understand what functionality a tunnel broker needs to implement, it is necessary to have a look at the different types of clients that need to be connected to the tunnel broker.

First of all, one needs to identify the network topology that a potential client will most likely reside in. It is assumed that any tunnel broker client only has native global IPv4 connectivity and no global IPv6 connectivity. From a practical viewpoint, having global IPv6 connectivity additionally to the tunnel broker IPv6 connectivity is possible. However, this scenario is not a standard scenario where an IPv6 tunnel broker would be employed. Additionally, effects that are imposed by having two types of global connectivity still need to be investigated. No serious problems are to be expected but tests have not yet been conducted to verify this.

One differentiates between two types of clients that reside in two different network topologies for this particular OpenVPN IPv6 tunnel broker:

- Hermit client: a lone client that will be assigned a /128 address
- Subnet client: a client that will be assigned a /64 prefix and that may act as a router for a subnet where it may announce this /64 prefix to other hosts that use the client as their default router

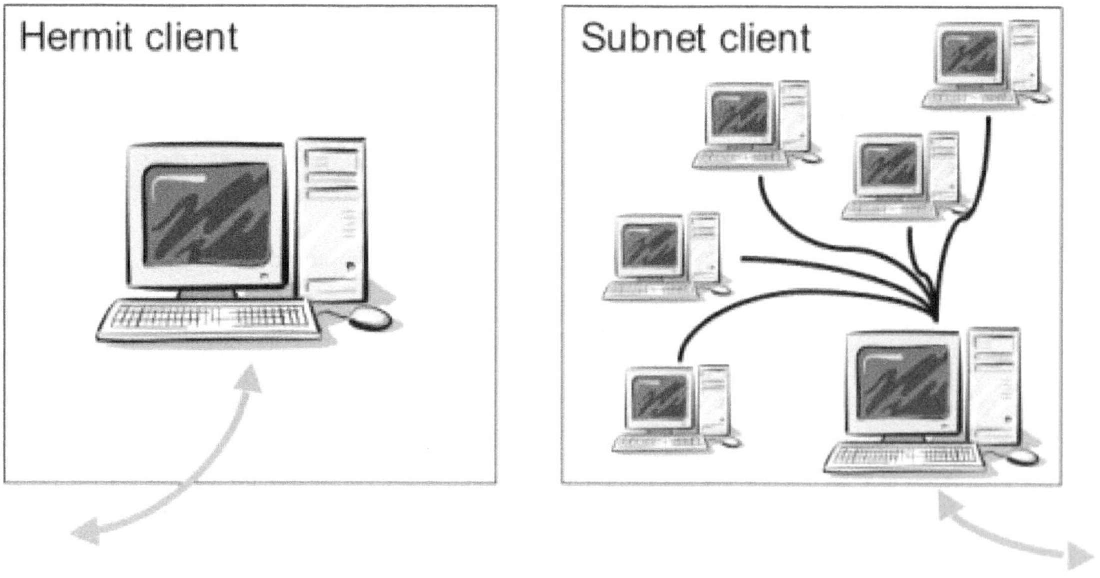

Figure 5-7 Types of Tunnel Broker Clients

5.2.10.3 OpenSSL CA

For many tunnel brokers, having some form of access control and authorisation is mandatory. OpenVPN offers a very flexible and secure way of authorising access using X.509 certificates and keys. OpenVPN uses functionality provided by the OpenSSL library (e.g. TLS key exchange). The OpenSSL CA is needed to sign certificates for clients that would like to connect to the tunnel broker.

When a new client subscribes to the tunnel broker service, the following things have to be done:

1. Create an X.509 key and certificate for the client.
2. CA verifies the identity and authorisation of the client to actually use the tunnel broker and then signs the certificate of the client.
3. The CA's certificate is given to both the client and the server. It is used to verify the signature of the X.509 certificates of both client and server when they execute a TLS key exchange.

The CA is the trusted intermediary instance that both the server and the client trust.

When a client starts an OpenVPN-connection to the server, the following steps are exercised by client and server:

1. TLS handshake and key exchange is started.
2. Both server and client verify the Common Names of each other's public certificates. Only on a positive verification of the Common Names do the server or client continue the negotiations. (The Common Names verification can be seen as an initial sanity check.)
3. After the Common Names verification, the key exchange is started. Server and client verify each other's keys using the CA's certificate to find out if the signatures of the certificates are valid. If yes, both client and server proceed.
4. The server uses the client's certificate to cipher the stream that is sent to the client and it uses OpenSSL functionality to multiplex the tunnel into a UDP/IPv4 stream. The client uses his private key to decrypt the ciphered stream after demultiplexing it. The client's use of the server's certificate is analogue.

This summarises where the OpenSSL CA and the X.509 certificates and keys created by the CA play a key role.

Note: Usually the basic configuration of an OpenVPN based tunnel broker uses encrypted tunnel streams. However, it is possible to use the null cipher instead of the blowfish block stream cipher. This solves some performance and overhead issues.

5.3 Translation Methods

Translation methods are deployed where IPv6-only devices wish to communicate with IPv4-only devices, or vice-versa and no IPv4-in-IPv6 is used.

5.3.1 SIIT, NAT-PT and NAPT-PT

A translator located in the network layer in the protocol stack is called a "header translator". Such mechanisms translate IPv4 datagram headers into IPv6 datagram headers or vice versa. A model that can be used when implementing this mechanism is presented in RFC 2765 [RFC2765]: "SIIT – Stateless IP/ICMP Translation Algorithm".

Network Address Translation with Protocol Translation (NAT-PT), defined in RFC 2766 [RFC2766], is a service that can be used to translate data sent between IP-heterogeneous nodes. NAT-PT translates an IPv4 datagram into, as far as possible, a semantically equivalent IPv6 datagram or vice versa. For this service to work it has to be at the interconnection point between the IPv4 network and the IPv6 network.

Just like existing NATs in the IPv4 world translate between (usually) private IPv4 addresses and globally routable IPv4 addresses, the NAT part of NAT-PT translates between a globally routable IPv4 address to an IPv6 address or vice versa as well as from a private IPv4 address to a global IPv6 address. The PT part of the NAT-PT handles the interpretation and translation of the semantically equivalent IP headers, either from IPv4 to IPv6 or from IPv6 to IPv4. Like NAT, NAT-PT also uses a pool of addresses, which it dynamically assigns to the translated datagrams.

Dual-stack and tunnel-based mechanisms do not alter any of the data contained in the IP datagram. This is true both for IPv4 and IPv6 since the communication is end-to-end using only one protocol. NAT-PT (and NAPT-PT as described below) on the other hand translates the header of the datagram from IPv6 to IPv4 or vice versa. The result is a new header which is semantically equivalent to the original header but not equal. It is therefore likely that some of the information is lost during translation. For example it may happen that a service, which is only available for one protocol, is lost when converted to another protocol.

RFC2766 also specifies a service called Network Address Port Translation + Packet Translation (NAPT-PT). This service enables IPv6 nodes to communicate transparently using only one IPv4 address. NAPT-PT maintains a set of port numbers, which it dynamically assigns to sockets located on the recipient side of the NAPT-PT node.

NAT-PT shares many of the problems normal NAT or the TRT mechanism have, e.g. handling or rather failing to handle IP addresses embedded in application protocol payloads.

The IETF is currently deprecating NAT-PT (see [AD05] for the rationale), but may rework it to a more acceptable format. It should be seen as a transition method of last resort. It is highly preferable that at least one 'side' of the networking scenario is dual-stack so that a common, non-translated, network protocol can be used (IPv4 or IPv6). If this is not possible, and performance permits, an ALG should be preferred (see below).

5.3.2 Bump in the Stack

The Bump in the Stack (BIS) [RFC2767] (see Figure 5-8) translation mechanism is similar to taking the NAT-PT approach with SIIT and moving it to the OS protocol stack within each host. Unlike SIIT however, it assumes an underlying IPv6 infrastructure. Whereas SIIT is a translation interface between

IPv6 and IPv4 networks, BIS is a translation interface between IPv4 applications and the underlying IPv6 network (i.e. the network interface driver). The host stack design is based on that of a dual-stack host, with the addition of three modules, a translator, an extension name resolver, and an address mapper.

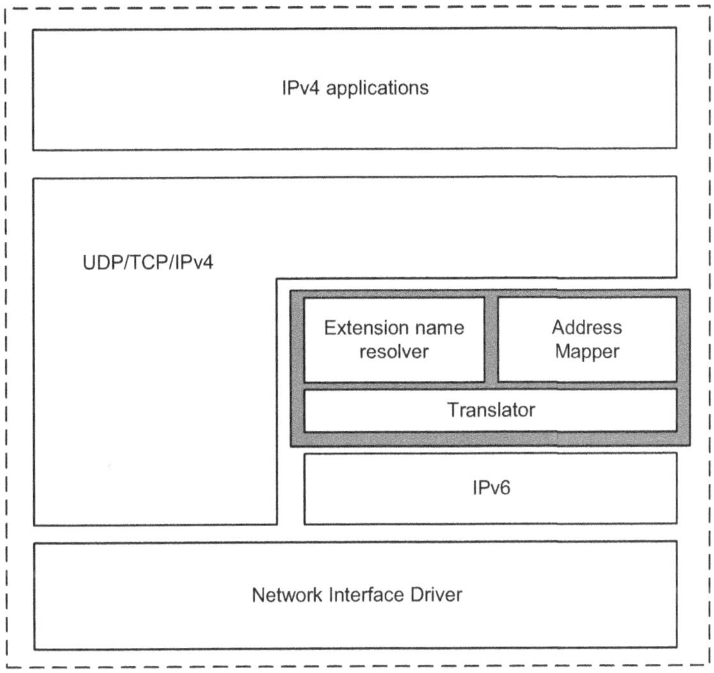

Figure 5-8 The BIS Protocol Stack

The translator rewrites outgoing IPv4 headers into IPv6 headers and incoming IPv6 headers into IPv4 headers (if applicable). It uses the header translation algorithm defined in SIIT. The extension name resolver acts as the DNS-ALG in the NAT-PT mechanism. It snoops IPv4 DNS queries and creates another query asking to resolve both 'A' (IPv4) and 'AAAA' (IPv6) records, sending the returned 'A' record back to the requesting IPv4 application. If only 'AAAA' records are returned, the resolver requests the address mapper to assign an IPv4 address corresponding to the IPv6 address. The address mapper maintains a pool of IPv4 addresses and the associations between IPv4 and IPv6 addresses. It will also assign an address when the translator receives an IPv6 packet from the network for which there is no mapping entry for the source address. Because the IPv4 addresses are never actually transmitted on the network, they do not have to be globally unique and a private address pool can be used.

The BIS mechanism may be useful during initial stages of IPv4 transition to IPv6 when IPv4 applications remain unmodified within IPv6 domains. However, BIS is limited in its translation capabilities. It allows IPv4 to IPv6 host communication but not vice versa. It does not send or receive any IPv4 packets to/from the network. Thus, even an IPv4 application attempting communication with another IPv4 application using BIS, will fail without additional translation mechanisms somewhere in the communication path. As with NAT-PT and SIIT, BIS will not work for multicast communications and will not work for applications that embed IP addresses in their payloads. An ALG is required for any application that exhibits this behaviour.

The BIS method is not widely used; indeed we are not aware of any 6NET sites that see a need for its deployment.

5.3.3 Bump in the API

The Bump in the API (BIA) [RFC3338] translation mechanism is very similar to that of BIS. However, instead of translating between IPv4 and IPv6 headers, BIA inserts an API translator between the socket API and the TCP/IP modules of the host stack (see Figure 5-9).

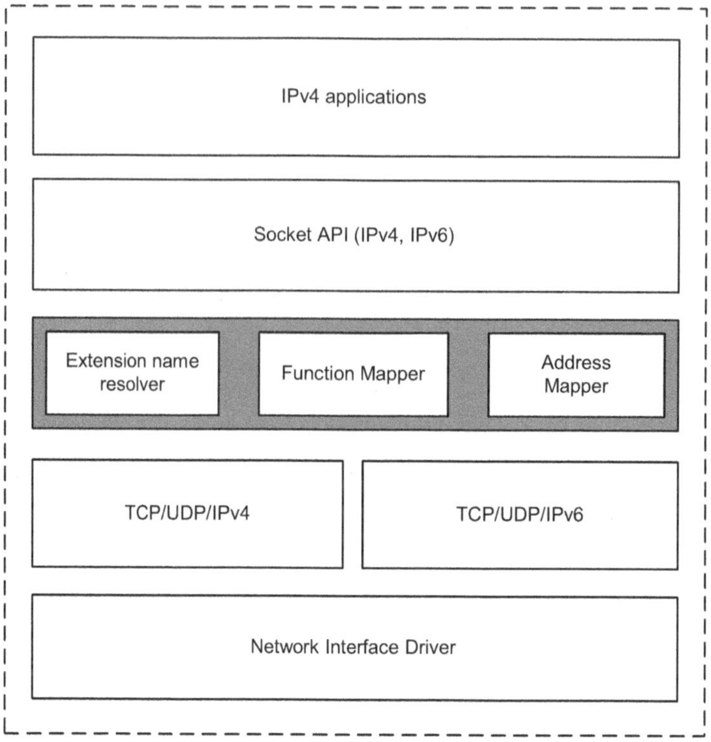

Figure 5-9 The BIA Protocol Stack

Thus, IPv4 socket API functions are translated into IPv6 socket API functions and vice versa. In this way, IPv4/IPv6 translation can be achieved without the overhead of translating every packet header. Like BIS, BIA is based on the addition of three modules: the extension name resolver, the function mapper and the address mapper. Both the extension name resolver and the address mapper modules operate in exactly the same way as the corresponding modules in BIS. The function mapper is the entity that maps IPv4 socket calls to IPv6 socket calls and vice versa. The function mapper does this by intercepting IPv4 socket API function calls and invoking corresponding IPv6 socket API function calls in their place. These IPv6 socket function calls are used to communicate with the peer IPv6 host and are transparent to the IPv4 application that invoked the original IPv4 socket function calls.

The BIA mechanism is intended for systems that have an IPv6 stack but contain applications that have not been upgraded to IPv6. Thus, BIA may be useful in early stages of transition when there are many unmodified IPv4 applications within IPv6 domains. BIA allows IPv4 to IPv6 host communication, but does not specify the reverse case. However, it could be easily extended to cater to IPv6 to IPv4 host communication (this is also applicable to BIS). The advantage BIA has over BIS is that it is independent of the network interface driver and does not introduce the overhead of per-packet header translation. However, BIA exhibits similar limitations to BIS. It will not support multicast communication without some additional functionality in the function mapper module, and it will not work for applications that embed IP addresses in their payloads.

The BIA method is, like the BIS method, not widely used. No 6NET sites see a deployment requirement for it.

5.3.4 Transport Relay

A translator located in the transport layer is called a transport relay. The relay is located somewhere between the communicating nodes and enables IPv6-only hosts to exchange traffic (UDP or TCP) with IPv4-only hosts. If two nodes, for example a client and an application server, use different protocol stacks, they couldn't communicate directly with each other, and traffic has to be passed over a relay. In case of TCP the relay terminates the IPv6 transport protocol session from the client, and thus acts as a transport destination endpoint to the client. At the same time it initializes a second IPv4 transport session with the server, and copies received data from each session to the other. In the case of UDP the datagram is just translated and forwarded to the target node.

5.3.4.1 Transport Relay Translator

The Transport Relay Translator (TRT) [RFC3142] enables IPv6-only hosts to exchange traffic (TCP or UDP) with IPv4-only hosts. No modification on hosts is required, the TRT system can be very easily installed in existing IPv6 capable networks.

A transport relay translator which runs on a dual-stack node can use one protocol when communicating with the client and one protocol when communicating with the application server. In such a setting the relay is able to translate in the transport layer all data sent between the client and application server. For TCP such a translation includes recalculating the checksum, keeping the necessary state information about which client socket is connected to which server socket and removing this state when the client ends its communication. With UDP the checksum is mandatory when using IPv6 but not when using IPv4. UDP is a connectionless protocol and in theory it is impossible for a relay to know which UDP datagrams belong to the same session. A UDP relay implementation will typically assume that a UDP datagram that follows another with the same source and destination within a certain time interval, belong to the same session.

The TRT system can work with most of the common Internet applications: HTTP, SMTP, SSH, etc. The transition mechanism operation is relatively simple:

The IPv6 host uses a DNS-ALG as its nameserver to resolve its DNS queries. The IPv6 host, when asking its nameserver for the IPv6 address (AAAA record) of an IPv4-only host, will receive an IPv6 address (AAAA record) from the DNS-ALG which was specially constructed from the IPv4 address (A record), instead of an error message with the answer that no IPv6 address could be found corresponding to the query. The constructed addresses consist of a special network prefix associated with the transport relay and a host ID (the lower 64 bits) that embeds the IPv4 address of the remote host. Such a DNS-ALG has been developed as part of the 6NET project and has been tested extensively with very good results.

The network is set up such that packets destined for addresses with the special network prefix are routed to the TRT relay node. The TRT then intercepts transport sessions and acts towards the client node as the destination endpoint of an IPv6 session and acts towards the server node as the source for an IPv4 session, copying all data it receives from each session to the other.

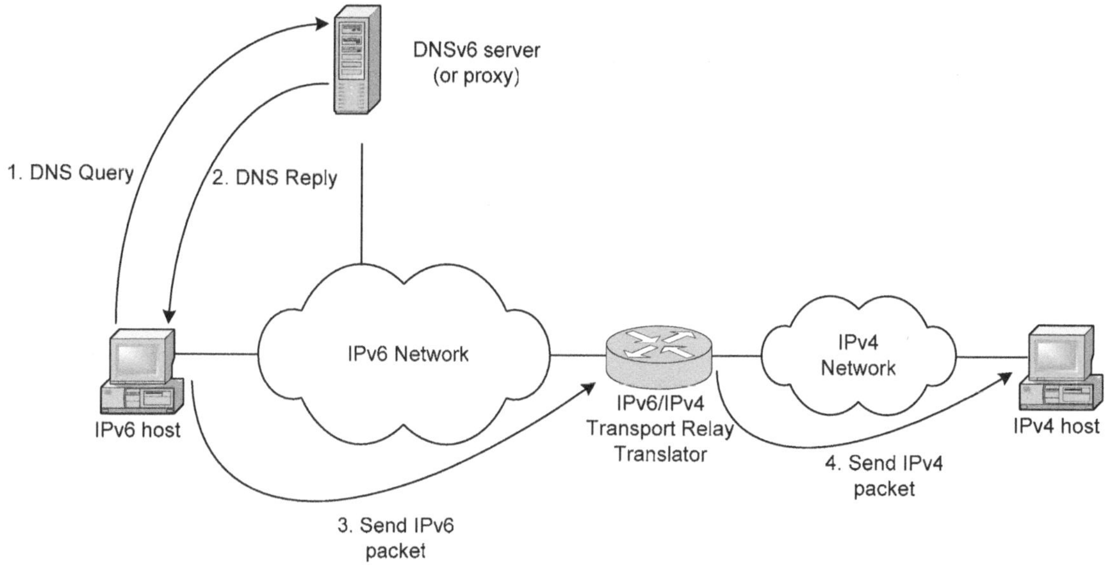

Figure 5-10 Transport Relay Translator in Action

A UDP relay can be implemented in a similar manner to a TCP relay. An implementation can recognise a UDP traffic pair like a NAT system does, by recording address/port pairs into a table and managing table entries with timeouts.

There are both advantages and disadvantages in employing the TRT mechanisms. The advantages include:

- There is no problem with fragmentation. If different fragmentation has to be used in the IPv6 and IPv4 parts of the TRT "connections", there is no problem: the Path MTU discovery algorithm or fragmentation mechanism of the TRT relay server can handle the situation.
- There is no problem with ICMP packets. If any error occurred in any part of the TRT connections the ICMP/ICMPv6 packet is sent back to the TRT relay server, where the error can be handled properly or be reported towards the other end of the "connection".
- It is not necessary to modify the IPv6 stack of the initiating host, neither is it necessary to modify the application to support relaying.
- It is relatively easy to set up.
- It can be enough to have only one TRT relay server for a whole site. And this router has to have only one global IPv4 address.

The disadvantages include:

- There can be problems with applications using embedded IP addresses (e.g. FTP, H.323). The TRT relay has to be smart enough to "look inside" the packets if such an application has to be supported. In this case the TRT relay server becomes a kind of application proxy.
- It supports only unicast TCP/IP traffic, however it is theoretically possible to implement multicast support as well.
- TRT is more difficult to scale than the stateless translation methods. The TRT relay server has to keep track of all the TRT connections to properly handle all error conditions. The scaling problem can be eased using anycast technology to reach the closest TRT relay server.

- The TRT relay server can generate a major security problem, since it can be used as an intermediate hop to reach IPv4 servers. The served community of a TRT relay server has to be carefully controlled by packet filtering or access control lists. To reduce the problem site local addresses could be used for accepting incoming IPv6 packets (Note that within the IETF there are currently plans to deprecate site-local addresses and replace them with a new addressing scheme for "private" addressing within a site).
- TRT requires a specially configured DNS server to run.
- Due to the nature of the TCP/UDP relaying service, it is not recommended to use TRT for protocols that use authentication based on source IP address (e.g., rsh/rlogin).
- IPSec cannot be used across a TRT relay.

The TRT relay is used in the Tromso scenario within the 6NET project, as described in Chapter 13.

5.3.5 SOCKS

SOCKS [RFC1928] is another example of a transport relay but it is usually referred to as a "proxy protocol for client/server environments".

A SOCKS proxy works in a similar fashion as a traditional transport relay, but there are minor differences, which we will now describe.

When a client wants to connect to an application server it first sets up a connection to a well known, preconfigured proxy server using a special proxy protocol. The client informs the proxy about the IP address and the port number of the application server it wants to communicate with. The proxy server is now responsible to set up a connection to the application server. As soon as this connection is up and running the proxy relays packet between the client and application server hiding the actual connection.

SOCKS includes two primary components: a SOCKS server and a SOCKS client library. The server component is located in the application layer while the client component is located between the client application and the transport layer.

Before an application client can use SOCKS it has to be modified ("socksified"). This can be done in two different ways: If the source code is available it can be compiled together with the SOCKS client library using a set of pre-processor directives. If one has instead only precompiled binaries for an application, but the operating system supports dynamic linking of shared libraries one can change some environment variables in the operating system so that the client uses SOCKS instead of the default network libraries.

RFC 3089 [RFC3089] presents a SOCKS-based IPv6/IPv4 gateway mechanism that supports both IPv6 to IPv4 communication and IPv4 to IPv6 communication. This RFC also contains a link to two different implementations of the mechanism described.

No 6NET partners are currently using SOCKS for IPv6 transition purposes.

5.3.6 Application Layer Gateway

An Application Layer Gateway (ALG) is a common mechanism to allow users behind firewalls or behind a NAT gateway to use applications that would otherwise not be allowed to traverse the firewall or NAT gateway. A common example for an ALG is a classical HTTP proxy like "squid" or "wwwoffle".

The principle of an ALG can easily be explained using an HTTP proxy as an example. Normally, a web browser would directly open a connection to a web server if a direct connection between the client and the server can be established. However, when using an ALG, the client opens a connection to the ALG (in this case the HTTP proxy), which (if the required content is not already cached locally from a previous request) then itself establishes a connection to the webserver acting as a relay for outgoing requests and incoming data. In most cases, the use of an ALG is almost transparent for the user. Applications that use ALGs have to be configured to do so beforehand. A web browser has to be configured to use a certain HTTP proxy, for example. There are also applications that allow automatic configuration of ALGs.

In IPv6-only networks, the ALG functionality can be used to enable hosts to establish connections to services in the IPv4-only world and in some cases the other way around as well. This can be achieved by setting up ALGs on dual-stack hosts, which have both IPv6 and IPv4 connectivity. The only difference between a normal application proxy and an ALG in this case is that it will use IPv6 transport in the internal network to receive requests but IPv4 to relay the requests to outside IPv4-only communication partners.

ALGs are the "translation" method of choice for most 6NET sites, simply because many common applications naturally support this mode of operation (web proxies, SMTP MXs, IRC servers, etc).

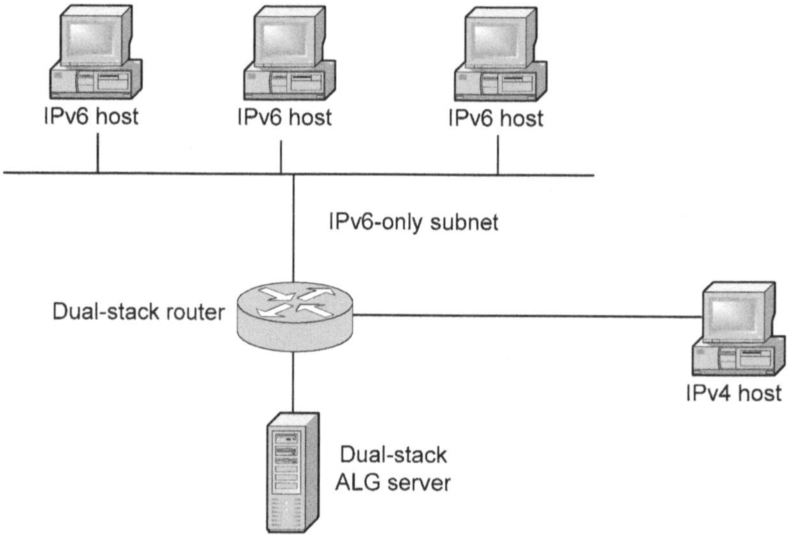

Figure 5-11 ALG Scenario

5.3.7 The 'Trick or Treat' DNS-ALG

The 'Trick or Treat' DNS-ALG called 'totd' is a lightweight DNS proxy (not a full DNS server); it does not recursively resolve queries itself. It is lightweight in that it consists of less than 5000 lines of C code. It has been downloaded over a 100 times per month from its main ftp server alone (it is also distributed with various open source operating systems) for several years now, so we believe that it is in fairly widespread use. We have received just a few bug reports from users and believe we fixed these bugs in the latest version while adding little new code. We believe therefore that the totd code is fairly well tested and quite stable.

The "totd" DNS-ALG has been developed as part of the 6NET project in order to be used in conjunction with transition mechanisms that require or benefit from special support from DNS. In addition, it has been used to test DNS-related ideas proposed in the IPv6 working groups of the IETF, and act as proof-of-concept implementation for these. Such proof-of-concept code is not compiled in by default in the latest version of the totd proxy. Here, we describe the stable core functionality of totd that is related to IPv6 transitioning.

The "totd" DNS-ALG is a proxy that forwards queries to one or more real nameservers that will recursively resolve queries. Such nameservers are called forwarders in totd terminology. If there are multiple forwarders specified, it will try them in the order listed. As a proxy, totd sits between client resolvers and real forwarder nameservers and as such receives requests from clients which totd normally forwards to a real nameserver to resolve. When it subsequently receives a response from the nameserver it simply forwards it back to the client. Such DNS proxy functionality with transport support for both IPv4 and IPv6 is already quite useful. However, the main reason for totd's existence is its ability to perform translation tricks on the DNS queries and responses that it forwards.

5.3.7.1 Support for NAT-PT and TRT

The totd DNS proxy can treat each AAAA query in a special way. This behaviour is enabled when one or more prefixes are configured. Such a prefix is configured on the command line, in the totd config file, or dynamically using a web form if the optional small webserver is compiled in.

If the nameserver that totd forwards the AAAA query to, does not return an IPv6 address for the AAAA query, totd will make a second query but this time for an A record of the hostname of the original query. The resulting IPv4 address is then used to construct a fake IPv6 address, by replacing the lower 32 bits of the specified prefix with this IPv4 address. The resulting IPv6 address is sent as response to the original AAAA record query. In addition, totd treats PTR type queries (reverse name lookup) in the ip6.int. and ip6.arpa. domains specially. If the query matches a specified prefix, totd will forward a PTR query for an IPv4 address (using the lower 32 bits of the address to construct an IPv4 address) instead and use that to construct a faked response to the original PTR query.

If multiple prefixes are configured, totd will cycle through them in round robin fashion. In this way totd can balance the load for multiple NAPT-PT/TRT translators in a network and support to some extent redundancy in the setup of transitioning mechanisms in a network. The totd proxy has no way to check itself whether the prefixes it uses are actually 'live', i.e. can be used to contact remote (IPv4-only) machines. However, a separate monitoring tool or the transitioning mechanisms itself may have support for this. For this reason, the latest version of totd can be configured dynamically using a small built-in webserver. A totd proxy can listen on some TCP port for http requests that tell it do add or delete a prefix from its list of prefixes. A network administrator can then use a web browser to reconfigure a running totd, or (more likely) use tools to do so from automated scripts.

5.4 *Configuration Examples: Dual Stack*

This section, as well as the following two, includes installation and configuration examples for most of the implementations of the tools and mechanisms previously described in this chapter.

Generally, adding IPv6 functionality to existing IPv4 interfaces – if it is supported in the operating system/on the platform – is often a simple task. Nevertheless, as one basically adds a complete new IPv6 network living next to the existing IPv4 network, one has to think about internal and maybe external routing structures. These may differ from those used in IPv4, as not all of the current IGPs (like OSPFv2) are capable to route IPv6 traffic. Instead it may happen that new protocols (e.g. OSPFv3) need to be deployed.

Information on how to switch on IPv6 on any platform is included in Appendix B. As IPv6 becomes more and more common it is likely that this information will become unnecessary. Very soon all operating systems and router platforms will have IPv6 switched on by default.

Configuration examples for routing protocols are covered in Chapter 6. We would like the reader to refer to that chapter to learn how to set up inter or intra-domain routing with either iBGP, OSPFv3, IS-IS or RIPng for most platforms.

5.4.1 Dual-stack VLANs

Using VLANs for IPv6 site deployment is not really a transition tool but it is a method that is becoming more commonly used for dual stack IPv6 deployment in site networks because it is so easy if the network already makes use of the VLAN technique. One just injects (new) IPv6 subnets/links into the existing IPv4 VLANs. In a smaller size network, there may be 10-15 VLANs, each just carrying traffic for one IPv4 subnet. In such situations, one can take advantage of the VLAN segregation of traffic to connect IPv6 routers such that a single IPv6 prefix (a /64 prefix) is injected into each IPv4 VLAN that requires dual-stack networking. Hosts in such subnets can then autoconfigure IPv6 addresses in addition to their IPv4 addresses or make use of DHCPv6 if the service is implemented. In this case, the IPv6 routing hierarchy may be IPv6-only, and exist in parallel to the IPv4 network infrastructure. The IPv6 link offsite may also be separate.

It is important in such an instance that IPv6 filters and access control lists are deployed to prevent IPv6 being a back door for hackers to enter the (IPv4) network.

See [Cho04b], an IETF I-D produced within the 6NET project, for more details.

5.4.1.1 Configuring an interface on a Linux host to become part of a VLAN

The following example shows how a physical interface of a Linux host (i.e. eth0) is trunked to become part of a tagged VLAN. The only prerequisite is that support for VLANs needs to be switched on before compiling the kernel.

```
# ip link set <trunked interface> up;
# /usr/sbin/vconfig add <trunked interface> <VLAN-ID>
# ip link set <trunked interface>.<VLAN-ID>
```

5.4.1.2 Configuring a BSD system to act as a VLAN tagging router

In this section we describe a configuration example for BSD to deploy IPv6 networking across a number of IPv6 links on an enterprise (in this case, eight links), for a scenario similar to the one described above. Here the precise configuration may of course vary depending on the existing site VLAN deployment. This section highlights that the VLAN configuration must be manually configured; the support is not "automatic".

In this example, the configuration is for an IPv6 BSD router connected directly to a site's external IPv6 access router. The BSD router has one interface (dc0) towards the site IPv6access router, and three interfaces (dc1, dc2, dc3) over which the internal routing is performed (the number of interfaces can be varied, three are used here to distribute the traffic load). The IPv6 documentation prefix (2001:db8::/32) is used in the example.

```
--- Example IPv6 VLAN configuration, FreeBSD ---

#
# To IPv6 enable a vlan
#
# 1. Add a new vlan device to cloned_interfaces called vlanX
#
# 2. Add an ifconfig_vlanX line, the number in quotes is the vlan tag ID
#
# 3. Add vlanX to ipv6_network_interfaces
#
# 4. Add an ipv6_ifconfig_vlanX line, with a new unique prefix
#
# 5. Add vlanX to rtadvd_interface
#
# 6. Add vlanX to ipv6_router_flags

### Interfaces ###

# Bring physical interfaces up
ifconfig_dc0="up"
ifconfig_dc1="up"
ifconfig_dc2="up"
ifconfig_dc3="up"

# Create VLan interfaces
cloned_interfaces="vlan0 vlan1 vlan2 vlan3 vlan4 vlan5 vlan6 vlan7 vlan8"

# Upstream link to IPv6 Access Router
ifconfig_vlan0="vlan 37 vlandev dc0"
```

```
# Downstream interfaces, load balance over interfaces dc1,dc2,dc3
ifconfig_vlan1="vlan 11 vlandev dc1" # Subnet1
ifconfig_vlan2="vlan 17 vlandev dc2" # Subnet2
ifconfig_vlan3="vlan 24 vlandev dc3" # Subnet3
ifconfig_vlan4="vlan 25 vlandev dc1" # Subnet4
ifconfig_vlan5="vlan 34 vlandev dc2" # Subnet5
ifconfig_vlan6="vlan 14 vlandev dc3" # Subnet6
ifconfig_vlan7="vlan 19 vlandev dc1" # Subnet7
ifconfig_vlan8="vlan 13 vlandev dc2" # Subnet8

### IPv6 ###

# Enable ipv6
ipv6_enable="YES"

# Forwarding
ipv6_gateway_enable="YES"

# Define Interfaces
ipv6_network_interfaces="vlan0 vlan1 vlan2 vlan3 vlan4 vlan5 vlan6 vlan7 vlan8"
# Define addresses
ipv6_ifconfig_vlan0="2001:db8:d0:101::2 prefixlen 64" # Uplink
ipv6_ifconfig_vlan1="2001:db8:d0:111::1 prefixlen 64" # Subnet1
ipv6_ifconfig_vlan2="2001:db8:d0:112::1 prefixlen 64" # Subnet2
ipv6_ifconfig_vlan3="2001:db8:d0:121::1 prefixlen 64" # Subnet3
ipv6_ifconfig_vlan4="2001:db8:d0:113::1 prefixlen 64" # Subnet4
ipv6_ifconfig_vlan5="2001:db8:d0:114::1 prefixlen 64" # Subnet5
ipv6_ifconfig_vlan6="2001:db8:d0:115::1 prefixlen 64" # Subnet6
ipv6_ifconfig_vlan7="2001:db8:d0:116::1 prefixlen 64" # Subnet7
ipv6_ifconfig_vlan8="2001:db8:d0:117::1 prefixlen 64" # Subnet8

# Router advs
rtadvd_enable="YES"
rtadvd_interfaces="-s vlan0 vlan1 vlan2 vlan3 vlan4 vlan5 vlan6 vlan7 vlan8"

### Routing ###

# Multicast
mroute6d_enable="YES"
mroute6d_program="/sbin/pim6sd"
```

```
# RIP-ng
ipv6_router_enable="YES"
ipv6_router_flags="-N
dc0,dc1,dc2,dc3,vlan1,vlan2,vlan3,vlan4,vlan5,vlan6,vlan7,vlan8"


--- End of configuration ---
```

5.5 Configuration Examples: Tunnelling Methods

5.5.1 Manually Configured Tunnels

The necessary configuration to manually configure IPv6-to-IPv4 tunnels in different operating systems and router platforms is presented in the following subsections.

5.5.1.1 Cisco IOS

Manually configuring an IPv6-in-IPv4 tunnel on a Cisco IOS platform is not much different from setting up an IP-over-IP tunnel. One creates the interface by simply changing to the configuration mode by typing:

```
# configure terminal
```

In configuration mode, one can create the interface:

```
(config)# interface Tunnel 0
```

Note that the number of the Tunnel can be any number from 0 up to about 65000. To configure the interface with an IPv6 address on has two possibilities:

```
(config-if)# ipv6 address <full ipv6-address>/<subnet-length>
```

or

```
(config-if)# ipv6 address <prefix>/<prefix-length> eui-64
```

The first possibility will result in the interface being configured with the exact address one has specified. Note that the length of the subnet can be set as 128. Using the second possibility one specifies a prefix, which may be up to 64 bits long. The full IPv6 address the interface will then be configured with includes (for example) the MAC address of the hardware in the interface identifier as specified in the EUI-64 standard.

The tunnel source can either be specified with the name of the IPv4 source or by directly stating the IPv4 address of the local tunnel endpoint, e.g.:

```
(config-if)# tunnel source 128.176.191.82
```

or

```
(config-if)# tunnel source FastEthernet0/0
```

The tunnel destination is set up by:

```
(config-if)# tunnel destination <IPv4 address of remote tunnel endpoint>
```

Finally one has to set the tunnel mode to "ipv6ip" to specify the correct encapsulation and decapsulation.

```
(config-if)# tunnel mode ipv6ip
```

With the "ipv6 route" command one can configure routes for tunnel interfaces just like with any other interface.

5.5.1.2 Juniper (JunOS)

If you have Tunnel PIC installed in your Juniper router, you can configure IPv6 over IPv4 tunnels. To do this, you configure a unicast tunnel across an existing IPv4 network infrastructure.

Configuration example:

```
Router #1:
    [edit]
    interfaces{
            gr-1/0/0{
                    unit0{
                            tunnel{
                                    source 128.176.191.82;
                                    destination 128.176.184.7;
                            }
                            family inet6{
                                    address 2001:db8:ffff::ffff:1/112
                            }
                    }
            }
    }
Router #2:
    [edit]
    interfaces{
            gr-1/0/0{
                    unit0{
                            tunnel{
                                    source 128.176.184.7;
                                    destination 128.176.191.82;
                            }
                            family inet6{
                                    address 2001:db8:ffff::ffff:2/112
                            }
                    }
            }
    }
```

Configured tunnels require IPv6 routing. For that purpose one can either create static routes or add the tunnel interface to OSPFv3 or RIPng.

5.5.1.3 Extreme (ExtremeWare IPv6)

You can configure a tunnel between a dual stack host and a dual stack router or between two dual stack routers.

IPv6-in-IPv4 tunnelling requires an active IPv4 interface on the switch. The address of this interface is used for the configuration of the tunnel. If that particular IPv4 interface goes down, tunnelling fails even if other IPv4 interfaces are available on the switch.

To avoid this situation, we create an IPv4 VLAN with loopback enabled. Even if all of the ports on the VLAN go down, the VLAN stays up and so does the tunnel. At the cost of an additional VLAN on each IPv6-in-IPv4 router and advertisement of the additional IPv4 address, you ensure greater tunnel stability.

Configuration of Switch A:

```
create vlan to_router_b
configure vlan to_router_b add ports 1-10
configure vlan to_router_b ipaddress 128.176.191.82/24
enable loopback-mode to_router_b
create tunnel 6in4_to_b ipv6-in-ipv4 destination 128.176.184.7 \
                                            source 128.176.191.82
configure tunnel 6in4_to_b ipaddress ipv6 2001:db8:ffff::ffff:1/112
enable ipforwarding ipv6 6in4_to_b
```

Configuration of Switch B:

```
create vlan to_router_a
configure vlan to_router_a add ports 1-5
configure vlan to_router_a ipaddress 128.176.184.7/24
enable loopback-mode to_router_a
create tunnel 6in4_to_a ipv6-in-ipv4 destination 128.176.191.82 \
                                            source 128.176.184.7
configure tunnel 6in4_to_a ipaddress ipv6 2001:db8:ffff::ffff:2/112
enable ipforwarding ipv6 6in4_to_a
```

5.5.1.4 6WIND (SixOS)

While essentially being nothing more than a PC running some version of FreeBSD, 6WIND routers come with their own command line interface (CLI). Note that 6WIND no longer sell their hardware but we still give configuration examples here since existing 6WIND routers can obviously be used in IPv6 deployments. For the purpose of this example we assume one has just logged on to the rooter as user “admin”.

1. First one has to go into the configuration mode for the running configuration:

```
sixwind{} edit running
```

2. Change to the "migration context":

```
sixwind{running} mig
```

3. Setup the IPv6-in-IPv4 tunnel:

```
sixwind{running-mig} 6in4 <tun-#> <local v4> <remote v4> <local v6> \
                                                          <remote v6>
```

As an actual example:

```
sixwind{running-mig} 6in4 0 128.1.2.3 68.2.3.4 2001:pTLA:y::xxx:2 \
                                                 2001:pTLA:y::xxx:1
```

With this configuration the 6WIND router will create two /128 routes for both of the IPv6 addresses of the tunnel endpoints.

4. Leave the "migration context":

```
sixwind{running-mig} exit
```

We assume that the tunnel is going to be the only IPv6 connection for the 6WIND router (e.g., if it is the IPv6 access router for the site). Therefore the IPv6 default route needs to be set to this tunnel.

5. Change to the "routing context":

```
sixwind{running} rtg
```

6. Configure the IPv6 default route:

```
sixwind{running-rtg} ipv6_defaultroute <local v6 IP>
```

In our example:

```
sixwind{running-rtg} ipv6_defaultroute 2001:pTLA:y::xxx:1
```

7. Leave the "routing context":

```
sixwind{running-rtg} exit
```

8. Apply the configured changes to the running configuration:

```
sixwind{running} addrunning
```

9. Exit the configuration mode:

```
sixwind{running} exit
```

Note: If you have performed step 8 immediately before typing in "exit" here everything should be fine. Should you have configured other changes after step 8 before exiting the configuration context the router will ask you if you want to apply these changes to the running configuration as well. Type "y" if you want the changes to be added to the running configuration, otherwise answer "n", in which case all changes after the last "addrunning" command will be lost.

10. Save changes to the startup configuration so the tunnel will still be configured after the next reboot:

```
sixwind{} copy conf running start
```

5.5.1.5 Windows XP

Configuring static tunnels on Windows XP hosts can be performed by the following steps:

1. Create an IPv6-in-IPv4 tunnel, named myTunnel:

```
C:\>netsh interface ipv6 add v6v4tunnel myTunnel 195.251.29.15 \
                                              195.251.29.243 enable
```

2. Add an IPv6 address to the tunnel:

```
C:\>netsh interface ipv6 add address "myTunnel" 2001:db8:1::1
```

3. Add a default route to the remote IPv6 address of the tunnel, e.g. 2001:db8:1::2, so that all IPv6 traffic goes through the tunnel:

```
C:\>netsh interface ipv6 add route ::/0 "myTunnel" 2001:db8:1::2
```

5.5.1.6 Windows 2000

Microsoft IPv6 Technology Preview software should initially be installed to the Windows 2000 host. After rebooting the system, three IPv6 enabled interfaces are created automatically. The "Tunnel Pseudo-Interface" can be use for creating static tunnels between to hosts, as follows:

1. Assign an IPv6 address to tunnel interface:

```
C:\>ipv6 adu 2/2001:db8:1::1
```

2. Create a static route entry that it points to remote IPv4 address of the tunnel:

```
C:\>ipv6 rtu ::/0  2/::194.177.210.38
```

5.5.1.7 Linux

The easiest way to set up a tunnel on a Linux host is using the "ip" command. Modern distributions usually include IPv6 functionality not only with this command but in general as well.

To set up an IPv6-in-IPv4 tunnel usually a "sit" interface is created:

```
# ip tunnel add sit1 remote <IPv4 address of remote tunnel endpoint> \
local <local IPv4 address>
```

Note that "sit1" is the name of the sit interface. The "local IPv4 address" is the address of the network interface to be used for the incoming IPv4 traffic which contains the encapsulated IPv6 datagrams.

After configuring the interface it has to be brought up:

```
# ip link set sit1 up
```

To equip interface sit1 with an IPv6 address other than the autoconfigured link-local address one can use the following command:

```
# ip add addr <IPv6 address>/<subnet-length> dev sit1
```

After these commands the output from "`ifconfig sit1`" should look somewhat like:

```
sit1Link encap: IPv6-in-IPv4
          inet6 addr: 2001:db8:1::fff0:2/112 Scope:Global
          inet6 addr: fe80::80b0:b807/128 Scope:Link
          UP POINTOPOINTRUNNING NOARP     MTU:1480     Metric:1
          RX packets:0 errors:0 dropped:0 overruns:0 frame:0
          TX packets:0 errors: 0 dropped:0 overruns:0 carrier:0
          collisions:0 txqueuelen:0
```

Creating tunnels and adding IPv6 addresses can also be achieved with the command "ifconfig", but this is an old fashioned style and should not be used in newer Linux distributions.

5.5.1.8 Solaris 8+

The steps to manually configure a tunnel interface on a Solaris 8 workstation are the following:

1. Create the file `/etc/named/hostname6.ip.tun0`, which is executed every time the workstation boots. Each line of the file is used as input by the `ifconfig` command, and thus, the appropriate command syntax is required.

2. The first line in the `/etc/named/hostname6.ip.tun0` file contains the IPv4 source and the destination addresses of the tunnel. For example, if the source and destination addresses are 150.140.21.45 and 194.177.63.238, respectively, the first line should be:

```
tsrc 150.140.21.45 tdst 194.177.63.238
```

3. The second line in the `/etc/named/hostname6.ip.tun0` file configures the IPv6 addresses of the tunnel endpoints. The first IPv6 address belongs to the local host and the second to the peer host. For example:

```
addif 2001:db8:2D00:1::1 2001:db8:3D00:1::2 up
```

4. Restart the script `/etc/init.d/inetinit`

5. Set the IPv6 default route to the remote tunnel endpoint (if the tunnel is the only IPv6 connection of the host:

```
# add -inet6 default 2001:db8:3D00:1::2
```

5.5.1.9 FreeBSD, NetBSD and Darwin/Mac OS X

Tunnels are configured via the "ifconfig" command with little to no variation on all operating systems that have incorporated the KAME project's IPv6 stack, including FreeBSD, NetBSD and Darwin/Mac OS X (OpenBSD could most likely be added to this list as the same instructions would most likely work on it, too, but this has not yet been verified by the authors).

The next installation steps should be followed in case of using ifconfig:

1. Check whether a "gif" interface exists using ifconfig:

```
# ifconfig gif0
```

The result is either:

```
ifconfig: interface gif0 does not exist
```

or

```
gif0: flags=8010<POINTOPOINT,MULTICAST> mtu 1280
```

2. Create the interface:

```
# ifconfig gif0 create
```

and audit its state:

```
# ifconfig gif0
  gif0: flags=8010<POINTOPOINT,MULTICAST> mtu 1280
```

This method works in FreeBSD and NetBSD, but not on Mac OS X even though it is documented in the manual pages for ifconfig on Darwin 6.8/Mac OS X 10.2.8 (aka Jaguar) as well as on Darwin 7.2.0/Mac OS X 10.3.2 (aka Panther) and in the usage information printed by the ifconfig command itself. However, Mac OS X comes with gif0 created as standard so if only a single tunnel is needed this poses no problem.

3. Assign the two (remote and local) IPv4 addresses of the tunnel endpoints, e.g.:

```
# ifconfig gif0 tunnel 130.1.2.3 134.5.6.7
```

4. Assign the local IPv6 addresses of the tunnel:

```
# ifconfig gif0 inet6 alias <Local_IPv6_TUNNEL_ ADDR> \
                           prefixlen <Length of prefix for tunnel address>
```

For example:

```
# ifconfig gif0 inet6 alias 2001:DEAD:BEAF:ABBA::1 prefixlen 64
```

Note that the "alias" keyword is not necessary on all BSD OSes, but it never hurts to include it. The prefix length may be omitted when it its equal to 64 since 64 is the default. When the user has only one or a few tunnels, it is recommended to use a 64 bit prefix length as that will typically also be used for other (less virtual) interfaces. However, longer (more specific) prefix lengths are not a problem and may be an attractive choice for tunnel brokers hosting many tunnels from a limited address space. It is wise to avoid prefixes longer than 126 bits as some implementations have reportedly had problems with 127 and 128 bit long prefixes, even though the authors are not currently aware of any such problems in recent releases of any operating system. Still, taking a prefix of 120, 126 or even 112 bits in length barely wastes address space and may be worthwhile to avoid any potential problems. For more details on this please refer to RFC 3627 [RFC3627].

In the above commands it is also possible to specify both the source and destination IPv6 addresses of the tunnel but it is not necessary as the routing subsystem does not need to know the remote end's global address (it is enough to be able to talk to the next hop using link-local addressing). Though for administrative reasons it may be attractive to assign the destination address too. Some non KAME derived implementations even *require* the global IPv6 addresses of both tunnel endpoints to be set. This is accomplished by substituting the above command with, for example:

```
# ifconfig gif0 inet6 alias 2001:DEAD:BEAF:ABBA::1 \
                                     2001:DEAD:BEAF:ABBA::2 prefixlen 128
```

Actually, as routing over an interface can work without assigning global addresses at all, it should not be necessary to assign any of them. Indeed, KAME derived IPv6 stacks do not require global IPv6 addresses to be assigned to a tunnel interface (as tested by the author with NetBSD and FreeBSD 3.x). In that case, one needs to explicitly add a route over the tunnel interface to the link-local address of the remote tunnel end (or run a routing protocol that will figure it out for itself using the well-known multicast address). For example, to add a default route over a tunnel interface to a remote end with link-local address fe80::2, one would add a route like this:

```
# route add -inet6 default fe80::2%gif0
```

or

```
# route add -inet6 default -ifp gif0
```

Such unnumbered tunnels will typically only make sense when both tunnel endpoint use a KAME derived IPv6 stack as other implementations usually don't support unnumbered tunnels.

Alternative with FreeBSD

As an alternative to the above way of creating a manual IPv6-in-IPv4 tunnel, FreeBSD also offers the possibility to set up a tunnel by only modifying the contents of `/etc/rc.conf` file such that the tunnel is automatically created and configured at boot time. Add the following lines to the `rc.conf` file:

```
gif_interfaces="gif0"
gifconfig_gif0="130.1.2.3 134.5.6.7" \
                    ipv6_ifconfig_gif0="2001:DEAD:BEAF:ABBA::1 \
                    2001:DEAD:BEAF:ABBA::2 prefixlen 128"
```

Alternative with NetBSD

With NetBSD, one can easily configure a tunnel interface by making a corresponding `/etc/ifconfig.<ifn>` file, where `<ifn>` is the name if the interface (i.e. gif0).

For the example above one would create a file `/etc/ifconfig.gif0` containing the following lines:

```
create
    tunnel 130.1.2.3 134.5.6.7
    inet6 2001:DEAD:BEAF:ABBA::1 2001:DEAD:BEAF:ABBA::2 prefixlen 128
```

5.5.2 6over4

5.5.2.1 Microsoft Implementations

6over4 is included in the Microsoft Research IPv6 stack, Windows XP and the .NET Server family but is disabled by default. By the very nature of the 6over4 transitioning method, an IPv4 multicast enabled infrastructure must be available for 6over4 to be able to work.

To enable 6over4 type:

```
C:\>netsh interface ipv6 set global 6over4=enabled
```

at the command prompt. This will create a new 6over4 tunnelling pseudo-interface for each IPv4 address assigned to the host.

5.5.3 6to4

5.5.3.1 Cisco IOS (as Client and Relay)

A Cisco router running a version of IOS that includes 6to4 support can either become a 6to4 client, if it only has IPv4 connectivity or, if the router already has global IPv6 connectivity, become a 6to4 relay.

Client configuration

To configure a Cisco router as a 6to4 client is rather easy and can be done by setting up a tunnel as follows:

```
interface Tunnel64
        no ip address
        no ip redirects
        ipv6 unnumbered FastEthernet0
        tunnel source FastEthernet0
        tunnel mode ipv6ip 6to4
```

One also has to set up the following route:

```
ipv6 route 2002::/16 Tunnel64
```

Configuration as a 6to4 relay

If the tunnel and route is configured as described above on a router, which also has outside connectivity to the rest of the IPv6 Internet, this router automatically functions as a 6to4 relay and can thus provide outside connectivity to all hosts connected to it by 6to4.

5.5.3.2 Extreme (ExtremeWare IPv6)

Dual stack Extreme switches (with a globally unique IPv4 address) can be configured to communicate with other isolated IPv6 domains using the 6to4 automatic tunnelling mechanism. Supposing that the two (layer 3) switches A and B are access routers of such domains willing to make use of 6to4, they should be configured as follows below.

Like configured tunnels 6to4 tunnelling requires an active IPv4 interface on the switch. With 6to4 the address of this interface is embedded in the IPv6 address of the tunnelling interface. If that particular IPv4 interface goes down, tunnelling fails even if other IPv4 interfaces are available on the switch.

To avoid this situation, we create an IPv4 VLAN with loopback enabled. Even if all of the ports on the VLAN go down, the VLAN stays up and so does the tunnel. At the cost of an additional VLAN on each 6to4 router and advertisement of the additional IPv4 address, you ensure greater tunnel stability.

Switch A:

```
create vlan to_router_b
configure vlan to_router_b add ports 1-10
configure vlan to_router_b ipaddress 128.176.191.82/24
enable loopback-mode to_router_b
create tunnel 6to4_to_b 6to4
configure tunnel 6to4_to_b ipaddress 2002:80b0:b807::1/16
enable ipforwarding ipv6 6to4_to_b
```

Switch B:

```
create vlan to_router_a
```

```
configure vlan to_router_a add ports 1-5
configure vlan to_router_a ipaddress 128.176.184.7/24
enable loopback-mode to_router_a
create tunnel 6to4_to_a 6to4
configure tunnel 6to4_to_a ipaddress 2002:80b0:bf52::1/16
enable ipforwarding ipv6 6to4_to_a
```

5.5.3.3 Windows XP

First, IPv6 functionality should be enabled on the Windows XP host as described in Appendix B. If there is no native IPv6 on the LAN the host is connected to, the operating system configures a "6to4 Tunnelling Pseudo-Interface" and adds a default route pointing to Microsoft's Research 6to4 relay router, i.e. 6to4.ipv6.microsoft.com. This allows you to initially test the newly enabled IPv6 stack and its functionality through the "tracert6" command while pointing to the above host. Unfortunately, this automatically enabled configuration will not allow you to establish a connection to any other IPv6 host or networks.

In order to establish connectivity with other IPv6 networks, such as 6NET, the 6to4 tunnel should be configured to point to a free 6to4 relay router. For example, the following command

```
C:/>netsh interface ipv6 6to4 set relay x.y.w.z
```

points the host's 6to4 tunnel to the 6to4 relay router with the IPv4 address x.y.w.z.

In order for this 6to4 client to serve a whole subnet as IPv6 default router, the /48-prefix, the host configured itself with needs to be advertised on the normal LAN interface. Also the default route needs to be specifically set to be published:

```
C:/>netsh interface ipv6 add route 2002:<IPv4 address in hex>::/48 \\
          <number of normal LAN interface> publish=yes \\
          validlifetime=<valid lifetime of route> \\
          preferredlifetime=<period for which the route is preferred>
C:/>netsh interface ipv6 set route ::/0 \\
                <name or number of 6to4 interface> publish=yes
```

5.5.3.4 Windows 2000

A Windows 2000 host can be manually configured to access IPv6 sites through the 6to4 tunnelling mechanism. The "ipv6" utility, which is included in the "Microsoft IPv6 Technology Preview" software, is used for setting the appropriate configuration to the 6to4 tunnel interface. The required steps for acquiring connectivity with other (6to4) IPv6 hosts are the following:

1. Configure the host 6to4 address for the "Tunnel Pseudo-Interface", using the colon-hexadecimal encoding of the IPv4 address of the Ethernet interface. For example, if the IPv4 host address is 195.251.29.19, the 6to4 IPv6 address should be 2002:c3fb:1d13::c3fb:1d13 and the full command is

```
C:/>ipv6 adu 2/2002:c3fb:1d13::c3fb:1d13
```

Note that the "Tunnel Pseudo-Interface" is used for statically configured tunnels, automatic tunnelling and 6to4 tunnels.

2. Add the appropriate entry in the routing table through the command that points all the IPv6 packets with 6to4 address to the "Tunnel Pseudo-Interface" by executing the command:

```
C:/>ipv6 rtu 2002::/16 2
```

3. In order to enable communication to an IPv6 network, a tunnel should be created to a 6to4 relay router. In the following example the command adds an IPv6 default route to a 6to4 relay at 194.177.210.38 through the interface 2:

```
C:/>ipv6 rtu ::/0 2/::194.177.210.38 pub
```

5.5.3.5 Linux

Manual Configuration using the command "ip"

To not depend on any distribution specific setup scripts one can create a 6to4 tunnelling interface by hand using the command "ip" and tunnel mode "sit" just like with manually configured tunnels. The only difference here is that there is no need to give any information about remote tunnel endpoints.

1. Create a new tunnel interface:

```
#/sbin/ip tunnel add <tunnelname> mode sit ttl <default ttl> remote any \
                                          local <local IPv4 address>
```

Example:

```
#/sbin/ip tunnel add tun6to4 mode sit ttl 0 remote any \
                                          local 128.176.184.7
```

Note: A TTL must be specified. Otherwise the TTL is inherited (value 0).

2. Bring the new interface up:

```
#/sbin/ip link set dev tun6to4 up
```

3. Add the local 6to4 address to interface. This is the address computed from the local IPv4 address used in the creation of the tunnel interface. Note that it is important to use the prefix length 16.

```
#/sbin/ip -6 addr add <local 6to4 address>/16 dev tun6to4
```

In this example the line would be:

```
#/sbin/ip -6 addr add 2002:80b0:b807::1/16 dev tun6to4
```

4. At last only the (default) route has to be configured accordingly. In this case we want to get the host connected to the rest of the IPv6 internet and thus configure the default route to point to the "all-6to4-(relay)-routers" IPv4 anycast address:

```
# /sbin/ip -6 route add 2000::/3 via ::192.88.99.1 dev tun6to4 metric 1
```

Using network-scripts with Redhat

Initially, IPv6 functionality should be enabled on the RedHat host (see Appendix B). Furthermore, in order to set up a 6to4 tunnel, one has to follow the next steps:

1. In the /etc/syconfig/network-scripts/ifcfg-eth0 file include:

```
IPV6TO4INIT=yes
```

   which forces the system to initialize a tunnel (sit1) using the configuration defined in the file "ifcfg-sit1".

2. Modify the /etc/sysconfig/ifcfg-sit1 file as follows:

```
DEVICE=sit1                      #Defines the name of the tunnel
BOOTPROTO=none                   #Disables the boot protocol
ONBOOT=yes                #Forces the interface to start on boot
IPV6INIT=yes                     #Initialising IPv6
IPV6TUNNELIPV4=x.y.z.w   #Set the remote IPv4 address of the tunnel
IPV6ADDR=2002:aabb:ccdd::aabb:ccdd/0 #Set local IPv6 address of the \
                                 tunnel
```

The above settings will create a 6to4 tunnel pointing to a 6to4 relay router. In the above configuration, x.y.z.w is the IPv4 address of a 6to4 relay router and 2002:<IPv4 address as hex>::<IPv4 address as hex> is the local 6to4 IPv6 address of the host. Note that the IPv6 address, e.g. 2002:aabb:ccdd::aabb:ccdd, is followed by a "/0" suffix in order to force the creation of a default route for all the 6to4 traffic through the sit1 tunnel.

In the file /etc/sysconfig/network include the following line:

```
IPV6_GATEWAYDEV=sit1
```

This sets the 6to4 tunnel interface sit1 as the default gateway for all IPv6 traffic.

5.5.3.6 FreeBSD, NetBSD and Darwin/Mac OS X 6to4 Client

FreeBSD, NetBSD and Darwin/Mac OS X (as well as probably OpenBSD9 use the stf0 (six-to-for) interface to configure 6to4. Good instructions on how to configure a stf-interface can be found at the following two weblocations:

http://www.netbsd.org/Documentation/network/ipv6/#typical2

and

http://onlamp.com/pub/a/onlamp/2001/06/01/ipv6_tutorial.html

6to4 with NetBSD's 6to4-script (Perl)

The easiest way to configure 6to4 on NetBSD (may also work on the other OSes) is to install the Perl script called "6to4", that comes with NetBSD itself. The script uses a configuration file called 6to4.conf in which all the needed configuration information is collected and properly commented. On can install the 6to4 script either manually or from NetBSD's pkgsrc system where it is found in /usr/pkgsrc/net/6to4.

5.5.3.7 BSD with Zebra

In this example the router is configured to advertise the 6to4 anycast prefix 192.88.99.0/24 using OSPFv2 [RFC3068], and to advertise the 6to4 prefix 2002::/16 [RFC3056] via BGP.

With FreeBSD, the file "/etc/rc.conf" is use for system-level configuration. Here one should add:

```
ifconfig_xl0_alias0="inet 192.88.99.1 netmask 0xffffff00"
stf_interface_ipv4addr="192.88.99.1"
stf_interface_ipv6_ifid="::"
ipv6_gateway_enable="YES"
```

The first listed command configures the IPv4 anycast prefix as an alias for the xl0 interface. Note that in real deployments, xl0 will have to be replaced by an address corresponding to the used physical interface with IPv4 connectivity. The second command specifies the address with which the IPv6 6to4 address for the relay router is created (the bits 16-47 of the IPv6 address). The third command sets all the site and interface-id bits to zero. The last command finally enables IPv6 forwarding on the router.

However, the file "rc.conf" can't be used to configure everything. For that reason some manual tuning of the file "rc.local" is also needed; the script is run after the processing of rc.conf has finished.

```
ifconfig stf0 inet6 2002:c058:6301:: prefixlen 16 anycast

/usr/local/sbin/zebra -d
/usr/local/sbin/bgpd -d
/usr/local/sbin/ospfd -d

/usr/local/bin/vtysh -b
```

The first command adds an "anycast" flag to the IPv6 6to4 address, so that it is not used as a source address in outgoing packets. The next three commands start zebra routing processes in the background. Finally the last command leads to "/usr/local/etc/Zebra.conf" being read and fed to the respective routing process as a configuration file.

The relevant parts of the Zebra configuration file /usr/local/etc/Zebra.conf" are:

```
router bgp 1741
 no bgp default ipv4-unicast
 neighbor 2001:708::2 remote-as 1741
 neighbor 2001:708::2 description 6net-rtr
 neighbor 2001:708:0:1::625 remote-as 1741
```

```
 neighbor 2001:708:0:1::625 description v6-rtr
!
 address-family ipv6
 network 2002::/16
 neighbor 2001:708::2 activate
 neighbor 2001:708::2 soft-reconfiguration inbound
 neighbor 2001:708:0:1::625 activate
 neighbor 2001:708:0:1::625 soft-reconfiguration inbound
 exit-address-family
!
router ospf
 ospf router-id 128.214.231.106
 network 128.214.231.104/29 area 3248883125
 network 192.88.99.0/24 area 3248883125
!
```

Here, the BGP sessions have been configured using AS1741 for two routers in the same autonomous system. The configuration syntax is similar to one used with Cisco IOS. The main difference is the Statement "network 2002::/16" under IPv6 address-family, which will originate a BGP advertisement for the 6to4 prefix.

The prefix 192.88.99.0/24 is advertised using OSPFv2 under a stub area. The simplest way is to use area 0 though. IPv4 BGP has been configured to advertise 192.88.99.0/24, but this will not work unless there exists an IGP route to it. Using static routes would be an option, but in this case the traffic would be blackholed should the relay router go down. For this purpose, OSPF was chosen so the BGP advertisements would cease immediately if the OSPF process on the relay router halts for any reason.

5.5.4 ISATAP

To use ISATAP within a site, one will need one or more IPv6 hosts supporting ISATAP, and also a dual stack router supporting it. The following paragraphs on configuration examples cover both host and router setup on multiple platforms. Different implementations of the mechanism should interoperate so that host and router platforms can be mixed as needed.

For general security consideration when setting up ISATAP within a site please refer to Chapter 9. Implementation specific security issues are being addressed in this chapter where needed.

5.5.4.1 Cisco IOS Platform (as Router/Server)

The setup of a Cisco router as ISATAP server one needs to define a tunnel interface as follows:

```
interface Tunnel0
    no ip address
    no ip redirects
    ipv6 address 2003:abc:def:123::/64 eui-64
```

```
    no ipv6 nd suppress-ra
    tunnel source FastEthernet0
    tunnel mode ipv6ip isatap
```

If an ISATAP supporting client is set up to know about this Cisco router it will be able to automatically configure its interface with the prefix above. The last 64 bits will be based on the EUI-64 address and include the IPv4 address of the client as specified in the ISATAP draft [TGTT05]. According to present experience with ISATAP it does not matter which interface is specified as the tunnel source as long as it has an IPv4 address reachable by the clients. One can also specify an address directly.

5.5.4.2 6WIND (as router/server)

The following configuration example was tested on a 6WINDgate 6231 running version 6.3.0b12 of SixOS.

Configuring a 6WIND router to become an ISATAP router is really rather easy and consists mainly of only two commands, one specifying the IPv4 address of the tunnelling interface the other defining the prefix to use for the global IPv6 addresses in the ISATAP subnet. This configuration enables the router to give itself a valid global (ISATAP style) IPv6 address as well as to send out router advertisements to possible clients.

For the following example we assume that one has logged on to the router as user "admin" or as a user with similar permissions.

1. The first step in the configuration is of course to switch to the configuration context for the configuration file one wants to edit which in the case of this example is the running configuration. Within the configuration context one has to enter the migration context:

```
sixwind{} edit running
sixwind{running} mig
```

2. Now follows the actual ISATAP configuration. First one has to configure an "ISATAP router", that is a separate routing process for the outgoing IPv4 interface one uses for the tunnelling. It is possible to define several of these processes each with a different number and possibly different IPv4 addresses.

The theoretic command for this configuration is:

```
sixwind{running-mig} isatap_router 'number' 'address_v4' ['address_v4']
```

As 'number' one specifies the number of the ISATAP process, 'address_v4' is the IPv4 address of the interface the automatic tunnels end on. The optional 'address_v4' feature is given as either "up" or "down" and defines configured process is switched on or off. If no state is given the default is "down".

Later on the state of an ISATAP routing process can also be changed by the command

```
sixwind{running-mig} isatap_router 'number' 'state'
```

In our example however we immediately specified the state as "up":

```
sixwind{running-mig} isatap_router 1 128.176.191.74 up
```

3. Next a prefix has to be defined which is announced into the ISATAP subnet. This prefix should have length 64 and it should be taken care that there is not yet a route defined for this prefix, e.g. by having configured another interface of the router with an address within this prefix.

The theoretic command for this configuration step is:

```
sixwind{running-mig} isatap_prefix 'number' 'address_v6/len'
```

specifies the ISATAP routing process this prefix corresponds to and thus should be the same as in the command above. In our example the prefix was configured as follows:

```
sixwind{running-mig} isatap_prefix 1 2001:db8:10:110::/64
```

4. At last after exiting from the migration context the new configuration has to be applied to the running configuration and one can also add it to the startup configuration to not loose it during a reboot:

```
sixwind{running-mig} exit
    sixwind{running} addrunning
    sixwind{running} exit
    sixwind{} copy running start
```

5.5.4.3 Windows XP host (as client)

Manual Configuration as ISATAP Client

Since Service Pack 1 ISATAP, like all IPv6 functionality, is configured using the "netsh" command in the command shell. Only the IPv4 address of an ISATAP server is needed to configure a Windows XP host as an ISATAP client. (Of course it is required that IPv6 be installed on the host before using "ipv6 install"). The full command to set up ISATAP after that is:

```
C:\>netsh interface ipv6 isatap set router \
                                            <IPv4 address of ISATAP router>
```

This is it. With the command "ipconfig /all" one can verify that the host has indeed received router advertisements from the server and configured its interface accordingly with an IPv6 ISATAP address. Using the command "tracert" or typing

```
C:\>netsh interface ipv6 show route
```

further shows, that the default route is now also configured for the ISATAP interface (number 4), even though 6to4 probably still also is configured.

Automatic Configuration as ISATAP Client

When the IPv6 protocol is started (e.g. at boot or installation) and realizes that there is no native IPv6 connectivity on the link, it tries to resolve the hostname "ISATAP" (on Windows XP without SP1 "_ISATAP"). If this hostname resolves into an IPv4 address the host will configure itself as an

ISATAP client for this server and set the default route accordingly. Please note that the host will also configure 6to4 but just as a backup to the ISATAP connection or to communicate with other 6to4 sites.

5.5.4.4 .NET/Windows 2003 Server (as Client and Router/Server)

Windows 2003 Server can be configured as both ISATAP client and server.

Windows 2003 Server as ISATAP Client

Configuring a .NET/2003 server as an ISATAP client works just like with Windows XP either manually with the command netsh or automatically by resolving the name "ISATAP". The only difference is that once ISATAP is installed the 6to4 configuration is deleted.

Windows 2003 Server as ISATAP Server

For a host running Windows 2003 server to become an ISATAP router it is of course necessary for the advertised ISATAP prefix to be routed to the server. Additionally the default route of the host needs to be configured to be published. Otherwise Windows clients will not automatically set their default route to their ISATAP interface.

To configure the default route to be published the following command is used:

```
C:\>netsh interface ipv6 set route ::/0 \\
                    "<name or number of default interface>" publish=yes
```

If the Windows server is a dual stack host integrated in a native IPv6 subnet, the default interface will most likely be the normal LAN interface (4). Otherwise it might be a configured tunnel or 6to4 interface.

```
C:\> netsh interface ipv6 set interface \\
                    "<interface name or number>" forwarding=enabled
```

Now the ISATAP interface has to be configured. In order to do so however it first needs to be enabled. This is achieved by configuring the Windows server as an ISATAP client for itself:

```
C:\> netsh interface ipv6 isatap set router <IPv4 address>
```

The IPv4 address refers to the physical interface used for the tunnelling.

The ISATAP interface now also has to be set to forward packets. Additionally it has to be configured do send out router advertisements:

```
C:\>netsh interface ipv6 set interface 2 forwarding=enabled \\
                                                  advertise=enabled
```

At last the route and thus the prefix to be advertised on the ISATAP interface is configured. Like the default route this route has to be explicitly configured to be published.

```
C:\> netsh interface ipv6 add route <ISATAP prefix/64> 2 \\
          publish=yes validlifetime=<valid lifetime of route> \\
```

```
        preferredlifetime=<period for which this route is preferred>
```

The time periods can be specified in seconds (s), minutes (m), hours (h) or days (d) (e.g. 1d2h3m4s). The default for validlifetime is eternity. If no preferredlifetime is given, the default is the value for validlifetime.

5.5.4.5 Linux (as Client and Router/Server)

ISATAP has been included in the Linux kernel by the USAGI project [USAGI]. It can thus be patched into any present kernel sources and compiled as is described further down. One also needs the iproute package from USAGI.

Patching the Kernel

First one has to download the newest USAGI patch for the kernel one wants to patch, which are available on USAGI's pages at

ftp://ftp.linux-ipv6.org/pub/usagi/

Of course it is best to use stable versions.

Once downloaded and unpacked one can patch the existing kernel sources in /usr/src/linux by typing:

```
#patch -p1 <usagi-linux2<4,5 or 6>-stable-<snapshot>-<kernel-ver>.diff
```

After the sources have been patched the kernel needs to be configured by typing

```
# make xconfig
```

The section 'networking options' contains the new features. Here 'IPv6: ISATAP interface support (EXPERIMENTAL)' needs to be chosen. Please note that there were times when the ISATAP protocol was not favoured all the time and that ISATAP support is not available in all kernel versions.

Building USAGI iproute Packages

The USAGI project has its own iproute package. This is included in usagi-tools-* which can also be found at the above URLs.

Configuring a Linux Host as an ISATAP Gateway

If a Linux host is used as an ISATAP router this router becomes a kind of access router for an ISATAP subnet. This subnet has to be provided with a prefix just like any other subnet and this prefix has to be routed.

During a test setup, the host lemy.uni-muenster.de has been configured as an ISATAP router. At the same time this host was already a normal access router to another IPv6 subnet with the prefix 2001:638:500:200::/64 and connected to the rest of the IPv6 internet by an IPv6-in-IPv4 tunnel.

For simplicity the /64 prefix was shortened to /63, so 2001:638:500:201::/64 could be used for the ISATAP subnet.

After compiling the kernel and rebooting the host the first thing to do is to configure an ISATAP interface (is0). In the test setup the IPv4 address of the interface where the packets come through (eth0 on host lemy.uni-muenster.de) was 128.176.184.113. So the interface was configured by typing:

```
#/sbin/ip tunnel add is0 mode isatap local 128.176.184.113 ttl 64
```

To enable the interface:

```
#/sbin/ip link set is0 up
```

Now the interface has to be configured with an IPv6 ISATAP address. An ISATAP address includes the IPv4 address of the host and has the format:

<prefix/64>:0:5efe:<IPv4 address in hex format>

In this case host lemy.uni-muenster.de has the IPv4 IP 128.176.184.113 and is configured with an address for the prefix 2001:638:500:201::/64. So the ISATAP address for lemy is:

2001:638:500:201:0:5efe:80b0:b871

To add this address to the interface configuration type:

```
#/sbin/ip addr add 2001:638:500:201:0:5efe:80b0:bf71/64 dev is0
```

Now the host has to actually be configured to become a router and send out router advertisements. Usually 'radvd' is used for router advertisements. It can be found at

http://v6web.litech.org/radvd/

In this case the configuration file for radvd (usually /etc/radvd.conf) has the following entries:

```
interface is0
{
    AdvSendAdvert on;
    UnicastOnly on;
    AdvHomeAgentFlag off;
    prefix 2001:638:500:201::0/64
    {
          AdvOnLink on;
          AdvAutonomous on;
          AdvRouterAddr off;
    };
};
```

Now the router configuration is done. To have this setup come up at boot one can add the "/sbin/ip" lines from above to /etc/rc.local.

Configuring a Linux Host as an ISATAP client

To configure a Linux host as an ISATAP client one has to know the IPv4 address of the host acting as the ISATAP gateway (in this case lemy.uni-muenster.de = 128.176.184.113) and the IPv4 address of the client in question (here 128.176.245.58). With this information configuration is performed by two commands:

```
#/sbin/ip tunnel add is0 mode isatap local 128.176.245.58 v4any \
                                                128.176.184.113 ttl 64
# /sbin/ip link set is0 up
```

Now the client should be connected to the rest of the IPv6 world, as long as the ISATAP server has global IPv6 connectivity.

5.5.5 OpenVPN Tunnel Broker

This following sections describe the process of setting up an OpenVPN based IPv6 tunnel broker to enable ISP-independent IPv6 connectivity that is authenticated, secure, stable, and IPv4 source address independent.

Though the OpenVPN client runs on many different platforms and hence a tunnel broker that is based on OpenVPN should be able to accommodate quite a large number of different client OSes, this section will only deal with Linux and Windows clients for now, since those are the client OSes that haven been tested as tunnel broker clients.

5.5.5.1 Installation of Tunnel Broker components

To set up an OpenSSL certification authority it is sufficient to install the OpenSSL package on your Linux distribution (check that the openssl-binary is present and executable as root). The more difficult step is to create an appropriate configuration file and to create the necessary CA certificates and keys. This section will present a sample openssl.cnf configuration file that is self explanatory and that may be edited to fit individual needs. It will also list the necessary steps to create all CA keys and certificates.

Installation of the OpenSSL CA

First, you need to create an openssl.cnf file. The following listing shows an example openssl.cnf that was used for an OpenSSL CA:

```
#
# OpenSSL example configuration file.
#
HOME                    = .
RANDFILE                = $ENV::HOME/.rnd
oid_section             = new_oids

[ new_oids ]

[ ca ]
default_ca      = CA_default

[ CA_default ]
dir             = /usr/local/etc/openvpn/ssl       # Adjust this!
certs           = $dir
crl_dir         = $dir
database        = $dir/index.txt
new_certs_dir   = $dir
```

```
certificate     = $dir/tmp-ca.crt              # Adjust this!
serial          = $dir/serial
crl             = $dir/crl.pem
private_key     = $dir/tmp-ca.key              # Adjust this!
RANDFILE        = $dir/.rand

x509_extensions = usr_cert

name_opt        = ca_default
cert_opt        = ca_default
default_days    = 365                          # Adjust this!
default_crl_days= 30
default_md      = md5
preserve        = no
policy          = policy_match

[ policy_match ]
countryName             = match
stateOrProvinceName     = match
organizationName        = match
organizationalUnitName  = optional
commonName              = supplied
emailAddress            = optional

[ policy_anything ]
countryName             = optional
stateOrProvinceName     = optional
localityName            = optional
organizationName        = optional
organizationalUnitName  = optional
commonName              = supplied
emailAddress            = optional

[ req ]
default_bits            = 1024
default_keyfile         = privkey.pem
distinguished_name      = req_distinguished_name
attributes              = req_attributes
x509_extensions = v3_ca
string_mask = nombstr

[ req_distinguished_name ]
```

```
countryName                    = Country Name (2 letter code)
countryName_default            = DE              # Adjust this!
countryName_min                = 2
countryName_max                = 2

stateOrProvinceName            = State or Province Name (full name)
stateOrProvinceName_default    = Nordrhein-Westfalen   # Adjust this!

localityName                   = Locality Name (eg, city)
localityName_default           = Muenster              # Adjust this!

0.organizationName             = Organization Name (eg, company)
0.organizationName_default     = ZIV, WWU Muenster     # Adjust this!

organizationalUnitName         = Organizational Unit Name (eg, section)
organizationalUnitName_default = JOIN-Projekt          # Adjust this!

commonName                     = Common Name (eg, YOUR name)
commonName_max                 = 64

emailAddress                   = Email Address
emailAddress_max               = 64

[ req_attributes ]
challengePassword              = A challenge password
challengePassword_min          = 4
challengePassword_max          = 20

unstructuredName               = An optional company name

[ usr_cert ]
basicConstraints=CA:FALSE
nsComment                      = "OpenSSL Generated Certificate"
subjectKeyIdentifier=hash
authorityKeyIdentifier=keyid,issuer:always

[ v3_req ]
basicConstraints = CA:FALSE
keyUsage = nonRepudiation, digitalSignature, keyEncipherment

[ v3_ca ]
subjectKeyIdentifier=hash
```

```
authorityKeyIdentifier=keyid:always,issuer:always
basicConstraints = CA:true

[ crl_ext ]
authorityKeyIdentifier=keyid:always,issuer:always
```

Please note that you need to include "-config openssl.cnf" (where openssl.cnf is to be given with full path if not located in current directory) in every call of the openssl-binary.

Also note that you must initialise the files index.txt and serial when setting up the CA. You can create index.txt as an empty file and serial with the content "01". Additionally, you need a DH-hash that you can create with the command

```
#openssl dhparam -out /usr/local/etc/openvpn/ssl/dh1024.pem 1024
```

After creating the openssl.cnf file you must then create the keys and certificates for your CA.

It is important to note that this section shows a rather lax use of a CA. Ideally, you should take the process of running a CA rather seriously, especially if you want to hold people liable for the abuse of your tunnel broker. If you already have an established CA, please try to use it for creating client and server certificates. This will add to the security of your tunnel broker. Please use "your own private little CA" just for experimental purposes or if you think that you can afford to keep the security rather lax.

To create your own CA keys and certificates, run the following command:

```
# openssl req -days 365 -new -x509 -keyout tmp-ca.key \
                                   -out tmp-ca.crt -config openssl.cnf
```

This command will create the secret key called "tmp-ca.key" and the certificate "tmp-ca.crt". Please note that the notation "tmp-ca.*" is intentional to make administrators aware that they are dealing with an experimental or temporary CA. Please make sure that the permissions for the secret key do not allow it to be read by any other user than the one who created it ("chmod 600 tmp-ca.key").

With these basic steps the setup of the OpenSSL CA is completed.

Installation of the OpenVPN server

At the time this was written, a very recent CVS version of the OpenVPN software was needed to have all functionality that was necessary for running the OpenVPN based IPv6 tunnel broker. The OpenVPN software can be found at

http://openvpn.sourceforge.net/

Please follow the installation instructions for the CVS version on the OpenVPN site. The installation is not expected to pose any problems.

It is assumed that the OpenVPN sources are compiled with the given installation prefix /usr/local which means that the configuration files can be found in /usr/local/etc/openvpn. Naturally, any other prefix works just as well but for the sake of readability, the /usr/local prefix will be used for the remainder of this section.

Installation of user database

The installation of a user database is completely optional. The more users need to be accommodated by the tunnel broker, the more sophisticated the user database should be. For testing purposes, a simple text file may suffice.

Since there are significant differences between each local user database requirement, this section will not deal with the setup of the database in detail.

5.5.5.2 Routing configuration

An important task when setting up and maintaining a tunnel broker is the organisation of the routing. Not only does one have to set up routes to the OpenVPN server which itself has to act as a router, one also needs to dynamically add routes upon a client connection and remove them afterwards. The routing itself is not very complicated but there are a few things that need to be taken into account when planning the routing.

- A /56 prefix is at the tunnel broker's disposal to assign addresses for clients (either single IPv6 addresses or complete prefixes).
- Subnet clients must be able to freely assign addresses from the /64 prefix they get assigned.
- All clients must be identifiable by their respective addresses (hermit clients) or prefixes (subnet clients).

A concept that would meet all of the above prerequisites might have the following form:

- The prefix used for the tunnel broker is 2001:638:500:f100::/56.
- All hermit hosts receive a /128 address coming from the prefix 2001:638:500:f1ff::/64.
- All subnet hosts receive /64 prefixes ranging from 2001:638:500:f101::/64 to 2001:638:500:f1fe::/64.
- The prefix 2001:638:500:f100::/64 is solely used for routing purposes for subnet hosts. Example: for a subnet client that is provided with the prefix 2001:638:500:f1ab::/64, the routing address 2001:638:500:f100::f1ab:1/112 is used for the P-t-P interface on the OpenVPN server's side, the address 2001:638:500:f100::f1ab:2/112 is used on the OpenVPN client's side. This way routes can be assigned uses those routing addresses as Next-Hop. No addresses from 2001:638:500:f1ab::/64 are used and hence the client can freely assign addresses from this prefix locally.
- All clients are assigned the same addresses or prefixes every time they connect. There is a 1:1 mapping between address/prefix and X.509 certificate. This helps to identify tunnel broker clients by they IPv6 addresses.

Please note that we use /64 prefixes, as we expect to connect a single subnet to the tunnel broker. If a set of subnets wants to connect a /48 prefix per client has to be used.

The following figure depicts a sample address assignment and routing configuration for a subnet client.

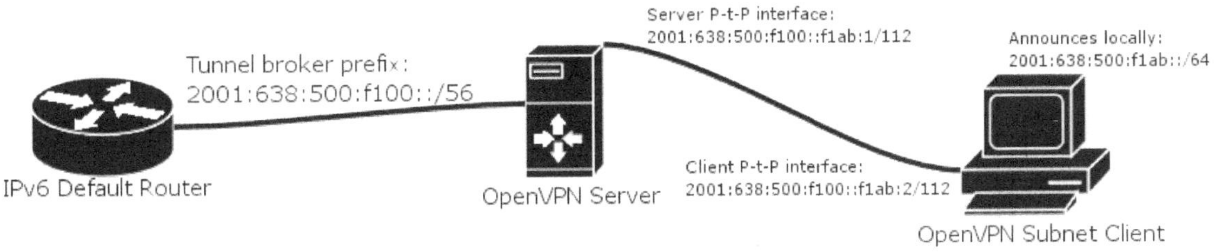

Figure 5-12 Sample Address Assignment and Routing Configuration

To show how the routing is arranged for several subnet clients, please see the following figure.

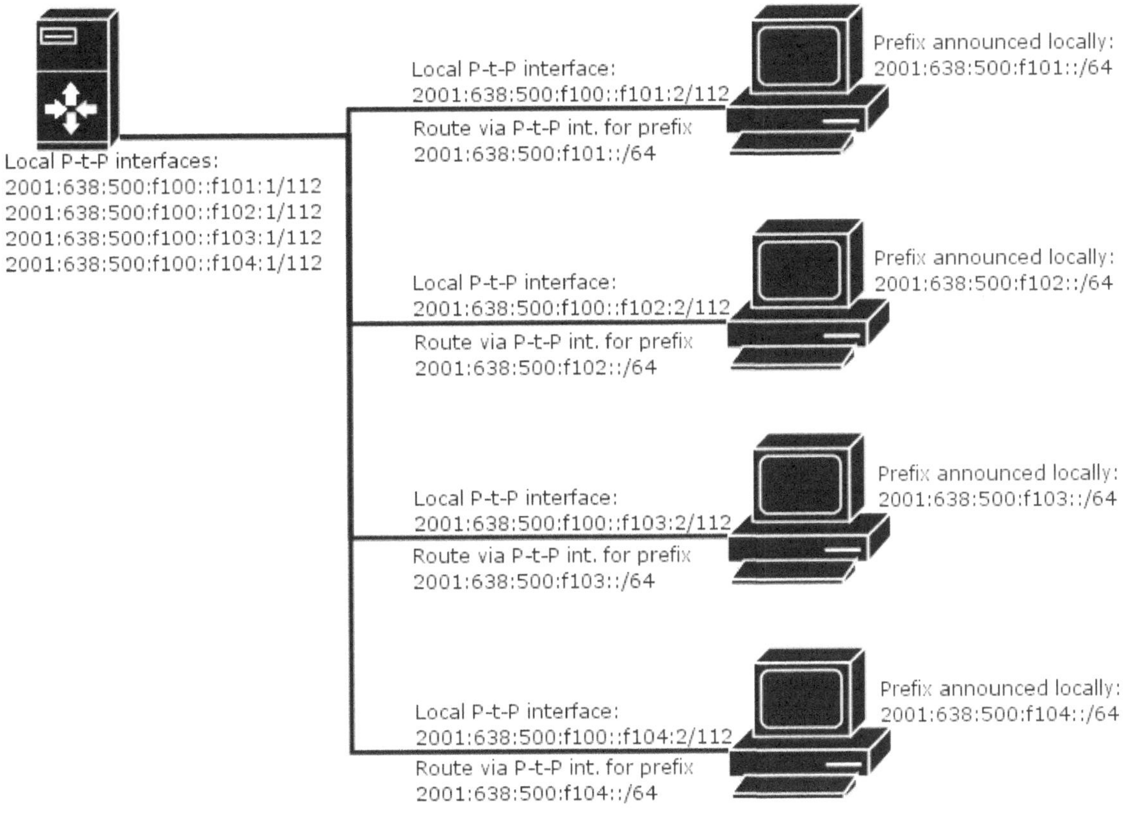

Figure 5-13 Sample Subnet Routing

The hermit client case is trivial: the server's local interface gets a fe80::1/64 IP address to have a next-hop address for the client on the other side. A route to the /128 IPv6 address of the client is added via the corresponding tunnel interface.

5.5.5.3 Sample server configuration

The server needs three mandatory configuration files per client (note: each client has his own server instance with its own configuration; also, each server occupies exactly one UDP port):

- basic configuration file
- TLS verification script
- "up" script to initialise tunnel interface and routing

A sample configuration file looks like this:

```
daemon server-user.name.ID
dev tun
tun-ipv6

up /usr/local/etc/openvpn/server-conf/user.name.ID.up
tls-server

log-append /usr/local/etc/openvpn/server-logs/user.name.ID.log

dh /usr/local/etc/openvpn/ssl/dh1024.pem
ca /usr/local/etc/openvpn/ssl/tmp-ca.crt
cert /usr/local/etc/openvpn/ssl/servers/user.name.ID.crt
key /usr/local/etc/openvpn/ssl/servers/user.name.ID.key
tls-verify /usr/local/etc/openvpn/server-conf/user.name.ID.tls-verify

port 5000

persist-tun
ping 15
ping-restart 45
ping-timer-rem
persist-key

verb 3
```

The first part of the configuration file configures the OpenVPN server itself (act as a daemon, use a tun P-t-P interface and optimise multiplexing for IPv6 tunnelling). The second part tells the server where to find the "up" script and the server should authorise connection via TLS. The third part defines where to write log messages. The fourth part tells the server where to find the Diffie Hellmann hash, the CA certificates, the client's public key, the server's private key and the TLS verification script that check's the client certificate's Common Name. The fifth part tells the server which UDP port to use. The sixth part is very important to guarantee the OpenVPN tunnel's stability when used on dial-up links. It tells the tunnel to try to be as persistent as possible by checking the status of the tunnel with regular pings and other techniques. These options also suffice in many cases to help a client to traverse a NAT gateway because the gateway might be able to recognise that there is constant traffic coming in over the same port. The seventh and last part sets the verbosity level of the log messages.

Another important configuration file is the "up" script that is run by the OpenVPN software after the tunnel has been established. The "up" script configures the local tunnel interface and handles the route setup.

```
#!/bin/bash

INTERFACE=$1; shift;
TUN_MTU=$1;   shift;
UDP_MTU=$1;   shift;
LOCAL_IP=$1;  shift;
REMOTE_IP=$1; shift;
MODUS=$1;     shift;

ip link set ${INTERFACE} up
ip link set mtu ${TUN_MTU} dev ${INTERFACE}

ip -6 addr add 2001:638:500:f100::f101:1/112 dev ${INTERFACE}
ip -6 addr add fe80::f101:1/64 dev ${INTERFACE}
ip -6 route add 2001:638:500:f101::/64 dev ${INTERFACE}
exit 0
```

5.5.5.4 Sample subnet client configuration

This paragraph will present a sample subnet client configuration. Since a hermit client's configuration is almost the same, it is easy to deduct the configuration for it from this subnet client's sample configuration.

The basic configuration file of the client that corresponds to the server in the above paragraph looks like the following:

```
daemon client-user.name.ID
dev tun
tun-ipv6

remote corello.uni-muenster.de

up /etc/openvpn/user.name.ID.up

tls-client
ca /etc/openvpn/tmp-ca.crt
cert /etc/openvpn/user.name.ID.crt
key /etc/openvpn/user.name.ID.key

tls-verify /etc/openvpn/tls-verify

port 5000
```

```
persist-tun
ping 15
ping-restart 45
ping-timer-rem
persist-key

verb 3
exit 0
```

The configuration is similar to the server configuration. The only differences are that a remote server is defined that the OpenVPN client tries to connect to and that no DH hash is used. Usually all configuration files are placed in /etc/openvpn.

The "up" script of a subnet client also sets up the tunnel interface and it creates a default route via the tunnel interface. Additionally, it enables IPv6 packet forwarding and it adds a route for the /64 prefix that is assigned to the client via an internal interface (in most cases eth0):

```
#!/bin/bash

INTERFACE=$1; shift;
TUN_MTU=$1;   shift;
UDP_MTU=$1;   shift;
LOCAL_IP=$1;  shift;
REMOTE_IP=$1; shift;
MODUS=$1;     shift;

ip link set ${INTERFACE} up
ip link set mtu ${TUN_MTU} dev ${INTERFACE}

ip -6 addr add 2001:638:500:f100::f101:2/112 dev ${INTERFACE}
ip -6 addr add fe80::f101:2/64 dev ${INTERFACE}
ip -6 route add default dev ${INTERFACE} metric 1

sysctl -w net.ipv6.conf.all.forwarding=1
ip -6 addr show dev eth0 | grep 2001:638:500:f101::1/64 \
    >/dev/null 2>&1 || ip -6 addr \
    add 2001:638:500:f101::1/64 dev eth0
```

5.5.5.5 Management

The management of the tunnel broker may be complicated to handle manually. Therefore 6NET partners have written a very basic bash script that handles certificate creation, certificate signatures, server and client configurations and the creation of an archive file that may be given to users to set up the OpenVPN client on their machines. However, the script as of now can only be used to create client accounts, it cannot remove accounts and it does not handle the storage of client information in a user database. Therefore, the script should only be used as a reference for tunnel broker administrator how to set up local management. The script is released under the GNU GPL and may be modified to fit individual needs.

create-client-conf.sh is a script that is used to:

- create a client ID (e.g. user.name.ID),
- create an X.509 key and certificate for the client,
- sign the certificate using the CA's key,
- read routing relevant information from command line (hermit or subnet client, Linux or Windows host, prefix to use),
- create the server's configuration files and scripts,
- put all client relevant configuration files into an archive that is given to the user.

To facilitate debugging of the tunnel on the client's side, join-openvpn-sanity-check.sh can be run on a Linux subnet client. The script collects a number of different information and tries to analyse if the information makes sense. It tests the setup for potential errors and reports these errors back to the user. The script does not modify the system; it is "read-only". It also does not send information somewhere; it merely displays information on the console that can be used by the user to identify the source of a problem.

Both scripts may be freely downloaded and distributed under the terms of the GNU GPL, however it is important to note that the scripts should only be used as a reference for a local installation rather than as a full featured "all-in-one" package.

Note: Please make sure to read the README and INSTALL files that are included in the tarball because they contain important setup information for the scripts.

5.5.5.6 Client user guide

The installation of the OpenVPN based IPv6 tunnel broker client consists of three different steps:

1. Subscription to the service and receiving of configuration files from tunnel broker.
2. Installation of the OpenVPN client.
3. Installation of the OpenVPN configuration files provided by the tunnel broker.

The subscription part is the non technical part. The technical part starts with the installation of the OpenVPN client. The client should be the newest version and should match the version of the server if possible. It can be downloaded at http://openvpn.sourceforge.net/. Please install the package according to the documentation that can be found on the OpenVPN homepage (quick guide: under Windows, simply double click the EXE file; under Linux, make sure that you have tun-driver and IPv6-support in your kernel and that you have OpenSSL-devel and LZO-devel packages installed and do a "./configure ; make ; make install" -- for details, please refer to OpenVPN's documentation).

The configuration files that are provided by the tunnel broker must be copied to either /etc/openvpn (Linux) or to the config subdirectory of your OpenVPN installation (Windows). Starting the client is trivial.

For Linux type:

```
#openvpn --config /etc/openvpn/<your.ID>.conf
```

For Windows, run OpenVPN either as a service or from the cmd.exe shell.

5.5.6 DSTM

5.5.6.1 A DSTM Experiment with FreeBSD 4.5

The DSTM server/TEP implementation by ENST [ENST] is available on the ENST's web site:

http://www.ipv6.rennes.enst-bretagne.fr/dstm/

The implementation requires that the server and gateway (TEP) be installed on the same host if the allocations made by the server should be coherent with the tunnels set up on the TEP. An external TEP (For example a 6Wind router with DSTM code) can also be used (But, this scenario has not been tested). In that case the TEP manages the tunnels directly and does not interact with the server, which then only is responsible for distributing the leases of IPv4 addresses. It must only be insured that the leases expire/renew durations are coherent with respect to the TEP configuration. In this configuration example however the TEP and the server are the same program. Thus the tunnel extremities are on the machine running the server and there is no way to use two different Linux/FreeBSD nodes separating the server from the TEP.

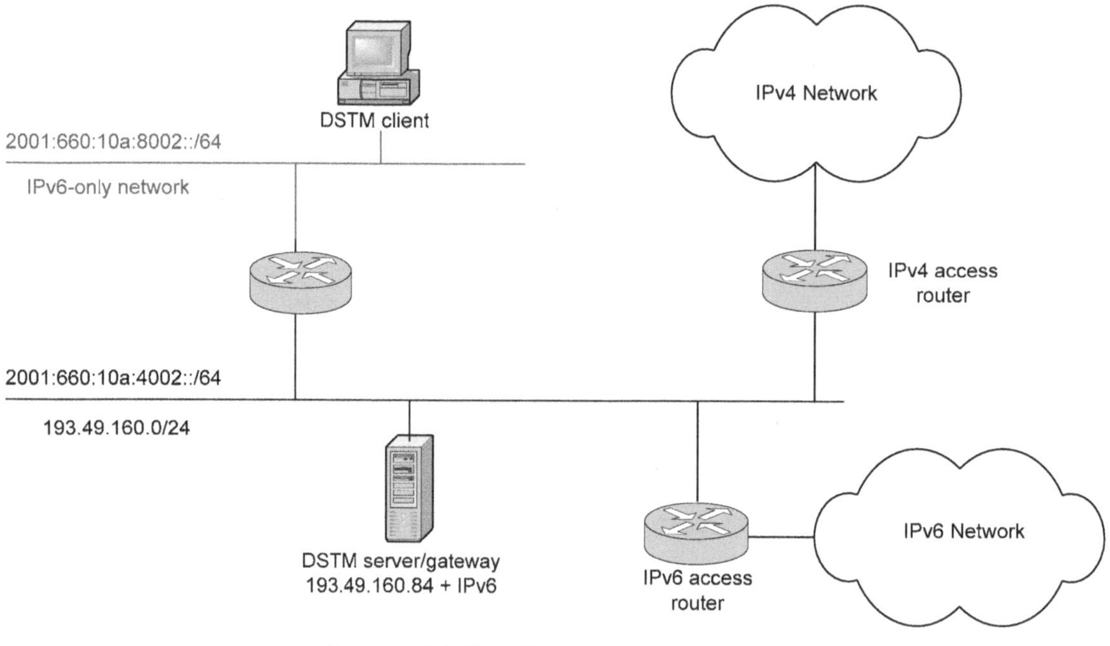

Figure 5-14 Test Network Infrastructure

When installing DSTM one has to be aware of the fact that the TEP has to be the router declared as having access to the IPv4 address pool from the IPv4 world, and that the DSTM server program does not manage route advertisements. Therefore, on the server site, one must provide by some way routes and route advertisements for the IPv4 addresses of DSTM clients toward the TEP node. For example on the site entry router, one can set a route for the remote IPv4 address pool allocated to DSTM clients toward the TEP IPv4 address, and make sure that this IPv4 route is announced or aggregated. Also there are routing loops between the TEP and the site IPv4 default router thus, on the TEP node; one should set a static discard route to suppress all traffic to down clients.

The DSTM implementation uses RPCv6, TSP and TSP–SSL (For VPN scenario) for the communication between DSTM Server/TEP and DSTM clients. Until now, the current implementation has no support for DHCPv6

DSTM Installation

To Install DSTM, one needs to perform the system installation which includes the application of an RPC patch from the ENST website and then commencing with the installation of DSTM system modules. To install DSTM system modules the source code should be unpacked and after going to dstmd directory, the 'make system' and 'make systeminstall' commands should be executed to compile the system modules.

Note that the website mentioned above explains the installation procedure in more detail.

After system installation one needs to configure the DSTM server/TEP and the DSTM clients as follows:

Configuration of the DSTM server/TEP

In this example the following lines where the output from the command "ifconfig" before starting on the configuration of the DSTM server:

```
xl0: flags=8843<UP,BROADCAST,RUNNING,SIMPLEX,MULTICAST> mtu 1500
        inet 193.49.160.84 netmask 0xffffff00 broadcast 255.255.255.0
        inet6 fe80::260:8ff:fe59:6623%xl0 prefixlen 64 scopeid 0x1
        inet6 2001:660:10a:4002:260:8ff:fe59:6623 prefixlen 64 autoconf
        ether 00:60:08:59:66:23
        media: Ethernet 10baseT/UTP (10baseT/UTP <half-duplex>)
gif0: flags=8050<POINTOPOINT,RUNNING,MULTICAST> mtu 1280
        inet6 fe80::260:8ff:fe59:6623%gif0 prefixlen 64 scopeid 0x7
```

The following lines should be added to /etc/rc.local:

```
ifconfig gif0 create
ifconfig gif1 create
ifconfig gif2 create
ifconfig gif3 create
sysctl -w net.inet.ip.forwarding=1          # enables IPv4 routing

route add -net 195.98.237.144/28 193.49.160.126 -reject
```

The following lines should be added to /etc/rc.conf:

```
hostname="DSTM-server.renater.fr"           # Name of the workstation
ifconfig_xl0="inet 193.49.160.84 255.255.255.0"    # IP configuration
ipv6_enable="YES"                     # Enables IPv6
portmap_enable="YES"                        # Enables portmap (used by DSTM)
portmap_program="/usr/sbin/rpcbind"   # Portmap program
defaultrouter="193.49.160.126"        # Default gateway
```

In /usr/local/etc/rpcdstmd.conf one should add:

```
subnet 195.98.237.144 netmask 255.255.255.224 {  # IPv4 address pool used
   default-lease-time 1200;
   tep6 2001:660:10a:4002:260:8ff:fe59:6623;# IPv6 address of the
                                              # TEP (itself here)
   tep4 193.49.160.84;                      # IPv4 address of the TEP
                                              # (itself here)
   range 195.98.237.146 195.98.237.158;      # Part of the pool used for
                                              # allocations
}
```

To launch the server one has to execute:

```
# touch /var/db/rpcdstmd.lease
# /usr/src/sbin/dstmd/server/rpcdstmd -notsp -rpcport 6000
```

Configuration of the DSTM client

Output from command "ifconfig":

```
xl0: flags=8843<UP,BROADCAST,RUNNING,SIMPLEX,MULTICAST> mtu 1500
        options=3<rxcsum,txcsum>
        inet6 fe80::2c0:4fff:fe83:22c4%xl0 prefixlen 64 scopeid 0x1
        inet6 2001:660:10a:8002:2c0:4fff:fe83:22c4 prefixlen 64 autoconf
        ether 00:c0:4f:83:22:c4
        media: Ethernet autoselect (100baseTX <full-duplex>) status: active
```

The following lines should be added to the file /etc/rc.config on the client host.

```
hostname="DSTM-client.renater.fr"
ipv6_enable="YES"
```

Lines to add to /etc/rc.local:

```
ifconfig gif1 create                # creates one tunnel interface
sysctl -w net.inet.ip.dti_magic=10  # sets up the DTI timer (time the kernel
                                    # sleeps waiting dstmd daemon to do
                                    # something)
```

To launch the daemon type:

```
# dstmd -rpcserver <DSTM-server> -port 6000
```

It is necessary to specify the name or the address of the DSTM server and sometimes the port.

Tests results and Issues

When installation and configuration is accomplished, it is possible for every DSTM client to communicate with IPv4 hosts using IPv4 enabled applications.

The performance testing of DSTM was done over a Very High Speed Network (1Gbps) and comparison was made between normal IPv4 communication and DSTM IPv4 communication over the network. When DSTM performance was measured after measuring IPv4 performance, then it was found that RTT (Round Trip Time) decreased just about 2 percent and throughput decreased just around 7 percent if the payload size was kept below 1212 bytes (limit after which fragmentation starts with DSTM configurations). If the payload size was bigger, throughput decreased a bit more due to the increase of load with the DSTM mechanism.

There are also some other issues:

- Some times in older kernel versions the make script in the dstmd/bsd folder works only after a slight and minor modification.
- One has to rebuild the full kernel after making the RPCv6 patch and if one uses the patch, then it is also very sensitive to system version.
- RPCv6 mechanism cannot cross firewall and cannot be used for VPN scenario.
- With KAME, the correct number of gif (interfaces) must be put in the system configuration file (no dynamic gif).
- All IPv4 communication must be initiated by the DSTM client, because the DSTM client is the one that requests the tunnel to be set up (Although there exists an implementation that was not tested yet making it possible for remote IPv4-only hosts to initiate a communication with a DSTM client in an IPv6-only network).

5.5.6.2 DSTM using TSP-SSL (in a VPN scenario) on FreeBSD

Installation and Setup

Please refer to the previous section about how to install DSTM on a FreeBSD host.

In order to use SSL with TSP, some certificates are needed:

- Certificates with authority to sign other certificates (CA).
- Certificates (cert) and corresponding private keys, signed by some known CA.

For both server and client the following files and certificates are needed:

1) *local cert*: A file containing a certificate for the local machine and the corresponding private key. In the following example configuration this file will be /etc/dstmd/cert.pem. The certificate is signed by some CA. This CA must be known by any correspondent (the other side of a TSP connection) in its CA file (see below).

   Both the certificate and key are in PEM format, the certificate is the first data in the file.

   The file contains:

```
Comments
          -----BEGIN CERTIFICATE-----
          certificate
          -----END CERTIFICATE-----
```

```
Comments
-----BEGIN RSA PRIVATE KEY-----
Private key
-----END RSA PRIVATE KEY-----
```

The certificate's key may be protected (crypted) with a password/pass phrase. If the certificate's key is not encrypted, some measures should be taken to protect the file /etc/dstmd/cert.pem as a whole, i.e:

```
# chown root /etc/dstmd/cert.pem; chmod 400 /etc/dstmd/cert.pem
```

2) *password file*: If the certificate's key is encrypted, put the pass phrase needed to decode it in some other file (in clear text), e.g. /etc/dstmd/pass and protect it:

```
# chown root /etc/dstmd/pass; chmod 400 /etc/dstmd/pass
```

3) *CA*: A file containing all CAs used for signing certificates of correspondents, and also the CA signing the CA of this file (if there is a chain of certification), concatenated in some file, e.g.

```
# cat .../*CA*pem > /etc/dstmd/cacert.pem
```

Each CA is in PEM format, the file contains:

```
Comments
           -----BEGIN CERTIFICATE-----
           First CA
           -----END CERTIFICATE-----
           Comments
           -----BEGIN CERTIFICATE-----
           second CA
           -----END CERTIFICATE-----
```

4) *Accepted cert list*: If you want to restrict access to only some certificates.

One local cert is needed for the server and one for each client, but they may be the same - if the security risk of sharing is accepted. Note: cert key may protected by a password; if you use a password, it must be passed (clear text) to dstmd/rpcdstmd in a file (protected! use chmod 400). If you do not use a password, the key/cert file should be protected (chmod 400).

To obtain a certificate, either use a certificate issued by some authority (it seems that standard certificates are sufficient, no special "role" is needed), or use the easiest way and create one using the program openssl as described in the 'How to create CA and certs, using openssl' section of the README-SSL file provided with the SSL version of DSTM available on ENST's website.

Configuration of the DSTM Server/TEP

The DSTM server/TEP is configured exactly as described above (when using RPCv6). The difference when using TSP only arises when starting the server, for which one needs to execute the following command:

```
#rpcdstmd -tspport 7000
```

For using SSL with TSP start rpcdstmd with the following additional options:

```
-key /etc/dstmd/cert.pem -ca /etc/dstmd/cacert.pem
```

If the files exist and should be used also specify the following options:

```
-pass /etc/dstmd/
-cert /etc/dstmd/accepted.pem
```

Configuration of the DSTM Client (with TSP)

Again the only difference to using DSTM with RPC is the command to start the daemon:

```
#dstmd -tspserver 2001:688:1f9b:1003:207:e9ff:fe11:bfb8 -port 7000
```

When also using SSL of course also the necessary certificate options need to be specified:

```
-key /etc/dstmd/cert.pem -ca /etc/dstmd/cacert.pem
-pass /etc/dstmd/pass          (if /etc/dstmd/pass exists)
-cert /etc/dstmd/accepted.pem  (if /etc/dstmd/accepted.pem exists)
```

Testing Results and Issues

Installation was easy as an RPC patch was not needed and moreover DSTM is now a module so there was no need to recompile the kernel. The use of SSL greatly increases security but will also lead to a rather significant performance loss due to the added load of certificate verification when setting up new connections.

Please refer to the previous section of the configuration example on using DSTM with RPC on FreeBSD systems for more implementation results.

5.5.6.3 Linux (RedHat 7.3, 8.0, 9.0)

Availability

DSTM (currently version 2.1) for Linux is available from ENST and is virtually identical to the FreeBSD version available from the same source. The Server and TEP components must be co-located to work under this implementation and the client must be installed on any host that requires DSTM, the components communicate via RPCv6. The mechanism is available from the link below.

http://www.ipv6.rennes.enst-bretagne.fr/dstm/

Initial Installation and Configuration

To install DSTM the files must first be unzipped/untarred into an appropriate directory and the system modules compiled and installed. Regardless of the module required, the same basic configuration steps must be taken. First the system module must be compiled using the 'make system' and 'make installsystem' commands. Mostly there is no need of a kernel rebuild but the modules work only on a 2.4.* kernel where ipv6 is a module. Otherwise for new kernel versions, see 'linux/00README' and the module ipv6f and sometimes kernel rebuild will be needed after applying the given kernel patch. Also for the new kernels the module stuff (insmod etc.) has changed and hence must be updated.

The RPCv6 patch is not required even when using RPC. When using TSP + SSL one needs certificates, when only using TSP certificates are not needed.

Server/TEP Installation and Configuration

Installing the Server/TEP module (rpcdstmd), is done by moving to the '/dstmd/server' directory and running the 'make' and 'make install' commands.

The server is configured via the rpcdstmd.conf file that takes the following format:

```
subnet 194.80.38.225 netmask 255.255.255.240 {      # IPv4 address pool used
    default-lease-time 1200;                         # Default lease time
    tep6 2001:630:80:7100::1;                        # IPv6 address of the TEP
    tep4 194.80.38.38;                               # IPv4 address of the TEP
    range 194.80.38.227 194.80.33.230;               # Part of the pool used for
                                                     # allocations
}
```

There is some minor additional setup to be done at this point before the server can be started. First, IPv4 forwarding must be enabled:

```
# sysctl -w net.ipv4.ip_forward=1
```

Also, a lease file must be created:

```
# touch /var/db/rpcdstmd.lease
```

The needed modules are now automatically loaded and tunnels re created if needed, so there is no need for "-load" or "-create" options when running the server.

When running the server with RPC support one can execute:

```
# /usr/src/sbin/dstmd/server/rpcdstmd -notsp -rpcport 6000
```

To start the server with TSP support the command is the following:

```
# /usr/src/sbin/dstmd/server/rpcdstmd -tspport 6000
```

When using both SSL and TSP the program rpcdstmd has to be started with the following additional options:

```
-key /etc/dstmd/cert.pem -ca /etc/dstmd/cacert.pem
```

Of course the filenames "cert.pem" and "cacert.pem" need to be substituted with the real certificates on the system.

Also add the options:

```
-pass /etc/dstmd/pass
    -cert /etc/dstmd/accepted.pem
```

if either file exists and should be used.

Sometimes when the modules like dti.o are required, they do not load while launching the server then the modules should be loaded by using "insmod dti.o" or the "modprobe" after changing to the dstmd/linux/dtmod directory.

Client Installation and Configuration

To install the DSTM client module (dstmd) the 'make', 'make install' commands should be run from the '/dstmd' directory but no further configuration is necessary.

To run dstmd, a number of command line options must be included. One has to specify the server name (or IPv6 address) and port number that identifies the server and also an option to load the rpc module is necessary under Linux.

```
# dstmd -rpcserver penguin.trans.ipv6-uk.net -port 6000
```

When using TSP one can use the following command:

```
# dstmd -port 3545 -tspserver 2001:688:1fa1:2::100
```

When also using SSL with TSP one has to start the dstmd with the additional options:

```
-key /etc/dstmd/cert.pem -ca /etc/dstmd/cacert.pem
```

Also add the following options when either file is present and should be used:

```
-pass /etc/dstmd/pass
-cert /etc/dstmd/accepted.pem
```

In order to use IPv6 transport for DNS queries one should put IPv6 address(es) in the nameserver lines in the file /etc/resolv.conf on a client host. Otherwise one should at least not specify a hostname for the rpcserver option of the dstmd client if one uses IPv4 name resolution.

When the module dstm.o is required, it sometimes does not load automatically when launching the client. I those cases the module can be loaded by hand through the use of either the command "modprobe" or "insmod" (after changing to dstmd/linux/dstmmod).

Operational and Installation Issues

When installing DSTM under Linux (RedHat 7.3 or later) there were a number of issues encountered. Primarily, the kernel source (exact same version) is required in order to install properly and under RedHat (and perhaps other Linux derivatives) this is not in the default location. This can be resolved by providing a command line redirect. Also, when compiling the system module, the 'make system' and 'make installsystem' commands should be run, not 'make systeminstall' as listed.

Installation of DSTM on a Linux host with kernel 2.6.x, things where a little more complicated as IPv6 was not a module which made it necessary to patch the kernel itself and rebuild it completely. Even in this case though the modules dti.o or dstm.o sometimes fail to load automatically.

When installing the DSTM client (dstmd), the make install command fails due to dstmd.8 not being in /usr/local/man/man8. Under RedHat there is no /usr/local/man/man8 directory so this must be created and the dstmd.8 file copied there manually.

Also, when installing the server (rpcdstmd) the instructions specify to use 'make depend', 'make' and 'make install', we found the 'make depend' command did nothing and so is unnecessary.

When installation and configuration is accomplished it should be possible for every DSTM client to communicate with IPv4 hosts using IPv4 applications. Moreover if the DSTM server is used with SSL options then the IPv4 address allocation takes place only after verifying the certificates. DSTM clients without a valid certificate are denied for address allocation. This greatly increases security but also slows down the process of address allocation and hence initialisation of IPv4 communication. It also makes it a little more complicated for the user end as one need to come by the SSL certificates beforehand.

As with the FreeBSD implementation, IPv4 communication can only by initiated by a DSTM client, because the DSTM client is the one that requests the tunnel to be set up. There exists however a DSTM implementation that was not tested yet which permits communication to be initiated by outside (IPv4-only) hosts.

Conclusions

While the Linux version of DSTM is essentially the same as in FreeBSD, the installation and configuration is less complicated than the FreeBSD version and should be given preference. For example, the RPC patch is not required and various configuration options are simplified under Linux.

In addition to the version evaluated here from ENST, there is a gateway/TEP mechanism available in the 6wind routers and there is now a DSTM Client for Windows XP from 6talk.net that should work with this implementation. However, while we can confirm that the 6wind gateway works with this to some extent, neither has been evaluated here.

5.6 Configuration Examples: Translation Methods

5.6.1 NAT-PT

5.6.1.1 NAT-PT for Linux (RedHat 9.0)

Availability

This implementation of NAT-PT was developed by ETRI using Linux kernel 2.4.0-test9 but should work on any kernel 2.4.x or above (it has been tested successfully on RedHat7.3, 8.0, 9.0 and various USAGI kernels). It includes both DNS and FTP ALGs functionality and is available from the following link:

http://www.ipv6.or.kr/english/natpt-overview.htm

Install and Configuration

To install NAT-PT, the files must be unzipped/untarred into an appropriate directory and some minor configuration must be done.

The primary configuration option for NAT-PT is the IPv4_addresses.list file which must be populated with the IPv4 address pool to be used and a static binding made for the DNS. This file takes the form of a basic list shown as follows:

```
194.80.38.226
194.80.38.227
194.80.38.228
194.80.38.229
DNS 194.80.38.225 2001:630:80:7100::10
```

Additionally, minor changes may be made to the nat-pt_global.h and nat-pt.c files to configure the network prefix and the IPv4 and IPv6 network interfaces respectively though in our case this was unnecessary.

The application is compiled using 'make' or 'make clean' and run using nat-pt. DNS must also be properly configured in order for NAT-PT to create dynamic address bindings.

Host Configuration

No major changes are needed for host configuration however the DNS may need setting up. The resolvers (DNS clients) on the IPv6 hosts must be configured to send DNS requests to an IPv6 address. This can either be the 'real' address of a native IPv6 DNS server, or the mapped address of an IPv4 DNS server.

Issues

A number of issues were encountered when compiling the NAT-PT device, primarily due to a missing 'include' file, bpf.h. This file appears in 5 files; nat-pt_global.h, nat-pt.c, alg_manager.c, utils.c and dns_alg.c and each reference must be updated in order to make the compile successful. Additionally, in nat-pt.c a constant from the 'clock' library CLK_TCK is used erroneously and should be replaced with an appropriate value such as 100.

As a note of warning, this implementation is no longer being developed and it has been noted that the service is some way off a production quality service. As such, we recommend it should be used as an experimental service only.

5.6.1.2 ULTIMA for FreeBSD

Availability

Ultima is a NAT-PT implementation from BT Labs, it supplies a NAT-PT device with DNS, FTP and SIP ALG functionality. In this case, it was installed on FreeBSD 5.2 but should run on any version above FreeBSD 4.2. It cannot be directly downloaded from the Internet but is available by request on a case by case basis, below is a link the BTExact website highlighting the Ultima transitioning toolkit and other IPv6 activities at BT:

http://www.ipv6.btexact.com/activities/projects.html#ultima

Install and Configuration

Installation of Ultima takes place in two steps the basic device configuration and the http interface setup (which is rather less well documented). Installation of the device itself however is very straight forward, simply unzip the file into an appropriate directory and run the ultima_install program.

Setup is via a text based interface which is both comprehensive and simple to use and can also be run at any time to reconfigure the device. It follows these basic steps.

`IPv4 interface`	Specify IPv4 interface of device
`IPv6 interface`	Specify IPv6 Interface of device
`IPv6 prefix`	Specify IPv6 prefix of Ultima
`Address Pool configuration`	Configure IPv4 address pool, selecting this option allows the addition or removal of IPv4 addresses in the address pool and the addition or removal of static address mappings. At least one static mapping is required for the DNS
`Lan/wan and DNS options`	Allows selection of lan or wan operating modes (basically turns on or off rtadv. Configures DNS ALG to allow IPv4 or IPv6 queries to get forwarded or blocked on either interface
`http interface password`	Configures http interface password (see below)

The http interface setup is rather more complicated and requires both Apache and openSSH ports to be installed onto the machine in addition to numerous other PERL modules. Afterwards, the interface package can be compiled and installed. Once installed, NAT-PT can be operated remotely via a browser. This was not attempted in our case.

Host Configuration

No major changes are needed for host configuration however the DNS options may need to be configured appropriately.

Issues

The installation procedure threw up several complications in that the supplied 'ultima_NAT-PT.zip' package cannot be opened in FreeBSD with the usual methods as the package seems to be windows based with MS Word documentation supplied as opposed to the usual README text files. To unzip the files, PKZip was used but they could easily be unzipped in Windows and transferred to UNIX.

Additionally, the file permissions had to be changed as they were not set to be executable by any user by default (ultima_install, ultima, get_passwd, check_prefix, check_IPv4_address) so the device could not be configured or run.

5.6.2 ALG

5.6.2.1 WWWoffle

This configuration example assumes that wwwoffle is configured to listen on all IPv4 and IPv6 sockets of the server it is installed on. The sample configuration that comes with wwwoffle source packages may be used as a reference.

Note that this configuration does not cover all cache-specific options. The following parts of the wwwoffle configuration file are excerpts that cover only the IPv6-specific parts of the configuration.

StartUp Section

This section sets options that are parsed by wwwoffle on startup.

```
StartUp
{
     # Bind to all available IPv4-addresses.
     bind-ipv4          = 0.0.0.0

 # Bind to all available IPv6-addresses.
 bind-ipv6          = ::

 # Let proxy listen on port 8080.
 http-port          = 8080

 # Let HTTP-server for wwwoffle-control run on port 8081.
 wwwoffle-port      = 8081

 # Spool-directory for cache.
 spool-dir          = /var/spool/wwwoffle

 # Do syslogging.
 use-syslog         = yes
```

```
# Set password for control pages to "secrect".
password           = secret

# Max.-number of server-threads.
max-servers        = 8

# Max.-number of servers when fetching pages.
max-fetch-servers = 4
    }
```

Please note that the performance-specific options need to be adjusted to fit individual needs. Most options that do not directly concern IPv6 are left to their default values.

LocalHost Section

This section contains aliases and IPs under which the wwwoffle server is known. Requests to any of those aliases or IPs are not cached. Configuring this section is trivial. Valid entries are names and IPs without wildcards. The first entry will be used as the proxy's name which is relevant for some features of the wwwoffle configuration page.

```
LocalHost
{
 proxy.mynetwork.org
 proxy.ipv6.mynetwork.org
 localhost
 127.0.0.1
 ::ffff:127.0.0.1
 ip6-localhost
 ::1
 128.176.184.159
 2001:638:500:200::ff00
 2001:db8:100:7efa::2
 2001:666:3ffe::22
}
```

Other Sections

In general, all other sections are configured as they would be for an IPv4-only wwwoffle. Additionally, for options which hold an IPv4 address, IPv6 addresses may be used as well in the same manner as in the previous section.

Client-Side Configuration

All clients in the IPv6-only subnet should be configured to use the wwwoffle server as a proxy. This is done by configuring all web and ftp clients and similar applications accordingly.

5.6.2.2 WWW6to4 HTTP Proxy

The www6to4-1.5 HTTP proxy is a small program that is meant to act as a dual-stack front end to an IPv4 only browser. It has a few other features but those are entirely optional and not discussed here. This proxy is meant to run on a client machine and not to server a large number of clients and keep a cache for them. For the latter one is much better off with a full-fledged proxy like squid or wwwoffle.

The program is primarily distributed in source form, but binary packages for NetBSD and Debian Linux can also be found. Compilation from source normally involves no more than typing 'make' in the source directory. To run it, one needs a configuration file www6to4.conf including at least the following two lines:

```
listen-to                127.0.0.1,::1
listen-port              8000
```

If the www6to4.conf configuration file is located in the /etc-directory, www6to4 can simply be started with:

If the configuration file is located somewhere else its location needs to be given at the command line:

```
www6to4 -c <path to configuration file>/www6to4.conf
```

Note that there is no reason why www6to4 runs as root, it can run as an ordinary user or even as user 'nobody'.

Once www6to4 is running, all that is left to do for the user is to configure his or her web browser to use it as its the proxy (localhost:8000).

www6to4 is not an ftp proxy, it will proxy for http and https only. However, www6to4 is capable of 'forwarding' ftp URL's to another proxy that does understand ftp. In that case a so-called 'forward-file' needs to be configured by adding the following line to the www6to4.conf file:

```
forwardfile              <path_to>/www6to4_forward.conf
```

The www6to4_forward.conf should then contain a line like the following example:

```
ftp://*           proxy.mydomain.tld:8000
```

The following functionality was requested and added by the 6NET project to www6to4. The program www6to4 has now a new option called "-forwardingonly". This is useful in IPv6-only networks, where one wants to connect directly to IPv6 servers over IPv6, but where requests to IPv4 servers need to be forwarded to another (per site) dual-stack proxy. The new option provides exactly this functionality; it looks up the DNS IPv6 address records (AAAA) for the requested HTTP server and only if no such records are found will it forward the request according to the rules in the forward file (typically named /etc/www6to4_forward.conf). The forward file then needs to contain the following lines:

```
ftp://*           proxy.mydomain.tld:8000
http://*          proxy.mydomain.tld:8000
```

These lines tell the www6to4 program to forward any ftp or http request to proxy.mydomain.tld at port 8000.

5.6.2.3 Postfix Configuration

Server side configuration

In most cases, postfix' configuration files are located in /etc/postfix. Basically, only the file main.cf needs to be modified. When modifying main.cf, it is important to be aware of potential security risks that may occur if these modifications are not done carefully. One should under all circumstances avoid creating open relays that allow spam and bulk mailers to abuse the ALG as a relay server.

To be able to relay mail from the IPv6-only subnet, this subnet has to be added to the trusted subnets (the class of subnets that are allowed to relay mail via this server). By default, postfix trusts all machines that are in the same subnet as the postfix server. This behaviour is configured by setting

```
mynetworks_style = subnet
```

in main.cf. We assume that the IPv6-only subnet has the prefix 2001:db8:10:110::/64. To allow hosts in this subnet to relay via this postfix server, we add the prefix to "mynetworks" in main.cf.

```
mynetworks = [2001:638:500:200::]/64, [2001:db8:10:110::]/64, \
                                         [::1]/128, 127.0.0.0/8
```

Note that in this case, 2001:638:500:200::/64 is the subnet that the postfix server is located in.

Using the two options above allows relaying from the IPv6-only subnet for which the postfix server acts as an ALG.

Client Side Configuration

The postfix server above may be used as a normal SMTP server by any email clients in the IPv6-only subnet. This has to be configured for each application separately.

Mail Transfer Applications (MTAs)

MTAs such as postfix and sendmail can be configured to use an SMTP smarthost. In postfix's case, this is done by adding the following option to main.cf:

```
relayhost = [2001:638:500:200:0:0:0:ff00:25]
```

This lets postfix relay all outgoing mail via 2001:638:500:200::ff00:25. 2001:638:500:200::/64 is the subnet that the postfix server is located in.

Using the two options above allows relaying from the IPv6-only subnet for which the postfix server acts as an ALG. This is a save configuration in terms of relay protection as long as only the IPv6-only subnet is allowed to use the postfix server as a relaying smarthost.

5.6.2.4 SMTP Relaying with Sendmail

From IPv6 to IPv4

One can set up a single dual-stack mail server to act as a so called 'smart host' (smart mail relay) for IPv6-only hosts. A sendmail configuration file 'sendmail.cf' is typically generated from an m4 macro file. One should add the following lines to this m4 macro file:

```
DAEMON_OPTIONS(`Family=inet, address=0.0.0.0, Name=MTA')dnl
DAEMON_OPTIONS(`Family=inet6, address=::, Name=MTA6, Modifiers=O')dnl
```

IPv6 is marked optional in the above setting so that the 'sendmail.cf' generated from it can be used on IPv4-only kernels as well.

Once the dual-stack mail server has been set up, IPv6-only hosts can configure it as their 'smart host'. For sendmail a smarthost can be configured by adding the following line to its existing 'sendmail.cf' configuration file:

```
DSmail64.mydomain.tld
```

Here 'mail64.mydomain.tld' is the domain name of the dual-stack mail server that has been set up.

From IPv4 to IPv6

Two methods can be used to relay email through a dual-stack sendmail server to an IPv6-only mail server. The first method is by defining IPv6-only relays in the configuration file of the dual-stack sendmail. An example of this is to set the so-called 'LUSER_RELAY' in the dual-stack sendmail to the IPv6-only mail server in such a way that all email destined for email accounts not known at the dual-stack server are relayed to the IPv6-only mail server. This configuration for the dual-stack sendmail can be generated by adding a line lithe the following to the m4 macro file it is generated from:

```
define(`LUSER_RELAY', `relay:mail6.mydomain.tld')
```

The second method to relay email through a dual-stack sendmail server to an IPv6-only mail server (from IPv4-only hosts) is by setting up the MX records for the domain in question appropriately. Let us take as example the domain 'mydomain.tld' and assume that an (optional) IPv4-only mail server 'mail4.mydomain.tld', a dual-stack mailserver 'mail64.mydomain.tld' and an IPv6-only mail server 'mail6.mydomain.tld' have been set up for this domain.

An appropriate DNS configuration should then list MX records in the following order of priority:

```
mydomain.tld.       IN MX   0 mail6.mydomain.tld.
mydomain.tld.       IN MX   10 mail64.mydomain.tld.
mydomain.tld.       IN MX   20 mail4.mydomain.tld.
```

In other words, the IPv6-only mail server(s) should have lowest priority code (meaning highest priority mail server), followed by the dual-stack mail server(s) and finally the IPv4-only mail server(s), if any, should be given the highest code(s) (and thus the lowest priority). Of course, mail6.mydomain.tld should have an AAAA DNS record, mail64.mydomain.tld should have both an AAAA and an A DNS record, while mail4.mydomain.tld would only have an A record in DNS.

IPv4 clients will then send email to (one of) the IPv4 capable mail servers, which will relay it to (on of the) IPv6-only server(s). In the example above, an IPv4 client will send its mail to the first mail server on the list that has an IPv4 address: the dual-stack server mail64.mydomain.tld. Only if mail64.mydomain.tld is unreachable or down will it (try to) send the email to mail4.mydomain.tld. After mail64.mydomain.tld has received the email it will relay it to the higher priority mail server mail6.mydomain.tld, which is IPv6-only.

IPv6 capable clients will try to send their email for domain mydomain.tld directly to the IPv6-only mail server mail6.mydomain.tld. If this is (temporarily) unreachable those clients will instead use the dual-stack server mail64.mydomain.tld.

Note that most sites will want to have a backup mail server for both IPv6 and IPv4. This means that at least two of the mail servers need to be IPv6 capable and two of them need to be IPv4 capable as in the example above.

5.6.2.5 The totd DNS-Proxy (NetBSD/FreeBSD/Solaris/OS X/Linux)

The Totd DNS proxy is available both in source and binary form. Its binary distributions include NetBSD packages, FreeBSD ports, Debian Linux packages and a Redhat Linux RPM. Searching the Web for "DNS proxy totd" will provide you with links to most of these. Installing the binary distributions of totd is operating system specific and is not described here further. A totd binary can easily be produced on many Unix-like systems by compilation from source. The source is available from the 6NET project site but also directly from the author's ftp site at:

ftp://ftp.dillema.net/pub/users/feico/totd-latest.tar.gz

The md5 hashes of the current totd source distributions are:

```
MD5 (totd-1.2.tar.gz) = 4e682bb293c771a2f6ffc30aded20e0e
MD5 (totd-1.3-1.src.rpm) = ab16e70c4d5ca2df0ac014ef53885133
MD5 (totd-1.3.tar.gz) = bc6b85a5bddb72fc3fb20fa9fe50d3a0
MD5 (totd-1.4.tar.gz) = f732aaad9b9507cd9985224fc40f5bab
MD5 (totd-1.5.tar.gz) = b7da63fc1ea1b2e2ce959732826bc146
```

After unpacking the sources in any directory on the totd server, it can be configured and compiled by issuing the following commands. Preferably, compilation is done as an unprivileged user.

```
# ./configure --prefix=/usr/local
# make depend
# make
```

Then, as root, totd may be installed with the command:

```
# make install
```

The configuration file /usr/local/etc/totd.conf has to be edited to include the following lines:

```
forwarder 2001:db8:10:100:201:2ff:feb5:3806
prefix fec0:0:0:ffff::
port 53
```

Explanation of the lines above:

- forwarder:
  With this keyword you specify an IP address (either IPv4 or IPv6) of a nameserver for totd to forward its queries to. At least one forwarder needs to be specified in order for totd to have non-trivial behaviour.
- prefix:
  Specifies a 64 bit IPv6 address prefix to use for the 'address translation trick' described in more detail in Section 5.3.7. Prefix(es) can also be specified on the command line (or even using http if the optional web server is compiled into totd, see below).
- totuser:
  The port totd listens on for incoming requests. Normally port 53 which is the default.

By default, totd will listen on wildcard sockets for incoming requests and as such will accept requests from everywhere. It is possible to let totd only accept requests from certain network interfaces (not supported on Linux). For example, to let totd only accept requests from the loopback interface, add the following line to the totd.conf:

```
interfaces lo0
```

If you want to run totd on a privileged port, e.g. the default port 53, you either have to run totd as root or start as root but let it switch to another user and group after it has opened the sockets its needs. In the former case, totd is able to rescan the interface list and deal with interface and address changes on the fly. In the latter case, totd will not be able to rescan interfaces and react to such changes but needs to be restarted to handle such changes.

If totd is started using the -u and -g arguments, it will (try to) switch to the given user and group and drop all other (root) privileges. For example, totd can be started as root using:

```
# totd -u totuser -g totuser
```

where totuser must be a specially created user account with few privileges just to be used by totd. Such an account can be created on many Unix-like systems with:

```
# useradd -c "totd User" -s /bin/false totuser
```

Note: It is prudent to additionally change the password of totuser if the Linux server which will be running totd does not disable accounts that did not get an initial password. This can be achieved by using the following command

```
# passwd totuser
```

For additional security, totd can be run in a so-called chroot() cage such that even when compromised can not access filesystem outside the given directory. Start totd then using the -t option, like:

```
# totd -u totuser -g totuser -t /home/totuser
```

Once totd is started, you can test it by issuing a DNS query for an IPv4-only machine:

```
# dig -t aaaa www.ietf.org

        ; <<>> DiG 9.2.2 <<>> -t aaaa www.ietf.org
        ;; global options:  printcmd
        ;; Got answer:
        ;; ->>HEADER<<- opcode: QUERY, status: NOERROR, id: 45840
        ;; flags: qr rd ra; QUERY: 1, ANSWER: 2, AUTHORITY: 5, ADDITIONAL: 6

        ;; QUESTION SECTION:
        ;www.ietf.org.                 IN      AAAA

        ;; ANSWER SECTION:
        www.ietf.org.          3600    IN      AAAA    fec0:0:0:ffff::41f6:ff33
        www.ietf.org.          3600    IN      AAAA    fec0:0:0:ffff::8497:64b
```

For more complicated setups where multiple prefixes are used or prefixes need to be added and removed dynamically without manual intervention in order to support failover between separate transition mechanisms, totd can be compiled to include a small webserver. Then totd allows reconfiguration using http requests.

This functionality is provided by SWILL which is shipped with totd in its original form. Note that the SWILL library is covered by the GNU LESSER GENERAL PUBLIC LICENSE.

For this, compile totd as follows:

```
# ./configure --prefix=/usr/local  --enable-http-server
# make depend && make && make install
```

Even when compiled in, totd by default does not accept http requests for security reasons. You need to specify a port on the command line on which totd should listen for http requests. For example:

```
# totd -http-port 6464
```

In addition, you need to tell totd via its config file what addresses it should accept http requests from (the default is none) by adding a line like:

```
allow ::1
```

There is no other support for protecting this mechanism from abuse by third parties; no http authentication or https support is provided. We believe that where secure remote reconfiguration access is needed, the system administrator will choose to tunnel the http requests through some secure channel (e.g. a ssh tunnel or an IPSEC protected link).

Requesting index.html gives a HTML page with the current state and statistics of totd. You can also use it to dynamically update the prefixes used by totd. Prefixes are added and removed by requesting add_prefix.html and del_prefix.html combined with the variable 'prefix' set to the prefix in question.

Example URL for adding a prefix:

http://localhost:6464/add_prefix?prefix=fec0:0:0:ffff::

You can use a tool like curl (http://curl.haxx.se) to automatically from some script, from a remote (management) machine, add and delete prefixes to a running totd this way.

5.6.3 TRT

5.6.3.1 pTRTd and totd on a Linux router

Prerequisites

For this example it is assumed that there is a Linux router which has two interfaces (eth0 and eth1) and which serves as an edge router to an IPv6-only subnet on eth1 which has the following prefix:

2001:db8:10:110::/64

The Linux router itself has the IPv6 address 2001:db8:10:100:250:4ff:feec:b3b3. To provide connectivity to IPv4 hosts for the subnet mentioned above, it will be shown how a TRT setup using pTRTd and totd is implemented. It is also assumed that there is a DNS server available under the IP

2001:db8:10:100:201:2ff:feb5:3806. This server will be used to resolve DNS queries done by clients with IPv6-only connectivity and forwarded by totd.

Overview of installation steps

The following steps summarize the configuration work that has to be performed to provide TRT functionality on the Linux router for the 2001:db8:10:110::/64 subnet:

- Installation of totd on a dedicated host. Not that this host does not necessarily have to be a dual-stack host nor does it have to be the same host that pTRTd will run on.
- Configuration of totd to use existing DNS and to prepend a specific prefix to converted IPv4 addresses.
- Starting totd.
- Check that all prerequisites for the installation of pTRTd on the Linux router are met.
- Installation of pTRTd and starting it.

Installation of totd

Totd does not necessarily need to be installed on a dual-stack host or on the (Linux/Unix flavour) router that will be running pTRTd. However, the server hosting totd has to have IPv6-connectivity because it has to be reachable from an IPv6-only subnet. If there is an IPv6 capable DNS available to the totd sever, there is no need for it to have IPv4 connectivity. Otherwise, IPv4 connectivity is needed for contacting a DNS with only an IPv4 stack.

Installation of pTRTd

There are a few requirements that have to be fulfilled before pTRTd can be used:

- tun/tap driver support needs to be present in the Linux kernel (Version 2.2 or higher) either as a module or compiled into the kernel itself.
- A working totd server has to be present to provide translated IPv4 addresses. Totd has to be configured to prepend the prefix fec0:0:ffff:: to converted IPv4 addresses. Note that fec0:0:ffff:: is a site-local prefix. It may not make sense to use global prefixes. Please also note, that site-local prefixes are deprecated meanwhile. We keep this language here for the sake of consistency.
- /sbin/ip has to be present to allow pTRTd to set up an interface and a route.

Compilation and installation of pTRTd is trivial. After unpacking the sources on the Linux router, configuration and compilation of pTRTd is done by issuing the following commands:

```
# ./configure --prefix=/usr/local
# make
```

As root, pTRTd may be installed to /usr/local by running:

```
# make install
```

The usage of pTRTd is as follows:

```
# ptrtd [-i [<driver>:]<interface>] [-p <prefix>] [-l <prefix length>]
```

<prefix> defaults to fec0:0:0:ffff::/64 which means that there is no need to give the "-p" option if totd was configured to use this prefix. In general, there should be no need to give any options when starting pTRTd if TRT is set up according to this description. PTRTd is run by simply starting the daemon:

```
# /usr/local/sbin/ptrtd
```

If possible, one should perform a few checks to see whether or not pTRTd came up properly:

- "ps -ef | grep ptrtd" shows whether pTRTd is indeed up and running.
- "ip link show" verifies that a tap0 interface came up after starting pTRTd.
- "ip route show" checks whether or not there is a route which routes fec0:0:0:ffff::/64 via the tat0 interface mentioned above.

Configuring clients in the IPv6-only subnet

It is necessary to configure all clients in the IPv6-only subnet to use the totd server as DNS or otherwise no proper translation of IPv4 addresses is done.

To test the configuration, one can use an IPv6 enabled application and try to contact a server that is normally only reachable via IPv4, e.g. start an IPv6 capable browser like Mozilla and point it to a web server that only has an IPv4 address. Ideally, the browser is configured not to use any proxies for testing purposes. If it still can display the pages served by the IPv4-only server, the TRT installation was successful.

5.6.3.2 NTPD Time Server as a Proxy

Latest versions of the ntpd time server support IPv6. Building, installing and configuring ntpd with IPv6 support requires nothing special; it will simply listen for requests over both IPv4 and IPv6 and it can talk to either IPv4 or IPv6 ntpd servers.

5.6.3.3 The Faith TRT for FreeBSD and NetBSD

The transport relay translator faithd [RFC3142] is an IPv6-to-IPv4 TCP relay. Faithd relays TCP (not UDP, RTP or other transport protocols) from IPv6 to IPv4 (not the other way around). The faith daemon needs to be run on a dual-stack router between you local IPv6 site and outside IPv4 network. The daemon needs to be invoked per TCP service (TCP port number).

Example Setup

This example setup consists of two hosts on the same link running NetBSD software which are connected to a gateway. One of the hosts will be the TCP translator of the connections that the other host tries to establish. Once the TCP translation has been performed, the TCP connection will follow the normal way through the gateway.

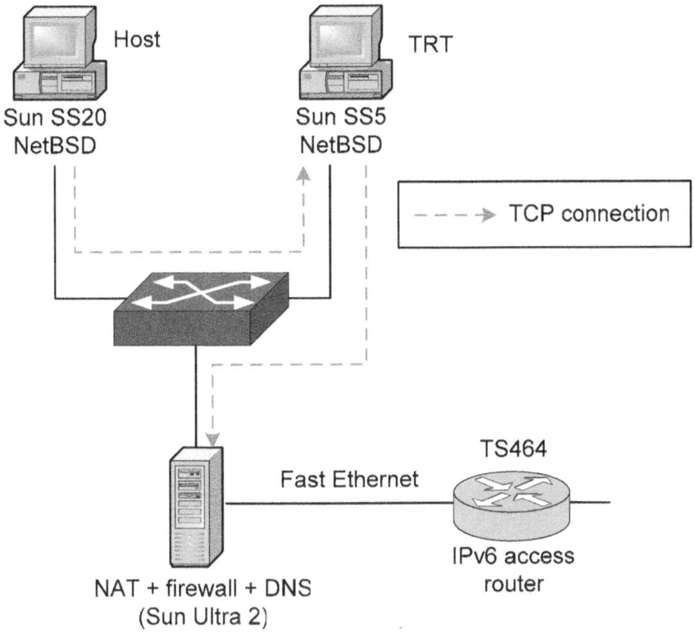

Figure 5-15 Example Setup of Faithd TRT

Installation

The installation of the TRT consists in running a daemon called faithd included with the NetBSD software. This daemon must be run for every service we want to provide. To be able to run the daemon, previously is necessary to enable an interface called faith.

When the faithd daemon receives TCP(v6) traffic from the faith interface it will perform the translation to TCP(v4). The destination of the TCP(v4) connection will be determined by the last 4 octets of the original IPv6 destination. It is necessary to reserve a prefix to perform this service. For example, if the prefix 2001:db8:10:110:: is reserved and the IPv4 destination is 10.1.1.1, the original destination should be 2001:db8:10:110::0a01:0101. The address translation can be performed by hand but of course you are better off using a DNS proxy such as totd.

The faith interface captures IPv6 traffic for implementing IPv6 to IPv4 TCP translations. To be able to use this interface is necessary to recompile the kernel, enabling the pseudo-interface faith.

The following example shows how to use faithd to provide a TCP relay for the ssh service using 2001:db8:10:110::/64 as faith prefix.

Perform the following steps on the router that will run the faith relay service:

1. If there already is an IPv6 TCP server for the "ssh" service, i.e. sshd, disable this daemon.
2. Execute the following as root to enable faith support:

```
# sysctl -w net.inet6. ip6.accept_rtadv=0
# sysctl -w net.inet6.ip6.forwarding=1
# sysctl -w net.inet6.ip6.keepfaith=1
```

3. Route packets when destination address within the faith prefix to the "faith0":

```
# ifconfig faith0 up
# route add -inet6 2001:db8:10:110:: -prefixlen 64 ::1
# route change -inet6 2001:db8:10:110:: -prefixlen 64 -ifp faith0
```

4. Start "faithd" as root as follows:

```
# faithd ssh /usr/sbin/sshd sshd -1
```

More examples that where successfully tested by the authors:

```
# faithd ftpd /usr/libexec/ftpd ftpd -l
# faithd sshd
# faithd telnet
# faithd telnet /usr/libexec/telnetd telnetd
# faithd smtp
# faithd www
# faithd https
# faithd irc
# faithd icqs
# faithd pop3
# faithd nntp
```

If inetd(8) on your platform has support for faithd, it is possible to setup faithd service (almost) like any other service started from inetd and configure it in /etc/inetd.conf. At least recent FreeBSD releases have included support for this.

On NetBSD one can make the above example setup permanent with automatic configuration at boot time. One simply creates a configuration file /etc/ifconfig.faith0 including the following lines:

```
# pseudo interface for IPv6/IPv4 transport relay
create
inet6 2001:db8:10:110:: prefixlen 64
```

Also add the flowing line(s) to /etc/sysctl.conf:

```
net.inet6.ip6.keepfaith=1
net.inet6.ip6.forwarding=1
# in case you don't want to do regular IPv4 forwarding at all:
net.inet.ip.forwarding=0
```

In addition it is strongly recommended to limit access to the translator. One way to do so is (at least on NetBSD) by creating a /etc/faithd.conf file restricting allowed connections. In the following example we assume that 2001:db8:10::/48 is the address space in use at the site:

```
# permit anyone from our site to use the translator, to connect to
# the following IPv4 destinations:
# any location except 10.0.0.0/8 and 127.0.0.0/8
```

```
# Permit no other connections.
#
2001:db8:10::/48 deny 10.0.0.0/8
2001:db8:10::/48 deny 129.168.0.0/16
2001:db8:10::/48 deny 127.0.0.0/8
2001:db8:10::/48 permit 0.0.0.0/0
```

Problems

The main problem in this platform is the scalability. The address resolution used in this case is made by the *hosts* table. That means that every server we want to access should be one entry of the hosts table. We can try to solve this problem using a special DNS server called totd, which has not been used in this platform.

One important problem with the TRT to be able to provide HTTP is the absolute links in the web pages, because the TRT can not parse them. One solution to that problem could be an ALG (Application Layer Gateway) which will manage with the absolute links properly. That problem makes TRT not recommended in HTTP services.

Chapter 6

Routing

In this chapter we briefly explain IP routing, paying particular attention to IPv6-specific features. The first section contains a general overview of the Internet routing architecture and explains several important concepts. In the subsequent sections we describe the various routing protocols available to the IPv6 implementor and how these may be configured and deployed in various router platforms such as Cisco and Juniper.

6.1 Overview of IP Routing

Conceptually, IP routing is remarkably simple. It provides a mechanism for connectionless communication between any two hosts that are connected to the global Internet. In the simplest but very common setting, every router along the path between the two hosts is really required to perform just one action for every received datagram, namely next-hop forwarding based on the destination address. Also, all datagrams arriving asynchronously on all router interfaces are essentially handled on the best-effort, first come – first served basis.

Of course, even this is far from easy, if for nothing else then for the sheer number of networks involved. Yet compared both to various extensions of IP (QoS provisioning, traffic engineering, even multicast) and to competitive technologies like ATM, plain IP routing is rather straightforward. Having this relatively "dumb", stateless and policy-free network near the bottom of the protocol stack have had two important consequences:

1. IP routing technology scaled so far extremely well without any strict control mechanisms.
2. The protocol layers above IP (applications in particular) have enough degrees of freedom to implement many different policies and approaches.

In the following subsections we give an overview of the key elements and concepts of IP routing. Most of them are common to IPv4 and IPv6, but we will specifically point out those (relatively few) cases where both protocols differ.

6.1.1 Hop-by-hop Forwarding

IP communication between two hosts A and B that are not on the same LAN segment must pass through one or more routers as indicated in Figure 6-1.

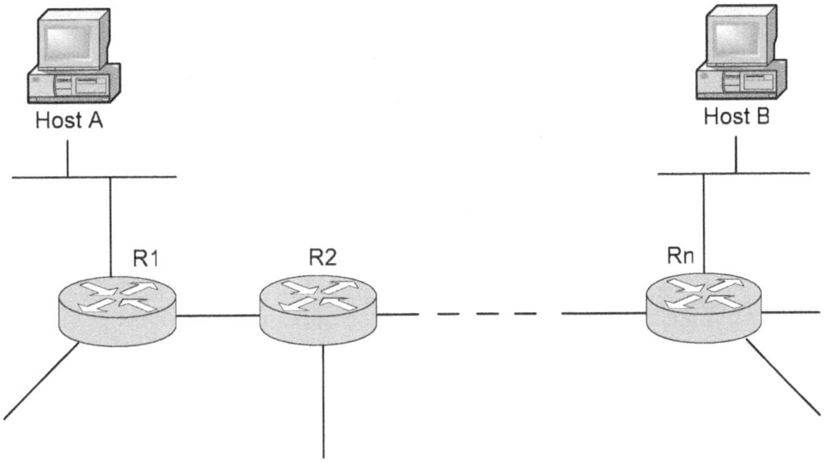

Figure 6-1 Classical IP Forwarding

Under the classical model of IP forwarding, every datagram generated by one of the end hosts (say, A in Figure 6-1) travels through the sequence of routers almost unchanged. What changes from one hop to the next one are the link layer headers that encapsulate the IP datagram. The link layer headers for any two consecutive links can either be completely disparate (if the underlying link technologies are not the same) or at least differ in link layer addressing information.

We said that the datagram is delivered by the IP network from one end host to the other one almost unchanged. The routers along the forwarding path indeed do modify certain fields in the IP header but such changes are minor and well defined – for example, the hop limit in the IPv6 header (or TTL in IPv4) must be decremented at every hop. Specifically, the source and destination IP addresses in the datagram header are not changed along the way and refer to the two end hosts.

As a matter of fact, the prevailing practice of the last decade or so made the above model of transparent end-to-end communication rather rare. The current IPv4 Internet is full of various layer violating devices (firewalls, NAT gateways, proxy servers etc.) and a vast majority of connected hosts use private IPv4 addresses these days. Such an environment is hostile to certain classes of applications (peer-to-peer, IP telephony etc.) and has also considerable drawbacks from the viewpoint of network reliability and management. As discussed in [RFC2775], several factors are behind this significant architectural shift. One of them has been the lack of global IPv4 addresses and this is where IPv6 could really help. However, layer violating devices are often deployed for other purposes, most notably security, and so devices like firewalls are likely to persist in the IPv6 Internet as well (see Chapter 9, Security).

6.1.2 Routing Tables

Routing decisions are based on data about reachability of various network prefixes that are either manually configured or collected from routing protocols. This decision making is usually trivial for end hosts (all traffic is sent to the default router) but becomes increasingly complicated as we move towards the Internet core.

Reachability information concerning a specific network prefix is known as a route. Actual content of a route depends both on the routing platform and the protocol that generated it, but typically we can expect to find the following data:

1. Destination prefix consisting of a network address and prefix length.

2. IP address of the next hop, defining the router that receives the outgoing datagrams whenever this route is used.
3. Preference of the route, also known under the (slightly confusing) name administrative distance. This can be used for assigning priorities to routing protocols so that routes learned from one protocol are preferred a priori to those learned from another protocol.
4. Source of the route, i.e., the protocol the route was learned from or a special local source (automatic routes for directly connected networks, static routes etc.). In the case of dynamic routing protocols, the neighbouring router that sent us the route may also be recorded.
5. Other protocol independent data, for example age of the route.
6. Dynamic protocol specific data – metric etc.

Individual routes are organised into sets known as routing tables. The common router platforms have separate tables for IPv4 and IPv6.

Example 6.1. Cisco IOS

Cisco command line interface handles the two routing tables implicitly: commands containing ip route and ipv6 route affect IPv4 and IPv6 unicast routing tables, respectively. For example, the entire routing table can be displayed by entering show ip route for IPv4 and show ipv6 route for IPv6.

Example 6.2. JUNOS

Juniper routers deal with different routing tables explicitly. They are identified by names consisting of a protocol family identifier and a non-negative integer (separated by a period). Thus inet.0 and inet6.0 are the main unicast routing tables for IPv4 and IPv6, respectively. The command show route displays all routing tables. A specific routing table can be selected by appending keyword table and the name of the desired table. For example, enter show route table inet6.0 to get the IPv6 routing table.

Example 6.3. Linux

Linux has separate routing tables for IPv6 and IPv4 that are directly accessible via the /proc filesystem:

- /proc/net/ipv6_route – IPv6 routing table
- /proc/net/route – IPv4 routing table

These tables can be displayed and managed either by traditional Unix commands like netstat and route (of course, with few Linux-specific idiosyncrasies), or by the more powerful ip command that comes with the iproute2 suite. The IPv6 routing table can be displayed using the command ip -6 route.

6.1.3 Policy Routing

In certain special situations it may be legitimate to base routing decisions not only on the destination IP address but also on other fields in the IP or TCP/UDP header, for instance source IP address or destination port. Such an approach is known as policy routing. Typical applications of policy routing are load balancing (distributing traffic among several connections), QoS provisioning or, indeed, imposing some kind of policy (e.g., to satisfy acceptable use conditions of certain networks).

Modern router architectures usually implement policy routing as part of the facilities for packet filtering (access lists). Incoming packets are processed using a sequence of rules. Each rule consists of match conditions and an action that is applied if the incoming packet matches the conditions. Simple actions can for example just select an explicit next hop or output interface. Some modern router systems offer sophisticated policy routing frameworks where multiple routing tables can be defined and selected by the actions.

Example 6.4. Cisco IOS

In Cisco IOS, routing policies are specified using route maps. Say we want to take all IPv6 datagrams received on the interface GigabitEthernet0/1 whose source address falls under the prefix 2001:798::/40 and send them to a special next hop. We can accomplish this using the following configuration commands:

```
ipv6 access-list 6net-src                                  (1)
 permit ipv6 2001:798::/40 any

route-map 6net-policy permit 10                            (2)
 match ipv6 address 6net-src
 set ipv6 next-hop fe80::211:85ff:fe61:2a0f

interface GigabitEthernet0/1
 ipv6 policy route-map 6net-src                            (3)
```

1. This access list defines the prefix for which the special next hop is to be applied.
2. This route map has a single rule: If the IPv6 datagram matches the access-list 6net-src, then the next hop is set to the given address.
3. This command attaches the route map to the desired interface.

6.1.4 Internet Routing Architecture

For a vast majority of networks connected to the global Internet, routing is not a big issue. They have just a single uplink to their service providers and so a simple static setup is all they need. However, as we move upstream towards the Internet core, the network topology becomes more complex and the routers must have more information in order to be able to forward datagrams to appropriate next hops. This information is usually collected and managed dynamically by means of routing protocols.

We will see in the following sections that individual routing protocols differ in many aspects, yet the basic idea is common to all of them: Every router advertises itself to its neighbours as a candidate next hop for a certain set of network prefixes. The neighbours process this information and pass it in a properly modified form to their own neighbours, and so on.

Unlike traditional voice networks, Internet has no centralised control. The routing advertisements thus cannot be propagated and trusted too far from their origin since otherwise the network would be vulnerable to misconfigurations and malicious attacks. Therefore, the globally routable Internet is divided into manageable chunks called Autonomous Systems (also known as routing domains). An autonomous system must appear to the rest of the Internet as a well behaved unit with a consistent routing policy. It is also important that this policy be sufficiently distinct from the neighbouring autonomous systems. For example, single connected networks of any size have no space for their own routing policy and must be integrated into an upstream AS.

Note

This need not always be true for IPv6 since most networks use the same autonomous system for both IPv4 and IPv6 and their IPv6 setup and routing policy is often much less sophisticated.

With autonomous systems in place, all globally reachable IP routers are organised in a two-tier hierarchy illustrated in Figure 6-2.

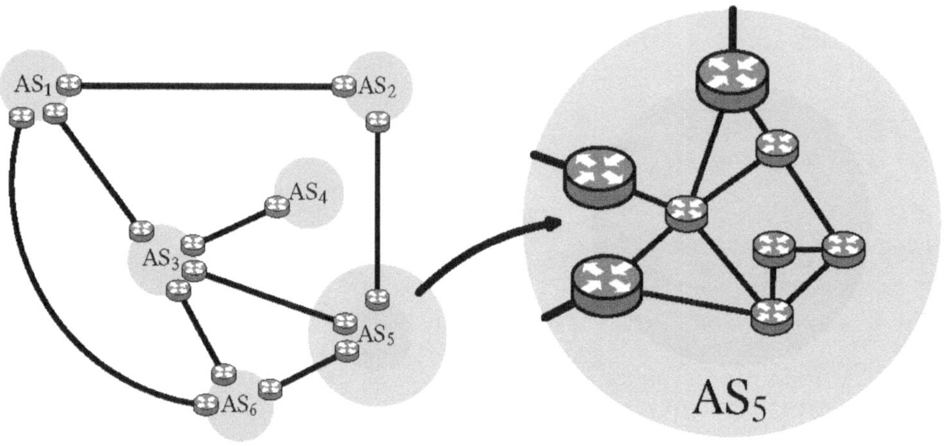

Figure 6-2 Internet Routing Architecture

In the top tier, the routable Internet is represented as a general graph whose nodes are autonomous systems and edges correspond to existing physical or logical links between autonomous systems.

Note

Historically, due to the limitations of the older EGP routing protocol, this top-tier topology had to be a tree (loop free). All traffic from a peripheral AS had to go first upstream to the root AS (so-called core routers) and then downstream to the destination AS. The BGP protocol that is now universally used throughout the Internet imposes no such restriction – the top-tier topology may contain loops.

Routing in the top tier (inter-domain routing) determines the optimal next hop for a given prefix by comparing the lengths of alternative AS paths (sequences of autonomous systems that have to be traversed before the destination AS is reached) – the shortest AS path is always preferred.

In the bottom tier, the scope of the routing task is essentially limited to a single autonomous system, as illustrated by the expanded view of AS5 in Figure 6-2. The interior routers exchange information about the topology of the local AS by means of intra-domain routing protocols. This enables them to deliver datagrams directly to any destination inside their autonomous system. For external destinations, intra-domain routing procedures only have to select an appropriate exit point (border router) and deliver the datagram to it. Intra-domain routing protocols mostly use finer grained metrics than just a number of hops for selecting the best next hop.

The autonomous system border routers (ASBR) are depicted in Figure 6-2 as "connectors" between pairs of autonomous systems. Their role is important in that they glue together the two tiers of the routing hierarchy and mediate relevant routing data in both directions.

Currently, inter-domain routing for both IPv4 and IPv6 is absolutely dominated by a single routing protocol: BGP version 4. The choice for intra-domain routing is richer, with at least four commonly used protocols – RIP, OSPF, IS-IS and Cisco-proprietary EIGRP – all of them now available for IPv6 as well.

6.1.5 Is IPv6 Routing Any Different?

Although the contents of IPv4 and IPv6 routing toolboxes are practically identical, we can still observe significant differences in the behaviour of the IPv6 routing system, compared to its IPv4 counterpart.

First of all, IPv6 Internet is still by several orders smaller. According to the CIDR report (data from February 2005), inter-domain routing tables contain more than 150 thousand IPv4 network prefixes but only about 700 IPv6 prefixes. The complexity of IPv6 routing is thus incomparable to its IPv4 counterpart.

IPv6 routing still suffers from two characteristic problems:

1. Network interfaces with multiple global IPv6 addresses are prone to asymmetric routing, which is often undesirable. This is mostly due to improper implementation of source address selection.
2. The IPv6 Internet is still, by and large, an overlay network over IPv4 and its tunnels distort the inter-area link metrics (number of hops in AS paths) and mislead routing algorithms.

Both problems can be expected to disappear after IPv6 becomes more mainstream and the implementations stabilise. One highly visible difference is likely to persist though: most routing domains in the default-free zone filter out all incoming prefixes that are longer than /32. Such a strict aggregation of prefixes is absolutely crucial for long term viability of global IPv6 routing. Note that the set of /32 IPv6 prefixes still has the same size as the set of all IPv4 addresses, so the aggregation rules may perhaps become even stricter in the future.

6.2 *Implementing Static Routing for IPv6*

6.2.1 Cisco IOS

6.2.1.1 Prerequisites

The minimum required IOS release for the static routing feature in each train is generally the one where IPv6 became first available, that is 12.0(21)ST, 12.0(22)S, 12.2(2)T, 12.2(14)S, 12.3(2)T, 12.3(1)M.

Before configuring the router with a static IPv6 route you must enable the forwarding of IPv6 packets using the ipv6 unicast-routing global configuration command. Then enable IPv6 on at least one interface by configuring an IPv6 address on it, which can be accomplished with the command ipv6 address in the respective interface's context.

6.2.1.2 Configuring Static Routes

Using static routes in IPv6 is similar to configuring static routes for IPv4 with a few differences. A new command, ipv6 route, is used to configure IPv6 static routes and some of the IPv4 keywords are not yet supported. The command structure is as follows:

```
Router(config)# ipv6 route ipv6-prefix/prefix-length \\
{ipv6-address | interface-type interface-number \\
[ipv6-address]} [administrative-distance]
```

Note that a floating static route must be configured with a greater administrative distance parameter than any dynamic routing protocol because routes with smaller administrative distances are preferred. By default, static routes have smaller administrative distances than dynamic routes.

Examples

a) In the following example the IPv6 default route is configured to point to serial interface 2/0:

```
Router(config) # ipv6 route ::/0 serial 2/0
```

b) This example shows a normal route configured to go through serial interface 0:

```
Router(config) # ipv6 route 2001:0db8::/32 serial 0
```

c) In this example an additional (optional) IPv6 address is configured for the next hop:

```
Router(config) # ipv6 route 2001:0db8::/32 ethernet 0 fe80::1
```

d) The following example shows how a static route can be configured with just the next hop IPv6 address omitting any interface specification:

```
Router(config) # ipv6 route 2001:0db8::/32 2002:806b:f0fe::1
```

6.2.1.3 Verifying Static IPv6 Route Configuration and Operation

To verify that static routes have been correctly configured one can use the show ipv6 route command, which has the following syntax:

```
router # show ipv6 route [ipv6-address | \\
ipv6-prefix/prefix-length | protocol]
```

Examples

a) In the following example the show ipv6 route EXEC command is used to verify the configuration of a static route through a point-to-point interface:

```
Router# show ipv6 route
IPv6 Routing Table - 9 entries
Codes: C - Connected, L - Local, S - Static, R - RIP, B - BGP
U - Per-user Static route
I1 - ISIS L1, I2 - ISIS L2, IA - ISIS interarea
O - OSPF intra, OI - OSPF inter, OE1 - OSPF ext 1, OE2 - OSPF ext 2
S 2001:0DB8::/32 [1/0]
via ::, Serial2/0
```

b) In this case, the show ipv6 route EXEC command is used to verify the configuration of a static route on a multi-access interface. An IPv6 link-local address (FE80::1) is the next hop router.

```
Router# show ipv6 route
IPv6 Routing Table - 11 entries
Codes: C - Connected, L - Local, S - Static, R - RIP, B - BGP
U - Per-user Static route
I1 - ISIS L1, I2 - ISIS L2, IA - ISIS interarea
O - OSPF intra, OI - OSPF inter, OE1 - OSPF ext 1, OE2 - OSPF ext 2
S 2001:0DB8::/32 [1/0]
via FE80::1, Ethernet0/0
```

c) In this example, the show ipv6 route EXEC command is used with static as the value of the protocol argument to display information about static routes installed in the IPv6 routing table:

```
Router# show ipv6 route static
IPv6 Routing Table - 330 entries
Codes: C - Connected, L - Local, S - Static, R - RIP, B - BGP
U - Per-user Static route
I1 - ISIS L1, I2 - ISIS L2, IA - ISIS interarea
S 2001:0DB8::/32 [1/0]
via ::, Tunnel0
S 2001:db8:C00:8011::/48 [1/0]
via ::, Null0
S ::/0 [254/0]
via 2002:806B:F0FE::1, Null
```

d) In the following example, the debug ipv6 routing privileged EXEC command is used to verify the installation of a floating static route into the IPv6 routing table when an IPv6 RIP route is deleted. The floating static IPv6 route was previously configured with an administrative distance value of 130. The backup route was added as a floating static route because Routing Information Protocol (RIP) routes have a default administrative distance of 120 and the RIP route should be the preferred route. When the RIP route is deleted the floating static route is installed in the IPv6 routing table.

```
Router# debug ipv6 routing
*Oct 10 18:28:00.847: IPv6RT0: rip two, Delete 2001:0DB8::/32 from table
*Oct 10 18:28:00.847: IPv6RT0: static, Backup call for 2001:0DB8::/32
*Oct 10 18:28:00.847: IPv6RT0: static, Add 2001:0DB8::/32 to table
*Oct 10 18:28:00.847: IPv6RT0: static, Adding next-hop :: over Serial2/0 for
2001:0DB8::/32, [130/0]
```

6.2.2 Juniper JunOS

The only difference in specifying static routes for IPv6 and IPv4 on Juniper platforms is that for the new version of the Internet Protocol one needs to explicitly specify the IPv6 routing table (inet6.0, inet6.2) in the statements. Other than that, syntax and options are very much the same and therefore are not explained in this section.

6.2.2.1 Examples

a) Configure an IPv6 default route through the next-hop router 2001:638:500::1:

```
[edit]
user@host# set routing-options rib inet6.0 static \\
                      route abcd::/48 next-hop 2001:638:500::1

[edit]
user@host# show
routing-options {
   static {
        route abcd::/48 next-hop 2001:638:500::1;
    }
}
```

b) Install an IPv6 static route into both inet6.0 and inet6.2 routing tables:

```
[edit routing-options rib table1.inet6.0 static]
rib-group groupA;

[edit routing-options rib-groups]
groupA {
```

```
    import-rib [table1.inet6.0 inet6.0 inet6.2]
}
```

c) Propagate IPv6 static routes into the routing protocols:

```
[edit routing-options rib inet6.0 static (defaults | route)]
discard;
```

d) Resolve an IPv6 static route to non-next-hop router 2001:638:500:101::1/64 using next-hop router 2001:638:500::1:

```
[edit]
user@host# set routing-options rib inet6.0 static route \\
                    2001:638:500:101::1/64 next-hop 2001:638:500::1 resolve

[edit]
user@host# show route 2001:638:500:101::/64
inet6.0: 26 destinations, 27 routes (25 active, 0 holddown, 1 hidden)
+ = Active Route, - = Last Active, * = Both

2001:638:500:101::/64     *[Static/5] 00:01:50
                          > to 2001:638:500::2 via ge-0/1/0.0

user@host# show route 2000::1
inet6.0: 26 destinations, 27 routes (25 active, 0 holddown, 1 hidden)
+ = Active Route, - = Last Active, * = Both

2000::/126             *[BGP/170] 00:05:32, MED 20, localpref 100
                       AS path: 2 I
                       > to 2001:638:500::2 via ge-0/1/0.0
```

6.2.3 Quagga/Zebra

Command Syntax:

```
Router(config)# ipv6 route <network> <gateway> [<distance>] {}
```

`network` is the destination prefix. `gateway` indicates the gateway for that prefix. As `gateway` you can either specify an IPv6 address or interface name. If the interface name is `null0` then Zebra installs a blackhole route. `distance` is an optional parameter to install the route with a specified distance.

Command Syntax:

```
Router(config)# table <tableno> {}
```

Select the primary kernel routing table to be used. This only works for kernels supporting multiple routing tables (like GNU/Linux 2.2.x and later). After setting `tableno` with this command, static routes defined after this are added to the specified table.

Command Syntax:

```
Router# show ipv6 route [<route>]{}
```

This command can be used to display routes in the current selected routing table. To show a specific route, specify it at the end.

6.3 RIP

RIP (Routing Information Protocol) is a true vintage class among the routing protocols that are still in common use. Its ancestry goes back to the ARPANET routing algorithm that was designed in 1969 [MFR78]. In the mid-1970s, a similar protocol was implemented for the Xerox PARC Universal Protocol (PUP) under the name Gateway Information Protocol (GWINFO). Later, GWINFO was included in the Xerox Network System (XNS), but its name was changed to Routing Information Protocol. However, the most important milestone in the RIP history was the release of the 4.2BSD Unix in August 1983. This operating system included the routed daemon, essentially a generalisation of the Xerox RIP capable of handling IP addresses and networks. The routed daemon then become a de facto standard for intra-AS routing in the emerging Internet. It was not until 1988 that RIP became a proposed standard in IETF [RFC1058].

The second version of RIP [RFC1723] added support for classless IPv4 addresses (CIDR) along with other significant improvements. The strongest point of the RIP protocol is its simplicity, which makes it easy to implement and configure. As a result, interoperable implementations have long been available for virtually all IPv6 routing platforms and so RIPng used to be a popular choice, especially in mixed environments. Although this niche is gradually being taken over by the more advanced intra-AS routing protocols (IS-IS and OSPFv3), RIPng does still have some appeal, especially for small networks.

On the other hand, the most serious weakness of RIP, and one that is unlikely to go away, is its hard limit on path length: only 16! RIP considers destinations that are 16 or more hops away to be unreachable. This may seem very restrictive but there are good reasons for keeping the maximum allowable path length low.

6.3.1 RIPng Protocol

The IPv6 version of the RIP protocol (also known as RIPng) is defined in [RFC2080]. It is directly based on the version 2 of RIP for IPv4 [RFC1723].

6.3.1.1 Protocol Data

Each router running the RIPng protocol keeps the information about all known networks in the internal data structure called RIPng route table. It is essentially the RIPng-specific incarnation of the distance vector with few additional items that are necessary for RIPng operation and cooperation with other routing protocols. For every network, the routing table contains the following data:

- destination prefix
- metric
- next hop
- route tag
- route change flag
- route expiration timer
- garbage collection timer

The first three items together are known as a route and carry information about the reachability of a network from the viewpoint of the particular router. The destination prefix consists of an IPv6 network address and prefix length and identifies the network that the route table entry is about. The metric is the distance to that network, or rather the current estimate of the distance. For directly connected networks, the metric is set to the cost of that network. Finally, next hop contains the IP address of the router that is next on the (provisional) optimum path to the destination network. For directly connected networks, the next hop is irrelevant, usually empty.

The route tag is not of an immediate interest for RIPng; the standard only requires that the route tag be preserved and redistributed with the route. It is typically used for tagging routes that were imported from other routing protocols, for example BGP.

The route change flag and both timers are internal parameters that control the route processing. Their role in RIPng operation will be explained in the next subsection.

The routers running RIPng exchange entire route tables or their portions between each other. Such an exchange takes place in the following three cases:

1. About every 30 seconds, each router sends regular updates to all neighbours.
2. Whenever a router detects a change in network topology (e.g., a link going down), it sends to all neighbours a triggered update containing only the routes that are affected by the topology change.
3. Routers may also send their routing table or part of it after receiving an explicit Request message from another router or host.

The routes are exchanged in the form of a data structure known as route table entry (RTE).

The current version of the RIPng protocol [RFC2080] defines two types of messages: Request and Response. Both types have the same format as shown in Figure 6-3 and every message contains one or more RTEs.

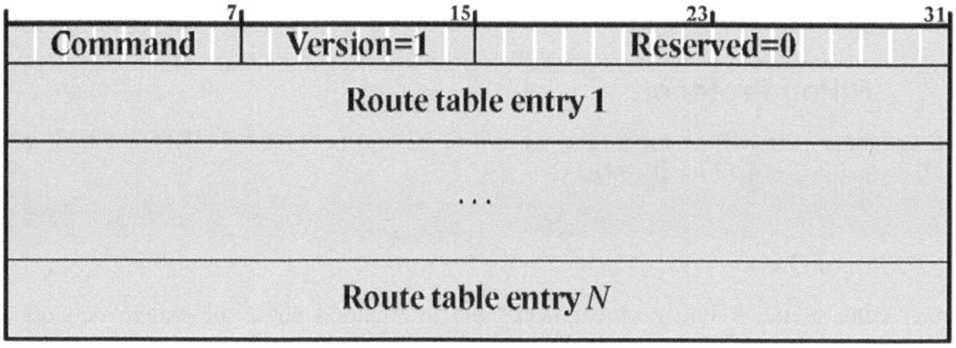

Figure 6-3 RIPng Message

6.3.1.2 Protocol Operation

If we start a packet sniffer on a network segment with active RIPng router, most of the time we will only see the unsolicited Response messages similar to the one shown above. All routers send these updates with a period of 30 seconds, but independently of each other, i.e., with random phase shifts.

> **Note**
>
> Actually, for networks with many RIPng routers it is quite important to keep the routers unsynchronised, since otherwise a large number of Response messages sent within a short interval may adversely influence the network performance. Interestingly enough, weakly coupled periodic processes that are originally asynchronous often tend to synchronise. S. Floyd and V. Jacobson [FJ94] showed this can also happen to a set of routers exchanging

periodic messages. To counter this phenomenon, the RIPng specifications requires the implementations either to derive the period of the messages from a precise clock that is not influenced by system load, or each time add a random offset to the nominal 30-second period so that the period is uniformly distributed between 15 and 45 seconds.

The essential part of the RIPng router operation involves the following two procedures:

1. Listen to the route advertisements sent by its neighbours and update its own routing table so that it contains the best routes (with shortest metrics) heard so far.
2. Every 30 seconds, send the current route table to all neighbours.

6.4 Implementing RIPng for IPv6

IPv6 RIP or RIPng (RIP Next Generation) is generally very similar to RIP (for IPv4) and functions in the same way, offering the same benefits. RIP enhancements for IPv6 (RIPng) is detailed in RFC 2080 [RFC2080] and includes support for IPv6 addresses and prefixes, and the use of all-RIP-routers multicast group address FF02::9 as the destination address for RIP update messages.

The RIPng IGP uses the Bellman-Ford distance-vector algorithm to determine the best route to a destination. RIPng uses the hop count as the metric and allows hosts and routers to exchange information for computing routes through an IP-based network. RIPng is intended to act as an IGP for moderately sized autonomous systems (ASs).

RIPng is a User Datagram Protocol (UDP)-based protocol and uses UDP port 521.

RIPng has the following architectural limitations:

- The longest network path cannot exceed 15 hops (assuming that each network, or hop, has a cost of 1).
- RIPng depends on counting to infinity to resolve certain unusual situations. When the network consists of several hundred routers, and when a routing loop has formed, the amount of time and network bandwidth required to resolve a next hop might be great.
- RIPng uses only a fixed metric to select a route. Other IGPs use additional parameters, such as measured delay, reliability and load.

A RIPng packet header contains the following fields:

- Command—Indicates whether the packet is a request or response message. Request messages seeks information for the router's routing table. Response messages are sent periodically or when a request message is received. Periodic response messages are called update messages. Update messages contain the command and version fields and a set of destinations and metrics.
- Version number—Specifies the version of RIPng that the originating router is running. This is currently set to Version 1.

The rest of the RIPng packet contains a list of routing table entries with the following fields:

- Destination prefix—128-bit IPv6 address prefix for the destination.
- Prefix length—Number of significant bits in the prefix.
- Metric—Value of the metric advertised for the address.

- Route tag—A route attribute that must be advertised and redistributed with the route. Primarily, the route tag distinguishes external RIPng routes from internal RIPng routes in cases where routes must be redistributed across an exterior gateway protocol (EGP).

6.4.1 Cisco IOS

In the Cisco IOS software implementation of IPv6 RIP each IPv6 RIP process maintains a local routing table, referred to as a Routing Information Database (RIB). The IPv6 RIP RIB contains a set of best-cost IPv6 RIP routes learned from all its neighbouring networking devices. If IPv6 RIP learns the same route from two different neighbours, but with different costs, it will store only the lowest cost route in the local RIB. The RIB also stores any expired routes that the RIP process is advertising to its neighbours running RIP. IPv6 RIP will try to insert every non-expired route from its local RIB into the master IPv6 RIB. If the same route has been learned from a different routing protocol with a better administrative distance than IPv6 RIP, the RIP route will not be added to the IPv6 RIB but the RIP route will still exist in the IPv6 RIP RIB.

6.4.1.1 Prerequisites

For the minimum required IOS version for IPv6 RIP features please refer to:

http://www.cisco.com/univercd/cc/td/doc/product/software/ios123/123cgcr/ipv6_c/ftipv6s.htm#wp1004964

As with all IPv6 features within IOS the same configuration prerequisites apply to configure IPv6 RIP features. Therefore IPv6 forwarding must be enabled and an IPv6 address must be configured for at least one interface, in this case specifically those which take part in RIP routing.

6.4.1.2 How to Implement RIP for IPv6

When configuring supported routing protocols in IPv6, you must create the routing process, enable the routing process on interfaces and customize the routing protocol for your particular network.

Note: The following sections describe the configuration tasks for creating an IPv6 RIP routing process and enabling the routing process on interfaces. The following sections do not provide in-depth information on customizing RIP because the protocol functions the same in IPv6 as it does in IPv4.

To configure IPv6 on a Cisco IOS platform one has to perform two tasks. The first is to create an IPv6 RIP routing process with a specific name. The syntax of the corresponding command is:

```
router(config)# ipv6 router rip name
```

This command enters the configuration context for this routing process to optionally configure it further. In its simplest form one has to do nothing here but exit the context again.

The second task in configuring IPv6 RIP is to enable the process on the interfaces involved in RIP routing. In order to accomplish this it's necessary to enter the corresponding interface's context and use the following command.

```
router(config-if)# ipv6 rip name enable
```

By `name` one refers to the respective IPv6 RIP routing process.

Examples

a. The following example command creates an IPv6 RIP routing process by the name of "ciscotest"

```
Router(config)# ipv6 router rip ciscotest
```

b. The routing process configured in example a) is now enabled on Ethernet interface 0/0:

```
Router(config)# interface Ethernet 0/0
Router(config-if)# ipv6 rip ciscotest enable
```

6.4.1.3 Customizing IPv6 RIP

This optional task explains how to configure the maximum numbers of equal-cost paths that IPv6 RIP will support, adjust the IPv6 RIP timers and originate a default IPv6 route.

The corresponding commands are either entered in the configuration context of IPv6 RIP routing processes or applied to specific interfaces in their configuration contexts.

The optional command for defining the maximum number of equal-cost routes that IPv6 RIP can support applies to the whole routing process:

```
Router(config-router)# maximum-paths number-paths
```

The number-paths argument is an integer from 1 to 4. The default for RIP is 4 paths.

RIP update times are also relevant for the routing process in general. By default, updates occur every 30 seconds and timeout after 180 seconds, hold-down lasts 0 seconds and garbage collection is activated after 120 seconds. To change these values use the following command:

```
Router(config-router)# timers update timeout holddown garbage-collection
```

To originate the IPv6 default route (::/0) into the updates of a specified RIP routing process from a specified interface enter the following command in the configuration context of that interface:

```
Router(config-if)# ipv6 rip name default-information {only | originate}
```

Note: To avoid routing loops after the IPv6 default route (::/0) is originated out of any interface, the routing process ignores all default routes received on any interface.

Specifying the only keyword originates the default route (::/0) but suppresses all other routes in the updates sent on this interface.

Specifying the originate keyword originates the default route (::/0) in addition to all other routes in the updates sent on this interface.

Examples

a) This example shows how the RIP process is configured to support only one equal cost path:

```
Router(config-router)# maximum-paths 1
```

b) With the following command the update timer is reduced to 5 seconds, timeouts occur after 15 seconds while holddown lasts 10 seconds and garbage collection is activated after 30 seconds:

```
Router(config-router)# timers 5 15 10 30
```

c) In this example Ethernet interface 0/0 is configured to originate the IPv6 default route in addition to all other routes for IPv6 RIP process "ciscotest":

```
Router(config)# interface Ethernet 0/0
Router(config-if)# ipv6 rip ciscotest default-information originate
```

6.4.1.4 IPv6 prefix lists to filter routes on outgoing or incoming RIP updates

IPv6 prefix lists are used to specify certain prefixes or a range of prefixes that must be matched before a permit or deny statement can be applied. Two operand keywords can be used to designate a range of prefix lengths to be matched. A prefix length of less than, or equal to, a value is configured with the le keyword. A prefix length greater than, or equal to, a value is specified using the `ge` keyword. The `ge` and `le` keywords can be used to specify the range of the prefix length to be matched in more detail than the usual `ipv6-prefix/prefix-length argument`. For a candidate prefix to match against a prefix list entry three conditions can exist:

- the candidate prefix must match the specified prefix list and prefix length entry;
- the value of the optional `le` keyword specifies the range of allowed prefix lengths from the `prefix-length` argument up to, and including, the value of the `le` keyword;
- the value of the optional `ge` keyword specifies the range of allowed prefix lengths from the value of the `ge` keyword up to, and including, 128.

Note: The first condition must match before the other conditions take effect.

An exact match is assumed when the `ge` or `le` keywords are not specified. If only one keyword operand is specified then the condition for that keyword is applied, and the other condition is not applied. The `prefix-length` value must be less than the `ge` value. The `ge` value must be less than, or equal to, the le value. The le value must be less than or equal to 128.

An IPv6 prefix list is created by specifying its first entry in the global configuration environment. The command syntax to either deny specific routes or permit them is as follows:

Command syntax:

```
Router(config)# ipv6 prefix-list prefix-list-name \\
        [seq seq-number] {deny ipv6-prefix/prefix-length \\
        | description text} [ge ge-value] [le le-value]

Router(config)# ipv6 prefix-list prefix-list-name \\
        [seq seq-number] {permit ipv6-prefix/prefix-length \\
        | description text} [ge ge-value] [le le-value]
```

The optional `seq` parameter specifies the sequence number of the corresponding entry in the specified prefix-list.

To enter more than one filter to any prefix list repeat the above commands specifying the same `prefix-list-name` as often as needed with the appropriate parameters.

IPv6 prefix lists can be applied to specific IPv6 RIP routing updates that are received or sent on the specific interface with the following command:

Command syntax:

```
Router(config-router)# distribute-list prefix-list \\
        prefix-list-name {in | out} [interface-type interface-number]
```

Note: If an interface is not specified with the distribute-list prefix-list command, the specified prefix list is applied to IPv6 routing updates that are sent or received on all interfaces in the router running the specified process.

The `in` keyword applies the prefix list to incoming routing updates on the specified interface.

The `out` keyword applies the prefix list to outgoing routing updates on the specified interface.

Examples

a) In this example, the default IPv6 route will be denied.

```
Router(config)# ipv6 prefix-list eth0/0-in-flt seq 10 deny ::/0
```

b) In this example, all routes are permitted. This entry is following the deny rule in Step a) in order to permit all other routes, except the IPv6 default route. Without this permit rule all prefixes would be blocked.

```
Router(config)# ipv6 prefix-list eth0/0-in-flt seq 20 permit ::/0 le 128
```

c) In the following example, the ipv6 prefix-list "eth0/0-in-flt" is distributed to IPv6 RIP routing process "ciscotest". It is specifically used to filter routes coming in through interface Ethernet 0/0. The result is that all routes but the IPv6 default route are accepted.

```
Router(config)# ipv6 router rip ciscotest
Router(config-router)# distribute-list prefix-list eth0/0-in-flt \\
                                   in Ethernet 0/0
```

6.4.1.5 Route Tags and Redistribution of Routes into an RIP Routing Process

This task explains how to set route tags using a route map and redistribute tagged routes into an IPv6 RIP routing process.

Defining route maps and tagging routes for IPv6 is not much different from the same task in IPv4. The only difference is the fact that route maps match to IPv6 prefix lists.

Command syntax:

```
Router(config)# route-map map-tag [permit | deny] [sequence-number]
Router(config-route-map)# match ipv6 address prefix-list prefix-list-name
Router(config-route-map)# set tag value
```

Note: IPv6 RIP does not support route tags when the number of parallel routes is configured to be greater than one. Use the `maximum-paths` command to configure the number of parallel routes.

Redistribution of routes defined in a route map is then set in the respective IPv6 RIP process with the redistribute command:

```
Router(config-router)# redistribute protocol [process-id] \\
{level-1 | level-1-2 | level-2} [metric metric-value] \\
[metric-type {internal | external}] [route-map map-name]
```

The `protocol` argument can be one of the following keywords: `bgp`, `connected`, `isis`, `rip`, or `static`.

The `rip` keyword and `process-id` argument specify an IPv6 RIP routing process.

Note: The `connected` keyword refers to routes that are established automatically by assigning IPv6 addresses to an interface.

Examples

This example shows how a route map with the name `bgp-to-rip` is defined to match a previously defined IPv6 prefix list with the name `bgp-to-rip-flt`. This route map is then used to tag those routes with the tag "4" and to subsequently be used to redistribute them in an RIP routing process:

```
Router(config) # route-map bgp-to-rip permit 10
Router(config-route-map)# match ipv6 address prefix-list bgp-to-rip-flt
Router(config-route-map)# set tag 4
Router(config-route-map)# exit
Router(config)# ipv6 router rip ciscotest
Router(config-router)# redistribute bgp 65001 route-map bgp-to-rip
```

6.4.1.6 Verifying IPv6 RIP Configuration and Operation

This task explains how to display information to verify the configuration and operation of IPv6 RIP. The commands, which are specific to RIP in this context are show ipv6 rip and debug ipv6 rip, but as with static routes show ipv6 route is also useful in this task. To display information about current IPv6 RIP processes use the following command:

```
Router> show ipv6 rip [name] [database | next-hops]
```

Note that this command may be used as an unprivileged user.

Debugging messages to IPv6 RIP routing transactions may be displayed with the following command syntax:

```
Router# debug ipv6 rip [interface-type interface-number]
```

The debugging information may be constrained to just those transactions taking place on a specific interface. The command may only be executed by privileged users.

For the syntax of the show ipv6 route command please refer to section 6.2.1.

Examples

a) In the following example, output information about all current IPv6 RIP processes is displayed using the `show ipv6 rip` user EXEC command:

```
Router> show ipv6 rip
RIP process "cisco", port 521, multicast-group FF02::9, pid 62
Administrative distance is 120. Maximum paths is 1
Updates every 5 seconds, expire after 15
Holddown lasts 10 seconds, garbage collect after 30
Split horizon is on; poison reverse is off
Default routes are generated
Periodic updates 223, trigger updates 1
Interfaces:
Ethernet0/0
Redistribution:
Redistributing protocol bgp 65001 route-map bgp-to-rip
```

b) In the following example, output information about a specified IPv6 RIP process database is displayed using the `show ipv6 rip` user EXEC command with the `name` argument and the `database` keyword. In the following output for the IPv6 RIP process named `ciscotest`, timer information is displayed, and route 4002::16/64 has a route tag set:

```
Router> show ipv6 rip ciscotest database
RIP process "ciscotest", local RIB
2000::/64, metric 2
Ethernet0/0/FE80::A8BB:CCFF:FE00:B00, expires in 13 secs
4000::/16, metric 2 tag 4, installed
Ethernet0/0/FE80::A8BB:CCFF:FE00:B00, expires in 13 secs
4001::/16, metric 2 tag 4, installed
Ethernet0/0/FE80::A8BB:CCFF:FE00:B00, expires in 13 secs
4002::/16, metric 2 tag 4, installed
Ethernet0/0/FE80::A8BB:CCFF:FE00:B00, expires in 13 secs
::/0, metric 2, installed
Ethernet0/0/FE80::A8BB:CCFF:FE00:B00, expires in 13 secs
```

c) In the following example, output information for a specified IPv6 RIP process is displayed using the show ipv6 rip user EXEC command with the `name` argument and the `next-hops` keyword:

```
Router> show ipv6 rip ciscotest next-hops
RIP process "ciscotest", Next Hops
FE80::A8BB:CCFF:FE00:A00/Ethernet0/0 [4 paths]
```

d) In the following example, output information for all IPv6 RIP routes is displayed using the `show ipv6 route` user EXEC command with the `rip` protocol keyword:

```
Router> show ipv6 route rip
IPv6 Routing Table - 17 entries
Codes: C - Connected, L - Local, S - Static, R - RIP, B - BGP
U - Per-user Static route
I1 - ISIS L1, I2 - ISIS L2, IA - ISIS interarea
O - OSPF intra, OI - OSPF inter, OE1 - OSPF ext 1, OE2 - OSPF ext 2
R 2001:1::/32 [120/2]
via FE80::A8BB:CCFF:FE00:A00, Ethernet0/0
R 2001:2::/32 [120/2]
via FE80::A8BB:CCFF:FE00:A00, Ethernet0/0
R 2001:3::/32 [120/2]
via FE80::A8BB:CCFF:FE00:A00, Ethernet0/0
```

e) In the following example, debugging messages for IPv6 RIP routing transactions are displayed using the `debug ipv6 rip` privileged EXEC command:

```
Router# debug ipv6 rip
RIPng: Sending multicast update on Ethernet0/0 for ciscotest
src=FE80::A8BB:CCFF:FE00:B00
dst=FF02::9 (Ethernet0/0)
sport=521, dport=521, length=112
command=2, version=1, mbz=0, #rte=5
tag=0, metric=1, prefix=2000::/64
tag=4, metric=1, prefix=4000::/16
tag=4, metric=1, prefix=4001::/16
tag=4, metric=1, prefix=4002::/16
tag=0, metric=1, prefix=::/0
RIPng: Next RIB walk in 10032
RIPng: response received from FE80::A8BB:CCFF:FE00:A00 on Ethernet0/0
for ciscotest
src=FE80::A8BB:CCFF:FE00:A00 (Ethernet0/0)
dst=FF02::9
sport=521, dport=521, length=92
command=2, version=1, mbz=0, #rte=4
tag=0, metric=1, prefix=2000::/64
tag=0, metric=1, prefix=2000:1::/32
tag=0, metric=1, prefix=2000:2::/32
```

Note: By default, the system sends the output from debug commands and system error messages to the console. To redirect debugging output, use the logging command options within privileged EXEC mode. Possible destinations include the console, virtual terminals, internal buffer and UNIX hosts running a syslog server. For complete information on debug commands please refer to the appropriate Cisco IOS manual.

6.4.1.7 Complete Configuration Example for IPv6 RIP

In the following example, the IPv6 RIP process named `ciscotest` is enabled on the router and on Ethernet interface 0/0. The IPv6 default route (::/0) is advertised in addition to all other routes in router updates sent on Ethernet interface 0/0. Additionally, BGP routes are redistributed into the RIP process named `ciscotest` according to a route map where routes that match a prefix list are also tagged. The number of parallel paths is set to one to allow the route tagging, and the IPv6 RIP timers are adjusted. A prefix list named `eth0/0-in-flt` filters inbound routing updates on Ethernet interface 0/0.

```
ipv6 router rip ciscotest
 maximum-paths 1
 redistribute bgp 65001 route-map bgp-to-rip
 timers 5 15 10 30
 distribute-list prefix-list eth0/0-in-flt in Ethernet0/0
!
interface Ethernet0/0
 ipv6 address 2000::/64 eui-64
```

```
ipv6 rip ciscotest enable
ipv6 rip ciscotest default-information originate
!
ipv6 prefix-list bgp-to-rip-flt seq 10 deny 4003::/16 le 128
ipv6 prefix-list bgp-to-rip-flt seq 20 permit 4000::/8 le 128
!
ipv6 prefix-list eth0/0-in-flt seq 10 deny ::/0
ipv6 prefix-list eth0/0-in-flt seq 15 permit ::/0 le 128
!
route-map bgp-to-rip permit 10
 match ipv6 address prefix-list bgp-to-rip-flt
 set tag 4
```

6.4.2 Juniper JunOS

The JUNOS software implementation of RIPng is similar to RIPv2. However, RIPng is a distinct routing protocol from RIPv2 and differs in a few aspects from the older version of RIP. Aside from the general architectural limitations of RIPng as stated at the beginning of this chapter the following additional differences are specific to JunOS in comparison to RIPv2:

RIPng does not need to implement authentication on packets.

- There is no support for multiple instances of RIPng.
- There is no support for RIPng routing table groups.

6.4.2.1 Configuring RIPng

To configure Routing Information Protocol Next-Generation (RIPng), you include the following statements:

```
protocols {
    ripng {
        graceful-restart {
            disable;
            restart-time seconds;
        }
        holddown seconds;
        import [ policy-names ];
        metric-in metric;
        receive <none>;
        send <none>;
        traceoptions {
            file name <replace> <size size> <files number> <no-stamp>
                <(world-readable | no-world-readable)>;
```

```
            flag flag <flag-modifier> <disable>;
        }
        group group-name {
            export [ policy-names ];
            metric-out metric;
            preference number;
            neighbor neighbor-name {
                import [ policy-names ];
                metric-in metric;
                receive <none>;
                send <none>;
            }
        }
    }
}
```

6.4.2.2 Define RIPng Global Properties

When RIPng detects a route with a high metric associated, the router waits for a period of time before making any updates into the routing table. This minimises the effects of route flapping to the routing table. The period of time that RIPng waits is the hold-down timer.

To configure the hold-down timer for RIPng, include the `holddown` statement, which can be a value from 10 through 180. The default value is 180 seconds.

Graceful restart is disabled by default. You can globally enable graceful restart for all routing protocols under the `[edit routing-options]` hierarchy level.

You can configure graceful restart parameters specifically for RIPng. To do this, include the `graceful-restart` statement.

To disable graceful restart for RIPng, specify the `disable` statement. To configure a time period for the restart to finish, specify the `restart-time` statement.

6.4.2.3 Define RIPng Global and Neighbour-Specific Properties

To define RIPng properties can be entered either in the global RIPng configuration context and/or with each neighbour. They either apply to all or just to a specific RIPng neighbour.

```
[edit protocols ripng ]
import  [ policy-names ];
metric-in  metric ;
receive  receive-options ;
send  send-options ;

[edit protocols ripng group group-name]
neighbor neighbor-name {
```

```
    import [ policy-names ];
    metric-in metric;
    receive receive-options;
    send send-options;
}
```

By default, RIPng imports routes from the neighbours configured with the `neighbor` statement. These routes include those learned from RIPng as well as those learned from other protocols. By default, routes that RIPng imports from its neighbors have a metric of 1 added to the current route metric.

To change the default metric to be added to incoming routes, include the `metric-in` statement, which can be a value from 1 through 15. A value of 16 indicates infinity or unreachable.

You can enable and disable the sending or receiving of update messages. By default, sending and receiving update messages is enabled. To disable the sending and receiving of update messages, include the `receive` and `send` statements with the none keyword

To enable the sending and receiving of update messages, just include the `receive` and `send` statements.

To filter routes being imported by the local router from its neighbours, include the `import` statement and list the names of one or more policies to be evaluated. If you specify more than one policy, they are evaluated in order (first to last) and the first matching policy is applied to the route. If no match is found, the local router does not import any routes.

6.4.2.4 Defining RIPng Neighbour-Specific Properties

By default, RIPng does not export routes it has learned to its neighbours. To have RIPng export routes, apply one or more export policies. To apply export policies and to filter routes being exported from the local router to its neighbors, include the `export` statement and list the name of the policy to be evaluated.

You can define one or more export policies. If no routes match the policies, the local router does not export any routes to its neighbors. Export policies override any metric values determined through calculations involving the `metric-in` (see above) and `metric-out` values.

If you configure an export policy, RIPng exports routes it has learned to the neighbours configured with the `neighbor` statement.

If a route being exported was learned from a member of the same RIPng group, the metric associated with that route (unless modified by an export policy) is the normal RIPng metric. For example, a RIPng route with a metric of 5 learned from a neighbor configured with a `metric-in` value of 2 is advertised with a combined metric of 7 when advertised to RIPng neighbors in the same group. However, if this route was learned from a RIPng neighbor in a different group or from a different protocol, the route is advertised with the metric value configured for that group with the `metric-out` statement. The default value for `metric-out` is 1.

By default, the JunOS software assigns a preference of 100 to routes that originate from RIPng. When the JunOS software determines a route's preference to become the active route, the software selects the route with the lowest preference and installs this route into the forwarding table.

To modify the default RIPng preference value, include the `preference` statement, which can be a value from 0 through 4,294,967,295 (232 - 1).

6.4.2.5 Tracing RIPng traffic

To trace RIPng protocol traffic, you can specify options in the global `traceoptions` statement at the `[edit routing-options]` hierarchy level, and specify RIPng-specific options by including the `traceoptions` statement:

You can specify the following RIPng-specific options in the RIPng traceoptions statement:

- `all` - Trace everything.
- `error` - Trace RIPng errors.
- `expiration` - Trace RIPng route expiration processing.
- `general` - Trace general events.
- `holddown` - Trace RIPng hold-down processing.
- `normal` - Trace normal events.
- `packets` - Trace all RIPng packets.
- `policy` - Trace policy processing.
- `request` - Trace RIPng information packets.
- `route` - Trace routing information.
- `state` - Trace state transitions.
- `task` - Trace routing protocol task processing.
- `timer` - Trace routing protocol timer processing.
- `trigger` - Trace RIPng triggered updates.
- `update` - Trace RIPng update packets.

Note: Use the traceoption flags `detail` and `all` with caution. These flags may cause the CPU to become very busy.

6.4.2.6 Complete Configuration Example

Configure RIPng:

```
[edit policy-options]
policy-statement redist-direct {
    from protocol direct;
    then accept;
}
[edit protocols ripng]
metric-in 3;
group wan {
    metric-out 2;
    export redist-direct;
```

```
    neighbor so-0/0/0.0;
    neighbor at-1/1/0.0;
    neighbor at-1/1/0.42;
    neighbor at-1/1/1.42 {
        receive version-2;
    }
}
group local {
    neighbor ge-2/3/0.0 {
        metric-in 1;
        send broadcast;
    }
}
```

6.4.3 Quagga

There are no ripngd specific invocation options. Common options can be specified.

Currently ripngd supports the following commands:

Command Syntax:

`Router(config)# router ripng {}`

This command is used to enable RIPng.

Command Syntax:

`Router(config-ripng)# flush_timer time {}`

Set flush timer.

Command Syntax:

`Router(config-ripng)# network <network> {}`

Set RIPng enabled interface by network.

Command Syntax:

`Router(config-ripng)# network <ifname> {}`

Set RIPng enabled interface by `ifname`.

Command Syntax:

`Router(config-ripng)# route <network> {}`

Set RIPng static routing announcement of `network`.

Command Syntax:

`Router# router zebra {}`

This command is the default and does not appear in the configuration. With this statement, RIPng routes go to the `zebra` daemon.

To verify configuration or to debug it, several show and debug commands can be used:

Commands:

```
Router# show ip ripng {}
Router# show debugging ripng {}
Router# show ripng events {}
Router# debug ripng packet {}
Router# debug ripng zebra {}
```

You can apply an access list to the interface using the `distribute-list` command. `access_list` is an access list name. Direction is `in` or `out`. If direction is `in`, the access list is applied only to incoming packets.

```
Router(config-ripng)# distribute-list access_list (in|out) ifname {}
```

Example:

```
Router(config-ripng) # distribute-list local-only out sit1
```

6.5 *Implementing IS-IS for IPv6*

IS-IS in IPv6 functions the same and offers many of the same benefits as IS-IS in IPv4. IPv6 enhancements to IS-IS allow IS-IS to advertise IPv6 prefixes in addition to IPv4 and OSI routes.

6.5.1 Cisco IOS

Extensions to the IS-IS command line interface (CLI) allow configuration of IPv6-specific parameters. IPv6 IS-IS extends the address families supported by IS-IS to include IPv6, in addition to OSI and IPv4.

IPv6 IS-IS in IOS supports either single topology mode or multiple topology mode.

Single topology support for IPv6 allows IS-IS for IPv6 to be configured on interfaces along with other network protocols (for example, IPv4 and Connectionless Network Service). All interfaces must be configured with the identical set of network address families. In addition, all routers in the IS-IS area (for Level 1 routing) or the domain (for Level 2 routing) must support the identical set of network layer address families on all interfaces.

When single topology support for IPv6 is being used, either old or new style TLVs may be used. However, the TLVs used to advertise reachability to IPv6 prefixes use extended metrics. Cisco routers do not allow an interface metric to be set to a value greater than 63 if the configuration is not set to support only new style TLVs for IPv4. In single topology IPv6 mode, the configured metric is always the same for both IPv4 and IPv6.

IS-IS multitopology support for IPv6 allows IS-IS to maintain a set of independent topologies within a single area or domain. This mode removes the restriction that all interfaces on which IS-IS is configured must support the identical set of network address families. It also removes the restriction that all routers in the IS-IS area (for Level 1 routing) or domain (for Level 2 routing) must support the identical set of network layer address families. Because multiple SPFs are performed, one for each configured topology, it is sufficient that connectivity exists among a subset of the routers in the area or domain for a given network address family to be routable.

You can use the `isis ipv6 metric` command to configure different metrics on an interface for IPv6 and IPv4.

When multitopology support for IPv6 is used, enter the `metric-style wide` command to configure IS-IS to use new style TLVs because TLVs used to advertise IPv6 information in LSPs are defined to use only extended metrics.

6.5.1.1 Transition from Single Topology to Multi Topology Support for IPv6

All routers in the area or domain must use the same type of IPv6 support, either single topology or multi topology. A router operating in multi topology mode will not recognize the ability of the single topology mode router to support IPv6 traffic, which will lead to holes in the IPv6 topology. To transition from single topology to a more flexible multi topology support, a multi topology transition mode is provided.

The multi topology transition mode allows a network operating in single topology IS-IS IPv6 support mode to continue to work while upgrading routers to include multi topology IS-IS IPv6 support. While in transition mode, both types of TLVs (single-topology and multi topology) are sent in LSPs for all configured IPv6 addresses, but the router continues to operate in single topology mode (that is, the topological restrictions of the single topology mode are still in effect). After all routers in the area or domain have been upgraded to support multi topology IPv6 and are operating in transition mode, transition mode can be removed from the configuration. Once all routers in the area or domain are operating in multi topology IPv6 mode, the topological restrictions of single topology mode are no longer in effect.

6.5.1.2 Prerequisites

For the minimum required IOS version for IS-IS features please refer to:

http://www.cisco.com/univercd/cc/td/doc/product/software/ios123/123cgcr/ipv6_c/ftipv6s.htm#wp10 04964

Before configuring the router to run IPv6 IS-IS, globally enable IPv6 using the ipv6 unicast-routing global configuration command.

6.5.1.3 Restrictions for Implementing IS-IS for IPv6

In Cisco IOS Release 12.0(21)ST, Cisco IOS Release 12.0(22)S or later releases, and Cisco IOS Release 12.2(8)T or later releases, IS-IS support for IPv6 implements single topology IPv6 IS-IS functionality based on IETF IS-IS working group draft *draft-ietf-isis-ipv6* [Hop03]. A single shortest path first (SPF) per level is used to compute OSI, IPv4 (if configured) and IPv6 routes. The use of a single SPF means that both IPv4 IS-IS and IPv6 IS-IS routing protocols must share a common network topology. To use IS-IS for IPv4 and IPv6 routing, any interface configured for IPv4 IS-IS must also be configured for IPv6 IS-IS, and vice versa. All routers within an IS-IS area (Level 1 routing) or domain (Level 2 routing) must also support the same set of address families: IPv4 only, IPv6 only, or both IPv4 and IPv6.

Beginning with release Cisco IOS Release 12.2(15)T, Cisco IOS Release 12.2(18)S and Cisco IOS Release 12.3(1)M, IS-IS support for IPv6 is enhanced to also support multitopology IPv6 support as defined in IETF IS-IS WG *draft-ietf-isis-wg-multi-topology.txt* [PSS05]. Multitopology IPv6 IS-IS support uses multiple SPFs to compute routes and removes the restriction that all interfaces must support all configured address families and that all routers in an IS-IS area or domain must support the same set of address families.

The following IS-IS router configuration commands are specific to IPv4 and are not supported by, or have any effect on, IPv6 IS-IS:

```
mpls
traffic-share
```

If you are using IS-IS single topology support for IPv6, IPv4, or both IPv6 and IPv4, you may configure both IPv6 and IPv4 on an IS-IS interface for Level 1, Level 2, or both Level 1 and Level 2. However, if both IPv6 and IPv4 are configured on the same interface, they must be running the same IS-IS level. That is, IPv4 cannot be configured to run on IS-IS Level 1 only on a specified Ethernet interface while IPv6 is configured to run IS-IS Level 2 only on the same Ethernet interface.

6.5.1.4 Configuring Single Topology IS-IS for IPv6

This task explains how to create an IPv6 IS-IS process and enable IPv6 IS-IS support on an interface.

Configuring IS-IS comprises two activities. The first activity, creates an IS-IS routing process using protocol-independent IS-IS commands. The second activity, configures the operation of the IS-IS protocol on an interface.

Command syntax for the global protocol-independent configuration:

To enable IS-IS for the specified IS-IS routing process, and enter router configuration mode use the following command:

```
Router(config)# router isis area-name
```

Next, configure an IS-IS network entity title (net) for the routing process:

```
Router(config-router)# net network-entity-title
```

The `network-entity-title` argument defines the area addresses for the IS-IS area and the system ID of the router.

After configuring an IS-IS routing process it may be enabled on appropriate interfaces by the following command:

```
Router(config-if)# ipv6 router isis area-name
```

Examples

The following example shows the minimal configuration necessary to enable single topology IS-IS for IPv6 on a router. First the routing process is created, then this process is enabled on Ethernet interface 0/0/1.

```
Router(config)# router isis area2
Router(config-router)# net 49.0001.0000.0000.000c.00
Router(config-router)# exit
Router(config)# interface Ethernet 0/0/1
Router(config-if)# ipv6 address 2001:0DB8::3/64
Router(config-if)# ipv6 router isis area2
Router(config-if)# exit
Router(config)#
```

6.5.1.5 Configuring Multi Topology IS-IS for IPv6

This task explains how to configure multi topology IS-IS in IPv6. For these optional configuration steps it is assumed that IS-IS for IPv6 is already configured as described in the previous section. The commands described below may then be entered in the configuration context of the corresponding IS-IS routing process.

When multi topology IS-IS for IPv6 is configured, the `transition` keyword allows a user who is working with the single topology SPF mode of IS-IS IPv6 to continue to work while upgrading to multi topology IS-IS. After every router is configured with the transition keyword, users can remove the transition keyword on each router. When transition mode is not enabled, IPv6 connectivity between routers operating in single topology mode and routers operating in multi topology mode is not possible.

You can continue to use the existing IPv6 topology while upgrading to multi topology IS-IS. The optional `isis ipv6 metric` command allows you to differentiate between link costs for IPv6 and IPv4 traffic when operating in multi topology mode.

Command syntax to enable multi topology IS-IS:

The following command configures a router running IS-IS to generate and accept only new style TLVs:

```
Router(config-router)# metric-style wide [transition] \\
                                [level-1 | level-2 | level-1-2]
```

Now, one enters IPv6 address family configuration mode.

```
Router(config-router)# address-family ipv6 [unicast]
```

The unicast keyword specifies the IPv6 unicast address family which is the default in this case anyway.

Within the IPv6 address family multi topology IS-IS for IPv6 can be enabled with the following command:

```
Router(config-router-af)# multi-topology [transition]
```

The optional transition keyword allows an IS-IS IPv6 user to continue to use single topology mode while upgrading to multi topology mode (s.a.).

Examples

In the following example a previously configured (single topology) IS-IS session "area2" is switched to multi topology IS-IS.

```
Router(config)# router isis area2
Router(config-router)# metric-style wide level-1
Router(config-router)# address-family ipv6
Router(config-router-af)# multi-topology
Router(config-router-af)# exit
Router(config-router)# exit
Router(config)#
```

6.5.1.6 Customizing IPv6 IS-IS

This task explains how to configure a new administrative distance for IPv6 IS-IS, configure the maximum number of equal-cost paths that IPv6 IS-IS will support, configure summary prefixes for IPv6 IS-IS, and configure an IS-IS instance to advertise the default IPv6 route (::/0). It also explains how to configure the hold down period between partial route calculations (PRCs) and how often Cisco IOS software performs the SPF calculation when using multitopology IS-IS.

You can customize IS-IS multitopology for IPv6 for your network, but you likely will not need to do so. The defaults for this feature are set to meet the requirements of most customers and features. If you change the defaults, refer to Cisco IPv4 configuration guide and IPv6 command reference to find the appropriate syntax.

Command syntax for customization of single topology IS-IS for IPv6:

To inject the default route into an IS-IS routing domain the following command may be entered in the address family ipv6 context of the corresponding IS-IS process:

```
Router(config-router-af)# default-information originate [route-map map-name]
```

The `route-map` keyword and map-name argument specify the conditions under which the IPv6 default route is advertised.

If the `route-map` keyword is omitted, then the IPv6 default route will be unconditionally advertised at Level 2.

The following command defines an administrative distance for IPv6 IS-IS routes in the IPv6 routing table. Like the previous command it is entered in the `address family ipv6` context.

```
Router(config-router-af)# distance value
```

The `value` argument is an integer from 10 to 254 (values 0 to 9 are reserved for internal use).

As with RIP and BGP one may define the maximum number of equal-cost routes that IPv6 IS-IS can support:

```
Router(config-router-af)# maximum-paths number-paths
```

Optionally one can allow a Level 1-2 router to summarize Level 1 prefixes at Level 2, instead of advertising the Level 1 prefixes directly when the router advertises the summary.

```
Router(config-router-af)# summary-prefix ipv6-prefix/prefix-length \\
                          [level-1 | level-1-2 | level-2]
```

The `ipv6-prefix` argument in the summary-prefix command must be in the form documented in RFC 2373 [RFC2373] where the address is specified in hexadecimal using 16-bit values between colons.

The argument is a decimal value that indicates how many high-order contiguous bits of the address comprise the prefix (the network portion of the address). A slash mark must precede the decimal value.

Last but not least, the hold down period between PRCs and the interval between SPF calculations for multitopology IS-IS may also be manually set within the `address family ipv6` context:

```
Router(config-router-af)# prc-interval seconds \\
                          [initial-wait] [secondary-wait]
Router(config-router-af)# spf-interval [level-1 | level-2] \\
                          seconds [initial-wait] [secondary-wait]
```

The value of a multitopology IS-IS metric is not global but specific to an interface. Therefore it must be entered in that interface's configuration context:

```
Router(config-if) # isis ipv6 metric metric-value \\
                    [level-1 | level-2 | level-1-2]
```

Examples

a) In the following example the IPv6 default route will be unconditionally advertised at Level 2:

```
Router(config)# router isis area2
Router(config-router)# address-family ipv6
Router(config-router-af)# default-information originate
```

b) This example shows the administrative distance of IPv6 IS-IS routes in this domain set to "90":

```
Router(config-router-af)# distance 90
```

c) In the following example all Level 1 routes belonging to the specified prefix are summarized at level 2:

```
Router(config-router-af)# summary-prefix 2001:0DB8::/24
```

d) This example shows the manual setting of IS-IS timers for IPv6:

```
Router(config-router-af)# prc-interval 20
Router(config-router-af)# spf-interval 30
```

e) For the last configuration example the routing context is exited and the configuration context for Ethernet interface 0/0/1 is entered to configure the metric for a multitopology IS-IS process on the routes from this interface:

```
Router(config-router-af)# exit
Router(config-router)# exit
Router(config)# interface Ethernet 0/0/1
Router(config-if)# isis ipv6 metric 20
```

6.5.1.7 Redistributing Routes

IPv6 Routes from another routing process/protocol can also be redistributed to an IPv6 IS-IS routing process. The corresponding redistribute command is entered in the `address family ipv6` context of the IS-IS routing process:

```
Router(config-router-af)# redistribute protocol [process-id] \\
        [level-1 | level-1-2 | level-2] [metric metric-value] \\
        [metric-type {internal | external}] [route-map map-name]
```

The `protocol` argument can be one of the following keywords: `bgp`, `connected`, `isis`, `rip` or `static`.

IPv6 routes learned on one IS-IS level may also be redistributed to another level of the same process. The corresponding redistribute command in this case includes the keyword into:

```
Router(config-router-af)# redistribute protocol \\
        [level-1 [into level-2] | level-1-2 | level-2 \\
        [into level-1]]
```

By default, routes learned by Level 1 instances are redistributed by Level 2 instance.

Note: The `protocol` argument must be `isis` in this configuration of the redistribute command.

Examples

a) In the following example bgp routes from bgp process 64500 are redistributed into the IS-IS routing domain with metric value:

```
Router(config-router-af)# redistribute bgp 64500 \\
                    metric 100 route-map isismap
```

b) This example shows how IS-IS Level 1 routes are distributed in Level 2 domain:

```
Router(config-router-af)# redistribute isis level-1 into level-2
```

6.5.1.8 Disabling Consistency Checks

For single topology IS-IS IPv6, routers must be configured to run the same set of address families. IS-IS performs consistency checks on hello packets and will reject hello packets that do not have the same set of configured address families. For example, a router running IS-IS for both IPv4 and IPv6 will not form an adjacency with a router running IS-IS for IPv4 or IPv6 only. In order to allow adjacency to be formed in mismatched address families network, the adjacency-check command in

IPv6 address family configuration mode must be disabled. This command is designed for use only in special situations.

This said, Cisco IOS software historically makes checks on hello packets to ensure that the IPv4 address is present and has a consistent subnet with the neighbour from which the hello packets are received. To disable this check, use the `no adjacency-check` command in the router configuration mode. However, if multitopology IS-IS is configured, this check is automatically suppressed, because multitopology IS-IS requires routers to form an adjacency regardless of whether or not all routers on a LAN support a common protocol.

Note: Disabling the `adjacency-check` command can adversely affect network configuration. Enter the `no adjacency-check` command only when you are running IPv4 IS-IS on all your routers and you want to add IPv6 IS-IS to your network but it's necessary to maintain all your adjacencies during the transition. When the IPv6 IS-IS configuration is complete, remove the `no adjacency-check` command from configuration.

6.5.1.9 Verifying IPv6 IS-IS Configuration, Operation and Debugging

After IS-IS configuration one might want to verify if everything works as it should. Cisco IOS offers a few commands that help accomplish this task:

The first (non IS-IS specific) command that can be used is:

```
Router# show ipv6 protocols [summary]
```

It displays the parameters and current state of the active IPv6 routing processes.

To view a list of all connected routers running IS-IS in all or specific areas use the following command:

```
Router# show isis [area-tag] [ipv6 | *] topology
```

The `show clns` command is used to display end system (ES), intermediate system (IS) and multitopology IS-IS (M-ISIS) neighbours.

```
Router# show clns [area-tag] neighbors \\
               [interface-type interface-number] [area] [detail]
```

The same command may also be used to display adjacency information for IS-IS neighbours:

```
Router# show clns area-name is-neighbors [type number] [detail]
```

The last command displays the IS-IS link-state database:

```
Router# show isis [area-tag] database [level-1] [level-2] \\
               [l1] [l2] [detail] [lspid]
```

You can use several system debugging commands to check your IS-IS for IPv6 implementation. If adjacencies are not coming up properly, use the `debug isis adj-packets` command.

```
Router# debug isis adj-packets
```

If you are using IS-IS multitopology for IPv6 and want to display statistical information about building routes between intermediate systems, use the `debug isis spf-statistics` command.

```
Router# debug isis spf-statistics
```

To display a log of significant events during an IS-IS SPF computation, use the `debug isis spf-events` command.

```
Router# debug isis spf-events
```

Examples

a) In the following example output information about the parameters and current state of that active IPv6 routing process is displayed using the `show ipv6 protocols` EXEC command:

```
Router# show ipv6 protocols
IPv6 Routing Protocol is "connected"
IPv6 Routing Protocol is "static"
IPv6 Routing Protocol is "isis"
Interfaces:
Ethernet0/0/3
Ethernet0/0/1
Serial1/0/1
Loopback1 (Passive)
Loopback2 (Passive)
Loopback3 (Passive)
Loopback4 (Passive)
Loopback5 (Passive)
Redistribution:
Redistributing protocol static at level 1
Address Summarization:
L2: 33::/16 advertised with metric 0
L2: 44::/16 advertised with metric 20
L2: 66::/16 advertised with metric 10
L2: 77::/16 advertised with metric 10
```

b) In the following example, output information about all connected routers running IS-IS in all areas is displayed using the `show isis topology` EXEC command:

```
Router# show isis topology
IS-IS paths to level-1 routers
System Id Metric Next-Hop Interface SNPA
0000.0000.000C
0000.0000.000D 20 0000.0000.00AA Se1/0/1 *HDLC*
0000.0000.000F 10 0000.0000.000F Et0/0/1 0050.e2e5.d01d
0000.0000.00AA 10 0000.0000.00AA Se1/0/1 *HDLC*
IS-IS paths to level-2 routers
System Id Metric Next-Hop Interface SNPA
0000.0000.000A 10 0000.0000.000A Et0/0/3 0010.f68d.f063
0000.0000.000B 20 0000.0000.000A Et0/0/3 0010.f68d.f063
0000.0000.000C --
0000.0000.000D 30 0000.0000.000A Et0/0/3 0010.f68d.f063
0000.0000.000E 30 0000.0000.000A Et0/0/3 0010.f68d.f063
```

c) In the following example, detailed output information that displays both end system (ES) and intermediate system (IS) neighbors is displayed using the `show clns neighbors` command with the `detail` keyword.

```
Router# show clns neighbors detail
System Id         Interface     SNPA           State  Holdtime  Type Protocol
0000.0000.0007     Et3/3        aa00.0400.6408  UP     26        L1   IS-IS
Area Address(es): 20
IP Address(es): 172.16.0.42*
Uptime: 00:21:49
0000.0C00.0C35     Et3/2        0000.0c00.0c36  Up     91        L1   IS-IS
Area Address(es): 20
IP Address(es): 192.168.0.42*
Uptime: 00:21:52
0800.2B16.24EA     Et3/3        aa00.0400.2d05  Up     27        L1   M-ISIS
Area Address(es): 20
IP Address(es): 192.168.0.42*
IPv6 Address(es): FE80::2B0:8EFF:FE31:EC57
Uptime: 00:00:27
0800.2B14.060E     Et3/2        aa00.0400.9205  Up     8         L1   IS-IS
Area Address(es): 20
IP Address(es): 192.168.0.30*
Uptime: 00:21:52
```

d) In the following example, output information to confirm that the local router has formed all the necessary IS-IS adjacencies with other IS-IS neighbors is displayed using the `show clns is-neighbors` EXEC command. To display the IPv6 link-local addresses of the neighbours, specify the `detail` keyword.

```
Router# show clns is-neighbors detail
System Id Interface State Type Priority Circuit Id Format
0000.0000.00AA Se1/0/1 Up L1 0 00 Phase V
Area Address(es): 49.0001
IPv6 Address(es): FE80::YYYY:D37C:C854:5
Uptime: 17:21:38
0000.0000.000F Et0/0/1 Up L1 64 0000.0000.000C.02 Phase V
Area Address(es): 49.0001
IPv6 Address(es): FE80::XXXX:E2FF:FEE5:D01D
Uptime: 17:21:41
0000.0000.000A Et0/0/3 Up L2 64 0000.0000.000C.01 Phase V
Area Address(es): 49.000b
IPv6 Address(es): FE80::ZZZZ:F6FF:FE8D:F063
Uptime: 17:22:06
```

e) In the following example, detailed output information about LSPs received from other routers and the IPv6 prefixes they are advertising is displayed using the show `isis database` EXEC command with the `detail` keyword specified:

```
Router# show isis database detail
IS-IS Level-1 Link State Database
LSPID LSP Seq Num LSP Checksum LSP Holdtime ATT/P/OL
0000.0C00.0C35.00-00 0x0000000C 0x5696 325 0/0/0
  Area Address: 47.0004.004D.0001
  Area Address: 39.0001
  Metric: 10 IS 0000.0C00.62E6.03
  Metric: 0 ES 0000.0C00.0C35
0000.0C00.40AF.00-00* 0x00000009 0x8452 608 1/0/0
  Area Address: 47.0004.004D.0001
  Topology: IPv4 (0x0) IPv6 (0x2)
  NLPID: 0xCC 0x8E
  IP Address: 172.16.21.49
  Metric: 10 IS 0800.2B16.24EA.01
  Metric: 10 IS 0000.0C00.62E6.03
  Metric: 0 ES 0000.0C00.40AF
  IPv6 Address: 2001:0DB8::/32
  Metric: 10   IPv6 (MT-IPv6) 2001:0DB8::/64
  Metric: 5    IS-Extended cisco.03
  Metric: 10   IS-Extended cisco1.03
  Metric: 10    IS (MT-IPv6) cisco.03
IS-IS Level-2 Link State Database:
LSPID LSP Seq Num LSP Checksum LSP Holdtime ATT/P/OL
0000.0000.000A.00-00 0x00000059 0x378A 949 0/0/0
Area Address: 49.000b
NLPID: 0x8E
IPv6 Address: 2001:0DB8:1:1:1:1:1:1
Metric: 10 IPv6 2001:2:YYYY::/64
Metric: 10 IPv6 3001:3:YYYY::/64
Metric: 10 IPv6 3001:2:YYYY::/64
Metric: 10 IS-Extended 0000.0000.000A.01
Metric: 10 IS-Extended 0000.0000.000B.00
Metric: 10 IS-Extended 0000.0000.000C.01
Metric: 0 IPv6 11:1:YYYY:1:1:1:1:1/128
Metric: 0 IPv6 11:2:YYYY:1:1:1:1:1/128
Metric: 0 IPv6 11:3:YYYY:1:1:1:1:1/128
Metric: 0 IPv6 11:4:YYYY:1:1:1:1:1/128
Metric: 0 IPv6 11:5:YYYY:1:1:1:1:1/128
0000.0000.000A.01-00 0x00000050 0xB0AF 491 0/0/0
```

```
Metric: 0 IS-Extended 0000.0000.000A.00
Metric: 0 IS-Extended 0000.0000.000B.00
```

6.5.2 Juniper JunOS

Since IS-IS for IPv6 is configured and treated in the same way as IPv4 this section only details the specific IPv6 commands and differences. For general IS-IS configuration guidelines please refer to Juniper's official JunOS documentation.

6.5.2.1 Configuring IS-IS

To configure Intermediate System to Intermediate System (IS-IS), you include statements in the configuration:

```
protocols {
    isis {
        disable ;
        ignore-attached-bit ;
        graceful-restart {
            disable;
            helper-disable;
            restart-duration seconds ;
        }
        label-switched-path name level level metric metric ;
        level level-number {
            authentication-key key ;
            authentication-type authentication ;
            external-preference preference ;
            no-csnp-authentication;
            no-hello-authentication;
            no-psnp-authentication;
            preference preference;
            prefix-export-limit number ;
            wide-metrics-only ;
        }
        lsp-lifetime seconds ;
        no-authentication-check ;
        no-ipv4-routing;
        no-ipv6-routing;
        overload <timeout seconds >;
        reference-bandwidth reference-bandwidth;
        rib-group group-name ;
        spf-delay milliseconds ;
        topologies {
```

```
        ipv4-multicast;
        ipv6-unicast;
    }
    traffic-engineering  {
        disable ;
        shortcuts ;
    }
    traceoptions  {
        file name  <replace> <size size > <files  number > <no-stamp>
            <(world-readable | no-world-readable)>;
        flag flag  < flag-modifier > <disable>;
    }
    interface  interface-name  {
        disable ;
        bfd-liveness-detection {
            minimum-interval milliseconds ;
            minimum-receive-interval milliseconds ;
            minimum-transmit-interval milliseconds ;
            multiplier number ;
        }
        checksum;
        csnp-interval  ( seconds  | disable);
        lsp-interval  milliseconds ;
        mesh-group  ( value  | blocked);
        no-ipv4-multicast;
        no-ipv6-unicast;
        passive ;
        point-to-point;
        level  level-number  {
            disable ;
            hello-authentication-key  key ;
            hello-authentication-type  authentication ;
            hello-interval  seconds ;
            hold-time  seconds ;
            ipv4-multicast-metric number ;
            ipv6-unicast-metric number
            metric  metric ;
            passive ;
            priority  number ;
            te-metric  metric ;
        }
    }
```

```
    }
}
```

6.5.2.2 Disable IPv6 Routing

It is possible to disable Internet Protocol Version 6 (IPv6) routing for IS-IS. Disabling IPv6 routing results in the following:

- Router does not advertise the NLPID for IPv6 in JunOS software 0th LSP fragment.
- Router does not advertise any IPv6 prefixes in JunOS software LSPs.
- Router does not advertise the NLPID for IPv6 in JunOS software hello packets.
- Router does not advertise any IPv6 addresses in JunOS software hello packets.
- Router does not calculate any IPv6 routes.

To disable IPv6 routing on the router, include the `no-ipv6-routing` statement:

```
[edit protocols]
isis {
    no-ipv6-routing;
}
```

To re-enable IS-IS, delete the `disable` statement from the configuration:

```
[edit protocols]
user@host# delete isis no-ipv6-routing
```

6.5.2.3 Configure IS-IS IPv6 Unicast Topologies

You can configure IS-IS to calculate an alternate IPv6 unicast topology, in addition to the normal IPv4 unicast topology, and add the corresponding routes to inet6.0. The IS-IS interface metrics for the IPv4 topology can be configured independently of the IPv6 metrics. You can also selectively disable interfaces from participating in the IPv6 topology while continuing to participate in the IPv4 topology. This lets you exercise control over the paths that unicast data takes through a network.

To enable an alternate IPv6 unicast topology for IS-IS, include the `ipv6-unicast` statement:

```
[edit protocols]
isis {
    topologies {
        ipv6-unicast;
    }
}
```

To configure a metric for an alternate IPv6 unicast topology, include the `ipv6-unicast-metric` statement:

```
[edit protocols]
isis {
    interface interface-name {
        level level-number {
            ipv6-unicast-metric number;
        }
    }
}
```

To disable alternate IPv6 unicast topologies for IS-IS, include the no-ipv6-unicast statement:

```
[edit protocols]
isis {
    interface interface-name {
        no-ipv6-unicast;
    }
}
```

6.6 *Implementing OSPF for IPv6*

OSPF is a routing protocol for IP. It is a link-state protocol, as opposed to a distance-vector protocol like RIP. Think of a link as being an interface on a networking device. A link-state protocol makes its routing decisions based on the states of the links that connect source and destination machines. The state of a link is a description of that interface and its relationship to its neighbouring networking devices. The interface information includes the IPv6 prefix of the interface, the network mask, the type of network it is connected to, the routers connected to that network, and so on. This information is propagated in various type of link-state advertisements (LSAs).

A router's collection of LSA data is stored in a link-state database. The contents of the database, when subjected to the Dijkstra algorithm, result in the creation of the OSPF routing table. The difference between the database and the routing table is that the database contains a complete collection of raw data; the routing table contains a list of shortest paths to known destinations via specific router interface ports.

OSPF version 3, which is described in RFC 2740 [RFC2740], supports IPv6. Implementing OSPFv3 for IPv6 expands on OSPFv2 to provide support for IPv6 routing prefixes. This section describes the concepts and tasks you need to implement OSPFv3 for IPv6 on your network.

Note: OSPFv3 is a separate protocol from OSPFv2 and is therefore an IPv6-only routing protocol. If you are running a dual-stack environment with OSPF you need separate routing processes for IPv4 and IPv6 (OSPFv2 and OSPFv3 respectively).

6.6.1 LSA Types for IPv6

Due to the fact that with IPv6 it is possible to configure many different IP addresses on one interface LSA types for OSPv3 differ from those in OSPFv2 for IPv4.

The following list describes OSPFv3 LSA types, each of which has a different purpose:

- Router LSAs (Type 1)—Describes the link state and costs of a router's links to the area. These LSAs are flooded within an area only. The LSA indicates if the router is an Area Border Router (ABR) or Autonomous System Boundary Router (ASBR), and if it is one end of a virtual link. Type 1 LSAs are also used to advertise stub networks. In OSPF for IPv6, these LSAs have no address information and are network protocol independent. In OSPF for IPv6, router interface information may be spread across multiple router LSAs. Receivers must concatenate all router LSAs originated by a given router when running the SPF calculation.

- Network LSAs (Type 2)—Describes the link-state and cost information for all routers attached to the network. This LSA is an aggregation of all the link-state and cost information in the network. Only a designated router tracks this information and can generate a network LSA. In OSPF for IPv6, network LSAs have no address information and are network protocol independent.

- Interarea-prefix LSAs for ABRs (Type 3)—Advertises internal networks to routers in other areas (interarea routes). Type 3 LSAs may represent a single network or a set of networks summarised into one advertisement. Only ABRs generate summary LSAs. In OSPF for IPv6, addresses for these LSAs are expressed as *prefix, prefix length* instead of *address, mask*. The default route is expressed as a prefix with length 0.

- Interarea-router LSAs for ASBRs (Type 4)—Advertise the location of an ASBR. Routers that are trying to reach an external network use these advertisements to determine the best path to the next hop. ASBRs generate Type 4 LSAs.

- Autonomous system external LSAs (Type 5)—Redistributes routes from another AS, usually from a different routing protocol into OSPF. In OSPF for IPv6, addresses for these LSAs are expressed as *prefix, prefix length* instead of *address, mask*. The default route is expressed as a prefix with length 0.
- Link LSAs (Type 8)—Have local-link flooding scope and are never flooded beyond the link with which they are associated. Link LSAs provide the link-local address of the router to all other routers attached to the link, inform other routers attached to the link of a list of IPv6 prefixes to associate with the link, and allow the router to assert a collection of Options bits to associate with the network LSA that will be originated for the link.
- Intra-Area-Prefix LSAs (Type 9)—A router can originate multiple intra-area-prefix LSAs for each router or transit network, each with a unique link-state ID. The link-state ID for each intra-area-prefix LSA describes its association to either the router LSA or the network LSA and contains prefixes for stub and transit networks.

An address prefix occurs in almost all newly defined LSAs. The prefix is represented by three fields: PrefixLength, PrefixOptions, and Address Prefix. In OSPF for IPv6, addresses for these LSAs are expressed as *prefix, prefix length* instead of *address, mask*. The default route is expressed as a prefix with length 0. Type 3 and Type 9 LSAs carry all IPv6 prefix information that, in IPv4, is included in router LSAs and network LSAs. The Options field in certain LSAs (router LSAs, network LSAs, interarea-router LSAs, and link LSAs) has been expanded to 24 bits to provide support for OSPF in IPv6.

In OSPF for IPv6, the sole function of link-state ID in interarea-prefix LSAs, interarea-router LSAs, and autonomous-system external LSAs is to identify individual pieces of the link-state database. All addresses or router IDs that are expressed by the link-state ID in OSPF version 2 are carried in the body of the LSA in OSPF for IPv6.

The link-state ID in network LSAs and link LSAs is always the interface ID of the originating router on the link being described. For this reason, network LSAs and link LSAs are now the only LSAs whose size cannot be limited. A network LSA must list all routers connected to the link, and a link LSA must list all of the address prefixes of a router on the link.

6.6.2 NBMA in OSPF for IPv6

On NBMA networks, the designated router (DR) or backup DR (BDR) performs the LSA flooding. On point-to-point networks, flooding simply goes out an interface directly to a neighbour.

Routers that share a common segment (Layer 2 link between two interfaces) become neighbours on that segment. OSPF uses the Hello protocol, periodically sending hello packets out each interface. Routers become neighbors when they see themselves listed in the neighbour's hello packet. After two routers become neighbors, they may proceed to exchange and synchronize their databases, which creates an adjacency. Not all neighboring routers have an adjacency.

On point-to-point and point-to-multipoint networks, the software floods routing updates to immediate neighbors. There is no DR or BDR; all routing information is flooded to each networking device.

On broadcast or NBMA segments only, OSPF minimizes the amount of information being exchanged on a segment by choosing one router to be a DR and one router to be a BDR. Thus, the routers on the segment have a central point of contact for information exchange. Instead of each router exchanging routing updates with every other router on the segment, each router exchanges information with the DR and BDR. The DR and BDR relay the information to the other routers.

The software looks at the priority of the routers on the segment to determine which routers will be DR and BDR. The router with the highest priority is the elected DR. If there is a tie, then the router with the higher router ID takes precedence. After the DR is elected, the BDR is elected the same way. A router with a router priority set to zero is ineligible to become the DR or BDR.

When using NBMA in OSPF for IPv6, you cannot automatically detect neighbours. On an NBMA interface, you must configure your neighbours manually using interface configuration mode.

6.6.3 Cisco IOS

Much of the OSPF for IPv6 feature is the same as in OSPF version 2. OSPF version 3 for IPv6, which is described in RFC 2740, expands on OSPF version 2 to provide support for IPv6 routing prefixes and the larger size of IPv6 addresses.

In OSPF for IPv6, a routing process does not need to be explicitly created. Enabling OSPF for IPv6 on an interface will cause a routing process and its associated configuration, to be created.

Furthermore, in OSPFv3 on Cisco IOS, each interface must be enabled using commands in interface configuration mode. This feature is different from OSPF version 2, in which interfaces are indirectly enabled using the router configuration mode.

When using a non-broadcast multi-access (NBMA) interface in OSPF for IPv6, users must manually configure the router with the list of neighbors. Neighboring routers are identified by their router ID.

In IPv6, users can configure many address prefixes on an interface. In OSPF for IPv6, all address prefixes on an interface are included by default. Users cannot select some address prefixes to be imported into OSPF for IPv6; either all address prefixes on an interface are imported, or no address prefixes on an interface are imported.

Unlike OSPF version 2, multiple instances of OSPF for IPv6 can be run on a link.

6.6.3.1 Prerequisites

Before you enable OSPF for IPv6 on an interface, you should have an OSPF network strategy planned for your IPv6 network. For example, you must decide whether multiple areas are required.

On the routers on which you want to use OSPFv3 you need to have IPv6 unicast routing enabled and IPv6 address must be configured on the interfaces taking part in the routing process(es).

For the minimum required IOS version for features related to OSPFv3 routing please refer to:

http://www.cisco.com/univercd/cc/td/doc/product/software/ios123/123cgcr/ipv6_c/ftipv6s.htm#wp10 04964

6.6.3.2 Restrictions

Be careful when changing the defaults for commands used to enable OSPF for IPv6. Changing these defaults will affect your OSPF for IPv6 network, possibly adversely.

Authentication is not yet supported in all IOS releases. It is currently only available in 12.3(4)T. The feature will be more widely supported in OSPF for IPv6 in future releases.

6.6.3.3 Enabling OSPF for IPv6

To implement OSPFv3 on a Cisco IOS platform the protocol basically just needs to be enabled on an interface with an IPv6 address with the following command:

```
Router(config-if)# ipv6 ospf process-id area area-id [instance instance-id]
```

Now an OSPFv3 process with the specified id is created and the protocol is enabled. The next two sections on configuring NBMA interfaces and forcing SPF calculation are optional.

You can customize OSPF for IPv6 for your network, but you likely will not need to do so. The defaults for OSPF in IPv6 are set to meet the requirements of most customers and features. If you must change the defaults, refer to Cisco IPv4 configuration guide and Cisco IPv6 command reference to find the appropriate syntax. Be careful when changing the defaults.

Example

The following example configures a (new) OSPFv3 process with id 1 and area 0.

```
Router(config-if)# ipv6 ospf 1 area 0
```

6.6.3.4 Configuring NBMA Interfaces

You can customize OSPF for IPv6 in your network to use NBMA interfaces. Before you configure NBMA interfaces you must actually have your network configured as an NBMA network and identified each neighbor. You cannot automatically detect neighbours, but must manually configure your router to detect neighbours when using an NBMA interface. The commands to issue in the respective interface's configuration context are:

```
Router(config-if)# frame-relay map ipv6 ipv6-address dlci \\
            [broadcast] [cisco] [ietf] \\
            [payload-compression {packet-by-packet | \\
            frf9 stac [hardware-options] | data-stream stac \\
            [hardware-options]}]
```

The command defines the mapping between a destination IPv6 address and the data-link connection identifier (DLCI) used to connect to the destination address.

To configure a neighbour use the following command:

```
Router(config-if)# ipv6 ospf neighbor ipv6-address \\
[priority number] [poll-interval seconds] [cost number] \\
[database-filter all out]
```

Examples

a) In the following example, the NBMA link is frame relay. For other kinds of NBMA links, different mapping commands are used:

```
Router(config-if)#  frame-relay map ipv6 FE80::A8BB:CCFF:FE00:C01 120
```

b) The router on the frame relay link above is configured as an OSPFv3 neighbour:

```
Router(config-if) ipv6 ospf neighbor FE80::A8BB:CCFF:FE00:C01
```

6.6.3.5 Clearing the Database and/or Forcing an SPF Calculation

Occasionally, when something was changed or for debugging purposes one might want to clear the present routing table and/or force the OSPFv3 process to build it a new. This is done using the following command, which is issued at the global configuration level:

```
Router # clear ipv6 ospf [process-id] {process | force-spf | \\
         redistribution | counters [neighbor [neighbor-interface]]}
```

The command clears the OSPF state based on the OSPF routing process ID.

When the `process` keyword is used with the `clear ipv6 ospf` command, the OSPF database is cleared and repopulated, and then the shortest path first (SPF) algorithm is performed. When the `force-spf` keyword is used with the `clear ipv6 ospf` command, the OSPF database is not cleared before the SPF algorithm is performed.

Example

The easiest way to do this is issuing the command without any more options:

```
Router# clear ipv6 ospf force-spf
```

6.6.3.6 Verifying OSPF for IPv6 Configuration and Operation

When debugging or verifying OSPFv3 configuration the show ipv6 ospf command comes in handy. It may be issued with the interface keyword, even adding a specific interface name for which OSPF-related information should be displayed. Or it may be used without an interface to display general OSPFv3 information:

```
Router# show ipv6 ospf [process-id] [area-id] \\
                 interface [interface-type interface-number]
Router# show ipv6 ospf [process-id] [area-id]
```

Examples

a) This command displays OSPF-related interface information:

```
Router# show ipv6 ospf interface
```

b) This command displays general information about OSPF routing processes:

```
Router# show ipv6 ospf
```

6.6.3.7 Load Balancing in OSPF for IPv6

When a router learns multiple routes to a specific network via multiple routing processes (or routing protocols), it installs the route with the lowest administrative distance in the routing table. Sometimes the router must select a route from among many learned from the same routing process with the same administrative distance. In this case, the router chooses the path with the lowest cost (or metric) to the destination. Each routing process calculates its cost differently and the costs may need to be manipulated in order to achieve load balancing.

OSPF performs load balancing automatically in the following way. If OSPF finds that it can reach a destination through more than one interface and each path has the same cost, it installs each path in the routing table. The only restriction on the number of paths to the same destination is controlled by the `maximum-paths` command. The default maximum paths is 16, and the range is from 1 to 64.

6.6.4 Juniper JunOS

Though OSPFv3 for IPv6 and OSPFv2 are separate and different protocols all of the configuration keywords available for both protocols are the same and have the same meaning. This section will therefore only focus on the differences in their configuration.

6.6.4.1 Configure OSPFv3

To configure OSPF Version 3, you include the following statements. Note that not all configuration statements available for IPv4 are present for IPv6 as well. Those that are however, are used in exactly the same way.

```
protocols {
    ospf3 {
        disable;
        export [ policy-names ];
        external-preference preference;
        graceful-restart {
            disable;
            helper-disable;
            notify-duration seconds;
            restart-duration seconds;
        }
        overload {
            <timeout seconds>;
        }
        preference preference;
        prefix-export-limit;
        reference-bandwidth reference-bandwidth;
        rib-group group-name;
        spf-delay;
        traceoptions {
            file name <replace> <size size> <files number> <no-stamp>
                <(world-readable | no-world-readable)>;
            flag flag <flag-modifier> <disable>;
        }
        area area-id {
```

```
            area-range network/mask-length <restrict>;
            interface interface-name {
                disable;
                dead-interval seconds;
                hello-interval seconds;
                metric metric;
                passive;
                priority number;
                retransmit-interval seconds;
                transit-delay seconds;
            }
            nssa {
                area-range network/mask-length <restrict>;
                default-lsa {
                    default-metric metric;
                    metric-type type;
                    type-7;
                }
                (no-summaries | summaries)
            }
            stub <default-metric metric> <summaries | no-summaries>;
            virtual-link neighbor-id router-id transit-area area-id {
                disable;
                dead-interval seconds;
                hello-interval seconds;
                retransmit-interval seconds;
                transit-delay seconds;
            }
        }
    }
}
```

6.6.4.2 Restrictions and Prerequisites

When you configure OSPFv3 on an interface, you must also include the `family inet6` statement at the `[edit interfaces interface-name unit logical-unit-number]` hierarchy level.

OSPFv3 does not support routing instances or authentication. It also only supports the no-forwarding and vrf routing instance types.

At least one router on each logical link must be eligible to be the designated router for OSPFv3.

For OSPFv3, one OSPF-specific interface must be created per interface name configured under OSPFv3. OSPFv3 does not allow interfaces to be configured by IP address.

Traffic engineering is not supported for OSPFv3.

6.6.4.3 Full Configuration Example

The following configuration was provided by FCCN, the Portuguese NREN. In this case there is only one area, in which two of the router's interfaces are active.

```
ospfv3@junos# show policy-options:

policy-statement default6 {
    from {
        protocol [ static direct ];
        route-filter ::/0 exact;
    }
    then accept;
}

ospfv3@junos# show protocols:

ospf3 {
    export default6;
    area 0.0.0.0 {
        interface lo0.0;
        interface ge-0/0/0.5 {
            priority 80;
        }
        interface ge-0/2/0.2 {
            priority 80;
        }
    }
}

ospfv3@junos> show configuration interfaces ge-0/0/0 unit 5

vlan-id 5;
family inet {
    address 193.137.0.x/yy;
}
family iso {
    address 49.0001.0000.0000.0005.05;
}
family inet6 {
    address 2001:690:xxxx:1::1/64;
}
```

6.6.5 Quagga

OSPFv3 is a special daemon "ospf6d" within Quagga. To configure OSPFv3 via the command line one has to enter the OSPFv3 configuration context:

```
Router(config)# router ospf6 {}
```

The next step is to configure a router-id:

```
Router(config-rtr)# router-id <a.b.c.d> {}
```

After this step the interfaces, which are to participate in OSPFv6 routing need to be bound to the OSPFv3 routing process:

```
Router(config-rtr)# interface <ifname> area <area> {}
```

Zebra/Quagga will then start sending OSPF packets on this interface. area can be specified as 0.

6.6.5.1 Specific OSPFv3 Interface commands

Enter the configuration context for the interface you want to configure.

Command Syntax:

```
Router(config-if)# ipv6 ospf6 cost <cost> {}
```

Sets interface's output cost (default value is 1).

Command Syntax:

```
Router(config-if)# ipv6 ospf6 hello-interval <hellointerval> {}
```

Sets interface's Hello Interval (default 40).

Command Syntax:

```
Router(config-if)# ipv6 ospf6 dead-interval <Ddeadinterval> {}
```

Sets interface's Router Dead Interval (default value is 40).

Command Syntax:

```
Router(config-if)# ipv6 ospf6 retransmit-interval <retransmitinterval> {}
```

Sets interface's Rxmt Interval (default value is 5).

Command Syntax:

```
Router(config-if)# ipv6 ospf6 priority <priority> {}
```

Sets interface's Router Priority (default value is 1).

Command Syntax:

```
Router(config-if)# ipv6 ospf6 transmit-delay <transmitdelay> {}
```

Sets interface's Inf-Trans-Delay (default value is 1).

6.6.5.2 Route Redistribution

OSPFv3 on the Quagga platform offers the possibility to redistribute static, connected or RIPng routes. The corresponding commands are entered in the ospf6 area context of the corresponding routing process.

```
Router(config-rtr)# redistribute static {}
Router(config-rtr)# redistribute connected {}
Router(config-rtr)# redistribute ripng {}
```

6.6.5.3 Displaying OSPFv3 Information

Several show commands can be used to display OSPFv3 routing information to verify correct configuration and router behaviour.

Command Syntax:

```
Router# show ipv6 ospf6 [<instance-id>] {}
```

`instance-id` is an optional OSPF instance ID. To see router ID and OSPF instance ID, simply type "`show ipv6 ospf6 `".

Command Syntax:

```
Router# show ipv6 ospf6 database {}
```

This command shows an LSA database summary. You can specify the type of LSA.

Command Syntax:

```
Router# show ipv6 ospf6 interface {}
```

Use this command to see OSPF interface configuration like for example costs.

Command Syntax:

```
Router# show ipv6 ospf6 neighbor {}
```

Shows the state and chosen (Backup) DR of a neighbour.

Command Syntax:

```
Router# show ipv6 ospf6 request-list <ipv6 address> {}
```

Shows the request-list of a neighbour.

Command Syntax:

```
Router# show ipv6 route ospf6 {}
```

This command shows the internal (OSPF) routing table.

6.7 *Implementing Multiprotocol BGP for IPv6*

This section describes how to configure Multiprotocol Border Gateway Protocol (MBGP) for IPv6 [RFC2283],[BCKR05]. BGP is an Exterior Gateway Protocol (EGP) used mainly to connect separate routing domains that contain independent routing policies (autonomous systems). Connecting to a service provider for access to the Internet is a common use for BGP. BGP can also be used within an autonomous system and this variation is referred to as internal BGP (iBGP). Multiprotocol BGP is an enhanced BGP that carries routing information for multiple network layer protocol address families, for example, IPv6 address family and for IP multicast routes. All BGP commands and routing policy capabilities can be used with multiprotocol BGP.

6.7.1 Cisco IOS

Multiprotocol BGP is the supported Exterior Gateway Protocol (EGP) for IPv6. Multiprotocol BGP extensions for IPv6 supports the same features and functionality as IPv4 BGP. IPv6 enhancements to multiprotocol BGP include support for an IPv6 address family and network layer reachability information (NLRI) and next hop (the next router in the path to the destination) attributes that use IPv6 addresses.

BGP uses a router ID to identify BGP-speaking peers. The BGP router ID is 32-bit value that is often represented by an IPv4 address. By default, the Cisco IOS software sets the router ID to the IPv4 address of a loopback interface on the router. If no loopback interface is configured on the router, then the software chooses the highest IPv4 address configured to a physical interface on the router to represent the BGP router ID. When configuring BGP on a router that is enabled only for IPv6 (the router does not have an IPv4 address), you must manually configure the BGP router ID for the router. The BGP router ID, which is represented as a 32-bit value using an IPv4 address syntax, must be unique to the BGP peers of the router.

6.7.1.1 Prerequisites

As with any IPv6 routing feature you must first enable ipv6 unicast-routing before configuring Multiprotocol BGP.

For the minimum required IOS version for multiprotocol BGP features please refer to:

http://www.cisco.com/univercd/cc/td/doc/product/software/ios123/123cgcr/ipv6_c/ftipv6s.htm#wp10 04964

6.7.1.2 Enabling and Implementing Multiprotocol BGP for IPv6

When configuring multiprotocol BGP extensions for IPv6, you must create the BGP routing process, configure peering relationships, and customize BGP for your particular network.

Note:The following sections describe the configuration tasks for creating an IPv6 multiprotocol BGP routing process and associating peers, peer groups, and networks to the routing process. The following sections do not provide in-depth information on customizing multiprotocol BGP because the protocol functions the same in IPv6 as it does in IPv4.

Command syntax:

```
Router(config)# router bgp autonomous-system-number
```

The command configures a BGP routing process, and enters router configuration mode for the specified routing process.

```
Router(config-router)# no bgp default ipv4-unicast
```

This command is used to disable the IPv4 unicast address family for the BGP routing process. Otherwise routing information for the IPv4 unicast address family is advertised by default.

As mentioned above usually an IPv4 address configured on one of the interfaces is used as BGP router id. You can optionally change/set this id with the following command:

```
Router(config-router)# bgp router-id ip-address
```

Note: Configuring a router id using the bgp router-id command resets all active BGP peering sessions.

As with IPv4 the next step is to configure BGP neighbors/peers. By default, neighbors that are defined using the neighbor `remote-as` command in router configuration mode exchange only IPv4 unicast address prefixes. To exchange other address prefix types, such as IPv6 prefixes, neighbors must also be activated using the neighbor activate command in address family configuration mode for the other prefix types, as shown for IPv6 prefixes.

The first step however is to add a neighbor in the context of previously created routing process:

```
Router(config-router)# neighbor ipv6-address remote-as \\
                                        autonomous-system-number
```

The specified `ipv6-address` may be a unicast IPv6 address of any form, but configuring IPv6 multiprotocol BGP between two IPv6 routers (peers) using link-local addresses requires that the interface for the neighbor be identified by using the `update-source` router configuration command, and that a route map be configured to set an IPv6 global next hop. The `update-source` is defined in the global BGP configuration context, after the neighbour was created:

```
Router(config-router)# neighbor ipv6-address update-source \\
                                   interface-type interface-number
```

If there are multiple connections to the neighbor and you do not specify the neighbor interface by using the `interface-type` and `interface-number` arguments in the `neighbor update-source` command, a TCP connection cannot be established with the neighbor using link-local addresses.

Now enter the IPv6 address family:

```
Router(config-router)# address-family ipv6 [unicast]
```

The `unicast` keyword specifies the IPv6 unicast address family. By default, the router is placed in configuration mode for the IPv6 unicast address family if the `unicast` keyword is not specified with the `address-family ipv6` command.

Within this context one can enable the neighbor to exchange prefixes for the IPv6 address family with the local router.

```
Router(config-router-af)# neighbor ipv6-address activate
```

By default, route maps that are applied in router configuration mode using the `neighbor route-map` command are applied to only IPv4 unicast address prefixes. Route maps for other address families must be applied in address family configuration mode using the `neighbor route-map` command, as shown for the IPv6 address family. The route maps are applied either as the inbound or outbound routing policy for neighbors under the specified address family. Configuring separate route maps under each address family type simplifies managing complicated or different policies for each address family.

```
Router(config-router-af)# neighbor ipv6-address route-map map-name {in | out}
```

To configure a route map as it is needed when using a neighbour's link local address in the BGP configuration the special command `set ipv6 next-hop` is used in the route map configuration.

```
Router(config) # route-map map-name [permit | deny] [sequence-number]
Router(config-route-map)# match ipv6 address prefix-list prefix-list-name
Router(config-route-map)# set ipv6 next-hop ipv6-address [link-local-address]
```

The last command overrides the next hop advertised to the peer for IPv6 packets that pass a match clause of a route map for policy routing.

The `ipv6-address` argument specifies the IPv6 global address of the next hop. It doesn't need to be an adjacent router.

The `link-local-address` argument specifies the IPv6 link-local address of the next hop. It must be an adjacent router.

Note: The route map sets the IPv6 next-hop addresses (global and link-local) in BGP updates. If the route map is not configured, the next-hop address in the BGP updates defaults to the unspecified IPv6 address (::), which is rejected by the peer.

If you specify only the global IPv6 next-hop address (`ipv6-address` argument) with the `set ipv6 next-hop` command after specifying the neighbor interface (`interface-type` argument) with the `neighbor update-source`, the link-local address of the interface specified with the `interface-type` argument is included as the next-hop in the BGP updates. Therefore, only one route map that sets the global IPv6 next-hop address in BGP updates is required for multiple BGP peers that use link-local addresses.

As with IPv4 several BGP peers for which the same route maps and prefix lists apply can be configured as a peer group. This facilitates the configuration as well as optimizes the router's handling of the corresponding rules.

By default, peer groups that are defined in router configuration mode using the `neighbor peer-group` command exchange only IPv4 unicast address prefixes. To exchange other address prefix types, such as IPv6 prefixes, you must activate peer groups using the `neighbor activate` command in address family configuration mode for the other prefix types, as shown for IPv6 prefixes.

Members of a peer group automatically inherit the address prefix configuration of the peer group.

IPv4 active neighbors cannot exist in the same peer group as active IPv6 neighbors. Create separate peer groups for IPv4 peers and IPv6 peers.

Peer groups in general are defined in global BGP configuration mode. The following command creates a multiprocotol BGP peer group:

```
Router(config)# router bgp autonomous-system-number
Router(config-router)# neighbor peer-group-name peer-group
```

Activating this peer group for IPv6 neighbours and adding neighbours to it must be done in the IPv6 address family configuration context. One can first add neighbors to a peer group and then later activate all neighbours at once by activating the corresponding peer group.

```
Router(config-router)# address family ipv6 [unicast]
Router(config-router-af)# neighbor ipv6-address peer-group peer-group-name
Router(config-router-af)# neighbor {ip-address \\
                                  | peer-group-name | ipv6-address} activate
```

Examples

a) The following example enables IPv6 globally, configures a BGP process and establishes a BGP router ID. Also, the IPv6 multiprotocol BGP peer `2001:0DB8:0:CC00::` is configured and activated.

```
ipv6 unicast-routing
!
router bgp 65000
 no bgp default ipv4-unicast
 bgp router-id 192.168.99.70
 neighbor 2001:0DB8:0:CC00::1 remote-as 64600
address-family ipv6 unicast
 neighbor 2001:0DB8:0:CC00::1 activate
```

b) The following example configures the IPv6 multiprotocol BGP peer `FE80::XXXX:BFF:FE0E:A471` over Fast Ethernet interface 0 and sets the route map named `nh6` to include the IPv6 next-hop global address of Fast Ethernet interface 0 in BGP updates. The IPv6 next-hop link-local address can be set by the `nh6` route map (not shown in the following example) or from the interface specified by the `neighbor update-source` router configuration command (as shown in this example).

```
router bgp 65000
 neighbor FE80::XXXX:BFF:FE0E:A471 remote-as 64600
 neighbor FE80::XXXX:BFF:FE0E:A471 update-source fastethernet 0
address-family ipv6
 neighbor FE80::XXXX:BFF:FE0E:A471 activate
 neighbor FE80::XXXX:BFF:FE0E:A471 route-map nh6 out
route-map nh6 permit 10
 match ipv6 address prefix-list cisco
 set ipv6 next-hop 2001:5y6::1
ipv6 prefix-list cisco permit 2Fy2::/48 le 128
ipv6 prefix-list cisco deny ::/0
```

Note: If you specify only the global IPv6 next-hop address (`ipv6-address` argument) with the `set ipv6 next-hop` command after specifying the neighbor interface (`interface-type` argument) with the `neighbor update-source` command, the link-local address of the interface specified with the `interface-type` argument is included as the next hop in the BGP updates. Therefore, only one route map that sets the global IPv6 next-hop address in BGP updates is required for multiple BGP peers that use link-local addresses.

c) The following example configures the IPv6 multiprotocol BGP peer group named `group1`:

```
router bgp 65000
no bgp default ipv4-unicast
neighbor group1 peer-group
neighbor 2001:0DB8:0:CC00::1 remote-as 64600
address-family ipv6 unicast
 neighbor group1 activate
 neighbor 2001:0DB8:0:CC00::1 peer-group group1
```

d) The following example, configures the route map named `rtp` to permit IPv6 unicast routes from network `2001:0DB8::/24` if they match the prefix list named `cisco`:

```
router bgp 64900
no bgp default ipv4-unicast
neighbor 2001:0DB8:0:CC00::1 remote-as 64700
address-family ipv6 unicast
 neighbor 2001:0DB8:0:CC00::1 activate
 neighbor 2001:0DB8:0:CC00::1 route-map rtp in
ipv6 prefix-list cisco seq 10 permit 2001:0DB8::/24
route-map rtp permit 10
 match ipv6 address prefix-list cisco
```

6.7.1.3 Advertising Routes into IPv6 Multiprotocol BGP

This task explains how to advertise (inject) a prefix into IPv6 multiprotocol BGP.

By default, networks that are defined in router configuration mode using the `network` command are injected into the IPv4 unicast database. To inject a network into another database, such as the IPv6 BGP database, you must define the network using the `network` command in `address family ipv6` configuration.

```
Router(config-router-af)# network ipv6-address/prefix-length
```

The command advertises (injects) the specified prefix into the IPv6 BGP database. (The routes must first be found in the IPv6 unicast routing table.)

Routes are tagged from the specified prefix as "local origin."

Example

The following example injects the IPv6 network `2001:0DB8::/24` into the IPv6 unicast database of the local router. (BGP checks that a route for the network exists in the IPv6 unicast database of the local router before advertising the network.)

```
router bgp 65000
 no bgp default ipv4-unicast
address-family ipv6 unicast
network 2001:0DB8::/24
```

6.7.1.4 Redistributing Prefixes into IPv6 Multiprotocol BGP

This task explains how to redistribute (inject) prefixes from another routing protocol into IPv6 multiprotocol BGP.

To accomplish this task the `redistribute` command is used in the `address-family ipv6` configuration context of the corresponding BGP process.

```
Router(config-router-af)# redistribute protocol [process-id] \\
                  [level-1 | level-1-2 | level-2] [metric metric-value] \\
                  [metric-type {internal | external}] [route-map map-name]
```

The command specifies the routing protocol from which prefixes should be redistributed into IPv6 multiprotocol BGP.

The `protocol` argument can be one of the following keywords: `bgp`, `connected`, `isis`, `rip` or `static`.

Note: The `connected` keyword refers to routes that are established automatically by IPv6 having been enabled on an interface.

Example

The following example redistributes RIP routes into the IPv6 database of the local router:

```
router bgp 64900
no bgp default ipv4-unicast
address-family ipv6 unicast
 redistribute rip
```

6.7.1.5 Advertising IPv4 Routes Between IPv6 BGP Peers

This task explains how to advertise IPv4 routes between IPv6 peers. If an IPv6 network is connecting two separate IPv4 networks, it is possible to use IPv6 to advertise the IPv4 routes. Configure the peering using the IPv6 addresses within the IPv4 address family. Set the next hop with a static route or with an inbound route map because the advertised next hop will usually be unreachable. Advertising IPv6 routes between two IPv4 peers is also possible using the same model.

Example

The following example advertises IPv4 routes between IPv6 peers when the IPv6 network is connecting two separate IPv4 networks. Peering is configured using IPv6 addresses in the IPv4 address family configuration mode. The inbound route map named `rmap` sets the next hop because the advertised next hop is likely to be unreachable.

```
router bgp 65000
!
neighbor 6peers peer-group
neighbor 2000:yyyy::2 remote-as 65002
address-family ipv4
neighbor 6peers activate
neighbor 6peers soft-reconfiguration inbound
neighbor 2000:yyyy::2 peer-group 6peers
neighbor 2000:yyyy::2 route-map rmap in
!
route-map rmap permit 10
set ip next-hop 10.21.8.10
```

6.7.1.6 Verifying IPv6 Multiprotocol BGP Configuration and Operation

Various show and debug commands may be used to verify IPv6 Multiprotocol BGP operation and configuration. The show command can be used as an unprivileged user.

Command syntax:

The following comannd displays entries in the IPv6 BGP routing table:

```
Router> show bgp ipv6 [ipv6-prefix/prefix-length] \\
                                    [longer-prefixes] [labels]
```

To view a summary of all BGP connections, use the following command:

```
Router> show bgp ipv6 summary
```

IPv6 BGP dampened routes may be displayed with this command:

```
Router> show bgp ipv6 dampened-paths
```

For the debug command one needs higher privilege levels.

```
Router# debug bgp ipv6 dampening [access-list-name] \\
                                    [prefix-list prefix-list-name]
```

The command displays debugging messages for IPv6 BGP dampening packets.

If no prefix list is specified, debugging messages for all IPv6 BGP dampening packets are displayed.

```
Router# debug bgp ipv6 updates [ipv6-address] \\
                           [prefix-list prefix-list-name] [in | out]
```

The command can be used to display debugging messages for IPv6 BGP update packets.

If an `ipv6-address` argument is specified, debugging messages for IPv6 BGP updates to the specified neighbor are displayed.

Use the `in` keyword to display debugging messages for inbound updates only.

Use the `out` keyword to display debugging messages for outbound updates only.

Examples

a) In the following example, entries in the IPv6 BGP routing table are displayed using the `show bgp ipv6` user EXEC command:

```
Router> show bgp ipv6
BGP table version is 12612, local router ID is 192.168.99.70
Status codes: s suppressed, d damped, h history, * valid, > best, i -
internal
Origin codes: i - IGP, e - EGP, ? - incomplete
Network Next Hop Metric LocPrf Weight Path
*> 2001:0DB8:E:C::2 0 3748 4697 1752 i
*                  2001:0DB8:0:CC00::1
 0 1849 1273 1752 i
* 2001:618:3::/48 2001:0DB8:E:4::2 1 0 4554 1849 65002 i
*> 2001:0DB8:0:CC00::1
 0 1849 65002 i
*> 2001:620::/35 2001:0DB8:0:F004::1
  0 3320 1275 559 i
* 2001:0DB8:E:9::2 0 1251 1930 559 i
* 2001:0DB8::A  0 3462 10566 1930 559 i
* 2001:0DB8:20:1::11
  0 293 1275 559 i
* 2001:0DB8:E:4::2 1 0 4554 1849 1273 559 i
* 2001:0DB8:E:B::2 0 237 3748 1275 559 i
* 2001:0DB8:E:C::2 0 3748 1275 559 i
```

b) In the following example, the status of all IPv6 BGP connections is displayed using the `show bgp ipv6 summary` user EXEC command:

```
Router> show bgp ipv6 summary
BGP router identifier 192.168.7.225, local AS number 109
BGP table version is 21898, main routing table version 21898
175 network entries and 693 paths using 66927 bytes of memory
555 BGP path attribute entries using 29224 bytes of memory
539 BGP AS-PATH entries using 13620 bytes of memory
0 BGP route-map cache entries using 0 bytes of memory
0 BGP filter-list cache entries using 0 bytes of memory
Dampening enabled. 10 history paths, 31 dampened paths
BGP activity 2672/8496 prefixes, 21621/20928 paths, scan interval 15 secs
Neighbor V AS MsgRcvd MsgSent TblVer InQ OutQ Up/Down State/PfxRcd
2001:7yy:20:1::11     4     293    31525     14358 21898    0 0 14:29:34    77
2001:Cyy:E:0:1::1     4     4768       0         0     0    0 0 never   Active
```

```
FE80::2xx:4BFF:FE1A:E42
4 30 4442 4442 5 0 0 3d01h 3
FE80::2yy:6DFF:FE25:6000
4 20 4443 4444 5 0 0 3d01h 5
```

c) In the following example, IPv6 BGP dampened routes are displayed using the `show bgp ipv6 dampened-paths` user EXEC command:

```
Router> show bgp ipv6 dampened-paths
BGP table version is 12610, local router ID is 192.168.99.70
Status codes: s suppressed, d damped, h history, * valid, > best, i - internal
Origin codes: i - IGP, e - EGP, ? - incomplete
Network From Reuse Path
*d 2001:0DB8::/24 2001:Cyy:E:B::2 00:00:10 237 2839 5609 i
*d 2001:2xx::/35 2001:Cyy:E:B::2 00:23:30 237 2839 5609 2713 i
```

d) In the following example, debugging messages for IPv6 BGP dampening packets are displayed using the `debug bgp ipv6 dampening` privileged EXEC command:

```
Router# debug bgp ipv6 dampening
00:13:28:BGP(1):charge penalty for 2000:y:0:1::/64 path 2 1 with halflife-time 15 reuse/suppress 750/2000
00:13:28:BGP(1):flapped 1 times since 00:00:00. New penalty is 1000
00:13:28:BGP(1):charge penalty for 2000:y:0:1:1::/80 path 2 1 with halflife-time 15 reuse/suppress 750/2000
00:13:28:BGP(1):flapped 1 times since 00:00:00. New penalty is 1000
00:13:28:BGP(1):charge penalty for 2000:y:0:5::/64 path 2 1 with halflife-time 15 reuse/suppress 750/2000
00:13:28:BGP(1):flapped 1 times since 00:00:00. New penalty is 1000
00:16:03:BGP(1):charge penalty for 2000:y:0:1::/64 path 2 1 with halflife-time 15 reuse/suppress 750/2000
00:16:03:BGP(1):flapped 2 times since 00:02:35. New penalty is 1892
00:18:28:BGP(1):suppress 2000:y:0:1:1::/80 path 2 1 for 00:27:30 (penalty 2671)
00:18:28:halflife-time 15, reuse/suppress 750/2000
00:18:28:BGP(1):suppress 2000:y:0:1::/64 path 2 1 for 00:27:20 (penalty 2664)
00:18:28:halflife-time 15, reuse/suppress 750/2000
```

e) In the following example, debugging messages for IPv6 BGP update packets are displayed using the `debug bgp ipv6 updates` privileged EXEC command:

```
Router# debug bgp ipv6 updates
14:04:17:BGP(1):2000:y:0:2::2 computing updates, afi 1, neighbor version 0, table version 1, starting at ::
```

```
14:04:17:BGP(1):2000:y:0:2::2 update run completed, afi 1, ran for 0ms, neighbor version 0, start version 1, throttled to 1

14:04:19:BGP(1):sourced route for 2000:0:0:2::1/64 path #0 changed (weight 32768)

14:04:19:BGP(1):2000:y:0:2::1/64 route sourced locally

14:04:19:BGP(1):2000:y:0:2:1::/80 route sourced locally

14:04:19:BGP(1):2000:y:0:3::2/64 route sourced locally

14:04:19:BGP(1):2000:y:0:4::2/64 route sourced locally

14:04:22:BGP(1):2000:y:0:2::2 computing updates, afi 1, neighbor version 1, table version 6, starting at ::

14:04:22:BGP(1):2000:y:0:2::2 send UPDATE (format) 2000:0:0:2::1/64, next 2000:0:0:2::1, metric 0, path

14:04:22:BGP(1):2000:y:0:2::2 send UPDATE (format) 2000:0:0:2:1::/80, next 2000:0:0:2::1, metric 0, path

14:04:22:BGP(1):2000:y:0:2::2 send UPDATE (prepend, chgflags:0x208) 2000:0:0:3::2/64, next 2000:0:0:2::1, metric 0, path

14:04:22:BGP(1):2000:y:0:2::2 send UPDATE (prepend, chgflags:0x208) 2000:0:0:4::2/64, next 2000:0:0:2::1, metric 0, path
```

6.7.2 Juniper JunOS

To enable MBGP to carry network layer reachability information (NLRI) for IPv6 address family, include the family `inet6` statement:

```
family inet6 {
    (any | labeled-unicast | multicast | unicast) {
        prefix-limit {
            maximum number;
            teardown <percentage> <idle-timeout (forever | minutes)>;
        }
        rib-group group-name;
    }
}
```

6.7.3 Quagga/Zebra

`bgpd` supports Multiprotocol Extension for BGP. So if remote peer supports the protocol, `bgpd` can exchange IPv6 and/or multicast routing information.

Traditional BGP does not have the feature to detect remote peer's capability whether it can handle other than IPv4 unicast routes. This is a big problem using Multiprotocol Extension for BGP to operational network. [RFC2842] proposing a feature called Capability Negotiation. `bgpd` use this Capability Negotiation to detect remote peer's capabilities. If the peer is only configured as IPv4 unicast neighbor, `bgpd` does not send these Capability Negotiation packets.

By default, Quagga will bring up peering with minimal common capability for the both sides. For example, local router has unicast and multicast capabilitie and remote router has unicast capability. In this case, the local router will establish the connection with unicast only capability. When there are no common capabilities, Quagga sends an "Unsupported Capability" error and then resets the connection.

If you want to completely match capabilities with a remote peer please use `strict-capability-match` command.

Command Syntax:

```
Router# (no) neighbor <peer> strict-capability-match {}
```

This command strictly compares remote capabilities and local capabilities. If capabilities are different, an "Unsupported Capability error" is sent and the connection is finished.

You may want to disable sending capability negotiation `OPEN` message optional parameter to the peer when remote peer does not implement capability negotiation. Use `dont-capability-negotiate` command to disable this feature.

Command Syntax:

```
Router# (no) neighbor <peer> dont-capability-negotiate {}
```

Suppress sending capability negotiation as `OPEN` message optional parameter to the peer. This command only affects the peer is configured other than IPv4 unicast configuration.

When remote peer does not have capability negotiation feature, remote peer will not send any capabilities at all. In that case, BGP configures the peer with configured capabilities.

You may prefer locally configured capabilities more than the negotiated capabilities even though remote peer sends capabilities. If the peer is configured by `override-capability`, `bgpd` ignores received capabilities then override negotiated capabilities with configured values.

Comannd Syntax:

```
Router# (no) neighbor <peer> override-capability {}
```

Override the result of capability negotiation with local configuration. Ignore remote peer's capability value.

6.7.3.1 Sample BGP configuration

```
zebra configuration
===================
!
! Actually there is no need to configure zebra
!

bgpd configuration
==================
!
! This means that routes go through zebra and into the kernel.
!
```

```
router zebra
!
! MP-BGP configuration
!
router bgp 7675
 bgp router-id 10.0.0.1
 neighbor 2001:1cfa:0:2:2a0:c9ff:fe9e:f56 remote-as as-number
!
 address-family ipv6
 network 2001:506::/32
 neighbor 2001:1cfa:0:2:2a0:c9ff:fe9e:f56 activate
 neighbor 2001:1cfa:0:2:2a0:c9ff:fe9e:f56 route-map set-nexthop out
 neighbor 2001:1cfa:0:2:2c0:4fff:fe68:a231 remote-as as-number
 neighbor 2001:1cfa:0:2:2c0:4fff:fe68:a231 route-map set-nexthop out
 exit-address-family
!
ipv6 access-list all permit any
!
! Set output nexthop address.
!
route-map set-nexthop permit 10
 match ipv6 address all
 set ipv6 nexthop global 2001:1cfa:0:2:2c0:4fff:fe68:a225
 set ipv6 nexthop local fe80::2c0:4fff:fe68:a225
!
! logfile FILENAME is obsolete.  Please use log file FILENAME

log file bgpd.log
!
```

Chapter 7

Network Management

Network management and monitoring is a critical part of operating any production quality network, whatever the nature of the network. It is one of the essential building blocks of the 6NET network, and must be so for any IPv6 public network, especially in the Internet service provider area. If IPv6 backbone networks are not subject to the same (or even an improved) standard of management and monitoring as existing IPv4 networks, the existing IPv4 user base will be unwilling to migrate to IPv6.

Network Management covers many areas (also called network segments) of the network. Usual classification distinguishes Local area Networks (LAN) from Metropolitan (MAN) and Wide Area Networks (WAN). In this regard sets of very different functions have to be provided to the manager, from straightforward monitoring of link status, to traffic statistics gathering and analysis. These sets could roughly be classified in two categories: those needed for day to day network control operations and those dedicated to network behaviour analysis. The latter allows the manager to optimise the network or parts of it and to schedule the necessary evolutions.

This chapter brings together all the important network monitoring and management work conducted by the network management workpackage of 6NET. This chapter is designed as a "cookbook", summarising the issues required for managing and monitoring an IPv6 network, and suggests appropriate tools that can be used to support the network management and monitoring function. The end result should be that this will be both a useful guide to designers of new IPv6 networks, and as a reference for more experienced network managers.

7.1 Management protocols and MIBs in the standardisation process

As the main management standard used for IPv4 networks is SNMP (Simple Network Management Protocol), [RFC3416], it was an obvious goal to pursue to also make SNMP management available for and via IPv6. This section focuses on SNMP for IPv6, the corresponding MIBs (Management Information Base) and standardisation process and also gives a brief history on the evolution of the SNMP protocol in general.

7.1.1 SNMP for IPv6

Today many network vendors (6WIND, CISCO, HITACHI, JUNIPER etc.) support SNMP over IPv6 and can be monitored in an IPv6-only environment. One could note that equipment not supporting SNMP over IPv6 can be managed over IPv4 as most IPv6 networks are running dual stack.

The number of SNMP applications able to poll remote SNMP agents over IPv6 remains low. Most of the tools today use the netSNMP open source SNMP library. Recently however, some integrated management platforms (HP Openview, Ciscoworks 2000) have also become, or are in the process of becoming, IPv6 capable and serious progress has been made towards the support of SNMP functions, even if the transport remains IPv4 in most cases.

7.1.2 MIBs

There are almost one hundred MIBs to check, to verify if they could be used to manage IPv6 networks. Some will have to be further developed to support IPv6.

7.1.2.1 The Textual Conventions

In 1998, a textual convention was defined for IPv6 addresses only. But this implied the partition of IPv4 and IPv6 management information bases, in other words, it would take double the effort to get all MIBs ready for both versions of IP. Fortunately, another approach is underway based on a "unified MIB convention" where the same MIB can handle both IPv4 and IPv6. To be able to achieve this, the address data structure had to be changed. But it is worth the effort.

This new convention defines an IP address as a structure {inetAddressType, inetAddress}, where:

- inetAddressType is an INTEGER which specifies if the following address is, for example, an IPv4 or IPv6 one, and
- inetAddress is defined as an OCTET STRING(SIZE(0...255)), in order to be able to save the value of an IPv4 or IPv6 address, as the value of a DNS name (cf. RFC 2851 [RFC2851] updated by RFC 3291 [RFC3291]).

7.1.2.2 The Evolution of the MIBs

In 1996, the MIB II was updated in order to manage IPv4 networks. It was defined by the RFC 2011 (IP MIB) [RFC2011], RFC 2012 (TCP MIB) [RFC2012], RFC 2013 (UDP MIB) [RFC2013] and RFC 2096 (IP forwarding MIB) [RFC2096]. Three groups were defined: ip, tcp and udp. Each group contains simple objects and tables (see Figure 7-1).

In 2002, the approach, illustrated in Figure 7-1, unified all the tables: ipAddrTable became ipAddressTable, ipNetToMediaTable became ipNetToMediaTable, and all the simple objects defined in the IPv4 MIB II became the ipIfStatsTable. Similarly, tcpConnTable became tcpConnectionTable, and udpTable became udpListenerTable. It must be noticed that, in addition to this table, issued from the IPv4 management architecture, new tables were defined like the ipv6InterfaceTable. RFC 2851 [RFC2851] (now updated with RFC 3291 [RFC3291] and RFC 4001 [RFC4001]) describes textual conventions to represent both versions of IP in MIBs. The existing MIBs (RFC 2011, 2012, 2013 and 2096) were updated following this new textual convention. Respectively, these are RFC 2011bis [RFC2011bis] (currently in the RFC editors queue), RFC 4022 [RFC4022], RFC 4113 [RFC4113], and RFC 2096bis [RFC2096bis] (also still in the RFC editors queue).

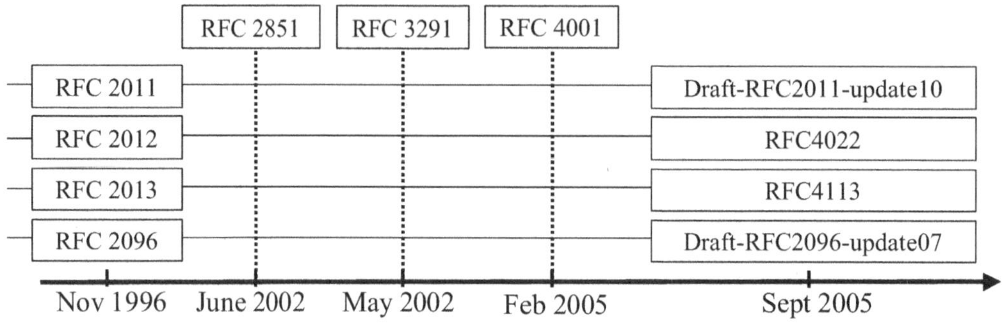

Figure 7-1 The Unified MIB II

(Numbers in parenthesis are oids)

7.1.3 The Other Standards

The SNMP standard was mainly used for the monitoring and fault management. Some other standards were defined to satisfy the need of configuration and AAA (Authentication, Authorization and Accounting) [RFC3539]. Those standards are COPS [RFC2748], WBEM (Web-Based Enterprise Manager) [WBEM] for the configuration point of view, RADIUS [RFC3162] and Kerberos V [RFC1510] for the AAA.

COPS and WBEM are available for IPv6 networks. The protocols themselves and their data models or policies are already defined to be able to manage such networks. But it seems that no implementation of those standards exist.

RADIUS was defined upon IPv6 in 2001 (RFC 3162). But as experience has shown that it cannot be used in large scale network, a new protocol was defined by the IETF called DIAMETER. However, there is IPv6 support in the RADIUS implementations 'Radiator' and 'FreeRadius'.

DIAMETER has been published as RFC 3588 [RFC3588]. An implementation already exists, from SUN Microsystems, based on the 7th version of the draft. A new one is under development within the IST Moby Dick project, defined upon the 10th version of the draft. An open source DIAMETER implementation project has also been started at SourceForge (for more information visit http://sourceforge.net/projects/diameter/), which aims to produce a reference implementation of the DIAMETER protocol.

KERBEROS V was partly implemented upon IPv6 since its 1.2 version, by the Massachusetts Institute of Technology.

7.1.4 Flow Monitoring (IPFIX, Netflow...)

Netflow is a flow-based traffic accounting protocol defined by Cisco Systems. It is widely used to support various applications such as usage-based billing, traffic analysis, or capacity planning. The latest version, Netflow v9, is used as a basis for the IPFIX (IP Flow Information eXport) protocol that is currently being standardized in the IETF (see [Cla05]). Only version 9 of Netflow is designed to export IPv6 flows towards the Netflow collector.

IPv6 support in Netflow v9 is now available in the 12.3T CISCO IOS train. But the transport used for the data export is still over IPv4 only. On the GSR series Netflow v9 is implemented but is not yet able to export IPv6 flows.

Netflow Collectors are also available for IPv6 either from Cisco (NFCv5.0) or from academic organizations (UTC, France).

7.1.5 Management of IPv6 Protocols and Transition Mechanisms

IPv6 is a new protocol and with it many services are being deployed. The network management entity has to be aware of the impact on network management when deploying these new services. For instance, transition mechanisms between IPv4 and IPv6 should be considered in the management infrastructure. Some work has already been done regarding the management of the IPv6/IPv4 coexistence protocols. RFC 4087 [RFC4087] describes a MIB for tunnel management.

Section 9.4 gives some recommendations for secured management of transition mechanisms but targets mostly security aspects of the different transition protocols rather than the management techniques.

Nevertheless, it should be noted that in general, there is little standardization effort made for the management of new services coming along with IPv6, as most of the work is concentrated on having the same level of management for IPv6 as for IPv4.

7.1.6 Remaining Work to be Done

As we can see, for the short-term the main problem is to get similar management standards for IPv6 as those for IPv4.

The implementation of the unified MIBs for TCP, UDP and BGP becomes more urgent. Today many manufacturers implement private MIBs based on RFC 2465 [RFC2465] or the drafts updating RFCs 2011, 2012 and 2013. The transport of SNMP over IPv6 is no longer a problem as most network equipment supports this feature today.

7.2 Network Management Architecture

In this section we describe the basic ideas of network management architecture design. It is aimed at giving help to anyone starting an IPv6 network, to help understand how to setup its management entities and information flows between these entities.

7.2.1 Conceptual Phase

7.2.1.1 Network Segments and Boundaries

Before deploying a new network, it is wise to think how to structure the network in order to facilitate the management. For instance in the 6NET project, three network segments were defined: a core network, access networks and user/site networks. Once the management boundaries are clearly defined, other elements can be added like VLANs, DMZ, intranets etc.

The other goal to achieve during this preliminary step is to clarify the domains responsibilities for every entity involved in the network management. For instance, in the example of 6NET, the core network was under 6NET NOC responsibility, the access networks under the NREN responsibility and the user/site network under the responsibility of the network administrator of the site.

7.2.1.2 Information Flows

After the preliminary planning stages it is useful to consider the information flows between the entities responsible for each domain to get a clear understanding on what information is needed to manage the domain, who is supposed to provide this information and who should receive it. Usually, the operation of the links is in the charge of the entity closer to the core, with every entity being responsible for its interfaces which are connected to links which have terminations in different domains.

From this information, operational procedures can be designed and written down (as an example, the reader can refer to deliverable D6.1.2 [D6.1.2], where this "theoretical exercise" has been applied to the 6NET network management). Looking back after completion of the project it can be stated that the process was useful and efficient. For many months nobody complained about the way the network – mainly the core network – was managed. Additionally, operational procedures for implementing test phases for experiments and tests were identified and implemented. This was not easy since the goal was to accommodate requirements both for production-like traffic and test constraints.

7.2.1.3 Security Aspects

One of the most complex things to decide is the security of management information and procedures. There are several things to take into account in this area:

- The security of the management information itself and the priority of its traffic.

  The management information should stay under the network administrator's control. Part of this information is usually not publicly available; it is reserved for administrators to control the normal network behaviour or to gather statistics data on the traffic flows... When there is congestion or an overload in (part of) the network, then it is efficient to have predefined the class of traffic the management information belongs to. It is a good way to insure the management information remains available to the administrator when the traffic is slowed down for whatever reason.

- The security of the operational procedures.

  Operational procedures are defined so the network management information and the access to the network resources are accessible almost at anytime. For general outage there is no real solution but these situations are becoming rare at least in developed countries. The operational procedures should be designed to take into account unusual events so the administrator knows in advance what he has to do (urgent actions to take, who to warn etc.). These procedures are usually only known by a restricted group of people and are written down.

- The security of the network equipments and their access.

  Access to the network equipments is obviously not granted to anyone. Security measures have to be implemented adequately. Moreover, a backup way (or ways) to access the network equipments in case of outage have to be predefined (for instance the IPv4 connectivity can be used to access dual stacked equipments when IPv6 routing is broken). Usually, for critical resources, phones lines or ISDN allow access to the equipment in case of outage. These accesses are part of the network management; they should be considered during the conceptual phase of building the network and then be checked on a regular basis when the network has been put into operation.

7.2.1.4 Maintenance

Maintenance procedures and their reserved time slots should be defined in advance so a wide set of people knows about them. Regular maintenance is usually scheduled out of working hours, to avoid disturbing the production traffic. Other maintenance procedures are for emergency cases (e.g. outages). They have to be foreseen in the operational procedures.

7.2.1.5 Management Information Accessible to Users

Various experiences have shown that it is very important to provide the users of the network with some management information. It is efficient since the user (including an administrator from another network segment/domain) can quickly understand where a problem comes from and try to get in touch with the appropriate person or entity, instead of asking people that cannot help in solving a problem and wasting time unnecessarily.

For this use, tools to provide management information have to be chosen and a relevant subset of the information should be selected. To this end, in the 6NET project a set of looking glasses, weather maps etc., were implemented. They allowed any user to understand with a simple click how the network performed and in case of problems in what part of the network the problem occurred. Obviously these facilities are not restricted to large networks, but can be applied to any LAN with real benefits. The only thing that changes in this case is the nature of management information the users can obtain.

7.2.1.6 Transition Mechanisms and Services

Most of the above applies with no major differences to either IPv4 or IPv6 networks. What are specific to IPv6 are the so-called transition mechanisms. In fact they are meant to provide internetworking between IPv4 and IPv6 resources. These mechanisms can be seen as services offered to the users. They need the administrator to pay attention to them depending on how they are implemented, managed and the secured. For instance, designing a 6to4 service requires decisions on which users should be allowed to use the service, where the 6to4 gateways are installed, whether there are any 6to4 relays available in the network or if another network's relays are allowed, At the present time, it is not yet completely clear how to manage such services and what information is relevant for the administrator. Since most of these mechanisms are based upon encapsulation techniques, the security issues are those associated with these kinds of well known mechanisms in IPv4. More information is available in 6NET deliverable D6.2.2v2 [D6.2.2] on operational procedures for secured management with transition mechanisms.

7.2.2 Implementation Phase - Management Tools Set

Once all the steps of the conceptual phase have been clearly understood and executed it is time to select the appropriate tools to gather the information needed as defined during the planning. To this respect the reader can refer to D6.2.4 [D6.2.4] where the management and monitoring tools we gained experience with are documented. A subset of those tools used for the management in the different segments of the 6NET network, is described in the following sections

7.3 Management Tools Deployed in 6NET

There are many tools to manage and monitor IPv6 networks. The management needs are not the same in the different parts of the network as discussed in the previous sections. For this reason this part of the chapter classifies the management tools according to the part of the network they best apply to (i.e. LAN or WAN).

In this section the following tools for wide area networks are presented:

- AS-path-tree (http://carmen.ipv6.tilab.com/ipv6/tools/ASpath-tree/)
- 6NET looking glass (http://tools.6net.org , http://w6.loria.fr)
- IPflow (http://www.rrt.cr-picardie.fr/~fillot/nf6/)
- IPv6 support for netflow v9 in IOS (http://www.cisco.com/go/netflow/)
- Mping (http://mping.uninett.no)
- RIPE TT server (http://www.ripe.net/ttm//ttm-ipv6.html)
- Cricket (http://cricket.sourceforge.net/)
- MRTG (http://people.ee.ethz.ch/~oetiker/webtools/mrtg/)

For local area networks the following tools are detailed:

- Argus (http://argus.tcp4me.com)
- Ethereal (http://www.ethereal.com)
- Multicast Beacon (http://dast.nlanr.net/Projects/Beacon/ and http://noc.man.poznan.pl/noc/ strony/aplikacje.html)
- Pchar (http://www.employees.org/~bmah/Software/pchar)
- Iperf (http://dast.nlanr.net)
- Ntop (http://www.ntop.org)

At the end examples are presented of tools that can be deployed in any part of the network:

- IPv6 management gateway (http://www.ipv6.man.poznan.pl)
- Nagios (http://www.nagios.org)
- Rancid (http://www.shrubbery.net/rancid/)

The reader can refer to 6NET deliverable D6.2.4 [D6.2.4] for detailed test results for all the management tools known by the 6NET project partners.

7.3.1 Management Tools for Core Networks (WAN)

7.3.1.1 AS-path-tree

ASpath-tree is a tool to perform IPv6 network operation analysis based on the snapshot of the BGP routing table on IPv6 routers running BGP. Originally ASpath-tree was designed to be used by an IPv6 site involved in the experimentation of the BGP protocol inside the 6Bone network, it now supports a set of features useful within any operational IPv6 network, which makes use of BGP.

The tool currently supports Cisco/Juniper/Zebra routers. Based on a single snapshot of the IPv6 BGP table, ASpath-tree automatically generates a set of html pages providing a graphical view of the routing paths towards the other IPv6 connected domains. Additionally it provides pages for the detection of anomalous route entries announced through BGP (invalid prefixes and unaggregated prefixes), anomalous AS numbers (i.e. reserved or private) in use and a set of summary information such as:

- The number of route entries (valid/total/suppressed/damped/history)
- The number of AS in table (total, originating only, originating/transit, transit only, private and reserved)
- The number of active AS paths
- The number of active BGP neighbours (i.e. announcing routing information)
- An analysis of the network size, in terms of AS distances
- The number of circulating prefixes (total, 6Bone pTLAs, sTLAs, 6to4, others)

Based on repeated snapshots of the IPv6 BGP table at different points in time, ASpath-tree automatically generates html pages reporting on BGP routing stability (last 24 hours) for:

- 6Bone pTLAs
- RIR's assigned prefixes

ASpath-tree is not a tool that monitors BGP peerings in the way that it does not send any kind of notification when peerings go down or up or when the number of routes received from a given peering is critical (too low or too large). Therefore it cannot be used for continuous operational monitoring of the routing in the network.

On the other hand, ASpath-tree is very useful to check that the routing table of the network matches the routing policy. It helps a lot for network routing engineering. It makes it possible for a network administrator to clearly see what is the routing map and if the announcements are coherent. In this period of IPv6 deployment, while more and more sites are moving to IPv6, network administrators have to check their routing policy frequently to be sure it is optimal.

Examples of implementations in 6NET:

6NET backbone: http://6nettools.dante.net/ASpath-tree/bgp.html (version3.3)

CERN: http://www-ipv6.cern.ch/ASpath-tree-v3_3/htdocs/bgp/bgp.html (version 3.3)

NIIF/HUNGARNET: http://6net.iif.hu/6netaspathtree/ (version 4.2)

JOIN/DFN: http://www.join.uni-muenster.de/bgp/bgp.html (version 4.1)

SWITCH: http://www.switch.ch/network/ipv6/bgp/ (version 3.3)

UNINETT: http://drift.uninett.no/ipv6/bgp/bgp.html (version 4.1)

RENATER: http://supervision-ipv6.renater.fr (for both IPv6 unicast and IPv6 multicast BGP trees)

PSCN: http://www.ipv6.man.poznan.pl/ (version 4.1.)

7.3.1.2 6NET looking glass

A looking glass is available for the 6NET core network. In essence a looking glass is a CGI script which allows one connect to a remote router from a simple web page, to run some predefined commands on the router and to show the result on another web page. Its pre-requisite is a simple user login on the router.

Example implementation in 6NET:

http://6nettools.dante.net/diafaneia/

7.3.1.3 IPFlow

IPFlow is a collector for Netflow version v1, v5, v6, v7, v8 and v9. It supports logging flow data to disk, data aggregation according to configuration, port scan detection, storage of aggregated data in RRDtool as well as a graphical display of flow statistics. The author is Christophe Fillot.

7.3.1.4 IPv6 support for Netflow v9 in IOS

The metering/exporting side of Netflow v9 has been implemented in Cisco IOS. Currently, 3640 and 7200/7500 routers are supported.

7.3.1.5 Mping

Mping collects ping statistics for multiple hosts at the same time. Performing an "mping" on all the hosts being listed by a traceroute command would give more statistical information than the traceroute itself. It can do percentiles and SDV statistics, sorted reports, histograms and curves. It does accumulation over days and months.

The Mping service consists of two parts: The Mping client, written in C, and the web interface extension, written in PERL. Unless otherwise specified, when referring to Mping we are referring to the Mping C-client.

Mping is a tool for measuring round-trip delay and packet loss, using the ICMP echo feature, in a TCP/IP based network. Multiple hosts - up to 500, both IPv4 and IPv6 at the same time - can be pinged in a round robin order. At runtime, the user can set the wait time between each packet sent, number of packets sent and the size of the packets. For each host specified, information about packet loss and minimum/average/maximum response time is displayed. Mping can also display the collected data as median, cube-sum, standard deviation or 10/50/90-percentile at the user's request.

Several techniques are implemented into the Mping service, to make sure that the collected data is "statistically" correct:

- Mping by default does not send more than 10 ICMP packets per second, thus measured data is independent from the time of measuring.
- Mping does not send all ICMP packets to one 'Gateway' at the same time, rather Mping tries to spread them out in a Round robin fashion, thus avoiding temporary network characteristics.
- Mping starts the pingsweeps at asynchronous intervals. A Poisson distribution is used, thus avoiding periodic network variance.

Techniques 1 and 2 are Mping C-client features, while 3 is implemented in the PERL web interface extension.

A web interface is used for browsing the collected data and for generating reports, graphs and traceroutes for the different hosts which are measured. The PERL code is modularised and easily extended to suite other needs. As an example, the language support is modularised and thus adding support for new languages is very easy.

Example implementation in 6NET:

UNINETT: http://mping.uninett.no

7.3.1.6 RIPE TT server

RIPE TT servers allow statistics to be gathered between any pair of deployed TT servers. The statistics include packet delay and loss, as well as a historical view of observed traceroutes. The system is available as a "black box" shipped from RIPE-NCC. It requires a roof-mounted GPS to be deployed for time synchronisation. Statistics are gathered at the RIPE NCC site and presented for views there by RIPE-NCC TT server owners (once you own a box, you can view any details). There is a purchase fee and a maintenance fee – these fees are currently under review and likely to be lowered (purchase at the moment is around 3,000 Euros, maintenance is likely to fall to 1,000 Euros p.a.).

IPv6 functionality was added to the existing RIPE NCC TT server after discussion between 6NET and the RIPE NCC, which started in Q1 2002. It was decided that RIPE NCC rather than 6NET would develop the new IPv6 functionality so that expertise could be gathered and maintained in RIPE NCC.

The 6NET project is running live TT server boxes on many project partner sites. These tools are being actively used for monitoring the backbone performance and routing paths.

As of July 2003 there are at least 14 IPv6-enabled RIPE NCC TT servers, of which six are located on 6NET project partner premises. They are:

- tt13: Surfnet, Utrecht
- tt42: NTUA, Greece
- tt73: University of Vienna, Austria
- tt76: University of Southampton, UK
- tt77: DFN, Germany
- tt85: SWITCH, Switzerland
- Other NREN sites include HEAnet (Ireland) and FCCN (Portugal).

All new TT servers shipping now have IPv6 support in them. There is ongoing work in addressing additional IPv6 issues, including IPv6 NTP. The progress of the TT server porting is followed in 6NET, with the tool used by partners for inter-site testing. 6NET will also seek to find international (e.g. US and Japan) sites that may host TT server systems for network performance analysis on international links.

7.3.1.7 Cricket

Cricket is a high performance, extremely flexible system for monitoring trends in time series data. Cricket was expressly developed to help network managers visualize and understand the traffic on their networks, but it can be used for all kinds of other jobs as well.

Network operators require awareness of how well their network performs. Every node in the network keeps statistics on many attributes that affect its performance. The operators would like to constantly monitor these attributes over time and keep track of their intensity. The tool can be used by anyone who wants to monitor and plot value variations of network attributes inside their management domain.

Example implementation in 6NET:

http://6net.iif.hu/cricket/grapher.cgi (HUNGARNET)

7.3.1.8 MRTG

The Multi Router Traffic Grapher (MRTG) is a tool to monitor the traffic load on network links. MRTG generates HTML pages containing graphical images, which provide a LIVE visual representation of the traffic on the links. MRTG is widely used, currently mostly over IPv4. IPv6 support has been tested on Linux only, but should work on other operating systems such as FreeBSD.

Examples of implementations in 6NET:

GARR: http://www.uniroma3.6net.garr.it/mrtg/graphs/gsr.html

RENATER: http://supervision-ipv6.renater.fr

PSNC : http://www.ipv6.man.poznan.pl/

7.3.2 Management Tools for End-sites (LAN)

7.3.2.1 Argus

Argus is a system and network monitoring application, which includes IPv6 support since version 3.2. It will monitor nearly anything it is asked to (TCP and UDP applications, IP connectivity, SNMP OIDS, etc). It comes with a nice and clean, easy to view web interface that will keep both the managers and the technicians happy. Argus contains built-in alert notification via email and pager (qpage) but is easily extendible to use any other program like i.e. winpopup etc. It will automatically escalate alerts until they are acknowledged by resending the alert at different intervals while optionally switching to other methods of notification or other recipients. Due to the fact that most of the testing modules are written in Perl, IPv6 functionality is included in most of them.

For installation one has to fulfil a few prerequisites to use the program with IPv6. Other than a running an operating system that supports IPv6 one also has to have both the Perl module Socket6.pm and fping6 installed. The standard fping is only IPv4 capable but the fping sources at fping.com can be compiled to either work with IPv4 or use IPv6. One binary only works with one protocol at a time. For configuration there is really nothing IPv6 specific to do. If you specify an IPv6 address or hostname that resolves to an IPv6 address, IPv6 will be used for the test.

For further documentation and downloading the program itself please refer to the project's homepage (http://argus.tcp4me.com).

Example implementation in 6NET:

JOIN: https://www.join.uni-muenster.de/cgi-bin/arguscgi?func=login (user:6net password:<any>)

7.3.2.2 Ethereal

Ethereal is a packet analyser with a graphical front end that supports drill-down. Ethereal fully supports the basic IPv6 protocols, and all TCP and UDP-based application protocols running over IPv6. It is widely used to develop and troubleshoot IPv6 applications and protocols. Proposed extension protocols that are used or developed within 6NET could be supported with additional or improved dissectors if required.

Ethereal is a useful network protocol analyser for Unix and Windows. Because it is free, it is IPv6 enabled and it runs on many system platforms; At PSNC it is often used when there is a need to examine the network flows. Ethereal offers a graphical interface and allows setting up different filters. In case of Linux systems, PSNC more often uses a standard tool – tcpdump, which is build in the system and is generally sufficient in its functionality. But in case of windows system, there is no built-in tool for analysing packets, so Ethereal is very useful.

7.3.2.3 Multicast Beacon and DBeacon

Multicast Beacon is the application for monitoring the parameters of multicast traffic. These parameters are: packet loss, delay, jitter, duplicate or order. The application consists of two parts: server and clients. The role of the server is collecting information received from clients and presenting them by means of a standalone GUI tool or HTTP interface. This is very usable for a large number of users interested in the collected results. They can observe the parameters via web browser, like Internet Explorer or Netscape Navigator

The beacon can be useful for multicast traffic monitoring in IPv6 networks. In PSNC a beacon server has been deployed to monitor an IPv6 multicast network called m6bone (http://www.m6bone.net). This network was used for IPv6 multicast tests before enabling multicast transmission in the 6NET core.

Multicast Beacon is now replaced by DBeacon, written in C++. DBeacon has better perforamce and easier to install. Moreover it makes it possible to monitor both ASM and SSM models. Another feature is the possibility to export flow results messages using multicast, making it possible to avoid having a central server.

An example of DBeacon matrix can be found at: http://mars.innerghost.net/matrix/

7.3.2.4 PCHAR

Pchar is a tool to characterize the bandwidth, latency, and loss of links along an end-to-end path through the Internet. It is based on the algorithms of the pathchar utility written by Van Jacobson, formerly of Lawrence Berkeley Laboratories.

Pchar measures the characteristics of the network path between two Internet hosts, on an IPv4 or IPv6 network. The program measures network throughput and round trip time by sending UDP packets of varying size into the network and waiting for ICMP messages in response. It modulates the IPv4 time to live (TTL) field or the IPv6 hop limit field to get measurements at different distances along a path.

Pchar presents the following details for each hop in the trip:

- the number of partial or lost datagrams and percentage of probe packets that were lost during the probes for that hop
- the estimated round trip time from the probing host through the current hop
- estimates of the round trip time and bandwidth for the current hop
- estimate of the average queuing along the path, up to and including the current hop

After the last hop (usually the target host), pchar prints statistics in the entire path, including the path length and path pipe (the latter is an estimate of the delay bandwidth product of the path).

In the other/second mode of operation called "trout" (short for "tiny traceroute") Pchar sends packets of random sizes (one packet per hop diameter) along the path to a destination. This mode is extremely fast but no attempt at estimating link properties is made.

Example implementation in 6NET:

In PSNC, Pchar is running on a host called plum.man.poznan.pl. It can be accessed directly using the following link: http://plum.man.poznan.pl/cgi-bin/pchar.cgi . The user-friendly web interface for the Pchar tool is implemented as a Perl script written in PSNC. Their implementation is IPv4 and IPv6 enabled and publicly available through the links mentioned above. Only basic options for this tool are used to simplify the user interface. During the testing phase and every day use PSNC have noticed that Pchar can return quite accurate results for the nearest neighbours, but for far away hosts it can give incorrect results. Generally, Pchar can estimate the correct bandwidth for the near neighbours before it reaches the bottleneck of this link. Unfortunately, it can then propagate any limitations and approximations caused by the link's bottleneck giving inexact and unreliable results.

7.3.2.5 Iperf

As Pchar described above, Iperf can be used to check the bandwidth available on an end-to-end path of the IPv6 Internet, as well as packet loss and latency. As the throughput that can be measured with Iperf is low compared to the link capacities of core networks, it is more likely that this tool better fits usage in end site networks that want to check the performance they can get on end-to-end paths.

The "-V" option can be used with Iperf to use the IPv6 protocol. This option has to be explicitly mentioned on the client and server side.

Server side:

```
$ iperf -s -V
```

Client side:

```
$ iperf -c <Server IPv6 Address> -V
```

7.3.2.6 ntop

ntop is a network traffic probe that shows the network usage, similar to what the popular top Unix command does for CPU usage of a system. ntop is based on libpcap and it has been written in a portable way in order to virtually run on every Unix platform and on Win32 as well.

ntop now fully supports IPv6, thanks to the effort of INRIA within the WP6 framework of the 6NET project. ntop can collect and make stats available on IPv6 flows and hosts in the network. Moreover, IPv6 flows can be exported with netflow v9 from with the nProbe feature, merged with the ntop tool.

ntop can also act as a netflow v9 collector for IPv6 flows exported from other equipment (eg. a CISCO router or another ntop application)

7.3.3 Tools for all Networks

7.3.3.1 IPv6 management gateway (old name: SNMP Transition tool)

The main purpose of the developed IPv6 Management Gateway is to enable the existing IPv4 network management platforms to monitor, configure and manage the native IPv6 network. The IPv6 Management Gateway translates SNMP and ICMP protocol messages between IPv4 and IPv6 networks.

Example implementation in 6NET:

> The IPv6 Management Gateway was used to support the monitoring of 6NET core routers and "ping hosts". Monitoring was performed using Ipswitch, Inc. "WhatsUp Gold", which supports only IPv4.
>
> The IPv6 Management Gateway translates SNMP, ICMP and TCP protocol messages between WhatsUp Gold (IPv4) and the 6NET network (IPv6). WhatsUp Gold is accessible at http://chives.man.poznan.pl. The IPv6 Management Gateway is implemented on plum.man.poznan.pl.

7.3.3.2 Nagios

Nagios is a host and service monitor designed to inform network operators about network problems. The monitoring daemon runs intermittent checks on hosts and services as specified in the configuration using external "plugins" which return status information to Nagios. When problems are encountered, the daemon can send notifications out to administrative contacts in a variety of different ways (email, instant message, SMS, etc.). Current status information, historical logs, and reports can all be accessed via a web browser.

Example of running implementations available in 6NET :

> NAGIOS software is used at NIIF/HUNGARNET for monitoring networking services. A separate NAGIOS station for monitoring IPv6 network service of HUNGARNET and 6NET has been setup.
>
> NIIF/HUNGARNET: http://6net.iif.hu/nagios/ (same user '6core' from tools.6net.org)

7.3.3.3 RANCID

RANCID, "Really Awesome New Cisco config Differ", is a tool to automatically retrieve configuration files from a router and store it in a CVS environment. With CVS changes over time in these configurations can be tracked. There are various front ends to watch these changes, e.g. "cvsweb" or "viewcvs".

Rancid is a program written in perl, which uses external programs to connect to a router (telnet, ssh, rsh, expect) and to store the retrieved data (CVS). When these external programs are IPv6-ready, it is easy to use rancid in an IPv6 environment.

7.4 Recommendations for Network Administrators

7.4.1 Network Management Architecture

These recommendations are explained in section 7.2 of this chapter.

7.4.2 End-site Networks

The following tools could be deployed for managing end-site networks:

- A single tool for traffic management, service availability (web, DNS, SMTP, IMAP...) and link/equipment status: Argus, Nagios or Ntop
- Optionally, one tool for evaluating end-to-end performance of the IPv6 network: Iperf or Pchar
- Rancid for managing the configuration of the equipment
- One tool for analysing packets on shared links for occasional troubleshooting: Ethereal or tcpdump
- One Multicast Dbeacon for IPv6 multicast management

7.4.3 Core Networks

The following tools could be deployed for managing core networks:

- For traffic management, the following tools could be deployed: MRTG, Cricket or Nagios
- Intermapper or Nagios can be deployed for monitoring and displaying equipment and link status.
- For routing management, two different tools can be deployed, which have completely different goals :
  - ASpath-tree can be deployed to monitor the routing policy and the global status of the routing table.

    - Home-made scripts have to be deployed for monitoring BGP peerings for two reasons. On one hand, very few routers have a MIB describing IPv6 BGP behaviour of the router. On the other hand, there are no clients available to perform the requests.

- For accounting management: IPflow can be used. But it appears that in most cases, network administrators prefer to deploy their own collector.
- Rancid for managing the configuration of the equipment

Chapter 8

Multicast

We will explain differences between IPv4 and IPv6 multicast. We will first look at the basics and go through the different types of addressing and allocations available. Then we will look at how to deploy IPv6 multicast intra-domain, followed by inter-domain.

8.1 Addressing and Scoping

The complete multicast architecture defined today in different RFCs and Internet Drafts is described in this section. It is very important to know all the different address types defined because the allocation mechanisms will depend of the architecture used.

RFC 3513 (IP Version 6 Addressing Architecture) defines the IPv6 multicast address. As shown in Table 8-1, IPv6 multicast addresses are derived from the FF00::/8 prefix. The octet following the initial obligatory "FF" value contains four flags and 4-bit value defining the scope of the multicast group.

Table 8-1 IPv6 Multicast Address Format

8 bits	4 bits	4 bits	------------ 112 bits ------------
FF	Flags	Scope	Group ID

The flags field is a set of 4 flag bits.

Table 8-2 The Flags Field

x	R	P	T

Only bit T is described in RFC 3513 and indicates if the address is permanent (value 0) or temporary (value 1). Bits P and R are described in RFC 3306 [RFC3306] and RFC 3956 [RFC3956]. The high order flag bit is not yet used. The use of the flags makes it possible to distinguish different address type that will be detailed in the following sections.

The meaning of the 4-bit scope value is summarized in Table 8-3.

Table 8-3 Multicast Address Scope

Scope	*Meaning*
0	Reserved
1	interface-local; restricted to single interface, de facto usable just for loopback
2	link-local; reach is limited to single physical (layer 2) network, like Ethernet segment or serial line connecting two nodes
3	Reserved
4	admin-local; the smallest scope which must be configured manually, i.e., it is impossible to derive this scope using some autoconfiguration mechanisms
5	site-local; spans single site, the definition of site is not clear yet
6	Unassigned
7	Unassigned
8	organization-local; spans multiple sites belonging to the same organization
9	Unassigned
A	Unassigned
B	Unassigned
C	Unassigned
D	Unassigned
E	global; the whole internet
F	Reserved

The scope field makes it possible to control the scope of the desired broadcast very easily. This was done in IPv4 with the TTL value. The scope field has a major impact on the allocation process as it has to be specified for every allocation. Using scoped addresses makes it easier to control address allocations than with global addresses.

The Remaining 112 bits of the multicast address hold the identification of the group. If the T-flag is set, the identifier is valid inside its scope only. It means that the same identifier may be used outside the scope or with different scope to address another group. If the address is not transient, the address is independent of the scope. Its meaning stays the same and the scope just limits the spread of the subgroup involved.

For example, the (permanent) group identifier 101 (hexadecimal) has been assigned to all NTP servers. If somebody sends a datagram addressed to this group, scope-differing addresses have the following meaning:

- ff01::101 – all NTP servers on the same interface
- ff02::101 – all NTP servers on the same link
- ff0e::101 – all NTP servers in the whole Internet

The scoping is an innovative principle providing a neat mechanism to restrict the multicast distribution. Datagram lifetime limitation (TTL) is used in IPv4 to solve the same problem. Address scoping is a much more exact tool. Using the appropriate part of the address you define the area of the network which the distribution may not exceed – the datagrams never cross the boundary of their scope. So for example you may be sure that the datagrams addressed ff02:something never leave the physical network to which they have been sent.

Some multicast addresses are reserved, having predefined meaning. Some others are simply prohibited, like the addresses containing all-zero group identifier and a zero T-flag. RFC 3513 defines the meaning of some multicast addresses, de facto replacements of former broadcasts. They allow the sending of packets to all nodes or all routers in a given scope:

- ff01::1 – all nodes on the same interface
- ff02::1 – all nodes on the same link (layer 2 network)
- ff01::2 – all routers on the same interface
- ff02::2 – all routers on the same link
- ff05::2 – all routers in the same site

Another group of multicast addresses with the common prefix ff02:0:0:0:0:1:ff00:0/104 is dedicated to identify the solicited-node during neighbour discovery. Some other RFCs specify various dedicated addresses for particular purposes. The current list of reserved multicast addresses is available at http://www.iana.org/assignments/ipv6-multicast-addresses .

8.1.1 Well Known / Static Addresses

Multicast addresses with bit T of the flag field set to 0 correspond to permanent multicast addresses, assigned by IANA (Internet Assigned Number Authority)

Table 8-4 Permanent IPv6 Multicast Address Structure

FF	xxx0	scope	group ID
8 bits	4 bits	4 bits	112 bits

When IPv6 multicast is widely deployed, we can imagine that some organisms will have some permanent broadcasts. Some TV channels or radio channels could be given the right to be allocated a permanent IPv6 multicast address derived from FF00::/12 multicast prefix.

RFC 2375 [RFC2375] defines the IPv6 multicast addresses already allocated. There are different kinds of "permanent" addresses. Some correspond to "low level" services (such as NTP, DHCP, cisco-rp-announce, SAP). The second kind corresponds to permanent "commercial" services (such as TV channels if they don't use SSM). RFC 3307 [RFC3307] defines the allocation guidelines for the permanent addresses. It is described later in this chapter.

8.1.2 Transient Addresses

Transient addresses are IPv6 multicast addresses with bit T of the flag field set to 1.

8.1.2.1 General Transient Addresses

General transient addresses are addresses with all flags set to 0 but the bit T set to 1. It seems that there is no real recommendation for the use of these addresses at that time. Those addresses can be used for one shot sessions or test sessions.

8.1.2.2 Unicast Prefix-based Address

RFC 3306 [RFC3306] defines a way to derive an IPv6 multicast address from an IPv6 unicast prefix.

Table 8-5 Unicast Prefix-based IPv6 Multicast Address Structure

FF	x011	scope	res	Plen	Prefix	group ID
8 bits	4 bits	4 bits	8 bits	8 bits	64 bits	32 bits

If someone needs an IPv6 multicast address, he/she can derive it from its unicast prefix. There are potentially 232 addresses per /64 prefix (per link). The question remains about the way to choose the last 32 bits of the prefix-based address. Nevertheless, the allocation problem is now on a smaller zone that is known and managed.

8.1.2.3 Embedded RP Addresses

RFC 3956 defines a way to embed the RP (Rendezvous Point) address in the IPv6 multicast address. The following scheme shows the structure of such an address:

Table 8-6 Embedded RP IPv6 Multicast Address Structure

FF	x111	Scope	res	RPad	plen	prefix	group ID
8 bits	4 bits	4 bits	4 bits	4 bits	8 bits	64 bits	32 bits

The allocation problem is reduced with embedded RP addresses because there can be a collision only between addresses derived from the same RP. An entity that is well defined and managed.

8.1.2.4 SSM Addresses

SSM addresses are unicast prefix based address with prefix length field and prefix field set to 0. Therefore, SSM multicast addresses are derived from FF3x::/96 prefix.

Table 8-7 SSM IPv6 Multicast Address Structure

FF	x011	scope	all zeros	group ID
8 bits	4 bits	4 bits	80 bits	32 bits

As for SSM, there is no collision in IPv6 since the SSM range is well defined, and channels (S1,G) and (S2,G) are different (note that in IPv4, the SSM range is not entirely fixed, and a "Multicast Router Discovery SSM Range Option" has been defined, so an SSM address could possibly, by misconfiguration, collide with an ASM address). Therefore allocation of IPv6 SSM addresses is a purely local (host) problem. Obviously, there is a need for a per host mechanism (in the OS), to allocate automatically an SSM address (more or less similar to allocating TCP or UDP port numbers on the caller side). There is one constraint due to the mapping to multicast Ethernet addresses: the allocation should try to have an equal probability to select the last 32 bits. Random selection should be enough, since a collision at the Ethernet multicast address level is not very serious. This allocation procedure could have a similar API to RFC 2771 [RFC2771]. The OS has to remember which SSM addresses have been allocated, and probably for how long. This is because SSM may have to be advertised for a long time, and the application (source) (and the OS) may reboot many times during the life of the SSM channel.

8.1.3 Summary

Table 8-8 Summary of IPv6 Multicast Ranges Already Defined (RFCs or I-D)

Prefix	Usage
FF0X::/16	Permanent IPv6 multicast addresses
FF1X::/16	General transient IPv6 multicast addresses
FF3X::/16	Unicast prefix based multicast addresses (transient)
FF3X::/96	SSM addresses (transient)
FF7X::/16	Embedded RP multicast addresses (transient)

8.2 Multicast on the Local Link

8.2.1 Multicast Listener Discovery (MLD)

Routers need to know which multicast groups the hosts on a link want to receive. When an application on a host joins a group, the host must inform the router that it is interested in that group. Multicast Listener Discovery (MLD) (RFC 2710 [RFC2710]) is the protocol used between hosts and routers on a link for this purpose.

MLD is the equivalent to IGMPv2, defined for IPv4. MLD messages are carried in ICMPv6 packets. There are three different MLD messages, namely query, report and done. These have the ICMPv6 values 130, 131 and 132, respectively. MLD also uses the IPv6 Router Alert header so that routers can easily know that they should check the content of the IP packets. Furthermore, since the protocol is used on the local link, IPv6 link-local addresses are used as source addresses. Consequently, the hop limit is 1.

On a given link, there should be only one MLD querier. If a router sees MLD queries from a router with a numerically lower address, it will not sending queries of its own, unless there is a long period with no more queries. In this way, the router with the numerically lowest address will act as MLD querier. Note that which router is the MLD querier is independent of which router actually forwards multicast packets to or from the link.

The MLD querier periodically sends general queries (ICMPv6 type 130) to the all-nodes multicast group (FF02::1). Hosts will then with some small delays, send replies (ICMPv6 type 131) for each of the groups they are interested in. A reply for a group is sent to the group (the destination address in the IPv6 header will be the group address). Since the Router Alert is present, it is easy for routers to separate them from normal multicast traffic for the group. Also, the hop limit is set to 1, so the packets will never be forwarded. If multiple hosts on a link are interested in the same group, they will receive each other's MLD replies. If a host sees another host reply, it will suppress its own so that the router doesn't receive duplicates.

When an application joins a multicast group it wants to start receiving multicast immediately. Because of this, a host should immediately send a report when it is interested in a new group, rather than wait for the next periodical query.

When a host is no longer interested in a group, it should send a done message (ICMPv6 type 132). This is sent to the all-routers multicast group (FF02::2). Due to the suppression of replies mentioned earlier, the router cannot know whether there are other hosts that are still interested. To check whether there are any other hosts interested, the MLD querier will send a specific query for that address. The specific query is sent to the group address. If no hosts respond with a reply, the router will then assume there is no more interest in the group. Note that the specific query is repeated so that a single lost query will not disrupt the service. Note that if for some reason a host does not send a done message (it might be disconnected or lose power), the router will still learn that there are no listeners, but this will take significantly longer.

8.2.1.1 MLDv2

Version 2 of the MLD protocol, MLDv2 [RFC3810], has additional support for source filtering. Source filtering is the ability for a host to report interest in listening to packets *only* from a set of specific source addresses, as required to support Source-Specific Multicast [RFC3569]. Alternatively, source filtering also provides the ability for a host to listen to all packets *except* those from a set of specific source addresses. MLDv2 is designed to be interoperable with MLDv1.

8.2.2 MLD Snooping

When multicast is supported at IPv6 level, it is often broadcasted at lower levels. For example an Ethernet switch will broadcast multicast traffic on all ports, even if only one host wants to receive it. As it is not acceptable that an entire Ethernet segment gets flooded, the MLD snooping solution was proposed and is already implemented in some Ethernet switches. This solution is similar to IGMP snooping proposed for IPv4.

When the switch implements IGMP snooping, it will detect all MLD messages exchanged on the link and will maintain a table indicating for each of the interfaces, what IPv6 multicast groups should be forwarded. This simple solution easily prevents multicast flooding on an Ethernet link, but this requires complex processing on switches, that were not initially designed for this kind of task.

8.3 Building the Multicast Tree: PIM-SMv2

The only protocol to build multicast trees is PIM-SMv2. It is specified in draft-ietf-pim-sm-v2-new-11.txt [FHHK05], and is at this time of writing almost published as an RFC (this new RFC will obsolete RFC 2362). PIM-SMv2 supports IPv4 and IPv6, and supports both the ASM and SSM model. PIM-SMv2 is usually called PIM-SSM when working in the SSM mode. The mode of PIM-SMv2 (ASM or SSM) is subject to the addresses used inside the backbone. Also, to work in the ASM mode, PIM-SMv2 requires enabling of one or more Rendezvous Points (RPs).

As PIM-SMv2 is defined for IPv4 and IPv6, there are no differences with tree building for IPv4 and IPv6. The reader can refer to other documents to have information about PIM-SMv2. The small changes reside in the definition of the RP. CISCO RP discovery, which is a CISCO protocol to automatically advertise an RP, is not defined for IPv6. On the other hand, Embedded-RP proposes a new group-to-RP mapping solution.

A PIM-SSM router only needs to implement the upstream and downstream (S,G) state machine from the specification. It needs to implement the (S,G) assert and state machine for multiple PIM routers sharing a common LAN. Also Hello messages, neighbour discovery DR discovery and packet forwarding rules must be implemented.

With this subset, the implementation is greatly simplified compared to the (*,G), (S,G,RPT), (*,*,RP) downstream and upstream state machine, the register state machine the (*,G), assert state machine, the bootstrap RP election, the Keep alive Timer and the SptBit from a PIM-SM router. Also, the forwarding rules are more complex in PIM-SM.

By putting source discovery and address allocation outside of the network, SSM multicast routing does exactly what its name indicates: multi-destination routing. Because the multicast network function is greatly simplified, debugging, securing and deploying an SSM multicast network is greatly simplified too.

Network operators may choose to deploy PIM-SSM only or PIM-SM, but if PIM-SM is deployed, PIM-SSM is implicitly deployed too. Note that PIM-SM and PIM-SSM can be used simultaneously since they use different address ranges.

8.4 Inter-domain Multicast

While deploying multicast in a single domain is now well understood, things are not so well defined in the inter-domain case. Moreover different problems and solutions are different for ASM and SSM and whether we consider IPv4 or IPv6. In this section we consider only PIM-SMv2 as the protocol for building multicast trees, since this is the only protocol that is both available and usable in inter-domain. In next section we present the inter-domain solutions for the ASM case and then for the SSM case.

8.4.1 The ASM Case

8.4.1.1 Recall of the IPv4 Model

Here we will describe how inter-domain any-source multicast is done with IPv4. This differs quite a bit from how it is done with IPv6. For source-specific multicast there is no difference.

For both IPv4 and IPv6, PIM-SM is the most common multicast routing protocol. PIM-SM ensures that when a host in a domain joins a group, a shared tree is built from the RP in that domain, and also when a host in the domain is sending, the RP in that domain receives the data and is aware of the source. Doing this, PIM-SM can provide connectivity between sources and listeners when they are using the same RP. So by only using PIM-SM, it is necessary that all sources and receivers use the same RP.

For IPv6 this is basically how inter-domain ASM multicast is done with the Embedded-RP solution. For IPv4 however, there is a protocol called MSDP [RFC3618] that provides for communication between RPs in different domains. Using MSDP each multicast domain can have its own RP for groups of global scope, and a listener in one domain is able to receive from a source in another.

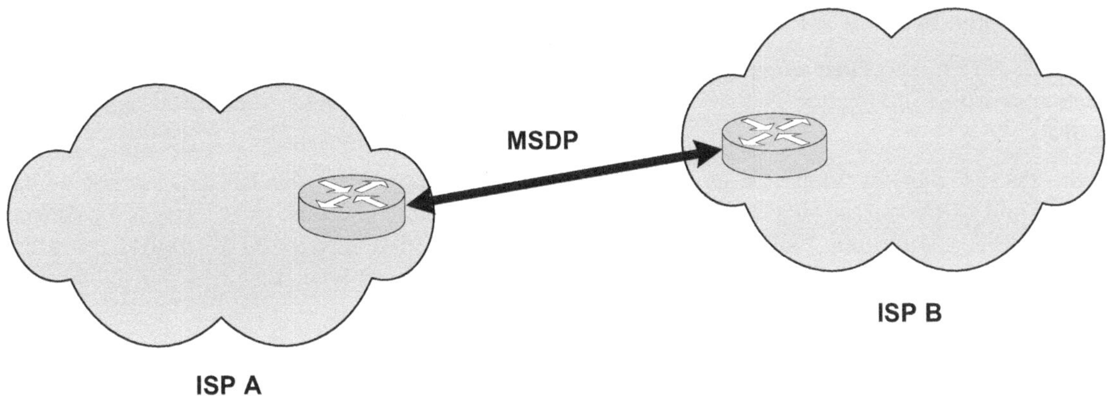

Figure 8-1 The MSDP Model

With MSDP, one sets up peerings between pairs of RPs. When an RP learns of a new source from PIM-SM, it will announce it to its MSDP peers. Also, a router receiving a source announcement from one peer, will forward it to its other peers. In this way the source announcements can be flooded throughout a network of peers. When an RP receives a source announcement for a group with local interest, someone in the RPs domain has joined the group, it will send a source specific join towards the source, building a SPT from the source in the other domain. Data received on the SPT can then be forwarded as usual.

By allowing each domain to have its own RP for all the global groups and using MSDP, one obtains a distributed model where no specific entity is needed to serve a group. This makes it easier to support multicast groups and sessions where no one in particular is responsible for it. One example might be the SAP [RFC2974] used for session announcements. This is a global service on a standardized group address. In contrast, for IPv6 there must for a given global group be a single RP, and the one operating the RP more or less owns the group or session. Note that MSDP is not scalable to a large number of inter-domain groups and sources since for each source there is a periodic flooding of a source announcement in the mesh of participating RPs. This is why MSDP has been considered by the IETF as an interim solution, waiting for another solution such as the now defunct BGMP architecture. MSDP has been deployed on a limited scale but there has been there as been problems with DDoS attacks. This explains why MSDP has not been specified for IPv6.

8.4.1.2 The Embedded RP Solution for IPv6

A simple proposition emerged to embed the RP address in the multicast address. This proposal is called Embedded-RP [RFC3956]. This seems impossible as both the RP address and the multicast address are 128 bits long. But making assumptions on the interface identifier of the RP, this solution is applicable.

An embedded-RP address structure is defined above:

Then an embedded-RP IPv6 multicast address for the RP having the address 2001:660:3307:125::3 will be FF7x:340:2001:660:3007:125:aabb:ccdd (aabb:ccdd being the group-ID chosen in this example); "x" can be any hexadecimal value as embedded-RP can be used for any address scope.

The embedded-RP solution requires that the RPs have unicast addresses with interface identifiers having all bits, except the 4 low order bits, set to zero.

Required modifications to PIM-SMv2

Embedded-RP requires that the group-to-RP mapping algorithm is changed. When a packet comes into the router with a destination address in FF70::/12 prefix, the RP address is retrieved as explained above.

Embedded-RP must be supported on all the routers of the shared tree, the RP and the DR of the sources and receivers. The support on the source tree is not required because the messages exchanged are PIM (S,G) prune/join. Nevertheless, one has to be aware that support on all routers eases the deployment and management of embedded-RP.

Impacts on the network

The IPv6 inter-domain multicast with embedded-RP is very different from what is done today in IPv4. The biggest change is that the PIM domains disappear with embedded-RP: the IPv6 multicast internet is a unique PIM "domain" where multiples rendezvous points are configured.

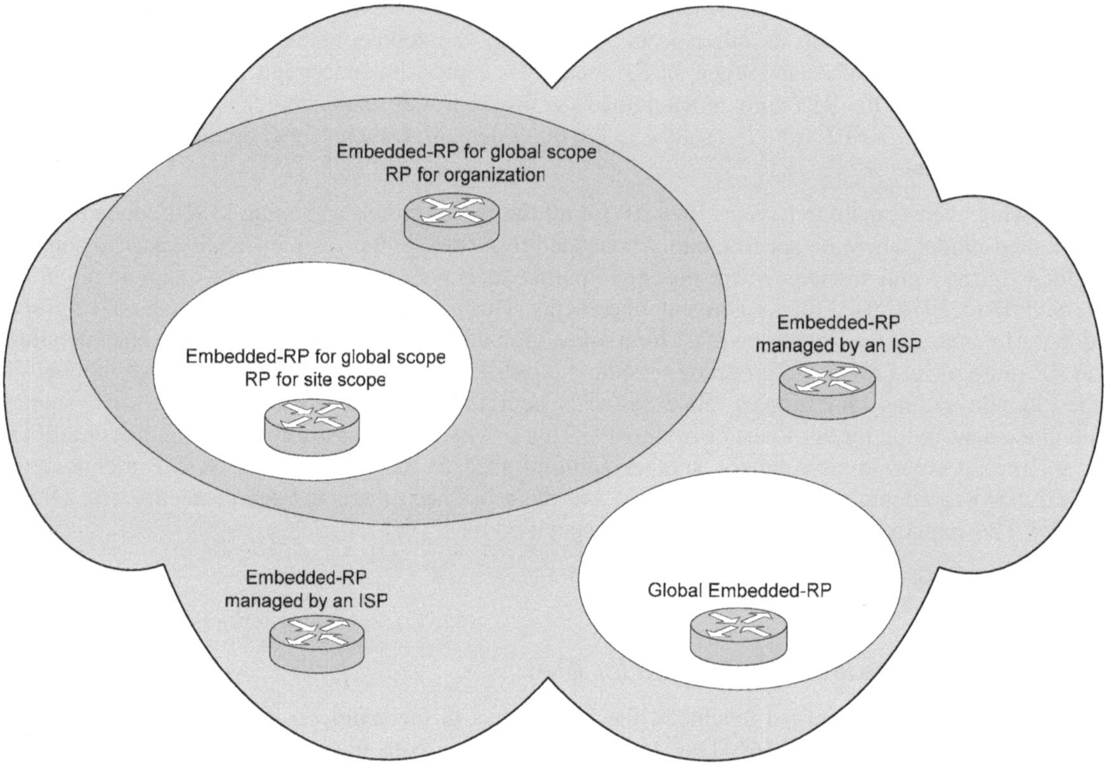

Figure 8-2 Embedded-RP Model

- A side benefit of embedded-RP is that the address allocation problem is much easier than with IPv4. It is difficult to say now if this model will be accepted and deployed. Even if tests showed that the technology worked fine, some questions remain about the impacts caused by differences with the model known and deployed today. Also some general problems of the ASM case remain. For example: the third party dependency, multicast packets from domain A to domain B have to go through the domain of the RP;
- there is no source control: any source on the Internet can send into any inter-domain group;
- multicast data packets are encapsulated towards the RP (at least initially).

8.4.2 The SSM Case

SSM (Source Specific Multicast) defines an IP multicast session with a single multicast source S, known by the set of multicast receivers. At the network level, only S is allowed to send in the channel identified by (S,G). G is generally allocated by a local process running on the host having the IP address S. (S,G) is a channel identifier where groups subscribe specifically with an SSM capable host to router protocol like MLD version 2. We focus here only on the routing part of SSM, i.e. how the source specific multicast tree is built between SSM receivers and the source. We describe an end-host solution which enables multi-source sessions over SSM only networks.

8.4.2.1 What is the inter-domain with SSM?

Strictly speaking, SSM is a subset/simplification of ASM and this is naturally the case for its implementation. The specification of PIM-SSM is now included in the PIM-SM specification, so from now on we will call PIM-SSM the behaviour of PIM-SM with SSM addresses (the FF3x::/32 prefix), and PIM-SM the behaviour with ASM addresses.

The additional components needed for inter-domain ASM are used for the in-band automatic source discovery function and for group address allocation. These functions are not needed with SSM because S from (S,G) is supposed to be previously known by each receivers and because (S,G) is supposed to be globally unique in the Internet as S has been allocated by IANA.

We have seen that with PIM-SM, Embedded-RP is a candidate solution for large scale multicast deployment as it resolves partially the multicast group address allocation and the rendezvous point discovery issues. With this solution, the IPv6 ASM multicast Internet is a unique "PIM" domain where multiple PIM-RPs are configured. SSM does not need any rendezvous point and address allocation scheme, and relies on a subset of PIM-SM to function. The IPv6 SSM multicast Internet is still a unique "PIM" domain, possibly not congruent with the unicast one with the help of MBGP but a lot easier to debug compared to PIM-ASM.

8.4.2.2 The ssmsdpifier - ASM application services over SSM

The main missing feature with SSM is automatic source discovery in multi source applications. If we consider that some domains might deploy SSM only (no ASM), it is necessary to have this feature implemented in end hosts. We have specified and implemented a new application protocol called SSMSDP (Source Specific Multicast Source Discovery Protocol). In this solution, a multi source session is identified by a control channel (C, G). Session receivers listen to this control channel. Sources send announcements to the controller (C). These announcements are then forwarded into the control channel. This allows receivers to learn about new sources and to join the corresponding SSM channel. The controller can be seen as some kind of RP but at the session level, and only for signalling.

The implementation of SSMSDP consists in a low level library aimed at offering at least the same functionality that ASM in the network does. We have developed a tool called "ssmsdpifier" based on this library. This tool allows the users to launch ASM applications (that is applications developed to run with ASM multicast), to be launched over SSM-only networks without patching/recompiling. Several well-known applications have shown to function without problems, including vic, rat and the multicast beacon.

Note that the lack of MLDv2 support in some operating systems (notably MS Windows) is currently limiting IPv6 SSM usage.

8.4.3 Future Work

A general purpose inter-domain IPv6 multicast service can be deployed using two different architectures: either ASM with embedded-RP, or SSM with a source discovery mechanism such as SSMSDP. It is hard to tell if a solution or the other will be widely accepted and deployed.

Embedded-RP is quite new, and it's not clear yet how the service best can be provided. One issue is how to provide failover or possibly load balancing mechanisms. In order to do this, anycast-RP mechanisms may be needed. For IPv6 MSDP is not available, but a possible solution is "Anycast-RP using PIM" described in the Internet draft draft-ietf-pim-anycast-rp-02.txt [FC05].

Another issue is address assignment. Users should not need to know what the RP address is and compute group addresses. Ideally applications or hosts should not care about RP addresses at all. But there should be some way the user or application can be told what group address to use, or at least a range to pick them from. Finally, another open issue is how to control usage of Embedded RPs. A provider or organization configuring a router as an Embedded RP, may wish to use it only for sessions for which at least some participants are customers or related to the organization.

There are also issues regarding SSM. One possible problem if SSM becomes widely used, is that routers in the Internet may end up with a lot of multicast state, since state must be stored for every single (S,G). This is a problem with current IPv4 ASM solutions as well. How to reduce this state might be a topic for new research into multicast protocols. There are some protocols solving this in the intra-domain case that cannot be used effectively inter-domain.

An issue with SSMSDP as specified and implemented today is that there is a single point of failure. There is now work going on to have redundant controllers to achieve both reliability and load sharing.

A common issue for both Embedded-RP and SSMSDP compared to the current IPv4 inter-domain multicast with MSDP, is that some entity must be responsible for providing the Embedded RP or the SSMSDP controller. There might be long lasting sessions that have no natural owner. Maybe someone from one organization starts a session and picks a group address using the organizations Embedded RP, or runs a SSMSDP controller. It might be that that session lasts for a long time with multiple participants, and that the creator wishes to leave. It may then be desired to use another RP or SSMSDP controller for the session. This would however require either a new group G or a new channel (S,G) to be chosen, and for the applications to migrate to that, ideally with no interruptions to the service.

Finally, to debug and manage inter-domain multicast, it is very useful to have support for mtrace. mtrace is sort of multicast traceroute. There are a few implementations for IPv4, while we are only aware of one for IPv6. There are attempts at specifying this in the IETF, but it is not clear whether it will be standardized and how quickly.

8.5 MRIB - Multicast Routing Information Base

When the multicast topology is the same as the unicast one, multicast protocols can rely on the unicast routing table. For example, PIM-SM in that case would rely on the unicast routing table to have information about where to send Joins and Prunes. Also RPF checks would be made according to the unicast routing table.

Unicast and multicast topologies can be different for several reasons (tunnels to bypass non-multicast capable equipment, different peering policies for unicast and multicast, different VLAN's for management purposes etc.) In this case the unicast routing table cannot be used by any of the multicast protocol. Multicast topology information needs to be stored in what is generally called the MRIB (Multicast Routing Information Base). It is another instance of the routing table that is used for multicast operations only.

The following figure illustrates the difference between the RIB and the MRIB. It shows 2 sites interconnected through an ISP that is not IPv6 multicast capable. The 2 sites decided to establish a tunnel to exchange IPv6 multicast traffic.

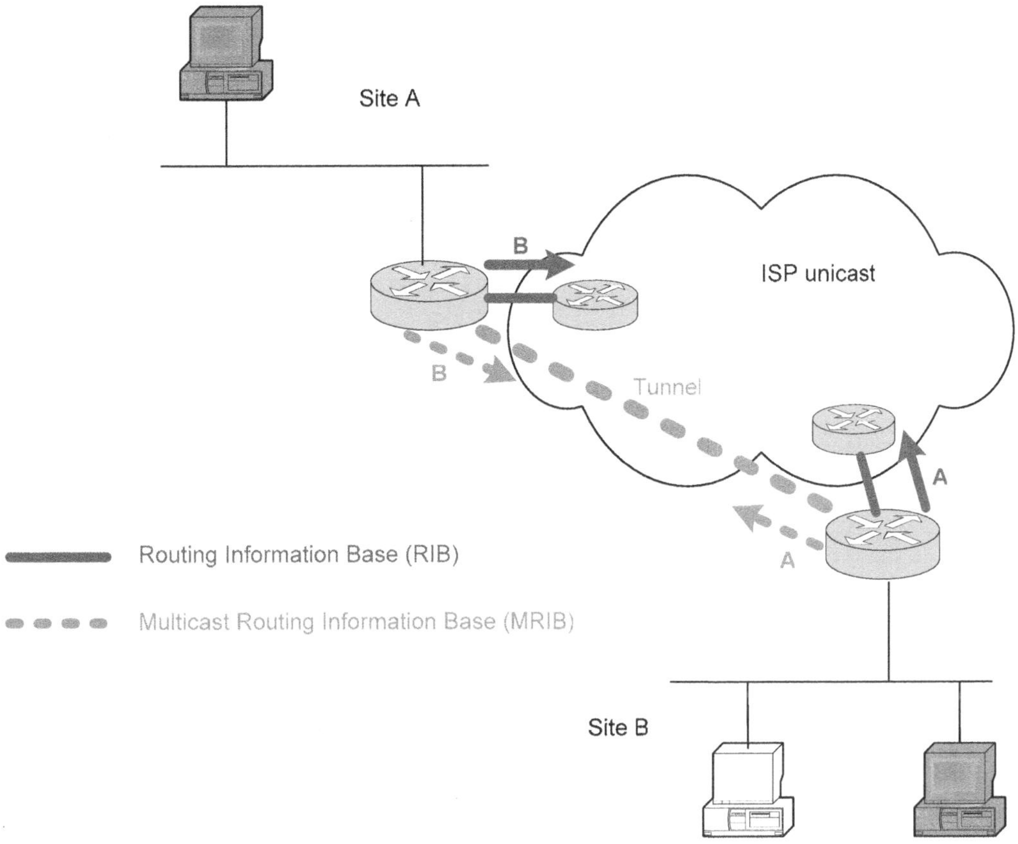

Figure 8-3 MRIB and RIB

Each site router needs to be configured with a RIB and an MRIB as topologies differ for unicast and multicast. On site B exit router, site A must be seen through the ISP for unicast while it must be seen through the tunnel for multicast. Then a route should be configured in the RIB for site A prefix with the ISP as next hop. Another route should be configured in the MRIB for site A prefix with the tunnel interface as destination.

Routes can be inserted statically in the MRIB. A routing protocol is needed to exchange the multicast routes between different domains, and sometimes also inside the same domain. MBGP [RFC2858] is a widely used protocol for this.

8.5.1 Extensions to BGP (MBGP)

BGP is usually used for inter-domain unicast routing and by using MBGP (multiprotocol BGP) one can exchange both unicast and multicast routes with BGP. MBGP adds additional attributes to BGP for specifying whether information is IPv4 or IPv6, and whether it is unicast, for multicast RPF checking or both. MBGP is sometimes, at least in multicast circles, called multicast BGP.

There is no difference between using MBGP for multicast in IPv4 and IPv6. Configuration should be quite similar, and it is used in the same way. Note that MBGP is needed not only when doing ASM, but also for SSM.

Chapter 9

Security

This chapter provides an overview of the current security issues in an IPv6 based networking environment and suggests a number of helpful security "guidelines".

First we will analyse how the IPv6 changed the security of IP networking environment. We will concentrate on the threat analysis compared with IPv4. Then we will discuss the major building block of a security architecture: IPv6 firewalls. Finally we will discuss the security implications of deploying various IPv4-IPv6 co-existnce and transitioning mechanisms.

9.1 What has been Changed in IPv6 Regarding Security?

In this section will enumerate the different threats that you can face when you operate a IP networking environment and we trying to provide some sort of solution in IPv6 in mind.

9.1.1 IPSec

IPSec is a framework of open standards developed by the Internet Engineering Task Force (IETF) that provide security for transmission of sensitive information over unprotected networks such as the Internet. IPSec acts at the network layer, protecting and authenticating IP packets between participating IPSec devices (peers), such as Cisco routers. IPSec provides the following network security services. These services are optional. In general, local security policy will dictate the use of one or more of these services:

- Data confidentiality—The IPSec sender can encrypt packets before sending them across a network.
- Data integrity—The IPSec receiver can authenticate packets sent by the IPSec sender to ensure that the data has not been altered during transmission.
- Data origin authentication—The IPSec receiver can authenticate the source of the IPSec packets sent. This service is dependent upon the data integrity service.
- Anti-replay—The IPSec receiver can detect and reject replayed packets.

With IPSec, data can be sent across a public network without observation, modification or spoofing.

IPSec functionality is essentially identical in both IPv6 and IPv4; however, IPSec in IPv6 can be deployed from end-to-end - data may be encrypted along the entire path between a source node and destination node. (Typically, IPSec in IPv4 is deployed between border routers of separate networks.) In IPv6, IPSec is implemented using the authentication extension header and the ESP extension header. The authentication header provides integrity and authentication of the source. It also provides optional protection against replayed packets. The authentication header protects the integrity of most of the IP header fields and authenticates the source through a signature-based algorithm. The ESP header provides confidentiality, authentication of the source, connectionless integrity of the inner packet, anti-replay and limited traffic flow confidentiality.

9.1.2 IPv6 Network Information Gathering

Usually an attacker begins his/her activity by network, host and service reconnaissance, most often by scanning. This is typically done via some sophisticated scanning methods (e.g. stealth scanning) to provide information to enable other forms of attacks. The IPv6 networking architecture provides some protection against scanning. The large number of potential hosts in a typical IPv6 LAN makes host and service identification ("fingerprinting", port scanning) quite difficult if not impossible. The exhaustive scanning of a /64 subnet is incredibly time consuming: If you have scanner that is capable of scanning 1 million addresses each second (note: the capability of today's scanners are couple of thousands address per seconds), then scanning would take 2^{64} addresses / 1000000 addresses-per-second /60 seconds-per-minute / 60 minutes-per-hour / 24 hours-per-day / 365.25 day-per-year = ~ 584,000 years!

A number of issues however could simplify the scanning process and setting important systems in danger:

Predictable addressing scheme

It is very common practice of system administrators to use specific, predictable, numbering schemes for important systems (e.g. routers, servers, etc.). The administrators should carefully select numbering pattern for their systems to help relieving with this problem.

Reducing the number of address by exploiting the structure of EUI-64 addresses

Usually the last 64 bits of the IPv6 addresses are constructed based on the modified EUI-64 algorithms as described in RFC 3513 from the IEEE 802 48 bit MAC address. In the algorithm there is padding with hexadecimal values 0xFF and 0xFE, that will reduce the problem space. The attackers can even further reduce the problem space if they guess or know in advance the vendor of the IEEE 802 network card, since the IEEE 802 addresses are constructed from a 24 bit vendor or company id and a 24 bit vendor supplied id to ensure uniqueness. (In this later case the attackers could scan the network in 17 seconds if they have a 1000000 addresses-per-second super scanner).

Scanning from inside the LAN

The possibility of information gathering on existing systems from poorly secured routers, gateways, DHCPv6 servers or other network devices. This problem is rather a system security one and the solution does not differ under IPv6: careful and timely security management, ensuring that the system is adequately protected from current threats.

Inappropriate filtering of incoming scanning messages

There is a need for particular ICMPv6 messages to be allowed in the protected network for the IPv6 protocol to operate correctly. As in IPv4, these packets can be used for information gathering therefore the security policy should be appropriately adjusted to cope with the new protocol features, allowing through only the necessary types of messages

Inappropriate filtering of multicast messages

Some IPv6 multicast addresses are used to reach group devices of the same type for convenience, e.g. all routers, all NTP servers etc. An attacker able to access these addresses could acquire access to the corresponding devices and perform attacks against them (e.g.

DoS). Careful border filtering should prevent the particular addresses from being announced or accessed outside the network's administrative borders.

Other forms of finding potential targets

The attacker also can find out potential targets by simply setting up services as honeypot to harvest addresses and after certain amount of time analyse the access logfiles of services to find out potential targets. The hosts can be identifiable this way from the log files, however if proper filtering is set up at the end-site the attacker will not get access to the potential targets.

Finally, a well known practice that is proven to be valuable under IPv4, filtering of unneeded services at the network's access points, can be equally useful under IPv6 for mitigating reconnaissance threats.

9.1.3 Unauthorised Access in IPv6 networks

Determining who has authorized access to a computer system is a policy decision. If this authorisation is enforced in TCP/IP at Layer 3 or Layer 4 then it is usually implemented in firewalls. Policy implementation in IPv6 at Layer 3 and Layer 4 is still implemented in firewalls with some design considerations.

The filtering of packets whose source (or possible destination) address should never appear in Internet routing tables (often called bogons) (e.g. non routable, non assigned etc.) is the minimal filtering that firewalls should provide. In IPv4 it is easier to filter out (deny) packets originating from bogon routes, while in IPv6 it is easier to allow legitimate packets as shown in table Table 9-1.

Table 9-1 Bogon Filtering Firewall Rules in IPv6

Rule	*Meaning*
deny 2001:db8::/32 any	Filter out documentation prefixes
allow 2001::/16 any	Allow RIR allocated prefixes 1
allow 2003::/16 any	Allow RIR allocated prefixes 2
allow 2002::/16 any	Allow 6to4 relay prefix
allow 3ffe::/16 any	Allow 6Bone prefixes - deprecated after 6th June 2006
deny any any	Deny everything else

More detailed discussion about IPv6 firewalls can be found in section 9.2 "IPv6 Firewalls".

Of course there is also the possibility of preventing unauthorised access to the IPv6 network below the network layer. A port-based authentication mechanism such as 802.1x [8021x] is a sound way to organise a secure network infrastructure. An 802.1x based infrastructure can integrate both wired and wireless segments of an organisation's network. For more information on using 802.1x with IPv6 wired and/or wireless networks please refer to [D4.2.2].

9.1.4 Spoofing in IPv6 Networks

Most of the occurrences of various Denial of Service (DoS) attacks which have employed forged or spoofed source addresses have proven to be a troublesome issue for Internet Service Providers and the Internet community overall. RFC 2827 [RFC2827] recommends a simple, effective, and straightforward method for using ingress traffic filtering to prohibit DoS attacks which use forged IP addresses propagated from 'behind' an Internet Service Provider's (ISP) aggregation point. The method, called "ingress filtering" can only prevent spoofing of the source address. An important benefit of implementing ingress filtering is that it enables the originator to be easily traced to its true source, since the attacker would have to use a valid, and legitimately reachable, source address.

The ingress filtering is usually implemented at ISP edge routers with various methods, either via firewall filters or by enforcing the uRPF (unicast reverse path forwarding) check. The behaviour of the ingress filtering is the following:

```
# uRPF processing

IF (packet's source address is from network residing behind the interface
where the packet comes from) {
    forward as appropriate
 } ELSE IF    (packet's source address is anything else) {
    deny packet
}
```

A similar technique can be implemented by the end-user of an ISP to prevent sending packets that do not belong to their network, usually called egress filtering.

These techniques can also be implemented in IPv6. IPv6 can make the ingress filtering easier, since only one prefix should be configured for the ingress filter, due to the hierarchical aggregation of IPv6 addresses. Usually only one /48 has to be configured, if you cannot setup automatically the anti-spoofing or uRPF (unicast Reverse Path Forwarding) check.

The egress filtering configuration is very similar to the ingress filtering configuration, the difference being that it is configured at the user's equipment.

We should note, that ingress and egress filtering might be more complex, albeit not impossible if multihoming and multiple address prefixes are employed at the user site. In this case the multiple address prefixes should be appropriately configured.

9.1.5 Subverting Host Initialisation in IPv6 Networks

In IPv4 environments it is rather easy to perform attacks against the ARP protocol, since hosts cannot prove ownership of their MAC addresses. Therefore it is easy to hijack the default router on the subnet. You can protect your network on a switch by enforcing a specific number of source MAC address for all frames received on a specific port. This protection is available on some switches (notably on modern Cisco Catalysts) as a feature called port security.

If we are using DHCP for initialising hosts, the attacker on the link can perform various attacks against the DHCP server: operating a false DHCP server and delivering DHCP messages faster than the original official DHCP server, exhausting resources of DHCP server by issuing large number of requests, exhausting leased IP address space by requesting too many IP addresses etc. You can protect your system against such an attack by a combination of port security, DHCP snooping, and DHCP message rate limiting. By using port security you can prevent rogue DHCP server operation and faking different MAC addresses on a certain port. The DHCP snooping provides security by filtering untrusted DHCP messages and by building and maintaining a DHCP snooping binding table. This binding table can be used to prevent IP spoofing by only allowing IP addresses that are obtained through DHCP snooping on a particular port.

The host neighbourship in IPv6 environments also can be attacked in a similar way to ARP. Possible attacking techniques could be: sending false Neighbour Advertisement messages, performing Denial of Service against the Duplicate Address Detection procedure, or sending fake Router Advertisements as described in RFC 3756 [RFC3756]. To mitigate attacks against the Neighbour Discovery procedure you can deploy Secure Neighbour Discovery (SEND) [RFC3971]. More detailed discussion about Secure Neighbour Discovery can be found in section 9.3.

9.1.6 Broadcast Amplification in IPv6 Networks

There have been several broadcast amplification attacks against IPv4 network infrastructures. The most famous was the smurf attack where the attacker sent out the packet with following content:

Table 9-2 Structure of the Smurf Attack Packets

Spoofed address of attack target	Subnet broadcast address of amplifier network	ICMP echo

There were two problems that allowed the smurf attack to work:

1. Ingress filtering was not implemented which allowed spoofing the source address field of the attack packet.
2. The host operating systems answered to a message destined to a broadcast address.

Such a problem cannot be foreseen in IPv6 environment for various reasons:

There is no broadcast address in IPv6 environment

This would stop any type of amplification/smurf attacks that send ICMP packets to the broadcast address. However global multicast addresses for special groups of devices, e.g. link-local addresses, site-local addresses, all site-local routers, etc. are available to reach groups of devices.

The IPv6 specification does not allow answering to multicast destinations

IPv6 specifications forbid the generation of ICMPv6 packets in response to messages to global multicast addresses except in two case as described in RFC 1885 [RFC1885]:

1. The Packet Too Big Message - to allow Path MTU discovery to work for IPv6 multicast
2. The Parameter Problem Message, Code 2 - reporting an unrecognized IPv6 option that has the Option Type highest-order two its set to 10.

9.1.7 Attacks Against the IPv6 routing Infrastructure

The primary purpose of IP routing attacks are to disrupt/corrupt router peering or routing information in order to cause denial of service attack or provide help to other type of attacks like DNS cache poisoning etc.

In an IPv6 environment the operators of the network can face similar attacks against the routing infrastructure. However in an IPv6 environment the network designers should be aware of certain idiosyncrasies of IPv6 routing.

In the cases of BGP, IS-IS and EIGRP the security algorithms of the routing protocol remains the same: keyed MD5 digest. So in these cases the same protection for the routing protocol should be used.

By contrast, in the case of OSPFv3 [RFC2740] and RIPng [RFC2080] the routing protocol has been adapted to IPv6 and relies on the IPSec protocol. So if you are using OSPFv3 or RIPng for routing you should also configure IPSec to protect these routing protocols.

The other types of attacks against the routing infrastructure as mentioned are very similar to IPv4 routing infrastructure attacks, therefore similar countermeasures should be implemented: e.g. infrastructure protection, limiting access to the router, SSH authentication etc.

9.1.8 Capturing Data in Transit in IPv6 Environments

Capturing unprotected data in IPv6 networking environment very much like sniffing in IPv4 environment. Ethereal, a tool already widely used by system/network administrators in various platforms and networks is such an example. Other similar tools sporting IPv6 capabilities and not limited to "passive sniffing" of the physical layer, are soon expected to appear, if they do not exist already. The conclusion is that this type of attack presents similar to IPv4 and real threat for services over IPv6.

However, the mandatory support of IPSec in IPv6 environment might help resolving the problem since the infrastructure to protect any kind of communication (e.g. SQL database queries) is built into the systems, and can be protected against sniffing

9.1.9 Application Layer Attacks in IPv6 Environments

These days the most common attacks against computer systems are targeted at the application layer. Often these attacks gain access to system resources by exploiting buffer overflows in the applications or by gaining elevated privileges by executing code with inappropriate checking.

These types of attacks are not bound to any underlying network protocol, so we can not expect any changes if we are deploying IPv6. The operators of the services, must be aware of the problems, and update their systems to prevent such an attacks to happen.

9.1.10 Man-in-the-middle Attacks in IPv6 Environments

Without application of IPSec, any attacks utilizing Man-in-the-middle techniques will have the same likelihood in IPv6 as in IPv4.

If we keep in mind that IPSec is strongly linked to IPv6, its usage alone would be enough to avoid any problems regarding connection hijacking attempts. Unfortunately, the dominant practice we see today in terms of IPv6 deployment already in place is that network operators do not make any use of IPSec. The use of certificates can also provide the needed end-to-end authentication at the application level (e.g. Web servers). Without such end-to-end security mechanisms, a man-in-the-middle hijack is a possibility.

9.1.11 Denial of Service Attacks in IPv6 Environments

Flooding attacks are identical between IPv4 and IPv6, so preventing them in a IPv6 network will be a future challenge. This requires powerful DoS detection tools, which can analyse IPv6 communication flows to find out DoS flows.

If the communication is authenticated by IPSec, the Denial of Service packets are not delivered to the final application, but the communication channels might still be filled, which can deny legitimate users access to services.

9.2 *IPv6 Firewalls*

In the 1990s, firewalls became the building block of each IP network. The recent growth of IPv6 usage has necessitated analysing whether the new protocol can provide enough security without the use of IPSec. This analysis is also important since the application of IPSec on the Internet is relatively scarce and probably will be limited due to deployment difficulties of the public key infrastructure, and in spite the fact that IPSec itself provides a good, modular framework. This section tries to analyse what is available and what is missing for effective IPv6 firewalling.

The Internet firewall is a system that implements and enforces the security policy between two networks: usually protects an internal private network (Intranet) from external Internet threats. Sometime firewalls are also implemented with more than two network interfaces, where the third, fourth interfaces are used for special purposes like DMZs (DeMilitarised Zones), etc.

The firewalls usually can be operated at different levels in the networking hierarchy:

IP level	Packet filtering firewalls
Transport level	Circuit oriented firewalls
Application level	Application level proxies. There is a higher level of support in the application level proxies, e.g. transparent proxies and modularisation

The most important principle of firewalls, however, is function in helping to enforce the security policy (administrative rules) that will protect certain assets. The majority of modern firewalls employ a mix of protective methods at different levels.

In IPv6 the levels are not changed, therefore we can expect that firewalls should support IPv6 at any level. A good firewall implementation should be IP version agnostic at transport or application levels.

We will focus our discussion to packet filtering firewalls for two reasons.

1. These types of firewalls are the basic elements for the more advanced firewalls. They have become necessary components due to the very large number of existing protocols on the Internet (e.g. a wide variety of H.323 related standards, instant messaging protocols, even FTP) that prevents the operation of proxy services for every one of them
2. Currently there are only very few application level firewalling solutions available on the market that offer IPv6 capabilities.

9.2.1 Location of the Firewalls

Traditionally the firewalls are installed next to the interconnecting device (usually routers) in order to choke the unwanted traffic as close to the originating point as possible. Nowadays the firewalls (usually more then one at each network) are installed in front of the device or network, which must be protected. What are the implications of enabling IPv6 on these firewalls [Moh01], [Moh04].

- The firewalls should support Neighbour Discovery ICMPv6 message processing – This issue is rarely discussed with IPv4 firewalls: The IPv4 firewalls must support ARP protocol. The Neighbour Discovery Protocol (RFC 2461) is an extension of ARP for IPv6, therefore IPv6 firewalls must support Neighbor Discovery Protocol filtering "out of the box".
- The IPv6 firewalls should not filter out packets with proper fragmentation header. A common practice in IPv4 firewalls, to guard against the tear-drop attack or other cases of heavily

fragmented packets, is to reassemble the IP fragments at the firewalls themselves and send the complete and sanitised resulting packets to the end systems. Unfortunately this is not possible in IPv6, since fragmentation and reassembly can happen only on the originating and destination node. However, some protection which might be possible in IPv6 is discussed later.

- IPv6 firewalls must support extension headers.

The rest of the requirements are depending on the location of the firewall boxes and routers.

9.2.1.1 Internet-router-firewall-protected network architecture

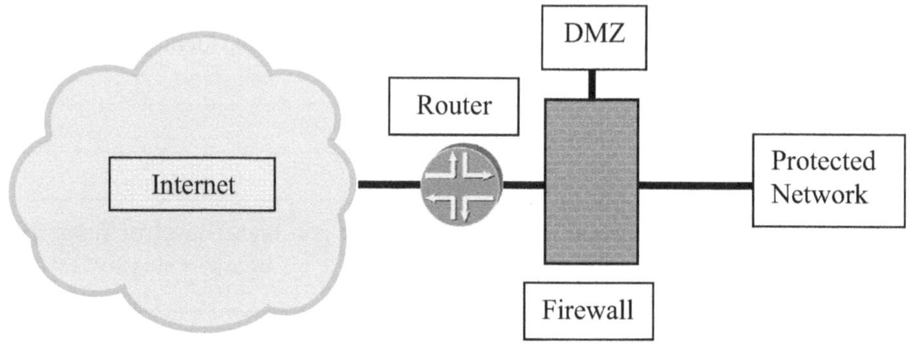

Figure 9-1 Internet-router-firewall-protected Network Setup

Additional requirements:

- In this setup the Firewall must support Stateless Address Autoconfiguration mechanisms (RFC 2462) if the Autoconfiguration option is used on the Protected Network. If the Firewall is operated transparently to the IP layer, then it should allow the Router Solicitation messages coming from hosts and their respective answer coming from the Router. It should also allow periodic Router Advertisement messages to go from the Router to the Protected Network. If the Firewall is operated non-transparently to the IP Layer, then it should be able to answer Router Solicitation messages and periodically announce Router Advertisement messages. These settings are also important if the network is operated with DHCPv6 (or other Statefull Address Assignment methods), since the Stateless RA messages will inform nodes on the network about the configuration method that is to be followed.
- If IPv6 multicast is implemented in the Protected Network, then the Firewall must support the Multicast Listener Discovery Protocol in order to keep track of the interested nodes in the Protected Network for a particular multicast group.

9.2.1.2 Internet-firewall-router-protected network architecture

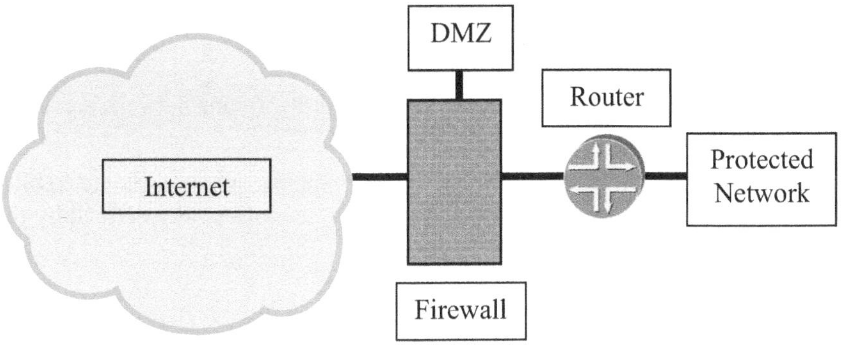

Figure 9-2 Internet-firewall-router-protected Network Setup

Additional requirements:

- The Firewall must support the dynamic routing protocol filtering, that is used by the access router (Router) and Internet Service Provider (e.g. OSPFv3, IS-IS, RIPng, or BGP). This might be challenging if IPSec is used for securing the routing protocols. As a general rule we recommend to use either static routing or BGP for such a setup, since BGP is using MD5 hash and TTL hack for securing routing updates that are IP version agnostic.

This setup might be inconvenient, since the Firewall should support a number of different access technologies, therefore it may need to support a wide variety of interfaces. This problem is expected to be less common in the future since many providers prefer handing over the Internet service over Ethernet media.

9.2.1.3 Internet-firewall/router (edge device)-protected network architecture

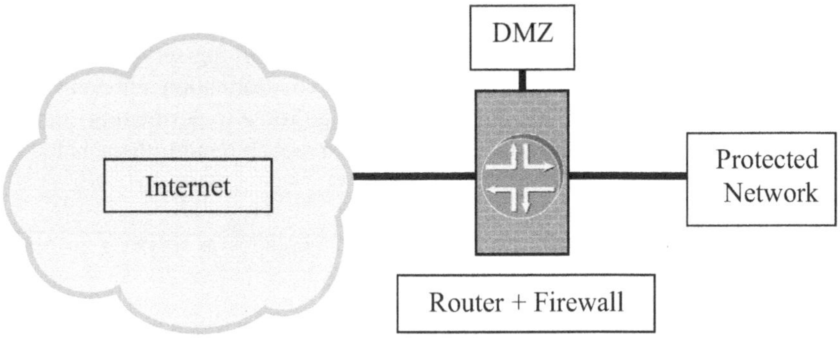

Figure 9-3 Internet-edge-protected Network Setup

Additional requirements:

- Must both support what is necessary for the previous two architecture (Router Solicitation, Router Announcement, and Dynamic routing filtering)

This is a rather powerful architecture, since it allows concentrating both the routing and the security policy in one device; however this concentration makes the particular architecture less susceptible to the security problems:

- More functionality should be integrated into one device. That makes it more complex and opens the possibility of more security problems
- Since it is only one device the principle of security: protect your network/service with more than one asset, cannot be fulfilled.

This setup is very common in home or small office environments, where a single xDSL, or cable router provides connectivity and in the same time enforces the security policy defined by the network administrator.

9.2.2 ICMP Filtering

It is very common (although questionable) practice to filter completely the ICMP messages in IPv4. This is no longer possible with IPv6. As the name that it stands for suggests, Internet Control Message Protocol for IPv6 (RFC 2463) is the control and foundation protocol for the operation of IPv6, not an auxiliary protocol that can be easily omitted. Our recommendation is the following:

ICMPv6 echo request and reply (Types 128 and 129):

- You should consider enabling at least outgoing ICMPv6 echo request and their answers, the ICMPv6 echo reply packets to facilitate debugging. Of course, it is wise to rate limit ICMPv6 debugging packets to a certain level.
- You may consider enable incoming ICMPv6 echo request packets and their answers to your well know IPv6 service machines. You should be sure, however that your IPv6 service machine can handle ICMPv6 requests over a certain rate. Of course, it is wise to rate limit ICMPv6 debugging packets to a certain level.

ICMPv6 destination unreachable (Type 1):

- You should consider enabling incoming ICMPv6 destination unreachable messages as answers, to outgoing IPv6 packets that have been sent for debugging purposes.
- You may generate proper ICMPv6 destination unreachable messages for all filtered packets. This is useful for debugging. It is a common practice in IPv4, to refrain from generating ICMPv6 destination unreachable messages to hide the networking/service structure. You can apply the same rule to IPv6. If you generate ICMPv6 destination unreachable messages, however, do it properly, setting the right reason code: no route to destination, administratively prohibited, beyond scope of source address, address unreachable, port unreachable.

ICMPv6 packet too big (Type 2):

- You must enable incoming ICMPv6 packet too big messages as answers to outgoing IPv6 packets for the Path MTU discovery to operate properly.
- You must generate ICMPv6 packet too big messages properly if your MTU is different anywhere within your network from the MTU on the link between you and your provider. So be prepared, to forward ICMPv6 packet too big messages at the firewall.

ICMPv6 time exceeded (Type 3)

- You must/should enable incoming ICMPv6 time exceeded messages to be able discover destination systems not reachable due to a low TTL value in the outgoing packets.
- You must generate correct ICMPv6 time exceeded messages since they are essential for proper operation of Internet.

ICMPv6 parameter problem (Type 4):

- You should consider enabling incoming ICMPv6 parameter problem messages as answers to outgoing IPv6 packets for debugging purpose.
- You must generate correct ICMPv6 parameter problem messages since they are essential for proper operation of Internet.

ICMPv6 Neighbour Solicitation and Neighbour Advertisement (Type 135 and 136):

- You must enable incoming and outgoing ICMPv6 Neighbour Solicitation, Neighbour Advertisement packets, with proper link-local addresses or multicast addresses for the Neighbour Discovery function to operate properly.

ICMPv6 Router Solicitation and Router Advertisement (Type 133 and 134):

- If the Stateless Address Autoconfiguration function is used, you must enable outgoing ICMPv6 Router Advertisement packets, with proper link-local addresses and multicast addresses (All node multicast addresses should be ff02::1).
- If the Stateless Address Autoconfiguration function is used, you must enable incoming ICMPv6 Router Solicitation packets, with proper link-local addresses and multicast addresses (All router multicast addresses should be ff02::2).

ICMPv6 redirect (Type 137)

- You may disallow ICMPv6 router redirect messages passing, if you have only one exit router. However, router redundancy might be implemented by router redirect. It is important to know that redirect has link-local meaning only.

ICMPv6 MLD listener query, listener report and listener done (Type 130, 131 and 132):

- You should enable incoming and outgoing ICMPv6 MLD messages, with proper link-local addresses or multicast addresses if you want to use IPv6 multicast on a bigger scope than link-local. This is required if the "internet-router-firewall-protected network" architecture is used. In this case your firewall should act as an MLD router.

ICMPv6 renumbering (Type 138)

- You may disallow ICMPv6 router renumbering messages passing, since router renumbering is not widely adopted.

ICMPv6 node information query and reply (Type 139 and 140)

- You may disallow ICMPv6 node information query and reply processing, since node information query/reply is not widely adopted.

We summarise the ICMPv6 recommendations in Table 9-3.

Table 9-3 ICMPv6 Recommendations

ICMPv6	Usage
Echo request/reply	Debugging
Destination unreachable	Debugging – better indicators
TTL Exceeded	Error report
Parameter problem	Error report
NS / NA	Important for IPv6 Neighbour Discovery.
RS / RA	For Stateless Address Autoconfiguration
Packet too big	Important for PATH MTU discovery
MLD messages	Required for Multicast operations

Note: Each IPv6 specific ICMP feature is in **bold**, each required ICMP feature is in *italics*.

9.3 *Securing Autoconfiguration*

The current operational practice in an IPv4 environment is to somehow keep track of which machine is using which IPv4 address at a certain point in time either by statically allocating IPv4 addresses or by using DHCP and keeping lease logs. It is also very common to identify machines in the enterprise network management systems by their MAC addresses. It is thus crucial for the secure and efficient operation of IPv4 networks to log the IP address, MAC address and L2 port combinations. There are also some tools, implemented in L2 switches, to prevent DHCP abuse and ARP poisoning called DHCP snooping and ARP inspection respectively. Let's see what is possible in IPv6, and what countermeasures are possible to prevent abuse. There are different possible ways to assign IPv6 addresses as described in the following sections.

9.3.1 Using Stateless Address Autoconfiguration

In this method the globally aggregatable unicast address is derived from the prefix advertised by the routers and the IEEE EUI-64 identifier (RFC 2462). Since the EUI-64 identifier is generated from the MAC address if it was available, then mapping the IP address to a MAC address is very easy to do. Only MAC addresses and L2 port mapping should be implemented. Enforcing the usage of the EUI-64 identifiers as part of IPv6 addresses could be easily enforced by firewalls. Some firewalls already allow checks MAC address and EUI-64 address consistency of the outgoing packets. This way the accountability of the outgoing communications can be easily provided. However, you should configure carefully your firewall rules if you also use statically assigned addresses.

9.3.2 Using Privacy Extensions for Stateless Address Autoconfiguration

Addresses of this type were developed due to concerns that the same Interface identifier could be used anytime in multiple communication contexts. In this case it becomes possible for that identifier to be used to correlate seemingly unrelated activity. But privacy extended addresses are considered harmful [DS04] for several reasons:

- They complicate debugging, troubleshooting
- They require frequent updates on the reverse DNS entries
- They allow easier in-prefix address spoofing
- In the current form temporary and forged addresses cannot be distinguished
- They do not improve the prefix privacy

Therefore we do not recommend using privacy extended address as defined in RFC 3041. The updated standard addresses [NDK05] solve some of the problems above. There is also a new IPv6 feature called Cryptographically Generated Addresses (CGA) [RFC3972], which generates a random interface identifier based on the public key of the node. The goal of CGA is to prove ownership of an address and to prevent spoofing and stealing of existing IPv6 addresses.

To prevent using RFC 3041 type of addresses you can use the filtering technique described in the previous section.

9.3.3 Using DHCPv6

DHCPv6 is the "statefull address autoconfiguration protocol" and the "statefull autoconfiguration protocol" referred to in "IPv6 Stateless Address Autoconfiguration" (RFC2461).

DHCP can provide a device with addresses assigned by a DHCP server and other configuration information, which are carried in options.

DHCPv6 (RFC 3315) servers use DUIDs (DHCP Unique Identifier) to identify clients for the selection of configuration parameters and in association with IA clients (Identity association - a collection of addresses assigned to a client). DHCP clients use DUIDs to identify a server in messages where a server needs to be identified.

The DUID can be generated from several different sources:

1. DUID Based on Link-layer Address Plus Time (DUID-LLT)
2. DUID Assigned by Vendor Based on Enterprise Number (DUID-EN)
3. DUID Based on Link-layer Address (DUID-LL)

In the case of DUID-LLT and DUID-LL, the association between the IPv6 address and Link-layer address (usually MAC) still exist in the state information of the DHCPv6 server, so accountability is still possible. In the case of DUID-EN it is the responsibility of the administrator to build such a pairing.

If the addresses are assigned from a well identifiable sub-range in /64 the firewalls can ensure that only hosts using DHCPv6 for address configuration can connect outside of the protected network.

Unfortunately, currently there is no similar technique available on the market that will allow only real DHCPv6 servers to assign addresses to the requester hosts.

9.3.4 Static Address Assignment

The static address assignment is very similar to IPv4 static assignment therefore similar pitfalls might possible if it is used.

9.3.5 Prevention techniques

A technique similar to the one that prevents ARP cache poisoning (in IPv6 ND cache poisoning) is possible but it requires DHCPv6 snooping. Firewalls can enforce the DHCPv6 usage and make the DHCPv6 address assignment the default method, thus making DHCPv6 snooping easier to implement. Currently no DHCPv6 snooping support is available for any networking device.

IPv6 can provide an option to prevent ND cache poisoning in the case of stateless autoconfiguration via snooping the Neighbour Solicitation and Neighbour Advertisement messages: Neighbour Solicitation messages contain an informational pair [source_IPv6, source_MAC] that can be stored, while Neighbour Advertisement messages contain two informational pairs: [source_IPv6, source_MAC] and [destination_IPv6, destination_MAC] which can be also stored. Any case of a mismatch can be diagnosed from the previously stored ND entry and the switch can disable the abusing port. A "light version" of the above protocol can be implemented in Firewalls: detect and report ND entry changes i.e. different IP address with same MAC address etc.

9.3.6 Fake router advertisements

Router Advertisements are one of the well-known differences between IPv6 and IPv4. IPv4's common method to supply an address for a (default) gateway is either through DHCP or static configuration. In IPv6, geographic network routers that are connected to the same link may use the Neighbour Discovery protocol for a variety of purposes, such as discover each other's presence, determine each other's link-layer addresses, learn parameter values necessary for communicating and exchange information about prefixes they know about. However, such mechanism has a cost in terms of risk from the security viewpoint. The potential range of attacks that one could make taking the place of a network segment's default gateway is considerable.

Routers consider the information carried in router advertisements sent by other on-link routers as authoritative, even though such information is not cryptographically secured (e.g., digitally signed or key-MACed or encrypted). Therefore, routers update the affected communication parameters accordingly, without any verification. In the absence of any verification of the received information, malicious nodes may inject bogus values for optional fields of the ICMPv6 extension header, such as the advertised prefix, link layer address or MTU. Since legal router advertisements do not necessarily carry values for all of the possible options defined by the actual state of the Neighbour Discovery protocol, there is a good chances that optional values proposed by malicious router advertisements are not be corrected by successive legitimate router advertisements. As an example, if a malicious router advertisement announces an MTU of 17 bytes and legal router advertisements do not specify the MTU option, the MTU value will remain 17 until a later router advertisement, either legal or fake, announces a different value.

A similar case applies to fields such as current hop limit and reachable time, which can be exploited since they allow the sender to leave their value "unspecified". In this case the receiver continues using its current values for those parameters. Thus, if the current value had been set via a fake router advertisement message, followed by a sequence of legitimate router advertisements that did not specify any value for the parameters, the bogus values would be used continuously until an explicit change occurs, if ever. Since parameters such as retransmission time, current hop limit and reachable time are seldom changed once they have been set, an attacker can easily poison the network. IPv6 service could thus degrade (by generation of extra hops) or become inaccessible. Network administrators should be aware of this phenomenon, avoiding configurations where such advertisements are configured by default. The use of DHCPv6 systems may also assist in preventing such rogue configurations. While this problem doesn't represent a major threat, it can reduce end-user confidence about IPv6 services.

When a "fake router" starts to divert traffic, it will probably operate as an "evil proxy", modifying contents of outbound packets, or acting as the end-node on a communication stream. These two types of attacks can be mitigated using the IPSec protocol, whenever possible. Without knowing the keys of a specific end-to-end communication, there is no point in diverting it or intercepting it, except for DoS purposes.

But IPSec may not be an option if one end of the communication is not known in advance, if there are a large number of peers, or they are located in a different management domain. Once again, using DHCPv6, may provide the extra level of control needed to reduce advertisement problems.

A possible counter measure that system/network administrators can deploy could be a mechanism that queries ff02::2 constantly in order to identify any "alien router" on the network segment. This type of solution is not an ideal one because it can only warn about an anomaly, not really being able to prevent or correct it. But correctly diagnosing a problem is half way to solve it.

Another (weak) solution would be to set up the "real router(s)'" advertisements settings in such a way that they force themselves as preferred paths on the end-nodes. However, any serious attempt intended to hack a network segment will certainly have this possibility also embedded in its design.

Of course, all the types of attacks (hijacking, DoS, DDoS, etc.) using fake router advertisements will only be possible after an intruder compromises one node on the same segment their other targets are located.

9.4 IPv4-IPv6 Co-existence Specific Issues

A lot of work has been undertaken inside the 6NET project to investigate and report on the existing IPv6 mechanisms. This section looks closely on the potential risks deploying the mechanisms and reports on the security issues raised by the use of them with the overall aim to create awareness to the people that manage the migration to an IPv6 network.

The next sections reviews general issues arising by the use of tunnels especially automatic tunnels and operational issues of NAT-PT

Generally, any form of tunnelling poses a security threat to a network. If set up properly tunnels can effectively circumvent and undermine any security features present to guard the network like access control lists and firewalls. In a way they drill a hole through them since these security measures only "see" the outer layer of the packets, which might be well within the permitted parameters but have nothing at all to do with the contents/protocol/traffic inside. So if this traffic reaches a tunnel end-point inside the guarded network it is decapsulated and from there can potentially be very harmful since within a network itself, defence levels are usually much lower. Tunnels used for IPv6 deployment are no exception.

During the migration from IPv4 to IPv6 three different kinds of tunnels may be used: IPv6-in-IPv4, IP(v4)-in-IPv6 or other layer tunnels. In terms of general management of tunnels, RFC 4087 [RFC4087] describes managed objects used for managing tunnels of any type over IPv4 and IPv6 networks.

9.4.1 General Management Issues with Tunnels

Often the tunnel MTU is not specifically configured on the end-points when a tunnel is set up. The system then chooses a default MTU. In Cisco's IOS, for example, the default MTU will be derived from the interface MTZ of the interface towards the other end-point (by subtracting the encapsulation overhead). Even if this happens to result in the same MTU at both end-points at the time the tunnel is set up, the MTUs may diverge later (e.g. if one of the end-points starts to support jumbo frames on the egress interface, or routing changes cause the egress interface to move to one with a different MTU).

The resulting situation is a logical IP(v6) subnet where not all interfaces have the same MTU. This violates a fundamental assumption in IP networking and causes connectivity problems.

However, the symptoms are such that this situation is often hard to diagnose. In the direction from the end-point with the smaller MTU towards the receiver with a larger MTU interface, no problems will show but the other way around packets with larger size than the receiver's MTU will usually be ignored and counted as errors at the receiver. Typical tests with ping or traceroute will not show any problems because these tools use small packets. Protocols like BGP may work over the tunnel most of the time but may come to the point where the side with larger MTU must send a large amount of data and uses larger packets than the other side can take.

Unfortunately some devices (seen on Cisco routers under IOS) ignore attempts to configure a 1480-byte MTU on a tunnel towards a 1500-byte MTU interface, because this is already the default. In these cases we recommend to fix the devices so that they still accept the manually configures MTU. This will guard against problems arising when the "default MTU" changes.

MTU incompatibilities are detected by some routing protocols such as OSPFv3, which is very useful for debugging. However, such protocols usually are not used over inter-domain tunnels, where problems are most likely to occur. From this point of view it would seem useful if BGP-4 had an option to advertise link MTU in the single-hop case. Alternatively, MTU validation could be made part of a link liveliness detection protocol such as BFD (bidirectional forwarding detection).

Note that path MTU discovery ([RFC1191, [MHL05]) would make it possible for the end-points to discover the largest MTU that can be supported by the underlying network without fragmentation, but this doesn't solve the inconsistent MTU problem, because there is no guarantee that the path MTUs in both directions end up being the same. Also it isn't always implemented for tunnel interfaces (see IPv6-in-IPv4 tunnels).

9.4.2 IPv6-in-IPv4 tunnels

This category of tunnels covers the most basic and well-known transition mechanisms Manually Configured Tunnels, 6to4 and ISATAP. We will cover any specific operational, management and security issues of these mechanisms below. All of these mechanisms however have quite a few issues in common since they all encapsulate IPv6 packets in IPv4 packets.

9.4.2.1 General security issues with IPv6-in-IPv4 tunnels

Security Issues with IPv6-in-IPv4 tunnels in general lie mainly in the above mentioned problem of these tunnels circumventing and subverting security measures present for IPv4, specifically normal (IPv4-based/IPv6 unaware) firewalls on which IPv4-encapsulated IPv6 traffic only registers as IP protocol type 41 (IPv6). If one wants to use IPv6-in-IPv4 tunnels, this protocol type has to be permitted in the firewall's rules and in some cases also protocol type 58 (ICMPv6). This will effectively open a hole in the carefully configured and maintained security of the site as the traffic is let through without further inspection. This IPv6 traffic can be anything and, if the tunnel end-point also acts as an IPv6 router and forwards IPv6 traffic inside the site's IPv6 network, upon reaching the tunnel end-point inside the site could go anywhere undetected after decapsulation (though the potential damage is in most cases limited to the broadcast domains that the tunnel end-point resides in).

> *An example:*
>
> A site filters all incoming and outgoing (IPv4) http traffic unless it originates from or goes to a specific host (proxy). This protects otherwise unprotected web servers inside the network (i.e. web interfaces for configuration of network components) against attacks from the outside. The other way around this could (if the proxy were properly configured) prevent access to certain websites from inside the site. If the site now uses any IPv6-in-IPv4 tunnel mechanism to get (global) IPv6-connectivity, this tunnel most likely needs to pass the firewall to an end-point on the inside, which then becomes the site's IPv6 border router. Any (IPv6) http traffic may then travel anywhere from and to IPv6 nodes in the network, which again leaves IPv6 enabled (and connected) network nodes with IPv6 enabled web interfaces vulnerable to attacks from the outside, if they are executed via IPv6.

The best way to remedy this problem is to install an IPv6 capable firewall on the tunnel end-point that examines and properly filters the incoming IPv6 traffic after it has been decapsulated from the IPv4 wrapping. This firewall could mirror any rules present for IPv4 at the site's border for IPv6. This is the only way to let only specific IPv6 traffic in and out of the site through the tunnel.

If one only wants to filter specific traffic, one could theoretically employ bitwise filtering and look for specific bit patterns in the payload of the packets. This might make it possible to filter on at least IPv6 source and destination addresses; but this is very tiresome, prone to mistakes and not at all scalable. We do not assume that anyone would try to do this but want to state specifically that we recommended not using this method nor any other kind of packet filtering that will not work on the decapsulated IPv6 packets.

Even when using a proper IPv6 firewall on the decapsulated packets, one must be careful when setting up a tunnel because any host could potentially spoof the other end-point's IPv4 address and send IPv6-in-IPv4 encapsulated packets. The local tunnel end-point will not know that the source of these packets is not the real remote tunnel end-point and decapsulate the IPv6 traffic which can then (if not further inspected/filtered) freely enter the local IPv6 network. The attacker does not even need to know the IPv6 addresses being used on this network as it can send an ICMPv6 packet to all hosts on the tunnel link using its own IPv6 global address and retrieve the IPv6 addresses used in the network. This problem is not easily solved and in its essence is not really specific to IPv6-in-IPv4 tunnelling because it is based on IPv4 address spoofing. The best way to ward against this is doing strict RPF checking at the site's edge but even then, one cannot be completely sure. One more or less relies on other sites filtering packets with IPv4 source addresses that are not from their site at their edge preventing them from being sent out to the Internet. Concerning IPv6 the local tunnel end-point can add some additional security by dropping packets that turn out to be link-local after decapsulation. This is not always possible though, since some services or protocols rely on the use of link-local (unicast or multicast) addresses. These protocols (e.g. PIM, RIPng) can potentially be attacked by anyone. If encryption or authentication facilities are available for these services they should be used. For the other services, no real filtering can be done. We have already seen the example of a broken IPv6 multicast network because an attacker was sending bad PIM announcements, causing a bad PIM topology on the tunnel end-point. Even if a protocol run over the tunnel is not using link-local addresses (like BGP) the implementation of authentication/encryption is advised.

9.4.2.2 General management issues with IPv6-in-IPv4 tunnels

Management of IPv6-in-IPv4 tunnels depends more on the specific mechanism used to set up the tunnel(s). However, concerning monitoring, these tunnels have in common, that after configuration they behave like a point-to-point link and will only appear as one hop concerning pings and traceroutes. Unfortunately this "link-like" behaviour does not extend to features like notifications when a link goes down or up, as one can see them with real physical links. One will only recognize a tunnel going down by the fact that packets can no longer be transmitted but debugging and finding the reason for the failure is much harder, and needs to be performed by hand on the "IPv4 way" the tunnel takes, which of course may vary without anybody noticing. Therefore both for maintenance as well as of course performance reasons IPv6-in-IPv4 tunnels should only be set up over topologically short IPv4 distances

Since IPv6-in-IPv4 tunnels are purely IP they cannot be used for routing protocols like IS-IS. They can however be used for BGP without problems.

The MTU for a tunnel link is less than the path MTU for the tunnel since an IPv4 header must be added to all packets going through the tunnel. In general this might lead to undesired fragmentation effects. For IPv6 the use of path MTU discovery makes this a much smaller problem, but it is not always implemented (for tunnels). Some IPv6 implementations instead just always use the minimal IPv6 MTU without checking before. The minimal MTU is 1280 for IPv6-in-IPv4 encapsulated packets. This will avoid the problem of fragmentation in nearly all cases, since the IPv4 path MTU is often at least 1500 at the cost of adding unnecessary overhead when a larger MTU would be possible.

There might be IPv6 implementations that do not allow the same management operations for tunnel interfaces as for physical interfaces. We have seen at least one implementation that did not allow tcpdump on tunnel interfaces. There are probably other examples.

Purely hardware based routers will need specialised hardware to be able to encapsulate and decapsulate packets so that they can be used as tunnel end-points. Routers that do some operations in hardware and some in software will probably be able to handle this. One should be aware, though, that the software processing power might be limited, and the CPU used for the processing is probably also used for other tasks.

9.4.2.3 Manually configured IPv6-in-IPv4 tunnels

Other than the above mentioned general security and management issues for IPv6-in-IPv4 tunnels there are no specific problems with manually configured tunnels. Out of all transition mechanisms building upon these kinds of tunnels, manually configured tunnels however are considered to be the most stable and operationally secure due to the high level of control the administrator has over them. On the other hand, they do require the most work upon setup and both IPv4 addresses are hardcoded into the configuration which makes it impossible to use these kinds of tunnels between end-points with dynamic IPv4 addresses (i.e. over dial-in lines), at least without some kind of extra automatic setup procedure which we cover in a separate section on Tunnel Brokers.

We have already seen one implementation of tunnels that did not check if the source address of the IPv4 packet was the one configured by the administrator. Any host could potentially send IPv6 packets through the tunnel. It is always recommended to at least check, if the IPv4 source address of an IPv6-in-IPv4 packet is the IPv4 address of the other end-point, even if this doesn't guard against spoofed packets.

9.4.3 6to4

Special issues with 6to4 mainly relate to the way IPv6-in-IPv4 tunnels are set up automatically and the security issues arising when somebody operates a (public) 6to4 relay. For the following section a 6to4 host or router is a host with just a 6to4 pseudo interface. This host might or might not have native IPv6 connectivity. Similarly it might or might not announce its 6to4 prefix to a subnet and thereby act as IPv6 access/default router for this subnet. A 6to4 relay is a dual-stack host with a 6to4 pseudo interface, which forwards packets between the 6to4 domain (2002::/16) and the rest of the IPv6 Internet. A 6to4 relay is also a 6to4 host.

In terms of management and security a network for which a 6to4 host acts as a border router is not affected by the fact that the border router uses 6to4 to provide outside connectivity (either globally or just within the 6to4 domain) aside from the fact that this network's IPv6 connectivity of course depends on the 6to4 connectivity of the 6to4 host.

9.4.3.1 Security issues with 6to4

6to4 hosts or routers accept and decapsulate IPv4 traffic from anywhere. Constraints on the embedded IPv6 packets or where IPv4 traffic is automatically tunnelled to are minimal. Two kinds of attacks are therefore possible:

1. The 6to4 pseudo-interface can be attacked remotely with tunnelled link-local packets. If the interface is not insulated from the host's other interfaces (which is rarely the case in practice) attacks like this could result in a corrupted neighbour cache for the whole system.

   This threat can be averted by adding an access list to the pseudo-interface to filter out bad tunnelled packets:

   - deny from 2002::/16 to 2002::/16
   - allow from 2002::/16 to 2000::/3
   - deny everything else

2. As stated above 6to4 hosts decapsulate and possibly forward any traffic coming in to the pseudo interface. They cannot distinguish between malicious IPv4-encapsulated IPv6 traffic and valid traffic coming from 6to4 relays. This "functionality" can be used both for unidirectional source address spoofing and the reflection of Denial-of-Service attacks against native IPv6 nodes. The latter is not a very big problem since the traffic can not be multiplied and might even be adversely affected by going through bottlenecks like 6to4 relays,

decapsulation and encapsulation. The only problem here is, that an attacker can more easily cover his tracks. The unidirectional source address spoofing of course also exists without 6to4 but becomes harder because the attacker needs to know a valid (existing) IPv6 address. This is a lot easier with 6to4 present because here the attacker can just take any non-6to4 address.

Attacks like these two can also only be remedied by employing sufficient filters. For example all IPv6 nodes inside the site can be guarded from attacks, if the 6to4 pseudo interface does not accept traffic from the IPv6 prefix(es) used inside the site. This also means that the site's own 6to4 prefix should be filtered on input.

Additional security issues with 6to4 relays are due to the fact that 6to4 relays by nature have a native IPv6 connection in addition to IPv4 and relay rather freely between the two. Native IPv6 nodes anywhere can use the relay as a means to obscure their identity when attacking (possibly even IPv4 nodes). Attackers from IPv6 can attack IPv4 hosts with tunnelled packets sending spoofed 6to4 packets via a relay to the IPv4 hosts. The relay can obscure identity, if it relays any packets whilst not checking if the 6to4 address actually matches the IPv4 host the packet comes from. Note that for relays it is assumed that it is at least configured in a way as to not relay between different 6to4 addresses (except of course from or to other known 6to4 relays), thereby facilitating IPv4 to IPv4 attacks.

1. A 6to4 relay can be used for locally directed (IPv4) broadcast attacks. For example if the relay has an interface with address w.x.y.z/24 an attacker could send packets with a 6to4 address that translates into the address w.x.y.255. This is even possible to remote locations if "no ip directed broadcast" is not configured.

   This problem however is easily remedied by another entry in the access list, which prevents packets with destination similar to the above 6to4 address from getting in.

2. The issue mentioned above is actually only a special case of the general problem of 6to4 relays becoming a part of DoS attacks against IPv4 nodes which might be totally unaware of 6to4 but get hit by encapsulated packets nevertheless. If the attack further is executed with a spoofed source address (which is easily possible as stated above) the source of the attacks cannot be traced. A 6to4 relay can also be used for address spoofing and therefore anonymization of attacks coming from native IPv6 hosts

Generally, a 6to4 relay can be reasonably well protected if the validity of source or destination 6to4 addresses is always checked. That is, it should be checked if the enclosed IPv4 address is a valid global unicast IPv4 address. It could even be restricted to only accepting and forwarding 6to4 encapsulated traffic where the 6to4 destination or source address matches the actual IPv4 address the packets come in from or go to. As with the general rule about no forwarding between 6to4 addresses however, exceptions must be made for traffic coming from or going to known other 6to4 relays.

For more information about security considerations with 6to4 please refer to [RFC3964].

9.4.3.2 Management issues with 6to4

However well protected a 6to4 relay may be, the traffic going through should always be monitored, especially if the relay is configured with the well-known IPv4 anycast address for public 6to4 relays.

Other than monitoring no particular management is required for 6to4 since it was specifically designed for ease of use and low maintenance.

9.4.4 ISATAP

ISATAP is another automatic tunnelling mechanism based on the automatic creation of IPv6-in-IPv4 tunnels. As such – from a security point of view – it should not be used, if manually configured IPv6-in-IPv4 tunnels are an option. However, since ISATAP is specifically meant to be used only within a site and if correspondingly protected, it is a reasonably secure and low maintenance mechanism, to provide isolated dual-stack hosts with IPv6 connectivity to the site's main IPv6 network and thereby global IPv6 connectivity.

9.4.4.1 Security issues with ISATAP Clients and Servers

An ISATAP server or router should be protected in such a way as to only permit incoming tunnels from the hosts inside the site. This can be accomplished with simple IPv4 firewall rules. Additionally the site's normal IPv4 border router should permit incoming and outgoing protocol 41 (IPv4 encapsulated IPv6 traffic) only for source and destination addresses belonging to known tunnels. This is not only to protect the ISATAP servers but all ISATAP clients in the site as well, as all clients connected to the same ISATAP server are essentially on the same (IPv6) link and cannot be easily protected from one another.

If the list of ISATAP servers is in any way made automatically available via DNS, DHCP or other means it should be very well maintained.

Since ISATAP clients and servers perform actual neighbour discovery when first starting to communicate with the only difference being that the ISATAP routers do not send unsolicited router advertisements, the same procedures to secure neighbour discovery should be taken as in any native IPv6 network.

9.4.4.2 Management issues with ISATAP

Monitoring traffic between the ISATAP hosts at a site is difficult. All hosts using the same ISATAP router are on the same virtual link, so the packets do not really pass through any other routers (of course the packets might pass through IPv4 routers on the layer below but there they are hardly distinguishable from the normal IPv4 traffic). Monitoring of non-link-local traffic can thus really only be done on the ISATAP router but itself. Note that ISATAP clients within the site can send packets to each other directly using IPv6-in-IPv4 encapsulation and their link-local ISATAP addresses. This traffic does not go through the ISATAP server and can only be monitored at the sending and receiving nodes which is hardly feasible for all hosts of the site.

9.4.5 Teredo

Teredo (also known as IPv4 network address translator (NAT) traversal for IPv6) is designed to make IPv6 available to IPv4 hosts through one or more layers of NAT by tunnelling packets over UDP. It is a host-to-host automatic tunnelling mechanism that provides IPv6 connectivity, when dual-stack hosts are located behind one ore multiple NATs by encapsulating IPv6 packets in IPv4-based User Datagram Protocol (UDP) messages.

9.4.5.1 Security Considerations for Teredo

The threats posed by Teredo can be grouped into four different categories:

1. Opening a hole in the NAT
2. Using the Teredo service for a man-in-the-middle attack

3. DoS of the Teredo Service
4. DoS against non-Teredo nodes

These four types of threats as well as possible mitigating strategies are addressed below.

Opening a Hole in the NAT

Teredo is designed to make a machine reachable via IPv6 through one or more layers of NAT. That means that the machine which uses the service consequently gives up any firewall service that was available in the NAT box. All services opened for local use will become potential targets for attacks from the entire IPv6 Internet. It is recommended to use a personal (IPv6) firewall solution, i.e. a piece of software that performs the kind of inspection and filtering locally that is otherwise performed in a perimeter firewall as well as the usage of IPv6 security services such as IKE, AH, or ESP. Since Windows XP Teredo clients are most common these days, we would like to point out at this point that Windows XP (since SP2 or the advanced networking pack) comes with an acceptable IPv6 firewall.

Man-in-the-Middle Attacks

The goal of the Teredo service is to provide hosts located behind a NAT with a globally reachable IPv6 address. There is a possible class of attacks against this service in which an attacker somehow intercepts the router solicitation, responds with a spoofed router advertisement and provides a Teredo client with an incorrect address. The attacker may have one of two objectives: a) it may try to deny service to the Teredo client by providing it with an address that is in fact unreachable, or b) it may try to insert itself as a relay for all client communications, effectively executing a man-in-the-middle attack. It is not possible to use IPv6 security mechanisms such as AH or ESP to prevent these kinds of attacks since they cover only the encapsulated IPv6 packet but not the encapsulating IPv4 and UDP header. In fact it is very hard to find an effective signature scheme to prevent such an attack since the attacker does not do anything else than what the NAT legally does. The Teredo client should systematically try to encrypt outgoing IPv6 traffic using IPSec. That will at least make spoofing of the IPv6 packets impossible and prevent third parties from listening in to the communication. By providing each client with a global IPv6 address Teredo enables the use of IPSec.

Denial of the Teredo Service by Server Spoofing or an Attack of the Servers

Spoofed router advertisements can be used to insert an attacker in the middle of a Teredo conversation. The spoofed router advertisements can also be used to provide a client with an incorrect address pointing to either a nonexistent IPv4 address or to the IPv4 address of a third party. The Teredo client will detect the attack when it fails to receive traffic through the newly acquired IPv6 address of the so-called Teredo server. Using authentication this attack can be prevented.

Other than confusing clients with false server addresses the Teredo service can of course also be disrupted by mounting a Denial of Service attack against the real Teredo servers and relays sending a huge number of packets in a very short time. Since Teredo servers are generally designed to handle quite a large amount of network traffic this attack most likely will have to be quite brute force, if it should work at all. The attack is mitigated if the Teredo service is built redundantly and the clients are ready to "failover" to another server. That will of course cause the clients to renumber.

If a Teredo relay is attacked in such a way it should stop announcing the reachability of the Teredo service prefix to the IPv6 network. The traffic will be picked up by the next relay.

Denial of Service against non-Teredo Nodes

There is a widely expressed concern that transition mechanisms such as Teredo can be used to mount denial of service attacks by injecting traffic at locations where it is not expected. These attacks fall into three categories: a) using the Teredo server as a reflector in a denial of service attack, b) using the Teredo server to carry a denial of service attack against IPv6 nodes and c) using the Teredo relays to carry a denial of service attack against IPv4 nodes. A common mitigating factor in all of these cases is the "regularity" of the Teredo traffic which contains highly specific patterns such as the Teredo UDP port or the Teredo IPv6 prefix. In cases of attacks these patterns can be used to quickly install filters and remove the offending traffic.

9.4.6 GRE Tunnels

The use of IPv4 GRE (Generic Route Encapsulation) tunnels provides another means to transport IPv6 over an IPv4-only network. In most cases they are used because unlike IPv6-in-IPv4 tunnels where IPv6 is directly encapsulated in IPv4 datagrams GRE can be used for the Intermediate System to Intermediate System (IS-IS) routing protocol.

9.4.6.1 Security issues with GRE tunnels

If GRE tunnels are to go through an IPv4 firewall this firewall has to be opened for IP protocol type 47 for IPv4 datagrams coming from or going to the remote tunnel end-point.

GRE tunnel end-points are authenticated by a simple key that is transmitted during the setup of the tunnel. Since the key is transmitted in clear text format this doesn't really add much security and the key is also not used for encryption of any kind.

9.4.6.2 Management of GRE tunnels

The broader functionality of GRE tunnels comes at the cost of an even shorter MTU, since the GRE header also has to be included in each packet. Other than that, GRE tunnels can be managed like IPv6-in-IPv4 tunnels or point-to-point links respectvely.

9.4.7 OpenVPN Tunnels

OpenVPN is (as the name indicates) a VPN solution. Licensed under the GPL it creates cross platform (layer 2) point-to-point or Ethernet-bridge tunnels over which IPv6 can easily be transported. The software multiplexes IPv6 in IPv4 UDP packets using functionality provided by the OpenSSL library, which may optionally be encrypted. As a VPN solution one has of course to regard one end of the tunnel as the "server" end and one as the client but both ends use the same software. The tunnel end at the site that provides IPv6 connectivity acts as the server. For more information on how OpenVPN works, please refer to the project's homepage at: http://openvpn.sourcefourge.net

9.4.7.1 Security Issues with OpenVPN tunnels

In terms of security OpenVPN has the great advantage of providing authenticated and optionally even encrypted tunnels. It is based on OpenSSL for certification and either uses static pre-shared keys or TLS for dynamic key exchange. The use of X.509 certificates can be regarded as very secure. It can only be compromised, if the secret key is not kept safe.

The certificates are not bound to specific hosts. They can be used anywhere between any two hosts. So an owner of a certificate could put both public and private key on his laptop and with that set up an authenticated tunnel from anywhere where he has IPv4 connectivity. This, of course, is the desired functionality for any Virtual Private Network solution but in comparison to the usual IPv6-in-IPv4 tunnels this has quite a few advantages for the deployment of IPv6 on for example dial-in lines where users not usually have static IPv4 addresses. It provides the user with much more flexibility at the cost of security relying solely on the fact that the user keeps his keys safe and only uses them for himself.

9.4.7.2 Management Issues with OpenVPN tunnels

OpenVPN tunnels are very robust and work even on rather unstable/unreliable IPv4 connections between both end-points. They are known to survive even ISDN or DSL reconnects where the client comes back with a different IPv4 address. In this case just a new TLS handshake is performed to authenticate both sides and the tunnel is back online.

In and of itself the mechanism is not automated but it is an ideal basis for setting up a tunnel broker:

- The use of a CA enables a centralized management of access authorization and trust.
- Failure of the tunnel broker's hardware or the IPv4 link between tunnel broker client and server does not impose administrative work other than fixing hardware or link. The service continues seamlessly after the IPv4 link between client and server is re-established. The FQDN is used to identify a server and hence DNS entries may be changed to redirect tunnel broker clients to a working server in the case of a failure.
- The persistence of the IPv6 link is very good because of mechanisms inherent to the OpenVPN software.
- OpenVPN traverses most NATs without the need of additional configuration. If the NAT does not support this traversal, fowarding of a single UDP port to the OpenVPN client suffices to establish connectivity.

9.4.8 Dual-stack

Dual-stack is the conceptually easiest and for quite some time to come the best way of deploying IPv6. The drawback to this scenario is the fact that it involves the maintenance of two separate IP infrastructures including management and security.

9.4.8.1 Security considerations for dual-stack networks or hosts

The most important paradigm for security in dual-stack networks or on stand-alone dual-stack hosts is that (if this network or host is also provided with global IPv6 connectivity) security for every IPv6 host must mirror exactly the security provisions in place for IPv4. Every firewall rule and every access list that is restricting access to a host needs to be "translated" into corresponding rules and access lists for IPv6. This is not always easy, especially if the network topology is not the same for IPv6 and IPv4. In that case access lists and firewall rule sets cannot be mirrored at all but need to be composed in such a way that they culminate in the exact same level of security for IPv6 for every host as for IPv4.

A special case is, when there's not even global IPv4 connectivity in a network, because that network sits behind a NAT and is addressed with private addresses. For IPv6 on the other hand all hosts could be addressed with globally unique (and reachable/routed) addresses, if connectivity is for example provided through a tunnel. In this case security for IPv6 needs to be designed from scratch although present firewall rules for the NAT itself can provide a basis, if they are translated to corresponding IPv6 rules.

9.4.8.2 Management (and performance) issues with dual-stack networks

An important aspect of dual-stack deployment is performance. Dual-stack hosts are configured to always prefer IPv6 when a hostname resolves into both an A (IPv4 address) and an AAAA (IPv6 address) record. The deployment of dual-stack services (e.g. FTP mirror) with different performance for IPv4 and IPv6 must be avoided because the IP layer does not remain transparent. We have seen the deployment of a dual-stack FTP mirror with a poor IPv6 performance, causing all the people used to upgrade their applications on this mirror having deployed IPv6 FTP clients to get a 80kBps bandwidth instead of 4Mbps for their downloads. This issue can of course only be controlled for services one deploys oneself. For remote services the only thing one can do is to keep the reason for these problems in mind (and to educate unknown users accordingly). It is important that people know that this does not happen because IPv6 is slower in and of itself.

One further management issue in deploying an IPv6/IPv4 dual-stack network lies in configuring both internal and external routing for both protocols. If one has for example used OSPFv2 for intra site routing before, adding IPv6 to the Layer 3 network one will either make the transition to OSPFv3 or IS-IS necessary or one will at least be forced to run one of these IGPs in addition to OSPFv2.

9.4.9 DSTM

DSTM (Dual Stack Transition Mechanism) is a tunnelling solution for IPv6-only networks, where IPv4 applications are still needed on dual-stack hosts within an IPv6-only infrastructure. IPv4 traffic is tunnelled over the IPv6-only domain until it reaches an IPv6/IPv4 gateway, which is in charge of packet encapsulation/decapsulation and forwarding between the IPv6-only and IPv4-only domains. The solution proposed by DSTM is transparent to any type of IPv4 application and allows the use of layer 3 security.

9.4.9.1 Security Considerations with DSTM

The DSTM mechanism can use all of the defined security specifications for each functional part of its operation. E.g. for DNS, the DNS Security Extensions/Update can be used.

Concerning address allocation, when connections are initiated by the DSTM nodes, the risk of Denial of Service attacks (DoS) based on address pool exhaustion is limited in the intranet scenario. With the intranet scenario, if DHCPv6 is deployed, the DHCPv6 Authentication Message can be used for security. When using TSP for address allocation, the SSL encryption and authentication can be used since TSP messages are in plain text.

When exchanging the DSTM options using DHCPv6, the DSTM Global IPv4 Address option may be used by an intruding DHCP server to assign an invalid IPv4-mapped address to a DHCPv6 client in a denial of service attack. The DSTM Tunnel Endpoint option may be used by an intruding DHCP server to configure a DHCPv6 client with an endpoint that would cause the client to route packets through an intruder system. To avoid these security hazards, a DHCPv6 client must use authentication to confirm that it is exchanging the DSTM options with an authorized DHCPv6 server. The DSTM Ports option may be used by an intruding DHCP server to assign an invalid port range to a DHCP client in a denial of service attack. To avoid this security hazard, a DHCP client must use authenticated DHCP to confirm that it is exchanging the DSTM options with an authorized DHCP server.

The main difference between the intranet scenario and the VPN scenario of DSTM is security. In the VPN scenario, DHCPv6 must not be used for address allocation but TSP (tunnel set up protocol) with SSL encryption can be used for this purpose.

In the VPN scenario, the DSTM server must authenticate the outside DSTM client. This authentication cannot rely on the IPv6 address since the address depends on the visiting network but can be based on some shared secret.

In the VPN scenario, the mapping between the IPv4 and the IPv6 address of the DSTM node in the TEP is also a security concern. If the mapping is established dynamically (no configuration by the DSTM server), it could be possible for every intruder knowing a valid temporary IPv4 address to use the TEP as an IPv4 relay or to access internal IPv4 resources. So, in the VPN scenario, the mapping in the TEP must be managed by the DSTM server which authenticates the DSTM host and its IPv6 address. This is an important requirement that avoids the use of IPv4 resources by non authorized nodes.

Finally, for IPv4 communications on DSTM nodes, once the node has an IPv4 address, IPSec can be used since DSTM does not break secure end-to-end communications at any point. The tunnel between the DSTM host and the TEP can be ciphered, but it is our view that this is more of an IPv6 feature (like the use of IPv6 mobility) than a DSTM feature

9.4.10 NAT-PT/NAPT-PT

As noted in RFC 2766 [RFC2766], NAT-PT and end-to-end security do not work together. When an IPv6-only node (X) initiates communication to IPv4-only node Y, the packets from X have certain IPv6 source and destination addresses which are both used in IPSec (AH or ESP) and TCP/UDP/ICMP checksum computations. Since NAT-PT translates the IPv6 address of X into an IPv4 address that has no relationship to X's IPv6 address, there is no way for recipient Y to determine X's IPv6 address and in that way verify the checksums.

9.4.10.1 Prefix Assignment

RFC2766 does not explain how the IPv6 nodes learn about the prefix that is used to route packets to the NAT-PT box. If the prefix is pre-configured in IPv6 nodes, the IPv6 node would prepend the preconfigured prefix to the address of any IPv4-only node with which it wants to initiate communications. However, with a prefix, there might be a reachability problem if the NAT-PT box were to shut down unexpectedly. If an attacker would somehow be able to give the IPv6 node a fake prefix, the attacker would be able to steal all of the node's outbound packets to IPv4 nodes.

Even though this is not specified in RFC 2766, DNS servers and DNS-ALGs should be used for outgoing connections to return the prefix information to the IPv6 node as a means to avoid the problem of a statically preconfigured prefix. When an IPv6-only node wishes to initiate communications with an IPv4-only node, its resolver would send an AAAA query. This query can be passed through the DNS-ALG which itself looks for an A record. In this case the DNS-ALG can prepend the appropriate prefix for NAT-PT itself and thus return a full AAAA record to the IPv6-only node.

9.4.10.2 Security Issues Arising when Using a DNS-ALG

A DNS-ALG is required when IPv4-only nodes should be allowed to initiate communication within a NAT-PT scenario. Since the DNS-ALG will translate simple "A record" requests into "AAAA record" requests and vice versa DNSSEC will not work in this case. However, as pointed out in draft-durand-v6ops-natpt-dns-alg-issues [Dur03], if the host sets the "AD is secure" bit in the DNS header, it is possible for the local DNS server to verify signatures. Also another option to increase security is for the DNS-ALG to verify the received records, translate them and sign the translated records anew. A third option would be if the host had an IPSec security association with the DNS-ALG to protect DNS records.

In case the DNS-ALG also monitors the state of a number of NAT-PT boxes and use only the prefixes of those that are running. The method by which a DNS-ALG determines the state and validity of a NAT-PT box must of course also be secure. The DNS-ALG and each NAT-PT box should be configured with a pairwise unique key that will be used for integrity-protected communications. Note that messages from a DNS-ALG are not integrity-protected and can therefore be modified. To prevent such a modification, a DNS-ALG can sign its packets. The DNS-ALG's public key can be made available like that of any other DNS server (see RFC 2535 [RFC2535]) or presented form of a certificate that has a well known root CA. A shared key technique may not be as practical.

9.4.10.3 Source address spoofing attack

There are two cases in which an attacker will use NAT-PT resources, one where the attacker is in the same stub domain as the NAT-PT box and the second where the attacker is outside the NAT-PT stub domain.

Suppose that an attacker is in the same stub domain as the NAT-PT box and sends a packet destined for an IPv4-only node to the other side of the NAT-PT-gateway, forging its source address to be an address that topologically would be located inside the stub domain. If the attacker sends many such packets, each with a different source address, then the pool of IPv4 addresses may quickly get used up, resulting in a DoS attack (or rather Address depletion attack). A possible solution to this attack as well as to similar attacks like resource exhaustion or a multicast attack is to perform ingress filtering on the NAT-PT box (which is the border router). This would prevent an attacking node in its stub domain from forging its source address and thus from performing a reflection attack on other nodes in the same stub domain. The NAT-PT box should also drop packets whose IPv6 source address is a multicast address. Address Depletion attacks can be prevented by employing NAT-PT in a way that it translates the TCP/UDP ports of IPv6 nodes into the corresponding TCP/UDP ports of the IPv4 nodes/addresses. However, sessions initiated by IPv4 nodes are restricted to one service per server. Of course IPSec might be used to further increase security.

Suppose now that an attacker outside the NAT-PT domain sends a packet destined to an IPv6-only node inside the NAT-PT domain and forges its (IPv4) source address to be an address from the IPv4 address pool used for NAT-PT. The same attacks are then possible as in the scenario above. Again filtering can be used to prevent this. The NAT-PT gateway should drop all packets whose IPv4 source address is a broadcast/multicast address. It should also filter out packets from outside that claim to have a source address from inside the NAT-PT domain.

9.4.11 Bump in the API (BIA)

Security issues with BIA mostly correspond to those of NAT-PT. The only difference is that with BIA address translation occurs in the API and not the network layer. The advantage here is that, since the mechanism uses the API translator at the socket API level, hosts can utilise the security of the underlying network layer (e.g. IPSec) when they communicate via BIA with IPv6 hosts using IPv4 applications.

Another security issue NAT-PT and BIA have in common stems from the use of address pooling, which may open a denial of service attack vulnerability. One should employ the same sort of protection techniques as mentioned fore NAT-PT in this regard.

Note that since there is no DNS ALG necessary with BIA as it is with NAT-PT, there is no interference with DNSSEC when using this transition mechanism.

Chapter 10

Mobility

The Mobile IPv6 (MIPv6) protocol [RFC3775] is a proposed standard by the IETF to provide transparent host mobility within IPv6. The protocol enables a Mobile Node to move from one network to another without the need to change its IPv6 address. A Mobile Node is always addressable by its home address, which is the IPv6 address that is assigned to the node within its home network. When a Mobile Node is away from its home network, packets can still be routed to it using the node's home address. In this way, the movement of a node between networks is completely invisible to transport and other higher layer protocols.

Mobile Nodes participating in the MIPv6 protocol each have a persistent home address, which can be used to address the Mobile Node irrespective of its current point of attachment to the IPv6 network. The IPv6 network which matches the home address' prefix is known as the home network. Mobile Nodes also adopt a Home Agent - an IPv6 capable router directly connected to the home network. This process may either be static, or dynamic, via the MIPv6 Home Agent discovery mechanism. The Home Agent is responsible for the interception and forwarding of IPv6 packets to the Mobile Node which are incorrectly routed to the home network while the Mobile Node is away from home.

When a Mobile Node is attached to its home network it operates as any other network node, so no special routing is required. When a Mobile Node moves to a foreign network, it uses IPv6 autoconfiguration to discover the new network and to allocate a care-of address within the address space of that network. However, to ensure that IPv6 packets destined for the Mobile Node's home address reach the proper location as efficiently as possible, the routing information pertaining to the Mobile Node's home address must be updated in both the Home Agent and any relevant Correspondent Nodes. MIPv6 provides this functionality by the introduction of a bindings cache on the Mobile and Correspondent Nodes and binding update messages which are transmitted in a new IPv6 extension header called the mobility header.

Although MIPv6 implementations have been around since 1998 most have fallen out of date as the MIPv6 protocol has progressed over the years. However, there are a handful of available implementations that are fairly up to date with either MIPv6 draft version 24 or RFC 3775 (which is based on draft version 24). Yet these implementations can still differ slightly in their supported features and are not likely to be completely 100% interoperable in most cases.

10.1 Bindings Cache

The relationship between a Mobile Node's home address and its current care-of address is known as a binding. All Nodes participating in MIPv6 are required to maintain a table of these bindings in a binding cache. One entry is held in the binding cache for each Mobile Node with which communication is currently taking place. The binding cache holds four pieces of information per binding which are central to the operation of MIPv6, as illustrated by Table 10-1 (other fields are present to ensure correct ordering of control messages, but these are omitted for clarity). The home address forms the key field of the cache.

Table 10-1 Mobile IPv6 Bindings Cache

Home Address	Care of Address	Lifetime	Home Agent
2001:1:2:3:4::1234	2001:5:6:7:8::5678	110	Yes
2001:9:a:b:c::9abc	2001:d:e:f:0::def0	60	no

When a node wishes to transmit an IPv6 packet to a remote host, the home address field of the binding cache is searched for the IPv6 address of that host. If no match is found, the packet is transmitted according to the normal IPv6 routing tables. However, if a match is found, then the packet is encapsulated prior to transmission, to redirect the packet to the care-of address specified in the binding cache. This ensures optimal routing to the Mobile Node's current location. The form this encapsulation takes is dependant on the state of the Home Agent flag stored in the binding cache entry.

10.2 Home Agent Operation

If the Home Agent flag is set in a binding cache entry, then the node maintaining that cache is acting as a Home Agent for the Mobile Node. If this is the case, and the packet was entered through a forwarding context, then the packet is encapsulated using IPv6 in IPv6 tunnelling, as illustrated in the following table.

Table 10-2 IPv6 in IPv6 Encapsulation

IPv6 Header(Outer)	IPv6 Header (Inner)	Transport	Payload
Src Addr: Home Agent	Src Addr: Correspondent Node	TCP/UDP	Data
Dst Addr: Care of Address	Dst Addr: Home Address		
|------------- 40 bytes -----------|	|------------- 40 bytes -------------|		

IPv6 tunnelling is used by Home Agents to forward IPv6 packets routed to a Mobile Node's home network while it is away from home, as illustrated in Figure 10-1. Tunnelling has the advantage of preserving the complete original IPv6 packet, which is important as any modification to an IPv6 header could cause problems with higher layer protocols, such as TCP. Intercepted packets are tunnelled directly to a Mobile Node's current care-of address, where they are subsequently decapsulated by the Mobile Node.

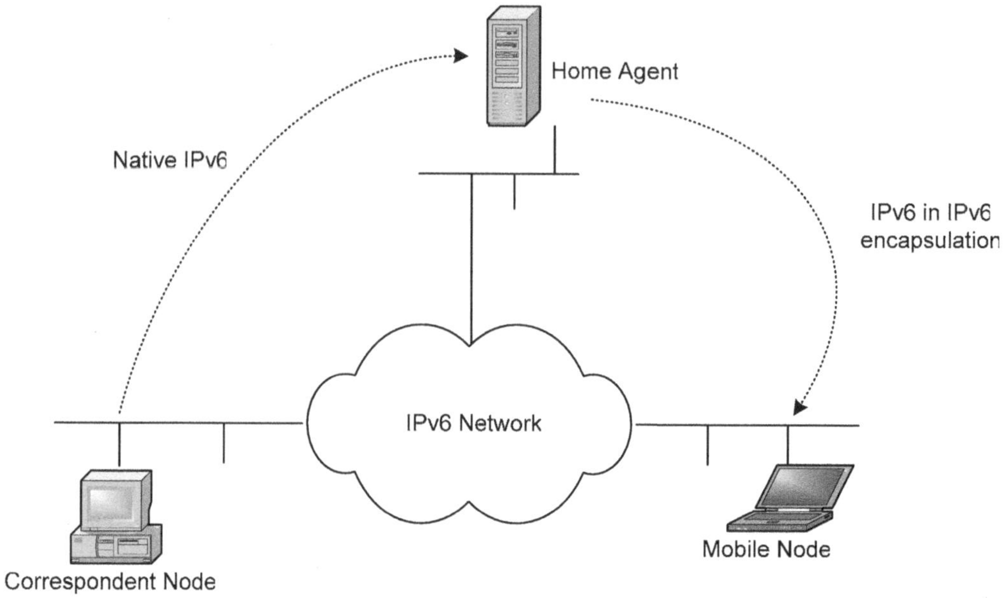

Figure 10-1 MIPv6 Routing to Mobile Nodes (Pre Route Optimisation)

10.3 Correspondent Node Operation

If the 'Home Agent' flag is cleared in a binding cache entry, or the packet was not received from a forwarding context, then an IPv6 routing header is used to redirect the IPv6 packet through the relevant care-of address, as shown in Figure 10-2.

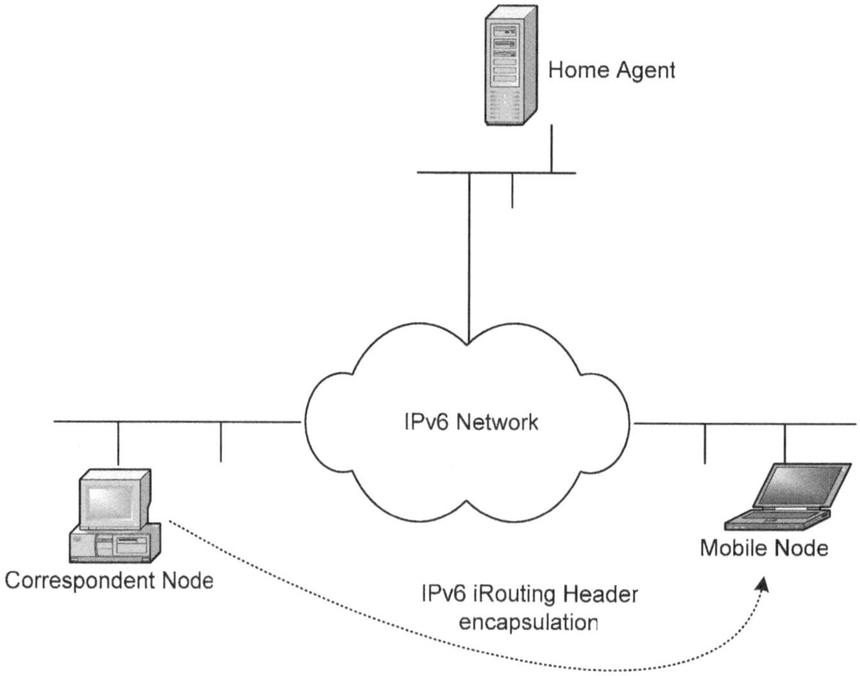

Figure 10-2 Mobile IPv6 Routing to Mobile Nodes (Post Route Optimisation)

As can be seen from Table 10-3, the use of the IPv6 routing header reduces the effective bandwidth required for the encapsulation of the packet in comparison to IPv6 in IPv6 tunnelling by 16 bytes. This reduction in packet size is possible due to spatial redundancy - i.e. if IPv6 tunnelling were used then the IPv6 source address of both the inner and outer IPv6 headers would be identical, resulting in a waste of bandwidth.

Table 10-3 IPv6 Routing Header Encapsulation

IPv6 Header		IPv6 Routing Header		Transport	Payload
Src Addr	Correspondent Node	Next Hop Address	Home Address	TCP/UDP	Data
Dst Addr	Care of Address				

|-------------- 40 bytes -------------| |--------------- 24 bytes ---------------|

10.4 Binding Cache Coherence

The use of the binding cache and IPv6 encapsulation provides a mechanism to enable optimal routing to Mobile hosts. This mechanism, however, relies on the bindings contained within that cache being accurate and up to date. Indeed, to protect against total machine failure (which is common in a mobile environment due to battery life constraints, etc.) and long periods of network disconnection by Mobile Nodes, binding cache entries for a Mobile Node must persist even after a period of total disconnection or loss of state by Mobile or Correspondent Nodes.

Mobile IPv6 maintains binding cache coherence through the use of binding update, binding acknowledgement and binding request messages. The remainder of this section describes these messages in detail, and how they interoperate to provide accurate and timely binding cache coherence.

Binding update, acknowledgement and request messages are all carried inside IPv6 destination options, each with their own destination option type. Utilising IPv6 destination options gives several advantages over less integrated methods of control messaging. Firstly, messages can be placed inline with the header of existing IPv6 packets, thereby reducing the packet transmission overhead of the message. Secondly, as no transport layer protocol is involved in the transmission of the message, fewer issues exist concerning the blocking of control messages by firewalls.

10.4.1 Binding Update Messages

Binding updates are transmitted by Mobile Nodes to Home Agents and Correspondent Nodes to create or update the entry in their binding cache relating to that Mobile Node's home address.

Binding updates can be generated at any time by Mobile Nodes, but are always transmitted upon the detection of an IPv6 packet which has travelled via an IPv6 in IPv6 tunnel from that node's Home Agent. The reception of such a packet indicates that the Correspondent Node that generated the packet currently has no binding for this Mobile Node (else the packet would have been delivered via an IPv6 routing header). In order to guarantee that 'stale' bindings are not indefinitely maintained by binding caches, Mobile IPv6 employs a soft state mechanism to purge out of date bindings. Every binding update contains a lifetime field, which specifies, in seconds, how long the binding is valid for. After this lifetime expires, the binding is removed from the binding cache. The lifetime value is set and refreshed by the corresponding lifetime field contained within binding update messages. A lifetime value of zero in a binding update indicates removal of the relevant binding.

10.4.2 Binding Acknowledgement Messages

Unlike binding updates, binding acknowledgements are sent to Mobile Nodes by Correspondent Node and Home Agents. They provide control feedback to Mobile Nodes in response to binding updates, and are used to provide reliable binding update delivery and to indicate any errors which are generated during the remote processing of binding updates. Mobile Nodes match binding acknowledgements with their corresponding binding updates by the comparison of sequence numbers.

10.4.3 Binding Request Messages

Correspondent Nodes and Home Agents detecting an entry in their binding cache which is nearing expiry may decide to send a binding request message to the respective Mobile Node. The receipt of a binding request message by a Mobile Node results in the transmission of a new binding update to the source of that binding request. This mechanism enables Correspondent Nodes to avoid short periods of sub-optimal routing, due to the expiry of an accurate binding.

10.4.4 Binding Update List

As a Mobile Node roams from network to network, it is essential that binding update messages are transmitted to that node's Home Agent and Correspondent Nodes as soon as possible, in order to facilitate a fast handoff. Mobile Nodes therefore cannot rely on the soft state timeout mechanism used in binding caches to refresh stale bindings maintained by Correspondent Nodes (typical binding lifetimes are of the order of minutes). An additional data structure, the binding update list, is therefore kept by Mobile Nodes, which maintains state on any Correspondent Nodes or Home Agents.

The binding update list contains one entry for every Correspondent Node or Home Agent to which a binding update has been sent. List entries contain information such as the address and time at which the binding update was transmitted, the state of any unacknowledged updates, the lifetime of the binding, a Home Agent flag, and the sequence number of the last transmission. Binding list entries are garbage collected from the binding update list as the respective binding expires.

The maintenance of the binding update list allows for significantly faster handoff performance. After a handoff has been detected and autoconfiguration has been completed, the binding update list is traversed, and a binding update message transmitted to every node contained within the list, thereby updating the binding caches of any active Correspondent Nodes.

10.5 Proxy Neighbour Discovery

Since packets destined for a Mobile Node may be incorrectly routed to its home network, placing Home Agents within an IPv6 edge router would allow the efficient interception of these packets, as they would likely travel through that router. However, the assumption that the packets will automatically reach this edge router cannot be relied upon. For example, consider the case of a Correspondent Node located on a Mobile Node's home network. If the Correspondent Node were to send a packet to that Mobile Node, its routing table would dictate that the Mobile Node was directly accessible, and did not require forwarding by a router. In this case, the Home Agent would not be able to intercept the packet.

Mobile IPv6 addresses this issue through a technique call proxy neighbour discovery (proxy ND). Neighbour Discovery [RFC2461] is a standard IPv6 protocol for the discovery of MAC addresses from IPv6 addresses, similar in concept to the ARP protocol for IPv4. Proxy ND involves an IPv6 node masquerading as another node at the MAC layer, by falsely responding to neighbour solicitations with its own MAC address. Home agents use proxy ND to ensure they intercept any IPv6 packets for a Mobile Node transmitted on its home network. To accomplish this, Home Agents also maintain a proxy neighbour discovery table, which contains the IPv6 addresses to which the Home Agent is acting as a proxy for. Entries to this table are added and removed as binding update messages with the 'Home Agent' flag set are added and removed from the binding cache.

10.6 Home Address Option

Mobile Nodes away from home have a choice of which global scope IPv6 address to use as a source for outgoing IPv6 packets. Either the node's home address could be used, or the current care-of address. However, neither of these choices are particularly desirable. If the current care-of address is used, then the source address for subsequent packets will change as a handoff takes place. This causes often irreparable problems for higher layer protocols such as TCP, which maintain transport layer identifiers and checksums based on network layer addresses. On the other hand, if the home address is used, then the outgoing IPv6 packet becomes susceptible to ingress filtering.

Ingress filtering is performed by many border routers to improve the security of the site to which they serve. Ingress filtering involves the inspection of the source address of all incoming IP packets, and verifying that the route to that address lies along the interface on which the packet was received. Any packets which fail this test are dropped as a security precaution. This can avoid many security attacks which use 'address spoofing'. Mobile Nodes sourcing their IPv6 packets with their home address on a foreign network can be mistakenly interpreted as a security threat by routers employing ingress filtering.

Mobile IPv6 defines a new IPv6 destination option, known as the home address option, which can provide a source address solution that is safe for transport protocols and is not susceptible to ingress filtering. This is achieved by a route optimised form of reverse tunnelling, which involves a level of minimal encapsulation when sending IPv6 packets from a Mobile Node. Table 10-4 illustrates the home address option.

Table 10-4 Mobile IPv6 Home Address Option

IPv6 Header		Home Address Option	Transport	Payload
Src Addr	Care of Address	Home Address	TCP/UDP	Data
Dst Addr	Correspondent Node			

|--------------- 40 bytes -------------| |--------- 18 bytes ---------|

The Mobile IPv6 specification states that Mobile Nodes should source their IPv6 packets using a care-of address, thereby avoiding ingress filtering. However, any upper layer protocols should assume the source address of outgoing packets is the home address. All outgoing packets from a Mobile Node include a home address option. Upon receipt by a Correspondent Node, the address contained within the home address option replaces the source address of the packet, before any upper layer processing takes place.

10.7 Home Agent Discovery

Mobile IPv6 provides a mechanism for Mobile Nodes to automatically detect the presence of Home Agents on its home network. This mechanism involves all Home Agents joining the link local Home Agents anycast address. Mobile Nodes wishing to discover a Home Agent sends a binding update (with the 'H' flag set) to this anycast address. This message will be delivered to at most one Home

Agent on the home network. Upon receipt of the message, the Home Agent responds with a binding acknowledgement, thereby informing the Mobile Node of the Home Agent's IPv6 address. The binding updates sent to the Home Agents anycast address are otherwise ignored by Home Agents.

10.8 The Mobility Header

A new IPv6 extension header, the mobility header, is designed to contain the MIPv6 signalling messages. The mobility header is used by Mobile Nodes, Home Agents and Correspondent Nodes for all messaging related binding creation and management. The format of the mobility header is illustrated in Figure 10-3.

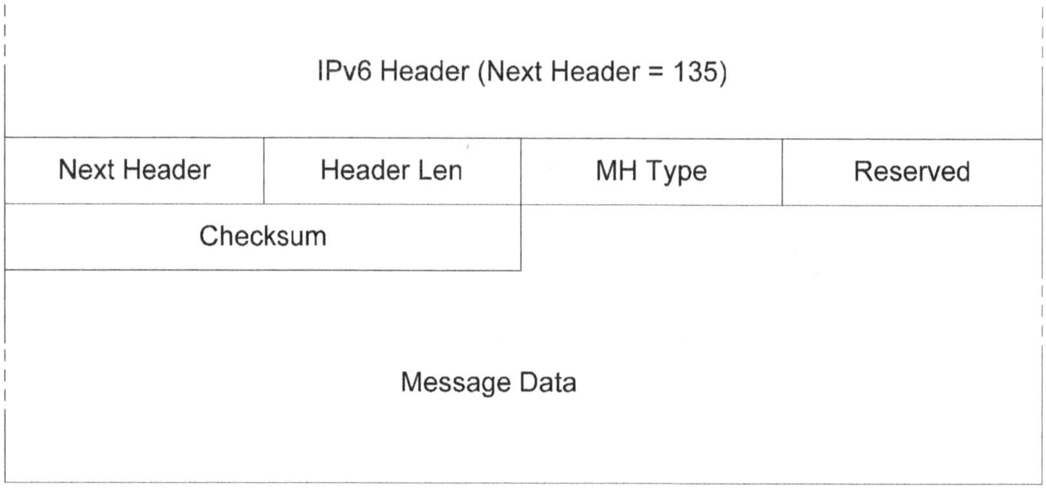

Figure 10-3 The Mobility Header Format

The mobility header is identified by a next header value of 135 (decimal) in the IPv6 header (or an alternative preceding header if there is one). The 'MH Type' field identifies the specific mobility message in question and can be one of the following:

- Home Test Init (HoTI)
- Care-of Test Init (CoTI)
- Home Test (HoT)
- Care-of Test (CoT)
- Binding Request (BR)
- Binding Update (BU)
- Binding Acknowledgement (BA)
- Binding Missing (BM).

Due to the use of the new mobility header, the piggybacking of MIPv6 signalling with data is no longer possible. However, a separate extension to the protocol that will allow piggybacking in the presence of the mobility header may become available in the near future.

10.9 The Return Routability Method

The Return Routability (RR) method is a new binding update (BU) authorisation mechanism, suitable for use between Mobile Node and Correspondent Node peers, which have no previous knowledge of each other. It is based on the principle of exchanging 'cookies' that verify the Mobile Node is 'alive' at its claimed address. The cookies are used by the Mobile Node to cryptographically protect the eventual BU message.

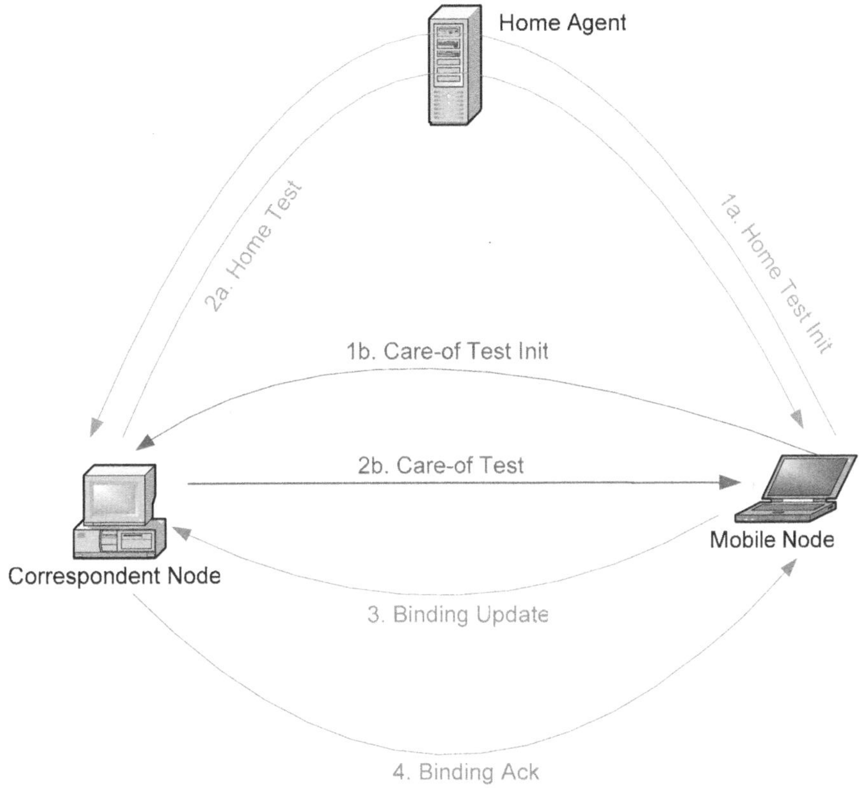

Figure 10-4 Return Routability Messaging

When a Mobile Node wishes to achieve route optimisation, it initiates the RR method as illustrated in Figure 10-4.

The HoTI and CoTI messages are sent simultaneously by the Mobile Node to the Correspondent Node.Upon the receipt of the HoTI and CoTI messages, the Correspondent Node computes two cookies based on the information contained in the messages, combined with its own secret key and nonce value. These cookies are inserted into the respective HoT and CoT messages, which are then sent back simultaneously to the Mobile Node.

Once the Mobile Node has received both the HoT and CoT messages, it has the cookies necessary to send the BU to the Correspondent Node. It hashes together the cookies to form a session key, which is then used to authenticate the BU that is sent to the Correspondent Node. When the Correspondent Node receives the BU, it can verify the information using its cookies and create a binding cache entry for the Mobile Node. The Correspondent Node may optionally acknowledge the BU with a BA.

10.10 Available Implementations

The implementations listed in Table 10-5 are not all of the implementation available. However, these are the implementations we know of that are both RFC 3775 compliant and are publicly available.

Table 10-5 Available MIPv6 Implementations

	MIPL	Cisco	Microsoft[1]	KAME	HP-UX
Platform	Linux 2.6.8.1	Cisco IOS	2000/XP/CE	FreeBSD	HP-UX-11i
Modes	MN/HA/CN	HA/CN	MN/HA/CN	MN/HA/CN	HA/CN
PND	Yes	Yes	Yes	Yes	Yes
IPv6-in-IPv6 tunnelling	Yes	Yes	Yes	Yes	Yes
DHAAD	Yes	Yes	Yes	Yes	Yes
Binding Management	Yes	Yes	Yes	Yes	Yes
HAO	Yes	Yes	Yes	Yes	Yes
Movement Detection	RAs	N/A	RAs and NDIS notifications	RAs	N/A
Smooth Handoff	Yes	Yes	Yes	Yes	N/A
IPSec	No (v1.1) Yes (v2.0)	No	Yes	Yes	Yes with HP-UX IPSec
Key exchange	MD5 or SHA-1	No	Manual	Manual	Unknown
Support for notebooks/ PDAs	Yes	N/A	Yes	Poor	N/A
MIPv6 built-in	No	Yes	No	Yes but not enabled by default	No. Is a component of TOUR 2.0
No. of patches	1	0	1 (XP and CE)	0	1
Set-up tools	mipdiag	command line tools	Auto-configuration and command line	Command line tools	Unknown
Licence	GNU	Commercial	Commercial	GNU	Commercial

MIPL 2.0 RC1 has been tested in Redhat 9 and Fedora Core 2, with kernel version 2.6.8.1 with TAHI MIPv6 conformance test suite version 3.0b (HA), 3.0b3 (CN) and 3.0b4 (MN).

The MIPL Mobile IPv6 for Linux code version 2.0 RC1 is the 13th public release and is the first for the 2.6 kernel series. It supports IPSec protection of the home registration signalling, but is still missing tunnel mode protection of the HoTI/HoT signalling and tunnelled payload data, as well as MPS/MPA support. These features are announced to be included in the next release so that the implementation then should be fully RFC 3775 compliant. Version 1.1 was the last release for the 2.4 kernel series.

[1] Not publicly available at time of writing but is expected to be soon.

10.11 Deployment Considerations

A general MIPv6 testbed would consist of:

- at least one Home Agent
- at least one Mobile Node
- at least one Correspondent Node
- several (>=2) IPv6 networks

At least one of the IPv6 networks must contain a Home Agent. Ideally, another two IPv6 networks should allow for the location of a Mobile Node (when away from home) and a Correspondent Node respectively. A very simple MIPv6 testbed like this is illustrated in Figure 10-5.

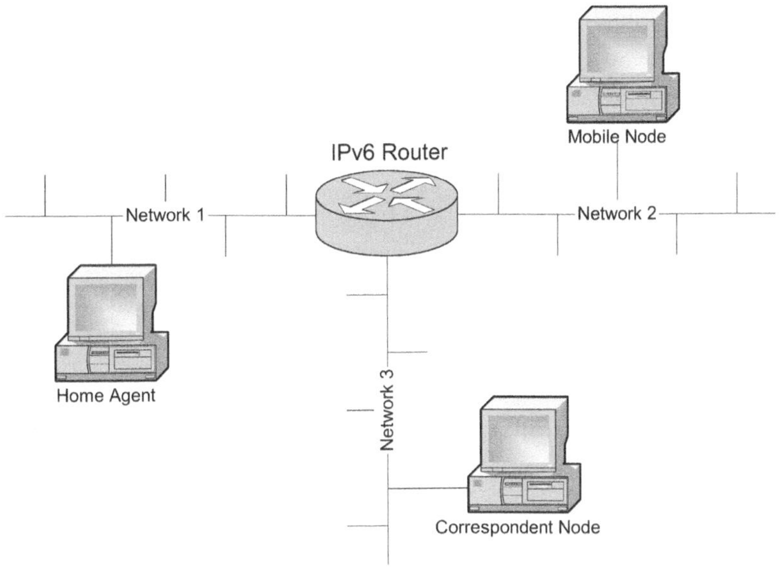

Figure 10-5 Simple Mobile IPv6 Testbed

The example in the figure shows three networks although, in theory, two networks would suffice (the Correspondent Node could be located in Network 1 or 2).

10.11.1 Hardware Requirements

In addition to the required network infrastructure (routers, cables, hubs, access points etc.) a MIPv6 testbed will require at least 3 separate machines: the Home Agent, the Mobile Node and the Correspondent Node. One could also use PC-based IPv6 routers (using open source systems like Linux and FreeBSD) instead of commercial IPv6 routers. This will certainly give more flexibility with regard to the addition of new IPv6 features and fine-tuning of network parameters (e.g. router advertisement intervals). Another possibility is to use a PC-based router that also offers Home Agent functionality.

The simplest way to simulate handoffs between networks is to unplug the Ethernet (or other media type) cable to which the MN is currently attached and replace it with a cable from the network you wish to move into. Of course, this means that the Ethernet cables pertaining to the different networks should be within easy reach (e.g. within a network room) if quick handoff latencies are desired.

Alternatively, you may wish to employ Wireless LANs to better facilitate roaming between networks (see case studies in Chapter 14). A simple configuration would be to have each network served by its own wireless access point (AP). In this way (assuming the APs are WiFi certified), one can perform handoffs simply by moving between APs without the need to unplug the WLAN network adapter from the Mobile Node.

10.11.2 Software Requirements

Before configuring the MIPv6 testbed, you will need to make some policy decisions:

- What kind of global network prefixes you are going to use in your network? 6BONE prefixes (3ffe::/16) are now deprecated so you will need to obtain a suitable production prefix from the 2001::/16 address block by contacting your ISP.
- How are you going to implement the IP routing? In a small network ripng would be a good choice. In both, Linux and in FreeBSD, you can use zebra (http://www.zebra.org) for accomplishing this.

Since the MIPv6 specification is relatively new (only recently received RFC status) and is still somewhat work in progress, implementations tend to be staggered in terms of what features they support. Thus, interoperability between implementations is somewhat of a hit and miss affair. Therefore, it is wise to first deploy the same MIPv6 implementation on all the machines in the testbed (so make sure that the implementation has HA, MN and CN functionality). Once confidence in one implementation is achieved, you may decide to deploy other implementations and see if they are interoperable.

Note that movement detection algorithms rely on receiving router advertisements from the default IPv6 router when first entering a network. Intelligent movement detection algorithms will also make use of media disconnect/connect notifications and issue router solicitation messages to speed up the reception of these router advertisement messages. Therefore, it is essential that the routers pertaining to the networks in the MIPv6 testbed issue periodic router advertisements so that a MN can configure itself with a new Care of Address when it connects to the network.

The following sections will try to throw some light on how a MIPv6 testbed can be accomplished by using open source software like FreeBSD and Linux in addition to commercial software such as Microsoft Windows XP/CE and Cisco IOS.

10.12 Cisco Mobile IPv6

The Cisco MIPv6 implementation began with a research collaboration with Lancaster University and the porting of their MIPv6 implementation for Linux. Since this date, Cisco integrates the MIPv6 Home Agent support in a "Technology Preview" release that is available for experiment.

The feature is not offered yet in a commercial Cisco IOS release as Mobile IPv6 is still an immature protocol.

The Cisco IOS release of the protocol has been demonstrated at several events, e.g. at the Madrid IPv6 Summit, March 2002 and N+I Tokyo, July 2002. The configuration comprised a Cisco 2600 acting as Home Agent, the Mobile Node was a Compaq iPAQ running Linux, and the Correspondent Node was an AlphaServer running Tru64.

At the time of writing, the Cisco IOS release supports version 24 of the IETF draft specification. Based on Cisco IOS 12.2T release train, the Technology Preview works on Cisco 2600, 3600, 3700 and 7200 routers series.

10.12.1 Available Feature Set

Home Agent Home agent functionality will allow a suitably configured IPv6 router to act as a home agent for one or more mobile nodes when they are away from home.

Timer changes MIPv6 requires that the range of some timers be changed, for example, the minimum interval between unsolicited router advertisements is reduced from the 3 seconds specified in RFC2461. These relaxations are supported.

Advertisement Interval option MIPv6 requires that routers be configurable to allow them to send an Advertisement Interval option in their Router Advertisements to help mobile nodes perform movement detection. This feature is supported.

Duplicate Address Detection A mobile node may request that a home agent perform Duplicate Address Detection (DAD) when processing its registration and, whilst acting as the mobile node's home agent, defend its address. This feature is supported.

Dynamic Home Agent Address Discovery Home Agents in a subnet learn of each others presence and capabilities by listening to Router Advertisements. A mobile node may obtain the list of home agents on its home subnet by sending a request to the anycast address for all MIPv6-home-agents. This feature is supported.

Access Control List Support for an ACL to control the subnets from which the router will accept Binding Updates and DHAAD requests. This may be used to 'black list' certain sub-networks, preventing mobile nodes roaming to them, and refusing to perform correspondent node route optimization with mobile nodes that are currently visiting such sub-networks.

10.12.2 How to Get it

At this date, the software is only available on the 'Ohanami' and can be obtained from Cisco CCO.

10.12.3 Installation

Appropriate Cisco IOS image must be downloaded on the router acting as Mobile IPv6 Home Agent. Minimum memory size must be compliant with the latest Cisco IOS 12.2T release, check CCO software centre to determine the appropriate memory size.

10.12.4 Configuration

10.12.4.1 Example Configuration

The following simple example configures a router as a Mobile IPv6 Home Agent on the interfaces Ethernet 1 and Ethernet 2. On the Ethernet2 interface, unsolicited router advertisements are configured to be transmitted every 0.05 seconds.

```
ipv6 unicast-routing
!
ipv6 mobile
!
interface Ethernet1
  ipv6 address 3000:1234:5678::1/64
  ipv6 mobile home-agent enable
interface Ethernet2
!
  ipv6 address 3000:1234:abcd::1/64
  ipv6 mobile home-agent enable
  ipv6 nd ra-interval msec 50
```

10.12.5 Configuration Commands

Global commands:

`[no] ipv6 mobile`

Enables Mobile IPv6. Default is disabled, all binding updates are ignored

`[no] ipv6 mobile mh-number <0-255>`

Changes the number used in the MIPv6 mobility header. The default is 62 which is also used by KAME.

`[no] ipv6 mobile bindings filter <acl>`

Configures a binding update filter using an ACL. When an ACL is configured all DHAAD requests and binding updates are filtered by Home Address and Destination Address. Default is no ACL configured.

This feature may be used to deny home agent services to mobile nodes that have roamed to particular sub-networks. When the filter blocks a binding update, a binding acknowledgement is returned with error status "Administratively prohibited". Default is no filter so all binding updates are accepted. Note that the filter is also applied to Dynamic Home Agent Address Discovery messages. When blocked, these are silently discarded.

In configuration of the ACL, the src is the CoA and the dst is the HoA.

`[no] ipv6 mobile binding lifetime <secs>`

Configures the maximum lifetime of a binding cache entry. Default is infinite lifetime.

```
[no] ipv6 mobile binding max <int>
```

Specifies the maximum number of registration bindings which may be maintained concurrently. By default, binding maximum is unset indicating unlimited. If the configured number of home agent registrations is reached or exceeded, subsequent registrations will be refused with the error "Insufficient resources". No existing bindings will discarded until their lifetime has expired, even if binding maximum is set to a value below the current number of such bindings.

```
[no] ipv6 mobile binding refresh
```

Default is 5 minutes (300 seconds).

Interface commands:

```
[no] ipv6 mobile home-agent enable
```

Enables home agent operation on the interface. By default, home agent operation is disabled.

```
[no] ipv6 mobile home-agent preference <pref>
```

Specifies the value to be use for Preference in the Home Agent Information Option transmitted on the interface. A value in the range -32768 to +32767 may be specified. By default, a value for Preference of zero is assumed for home agent operation on this interface.

```
[no] ipv6 nd ra-interval <secs> | msec <msecs>
```

Specifies the interval between sending unsolicited multicast Router Advertisements on this interface. The value for this should be set to less than or equal to the IPv6 Router Lifetime if this is a default router for the link. The optional sufffix msec has been introduced to indicate that the interval has been specified in milliseconds, rather than the default of seconds. This allows specification of the new minimum value of 0.05 seconds. The interval should be set to a low value on interfaces providing service to visiting mobile nodes in order to aid rapid movement detection. Note that to prevent undesirable synchronisation with other IPv6 nodes, the value may be randomly adjusted within +/- 20%.

```
[no] ipv6 nd advertise-interval
```

Specifies whether an Advertisement Interval option should be transmitted in Router Advertisements. This option may be used to indicate to a visiting mobile node how frequently it may expect to receive RAs. It may use this information in its movement detection algorithm.

```
[no] ipv6 nd prefix <prefix> | default
                  [ [<valid-lifetime> <preferred-lifetime>] |
                    [at <valid-date> <preferred-date>]
                    [off-link] [no-rtr-address] [no-autoconfig] ]
```

By default, all prefixes configured as addresses on the interface will be advertised in Router Advertisements. This command allows control over the individual parameters per prefix, including whether the prefix should be advertised or not. The default keyword can be used to set default parameters for all prefixes. A date can be set for prefix expiry. The valid and preferred lifetimes are counted down in real time. When the expiry date is reached the prefix will no longer be advertised. The keyword no-rtr-address means do not send the full router address in prefix advert; do not set the R bit.

Show commands:

```
show ipv6 interface
```

Existing command; output extended to include home agent data where and when applicable.

```
show ipv6 mobile binding [home-address <addr>]
                         [care-of-address <addr>]
                         [interface <int>]
```

Displays details of all bindings which match all the search criteria. If no parameters are specified, all bindings are listed. The output is in a form where parts may be cut/pasted into subsequent commands, e.g., clear ipv6 mobile binding.

```
show ipv6 mobile globals
```

Displays the values of all global configuration parameters associated with MIPv6, and lists the interfaces on which home agent functionality is currently operating.

```
show ipv6 mobile traffic
```

Displays binding updates received and binding acknowledgements sent.

```
show ipv6 mobile home-agents [<interface> [<prefix>]]
```

Displays the Home Agents List for the specified interface or, if none is specified, displays the Home Agents List for each interface on which the router is acting as a home agent. If a prefix is specified then only those addresses matching that value will be displayed.

Clear commands:

```
clear ipv6 mobile binding [home-address <prefix>
                          | care-of-address <prefix>
                          | interface <int>]
```

Clears all bindings with the mobile nodes which match the parameters. The parameter can be a prefix for the Care-of-Address or the Home-Address so that entire networks can be cleared. Use /128 to clear an individual node. The interface parameter will clear all bindings on the specified interface.

Note that when this command is used to delete bindings, the mobile node will not be informed that its home agent is no longer acting on its behalf.

```
clear ipv6 mobile home-agents [<interface>]
```

Clears the Home Agents List on the specified interface. The list will subsequently be reconstructed from received Router Advertisements.

```
clear ipv6 mobile traffic
```

Clears the statistics about the received binding updates and transmitted binding acknowledgements.

Debug commands:

```
[un]debug ipv6 nd
```

Existing command; output modified to include relevant home agent data.

```
[un]debug ipv6 mobile bindings-cache
```

Enables debugging of the bindings cache. Currently this only displays "SHUTDOWN" when the bindings cache is shutdown.

`[un]debug ipv6 mobile forwarding`

Enables debugging of soft tunnel forwarding.

`[un]debug ipv6 mobile home-agent`

Enables Home Agent debugging.

`[un]debug ipv6 mobile registrations`

Enables debugging of registrations, i.e. binding updates and binding acknowledgements.

`[un]debug ipv6 mobile correspondent-node`

Enables Correspondent Node debugging. This currently displays when a Home Address Options has been received.

10.12.6 Operation

Mobile IPv6 clients must be compliant with ID version 24 (or RFC 3775).

10.13 Mobile IPv6 for Linux

Mobile IPv6 for Linux (MIPL) is an implementation that was originally developed as a software project course in the Helsinki University of Technology (HUT), with the goal to create a prototype implementation of Mobile IPv6 for Linux. After the course, the implementation was further developed in the context of the GO/Core project at HUT Telecommunications and Multimedia Lab. It is an open source implementation, has been released under GNU GPL and is freely available to anyone.

The MIPL implementation has been tested in interoperability and conformance testing events such as the ETSI IPv6 Plugtests and TAHI Interoperability events.

10.13.1 How to get it

In Linux, the standard IPv6 stack is included in the mainstream kernel distribution. However, you have to patch the kernel if you want Mobile IPv6 features. Therefore, a MIPL release is usually compatible only with a specific kernel revision (unless between Linux revisions the kernel code that has to be patched has not changed). MIPL v1.1, which is described in this section, requires Linux kernel version 2.4.26. MIPL v1.1 is based on MIPv6 specification as described in RFC 3775 [RFC3775]. The most recent MIPL release, MIPL 2.0 RC1 requires Linux kernel version 2.6.8.1. It is recommended to use MIPL 1.1, at the time of writing MIPL 2.0 RC1 is a preview release and therefore very much still work in progress.

The kernel 2.4.26 can be obtained from your favourite kernel mirror site, e.g. http://www.kernel.org

The MIPL patch mipv6-1.1-v2.4.26tar.gz can be obtained from http://www.mobile-ipv6.org

10.13.2 Installation

The following steps describe the MIPL installation (based on the README and INSTALL files of the package).

1. Unpack the MIPL tar file, for example in the `/usr/src` directory. This will create the directory `/usr/src/mipv6-1.1-v2.4.26`
2. Go to the Linux source directory (e.g. `/usr/src/linux`)
3. Apply the MIPL kernel patch:
   "`patch -p1 < /usr/src/mipv6-1.1-v2.4.26/mipv6-1.1-v2.4.26.patch`"
4. "`make xconfig`" (or `config` or whatever you prefer) to configure the kernel: you should have the following settings in your configuration:

   ```
   CONFIG_EXPERIMENTAL=y
   CONFIG_SYSCTL=y
   CONFIG_PROC_FS=y
   CONFIG_MODULES=y
   CONFIG_NET=y
   CONFIG_NETFILTER=y
   CONFIG_UNIX=y
   CONFIG_INET=y
   CONFIG_IPV6=m
   CONFIG_IPV6_SUBTREES=y
   ```

```
CONFIG_IPV6_IPV6_TUNNEL=m
CONFIG_IPV6_MOBILITY=m
CONFIG_IPV6_MOBILITY_MN=m
CONFIG_IPV6_MOBILITY_HA=m
CONFIG_IPV6_MOBILITY_DEBUG=y
```

The last setting is optional. `CONFIG_IPV6_MOBILITY_DEBUG` turns on debugging messages. It is advised to set this to '`y`' in order to help debug any problems since MIPv6 is still very much an immature protocol.

5. Compile the kernel and modules:

   - "`make dep && make clean && make bzImage modules modules_install`"

6. Install the new kernel:

   Copy the created bzImage to `/boot/vmlinuz-2.4.24` and edit `/etc/lilo.conf` (or `/boot/grub/menu.lst` if you use GrUB) reflecting the changes, then run `lilo` to apply the changes (not applicable if you use GrUB).

7. Add the MIPv6 device:

   - "`mknod /dev/mipv6_dev c 0xf9 0`"

8. Build the user space tools of MIPL:

   - "`cd /usr/local/src/mipv6-1.1-v2.4.26`"
   - "`./configure`"
   - "`make && make install`"
   - the "`mipdiag`" tool should be available now, which allows configuration and status query.

9. If your distribution does not provide a router advertisement daemon, get one from http://v6web.litech.org/radvd/ and compile it.
10. Reboot into the new kernel.
11. Start MIPL with:

    `/etc/init.d/mobile-ip6 start`

10.13.3 Configuration

The configuration files for MIPL are as follows:

`/etc/network-mip6.conf`	- Mobile IPv6 features
`/etc/radvd.conf`	- Router advertisement daemon
`/etc/modules`	- Configuration file for modules loading

The main configuration file is `/etc/sysconfig/network-mip6.conf` although the path may be different in your particular Linux distribution (e.g. in Debian the path is `/etc/network/network-mip6.conf`). The following table lists the configuration variables that can be set in this file and their meaning.

Table 10-6 MIPL Configuration Parameters

Variable name	Description
FUNCTIONALITY	Defines the mode of the node: "ha" – Home Agent "cn" – Correspondent Node "mn" – Mobile Node Note that ha and mn both have cn functionality included
DEBUGLEVEL	If debugging was enabled when configuring the MIPL module, this variables controls the verbosity of the output (default: 0)
TUNNEL_SITELOCAL	Should unicasts to node's site-local address be tunnelled when mobile node is not in its home network (default: no)
MIN_TUNNEL_NR	Minimum number of free tunnel devices kept in cache on MN or HA. Must be set to at least 1 for MN and HA. To ensure successful bindings even during high work loads it could be set to a bigger value on the HA (default: 1).
MAX_TUNNEL_NR	Maximum number of free tunnel devices kept in cache on MN or HA. Must be set to at least 1 for MN and HA. To improve performance set it higher than MIN_TUNNEL_NR (default =3).
HOMEADDRESS	The MN's home address (including prefix length). Only valid in mn mode.
HOMEAGENT	The home agent address (including prefix length). Only valid in mn mode.

10.13.3.1 Node Type

To configure a Home Agent, the following settings should be in `network-mip6.conf`:

```
FUNCTIONALITY=ha
MIN_TUNNEL_NR=1
MAX_TUNNEL_NR=5
TUNNEL_SITELOCAL=yes
```

For a Mobile Node, make sure you have the following entries in `network-mip6.conf`:

```
FUNCTIONALITY=mn
TUNNEL_SITELOCAL=yes
MIN_TUNNEL_NR=1
MAX_TUNNEL_NR=3
HOMEDEV=mip6mnha1
HOMEADDRESS=<the home address of the mn>
```

```
HOMEAGENT=<the address of the ha>
```

Note that if you only require CN functionality, you must configure the node as you would a MN.

During the early stages of deployment, it is recommended to increase the verbosity level of the kernel module in `network-mip6.conf` in order to be able to debug any problems:

```
DEBUGLEVEL=4
```

For a HA you must have forwarding enabled in order for the HA to be able to forward captured packets to the MN when it is away from home:

```
"echo 1 > /proc/sys/net/ipv6/conf/eth0/forwarding"
```

This is assuming that you are using eth0 as the outgoing interface. In addition you should probably need to add a default route to the outgoing interface.

6.3.2 Route Optimisation and Return Routability

It is possible to control the use of route optimisation and return routability via the proc file system. If you do not wish to use route optimisation (and thus return routability) user the following command:

```
"echo 0 > /proc/sys/conf/net/ipv6/mobility/accept_return_routability"
```

The MN will then communicate with the CN only through the tunnel on the HA. Route optimisation and return routability are enabled by default (setting is 1).

10.13.3.2 IPSec Authentication

Authentication and authorisation of Mobile IPv6 messages between the MN and HA with IPSec is not possible in 2.4 kernels as IPSec support is missing. However, it is possible to use a 3rd party IPSec implementation with MIPL 1.1 to support IPSec authentication between the MA and HA.

10.13.3.3 Radvd

In order for the MN to be able to discover when it returns home, the HA must be configured to send out router advertisements. Do this by configuring `/etc/radvd.conf` with suitable parameters e.g.:

```
# cat /etc/radvd.conf
interface eth0
{
   AdvSendAdvert on;
   MaxRtrAdvInterval 3;
   MinRtrAdvInterval 1;
   AdvIntervalOpt off;
   AdvHomeAgentFlag on;
   HomeAgentLifetime 10000;
   HomeAgentPreference 20;
   AdvHomeAgentInfo on;
   prefix 2001:db8:2700::2/64
   {
     AdvRouterAddr on;
     AdvOnLink on;
     AdvAutonomous on;
```

```
            AdvPreferredLifetime 10000;
            AdvValidLifetime 12000;
        };
    };
```

Start radvd with

"`/etc/init.d/radvd start`"

You can verify that RAs are being sent by running radvdump.

10.13.4 Usage Notes/Problems

Using earlier versions of MIPL we observed a few problems with medium to long term usage. In brief these concerned the kernel failing to add IPv6 routes and needing to be rebooted and unsolved negative binding acknowledgements sent by the HA on MN binding updates. However, with MIPL 1.0 and further versions we have not noticed these problems.

Multiple interface support works (we tested for example handovers between Bluetooth and 802.11 access networks with a MIPL client switching the priority of the interfaces), but sometimes when both interfaces receive router advertisements at short intervals (around 1 second), there are spurious switches between the interfaces, though the interface preference is not changed. This might be a problem with how the router advertisement lifetime is handled in the MIPL implementation. If the router advertisements are received at a slightly lower rate (2 seconds), these interface changes do not occur.

In our testbeds, we have not been able to test IPSec authentication between the MN and HA. This is because authentication and authorization of MIPv6 messages between the MN and HA is missing in 2.4 series kernels. This will not be supported by the MIPL team in the 2.4 kernels unless someone backports the IPSec in 2.6 kernels to 2.4 kernels. However, MIPL for 2.6 series kernels (MIPL v2.0 onwards) will have IPSec support from the start.

Another problem which was observed is that the routing table is sometimes not correctly updated. So old routes from visited networks remain in the routing table.

10.14 KAME Mobile IPv6

The KAME project developed a Mobile IPv6 implementation for the FreeBSD and NetBSD platforms. The code is implemented as part of the kernel. In addition to this, several user space programs have been developed for MIPv6 control, for extracting MIPv6 statistics and for dynamic home agent discovery

The implementation follows RFC 3775 and includes functionality for HA, MN and CN (mandatory for an IPv6 implementation that claims to be IPv6 compliant). In addition, KAME supports authentication of messages between a MN and its HA using IPSec.

10.14.1 How to get it

To get a proper Kame IPv6 stack proceed with the following steps (IPv6 is included in all standard BSD releases but for Mobile IPv6 the KAME Kernel is required):

- For FreeBSD, get and install FreeBSD 4.10-RELEASE or 5.3-RELEASE (more information is available at http://www.freebsd.org/doc/en_US.ISO8859-1/books/handbook/)
- For NetBSD, get and install NetBSD 2.0 (more information available at http://www.netbsd.org/guide/en/)
- Get the latest Kame SNAP from ftp://ftp.kame.net/pub/kame/snap/ or from mirror servers.

10.14.2 Installation

Since MIPv6 functionality is not enabled by default you need to enable the correct features and rebuild the kernel. Depending on the type of node you wish to install (MN, HA or CN) the entries in the kernel configuration differ.

The following features should be set in your kernel configuration file for MN functionality:

```
options          MIP6
options          MIP6_MOBILE_NODE
pseudo-device    hif   1
```

The following features should be set in your kernel configuration file for HA functionality:

```
options          MIP6
options          MIP6_HOME_AGENT
```

The following features should be set in your kernel configuration file for CN functionality:

```
options          MIP6
```

Compile and install the kernel. This will give you a kernel supporting the node type you configured. The next step is to compile the user space programs. This will also provide you with:

- `rtadvd` - a Mobile IPv6 suitable routing advertisement daemon
- `had` - a dynamic home agent discovery protocol daemon
- `mip6stat` - an application to gather MIPv6 related statistics
- `mip6control` - a control application for MIPv6 functions

The user space programs `had`, `mipstat` and `mip6control` are built automatically and should be installed in `/usr/local/v6/sbin` (check your path settings as well to make sure you load the kame versions of the applications instead of the standard ones `/usr/local/v6` has to be in your path before the path to the regular apps). The two supporting binaries "`mip6control`" and "`mip6stat`" should have been compiled by applying the ordinary kame tree "`make`" procedure.

To build `rtadvd`, you need to add the following line to its Makefile (this should be located at `/freebsd4/sbin/rtadvd/` in FreeBSD):

```
CFLAGS+=-DMIP6
```

Then recompile `rtadvd` and install it:

```
make clean
make
make install
```

10.14.3 Configuration

Configuration files you have to edit:

`/etc/rc.conf` - system wide configuration file

`/etc/rtadvd.conf` - configuration file for the router advertisement daemon.

For FreeBSD and NetBSD users, there is a special rc script that enables MIPv6 configuration to be specified in `/etc/rc.conf`.

If you are using FreeBSD, you must copy `rc` and `rc.mobileip6` in `/kame/freebsd4/etc` directory to the `/etc` directory.

If you are using NetBSD, you must copy the `/kame/netbsd/etc/rc.d/mobileip6` file to the `/etc/rc.d` directory.

After this you can configure your node using `rc.conf`.

10.14.3.1 Home Agent

For having the Home Agent functionality on the FreeBSD system you will need to do the following (note that a node cannot act as a MN and HA at the same time). Add the following entries in `/etc/rc.conf`:

```
ipv6_mobile_enable="YES"
ipv6_mobile_config_dir="/usr/local/v6/etc/mobileip6"
ipv6_mobile_nodetype="home_agent"
ipv6_mobile_home_prefixes=<your home prefix>
ipv6_mobile_home_link=<your interface name>
```

Where `ipv6_mobile_home_prefixes` is your home prefix and `ipv6_mobile_home_link` is the interface name you use for the home network.

A home agent needs to contain routing functionality. Therefore you need other configuration parameters as would be required for a normal IPv6 router:

```
ipv6_gateway_enable="YES"
```

```
ipv6_router_enable="YES"
ipv6_router="/usr/local/v6/sbin/route6d"
ipv6_ifconfig_"xx"=<address of your interface>
```

The Access Router functionality is started at boot time if you add the following entries in the `/etc/rc.conf`:

```
rtadvd_enable="YES"
rtadvd_daemon=/usr/local/v6/sbin/rtadvd
rtadvd_flags="-ms -c /etc/rtadvd.conf"
```

Then you will have to adjust the file `/etc/rtadvd.conf` according to your needs. Below is a sample file:

```
#
# $Id: rtadvd.conf,v 1.2 2001/04/13 21:42:09 cco Exp $
# $Name:  $
#

#       $KAME$
#
# Note: All of the following parameters have default values defined
#       in specifications, and hence you usually do not have to set them
#       by hand unless you need special non-default values.
#
#       You even do not need to create the configuration file. rtadvd
#       would usually work well without a configuration file.
#       See also: rtadvd(8)

# that is advertised on each and every interface
default:\
             :chlim#64:rltime#10:rtime#10:retrans#0:\
             :vltime#30:pltime#10:mtu#1500:

# sent only by simple routers
router:\
        :raflags#0:pinfoflags#192:mininterval#3:maxinterval#5:\
        :tc=default:

# sent only by the Home Agents
ha:\
        :hatime#100:hapref#10:raflags#32:pinfoflags#224:\
        :mininterval#1:maxinterval#5:tc=default:
```

```
# per-interface definitions.
#   Mainly IPv6 prefixes are configured in this part.  However, rtadvd
#   automatically learns appropriate prefixes from the kernel's routing
#   table, and advertises the prefixes, so you don't have to configure
#   this part, either.
#   If you don't want the automatic advertisement, (uncomment and) configure
#   this part by hand, and then invoke rtadvd with the -s option.

# this is a router
xl0:\

:addrs#1:addr="2001:db8:0190:0046:250:4ff:fe64:eb78":prefixlen#64:tc=router:

# this is a HA interface
xl1:\
        :addrs#1:addr="2001:db8:0190:0047:210:4bff:feb4:d3a1":prefixlen#64:tc=ha:
```

After rebooting, the FreeBSD box will act as a Home Agent and Access Router. For checking the status of your Home Agent you should use:

```
/usr/local/v6/sbin/mip6control
```

10.14.3.2 Mobile Node

To configure your node as a mobile node, add the following lines to `/etc/rc.conf`:

```
ipv6_mobile_enable="YES"
ipv6_mobile_config_dir="/usr/local/v6/etc/mobileip6"
ipv6_mobile_nodetype="mobile_node"
ipv6_mobile_home_prefixes=<your home prefix>
```

Replacing ipv6_mobile_home_prefixes with your home prefix.

10.14.3.3 Correspondent Node

To run a CN, no additional measures are required provided that the kernel was built with MIPv6 support (see above).

10.14.4 Remarks

In contrast to MIPL Kame supported IPSec from early on. MIPL version 1.1 is the minimum requirement for usage as a MN in conjunction with a Kame HA. Earlier versions of MIPL are incompatible with KAME HA. With MIPL 2.0 IPSec support should be included as well (not evaluated yet).

The KAME Mobile IPv6 stack had been developed for long time. Last year, for several reasons, it was decided to merge the implementation with that of the WIDE project , where another Mobile IPv6 code for BSDs had been developed by SFC in Keio University. Both partners agreed to unify and re-design their implementations. The resulting new MIP6 code is called shisa which confirmed its interoperability during the latest ETSI IPv6 plugtest event.

The current shisa implementation is based on RFC 3775, RFC 3776 [RFC3776], RFC 3963 [RFC3963] and draft-wakikawa-mobileip-multiplecoa-04 [WUEN05]. It works on FreeBSD 4.10, FreeBSD 5.3 and NetBSD 1.6.2. But note that FreeBSD 4.10 will not be supported in kame snap soon as announced on snap-users mailing list.

Chapter 11

Applications

A number of middleware and user applications were developed or ported by the 6NET project. These included the SIP-based telephony system (including a PSTN gateway), the AccessGrid conferencing tool (including an IPv4-IPv6 gateway), IPv6 versions of the IBM WebSphere e-business applications, an IPv6 version of the FLUTE multicast file transfer tool, and MIPv6-based video streaming for PDAs. The 6NET project also created IPv6 versions of the Globus Toolkit (GT3.x) which is used to develop Grid-aware applications (e.g., IPv6 WeatherStation and eProtein), and the Open H.323 Toolkit, used to develop an IPv6 version of GnomeMeeting. Other network management tools such as NetSNMP, MRTG, OpenEye, Smokeping and Weathermap have been developed or ported for traffic measurement and visualisation purposes.

Applications summary

These are the application being ported, tested or developed by 6NET
Our aim is to perform trials on the suitability and robustness of
IPv6 applications with a view to wide-scale deployment
Click on the column headers to change sorting order

name	category	class	summary	status	responsible	modified	passed test
TUR	Streaming Radio	A	Trondheim Underground Radio	Running. Publicly available. Multicast support planned by mid 2003.	UNINETT	2004-03-11	✓
VideoLAN	Streaming	A	Streaming video server and player	Works. A multicast demonstrator. A first implementation of RTSP is available for better stream control	SURFnet	2004-02-27	✓
Quake	Gaming	B	Multiplayer FPS action game	Works.	GARR	2004-02-27	✓
Kphone	Conferencing	A	SIP based Voice-over-IPv6 telephony application	Demo version released	FhG Fokus	2004-03-11	✓
WMA through ftunnel	Streaming	A	Streaming of Windows Media using ftunnel	working	SURFnet bv	2004-03-11	✓
SER	Conferencing Support	A	SIP server	Operational	FhG Fokus	2004-03-11	✓
VIC	Conferencing	A	Video Conferencing Tool	VIC is currently fairly stable, and provides good performance. Further work is required on use of direct video display and integration of more codecs.	UCL	2004-03-17	✓
MCast6	Streaming	A	Tool for multimedia streaming in a computer network	testing phase	PSNC	2004-05-13	✓

Figure 11-1 Partial Screenshot of the Applications Database

Deliverable D5.1 [D5.1] of the 6NET project listed the applications initially identified as candidates to run on the 6NET IPv6 network. Since the development and porting of applications to support IPv6 is not a static activity, it is very difficult, if not impossible, to capture the ever-evolving status of the different applications mentioned in a single document.

Therefore, the Applications workpackage of 6NET decided that the applications list and current status would be in the form of a web page. This approach enables application owners to keep the status of their porting effort up to date and additionally allows interested users to keep track of the status, knowing that it is more up to date than a project deliverable downloaded from a web site or indeed, this book.

The up-to-date list of 6NET applications is therefore available at the following address: http://apps.6net.org/WP5Apps (Figure 11-1 shows a partial screenshot). This site also provides the results of the trials performed on each application through Test Evaluation Forms (TEFs) according to the methodology described in Deliverable D5.5 [D5.5].

Instead of listing those applications available on the above website, this chapter outlines the important changes that IPv6 brings to network APIs in C and other programming languages. This will be of interest to deployers of IPv6 looking to develop new or port existing applications for their organisation.

11.1 The new BSD Sockets API

BSD Sockets is by far the most popular application programming interface (API). The name pays tribute to its authors – it was created at the University of California in Berkeley, originally for BSD Unix, but later it was ported to other branches of Unix and also to MacOS, MS Windows and even PalmOS. Applications of BSD Sockets are not limited to IP, although other uses have been rare. It is not an exaggeration to say that the application side of the Internet is built on this API.

It is well-known that to Unix, everything looks like a file. BSD Sockets API uses this paradigm for communication between programs. Its fundamental program object – the socket – represents a communication channel through which two programs can exchange data using standard file descriptors.

Even though the original BSD Sockets API was designed as protocol-independent, the astronomical size of IPv6 addresses was something that apparently exceeded even the wildest dreams of its developers. Data structures of the original BSD Sockets left some space for protocol addresses longer than the 32 bits of IPv4, not enough though to accommodate the quadruple of that size and other information that is needed for IPv6. It was thus necessary to update and extend the API. The IPv6 working group at IETF utilised this opportunity for an overall consolidation and streamlining of the API. Their most recent – and hopefully more or less final – result is RFC3493 [RFC3493]. The new API enables the programmer to write applications for both IPv4 and IPv6 using a single programming framework. In addition, the IPv6 working group defined an API for advanced IPv6 applications using raw sockets [RFC3542] although the vast majority of TCP and UDP based applications will only require the API defined in RFC 3493.

We are going to describe the data structures and function using the formalism of the C language, as they appear in Unix header files. Equivalent APIs are available for most of the common programming languages and we will show some examples at the end of this section.

A detailed explanation of BSD Sockets programming is outside the scope of this section, we will mainly concentrate on the changes introduced by the new API for IPv6. Therefore, we assume the reader has at least a basic idea about the original API, which has been covered, for example, in the classic book "Unix Network Programming" [Ste97]. Other valuable sources of information are the Unix on-line manuals.

11.1.1 Principles of the New API Design

Authors of the new API realised it was not sufficient to treat IPv6 as just another protocol family supported by the socket API. First, since most application and services are common to IPv4 and IPv6, the new API must not break their smooth operation. And second, because of the infamous chicken-and-egg problem (and general laziness of programmers), the amount of work needed for including IPv6 support in applications must be minimal. Therefore, the following goals have been explicitly set for the new API design:

1. All changes must retain binary and source compatibility with existing programs. In other words, on systems with upgraded libraries that include support for the new API, old binary programs work as before. And also, programs written for the old API can be compiled and run unmodified on systems with the new API.
2. The changes in the API must be as small as possible and in line with the traditional socket programming methods.
3. Where possible and appropriate, applications written for the new API should be able to communicate using both IPv6 and IPv4.

Does it mean that with the new API migration of applications to IPv6 becomes a trivial exercise? Unfortunately, not necessarily. Quite a number of applications, including popular ones, employ certain programming techniques and assumptions that make their conversion to IPv6 difficult. For example, they

- work internally with IPv4 addresses (for host identification etc.), or
- expect every network interface to have just a single IP address, or
- assume IP addresses to be 32 bits long.

On the other hand, IPv4 applications that are free of these flaws can usually be converted with minimum effort. In fact, there are even tools doing this automatically.

11.1.2 Data Structures

For IPv6, a new address family has been defined. The corresponding constant can be found in the header file <sys/socket.h> (in Linux it is actually in <bits/socket.h>, which is included from the above header file).

The original API stores IPv4 addresses in the in_addr structure defined as follows:

```
typedef uint32_t in_addr_t;
struct in_addr
  {
    in_addr_t s_addr;
  };
```

In fact, it is nothing more than a wrapper for an unsigned long number. An analogical structure for IPv6 addresses has to use an array, something like

```
struct in6_addr
  {
```

```
    uint8_t s6_addr[16];
  };
```

In reality, looking into the header file <netinet/in.h> we find the definition is more complicated. For efficiency reasons, it uses an union of several variants which can be used to force word alignment for all processor architectures. Normally this is nothing a user of the API should care about.

A more interesting situation is with socket addresses. The main functions of BSD Sockets are universal across all protocol families. The socket addresses as parameters of those functions are in the form of opaque pointers to an abstract structure sockaddr. Consequently, the pointers that are passed as arguments must be properly typecast.

As we know, addresses of the classical IP sockets consist of the pair (IP address, TCP/UDP port). The corresponding structure sockaddr_inis defined as follows:

```
struct sockaddr_in
  {
    unsigned short int sin_family;     /* Address family */
    uint16_t sin_port;                 /* Port number */
    struct in_addr sin_addr;           /* Internet address */
    unsigned char sin_zero[8];         /* Padding */
  };
```

The structure is padded to the size of the abstract structure sockaddr so that there is some space for increasing the address size. However, for IPv6 addresses these eight spare bytes are not enough. IPv6 socket address thus uses a new structure:

```
struct sockaddr_in6
  {
    unsigned short int sin6_family;  /* Address family */
    uint16_t sin6_port;              /* Port number */
    uint32_t sin6_flowinfo;          /* Traffic class and flow info */
    struct in6_addr sin6_addr;       /* IPv6 address */
    uint32_t sin6_scope_id;          /* IPv6 scope-id */
  };
```

Beyond reserving the space for IPv6 addresses, two new members have been added as well:

- sin6_flowinfo contains data from two IPv6 header fields, traffic class and flow label.
- sin6_scope_id specifies network interfaces belonging to the same address scope as the address in sin6_addr.

Needless to say, all multi-byte members of the structures (including the IPv6 address) must be stored in the Network Byte Order (NBO), which is in the context of microprocessor architectures known as big-endian. In order to write portable applications, it is absolutely crucial to use the byte order conversion functions htonl() and htons().

11.1.3 Functions

The BSD Socket API offers three types of functions:

- basic socket management functions
- functions translating domain names to IP addresses and vice versa
- functions that transform different address formats

11.1.3.1 Basic functions

We already said that the basic function for creating sockets and working with them are identical for all supported address families. In a C program, an IPv6/TCP socket can be created in the usual way:

```
s = socket(PF_INET6, SOCK_STREAM);
```

Analogically for UDP:

```
s = socket(PF_INET6, SOCK_DGRAM);
```

To make the long story short, all basic socket functions remain unchanged. Here is an alphabetical list with short descriptions (see the on-line manual pages for details):

bind()

Bind the socket to a local address.

close()

Close the socket.

connect()

Connect to a remote host.

getpeername()

Obtain the address of the remote end.

getsockopt()

Get the socket options.

listen()

Listen on the socket (wait for a connection request).

recv()

Read data from the connected socket. address.

recvfrom()

Read data from a specified source (mainly used with UDP sockets).

send()

Send data to a connected socket.

sendto()

Send data to a specified destination (mainly used with UDP sockets).

setsockopt()

Set socket options.

shutdown()

Terminate the communication in one or both directions.

The bind() function allows to specify the source address for datagrams sent to the socket. In most cases, though, this can be left to the operating system. A common practice for IPv4 is to use bind() in the following way:

```
int s;
struct sockaddr_in hic;
hic.sin_family = AF_INET;
hic.sin_port = 0;
hic.sin_addr.s_addr = INADDR_ANY;
bzero(&(hic.sin_zero), 8);
s = socket(PF_INET, SOCK_STREAM, 0);
bind(s,.(struct sockaddr *)&hic, sizeof(struct sockaddr));
```

The symbolic constant INADDR_ANY signals the operating system to select an appropriate source address, in much the same way as zero port number on the previous line asks for arbitrary free port number.

Due to the fact that in_addr is nothing but a scalar value written in a cryptic way, INADDR_ANY constant can be used in assignment expressions as we just saw in the example. This is no more true for IPv6, since in6_addr type contains an array. For this purpose, the global variable in6addr_any is defined in the header file <netinet/in.h>. It can be used in a similar way as INADDR_ANY

```
hic.sin6_addr.s6_addr = in6addr_any;
```

Another option is to use the symbolic constant IN6ADDR_ANY_INIT, although only in variable initialisation and not in assignment expressions:

```
struct in6_addr anything = IN6ADDR_ANY_INIT;
```

A similar issue arises in the case of the loopback interface whose address can be used as either source or destination address. Again, for IPv4 we have the symbolic constant INADDR_LOOPBACK corresponding to 127.0.0.1, whereas for IPv6 we have to choose one of the two alternatives:

- global variable in6addr_loopback
- symbolic constant IN6ADDR_ANY_INIT useful only for variable initialisation.

11.1.3.2 Name-address translations

Few network applications written for IPv4 can dispense with the use of the Domain Name System (DNS) and, for that matter, function gethostbyname(). In the IPv6 context, though, this function is useless. Every IPv6-enabled host is likely to have, apart from one or more IPv6 addresses, also an IPv4 address and both A and AAAA records may belong to the same domain name. The gethostbyname() function provides no option for specifying which record we are interested in, or whether we want both. In 1999, RFC 2553 [RFC2553] thus came up with new functions for DNS look-ups, namely getipnodebyname and getipnodebyaddr. Unfortunately, they turned out to have other shortcomings (lack of support for address scopes). As a result, in RFC 3493 (which obsoletes RFC 2553) these two functions were deprecated. All in all, we have been left with just one function for DNS look-ups, getaddrinfo(). This function has its origins in the IEEE POSIX standard 1003.1g and is protocol independent. Along with gethostbyname(), it is also a replacement for the getservbyname() function. The prototype looks as follows:

```
int *getaddrinfo(const char *nodename, const char *servname,
        const struct addrinfo *hints, struct addrinfo **res);
```

The function returns either zero, which indicates success, or various error codes. The result of the DNS query is passed to the calling program via the res argument, a pointer to a unidirectional list of structures of the addrinfo type defined in <netdb.h> as

```
struct addrinfo
{
  int ai_flags;                  /* Input flags.  */
  int ai_family;                 /* Protocol family for socket.  */
  int ai_socktype;               /* Socket type.  */
  int ai_protocol;               /* Protocol for socket.  */
  socklen_t ai_addrlen;          /* Length of socket address.  */
  struct sockaddr *ai_addr;      /* Socket address for socket.  */
  char *ai_canonname;            /* Canonical name.  */
  struct addrinfo *ai_next;      /* Pointer to next in list.  */
};
```

The ai_next member points to the next item in the list (the last one has NULL here). Memory must be allocated dynamically for this list and so we have to keep in mind (at least in C) to release this memory when it is no more needed. This is done using the freeaddrinfo() function.

Each structure in the list contains data that can be directly fed as arguments to the socket() function: ai_family (its value is either PF_INET or PF_INET6 in our case), ai_socktype (usually SOCK_STREAM or SOCK_DGRAM) and ai_protocol (usually IPPROTO_TCP or IPPROTO_UDP). The socket address is found in ai_addr, with ai_addrlen specifying its length.

The nodename argument to getaddrinfo() should contain the domain name we want to look up or, alternatively, an IPv4 or IPv6 address in the usual textual notation. Optionally, we can also fill in the servname argument, either with a service name as defined in /etc/services or a string representing a decimal port number.

Through the hints argument we can specify the data we are interested in. Its type is again addrinfo, although only the following members may be filled in: ai_flags, ai_family, ai_socktype and ai_protocol. Other members must contain NULL. In the case you are prepared to accept everything in a certain category, set the values in the hints argument according to the following table:

Table 11-1 Values for the Hints Argument

Criterion	Member	Value
Any address family	`af_family`	`AF_UNSPEC`
Any socket type	`af_socktype`	`0`
Any protocol	`af_protocol`	`0`

If we have no preferences at all, we can pass the NULL as the hints argument.

Even more detailed requirements can be specified in the ai_flags member of the hints argument. As usual, we can combine individual flags using the bitwise OR operation (|). The following flags are available:

AI_PASSIVE

This flag is significant only if NULL has been passed as the nodename argument. By setting this flag we indicate our intention to use the result of getaddrinfo() directly as an argument to the bind() function, i.e., on the local side of the socket. The socket address is then filled with INADDR_ANY for IPv4 and IN6ADDR_ANY_INIT for IPv6. Hence, if we want to use the result of getaddrinfo() for the remote end of the socket, e.g., in the connect() or sendto() functions, this flag should be cleared. In the returned result, the IP address part of the socket address (i.e., sin_addr in sockaddr_in or sin6_addr in sockaddr_in6) will be set to INADDR_LOOPBACK or IN6ADDR_LOOPBACK_INIT, respectively.

AI_CANONNAME

If this flag is set and argument nodename non-NULL, getaddrinfo() will attempt to look up the canonical domain name as well. This may come handy, for example, if you only know the DNS alias and want to learn the "official" name.

AI_NUMERICHOST

If this flag is set, getaddrinfo() will not use DNS at all. In this case, the nodename argument must be a string representing an IPv4 or IPv6 address.

AI_NUMERICSERV

Setting this flag indicates that the servname parameter is to be interpreted as a decimal port number.

AI_V4MAPPED

If this flag is set and ai_family member of the hints argument contains AF_INET6, getaddrinfo() will first check for AAAA records and if none are found, it will return the contents of the A records (if there are any) in the form of IPv4-mapped IPv6 addresses RFC3513 .

AI_ALL

If this flag is set together with AI_V4MAPPED, and hints.ai_family has AF_INET6, then getaddrinfo() will return data from all AAAA and A records, where the latter will again be in the form of IPv4-mapped IPv6 address. If the address family is not specified, i.e., either hints.ai_family is AF_UNSPEC or hints is NULL, the flags AI_V4MAPPED and AI_ALL are taken into the account only if the host operating system supports IPv6.

AI_ADDRCONFIG

By setting this flag we instruct getaddrinfo() to return IPv4 addresses only if the local host has at least one network interface configured with an IPv4 address and, similarly, to return IPv6 addresses only if the local host has at least one interface configured with an IPv6 address. In both cases, loopback addresses do not count.

In a sense, inverse operations to those offered by getaddrinfo() are implemented in the getnameinfo() function:

```
int getnameinfo(const struct sockaddr *sa, socklen_t salen,
                char *node, socklen_t nodelen, char *service,
                socklen_t servicelen, int flags);
```

The main purpose of this function is the translation of data in a socket address into a domain name and/or service name. Its return value is again either zero in the case of success or a corresponding error code.

The sa argument is a pointer to a structure of the sockaddr type. This structure may also contain an IPv6 address with an embedded IPv4 address, that is, either an IPv4-mapped or an IPv4-compatible address. If this is the case, the embedded IPv4 address is extracted and getnameinfo() then continues as if it received a structure with a native IPv4 address.

Function getnameinfo() records its results in buffers pointed to by the arguments node and service. The programmer must take care about allocating memory for these buffers in advance. Their sizes are passed to getnameinfo() via the arguments nodelen and servicelen. It is also possible to set either of the arguments node and service to NULL; getnameinfo() then ignores this argument.

Again, behaviour of getnameinfo can be modified by setting several bit-ORed flags in the last argument:

NI_NOFQDN

If you try to resolve, inside the *sa argument, an IP address to a domain name and this name is in the same domain as the local host, only the host name – without the domain – is returned. Otherwise a fully qualified domain name is returned. For hosts in external domains, this flag has no impact.

NI_NUMERICHOST

With this flag on, getnameinfo() will set *node to a string representing an IP address. To an IPv6 address, a zone identifier may also be appended as described [RFC4007], for example "fe80::1%eth0".

NI_NUMERICSCOPE

If this flag is set together with the previous one, the zone within an address scope will be expressed as a zone index (for example, an interface index) instead of a symbolic zone identifier(e.g., eth0).

NI_NUMERICSERV

Similarly, with this flag on, the *service string will be filled with a decimal port number instead of a symbolic service name, for example "80" instead of "www".

NI_NAMEREQD

If this flag is set and no domain name can be found for the IP address in *sa, getnameinfo will return a non-zero error code, instead of just copying the IP address into *node.

NI_DGRAM

This flag indicates a connectionless service (SOCK_DGRAM). By default, a connection-oriented service (SOCK_DGRAM) is assumed.

11.1.3.3 Address format conversions

When working with IPv4 and IPv6 addresses, one often needs to convert their human-readable textual representation into a binary numeric form and vice versa. The following two functions serve this purpose:

```
int inet_pton(int af, const char *src, void *dst);

const char *inet_ntop(int af, const void *src,
                      char *dst, socklen_t size);
```

The inet_pton function converts the textual representation into binary and inet_ntop the other way around. The binary form always uses the Network Byte Order.

The af argument specifies the address family (AF_INET or AF_INET6) and through the src and dst arguments the functions are given two pointers – src points to the buffer with the input value and dst to the buffer where the result is to be stored. Finally, the size argument of inet_ntop gives the size of the buffer allocated for the result. This buffer should be long enough to store a textual representation of any IPv4 or IPv6 address (depending on the chosen address family).

Function inet_pton returns 1 if the conversion was successful, 0 if the input value is considered wrong and -1 in the case of an unknown address family. In contrast, inet_ntop signals a failure by returning the NULL pointer, whereas if the conversion succeeds, the dst pointer is passed as the function return value, too.

11.1.4 IPv4 Interoperability

Users of IPv6 certainly want too keep the same level of connectivity to the Internet they used to have without IPv6. The application programmer can ensure, by means of the getaddrinfo() and AI_V4MAPPED flag, that a DNS name resolves at least into an A record if no AAAA records are available. An IPv6 application can also initiate the communication with an IPv4 node by using an IPv4-mapped IPv6 address in the sockaddr_in6 structure. The library implementing BSD Sockets API must then translate on the fly between IPv4 and IPv6 so that the IPv4 node receives only IPv4 datagrams and, conversely, translate the IPv4 datagrams coming from the IPv4 node into the IPv4-mapped IPv6 addresses.

As a result, applications utilising IPv6 sockets usually do not have to distinguish between native and IPv4-mapped IPv6 addresses. For those that do, the IN6_IS_ADDR_V4MAPPED macro is defined in <netinet/in.h>.

11.2 Other Programming Languages

In the previous section we described the BSD Sockets API using the syntax of the C programming language. However, the API is by no means limited to C, and most modern languages implement it as well. In fact, many of them make socket programming considerably easier. In the following subsections we demonstrate it on two popular interpreted languages – Python and Perl.

11.2.1 Python

Python implements the BSD Sockets API in the socket module in its basic system library. Python adds an object-oriented interface that makes the API particularly easy to use. Otherwise, the implementation follows RFC 3493 pretty closely. The module also defines all the constants specified in RFC 3493 like AF_INET or AI_V4MAPPED. Documentation is available online as a part of the Python Library Reference [Pyth-Lib].

As in C, sockets are created using the socket() function, which returns a socket object. Following the object-oriented paradigm, all other socket functions are implemented as methods and applied to the socket object via messages. This will be demonstrated in the example below.

Python implementation also uses a simpler form of socket addresses.:

- IPv4 sockets are represented as a pair (address, port)
- IPv6 sockets are represented as a four-tuple (address, port, flowinfo, scopeid), where flowinfo and scopeid correspond to the sin6_flowinfo and sin6_scope_id members of the sockaddr_in6 structure.

Finally, the handling of error conditions was integrated into the Python system of exceptions. Instead of signalling a failure by returning an error code, as in C, Python functions raise an exception that the application can handle in a specific way.

The following example consists of two simple programs that demonstrate the Python way of using the BSD Sockets API. They should work with Python version 2.2.1 or higher. The programs realise connectionless communication using IPv6 and UDP. Both programs first execute the getaddrinfo() function to obtain the socket address and create the socket. The sender application then periodically sends a short message to a named peer using the sendto() function. The receiver binds the socket address to the socket and thus starts listening on the predefined port 54321, and then enters an infinite loop waiting for the data and printing them on the terminal.

A usual disclaimer applies here: real-life programs should also care about possible errors and define appropriate exception handlers. Also, a more graceful termination might be recommended – our programs must be abruptly terminated by pressing Ctrl-C.

11.2.1.1 Sender

```
from socket import *
import time

peer = "www.cesnet.cz"
port = 54321
af,styp,proto,cn,sa = getaddrinfo(peer, port,
                                  AF_INET6, SOCK_DGRAM)[0]
s = socket(af,styp,proto)
while 1:
    s.sendto("IPv6 rocks!", sa)
    time.sleep(1)
```

11.2.1.2 Receiver

```
from socket import *
import time

maxlen = 512
port = 54321
af,styp,proto,cn,sa = getaddrinfo(None, port,
                                  AF_INET6, SOCK_DGRAM,
                                  0, AI_PASSIVE)[0]
s = socket(af,styp,proto)
s.bind(sa)
while 1:
    recv = s.recvfrom(maxlen)
    print "Node", recv[1][0], "said:", recv[0]
```

11.2.2 Java

At the time of writing, we have the possibility to work with two levels of Java, the official 1.4 and the next generation 1.5, provided as beta. These two JDKs allow working with IPv6. The level of IPv6 implementation in the JDK 1.5 is better.

11.2.2.1 JDK 1.4

With the J2SDK/JRE 1.4 release, IPv6 support has been added to Java Networking. This will make J2SE compliant with the following specifications (RFCs):

- RFC 2373 IPv6 Addressing Architecture
- RFC 2553 Basic Socket Interface Extensions for IPv6
- RFC 2732 Format for Literal IPv6 Addresses in URLs.

Since the J2SDK does not support raw sockets, RFC 2292 (Advanced Sockets API for IPv6) is not supported in this release.

Other interesting features of IPv6, such as tunnelling, auto configuration of addresses, Mobile IPv6, etc., are not supported at the Java API level, as they are handled automatically by the underlying OS or system support.

On systems with a dual stack, system properties are provided for selecting the preferred IP stack.

By default, the IPv6 stack is preferred because the IPv6 Socket can work with IPv4 and IPv6 peers on a dual stack system.

All the methods for programming TCP/IP applications are localized in the `java.net` package. In this package, the class `InetAdress` has been modified to support both IPv4 and IPv6 addresses.

Two new classes appears, `Inet4Address` and `Inet6Address`, each class inherits from `InetAdress` and implements the specific behavior of its protocol version. As Java is an object oriented language, an application need to deals with the `InetAddress` class. With the polymorphism, it will get the correct behaviour. New methods are introduced to be able to exploit the nature of IPv6 addresses.

Due to object oriented nature of Java, the socket classes work for both IPv4 and IPv6 addresses. In fact, the classes manipulate an `InetAddress`. The socket API can handle both IPv4 and IPv6 traffic.

The selection of IP stack depends to OS where the application run and the user's stack preference setting. To provide the same support on IPv4 as IPv6, the old socket API has been overloaded to support the two protocols options.

11.2.2.2 JDK 1.5

The JDK 1.5 increases the support of IPv6. It keeps all the functionalities introduced with the JDK 1.4 and provides some new features.

Arguably, the major enhancement resides in the introduction in the socket API of the method `setPerformancePreference`. This method allows the application to express its own preferences to tune the performance characteristics of this socket. Performance preferences are described by three integers whose values indicate the relative importance of short connection time, low latency, and high bandwidth. With this method, the network oriented notion of Quality of Service (QoS) is introduced. Any application can set its preferences to adapt its network traffic and provide the best QoS.

PART II

Case Studies

Chapter 12

IPv6 in the Backbone

In this chapter we present case studies of IPv6 in the backbone. First we look at the core 6NET backbone and the NRENs that were connected to it before the core network was decommissioned in January 2005.

Next, we detail case studies of IPv6 deployment by the NRENs themselves inside their own country backbone networks. The most common method to introduce IPv6 services into IPv4 networks will be through dual-stack networking. This complements the backbone transition and pushes the issue of deployment to the edge, e.g. to the universities.

In the timeframe of 6NET, many NRENs migrated to dual stack; the specific experiences of SURFnet, Funet and Renater are reported here.

12.1 6NET Backbone Case Study

A backbone IPv6 network connecting sixteen countries and running at 155 Mbps was established in 2002. This ran IPv6 over dedicated links, although for cost reasons, four links (to Greece, Hungary, Poland and Portugal) were provided by POS (Packet-over-SONET/SDH) over a Layer 2 VPN infrastructure.

Local access was provided through national IPv6 testbeds operated by partner NRENs (National Research and Education Networks) such as JANET (UK), RENATER (France) and SWITCH (Switzerland). Connectivity to the non-European 6NET partners in Japan and South Korea was provided via connections to London and RENATER respectively, and there are were connections to Abilene in the US (via SURFnet), Euro6IX (via the JANET- UK6X, GARR-TILab and SWITCH-Swisscom exchange points) and to the 6Bone.

The 6NET backbone, and interconnected national testbeds, collectively formed the largest native IPv6 network in the world. This provided plenty of scope for trialling the new technology, testing interoperability with existing networks, and demonstrating services and applications. In fact, it demonstrated that the IS-IS and BGP4+ routing protocols, IPv6 over IPv4 tunnelling, and DNS support were stable and usable. In addition, a multicast overlay network (M6Bone) was established and has been utilised for conferencing and radio broadcasting (e.g., Trondheim Underground Radio).

12.1.1 Network Topology

This section explains the topology of the network, Figure 12-1 presents the topology as it was in February 2003 for the 6NET core and NREN PoPs.

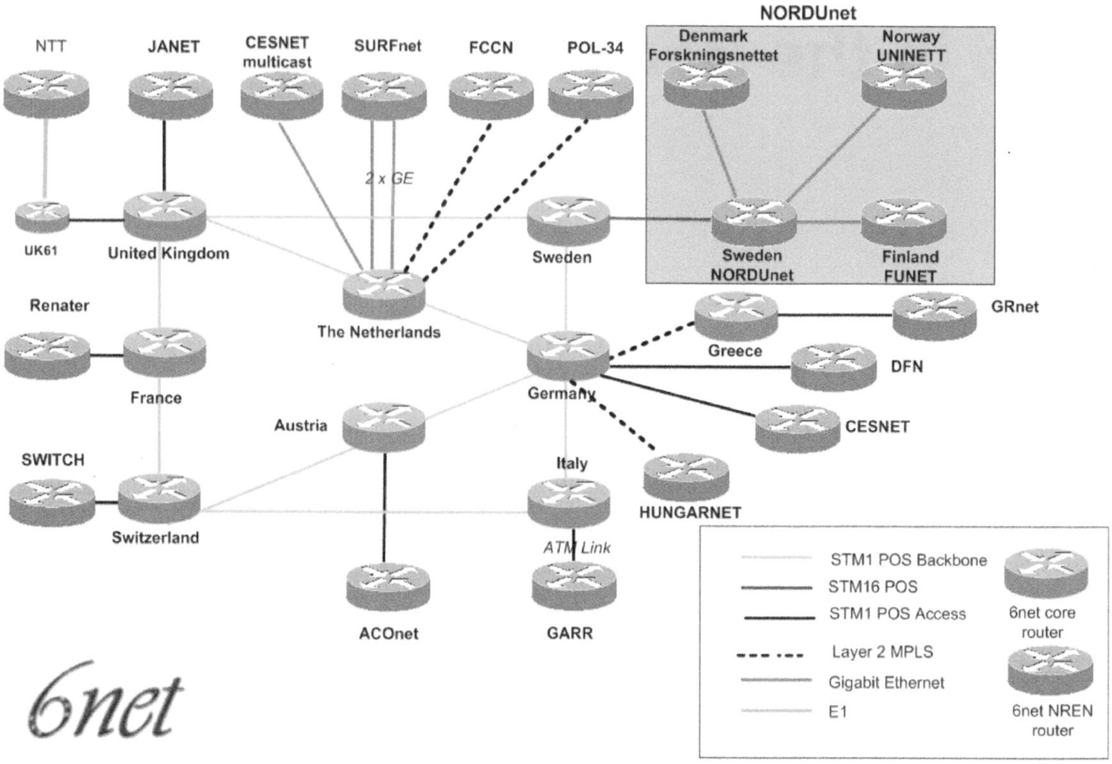

Figure 12-1 The 6NET Core and NREN PoPs

The 6NET network consisted of a set of international POS STM1/OC3 backbone circuits and a set of access circuits which mostly were native connections plus some tunnelled connections to 6NET partners. The 6NET core is represented by orange routers whilst blue routers represents the access routers of the NRENs.

In total, there were 16 partners directly connected to the 6NET core. POL34 was connected via a manual IPv4-to-IPv6 tunnel to the Swedish router. It also had a backup manual tunnel connection to the German Router. GRnet was connected to 6NET via a CCC/MPLS connection to the German router.

Previously, manual IPv4-to-IPv6 tunnels were configured for connecting HUNGARNET and CESNET. From January 2003 they were changed to STM1/OC3-155Mbps native connections. The rest of the access links were STM1/OC3-155Mbps, except NORDUnet with STM16/OC48-2.5Gbps, SURFnet with a 2xGE (2x1Gbps) access links and NTT with an E1 link to the UK router (2Mbps).

12.1.2 Addressing Scheme

Each NRENs used their IPv6 subTLA allocation. DANTE obtained an IPv6 subTLA for the pan-European IPv6 research backbone - divided into 6NET and GÉANT and other IPv6 purposes.

The IPv6 subTLA assigned to Dante is 2001:0798::/35. From this IPv6 address space a sub-section was used for 6NET. The allocated 6NET address space was ‘2001:0798::/40’.

The 6NET available address space '2001:0798:0::/40' was divided into logical sub portions to facilitate future expansions and enable simpler summarisation rules when required.

The address range can be seen as:

Table 12-1 6NET Prefix

35 bits	5 bits	8 bits	16 bits
DANTE subTLA	project	PoPs	SLA

/35 /40 /48 /64

For 6NET, the 5 bit <project> part consists of all zeroes. Other <project> allocations will be made by DANTE.

To summarize, the assigned IPv6 address consists of the following parts:

Structure = <xyz>.<PoP>.<SLA>

Where:

<xyz> = <40 bit provider prefix> = 2001:0798::/40

<PoP> = assigned address range per PoP

<SLA> = segmentation of use within the PoP

SLA =Site Level Aggregate

12.1.2.1 PoP Addressing

The 6NET locations that had a 6NET core router got their own prefixes. The 8 bits for the PoP part are used as follows:

00. core links
01. reserved core links

...

10. AT
11. BE
12. CH
13. CZ
14. DE
15. ES
16. FR
17. GR
18. HU
19. IE
20. IT
21. LU

22. NL
23. PL
24. PT
25. SE/NORDUNET
26. SI
27. SK
28. UK

Note: The start of the country PoP areas started at 10 for visual reasons when reading the IPv6 prefix addresses. The hexadecimal addresses A-F were not used. This gave the following prefixes for the PoPs:

Table 12-2 PoP Addressing

PoP Location	IPv6 PoP addressing: 2001:0798:<PoP>::/48
Core	2001:0798:00::/48
Sweden	2001:0798:25::/48
Netherlands	2001:0798:22::/48
Germany	2001:0798:14::/48
Austria	2001:0798:10::/48
Italy	2001:0798:20::/48
Switzerland	2001:0798:12::/48
France	2001:0798:16::/48
UK	2001:0798:28::/48
Greece	2001:0798:17::/48

The only 'special' address range, which is not really bound to a geographical location, is the 'core' address range. This address range is used for the connections between PoPs.

The SLA (Site Level Aggregate) is used for various prefixes, (mostly) within a PoP:

Table 12-3 SLA Usage

Range	Use
0000 - 00FF	Loopback addresses
0100 - 01FF	Intra-PoP point-to-points
0200 - 02FF	connections to NREN PoPs
0300 - 03FF	external 6NET connectivity
0400 - 04FF	PoP LANs

Note: Using this convention there is room for 256 prefixes with /64 address space for each point-to-point link or broadcast media.

The prefix length selected for point-to-point connections was /64. A /64 was chosen because it seems to be the best current practice. It makes the number plan easy because every interface gets a /64. There is no need for a /126, /127 or /128 because address conservation is not a deciding factor with IPv6.

The potential future use of a /127 address space (or other address space) which initially seems to use only minimal address range will not work in the long run. More study material can be found in RFC 3627 [RFC3627].

It is also possible to use /128 on point-to-point links. The drawback here is that in Cisco IOS you need to add a static route to the remote side.

For Switzerland with <PoP>=12 this would give the following prefixes:

Table 12-4 Switzerland Prefixes

Use	Prefix
Loopback addresses:	2001:0798:0012:0000::/56
Intra-PoP Point-to-points:	2001:0798:0012:0100::/56
Connections to NREN PoP:	2001:0798:0012:0200::/56
External 6NET connection:	2001:0798:0012:0300::/56
PoP LANs:	2001:0798:0012:0400::/56

12.1.2.2 Loopback Addresses

In networking environments, it is seen as good practice to give each device an IPv6 loopback address. This is an IPv6 address that is not directly assigned to any physical interface and will typically be reachable when the networking appliance (in this case a router) is up and running.

This loopback address is also used for operational and management actions on the equipment and for routing protocols like eBGP, which use these addresses for terminating the peering sessions.

Loopback addresses typically have a prefix mask of /128. This avoids unnecessary unused addresses although address conservation is not really an issue in IPv6.

In the initial 6NET core network, the 6NET PoP routers were the only pieces of equipment that needed a loopback address. Below is a list which details the addresses used.

The <SLA> for the loopback addresses is '0000'.

Table 12-5 Loopback Addresses

6NET PoP location	6NET PoP address space 2001:0798:<PoP>:<SLA= 0>::/64	IPv6 loopback address
Sweden	2001:0798:25::/64	2001:0798:25::1/128
Netherlands	2001:0798:22::/64	2001:0798:22::1/128
Germany	2001:0798:14::/64	2001:0798:14::1/128
Austria	2001:0798:10::/64	2001:0798:10::1/128
Italy	2001:0798:20::/64	2001:0798:20::1/128
Switzerland	2001:0798:12::/64	2001:0798:12::1/128
France	2001:0798:16::/64	2001:0798:16::1/128
United Kingdom	2001:0798:28::/64	2001:0798:28::1/128
Greece	2001:0798:17::/64	2001:0798:17::1/128

12.1.2.3 Point-to-Point Addressing

Intra-PoP Point-to-Point Links

Intra-PoP point-to-point links were numbered from the PoP prefix with a <SLA> = '01xx', where 'xx' is a sequence number. This allowed for 256 point-to-point links per PoP with a /64 prefix.

An example of intra-PoP point-to-point prefixes which have a <SLA>=01xx for the Germany PoP with <PoP>=14 would be:

2001:0798:0014:0100::/64

2001:0798:0014:0101::/64

2001:0798:0014:0102::/64

2001:0798:0014:0103::/64

6NET PoP to NREN PoP Point-to-Point Links

The 6NET core routers were connected to the NREN routers as previously described. A special address range was selected for this type of point-to-point connectivity:

2001:0798:<PoP>:<SLA=02xx>::/56, where 'xx' is a sequence number.

The addresses utilised on the point-to-point links between the 6NET core and the NREN PoP had a prefix-length /64. Initially there was only one NREN PoP router attached to a 6NET PoP router.

The host part of the address was '::1' for the 6NET core PoP side, and '::2' for the NREN PoP side.

Table 12-6 6NET PoP to NREN PoP Point-toPoint-Links

6NET PoP location	6NET PoP address space	1st Point-to-Point prefix 2001:0798:<PoP>:<SLA=0200>::/64
Sweden	2001:0798:0025:0200::/56	2001:0798:0025:0200::/64
Netherlands	2001:0798:0022:0200::/56	2001:0798:0022:0200::/64
Germany	2001:0798:0014:0200::/56	2001:0798:0014:0200::/64
Austria	2001:0798:0010:0200::/56	2001:0798:0010:0200::/64
Italy	2001:0798:0020:0200::/56	2001:0798:0020:0200::/64
Switzerland	2001:0798:0012:0200::/56	2001:0798:0012:0200::/64
France	2001:0798:0016:0200::/56	2001:0798:0016:0200::/64
United Kingdom	2001:0798:0028:0200::/56	2001:0798:0028:0200::/64
Greece	2001:0798:0017:0200::/56	2001:0798:0017:0200::/64

Inter-PoP point-to-point links were numbered from the Core prefix (2001:0798:00::/48) with a <SLA> = '00xx' , where 'xx' is a sequence number. For the initial rollout of 6NET, this resulted in the following table:

Table 12-7 Point-to-point links between 6NET PoPs

Connectivity Between	IPv6 prefix	IPv6 address side (1)	IPv6 address side (2)
UK (1) - FR (2)	2001:0798:0:1::/64	2001:0798:0:1::1/64	2001:0798:0:1::2/64
FR (1) - CH (2)	2001:0798:0:2::/64	2001:0798:0:2::1/64	2001:0798:0:2::2/64
CH (1) - IT (2)	2001:0798:0:3::/64	2001:0798:0:3::1/64	2001:0798:0:4::2/64
IT (1) - DE (2)	2001:0798:0:4::/64	2001:0798:0:4::1/64	2001:0798:0:4::2/64
DE (1) - NL (2)	2001:0798:0:5::/64	2001:0798:0:5::1/64	2001:0798:0:5::2/64
NL (1) - UK (2)	2001:0798:0:6::/64	2001:0798:0:6::1/64	2001:0798:0:6::2/64
UK (1) - SE (2)	2001:0798:0:7::/64	2001:0798:0:7::1/64	2001:0798:0:7::2/64
SE (1) - DE (2)	2001:0798:0:8::/64	2001:0798:0:8::1/64	2001:0798:0:8::2/64
DE (1) - AT (2)	2001:0798:0:9::/64	2001:0798:0:9::1/64	2001:0798:0:9::2/64
AT (1) - CH (2)	2001:0798:0:a::/64	2001:0798:0:a::1/64	2001:0798:0:a::2/64
DE (1) - GR (2)	2001:0798:0:b::/64	2001:0798:0:b::1/64	2001:0798:0:b::2/64

12.1.3 Naming Scheme

<cc>.6net.org

The domain name chosen for the 6NET backbone network was short and easy to remember. It was applied to all equipment that was considered part of the native 6NET core environment.

12.1.3.1 PoP Naming Convention

Every PoP had its own subdomain within 6NET. The subdomain name corresponded to the top level domain name of the country where the PoP was located. The following names were defined domains:

at – Austria

be – Belgium

ch – Switzerland

cz – Czech Republic

de – Germany

es – Spain

fr – France

gr – Greece

hu – Hungary

ie – Ireland

it – Italy

lu – Luxemburg

nl – The Netherlands

pl – Poland

pt – Portugal

se – Sweden

si – Slovenia

sk – Slovakia

uk – United Kingdom

All domain names in the 6NET backbone belonged to equipment located in the above PoPs, thus all the names had a suffix from the list and were prepended to the common suffix '6net.org'.

12.1.3.2 Router Naming Convention

The Router name was comprised of the 'domain name', the 'PoP name' and a sequential ordinal number. The equipment ordinal numbers started with 6. The possible extra routers would be called uk61, uk62 and so on.

Example:

The 6NET core router in the United Kingdom: <uk6.uk.6net.org>

12.1.3.3 Interface Naming Convention

Every IP interface (either physical, virtual or ATM-subinterface) had its own name, with the suffix corresponding to the equipment the interface belonged to, and a distinguished name describing the interface. The interface ordinal numbers corresponded to the ones in the equipment configuration and usually started with 0.

Overview:

Loopback (2 or more):	lo0 and lo1
Fast-Ethernet in some VLANs (1 or 2):	fe0, fe1
Giga-Ethernet in some VLANs:	ge0

POS or ATM interfaces for connections to other pops, called by the PoP name on the opposite side of the network link: the interface in the UK router connecting to the FR PoP is called fr.uk6.uk.net.sixnet.org.

Example:

Loopback interface on the United Kingdom router: <lo0.uk6.uk.6net.org>

12.1.3.4 Equipment Naming

The naming convention as seen above needs to be applied to the initial equipment utilised within 6NET. The application of the convention provides the following initial equipment names:

Core PoP routers:

Sweden:	se6.se.6net.org
The Netherlands:	nl6.nl.6net.org
Germany:	de6.de.6net.org
Austria:	at6.at.6net.org
Italy:	it6.it.6net.org
Switzerland:	ch6.ch.6net.org
France:	fr6.fr.6net.org
UK:	uk6.uk.6net.org
Greece:	gr6.gr.6net.org

12.1.3.5 Interface Naming

Each interface as seen in the naming convention had its own name.

Example: For the Austria 6NET core router

Fast Ethernet:	fe0 fe0.at6.at.6net.org
Gig Ethernet:	ge0 ge0.at6.at.6net.org
Loopback:	lo0 lo0.at6.at.6net.org
POS from Austria to Germany:	de.at6.at.6net.org

12.1.4 DNS

The DNS for the 6NET core network was operated by DANTE serving the following zones:

Forward zones:

- se.6net.org
- nl.6net.org
- de.6net.org
- at.6net.org
- it.6net.org
- ch.6net.org
- fr.6net.org
- uk.6net.org
- gr.6net.org

Reverse zones:

- 0.8.9.7.0.1.0.0.2.ip6.int
- 1.8.9.7.0.1.0.0.2.ip6.int
- 0.8.9.7.0.1.0.0.2.ip6.arpa
- 1.8.9.7.0.1.0.0.2.ip6.arpa

For the core network SWITCH and SURFnet are operated the slave DNS servers. SURFnet operated the central DNS server for the 6net.org zone.

12.1.5 IGP Routing

The options available for an IGP routing protocol within 6NET were: static routing, RIPv6 or IS-IS. The option 'static routing' would have very difficult to manage in practice, and would not have been very scalable. The dynamic routing options available were 'RIPv6' and 'IS-IS'.

RIPv6 is a distance vector routing protocol while 'IS-IS' is a link-state protocol. Although a distance vector routing protocol is easier to troubleshoot and the operation simpler to understand, it was preferred to utilise a link-state protocol due to its advantages in convergence, tuning and additional features (like opaque information, enhanced TLV (Type/Length, Value) information for Traffic Engineering, etc.).

Integrated IS-IS was used only to distribute the core router reachability. For everything else BGP4+ was used. No route exchange was used between IGP and EGP.

The 6NET ISIS topology is depicted in Figure 12-2.

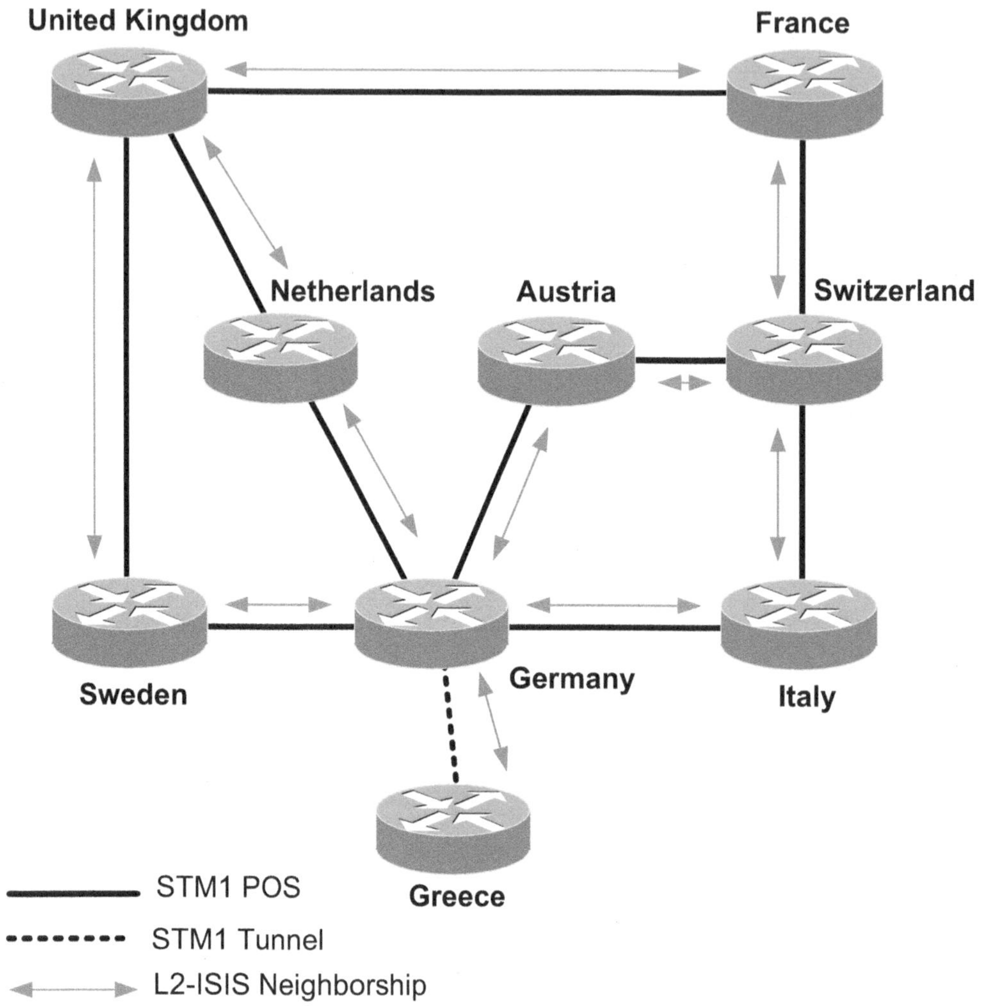

Figure 12-2 6NET IS-IS Topology

12.1.5.1 IS-IS structure

The hierarchical structure of ISIS enabled us to utilise two different levels of routing, allowing the routing protocol to scale through summarisation. The 6NET Core backbone initially consisted of a relatively small amount of routers and prefixes therefore, within 6NET a pure Level-2 routing domain was implemented with single area.

12.1.5.2 IS-IS authentication

Within the IS-IS routing protocol there are three basic password authentication mechanisms possible. The only authentication used was a password to authenticate the IIH packets for preventing accidentally forming wrong IS-IS adjacency.

12.1.5.3 IS-IS interface metrics

In order for a routing protocol to decide the best path from a one network to another it is important to assign a cost or metric to each interface. Typically, the metric is a direct correlation between value and the speed of the link. Other correlation can be delay, reliability, etc. Primarily, the link speed was used for the 6NET core according to the following table:

Table 12-8 Link Speed IS-IS Metric

Link Speed (Mbps)	IS-IS Metric
1	10000
10	1000
100	500
155	400
1000	300
2500	200
10000	100

12.1.5.4 Passive Interfaces

When a router interface is placed in the routing process it will send out IS-IS Hello packets in order to form an IS-IS neighbourship with peering IS-IS routers over that interface.

There are instances where it is desirable to include an interface in the IS-IS routing process to distribute the IPv6 prefix among the Level-2 area, but to never form an adjacency over that interface. To disable the sending of IIH packets the interface can be made passive with the command <passive-interface> under the IS-IS routing process. It is recommended to do this on stub LAN network interfaces.

In 6NET, all loopback interfaces and interfaces connecting to the NREN PoP routers and LAN stub interfaces were made passive.

12.1.5.5 6NET CLNS Addresses

The 6NET Core consisted of 9 routers that formed the International-backbone.

The following CLNS addresses were placed on the 9 routers:

Table 12-9 CLNS Addresses

Country	<domain>	<System ID>	<NSEL>
Sweden	49.0001	0025.0000.0001	00
Netherlands	49.0001	0022.0000.0001	00
Germany	49.0001	0014.0000.0001	00
Austria	49.0001	0010.0000.0001	00
Italy	49.0001	0020.0000.0001	00
Switzerland	49.0001	0012.0000.0001	00
France	49.0001	0016.0000.0001	00
United Kingdom	49.0001	0028.0000.0001	00
Greece	49.0001	0017.0000.0001	00

12.1.6 EGP Routing

At the time of deployment, BGP4+ was the only EGP supported for IPv6 when using Cisco IOS therefore the EGP used in 6NET was BGP4+.

12.1.6.1 Router-ID

When starting up a BGP process in an IPv6 only environment it is required to define a router-id on the BGP4+ router. The router-id has the same format as an IPv4 IP address.

For the 6NET environment the BGP router-id was identical to the initial IPv4 address placed on the Ethernet port for the initial management of the equipment.

12.1.6.2 eBGP

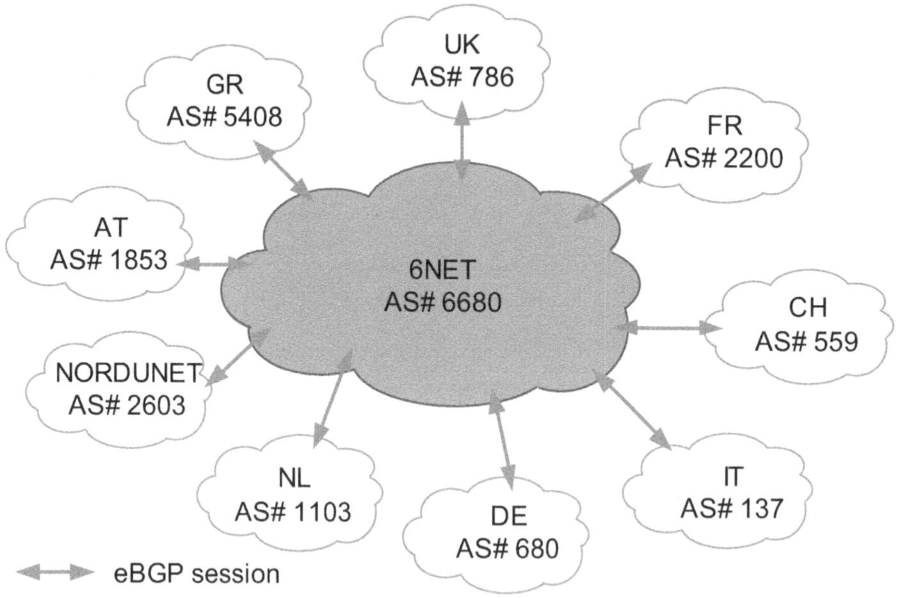

Figure 12-3 BGP peering with 6NET participants

BGP4+ was used between 6NET core and participant NRENs, 6NET and other organisations. Each NREN used their AS numbers. The 6NET core had a separate AS number from GÉANT as can be seen in Figure 12-3:

Neighbours with the same update policies can be grouped into peer groups to simplify configuration and to make updating more efficient.

Two initial peer groups were defined:

- Peer group for peerings between 6NET core PoP and NREN PoP:
  - 6NET_EXTERNAL_NREN_PEER
- Peer group for peerings between 6NET core PoPs:
  - 6NET_INTERNAL_6NET_PEER

12.1.6.3 iBGP

No Route-reflector was used due to the relatively small number of core routers. Instead full mesh BGP peering was configured inside the core. BGP peerings were secured with TCP MD5 authentication from the beginning to prevent the wrong peering by accident.

The external peers were grouped together to have same routing policy internally, with the groupname: 6NET_INTERNAL_NREN_PEER

The Next-hop-self functionality was not used in the 6NET rollout. The initial next-hop attribute checking of the NLRI was based on the IPv6 address from the NREN to which 6NET was peering.

12.1.6.4 BGP filtering

The complete 6NET IPv6 address range could be aggregated to '2001:0798::/40'. However, due to the aggressive filtering policies on the IPv6 Internet (see RFC 2772 [RFC2772]), initially the address range was aggregated to '2001:0798::/35'. To do this type of aggregation in a controllable way, some NLRI filtering was required. To enable the aggregation, 3 basic steps were required:

1. Configure static IPv6 route for '2001:0798::/35' to the null0 interface
2. Redistribute the static summary route to the IPv6 BGP table (this required NLRI filtering in order to redistribute only the summary prefix)
3. Use BGP NLRI filtering to the iBGP peers to exclude the summary prefix from being exchanged.

12.2 *SURFnet Case Study (Netherlands)*

SURFnet is the national computer network for higher education and research in the Netherlands. SURFnet connects the networks of universities, colleges, research centres, academic hospitals and scientific libraries to one another and to other networks in Europe and the rest of the world. The SURFnet network enables its users to communicate with other network users and to consult the Internet from their office or their home PC.

In the summer of 2001 the national research infrastructure of SURFnet, called SURFnet5, was constructed as part of the GigaPort project and in partnership with BT Nederland and Cisco Systems. After a public procurement process these partners were awarded a six year contract at the very end of 1999, with BT Nederland supplying the infrastructure and Cisco Systems providing the router equipment.

The building of the successor to SURFnet5, called SURFnet6, started at the end of 2004 and is performed in partnership with Nortel, Avici Systems, and Telindus. SURFnet6 will be a hybrid optical and packet switching infrastructure delivering IPv4, IPv6, and lambda services to SURFnet's constituency. The IPv6 implementation for unicast and multicast on SURFnet6 will be native and truly dual-stack, i.e. not using MPLS.

12.2.1 The SURFnet5 Dual Stack network

The SURFnet5 network consists of a core that is situated at two locations in Amsterdam, at the Points of Presence (PoPs) called "Amsterdam1"[1] and "Amsterdam2"[2]. Two Cisco 12416 routers are installed at each location implementing the core functionality. Fifteen concentrator PoPs are each connected to both core locations over two separate unprotected SONET/SDH framed lambdas running at 10 Gbit/s. The engineering of the lambdas is such that it ensures that one connection is always maintained in case of a single transmission or core router failure. At each of the fifteen PoPs a router of type Cisco 124xx is installed together with a Cisco 7507 router for the low speed, legacy connections at speeds up to 155 Mbit/s. The backbone of SURFnet5 makes use of IP-over-DWDM, using POS framing. BT owns and operates the DWDM transmission infrastructure. Figure 12-4 shows the logical topology of SURFnet5.

From the start of SURFnet5 all routers running Cisco's IOS have IPv6 implemented. During the early days of the network, IOS versions in the 12.0ST train were used in the GSR routers. During 2002 the transition to 12.0S was made. The current version, in March 2004, in the GSR routers is "IOS Version 12.0(26)S1" and in the 7500 routers is "IOS Version 12.2(14)S2".

SURFnet5 started as a dual-stack network and has been running as such until March 2004. During March 2004 IPv6 routing within the core of the network was migrated from dual-stack to 6PE. The reason for this migration was to achieve line rate IPv6 forwarding in the SURFnet5 network. SURFnet5 is a 10 Gbit/s network largely build on Engine4 line cards and these cards handle IPv4 on the fast path while IPv6 is handled by the processor of the line card. After a large replacement in 2003 of Engine2 line cards with Engine3 line cards, the edges of SURFnet5 became capable of handling IPv6 traffic at line rate. By implementing 6PE in the core of the network it was ensured that IPv6 traffic was also handled at line rate in the core and potential bottlenecks were removed.

[1] This PoP is located at SARA in the eastern part of Amsterdam.

[2] This PoP is located at Hempoint, a BT Nederland co-lo facility, in the western part of Amsterdam.

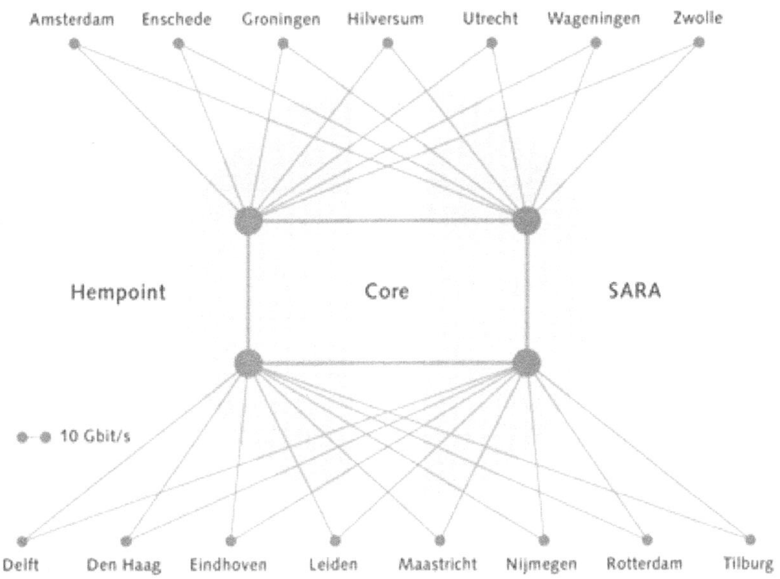

Figure 12-4 Logical topology for SURFnet5

The routing setup as implemented and running today runs without problems. A number of features are on SURFnet's requirements list, of which IPv6 multicast is high on the list. SURFnet already has hands-on experience with IPv6 multicast in the 6NET context using external MBGP for IPv6.

12.2.2 Customer Connections

Today, the vast majority of SURFnet's customer connections are at 1 Gbit/s using Ethernet technology. Three customers are connected at 10GE, connected to line cards in the backbone that do not support IPv6 at wire speed. In SURFnet6, the number of connected organizations using 10GE is expected to rapidly increase. Wire speed 10 Gbit/s IPv6 will be one of the features implemented in SURFnet6.

SURFnet5 supports customer connections on IPv4 as well as IPv6. For IPv4 unicast and multicast are supported, while for IPv6 this is currently unicast only. IPv6 can be delivered towards SURFnet's 180 customers in the field of research and higher education using either a native or tunnelled approach.

Native IPv6 connections are implemented either "dual stack" or "on a dedicated port". Dual stack implies that the customer connection runs IPv4 as well as IPv6 on the same local loop. A few customers, however, prefer IPv6 on a dedicated port, next to their IPv4 port for the simple reason that they have a dedicated router for IPv6 on their LAN.

Tunnelled connections to customers are only allowed in case the customer is not able to implement IPv6 in dual stack mode or on a dedicated port. In case we implement a tunnel connection with a customer, we always ask the customer to make plans for going native.

12.2.3 Addressing plan

SURFnet received an official IPv6 prefix from the RIPE NCC in August 1999 of length /35, which was enlarged to a /32 during the summer of 2002:

2001:0610::/32[1]

[1] For registration details on this prefix, see: http://www.ripe.net/cgi-bin/whois?2001:0610::/32.

This prefix is split up as follows:

Table 12-10 SURFnet Prefix

3 bits	13 bits	16 bits	3 bits	5 bits	8 bits
FP	TLA	sub-TLA	slow start	PoP (NLA 1)	site (NLA2)
/3	/16	/29	/35	/40	/48

Only the first /35 is currently used. The other 7 /35s are for future use right now. For each PoP a /40 prefix (NLA 1) is reserved and each /40 is again split into 256 /48 prefixes (NLA 2) to number the backbone links and customer networks. The breakdown of SURFnet's prefix on a per-PoP basis is shown in detail below.

The prefix 2001:0610::/40 is in use as the carrier network for SURFnet5, in which all links reside. For the links SURFnet uses /64 prefixes, in the format:

2001:0610:00xx:xyyy::zzz

In this format, xxx denotes the third octet of the link's or LAN's IPv4 prefix and yyy denotes the fourth octet of the link's or LAN's IPv4 prefix. The zzz denotes the actual address. An example of this is shown below in Table 12-11.

Table 12-11 SURFnet prefixes per POP

Prefix	NLA 1	PoP
2001:0610:0000::/40	0	(not used yet)
2001:0610:0100::/40	1	Amsterdam1
2001:0610:0200::/40	2	Amsterdam2
2001:0610:0300::/40	3	Hilversum
2001:0610:0400::/40	4	Leiden1
2001:0610:0500::/40	5	Utrecht
2001:0610:0600::/40	6	Chicago, USA
2001:0610:0700::/40	7	(not used yet)
2001:0610:0800::/40	8	(not used yet)
2001:0610:0900::/40	9	Delft
2001:0610:0A00::/40	10	(not used yet)
2001:0610:0B00::/40	11	Den Haag
2001:0610:0C00::/40	12	Rotterdam
2001:0610:0D00::/40	13	(not used yet)
2001:0610:0E00::/40	14	(not used yet)
2001:0610:0F00::/40	15	(not used yet)
2001:0610:1000::/40	16	(not used yet)

Prefix	NLA 1	PoP
2001:0610:1100::/40	17	Eindhoven
2001:0610:1200::/40	28	Maastricht
2001:0610:1300::/40	19	Nijmegen
2001:0610:1400::/40	20	Tilburg
2001:0610:1500::/40	21	(not used yet)
2001:0610:1600::/40	22	(not used yet)
2001:0610:1700::/40	23	(not used yet)
2001:0610:1800::/40	24	(not used yet)
2001:0610:1900::/40	25	Enschede
2001:0610:1A00::/40	26	Groningen
2001:0610:1B00::/40	27	(not used yet)
2001:0610:1C00::/40	28	(not used yet)
2001:0610:1D00::/40	29	Wageningen
2001:0610:1E00::/40	30	Zolle
2001:0610:1F00::/40	31	(not used yet)

12.2.4 Routing

During the build-up of SURFnet5, in the summer of 2001, IS-IS was used for IPv4 and IPv6. Since the transmission of SURFnet5, the 10G lambdas, is unprotected we used MPLS Traffic Engineering's extension Fast Re-Route as the protocol to protect the network against failures by making available an alternative path well within the 50 msec time frame. However, MPLS-TE was only supporting IPv4, yielding a situation in which the IPv4 topology was different from the IPv6 topology. At that time, IS-IS was not able to handle different topologies for the two protocols, and we had to move away from IS-IS for IPv6. We temporarily transitioned to RIPng for IPv6, while we stayed at IS-IS in combination with MPLS-TE FRR for IPv4.

In the mean time Cisco developed multi topology IS-IS, which enabled SURFnet to move away from RIPng back to the original plan. Before we went back to IS-IS for IPv6, we decided to abandon the MPLS-TE FRR ship for network management reasons, as we found the operations and maintaining of FRR too complex. At the same time, enhancements to IS-IS made it possible to fully rely on the routing protocols at the IP layer for the resilience in SURFnet5. During March 2004 the dual-stack approach was migrated to a 6PE implementation. The four core routers act as BGP route-reflectors in both the IPv4 as IPv6/6PE routing. All fifteen concentrator routers and border routers are BGP route-reflector clients hanging of these BGP route-reflectors.

12.2.5 Network Management and Monitoring

As a ground rule, SURFnet treats IPv6 on the network level equal to IPv4, as much as possible. This implies that procedures between SURFnet's NOC and SURFnet Network Services are streamlined to support this. Also, the external peering policy towards other non-European NRENs such as Abilene and CA*net 4 and towards the commodity Internet through SURFnet's upstream providers and through peerings at the Amsterdam Internet Exchange (AMS-IX) is the same for IPv4 and IPv6. At the

AMS-IX it means that IPv6 peering requests are handled exactly like IPv4 peering requests, as SURFnet's peering policy on the Exchange is identical for both protocols. In December 2004, SURFnet had approx. 65 IPv6 peering sessions enabled over the AMS-IX.

While SURFnet strives to be able to perform network management over IPv6 as well, today this is done only partly at this moment. SURFnet monitors the availability of the IPv6 customer connections as well as external connections. Also where software allows it (like SSH, Nagios and Rancid) IPv6 is used to manage the router equipment in SURFnet5.

12.2.6 Other Services

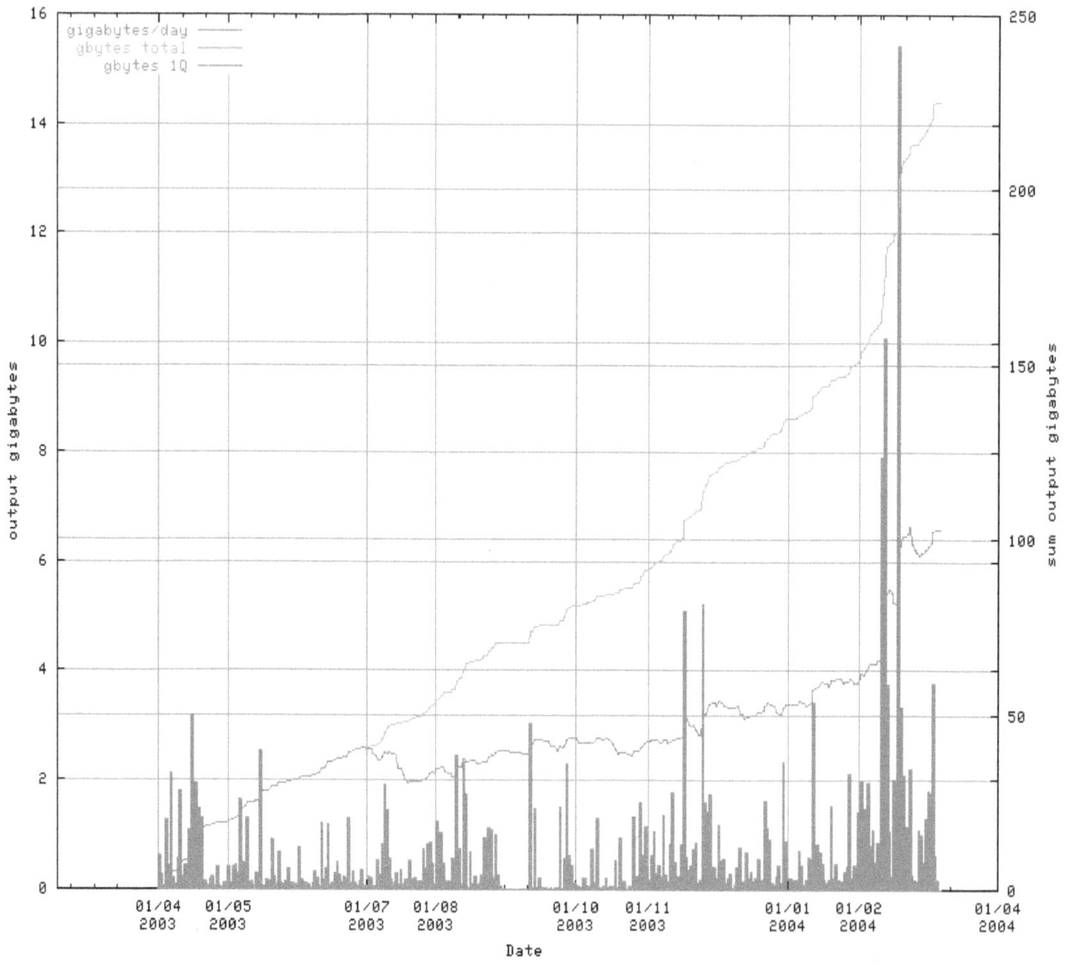

Figure 12-5 Anonymous-FTP over IPv6 volume

The following actions on applications and the like in the area of IPv6 are being or have been undertaken:

- The anonymous-FTP archive of SURFnet and NLUUG was enabled for IPv6 in the second quarter of 2002. See Figure 12-5 for the IPv6 volume transferred by this server.
- Four of SURFnet's Stratum 1 Network Time Protocol (NTP) servers are up and running and serving time over IPv6.

- All of SURFnet's three DNS server and three DNS resolvers are IPv6 aware as well as reachable over IPv6.
- Two Net News Transfer Protocol (NNTP) production feeders and three test feeders run IPv6 and have external peerings with Switch and Funet and other smaller peerings. In the test bed two news reader machines are used with IPv6 connectivity..
- The main web site of SURFnet[1] is enabled for IPv6.
- Several experimental services like video streaming (unicast, multicast) and internet telephony (SIP) run over IPv6 today.
- All SURFnet services are available over IPv6, either native or through a tunnel.

For new application services that are being developed and for which equipment or software is procured, we asked the potential suppliers on their readiness for IPv6.

[1] The English version is available at: http://www.surfnet.nl/en/.

12.3 FUNET Case Study (Finland)

In 2001, Funet's core network was upgraded to 2.5Gbit/s PoS links. Six Juniper routers (M20) were added to the previously all-Cisco network. There was not so much user demand for native IPv6 at this stage, but by the end of 2001, some plans for enabling dual-stack on these Juniper routers had been made.

During Q1/2002 various tests and trials were run.

After fixing all the issues, the Funet core had transitioned to complete dual-stack deployment in the core networks by Q2/2002. As of Q1/2005, dual-stack has worked well without any problems or performance impact.

12.3.1 History

The Funet experience involved some bleeding edge IPv6 deployment, leading to a subsequently stable service.

In Q2/2002, the minimum IPv6 working version 5.2R2 was installed on the Juniper routers. Later, versions 5.3R2, 5.3R3, and 5.4R3 were also used. Version 5.6R3 fixed a problem with IPv6 loopback access list breaking Neighbor Discovery, but since then (as of Q1/2005) no IPv6 issues have come up.

The IPv4 network used OSPFv2 and BGP for routing, but OSPFv3 for IPv6 was not ready. Funet didn't want to change the routing protocol, and for clarity, they wanted clearly separate IGP's for IPv4 and IPv6: OSPF and IS-IS. In addition, if IS-IS had been deployed for IPv4 and IPv6, multiple topologies would have to have been supported as IPv6 routing would have been different (in parts) from IPv4. So, IPv6-only IS-IS was clearly the best (and only, discounting RIPng) choice at that time.

Unfortunately, there were problems in the Juniper and Cisco devices with IPv6-only IS-IS. For example, the Juniper platform would not support IS-IS only for IPv6. The first, and worst, problem was that the Juniper routers would always also advertise IPv4 addresses used in loopbacks and point-to-point links. Cisco's IOS, unless you enabled IS-IS for IPv4 too (which was a non-starter for Funet), would discard all such attempts to form adjacencies: a total inoperability problem. Cisco's IS-IS implementation has an option 'no adjacency-check' to override this; however, an undocumented fact was that it would only work (at least in this case) when using level-2-only IS-IS circuit-type (which was not the default). A first step in interoperability was gained when these were enabled in IOS.

Some problems continued. IS-IS route advertisements from Ciscos to Junipers were accepted in the route database, but not put to the Junipers' routing table: this was caused by the above mentioned problem with adjacencies; this was reported, and fixed, in 5.2R2; a minimum workable version for Funet to use. The issue with Juniper always advertising IPv4 addresses in IS-IS was fixed, as (then undocumented) feature 'no-ipv4-routing' in 5.4R1. Also, one could not redistribute static discard routes to IS-IS (to generate a default route) until this was fixed in 5.3R3. You also could not set a metric when advertising a default route other than by redistributing a static discard route and applying a route-map in Cisco.

Fortunately, the rigorous tests in the lab network were enough to expose all of the above problems, which were fixed.

Also in 2002, most of Funet's Cisco routers were replaced by Junipers in an upgrade of the network.

In early 2003, Funet noticed significant bandwidth bottlenecks (in the order of dozens of megabits/second) with their remaining Cisco equipment - 7200's, 7500's, GSR's - regarding IPv6 forwarding capabilities, but the situation improved tremendously when software supporting CEFv6 come out later in 2003. This is very important for Funet as the IPv6 traffic level is at least 30-40 Mbit/s.

In early 2005, all IPv6 routing is done on production equipment; there are no longer any special "IPv6 routers", or any special IPv6-only links or connections. Almost all of these are Junipers (M10, M20, T320), about twenty, and two CSC's access routers are Ciscos (VXR with 12.2S software).

As of early 2005, Funet has not yet deployed IPv6 multicast support though the software capability has existed for a long time. Funet has waited for Embedded RP support (available in Junipers since 7.0R1 on Q4/2004), and availability of IPv6 multicast service from the upstream. It is expected that IPv6 multicast support is rolled out soon when the software becomes stable, within half a year or so.

Beyond that, no further IPv6 features have been identified missing in the core network.

The Funet IPv6 network is shown in Figure 12-6 (geography) and Figure 12-7 (topology).

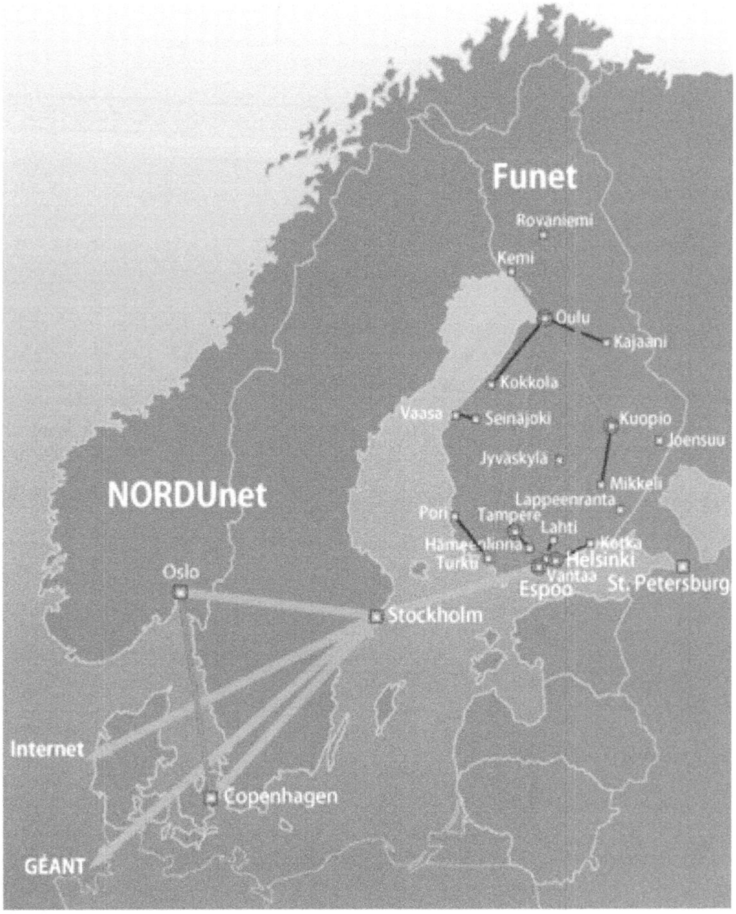

Figure 12-6 Funet Network by Geography

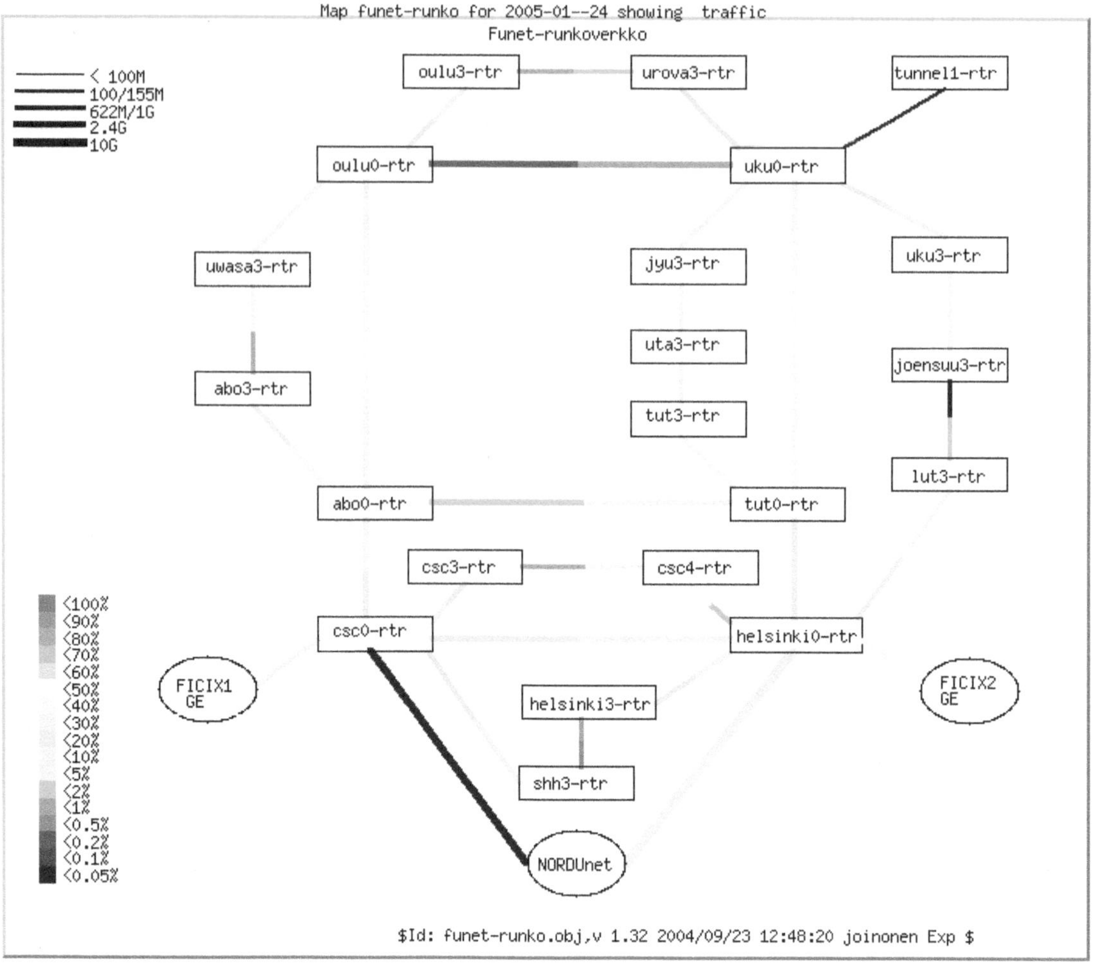

Figure 12-7 Funet Network by Topology

12.3.2 Addressing Plan

Funet has an IPv6 SubTLA address block of 2001:708::/32.

There are two different aspects to addressing: the customers and the network infrastructure.

12.3.2.1 Customers

There are six "SuperPoP" core routers; these are used when giving out /48 prefixes to customers, e.g.:

2001:708:0KLM::/48

"K" here is the number of the regional SuperPoP. This is not meant to be used for aggregation purposes, rather than to just create some mild hierarchy for the addresses, rather than allocate them in a sequential fashion.

"L" is the sequential number of customers within the SuperPoP. "0" is reserved.

"M" is reserved for expanding the number of customers in the SuperPoP and/or increasing the size of the assignment to the customers. To maintain future flexibility, this is still zero.

When assigning the prefix to the customers, Funet recommends they keep the first four bits (the first nibble) zero for now.

An example of a customer assignment is 2001:708:510::/48.

12.3.2.2 Network Infrastructure

Here, "KLM" has a slightly different meaning. "K" still means the SuperPoP, "L" means the PoP acting under the SuperPoP in an access network, and "M" is an identifier for the router in the PoP.

Loopback addresses are taken from the prefix:

2001:708:0:10:KLM::/112

So, a few loopback addresses will be:

tut0-rtr.funet.fi: 2001:708:0:10:300::1

tut1-rtr.funet.fi: 2001:708:0:10:301::1

uta3-rtr.funet.fi: 2001:708:0:10:313::1

These are configured using /128 prefix length. Note that the identifier of the router is also reflected in the naming ("uta_3_-rtr").

Point-to-point addresses in the core and the access networks are taken from one block - all addresses come from under a single /64:

2001:708:0:F000::/64

In particular:

2001:0708:0:F000::klmn:KLMm:z/112

klm and KLM identify the routers at the end of the point-to-point links, taken from the loopback addresses; in above, these would have been "300", "301", and "313". SuperPoP's or the smallest number goes first as klm. "n" and "m" are sequential numbers, used when necessary - for example if there are multiple links between routers which need to be numbered - defaulting to zero. "z" is the end-point of the point-to-point link: always "1" or "2". The same SuperPoP or smallest first rule applies here too. So, in consequence, the addressing becomes like:

uku0-jyu3:	2001:708:0:F000::4000:3230:[12]/112
uku0-oulu0:	2001:708:0:F000::4000:5000:[12]/112
uta3-jyu3:	2001:708:0:F000::3130:3230:[12]/112

The point-to-point links toward customers are always numbered from the customer's addresses, due to simplicity and policy reasons.

For peerings and miscellaneous use, a block of:

2001:708:0:F001::/64

is reserved.

In addition, some special use addresses are used inside 2001:708::/48, for example 2001:708::{1,2} (for a few routers), 2001:708::123 (NTP), 2001:708::53 (DNS) etc.

12.3.3 Routing

As was already noted, Funet network uses (as of Q1/2005) OSPFv2 for IPv4 and IS-IS (for IPv6 only) for IPv6. IPv4 infrastructure uses BGP with multiple (private) autonomous systems. Due to the (relatively) low number of IPv6 customers and traffic, the same kind of BGP topology has not been built for IPv6. Instead, IPv6 BGP has only been set up at the border routers, and the rest use IS-IS.

A longer term idea has been to switch from OSPFv2 to using IS-IS for both IPv4 and IPv6, but this has been a low priority task, and as of this writing, has not been done yet. At the same time, the same kind of BGP topology would probably be built.

12.3.4 Configuration Details

In this section, core and customer (edge) configuration examples are listed.

12.3.4.1 Configuring the Core

The configuration of the Juniper routers is given below.

```
interfaces {
    lo0 {
        unit 0 {
            family iso {
                address 49.0001.1931.6600.5180.00;     "IS-IS address from IPv4"
            }
            family inet6 {
                address 2001:708:0:BB:eeee:ffff:0000:1111/128; "Loopback"
            }
            family inet {
                [...]
            }
        }
    }

    so-X/X/X {
    unit 0 {
            [...]
        family iso;                                  "For IS-IS"
            family inet6 {
                address 2001:708:0:BB:aaaa:bbbb:cccc:dddd/112; "Core"
            }
            family inet {
                [...]
            }
        }
    }
}

protocols {
```

```
    isis {
        no-ipv4-routing;
        export ipv6-to-isis;
        level 1 disable;
        interface so-X/X/X.0 {        "Core connections"
        level 2 metric 2;
        }
    interface lo0.0 {
        passive;
    }
    }
}

policy-options {
    policy-statement ipv6-to-isis {
        from {
           protocol [ direct local static isis ];
           family inet6;
        }
        then {
            accept;
        }
    }
}
```

And respectively on Cisco:

```
interface POSX/Y
[...]
 ipv6 address 2001:708:0:BB:aaaa:bbbb:cccc:dddd/112
 ipv6 router isis
 isis circuit-type level-2-only
 isis metric 2
!
router isis
 passive-interface Loopback0
 !
 address-family ipv6
 redistribute static
 redistribute connected
 no adjacency-check
 exit-address-family
```

```
is-type level-2-only
net 49.0001.1931.6600.5181.00
metric-style transition
log-adjacency-changes
!
```

As can be seen, the model is such that all the routes of the router are redistributed in the IS-IS. An alternative approach would be to include all the interfaces in the IS-IS as passive interfaces.

This is not considered to have serious drawbacks, as none of these redistributed routes are advertised outside the autonomous system: the advertisement includes the aggregates only.

12.3.4.2 Connecting the Customers (edge)

Customers are connected using static routes. The configuration is very simple, like the below on Juniper:

```
interfaces {
    fe-X/X/X {
    unit Y {
        [...]
        family inet6 {
                rpf-check fail-filter RPF_FAIL_IPV6;
          address 2001:708:KLM:xxxx::2/64; # from the customer
        }
    }
    }
}
routing-options {
    rib inet6.0 {
        static {
            route 2001:708:KLM::/48 next-hop 2001:708:KLM:xxxx::1;
        }
    }
}

firewall {
    family inet6 {
        filter RPF_FAIL_IPV6 {
            term DEFAULT {
                then {
                    count count-rpf-fail-ipv6;
                    log;
                    discard;
                }
```

```
                }
            }
        }
}
```

And on Cisco this could look like:

```
interface Fa0/0
 [...]
 ipv6 address 2001:708:KLM:xxxx::2/64
!
ipv6 route 2001:708:KLM::/48  2001:708:KLM:xxxx::1
```

12.3.5 Monitoring

The addresses of all loopback and point-to-point addresses are entered into DNS in a special format. A script configured to allow zone-transfer of "ipv6.funet.fi" zone fetches this information and digs out the IP addresses which should be in use. The pinger periodically (once in five minutes) checks that the links (including the links to customers and the peers) are up and responding; if not, it sends an alert.

BGP and IS-IS adjacencies are also monitored using a tool which collects syslog warnings sent from routers to a central syslog server. If adjacencies or sessions flap, this can be noted in the monitoring page.

All routers and links are collected to a custom network map/monitoring tool, where the traffic levels and similar can be monitored easily.

A challenge in the dual-stack infrastructure is getting a feel how much traffic on the links is IPv4 and how much IPv6. As of this writing, there are no good mechanisms to get that. When IPv6 MIBs are complete and are implemented, getting such measurements may be easier.

The performance has not been rigorously tested, as the Junipers include a hardware IPv6 forwarding capability. When Cisco's performance issues were noticed, and CEFv6 was tested, Funet also briefly tested the backbone network's IPv6 forwarding capabilities; a PC with Gigabit Ethernet interface could not send enough traffic to cause any impact on the network, which was indeed what was expected.

12.3.6 Other Services

Funet has been using and advertising a 6to4 relay to everywhere (openly) since late 2001. This includes the advertisement of 2002::/16 and 192.88.99.0/24. The router in question is a FreeBSD system running zebra OSPF and BGP routing protocols.

IPv6 multicast has also been tested using separate infrastructure and tunnels, but this has been shut down as of Q1/2005, pending the upgrade of the core network to support IPv6 multicast.

A TCP/UDP relay (faith in FreeBSD) is used on server-side to experimentally enable IPv6 access to a few IPv4-only services.

An IPv6 newsfeed service is IPv6-enabled, and is generating 30+ Mbit/s of steady IPv6 traffic. Also, ftp.ipv6.funet.fi is also IPv6-operational.

12.3.7 Lessons Learned

It was noticed that especially if the network is built with Junipers, there is no need to worry about performance impacts, and building a dual-stack infrastructure in the core network is very easy and simple to maintain.

The more difficult part comes from getting the universities to use IPv6, either through tunnels or natively. This requires some education, but the main bottleneck is probably at the IT management at those organizations. The IT staff is typically overloaded with work, or otherwise reticent to start testing IPv6 or to provide that as a service to the university departments or other facilities.

As such, it seems that the researchers and departments, if they want to try out IPv6, should be more insistent in asking for it from their university's IT staff.

12.4 RENATER Case Study (France)

Within the framework of a pilot project by GIP RENATER, carried out by G6, the infrastructure of Renater2bis has been used to set up an IPv6 pilot network. The aim for the GIP RENATER was to begin to establish the means and mechanisms required to allocate the necessary resources to connect the test sites to the IPv6 pilot (NLA-ID allocation, reverse DNS delegation, IPv4 - IPv6 transition mechanisms, etc.)

The 2001:660::/35 prefix was used for addressing the pilot and connected academic sites. All industrial partners were addressed in the 3ffe:300::/24 address space. Dedicated ATM PVCs were used to transport IPv6 between the different IPv6 POPs. The original /35 prefix has been expanded to a /32 by the RIPE NCC (as part of common RIR policy) since the prefix was originally allocated.

12.4.1 Native Support

Thanks to this pilot experience, IPv6 is now offered as a native service on Renater3's backbone.

All Renater3's points of presence offer global IP connectivity to the regional networks and to the sites which contain both IPv4 unicast, IPv4 multicast and IPv6 unicast.

Both traffic types (IPv4 and IPv6) are carried in the backbone without any distinction, offering equal performance, availability, supervision and support levels. The Renater NOC was IPv6 trained to be able to achieve the same service for IPv6 and IPv4.

12.4.2 Addressing and Naming

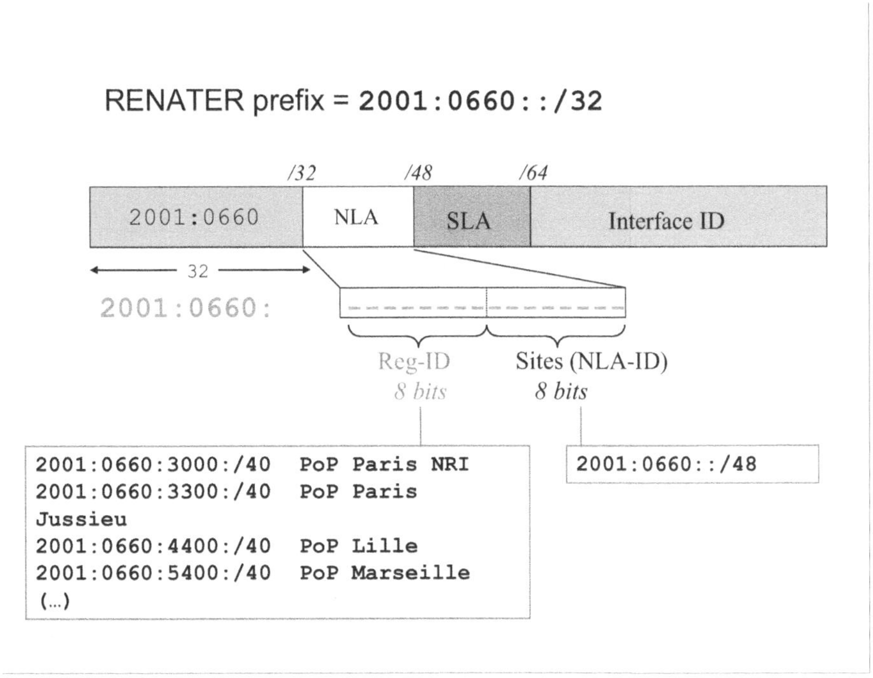

Figure 12-8 The Renater3 PoP Addressing Scheme

The addressing of the whole network is designed in a hierarchic way: this makes it possible to aggregate all routes, so reducing the routing table's size. Each point of presence of Renater3's backbone is allocated a /40 IPv6 prefix. Sites connected to a POP receive a /48 prefix derived from the /40 of the POP. For monitoring purpose, the /48 prefixes are not aggregated at the POP's in /40's. This way it is possible to have a view of sites routing announcements in the routing table. The addressing scheme is illustrated in Figure 12-8.

The GIP Renater manages the delegation of reverse zones of Renater3's SubTLA prefix (2001:0660::/32). It delegates to each site the reverse zone of the NLA-ID (/48) allocated to the site.

AFNIC, the French Network Information Center, is managing the .fr top-level domain name. They are connected to Renater3's Internet exchange point (SFINX) that supports IPv6.

12.4.3 Connecting to Renater 3

Using the experience gained with the IPv6 pilot of Renater2, procedures for connecting to Renater3 were designed and the teams were trained to be aware of the new processes. All the sites connected to the pilot have to be moved to Renater3, and be allocated a new prefix in the new address space. There was no D-day between the pilot and Renater3 as connectivity was not shut down for people connected through the pilot, to let them have time to do the procedures to connect to Renater3. Now all the sites have migrated to Renater3 and the pilot prefix is not used.

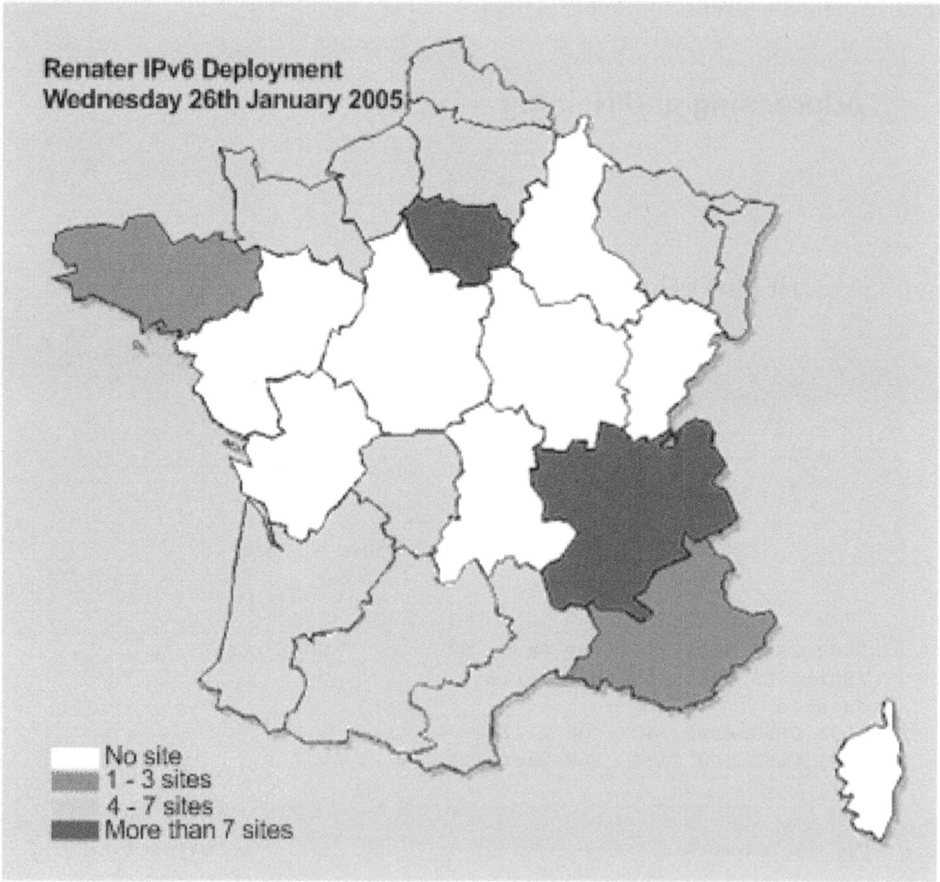

Figure 12-9 Density of IPv6 Connected Sites on Renater3

The procedures defined for IPv6 are very close to the ones defined for IPv4. This implies that a site can connect only if the network administrator fills some forms. An issue is that all these administrators are not IPv6 aware, and that some people in the site they manage need IPv6 connectivity. The prefix given to the site is aimed at addressing the whole network, and the administrator has to delegate a part of this prefix to the lab, which implies some IPv6 deployment forecast. This is not easy if the administrator is not IPv6 aware. This can lead to long delays to connect some sites to Renater3.

After 18 months, 50 sites are connected to the IPv6 service of Renater3 and 75 sites have received a prefix. The following map shows the density of IPv6 connected sites in the different French regions.

12.4.4 The Regional Networks

Renater3 is a national backbone with at least one POP in every French region. To connect to this POP, the sites use some access network (regional or metropolitan network). At the beginning of Renater3, none of these access networks were IPv6 enabled, meaning that the connection between the Renater3 POPs and the sites was done using tunnels or dedicated links (ATM PVCs, serial links, etc). As the core backbone is a Cisco GSR infrastructure, the choice was made not to set up tunnels on the core routers. Some dedicated equipment was deployed to concentrate the tunnels in the regions. Some of these routers are the ones used for the IPv6 pilot.

Eighteen months after the deployment of Renater3, there are 13 regional or metropolitan networks providing IPv6 connectivity to their customers, and 19 have received a prefix, so new networks should be connected soon. These networks used many different approaches for this IPv6 deployment: 6PE, VLANs, fully dual-stack, PVC ATM, tunnels, etc, and all these deployments are done in straight collaboration with Renater. It is clear that the deployment made in the core network is a real motivation for the other networks at the edges to follow.

12.4.5 International Connections

Renater3 offers IPv6 connectivity to national (RNRT) and Europeans (IST) projects. It is connected to GÉANT with a 10Gbps link where it exchanges traffic with the european NRENs. It has a connection to Asia via TEIN link, a 10Mbps ATM PVC is configured for IPv6, while the global link can offer 155Mbps. It also has an IPv6 connection to the transit network OpenTransit via one 2.5 Gbps link from the PoP of Lyon.

The IPv6 service is extended to the SFINX (Service for French Internet eXchange), which offers IP actors an interconnection point that carries both IPv4 and IPv6. IPv6 is exchanged in dedicated VLANs. This makes it possible to manage IPv6 traffic more easily. At this stage, 13 entities are connected to the SFINX using IPv6.

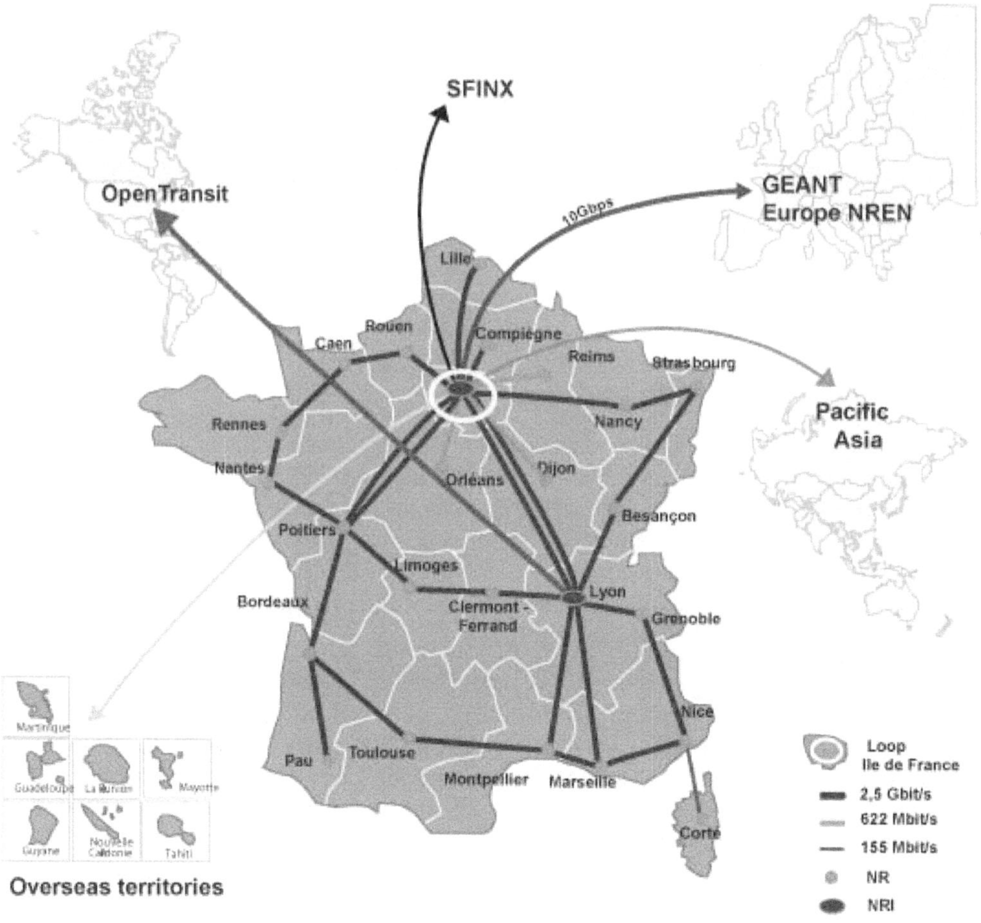

Figure 12-10 The Renater3 Network

12.4.6 Tunnel Broker Service Deployment

To overcome the lack of IPv6 in regional or metropolitan access networks, RENATER is deploying a tunnel broker service. The solution chosen is Hexago Migration Broker. Its main function is to connect sites or end-users who do not have IPv6 connectivity by creation of IPv6 dynamic tunnels. End-users can connect to the Tunnel Broker via a client software based on TSP (Tunnel Setup Protocol). This process will rely on MD5 authentication. The following scheme from Hexago shows the different use cases for the tunnel broker service.

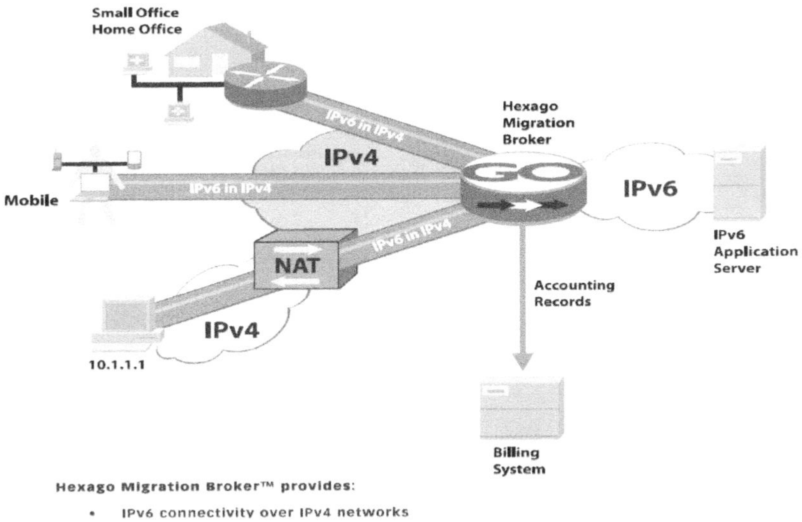

Figure 12-11 The RENATER Tunnel Broker

The tunnel broker will also be used for bringing IPv6 connectivity to meetings, conferences or any kind of event requiring IPv6 (IST, Launch events...).

12.4.7 Network Management

Being able to monitor the IPv6 service always stayed a priority since its deployment in Renater3 backbone. As it is offered now as a production service, same guarantees are required for IPv4 and IPv6.

12.4.7.1 Traffic monitoring

During the IPv6 pilot phase of Renater2, IPv6 was transported in dedicated ATM PVCs. The monitoring of IPv6 traffic was very easy as polling was made on separate interfaces. In Renater3, as IPv6 and IPv4 are transported on the same links and MIBs for monitoring IPv6 traffic are not yet implemented on Renater3 equipments, it is not possible to monitor IPv6 traffic the same way.

A script was developed to poll the routers using the CLI every 60 minutes. This feeds the Renater monitoring database and results can then be displayed using graphs or weathermaps.

Figure 12-12 IPv6 Traffic Weathermap

12.4.7.2 *Routing monitoring*

Due to the lack of MIBs capable of monitoring IPv6 routing on Renater3 equipments, some scripts were deployed capable of checking the status of BGP4+ peerings. Alarms are sent when peering go down.

ASPath-tree was also deployed to give an overview of the routing policy in Renater. It cannot be used for operational routing monitoring but is useful for checking routing policies and make new routing plans.

12.4.7.3 *Flow monitoring*

At this stage, the routers on Renater3 are not capable of exporting IPv6 flows using Netflow v9. Nevertheless, a lot of work has been made to make the Netflow collector of RENATER capable of collecting these IPv6 flows. A first version of the collector is about to be submitted for tests to the interested 6NET partners.

12.4.8 IPv6 Multicast

An experimental IPv6 multicast network (M6Bone) is running on the Renater3 infrastructure. It allows the connection of lots of sites, all over the world. This network allows all the sites connected to test and develop IPv6 multicasting. It is connecting today over 80 sites and networks in Europe, Asia and Africa, making the network one of the most advanced multicast IPv6 network in the world.

12.5 SEEREN Case Study (GRNET)

The South East European Research and Education Networking (SEEREN) infrastructure interconnects the Research and Education Networks (NRENs) of Albania, Bosnia-Herzegovina, Bulgaria, FYR of Macedonia, Greece, Hungary, Romania and Serbia-Montenegro amongst themselves and to the European backbone network. In this respect, it constitutes the South-Eastern European segment of the multi-gigabit pan-European Research and Education network, GÉANT.

The SEEREN infrastructure was officially inaugurated in January 2004, with first IPv4 services provided in November 2003. Since then, the project has been developing several services and tools on top of the infrastructure, including a virtual network operations centre and a one-stop-shop for the management tools [SEEREN]. The deployment of IPv6 services has been planned since Spring 2004.

12.5.1 SEEREN Network

The SEEREN physical and logical network topologies are depicted in Figure 12-13 and Figure 12-14, respectively. The MPLS-enabled core network infrastructure, which is provided by a consortium of operators in SE Europe, has Points of Presence (PoPs) in all the SE European capital cities. Interconnection between the SEEREN NRENs is achieved with the Carrier supporting Carrier (CsC) technique (see Figure 12-15), which enables an MPLS VPN-based service provider, called the carrier provider, to allow other IP (or MPLS) service providers, called customers carriers (SEEREN NRENs[1]), to use a segment of its backbone network.

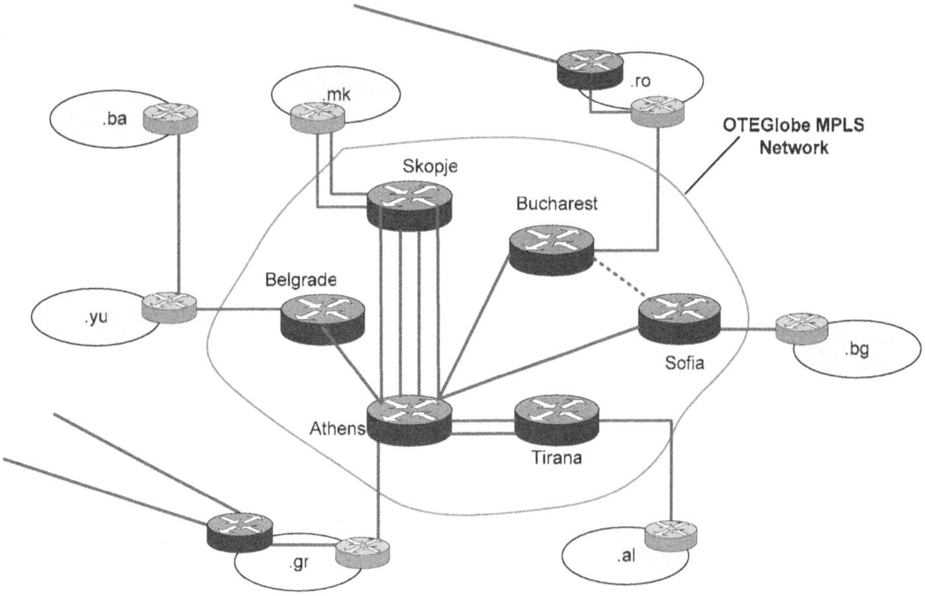

Figure 12-13 SEEREN Physical Network Topology

The access links of SEEREN NRENs range from 2Mbps up to 34Mbps, while connectivity is achieved by using diverse technologies from ATM to Ethernet over PPP (EoPPP). The SEEREN primary connection to GÉANT is a 95Mbps ATM PVC crossing GRNET. A secondary (backup) 34Mbps

[1] Each SEEREN NREN has deployed and manages one border router for its international connectivity. These routers consist of a "virtual" customer provider network.

ATM connection diverts traffic to RoduNET (Bucharest GÉANT PoP) in case of failure in the primary connection.

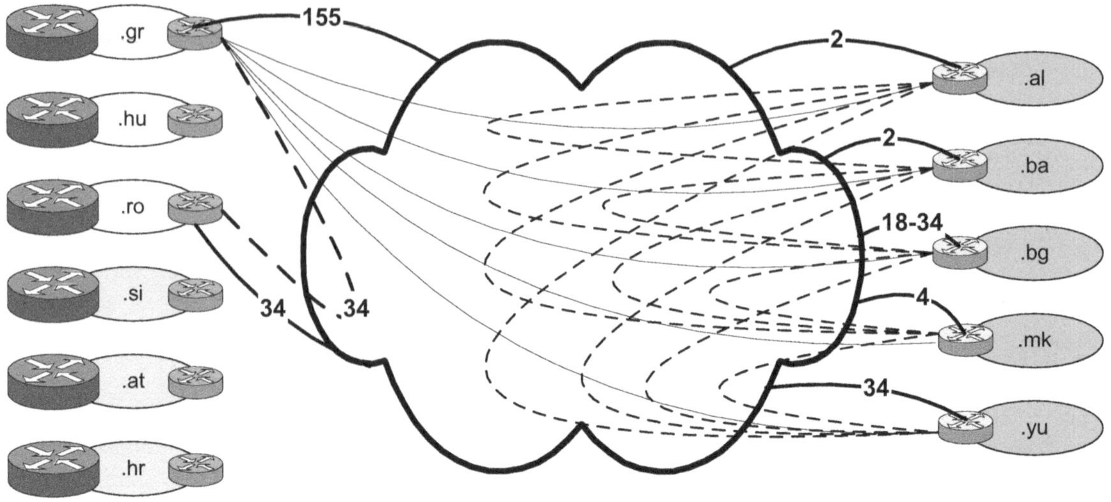

Figure 12-14 SEEREN Logical Topology

According to the CsC technique, in the data plane, the traffic exchanged between SEEREN NRENs border routers (CEs[1]) is encapsulated into MPLS frames and, then forwarded through the Carrier Providers MPLS network. The MPLS label is removed by the far-end along the path SEEREN CE router and forwarded as an ordinary IP packet. In the control plane, SEEREN CEs exchange with the Carrier Provider PEs only IGP routing information, i.e. CE loopback IP addresses and CE-PE interconnection subnets. The corresponding routing information populates a Carriers Provider virtual routing and forwarding (VRF) table. For each routing entry in the VRF a label is assigned by the carrier PE and advertised via eBGP or LDP to the directly connected SEEREN CE (see Figure 12-16).

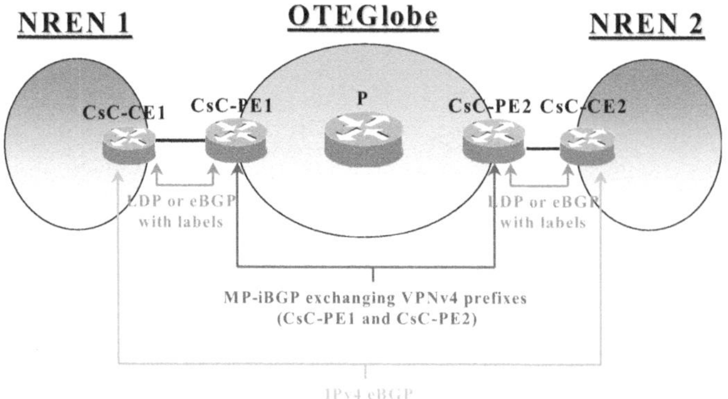

Figure 12-15 Label Exchange in the CsC Model

The CsC technique offers to the SEEREN NRENs multiple technical and economical advantages. SEEREN NRENs do not need to deploy, operate and maintain an international backbone infrastructure

[1] Each SEEREN NREN border router that is connected to the Carrier Provider's router is called customer edge (CE) router. The Carrier Provider's router connected to a Customer's router is called provider edge (PE) router.

but only need to exchange minimal routing information with its customers, e.g. only 15 routes are needed for the entire SEEREN network, even in cases where several instances of the entire Full Internet Routing Table is exchanged over the Provider's network. This allows SEEREN NRENs to define their routing policy (eBGP sessions) transparently over the carrier provider's network and the carrier provider to minimize the routing information stored in the VRF tables.

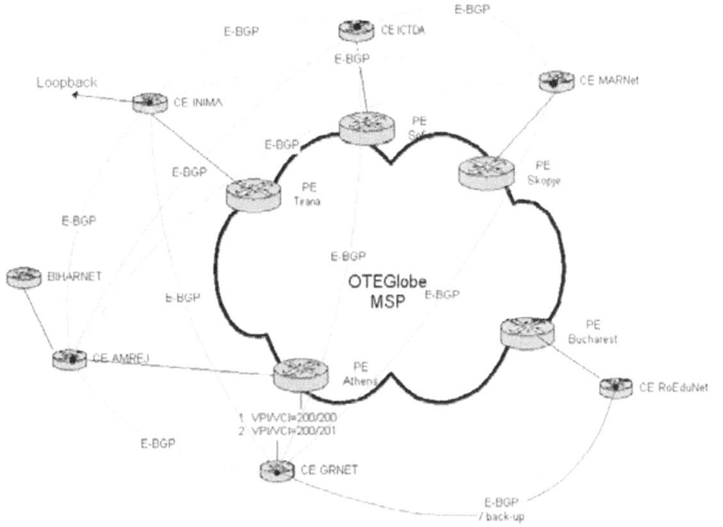

Figure 12-16 Routing Exchange in SEEREN

12.5.2 Implementation Details of CsC/6PE Deployment

The solution that was finally implemented in SEEREN infrastructure combined 6PE services at the NREN CE routers with transparent forwarding of IPv6 traffic over the Carrier Provider MPLS network. This solution did not require any software or hardware upgrades in the Carrier Provider network nor the creation of tunnels between the CE routers.

The 6PE deployment approach allows an ISP to support IPv6 services over an MPLS/IPv4 network. It has many technical implementation similarities to the MPLS VPN deployment solutions, where IP traffic is encapsulated into MPLS frames and sent over the MPLS core network.

At the SEEREN infrastructure, the NREN border routers act as 6PE routers and encapsulate IPv6 packets into MPLS frames. Concurrently, the NREN border routers act as CsC-CE routers and thus also encapsulate IPv4 (or IPv6) packets into MPLS frames. Consequently, the control and data plane of the CsC/6PE approach differs from the respective planes of either 6PE or CsC approaches.

In the CsC/6PE control plane, the 6PE routers (the NREN border routers) are dual stack, i.e. support IPv6 and IPv4 protocols, and communicate with the rest local NREN infrastructure with any common IPv6-enable routing protocol. The routing prefixes learned from the local networks are distributed among the 6PEs via multi-protocol MBGP (MP-iBGP). The BGP next-hop for each advertised IPv6 prefix derives from the IPv4 address of the connected 6PEs. Furthermore, the 6PE routers, now acting as CE routers in the CsC context, exchange routing and label information with the Service Provider (IPv4-only) PE routers. This process allows the 6PE routers to identify the labels for the IPv4 next-hop address for all destinations in the VPN, i.e. IPv4 addresses of CsC-CE routers. Finally, communication among CsC-PE routers is achieved via "pure" MPLS switching, where the (IPv4) IGP protocol is used for the distribution of appropriate MPLS labels for CsC-PE addresses.

In the data plane, IPv6 packets are sent from the local infrastructure routers to the NREN ingress 6PEs router. The latter imposes two labels on top of the IPv6 packet. The inner label identifies the IPv6 BGP next-hop and the outer label identifies the egress 6PE router. After the MPLS frame is received by the ingress CsC-PE router, the latter will replace the outer label in order to identify the VPN that the encapsulated packet belongs to. On top of the two labels, the ingress CsC – PE router will stack one additional label that identifies the MPLS-next hop along the path to the egress CsC – PE router. This label changes as the MPLS frame is switched inside the Service Provider MPLS core network. If MPLS penultimate hop poping operation is activated, the egress CsC-PE router receives an MPLS frame with two labels and removes the outer label as it forwards the frame to the 6PE router. Finally, the egress 6PE router removes the remaining label and forwards the IPv6 packet to the appropriate CE.

Chapter 13

IPv6 in the Campus/Enterprise

In this chapter we present case studies of IPv6 in the Campus/Enterprise. Since the vast majority of the 6NET partners were academic related, this case studies in this chapter are indeed related to Universities and academic departments. Nevertheless, there are many similarities between University/Campus based deployments and Enterprise deployments.

First, we we look at the Campus IPv6 deployment at the University of Münster. Next we describe two deployments at small and large academic departments (Tromsø and Southampton University respectively). A second University Campus deployment case study is given for Lancaster University and finally, we briefly describe some other deployment scenarios relating to the Campus/Enterprise class of network.

13.1 Campus IPv6 Deployment (University of Münster, Germany)

As the University of Münster is quite large, with a widespread network and is using at large set of different hardware and network techniques, several considerations had to be taken into account.

If one wants to integrate IPv6 in the network, the most desirable form of integration is always to run in dual-stack mode on each and every interface and node. However, while nowadays support for IPv6 is present in nearly every new product, there are still older hardware and technologies that do not easily support IPv6 capabilities or don't support them at all.

Especially in large sites, that have been in place for a long time, the network infrastructure has evolved over a number of years. Such networks often have a modern core, but still use old technology in some areas and on internal "stubby" edges. In such environments it is practically impossible to run full dual-stack mode. Several of the transition methods described in this cookbook can be used to reach such areas.

In addition, network administrators often hesitate to introduce IPv6, because they fear that they will destabilise their IPv4 infrastructure or because they are unfamiliar with IPv6 and IPv6 management. To overcome these fears it is helpful to start with IPv6 just in a few parts of the network and to leave the IPv4 infrastructure untouched.

A good method for this is using VLAN technology (802.1q). VLANs are very common and often used in modern networks, and it is especially easy to integrate IPv6 in these networks. If a dedicated IPv6 router is used, it can get access to only those VLANs where IPv6 is desired. So the IPv4 network remains unchanged, and all IPv6 traffic is routed and managed over a different set of hardware.. If no additional hardware is available, it might be sufficient to use only a small set of the existing routers to do IPv6 routing.

Since VLANs are spread throughout the whole University, it is possible to give IPv6 access to various areas. Still, there are some drawbacks. In those areas where no VLAN technology is available, but older remnants of e.g. ATM or FDDI infrastructure exist, other methods are needed to give IPv6 access to the hosts. This can be achieved with various tunnel technologies or a tunnel broker. Also, if there is a "secured" area, one should consider carefully if IPv6-access should be added to such a VLAN, because when bypassing the IPv4 infrastructure those security mechanisms might get bypassed. For example if there are ACL rules in use for IPv4, these should be applied also for IPv6. This is not always possible, because the two routing topologies are different. If IPv4 ACL rules rely on some kind of hierarchical routing infrastructure, they probably cannot be rebuilt directly for IPv6 in this case, or at least not easily so.

13.1.1 IPv4

In the University of Münster the "Centre for Information Processing", or "Zentrum für Informationsverarbeitung" (ZIV), has a key role as the Network Operation Centre (NOC) not only for the University itself, but also other facilities, e.g. the medical hospital and other educational institutes in Münster. That said, while ZIV is part of the university, it operates the network for several parties and is a kind of provider to multiple users. Therefore the network is not just a core network, but is more complex as it has several core networks and a transit network between them. Some smaller core networks connected to the transit network are not operated by the ZIV-NOC.

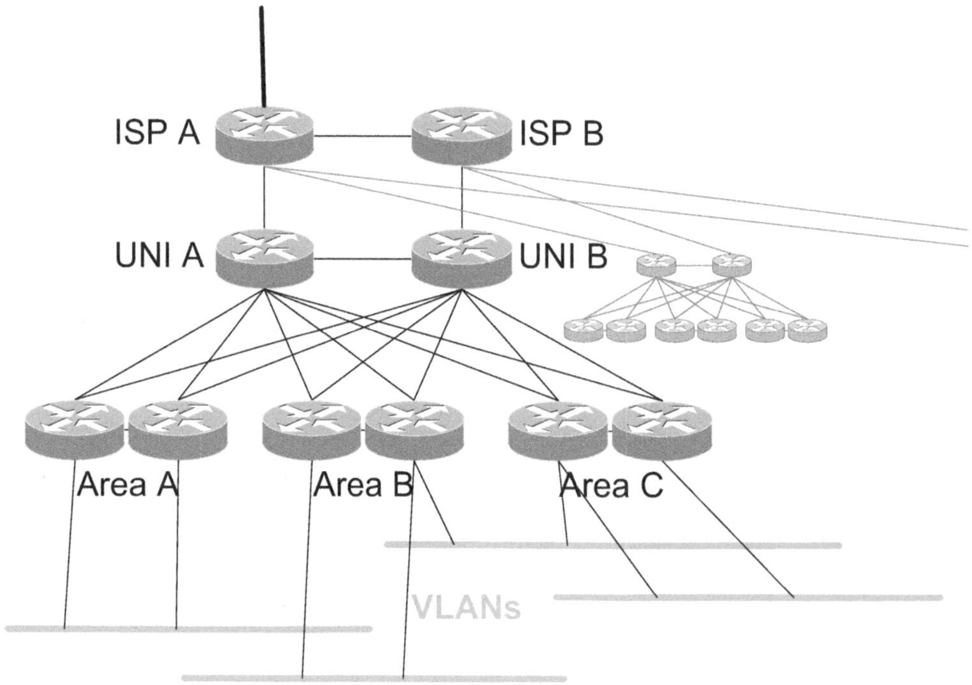

Figure 13-1 Ideal Overview of University's IPv4 Network

Figure 13-1 gives a rough overview of the current IPv4 network. All the routers shown are Cisco Catalyst 6509's with different kinds of engines (SUP2 or SUP720). Usually the connections shown are aggregated Gigabit Ethernet or 10Gigabit Ethernet connections. Redundancy is a key part of the whole network infrastructure and you will find redundant routers and structures in every core part of the network.

At the top of Figure 13-1 you see the transit routers ISPA and ISPB. One of them is connected to our upstream provider DFN. The network infrastructure below these two routers is the idealised form of the core network of the University. UNIA and UNIB act as border routers with redundant connections to the transit routers and likewise as the core routers of the internal network.

The University of Münster doesn't have a centralised campus but its buildings are spread out throughout the whole city centre. Thus the network is more like a metropolitan area network (MAN) than just a simple LAN. Several areas are equipped with a set of access switches that connect to the central core routers UNIA and UNIB. Reliability is provided by running the HSRP protocol between the routers.

VLANs are not necessarily limited to a single area but may span several access router located elsewhere.

Next to the core network of the university the ZIV manages a similar core network for the clinical facilities which is organised likewise (see the right side of Figure 13-1). Other sites connected to the transit routers are the Fachhochschule Münster and soon the Max-Planck-Institute. Other site networks may follow later on.

The scenario described here is an ideal one. As the University has quite a lot of areas, it is not affordable to allocate two high end routers to every location. To realise the described infrastructure we use virtualised router technology. (The reason for this extended virtualization is to create a hierarchical routing structure. This allows a strict correlation between a double set of routers and an area/site, which allows defining a security infrastructure and limits access based on the fact where a node is located in the network).

In addition, not every building is connected via this newer network infrastructure. There still exist remnants of old technologies used in the past, namely an ATM network and even some last parts of an FDDI ring. Some far off site buildings use ISDN or DSL to connect to the University's network.

Of course the management of this network is quite sophisticated. The most important components are Tivoli Netview management, an Oracle Database which contains every router, host, cable, number and data that is used for this network, and a web-based front-end system to update information in this database easily.

13.1.2 IPv6

The IPv6 infrastructure we started with took advantage of the fact that the University's core network uses VLAN technology extensively. This way we were able to add an IPv6 router independent from the rest of the IPv4 infrastructure. Therefore no harm could be done to running IPv4, be it the danger of higher resource usage (like CPU power) or caused by the necessity to use experimental IOS versions.

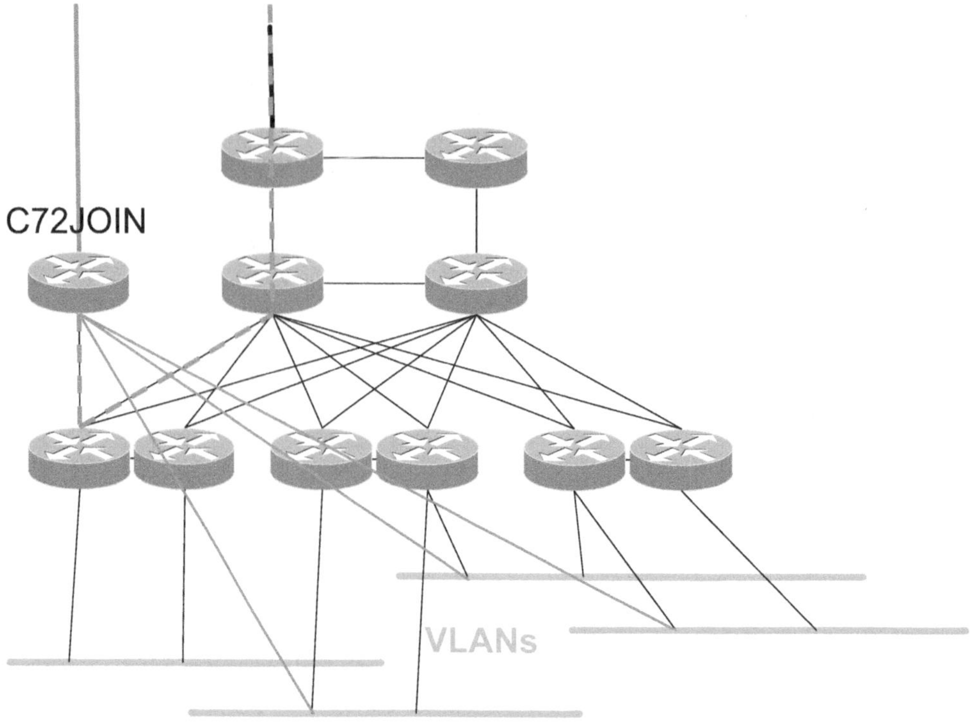

Figure 13-2 IPv6 Test Network

So we placed a dedicated Cisco 7206 router next the IPv4 infrastructure (see Figure 13-2). It is connected to the upstream network 6WiN via an IPv6-in-IPv4-Tunnel. It gets access to every VLAN we want to provide IPv6 services to. This IPv6 traffic is routed through the dedicated router and IPv4 uses the production network.

Management of the IPv6 network is limited. However, as it mainly consists of a single router, it is not so complex to monitor. We use mainly Argus and MRTG to obtain and visualize the network status.

Only a few VLANs are integrated into the IPv6 network. To give the user the opportunity to use IPv6, we offer most of the key services (DNS, Web, FTP, SMTP, NTP, NNTP, jabber, etc.) with dedicated servers we setup over time during the projects lifetime.

13.1.3 IPv6 Pilot

While being simple and effective, this method to distribute IPv6 doesn't match the requirements and features of the neighbouring IPv4 network at all. There is no redundancy and in comparison it is hardly managed.

A good start, to try to deploy an IPv6 pilot network, is to extend the IPv6 network to the current IPv4-only nodes and to run the network in dual-stack mode. With the goal to use this pilot for production usage one day, it is not only necessary to deploy IPv6 as dual-stack, but also to integrate IPv6 into all management procedures and to require that all concepts that are current practice in IPv4 will also be applied for IPv6. This means especially the requirement for the demand for redundancy, reliability and security.

Looking at the well-established procedures and methods used for the IPv4 network this is not so easy to accomplish and will require a lot of work, adaptation and education of NOC personnel.

13.1.3.1 Goal

The overall goal is to evolve the centralised single router IPv6 test network to a well managed IPv6 pilot that can be renamed to a highly reliable production network later on. The best way to achieve this is to establish a dual-stack network that uses the currently existing IPv4 network infrastructure for both IPv4 and IPv6 likewise.

The brief sketch in the chapter above might give you a hint the University's network is quite complex in its IPv4 structures and tries to serve complex needs. Taking into account that there is also a lot of old hardware in use, one can imagine that it is illusionary to add dual-stack to the whole network in one step.

13.1.3.2 Chosen hardware

We decided for a slow-start behaviour when introducing IPv6 into the production network. So in the beginning IPv6 will not be activated on every core router but only the most important ones, namely the transit routers. As some of the routers are only virtual and the virtual technology is quite new in the University's network, we will try to refrain from using these routes.

Still, we want to offer IPv6 in every VLAN that wants to use it. Which VLAN is allowed to receive IPv6 traffic is limited by the level of security that is active in that VLAN. As high security areas are secured with special (IPv4)hardware we cannot achieve the same level for IPv6 with current means.

In summary, in some VLANs the IPv4 router will not physically be the same as the IPv6 router. So the IPv4 network will differ from the IPv6 network, the NOC has to handle two different networks and we cannot achieve a full dual-stack mode from day one.

13.1.3.3 Setup

Currently the two transit routers ISPA and ISPB are the only Catalysts with a SUP720 engine. In contrast to SUP2, this engine is capable to forward IPv6 in hardware. So in the beginning we decided to use these routers as the core routers for the IPv6 network and to create the VLAN interfaces on these routers instead of using the routers at the customers end. Eventually the engines in others routers will be replaced with a SUP720 and every time this happens, we will extend the IPv6 network to these routers and will create the proper VLANs on those stub routers. In fact, currently one area is already equipped with such engines and the IPv6 core network spans these routers. In future, more and more of the older engines will be replaced by SUP720 engines.

13.1.3.4 External connectivity

For the time being, ISPA will take over the IPv6-to-IPv4-tunnel to 6WiN. Hopefully DFN is transforming 6WiN into a network that uses their IPv4 network. There are plans going on to use the G-WiN MPLS core to achieve this. This way, we could use the native IPv4-only connection for both IPv4 and IPv6. In addition we will add a second native connection to the IPv6 pilot project of T-Com in the near future.

13.1.3.5 Internal connectivity

As mentioned above the Catalyst 6500's with SUP720 will be used to form the IPv6 core network. In addition we have two Cisco 7206 routers at hand that can be used.

Most of the physical connection will use the same lines as for the IPv4 network. As the whole core network is trunked we have the option to use transit VLANs if necessary.

To connect the clients we use:

- Dual-stack in the core and for the VLANs
- A tunnel broker for satellite subnets without native IPv6 connectivity
- A tunnel broker and ISATAP for satellite clients without native IPv6 connectivity

ISATAP

The ISATAP server is already running on one of the Cisco 7206 routers. Clients have to configure the proper target IP or - if capable - can use the name isatap.uni-muenster.de.

Tunnel broker

The tunnel broker is an OpenVPN system as described in Chapter 5. Currently hosts get a /64 prefix (if more than one host is connected) or a /128 address (if only that host is connected). As soon as the university gets an extended address space it is intended to assign proper /48-prefixes to end sites, to meet the requirements of RFC3177.

Currently the used addresses and prefixes are hard configured in the script we deliver with the clients OpenVPN files. In the future we will use DHCPv6 prefix delegation to assign the /48 prefixes to clients.

IGP

The IPv4 network uses OSPFv2 as internal routing protocol. So far there was no need for an IGP for IPv6 as we only had one router with multiple VLANs attached. But for the extended IPv6 network we need an IPv6 IGP. We had some experience from running the 6WiN where we used IS-IS, so now there are several combinations what IGP's to use for these two networks.

- OSPFv2/OSPFv3
- OSPFv2/ISIS
- IS-IS single topology
- IS-IS multi topology

Running IS-IS with a single topology is not an option, as we do not intend to run IPv4 and IPv6 on the same topology. In any case, running IS-IS only would require that we substitute the current OSPFv2 with IS-IS. We feel that this is too much of an effort, at least for our size of network.

So the choice is only between OSPFv3 and IS-IS for IPv6. While we had some experience with IS-IS in the project, the University's NOC has more experience with OSPF. As OSPFv2 and OSPFv3 don't differ much, we felt it was best to go with the OSPFv2/OSPFv3 combination.

DNS

So far the standard University's nameservers (running BIND 8.3.x) are not used for IPv6, they serve IPv4 hosts only. Within the JOIN project we run a dedicated IPv6 nameserver (running BIND 9.3.1) that stores all AAAA resource records. It hosts a subdomain of the University domain uni-muenster.de. The University's main nameserver delegates the zone ipv6.uni-muenster.de to the dedicated IPv6 nameserver. This nameserver also hosts the reverse delegation for the IPv6 addresses. This is the default behaviour; there are a few (manual) exceptions.

As a result, you have to use different names when you want to access something via IPv4 or via IPv6. There is an additional domain (join.uni-muenster.de) which contains both AAAA and A records. Most times we use names out of this domain.

In order to deploy IPv6 in the University we have to add AAAA record to the now standard names in domain uni-muenster.de. This requires two prerequisites. First, we have to upgrade the University's nameservers to a newer version. While the currently running servers are able to store IPv6 records, they do not talk IPv6 transport and thus cannot answer to a request coming from an IPv6 host via an IPv6 packet.

To achieve this, the already running BIND 9.3.1 nameserver will become a secondary nameserver to the University's main servers. In addition, two additional new servers will be set up and the old server will get replaced eventually. Secondly, we have to add an AAAA record next to the A records in the domain uni-muenster.de and get rid of the two subdomains. This is the more complex part, as the zonefiles are generated with some scripts reading from a large database. The database and scripts have to be adapted.

Database

The main support tool our NOC has is the very extensive Oracle database. As mentioned before it contains every detail of the network, e.g. routers, hosts, cables and any kind of configuration data, especially IPv4 addresses. The NOC people feed the database via web pages that use homegrown ASP scripts. They retrieve and check data likewise. The database is also used to generate several statistics and lists. For our case it is important that the name server and the DHCP server are configured via scripts that read from this database.

To introduce IPv6 in the University's network it is necessary to integrate IPv6 addresses in this database, so that the University's NOC people can manage IPv6 as easily as IPv4. The database itself needs new fields to hold IPv6 addresses and prefixes and new pointers to relate these to hosts and routers. Web pages are required to manage IPv6 address space and to add IPv6 addresses. The scripts that generate lists need to get updated to use these new fields and to generate proper lists.

DHCPv6

All hosts in the University use DHCP to get an IPv4 address. All users have to register their hosts with their MAC address to the NOC and with this information the database and then the DHCP server is configured. With this policy, the NOC is in a position to maintain maximum control over IP addresses and who is using them. They want to keep this level of control for IPv6 too.

There are two methods to assign an address to a host in IPv6 automatically, via Router Advertisements (RA) or via stateful DHCPv6. As the interface ID that is used when configuring addresses with RAs is derived from the MAC address (EUI-64 format) we could use the data that is already available in the database. But, the fact the MAC address is visible in the network and that a hardware component of a host is identifiable, was a major concern of our NOC people. They had the strong wish to use other means to form an interface ID than the EUI-64 format. There are several ways to achieve this:

- configure IPv6 address manually
- use privacy addresses (RFC3041)
- use stateful DHCPv6 with non-EUI-64 address formats

The first option is clearly unacceptable as it disables autoconfiguration and complicates management. If we would use the second option, the IPv6 addresses are randomized and we would loose control of the addresses and there is no longer a relation between user and IP address. This is something our NOC people strongly rejected.

The last available option for us was to use stateful DHCPv6. Unfortunately as of today there is no production stateful DHCPv6 server available for us. So the decision was to start with RAs and addresses in EUI-64 format (this was still disliked, but the least painful option) and change to stateful DHCPv6 later on, when mature products are available.

Usage of SubnetID

As recommended for any enterprise site, the University of Münster received a /48 prefix from its provider DFN. We discussed a lot how to use the available address space and the SubnetID with the technical personnel of ZIV-NOC, based on our own discussion paper.

We came to the conclusion that a single /48 prefix is insufficient for our needs. There are multiple reasons. In the first place our University is very large and has ten thousands of students and personnel. Then the ZIV is not only giving connectivity to the University but is also managing the network and is giving broadband access to other parties, like the medical facilities and e.g. the Fachhochschule.

Thus ZIV-NOC is more a provider than just a University's NOC. Finally ZIV-NOC offers all students and personnel Internet access via ISDN. Following the rules in RFC 3177 [RFC3177] we should allocate a /48 to most of these users. With more than 50,000 students we would need more than a /32 prefix to achieve this. Something similar applies for VPN customers using the IPv6 tunnel broker system.

We tried to obtain more address space from our provider DFN. After lengthy discussions with DFN and RIPE, DFN was not able to fulfil our needs. The solution was to become a RIPE member, an LIR, and apply for our own /32 prefix. This way we would be allocated enough address space and additionally solve any multihoming issues, by having what amounts to Provider Independent (PI) IPv6 address space (we would be the provider).

At the time of writing, we have become RIPE members, but haven't been allocated a prefix so far. Therefore we will use the standard IPv6 documentary prefix 2001:db8::/32 (see RFC 3849 [RFC3849]) for examples in this section.

Usage of the provider /32 prefix

We split the 16 bit provider address range from bit 33 to 48 into four large chunks and defined a Format Prefix (FP) for each address range:

< 2 bits Format Prefix >< 14 bits free for use >

The Format Prefix is used in this way:

FP 00: 2001:db8:0000::/48 - 2001:db8:3fff::/48:	Standard broadband customer allocations
FP 01: 2001:db8:4000::/48 - 2001:db8:7fff::/48:	VPN access, e.g. OpenVPN tunnelbroker system
FP 10: 2001:db8:8000::/48 - 2001:db8:bfff::/48:	Remote Access Service (RAS), e.g. ISDN dial-in customers
FP 11: 2001:db8:c000::/48 - 2001:db8:ffff::/48:	Reservation for RAS or other

Usage of the last three blocks is hopefully very simple. Except for the first block, prefixes will become allocated consecutively starting with Zero (of each block). Currently we have about 8,000 RAS customers and about 15 OpenVPN tunnel broker customers. While the amount of RAS customers rises slowly, we expect a significant increase in the OpenVPN tunnel broker customers, once the tunnel broker system is integrated in the management plane of ZIV-NOC and we are able to give production IPv6 access via that system. The FP 11 block can be used for further RAS users if the FP 10 is ever exceeded or for any other usage if it arises. The only Format Prefix block that needs further subdividing is FP 00.

At least the addressing plan of the University's /48 prefix is very tight and it is highly likely that it will be exhausted at some point in time in the future. So instead of addressing consecutively like in the other three Format Prefix blocks, making reservations makes sense. Instead of making sparse reservations we choose to be generous here, as we do not expect to see that many broadband users for this Format Prefix block anyway. We split up the FP 00 address range into 64 chunks of /40 prefixes. Every customer will get a /48 prefix out of this chunk and the rest will be reserved for future use. Only half of the available FP 00 block will be used in this way, the second half (which equals a /35 prefix) will remain untouched and will be used only if this allocation method is too generous.

In addition, we spared the first /40 block for special prefixes, such as a /48 prefix for addressing of the backbone and a /48 prefix for specially needed subnets (like DNS servers and RPs).

In summary, the address plan for FP 00 looks like this:

2001:db8:0000::/40:	Assigned for special purposes
2001:db8:0000::/48	Used for addressing of the backbone
2001:db8:0001::/48 - 2001:db8:000f::/48	Reserved for backbone addressing
2001:db8:0010::/48	Used for special subnets (DNS, RP, etc.)
2001:db8:0011::/48 - 2001:db8:001f::/48	Reserved for further special subnets
2001:db8:0020::/48 - 2001:db8:00ff::/48	Free
2001:db8:0100::/40:	Assigned to University of Muenster (WWU)
2001:db8:0100::/48	Allocated to WWU network
2001:db8:0101::/48 - 2001:db8:01ff::/48	Reserved for further extension
2001:db8:0200::/40:	Assigned to Medical Clinic of Muenster (UKM)
2001:db8:0200::/48	Allocated to UKM network
2001:db8:0201::/48 - 2001:db8:02ff::/48	Reserved for further extension
2001:db8:0300::/40:	Assigned to Fachhochschule Muenster (FH)
2001:db8:0300::/48	Allocated to Fachhochschule network
2001:db8:0301::/48 - 2001:db8:03ff::/48	Reserved for further extension
2001:db8:0400::/40:	Assigned to Max-Planck-Institut Muenster (MPI)
2001:db8:0400::/48 - 2001:db8::4ff::/48	Allocated to MPI network
2001:db8:0500::/40:	Assigned to Studentenwerk Muenster
2001:db8:0500::/48 - 2001:db8::5ff::/48	Reserved
2001:db8:0600::/40:	Assigned to School network Muenster
2001:db8:0600::/48 - 2001:db8::06ff::/48	Reserved
2001:db8:0700::/48 - 2001:db8:1fff::/48	Free
2001:db8:2000::/48 - 2001:db8:3fff::/48	Unused

Usage of the University's /48 prefix

The address plan used for the /48 prefix for the University's network is older than our plans to apply for a /32 prefix. Nevertheless, as seen from a providers point of view, the University is still a single customer and a /48 should be enough. From this point of view we kept the /48 address plan and just freed and moved some reserved prefixes - those that are used to address the providers backbone - to other address ranges (see above).

In our University we have a sophisticated organisation structure for who is responsible for which institute or department in terms of computer and network support. Those units are named IVV (Informations-Verarbeitungs-Versorgungseinheit) and each of them takes care of one or more faculties.

The network partially reflects this organisation structure, so we decided to arrange the network addressing structure likewise. We refrained from dictating too strict an addressing framework, but decided to just use that IVV structuring and leave large blocks of the SubnetID range untouched for future use and let the IVV management decide how to use their SubnetID range.

Apart from this really simple method, we specifically refrained from using any kind of mapping any kind of information into the SubnetID field (like IPv4 addresses or VLAN IDs). The ZIV-NOC people hat strong concerns against such an approach, as change in the mapped structure would require renumbering of the network to keep the address plan intact. That was not accepted at all. One could say that using IVV unit IDs is the same kind of method, which is true. But in contrast, this organisational structure is vital for our network and our management to work, and it hasn't changed ever since it was created.

We ended up with the following address scheme for the SubnetID address range:

< 3 bits FP >< 4 bits IVV >< 9 bits free for use >

We defined a Format Prefix again. This time we used 3 bits yielding 8 different address blocks, but only the first 2 Format Prefixes are used. The last 6 FPs are spared for any future addressing plan, or if the current address range is too small. Currently we have 10 IVV units, so 4 bits - giving room for 16 of such units - will be more than enough. It is highly unlikely that there will be more IVV units in the future, much more likely that the number will be reduced.

How each IVV will use their remaining 9 bits of SubnetID address range depends on the administrators of each IVV. We decided to leave that decision in their hands. 9 bits for each IVV will be sufficient. Currently we serve about 600 subnets in the whole network. With 9 bits address range, each IVV can address 512 subnets. Even some hierarchical structure is possible. Some of the IVV assist more than one faculty, so our generic advice is to use the first 2 bits of the IVV address range to indicate the faculty. But that is not a requirement, just an advice.

The address plan in detail:

FP 000: 2001:db8:100:0000::/51:	Used for addressing
2001:db8:100:0000::/55:	IVV 1
2001:db8:100:0000::/57:	History/Philosophy
2001:db0:100:0080::/57:	Philology
2001:db8:100:0100::/57:	Speech Centre
2001:db8:100:0180::/57:	Free
2001:db8:100:0200::/55:	IVV 2 (Economic Science)
2001:db8:100:0400::/55:	IVV 3 (Law)
2001:db8:100:0600::/55:	IVV 4
2001:db8:100:0600::/57:	Physics
2001:db0:100:0680::/57:	Chemistry/Pharmacy
2001:db8:100:0700::/57:	Biology
2001:db8:100:0780::/57:	Free
2001:db8:100:0800::/55:	IVV 5

2001:db8:100:0800::/57:	Mathematics/Computer Science
2001:db0:100:0880::/57:	Psychology/sports science
2001:db8:100:0900::/56:	Free
2001:db8:100:0a00::/55:	IVV 6 (Geology)
2001:db8:100:0c00::/55:	IVV 7
2001:db8:100:0c00::/57:	Evangelic Theology
2001:db0:100:0c80::/57:	Catholic Theology
2001:db8:100:0d00::/57:	Educational/Social Science
2001:db8:100:0d80::/57:	Free
2001:db8:100:0e00::/55:	IVV 8 (Medical Science/UKM)
2001:db8:100:1000::/55:	IVV 9 (University Administration)
2001:db8:100:1200::/55:	IVV 10 (ZIV)
2001:db8:100:1400::/48 - 2001:db8:100:1fff:/48:	Unused
FP 001: 2001:db8:100:2000::/51:	Reserved for extension of addressing range
FP 010: 2001:db8:100:4000::/51:	Unused
FP 011: 2001:db8:100:6000::/51:	Unused
FP 100: 2001:db8:100:8000::/51:	Unused
FP 101: 2001:db8:100:a000::/51:	Unused
FP 110: 2001:db8:100:c000::/51:	Unused
FP 111: 2001:db8:100:e000::/51:	Unused

This current address plan is still under discussion. With a /32 and probably an extension of the /48 prefix at hand there is no need to be that sparing. For example, as mentioned above, we already swapped out some address ranges to external /48 prefixes. It is in question if we still really need 3 bits for Format Prefixes, but should instead use only 2 bits and give 10 bits to the IVV units.

Usage of the Medical Clinic's /48 prefix

ZIV-NOC is also responsible for the Medical Clinic's network and will also create the address plan for them. This has to be coordinated with clinic administration. It is most likely that they will get a similar addressing plan to the one above, because they have a similar organisational structure. So probably with some bits shifted, we will apply the same method. This is still under discussion.

Usage of the other /48 prefixes

Further /48 prefixes like those for the Fachhochschule are not in the responsibility of ZIV-NOC, as these are independent institutions and manage their network themselves.

Management

The main tool for management of the IPv4 network that is used by the University's NOC is Tivoli Netview. So far we use smaller tools like Argus and MRTG to monitor the IPv6 network. These smaller tools would be insufficient for a larger IPv6 network and it would require the University's NOC to learn and use a second tool next to Netview. It is better and more ergonomic to stick with one tool that can handle both, IPv4 and IPv6.

Unfortunately Netview does not support IPv6 yet. Still, it is adaptable and we can write own scripts to probe the IPv6 network, which can be inserted in the Netview command environment. So far, we haven't evaluated the amount of work to be done here, as we can use the "smaller" tools, as long as we run only a pilot network. So we still wait and hopefully there is then more time for IBM to react and integrate IPv6 functionality into Netview.

Services

During the lifetime of the 6NET project, JOIN helped to integrate IPv6 in several applications and set up such services to test them and to make all common services available over IPv6. After some time we now offer the following services within our University:

- Nameservice (DNS)
- Webservice (HTTP)
- Fileservice (FTP)
- Mail (SMTP)
- Time (NTP)
- News (NNTP)
- Jabber server (IMPP)
- Conference server (OpenMCU/Asterisk)

In order to launch a pilot we are in the lucky position to already have all major applications at hand with IPv6 support. A slight disadvantage might be that - except for the FTP service - all services run on dedicated hardware and are managed separately from the standard IPv4 application services in the University. While it is good to have all services at hand, it is a drawback to have to maintain two sets of hardware. One piece of advice might be not to set up IPv6 services on different hardware, but to try to integrate IPv6 in the already running applications/services from the start. This should be possible for nearly all modern applications. This could prove difficult or at least need additional work though, as one has to integrate IPv6 in the management structure of these applications as well (see our efforts to try to integrate IPv6 in the name service).

13.1.4 Summary

In order to integrate IPv6 in the University's premises we have to work on the following items:

- External connectivity
- Internal connectivity
    - Select/purchase Hardware
    - Select IGP
    - Choose VLANs to add IPv6 to
- Invent a suitable addressing scheme
- Integrate IPv6 in database
- Adapt DNS
- Add DHCPv6
- Adapt Monitoring Tools
- Educate NOC

Some of these items are easy to achieve, some of them are tough and long term work. One could say that integrating IPv6 in a larger network is not easy to do and needs a lot of work. Lots of resources - financial and personnel - are needed. If you do not have the proper equipment, one has to buy new hardware. Most of the time the latest equipment is already IPv6 capable one way or the other, but you might also need additional equipment if you plan to run dedicated hardware for IPv6 or if you plan to use some transition mechanisms (e.g. hosts for ALG gateways and/or tunnel broker systems). Personnel costs might be even higher, because you need manpower for programming, education and debugging.

In summary, depending on the size and the level of complexity of your network and depending on how elaborate the tools you use to monitor and manage that network, integration of IPv6 might become an time-consuming experience.

13.2 Small academic department, IPv6-only (Tromsø, Norway)

This section describes what has been done by Telenor Research in cooperation with the University of Tromsø and Invenia Innovation.

13.2.1 Transitioning Unmanaged Networks

This section has its focus on transitioning so-called unmanaged networks. Unmanaged networks are relatively small and simple networks that are not administered by competent technical personnel. Instead, such networks are setup and administered by their users. An example of an unmanaged network is the network in the home of a private person. Another example is the network of a small business. Such an unmanaged network typically consists of a single subnet connecting the equipment of the user. This subnet is connected via a small dedicated router to an Internet Service Provider. This router (also known as gateway) is normally not actively managed and it has been supplied and initially configured by the ISP. In some cases, however, the ISP may actively manage the gateway. In this setting, the home user has no control over the gateway. The user neither supplies nor configures nor manages the gateway that connects his network to the ISP. This restriction on the user may result in that the user adds an additional router between his home network and the gateway supplied by the ISP in order to gain control or add additional functionality. In the remainder, we will use the term gateway to refer to the router/gateway supplied by the ISP that provides the user with upstream connectivity.

Unmanaged networks were discussed by the last of the so-called deployment teams within the IETF v6ops working group. This deployment team has identified application requirements and relevant scenarios for transitioning unmanaged networks in "Unmanaged Networks Transition Scope". Their work meanwhile reached information standard status and was published as RFC 3904 [RFC3904]. This is a short summary:

The main application requirements with regards to introducing IPv6 in an unmanaged network can be summarized by:

1. Applications running fine over IPv4 should continue to run fine after IPv6 is introduced in the network.
2. New applications that are hard to realize over IPv4 should be able to benefit from the introduction of IPv6 in the network.
3. Deploying new IPv6 applications should be simple and not create problems.

The unmanaged network topology includes 3 parts: the ISP, the gateway and user equipment. Each of these can either support IPv4, both IPv4 and IPv6 or can support IPv6 only. This gives 27 (3*3*3) combinations of IPv6 support in unmanaged networks. The IETF deployment team selected 4 out of these 27 scenarios for further consideration:

A. Gateway supports IPv4 only.
B. ISP and gateway support IPv4 and IPv6, i.e. they are dual-stack.
C. Gateway supports IPv6, but the ISP supports only IPv4.
D. ISP supports IPv6 only.

We refer to the draft for a more elaborate description of these scenarios.

13.2.2 Implementation of a Pilot Network

Telenor Research in Tromsø, Norway designed and implemented an IPv6 network mostly based on radio links in cooperation with the Department of Computer Science at the University of Tromsø and Invenia Innovation AS. It covers most of the city. The purpose of establishing such a large pilot network is to experiment with an infrastructure that in design will be identical to what an ISP will have in the last phase of migration from IPv4 to IPv6. That is, an infrastructure where the ISP only supports IPv6 inside the network, but where customers will have legacy applications that can not run on anything but IPv4. Customers will have nodes running IPv6-only, IPv4-only and dual-stack.

In this experiment, the users have been staff from Telenor Research, faculty and technical staff from the Department of Computer Science, and students. The level of user competence has varied tremendously, from seasoned IPv6 administrators to complete novices with regards to IPv6 or (network) technology in general. The unmanaged networks were the home networks of these users. This experiment is therefore an example of Scenario D identified by the IETF deployment team on unmanaged networks.

The network has been designed to mimic the situation that an ISP will face and problems related to traffic at the user level is not in our focus. This leads to the following requirements:

- An IPv6-only core.
- All home networks must support a mix of IPv6-only, dual stack and IPv4-only hosts.
- IPv6-only should not need any modification.
- IPv6-only nodes must have access to services that run IPv4 only (outside of our network)
- Nodes running IPv4 only should have a functionality and performance as if the ISP supported IPv4 native.
- Nodes running IPv4-only must be given access to services on IPv6-only.
- The machinery for transition from IPv4 to IPv6 must be transparent.

13.2.2.1 *The core of the network*

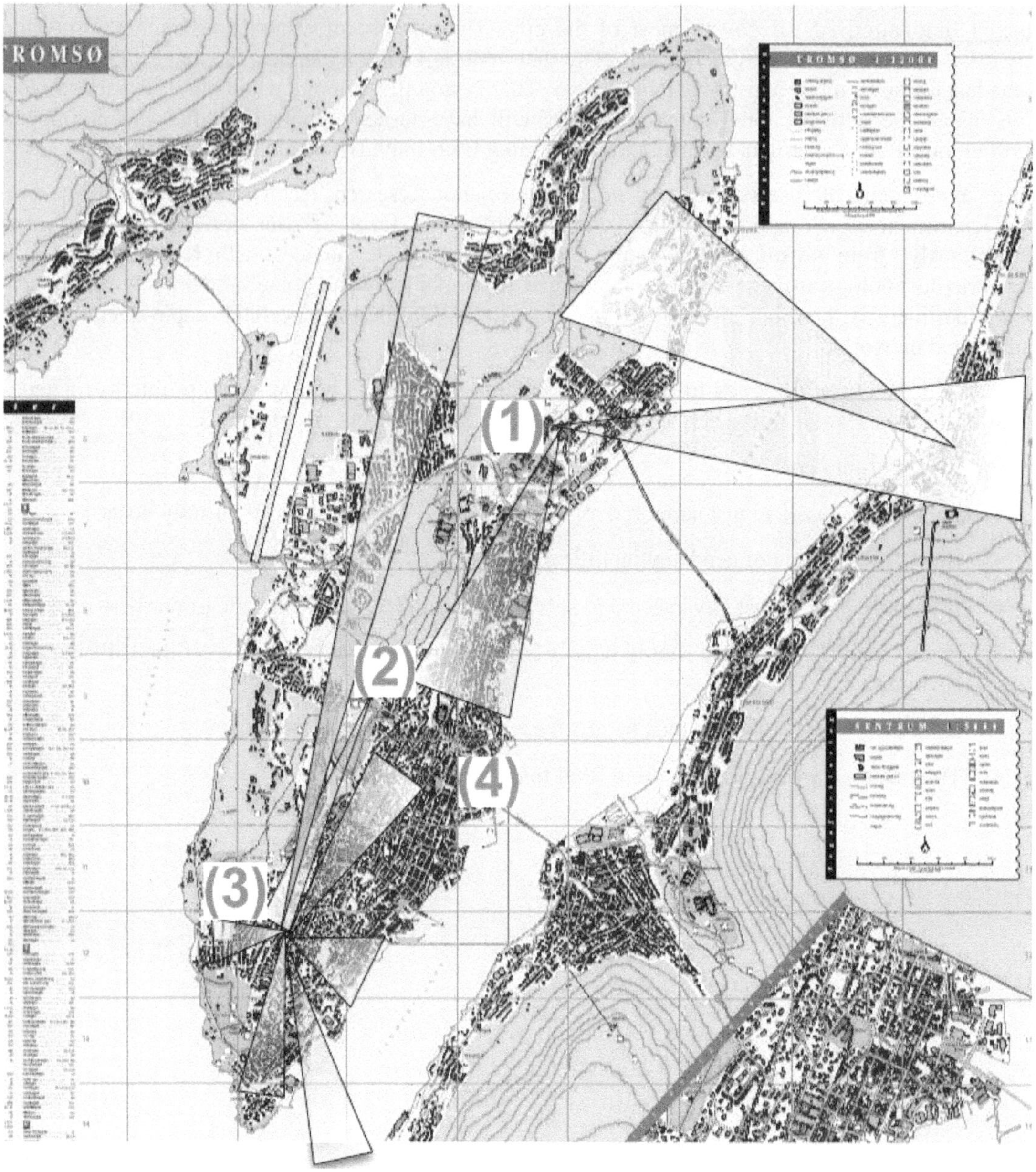

Figure 13-3 Overview of Tromsø and Transmission Points

Three main transmission points have been established in Tromsø; they are both connected to the 6NET IPv6-only network. From these three main points, a total of 12 new networks have been built. As of writing there are somewhere between 15 and 20 home networks spread out over these 12 networks, with an unknown number of machines connected.

In practice, connectivity to 6NET is provided by Uninett and the first transmission point is located at the University of Tromsø. This point is marked (1) in Figure 13-3. From there a fibre carries the traffic to the second transmission point (marked (2)). From there a single beam carries the traffic across town to a high mast (marked (3)) from where most of the city centre is covered. In addition, the

Student House ("Driv") downtown was connected to the network by means of a fibre; this point is marked (4).

A variety of antennas are in use, from large 24dBi dishes to small 6dBi omni-directional. The network is fully routed with a mix of Cisco and NetBSD routers. In addition, all home networks are routed and prefixes are allocated to homes as needed. The core is IPv6-only in order to ensure that no traffic "leaks" out of the home networks.

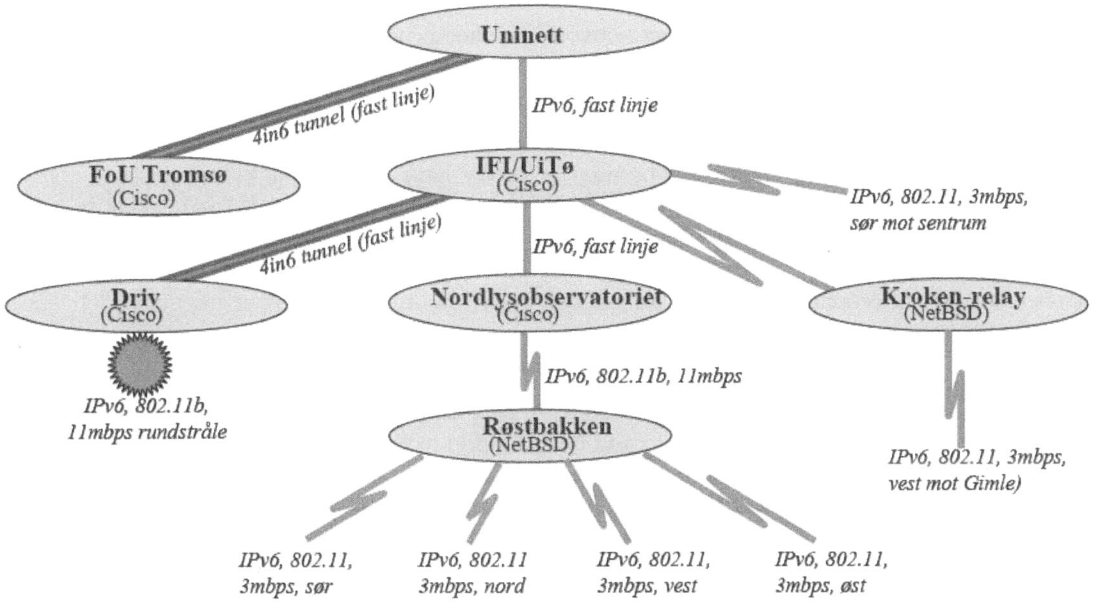

Figure 13-4 Topology Overview

13.2.2.2 The Home networks

All home networks are connected to the core by 802.11 WLAN. All networks use a small PC with two network cards that runs the NetBSD operating system as home gateway. Some of the home gateways run RIP, but most have default routing hard coded into their initial configuration. A prefix is manually allocated to each home network and routed to the NetBSD machine. The home networks use a /56 prefix. Almost all home networks are dual stack (on the inside, that is). A subset of the home networks has been used to experiment with complete IPv6-only operation.

All necessary software to facilitate the requirements of the network must be run on the NetBSD gateway. In particular, traffic of all kinds, including DNS that arrives at the router must be dealt with in a transparent manner. For the address allocation and routing of IPv6 packets the standard IPv6 autoconfiguration mechanisms were used. The gateway thus supplies user machines with the network prefix and the default route for IPv6. In addition, the gateway runs DHCPv4 which is used to assign non-routable private IPv4 addresses and IPv4 default route to user equipment. DHCPv4 is also used to configure the DNS server to use by user equipment. The DNS server configured is the non-routable IPv4-address of the home gateway. DHCPv4 was used to lacking DHCPv6 support or other DNS discovery mechanisms. Pure IPv6-only nodes that do not use or implement DHCPv4 therefore need to have their (IPv6) DNS server address configured manually.

On each home router a DNS proxy was run which would forward the DNS requests (over IPv6) to a real nameserver running at Telenor Research Laboratories in Tromsø. Each home network was given a domain beneath tft.tele.no. The DNS proxy is the totd proxy designed and implemented by Invenia Innovation within the 6NET project.

13.2.2.3 Interoperability

In this section, we describe how traffic makes its way from an application to the Internet. How it is treated depends on its type (IPv6, IPv4, TCP or UDP), its source, and its destination.

IPv6 from home network to IPv6 Internet

This traffic passes unaltered through the network. All home networks have global 2001::/16 prefix addresses and routing works as expected. There is no special treatment or translation of packets.

IPv6 from home network to IPv4 Internet

The IPv6 traffic to IPv4 services must be translated. We have opted for FAITH and NAT-PT. The former is a transport level connection translator, while the latter is a network level packet translator. While both translators are installed and operational, in practice, the transport level translator is used for daily use. The available NAT-PT implementation has a variety of non-trivial problems and does not seem ready for production use. It is installed and used in order to try to get a better understanding of its problems.

The problem with the faith implementation is that it only supports TCP. However, we have noticed that although there has not been support for UDPv4, no user request for it has been received. A lot of effort was saved this way. It is possible to add UDP support to FAITH and Invenia Innovation and the University of Tromsø have made an experimental implementation of such UDP support. This experiment was a successful proof-of-concept but further development needed for actual deployment was not performed due to limited interest compared to the effort involved and the number of problems to resolve. The most important application using UDP is DNS which is handled by the DNS proxy (Application Level Gateway). Most other UDP applications in use are multiparty games. At the moment there are few games with IPv6-capable clients that want to interoperate with their IPv4 counterparts.

In any way, DNS must be dealt with somehow in order for faith and NAT-PT to work transparently to the user. When a request is made, that results in an IPv4 address, the IPv6-only node would not know what to do with the result. To that end, we use the totd (Trick Or Treat) 6NET DNS proxy. This proxy needs to be accessible over both IPv4 and IPv6. Since the core is IPv6 only, this translation must occur at the "upper" edge of the network, i.e. at each home gateway.

Each home gateway then runs a totd DNS proxy, configured with the FAITH and/or NAT-PT network prefixes and the address of the 'real' recursive nameservers. In addition, the gateway is configured with a static route for these prefixes such that the traffic that requires translation is properly routed to the machines hosting the translators.

IPv4 from home network to IPv6 Internet

For HTTP/HTTPS and FTP connections we use the www6to4 ALG developed by Invenia Innovation AS. This simple ALG does not 'understand' the FTP protocol and can only forward it to another proxy that does. In our case, it forwards all FTP connections to a single central ftp proxy on a dual-stack machine located at the Telenor Research Lab. HTTP(S) traffic is handled directly by the www6to4 proxy itself. A more complex proxy could be developed or used that does understand ftp itself. However, the main advantage of www6to4 is its extremely small size, its simplicity of configuration and it has no complicated failure modes. As it is installed on each home gateway, these are important considerations.

In addition, transport level relays are used to translate connections for specific applications between specific source IPv4 address and IPv6 destination address. These relays are configured statically in each home gateway on user request. These relays are used mostly to allow IPv4-only email clients to connect to specific (IPv6) POP, IMAP or SMTP servers.

IPv4 from home network to IPv6 Internet

There is no direct IPv4 connectivity from the home network to the IPv4 Internet, and no network or transport layer translators are available currently for IPv4 to IPv6 translation. For this traffic two translations are required. First, as already explained the traffic is translated into IPv6 and routed to the main networking server. There it is again translated into IPv4 as described above.

IPv4 from Internet to IPv6 service at home

Support for this has been in a rather ad-hoc manner. Those who have servers at home need to give notice, and by means of 6tunnel (which is a Transport Relay Translator) incoming connections are then forwarded over IPv6 to the server on the home network. It works by reserving an address/port pair for each service on a dual-stack machine at the ISP. That is, the port is used to differentiate between the different sites (home networks) on the inside. This is not an elegant solution, but it works for simple protocols such as HTTP (not for FTP for example). There are obvious problems related to DNS since the target (where the service runs) and the relay do not have the same DNS entry (reverse lookup mismatch). There has been very little traffic over this mechanism and it is available mostly for completeness.

An alternative approach is to use the ALG proxy support (in apache 2, for example) to relay connections from the ISP to servers at the home networks. We have successfully tested this approach (although we inadvertently created a spam-relay for awhile due to inappropriate access control), but did not use it extensively.

IPv4 from Internet to IPv4 service at home

IPv4-to-IPv4 traffic is dealt with in the same manner as above, but with an additional translator running on the home gateway performing the translation from IPv6 to IPv4.

IPv6 from Internet to IPv4 service at home

This is dealt with by the same Transport Relay Translator discussed above.

IPv6 from Internet to IPv6 service at home

No special action is needed.

13.2.2.4 Summary

Only non-routable (private) IPv4 addresses are used on the home networks. This triggers the use of translators of various kinds. That the core only runs IPv6 complicates the matter further, but not beyond what can be maintained and run.

The components for IPv6 to IPv4 are:

- Translating IP directly (NAT-PT), and copying the user's data from one connection to another (FAITH). Cooperation with the totd DNS proxy is needed to get the connections needing translation to the translators.
- TRT (Transport Relay Translator) and one-to-one translation (6tunnel).
- Application specific solutions (for FTP).

The components for IPv4 to IPv6 are:

- TRT (Transport Relay Translator), 6tunnel

- Application specific translators (HTTP proxy and FTP)

13.2.3 Evaluation of the Pilot Network

The pilot network has been operational for more than two years now. In this section we describe our experiences and some problems we encountered with regards to the implementation and management of such a network.

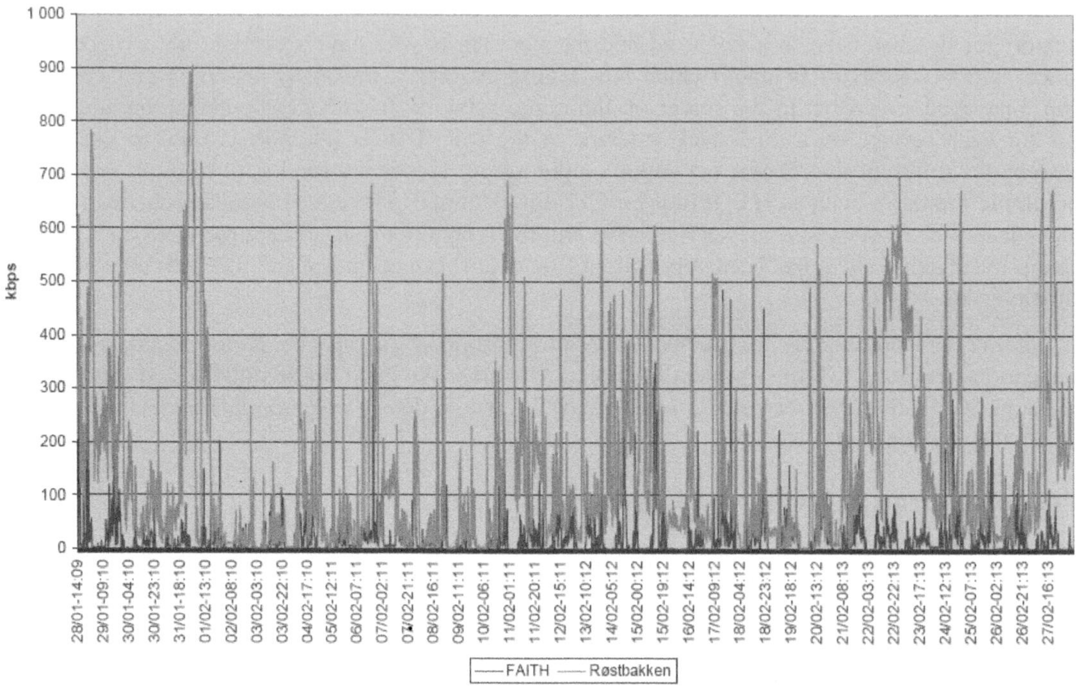

Figure 13-5 Traffic Statistics of Røstbakken Tower and faithd

The figure above gives an impression of the traffic patterns encountered in the core of our metropolitan network. The figure shows traffic measured at Røstbakken tower which is a central connection point for the majority of the home networks. In addition, the figure shows traffic measured at the most used IPv6 to IPv4 translator, namely the machine doing faithd TCP relaying that is located in the Telenor Research Laboratory. This does not give a complete image of the traffic on the whole network. Not only does it not capture the traffic from the northern part of the network, it also does not show the (IPv6-only) traffic produced by the IPv6-only network of the University of Tromsø that uses the same infrastructure.

13.2.3.1 NAT-PT

The NAT-PT implementation from KAME for FreeBSD that we used is not as mature as most other software from by the KAME project. Problems were exposed by HTTP connections to some websites failing when going through NAT-PT. We have not analysed the problems in more detail, nor extended the experiment to other applications. This decision was mainly motivated by the impression that the KAME project itself had abandoned further development of the NAT-PT code.

13.2.3.2 *Faithd*

Faithd only supports TCP connections and for each TCP port a separate process needs to be started. We have experimented with adding UDP support by making a python prototype (proof of concept). We did not continue to develop a production quality C implementation due to lack of interest by the users. In addition, we modified the original faithd to relay TCP connections for any port. This simplifies its configuration dramatically. Access control is then performed using firewall filtering. However, this modified faithd requires a small patch to the kernel code (NetBSD in our case). As our patches where not accepted by the NetBSD project team, kernel patching is required to use our faithd. This does not outweigh the advantage of easier configuration, and we therefore abandoned this modified faithd too.

13.2.3.3 *6tunnel*

Using 6tunnel for connecting to POP and IMAP servers does not allow SSL to be used. This is because unmodified SSL implementations use source and destination addresses as endpoint identifiers in their security associations. With 6tunnel in the middle modifying endpoint addresses, this fails.

13.2.3.4 *DNS*

Occasional problems were discovered where totd failed to deal with particular DNS server implementations. Some problems where dealt with in subsequent totd versions. One remaining problem is that some old nameserver implementations return a 'Server Failed' instead of the prescribed 'No Such Domain' response when asked for an IPv6 address record (that these nameservers have no knowledge of). Of course, these nameservers should be fixed, but in the meantime newer versions of totd work around the problem by always asking a nameserver for an IPv4 record even when it returns 'Server Failed'.

Another DNS-related problem, that totd cannot solve is that some services use hardcoded IPv4 addresses instead of DNS names to save some DNS lookups. This is one of the main reasons why we preferred using HTTP ALGs running on dual-stack machines over translating HTTP connections on the network or transport layer. A few popular sites like www.hotmail.com and some advertisement suppliers used hardcoded IPv4 addresses in URLs. This generated many user-generated problem reports.

Finally, some servers advertise an IPv6 address in DNS but offer services that are IPv4-only. Due to totd, applications will use IPv4 through a translator when no IPv6 address is found, but they can/will not fallback to IPv4 through a translator when the IPv6 connection fails for some reason. An example of such a server was mail.netbsd.org which was a dual-stack machine with IPv6 address in DNS, but ran an IPv4-only sendmail configuration. Sending email from an IPv6-only mail server to mail.netbsd.org therefore failed. This problem was fixed some time after the NetBSD maintainers were notified of the problem, but many sites are not so responsive to complaints from a (still) small user population.

13.2.3.5 *Hardware Failures*

We experienced several times problems with hardware used for IPv6 which worked fine when used for IPv4 only! Some problems could be fixed when identified like the one where a network card was too slow to initialize multicast reception to pick up replies to router solicitation it sent on startup. However, others remained a mystery and we had to 'fix' them by switching to other hardware. Luckily the failures were with low-end Ethernet cards that were cheap to replace.

13.2.3.6 IPv4-only applications at home

This required the most support and configuration due to the lack of a generic translation mechanism or ALG. ALGs for the most popular applications like Web browsing and ftp are available, but is often lacking for increasingly popular applications like multiparty gaming and P2P filesharing applications. A generic solution is to add tunnelling of IPv4 in IPv6. But in some cases the combination of reduced MTU due to tunnelling and non-routable addresses (going through one or more NATs) caused some applications to fail. However, in most cases, tunnelling works fine and transparent to the applications. We are therefore now introducing tunnelling at the time the experimental network is turning into a more permanent service to its users.

13.2.3.7 Security

We experienced the hard way, how several transition mechanisms can be (ab)used by third parties, mostly by spammers. We inadvertently created a spam relay twice. These relays where discovered quickly by spammers and used to forward almost 300,000 junk mails before we discovered what was happening. Proper access control, which takes into account the 'backdoors' created, is easily overlooked when introducing transition mechanisms. The most notable example of this was experienced when we started adding IPv4 over IPv6 tunnels from the home networks to the ISP (by the end of the pilot project), and a home gateway running an IPv4-to-IPv6 transport relay suddenly became globally accessible over IPv4. As formerly no global IPv4 addresses where used in the home network, no access control was deemed needed at the time the transport relay was setup. And, when a global IPv4 address was added later, the missing access control to the transport relay was overlooked creating a 'backdoor' to the main mail servers which believed the traffic through it to be from authorized home users.

13.2.3.8 Scalability

A variety of functionality to make IPv6 transitioning for a large number of unmanaged networks scalable and feasible is missing. Most notably we missed:

1. Dynamic DNS updating for autoconfigured addresses.
2. Automatic configuration on clients of IPv6 DNS resolver addresses (e.g. using DHCPv6, SLP or some well-known address).
3. Automatic configuration of transition mechanisms, especially those used on the home gateways.
4. Automatic configuration of the network prefix to use inside a home network.

The latter was sorely missed on a wireless based network with many links. It can be non-trivial to find out what antenna/link you are actually connecting too and what IPv6 addresses belong to it. We needed to define fairly elaborate technical and administrative procedures for new users to get their home gateway connected. We used the RIP routing protocol on home gateway routers and the routers of the core network. The main reason was not routing, but network debugging and making it easier to assist users remotely in getting connected.

13.2.4 Conclusions

Configuration of network equipment against a pure IPv6 ISP is still too complicated and out of reach of non-technical users. This is mostly due to the lack of autoconfiguration mechanisms for DNS localisation, prefix delegation and autoconfiguration of transition mechanisms.

The quality of service of the traditional IPv4 applications is significantly reduced because generic easy-to-setup transition support for many applications is still missing.

Our conclusion is then that we have shown that it is possible for ordinary users to live with an IPv6-only ISP, but at the cost of a significant reduction in user friendliness and quality of service. This means that it is still too early for an ISP to transition from IPv4 to IPv6-only. Currently, the best approach is a dual-stack ISP or maybe IPv6-only with IPv4 in IPv6 tunnelling. In our experience it seems that transition mechanisms are ok for centralised use, but that for IPv6-only ISP operation we should push for porting of applications to IPv6 instead of putting our hopes on better and easier to configure future implementation of translators.

13.3 Large Academic Department (University of Southampton)

In this section we begin by describing the systems components in this scenario of a large "departmental" network (1,500+ users with around 1,000 hosts) that wishes to transition to support IPv6. We describe the elements that need to be considered for the transition.

Southampton has been running IPv6 since 1996, but has only in the last two years adopted IPv6 as a production service in its network.

This scenario assumes no IPv6 is deployed beforehand, although in reality the transition at Southampton is already underway, in fact it is at the time of writing in a reasonably advanced stage. Thus after a review of the systems components, we present an overview of the status to date, current plans and next steps, and also the major remaining obstacles that have been identified.

Our motivation to deploy was in support of teaching, research projects, and communication with IPv6 networks (including those used by overseas students), while also encouraging innovation from staff and students – indeed already we have seen new streamed radio (Surge/Virgin[1]) and multicast video services (ECS-TV[2]) emerge.

This work has contributed to the IETF v6ops WG enterprise scenario descriptions and analysis. We have documented our campus experience in an Internet Draft [Cho04a] and also documented the IEEE 802.1q VLAN approach to introducing IPv6 [Cho04b] that has also been used at Muenster (see above). The [Cho04a] draft was built from a similar analysis as appears here.

13.3.1 Systems Components

The components fall into the following categories:

- Network components
- Address allocation components
- Services
- Host and device platforms
- User tools

We discuss these categories below.

In the light of the IETF v6ops WG activity on studying IPv6 network renumbering [RFC4192], we also cite components where hardcoded IP(v4) addresses may be found, that may need consideration in IPv6 networks. Further renumbering reporting can be found in D3.6.1 [D3.6.1] and D3.6.2 [D3.6.2].

13.3.1.1 Network

Physical connectivity (Layer 2)

The technologies used are:

- Switched Ethernet
- Gigabit Ethernet
- Wireless networking (802.11b)

[1] http://www.ipv6.ecs.soton.ac.uk/virginradio

[2] http://www.ecstv.ecs.soton.ac.uk

There is no use of ATM, FDDI or other "older" technologies. The network is purely Ethernet. IEEE 802.1q VLANs are supported by the network equipment.

Routing and Logical subnets (Layer 3)

The hybrid Layer 2/3 routing equipment is composed of Alcatel OSR and Omnicore L2/L3, with approximately 15 internal IPv4 subnets (in effect, routed VLANs). There is no specific internal routing protocol used. There is a static route via the site firewall to the main upstream provider (academic) running at 1Gbit/s, and there is also a static route to the secondary (low bandwidth) link offsite (commercial).

Hard coded IP information:

- The IPv4 address space assigned by academic provider
- There is hardcoded IP subnet information
- IP addresses for static route targets

Firewall

The firewall is currently a CheckPoint Firewall-1 solution running on a Nokia IP740 hardware platform. There is one internal facing interface, one external facing interface, and two "DMZ" interfaces, one for wired hosts and one for the Wireless LAN provision.

Hard coded IP information:

- Names resolved to IP addresses in FW-1 at "compilation" time
- IP addresses in remote firewalls allowing access to remote services
- IP-based authentication in remote systems allowing access to online bibliographic resources

Intrusion Detection (IDS)

The Snort package is used for intrusion detection.

Management

Some network management is performed by SNMP; there is no specific package for this. There is a greater emphasis on monitoring than explicitly in management.

Monitoring

A number of tools are used, to monitor network usage as well as systems availability, e.g. nocol, nagios and MRTG. The IBM AWM tool is used for network performance testing, along with iperf, rude and crude.

Remote Access

The components supporting remote access are:

- Livingston Portmaster 56K/ISDN dialup
- RADIUS server
- (Microsoft) VPN server

IPv6 access (e.g. for local testbed)

A native IPv6 service from the regional network (LeNSE) to the JANET (NREN) is used. This is facilitated by use of 6PE over MPLS.

Hard coded IP information:

- IP endpoints of upstream connectivity interface

13.3.1.2 Address allocation

The department receives its IPv4 and IPv6 address allocations from the University. For IPv4, the University has a /16 allocation which is not aggregated under the JANET NREN. For IPv6, the University receives its allocation as a /48 site prefix from JANET.

IPv6 network prefix allocation

The department currently has approximately 10 (non-contiguous) /24 IPv4 prefixes allocated to it by the campus computing services department (ISS).

For IPv6, JANET has the prefix 2001:630::/32 from RIPE NCC, as the national academic ISP in the UK. The University has been allocated 2001:630:d0::/48 by JANET. The department has been allocated a /52 size prefix 2001:630:d0::/52.

The department is a RIPE member and could obtain LIR status (as Muenster has done). However, we have not applied for an IPv6 prefix at this time.

In the initial deployment, we expect that IPv4 and IPv6 subnets will be congruent (and thus share and run over the same VLANs). We feel in an initial deployment that this approach simplifies management. We numbered our IPv6 links by topology, depending on which links were attached to which subrouter (in effect, an arbitrary scheme, given our small number of links – 15 or so).

The advantage for IPv6 is that subnets will not need to be resized to conserve or efficiently utilise address space as is the case currently for IPv4 (as subnet host counts rise and fall for administrative or research group growth/decline reasons).

Hard coded IP information:

- The IP prefix allocation from the university

IPv6 Address allocation

It is expected that the network devices will use a combination of address allocation mechanisms:

- Manually configured addresses (in some servers)
- Stateful DHCPv6 (probably in fixed, wired devices and some servers)
- Stateless address autoconfiguration (probably in wireless and mobile devices)
- RFC3041 privacy addresses (in some client devices)

For devices using stateless or RFC3041 mechanisms, a Stateless DHCPv6 server will be required for other (non-address) configuration options, e.g. DNS and NTP servers.

There is some concern over the use of RFC3041 addresses, due to the complexities it causes for tracking devices and knowing which network accesses are actually made by the same node over time.

13.3.1.3 Services

The component services hosted by the departmental network are:

Email

There are three MX hosts for inbound email, and two main internal mail servers. Sendmail is the MTA. POP and IMAP (and their secure versions) are used for mail access, using the UW-IMAP open source code. There is an MS Exchange server used by up to 200 users (generally those wanting shared access to mail spools, e.g. professors and secretaries).

MailScanner is used for anti-spam/anti-virus. This uses external services including various RBLs for part of its anti-spam checking.

Successful reverse DNS lookup is required for sendmail to accept internal SMTP connections for delivery.

Hard coded IP information:

- Blocked SMTP servers (spam sources)

Web hosting

Web content hosting is provided either with Apache 1.3.x (open source) or Microsoft IIS 5.0. Common components used to build systems with are MySQL, PHP 4 and Perl 5; these enable local tools such as Wikis to be run.

Hard coded IP information:

- .htaccess and remote access controls
- Apache "Listen" directive on given IP address

Databases

All database systems are presented via a web interface, including the financial systems. In some cases, e.g. student records, ODBC-like access is required to/from from the department systems to/from the campus systems. Databases include: finance records, people, projects and publications (offered using ePrints).

Directory services

A number of directory service tools are in use:

- NIS (6 servers, all Solaris)
- LDAP
- Active Directory
- RADIUS

DNS

The three DNS servers have recently been upgraded to BIND9. A DNS secondary is held at another UK university site.

PKI

The department has at least 10 SSL certificates from Thawte, including Web-signing certificates. No personal certificates are supported by the department (though users may have their own).

NTP

The JANET NREN offers several stratum 0 NTP servers. The department also has a GPS-based NTP server built-in to its own RIPE NCC test traffic server.

USENET news

The news feed is delivered using dnews.

Multicast

There is PIM-SM IPv4 multicast via a dedicated Cisco 7206 router. This supports applications including the IPv4 AccessGrid conferencing system. A number of bugs in the Alcatel equipment prevent heavy use of IPv4 multicast within the department network (thus an IPv6 multicast solution is highly desirable). An IPv4 multicast beacon is used for monitoring multicast.

Remote login

Remote login access is offered via ssh, with sftp for file transfer. Remote use of telnet and ftp is denied by the firewall.

File serving

The main file servers are SGI systems, hosting large (multi-TB) standalone RAID arrays. The files are offered via NFS and Samba to client systems.

The content distribution server is hosted on such a system (e.g. containing MS software licensed under the Campus Agreement).

13.3.1.4 Host and device platforms

Server platforms

The following server platforms are in use in the department:

- Windows 2003 server
- Windows 2000 server
- Windows NT
- Solaris 8
- Solaris 9
- RedHat Linux
- SGI Origin 300 (Irix 6.5.x)

Desktop/laptop platforms

The following client platforms are in use in the department:

- Windows 98, 2000, ME, XP
- Linux (various flavours)
- MacOS/X
- BSD (various flavours)

PDA platforms

The following PDA platforms are in use in the department:

- Windows CE/.NET
- PalmOS
- Familiar Linux
- Zaurus

13.3.1.5 User tools/systems

The following tools or systems are used by the department's user base.

Hardware

Various dedicated systems, for example:

- Networked printers
- Networked webcams

Mail client

Various, including:

- Outlook (various versions)
- Eudora
- Mutt
- Pine

Web browser

Various, including:

- MS Internet Explorer
- Mozilla
- Safari
- Opera

Conferencing systems

The following conferencing tools are in regular use:

- AccessGrid
- A dedicated H.323 system
- MS Netmeeting

Other collaboration tools

Collaboration tools in regular use include:

- IRC
- Jabber
- MSN Messenger
- cvs

USENET news client

Various, including:

- nn
- Mozilla

Host communications

Specific tools for remote host communications include:

- X11
- VNC
- PC Anywhere

13.3.2 Transition Status

Having described the components, we now outline the steps already taken towards transition at the site. The focus here is to provide increasing IPv6 functionality in a dual-stack environment, with the goal of allowing IPv6-only devices to be introduced and to operate successfully using only IPv6 transport (that does not mean they have to interoperate with all 'legacy' services, but they should be able to use DNS, NTP, SMTP and similar basic services).

Because the Alcatel switch/router equipment does not route IPv6, an alternative method was required to deliver IPv6 on the wire to existing IPv4 subnets. To enable this, IPv6 router advertisements were delivered using a parallel IPv6 routing infrastructure. These IPv6-only routers support IEEE 802.1q VLAN tagging; the BSD routers can inject a different IPv6 prefix onto each IPv4 subnet, using congruent VLANs. The router tags the packets travelling towards the internal network with a configured VLAN ID depending on the destination IPv6 prefix/link. This VLAN method is described by the authors in [Cho04b], and illustrated in Figure 13-6.

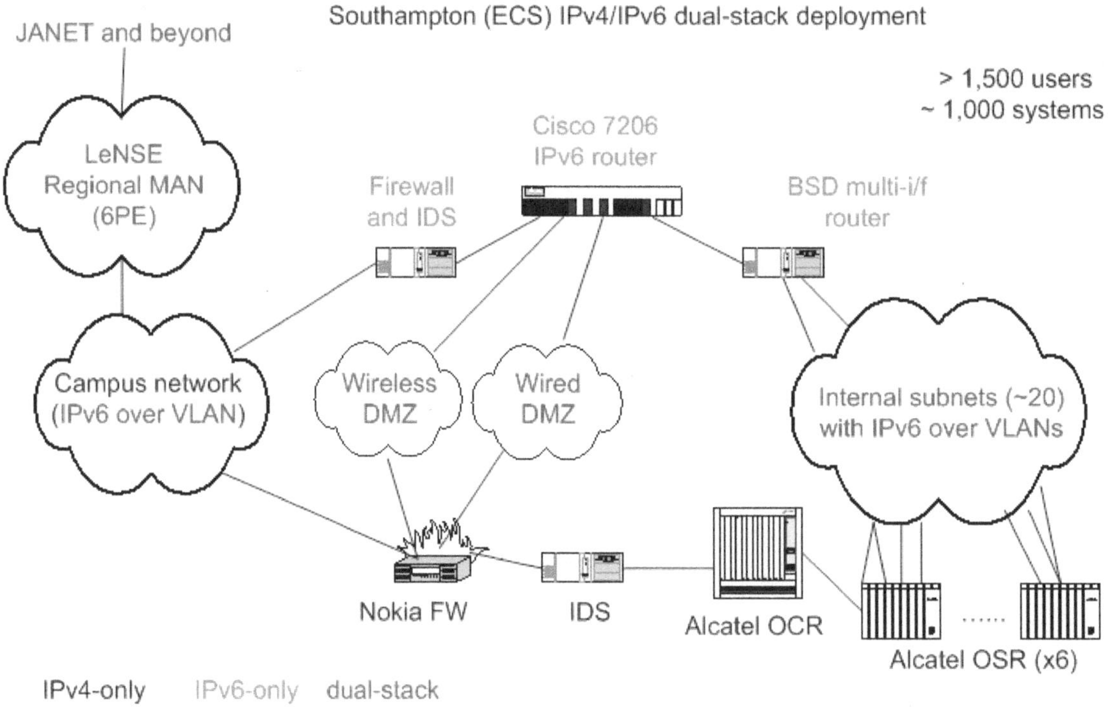

Figure 13-6 Use of IPv6 VLANs at Southampton

As traffic in the site grows, multiple routers can be dedicated to this task for internal routing, or a router with multiple interfaces. We currently have four routers with quad Fast Ethernet interfaces. BSD allows multiple-VLAN tagging per interface, so in light traffic conditions the interface count can be collapsed. We have found, however, that our BSD systems are beginning to struggle under the growing load of IPv6 traffic.

External IPv6 connectivity was configured using a Cisco 7206, for unicast and multicast (SSM and PIM-SM), with IPv6 multicast routed internally onto the VLANs using the BSD IPv6 multicast support. The connection to the JANET IPv6 service is delivered natively through the LeNSE regional network.

The longer term plan is to use IPv6 firewalling on the Nokia IP740; until then the firewall is an additional BSD system, on which ports are blocked by default. This is a partially stateful firewall.

Two IPv6-only DNS servers have been run in the past; now the main servers network/subnet is IPv6-enabled the department's three primary BIND9 DNS servers have been IPv6-enabled. This includes reverse delegation of our prefix under 0.d.0.0.0.3.6.0.1.0.0.2.ip6.int and 0.d.0.0.0.3.6.0.1.0.0.2.ip6.arpa (the .int is being phased out). The new DNS server information is currently as follows:

```
ns0.ecs.soton.ac.uk.    390    IN    A       152.78.70.1
ns0.ecs.soton.ac.uk.    390    IN    AAAA    2001:630:d0:116::53
ns1.ecs.soton.ac.uk.    390    IN    A       152.78.68.1
ns1.ecs.soton.ac.uk.    390    IN    AAAA    2001:630:d0:117::53
ns2.ecs.soton.ac.uk.    390    IN    A       152.78.71.1
ns2.ecs.soton.ac.uk.    390    IN    AAAA    2001:630:d0:121::53
```

The main Linux login server is IPv6-enabled, with ssh logins and sftp file transfer available through the firewall. Once IPv6 is present on the wire, all that was needed was the firewall hole to be opened up for the service, an IPv6 AAAA DNS entry added for the login server, and the sshd daemon with IPv6 support turned on. Offering only secure protocols (and not plain ftp or telnet) can be easier to do when starting afresh with a new protocol.

NTP has been provisioned for IPv6 by use of both the RIPE TTM server as an NTP server, and also a dedicated NTP server from Meinberg, that supports both IPv4 and IPv6.

Our SMTP and MX servers now exchange external email over IPv6. IPv6 DNS records were added for the hosts that provide these services. If the sending or receiving node we are communicating with supports IPv6, IPv6 transport for email is usually preferred.

Almost all of our web servers/sites have been made available using Apache 2, e.g. the main department web site at www.ecs.soton.ac.uk, and many of the 100 or so hosted domains that we run, e.g. the IST IPv6 Cluster site, as operated for the 6LINK project, or the IPv6 Forum web site www.ipv6forum.org.

The department's Wireless LAN (over 30 access points) is IPv6 enabled. Some Mobile IPv6 has been deployed and tested between the WLAN and the local community wireless network (SOWN), using the MIPL code (which lacks security elements, but is usable). The more advanced WLAN network we deployed uses 802.1x based access control, which is IP version neutral and thus can be used to secure the IPv4 and IPv6 WLAN access.

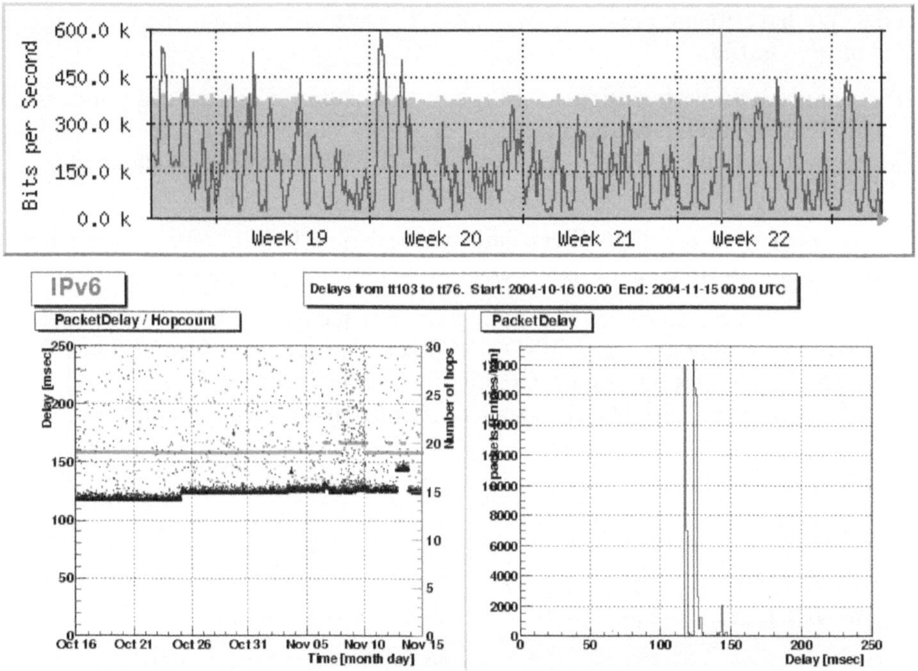

Figure 13-7 MRTG Monitoring Surge Radio Node (top) and RIPE TTM view (bottom)

Monitoring is achieved by a mixture of Netflow v9, Nagios, our RIPE TTM server and MRTG. An example of MRTG doing host monitoring and RIPE TTM output is shown in Figure 13-7.

The latest versions of Radiator and FreeRADIUS allow IPv6 transport for RADIUS.

Dual-stack Jabber and Internet Relay Chat (irc) servers are deployed.

An H.323 IPv6 conferencing system has been tested (GnomeMeeting for Linux), and we host a dual-stack Open H.323 MCU server for videoconferencing.

A key point to emphasise is that in making the transition to support IPv6 dual-stack pervasively in our network, we have not seen any adverse affect on IPv4 services. Making our DNS, MX and web servers all able to serve data over IPv4 or IPv6 has not had any noticeable adverse impact on robustness or reliability.

13.3.3 Supporting Remote Users

We offer a tunnel broker and a 6to4 relay for remote users, e.g. students in home networks or staff in wireless hotspots at conferences. At present tunnel broker users connecting get either a single IPv6 address or a /64 prefix. To offer more, in particular a /48 from our tunnel broker, we would need to use our RIPE membership to obtain LIR status and get a larger 'ISP' prefix.

We are assisting UKERNA to deploy a national academic IPv6 tunnel broker, using the Hexago broker which includes TSP support.

13.3.4 Next Steps for the Transition

Much has been achieved, but there is also still work to be done. Some imminent next steps include the following:

- A DHCPv6 service is required; implementations will be tested in the near future (from Cisco and Lucent). This will enable IPv6 DNS resolver discovery for hosts, but also be used for address allocation.
- Work on modifications to Snort to allow IPv6 IDS functions to be used.
- A dynamic DNS service is required for statelessly configuring hosts.

We are also deploying new network infrastructure over the summer of 2005, with a Cisco solution selected. One Cisco 6509 and around 30 Cisco 3750's will be deployed, with full dual-stack IPv6 support for unicast and multicast. We have already performed tests, e.g. for MLD snooping for IPv6 on the 3750's (with an advanced EFT image).

13.3.5 IPv6 Transition Missing Components

In the study for transition, we have identified a number of missing (unavailable) components for IPv6 transition, including:

1. No IPv6 Layer 3 functionality on the Alcatel OSR/Omnicore equipment (this will be resolved when the new Cisco IPv6-capable equipment is deployed in July 2005);
2. Lack of NFS/Samba IPv6 support;
3. Lack of MS Exchange, Outlook or Eudora IPv6 support;
4. No IPv6 intrusion detection system;
5. No IPv6 support for Active Directory;
6. No IPv6 dnews, so one would have to use inn as a Usenet news server;
7. Lack of supported IPv6 for Windows 98/2000/ME;
8. Lack of supported IPv6 for Irix;
9. Lack of supported IPv6 for various PDA platforms;
10. No method available to offer reverse IPv6 DNS for sendmail to verify autoconfiguring hosts (prepopulating a 64 bit subnet space is a problem, some wildcard method is required);
11. No available IPv6-enabled X11 (there is an xfree but it is encumbered by an unpopular copyright statement that most distributors find unacceptable).

This list is by no means a show-stopper for IPv6 deployment. Indeed, we take the view that by deploying IPv6 we are enabling a new environment. Some nodes will be able to take advantage of the new environment, and new applications that support IPv6, while others will happily still use 'legacy' IPv4 for basic functions such as email and web interactions.

The overall transition experience has been very positive to date.

13.4 *University Deployment Analysis (Lancaster University)*

IPv6 has been deployed within the Computing Department at Lancaster University for several years as part of our ongoing research activities and during that time, external connectivity has been provided via configured tunnels over the UK academic network to ULCC. However, as part of a recently initiated network upgrade process, Lancaster University's network operations group, ISS (Information System Services), decided to begin the native deployment of IPv6 across the main campus with the assistance of the Computing department. Indeed, one important motivator for IPv6 deployment at this time was due to the Computing Departments involvement in the 6NET project which represented a good opportunity to get useful additional support throughout the process.

Following the 6NET IPv6 management seminar in October 2004, which was attended by members of ISS, we began the collaborative process of planning the deployment of a dual stack IPv6 network. The goal of this was initially to provide native IPv6 connectivity to the Computing Department in the new InfoLab21 building before extending it to offer the service on a campus-wide basis. This type of widespread IPv6 deployment impacts on all aspects of the network from the underlying infrastructure to the services and applications run over it and so one of our first tasks was to conduct an analysis of what technologies will be affected by the deployment of IPv6 and what new or existing services will be needed. Once that was completed, the initial IPv6 deployment began and now that this too has been completed, we are ready to begin considering moving on to the next stage in the deployment process.

The aims in writing this section are therefore both to document the progress that has been made to date and to highlight the major issues that have been encountered and what solutions have been used to overcome them. In many cases, the issues that arose were the result of missing IPv6 support within deployed hardware or software and so we can (hopefully) expect this to be largely resolved in the near future as the wider deployment process continues. They are all currently however important considerations for those contemplating IPv6 deployments in the Enterprise, and particularly the campus scope, at this point in time.

13.4.1 IPv6 Deployment Analysis

This section presents a summary of the analysis that was conducted prior to IPv6 deployment at Lancaster and will begin with a brief discussion of our starting point in terms of the existing IPv6 deployment and production network. Thereafter, it will summarise the components of a production IPv6 network that were considered as essential for the deployment in the University campus. This includes areas such as addressing, network services, OS support and IPv6 application status.

13.4.1.1 Starting Point

As discussed briefly in the introduction, IPv6 has been used within the Computing Department at Lancaster University since around 1995 -1997. While this was primarily used as a research tool, it was also available both in the lab and office networks and over the departmental wireless network on a semi-production basis. The address space used for this was a subnet of the university prefix allocated to R&D activities. External connectivity was provided via configured tunnels to the 6Bone and on to other interested UK parties, including ULCC, UCL and the University of Southampton. This was coordinated under the Bermuda2 collaboration (www.ipv6.ac.uk/bermuda2/).

This deployment was still largely in place prior to the formal deployment of IPv6 across the University campus and so it is anticipated that when this occurs, the configured tunnels will be closed and the renumbering to production addresses (where appropriate) will take place.

At the outset of this project, the regional MAN, C&NLMAN (Cumbria & North Lancashire MAN) (http://www.canlman.net.uk/), and the University itself were both IPv4-only and the JANET Access Point had yet to be upgraded. As such, the most obvious IPv6 deployment approach was for it to begin at the innermost point in the network and be rolled-out to the edge. This gives us quite an interesting perspective to IPv6 deployment to see the progress from core to edge.

The deployment of IPv6 in the University campus was seen by ISS as part of a much larger network upgrade process moving away from a legacy 'flat' (ATM) network to a hierarchical subnet-based layout using VPNs. As such, the aim is that IPv6 deployment will ultimately be deployed in parallel to the new (IPv4) network giving a modern dual stack layout.

13.4.1.2 Addressing Considerations

One of the first aspects of the IPv6 deployment to be tackled was addressing both in terms of the allocation plan and the mechanism used. While an allocation plan had been in place for some years, the opportunity to refine this was taken and the format was changed to reflect a more logical allocation method over a physical plan based on buildings or departments to simplify management. A summary of the new plan is presented below.

Basic Configuration

Prefix allocated by JANET: 2001:0630:0080::/48

Special Addresses: 2001:630:80:0000::/64 - Reserved (DNS, services, etc.)

2001:630:80::1 Router

2001:630:80::4 DNS - primary

2001:630:80::7 DNS - secondary

General Address Format

Other than the above special addresses, Lancaster University IPv6 addresses observe the following format:

<48 UNI> <3 Res> <1 Site> <12 Subnet> <64 Host>

where:

<48 UNI> - 48 bit University prefix 2001:630:80::/48

<3 Res> - 3 bits reserved for future aggregation

<1 Site> - 1 bit identifying the site of the network (provisional)

<12 Subnet> - 12 bits for site subnet

<64 Host> - 64 bit host identifier

IPv6 Subnet Format

One issue that was of particular concern for ISS throughout was that flexibility be incorporated into the design in order to minimise the need for extensive or complicated reallocation in the future. As such, in addition to the high-order bits reserved for future use, the subnet allocation methodology follows whereby bits closest to the boundary between groups are allocated last in order to maximise the potential for reallocation.

Production subnets will use their 12 bits subnet allocation in the following way:

<4 Cat> <8 Physical>

The category group makes up the first 4 bits of the subnet identifier and is reserved for allocating subnets based broadly according to the roles they perform. An example of this would be to allocate subnets for office, public or wireless networks which can each then be further divided in the physical group.

The physical group (8 bits) can then be used to add geographical identifiers to the category. These will, for example, define the different colleges, academic departments and physical buildings that make up the university campus. In practice of course, there are likely to be multiple subnets allocated to larger buildings or departments as necessary.

Address Allocation Mechanism (DHCPv6 vs. SLAAC)

The DHCPv6/SLAAC (stateless address autoconfiguration) issue is still one that is a matter of continued debate among the community at large. After consultation with other 6NET members however, it was determined that there is a strong case to justify the ISS position that stateful DHCPv6 is the most suitable candidate for managed IPv6 address allocation in an enterprise-type network. The benefits of a centralised address allocation and service discovery method for network management make DHCPv6 a better choice than SLAAC for this type of network.

As such, the majority of Lancaster's IPv6 address allocation requirements will be handled via stateful DHCPv6 but there will be limited use of manually configured addresses (as in the special cases, see above) and SLAAC in certain cases and environments that favour it, such as wireless or mobile networks.

13.4.1.3 Operating System Considerations

Lancaster University uses a variety of Operating Systems including Microsoft Windows, Linux and Unix variants. In all cases, various versions are in use ranging from the most current, incorporating native IPv6 to older versions that will need to be upgraded as production IPv6 is not and will not be supported.

Microsoft

A range of Microsoft Operating Systems are in use ranging from NT4.0 to XP and Server 2003 and as such the degree of IPv6 support is obviously variable. Windows NT4.0 has no IPv6 support, Windows 2000 has no commercial IPv6 support but XP and Server 2003 does and so some upgrading may be necessary in this case.

Linux

The main versions of Linux in use at Lancaster are Redhat 7.3 – 9.0 and Fedora and so IPv6 support is generally available in most cases out of the box. IPv6 support was introduced in Linux from kernel version 2.4 onwards and since the versions in use range from 2.4 – 2.6, this should introduce no major problems.

Solaris

Solaris is the main UNIX variant used at Lancaster from version 2.5.1 right through to 9, but mainly version 7. Newer versions will not be seriously affected since IPv6 support was formally introduced from version 8 onwards. In older versions however, despite IPv6 patches being available, it would be highly preferable to upgrade to newer versions before IPv6 support is considered.

13.4.1.4 Core IPv6 Services

DNS

The Lancaster University DNS servers now run BIND9 and so can be used to provide native IPv6 transport (http://www.isc.org/index.pl?/sw/bind/). The deployment of IPv6 enabled DNS is now in progress and should be completed in the near future.

DHCPv6

As already discussed, ISS has made the decision to deploy stateful DHCPv6 to handle IPv6 address allocation in parallel with the existing DHCP service. Given the relatively 'new' nature of DHCPv6, the level of support is currently low but there are some implementations available including Sourceforge (open source), NEC, Dibbler, Cisco and HP. However, there are issues that arise with each and in any case ubiquitous DHCPv6 client support (in MS Windows for example) is some way off.

This is an important part of our IPv6 deployment plan and so we expect to begin experimentation and trialling of the various DHCPv6 implementations in the near future.

13.4.1.5 Network Services

Email

The University runs a number of email services based primarily on Exim, MS Exchange and Pine IMAP. Unfortunately, the availability of IPv6 over these services is variable. Exim has included IPv6 support for some time and all versions that are in use at Lancaster are IPv6 enabled. Pine IMAP has rudimentary IPv6 support provided via a patch but should not be considered production level. MS Exchange has no IPv6 support at this time.

Web Services

Lancaster utilises two key web services, Apache servers and web proxying via Squid. The newer versions of Apache, 2.x onwards, feature native IPv6 support but 1.3.x is also still in use and only supports IPv6 via a non-production patch (http://www.apache.org/). As such, some upgrading may be necessary to deploy IPv6 fully.

The Squid developers have enabled IPv6 in the current version, 2.5 as a patch against the latest version of the CVS sources (http://www.squid-cache.org/). While this is readily available, there has been little work in developing native IPv6 functionality in Squid and so this represents a significant issue that may necessitate further consideration.

File Sharing

Lancaster primarily uses MS Windows-based file sharing using Active Directory. Unfortunately this is not currently IPv6 enabled and so again introduces a significant issue when IPv6 deployment reaches this stage. There are no plans to upgrade our file sharing system in the immediate future but until this issue is resolved, it represents a significant problem for IPv6 deployment is this area.

In addition to the Microsoft service, Samba and NFS are available for non-Windows systems including Linux, UNIX and Solaris. To date IPv6 support is not included in either of these services.

Other Services

The above obviously only represents a small range of the services and applications deployed at Lancaster University and once the initial IPv6 deployments are complete a more thorough survey will be completed prior to the production roll out across campus.

Areas still to be addressed at this stage include security, management and remote access to name a few. There are now however many useful sources that list the current status of IPv6 applications including the deepspace6 site:

http://www.deepspace6.net/docs/ipv6_status_page_apps.html

13.4.2 IPv6 Deployment Status

This section will discuss in detail the IPv6 deployment efforts undertaken to date. This is concerned with first stage of IPv6 deployment which covers the rollout of native IPv6 connectivity from the JANET core network, across C&NLMAN, and out over the University backbone. As such, the majority of this section will be concerned with the issues encountered at the network level, enabling native IPv6 connectivity down to the Computing Department. The final part of this section however will summarise all the issues that have been encountered to date in our IPv6 deployment efforts.

13.4.2.1 Native Connectivity to the Computing Department

Lancaster University is connected to the UK academic network (JANET) via the C&NLMAN regional network, also administered in Lancaster. At the outset, this did not offer native IPv6 but was intended to be made dual stack as a precursor to a deployment within the University. This presented two distinct sets of problems, enabling IPv6 support within C&NLMAN and the subsequent deployment in the University campus. Since the focus of this section is the Enterprise/campus scope, this section focuses primarily on the later except in cases where the deployment of IPv6 in the provider network has implications for the campus deployment. We will first describe the basic topology of the network to outline how this was affected by the deployment of IPv6 and what modifications were necessary to achieve it.

Starting Point

The situation at Lancaster differs from that in other Enterprise networks because in our case ISS is responsible for the management and operation of both the regional MAN and the University network, thus reducing the number of parties involved in the process to two, the Computing Department and ISS. We exclude UKERNA here (who manage the JANET network) because while they are responsible for UK academic IPv6 prefix allocation and core deployments, they were not directly involved in the planning of our IPv6 deployment. This obviously has many advantages and has undoubtedly led to a reduction in the amount and time and effort spent during the planning the deployment process.

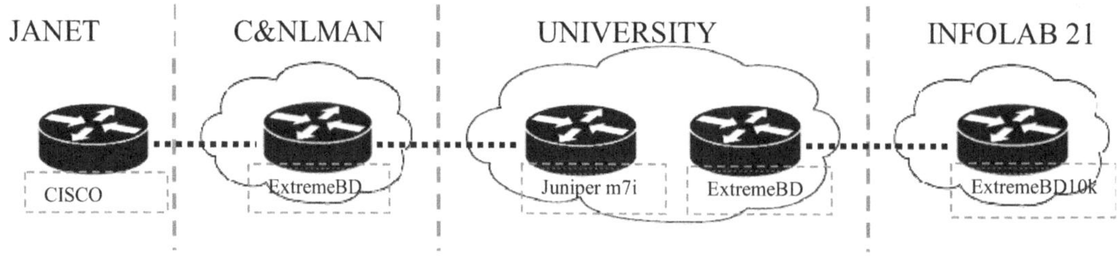

Figure 13-8 Basic Configuration of the Upgrade Path

As such, while the deployments in C&NLMAN and the University were considered separately (including addressing and routing considerations), the work was conducted almost in parallel, again leading to a reduction in the amount of time taken during the deployment. The original configuration of the network from the UKERNA access point to the InfoLab21 entry-point is shown below (Figure 13-8):

In our case, hardware is supplied from a number of vendors including Cisco, Juniper and Extreme and each device was first tested in a sandbox environment to both determine the extent of IPv6 functionality offered and to allow ISS to familiarise themselves with this aspect of their operation. Unfortunately, while the Juniper and Cisco equipment proved very capable of supporting IPv6, the Extreme devices did not, introducing problems at both the MAN and the University level. In the case of the Computing Department, a BlackDiamond 10k has recently been deployed on which limited IPv6 support is available and full support is promised shortly, unfortunately however the older BlackDiamond 6k devices deployed across the rest of the infrastructure do not currently offer IPv6 support and are unlikely to do so in the immediate future.

13.4.2.2 The IPv6 Deployment Process

An incremental approach was adopted by ISS for IPv6 deployment which involved the upgrade of first the UKERNA Access Point and the C&NLMAN infrastructure before moving on to address the University network.

Provider Network Deployment

With the UKERNA equipment being beyond our control (and upgraded separately: http://www.ja.net/development/ipv6/statustable.html), the most pressing issue was that of C&NLMAN connectivity. ISS determined that the most effective way to overcome the problem given the issues with Extreme networking equipment was to modify their existing configuration by introducing an additional device upstream of the BlackDiamond 6k to handle L3 (i.e. routing) functionality leaving the former as purely a L2 switch for which it is better suited in any case. The new device, a Juniper m7i, now handles the IP routing and is well suited to this role (with hardware support) thereby neatly sidestepping the problem. This process was completed as of December 2004 and so from that date native IPv6 connectivity was available into the University network.

University Backbone Deployment

The University upgrade followed a roughly parallel path to that of C&NLMAN as the infrastructure is similar. As such, the main issue faced was with the Computing Department employing a BlackDiamond 10k and so while the L3/L2 approach was followed across the majority of the University backbone, this device could not necessarily be circumvented in the same way.

Ironically, the BlackDiamond 10k claimed to have full IPv6 functionality but when this was explored by ISS, it soon became clear that a dual stack configuration opens significant security holes in the IPv4 stack and so was not a viable option (IPv6-only operation however was fine). An updated version of the firmware for this device is currently with ISS who are in the process of testing it ahead of the release and use within the network.

As a result, it was decided that the best solution to this was a temporary direct link into the Computing Department based on a Cisco 7206 that was available. This was connected directly to the Juniper m7i at the university BAR (Border Access Router) to circumvent the existing infrastructure until the remainder of the network (including the BlackDiamond 10k) has been upgraded and production IPv6 can be supported. This was achieved recently and as of April 2005 native IPv6 via the new infrastructure is now available into the Computing Department on a research basis. In the near future this will be used to replace the existing tunnelled connectivity, and be made available department-wide. Figure 13-9 shows the current configuration of the university infrastructure.

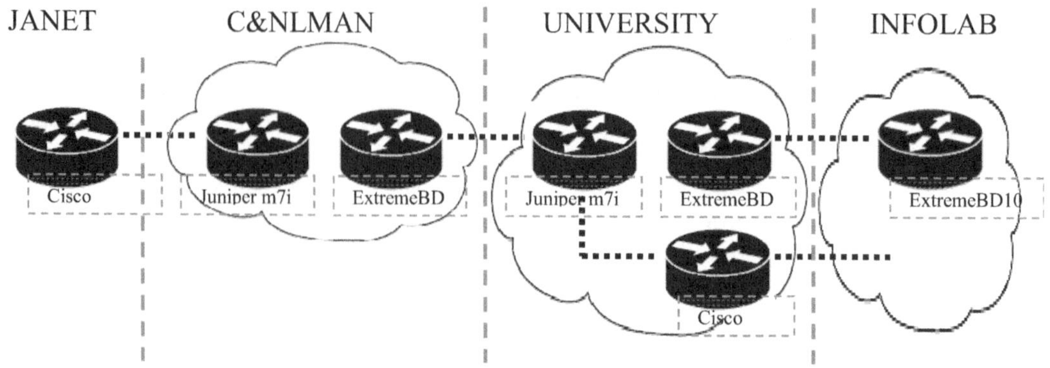

Figure 13-9 Alternative Configuration Providing Native IPv6 to the Computing Dept

Finally, as part of the continued upgrade process, the BlackDiamond 6k within the University network has now been replaced by a 10k. As such, once suitable firmware is available for the BlackDiamond 10k devices, the university infrastructure will be fully capable of supporting production dual stack from end-to-end across the backbone.

13.4.2.3 Outstanding Components

In order to complete an IPv6 deployment that is equivalent to the existing IPv4 infrastructure, a number of missing 'pieces' in the IPv6 deployment need to be upgraded to support IPv6. Unfortunately, this lack of support applies to every level of the deployment, from hardware to network services and applications. This section therefore provides a summary of the outstanding network components that need to be enabled with IPv6 or circumvented to allow the campus deployment process to continue.

In terms of hardware, the lack of IPv6 support on the BlackDiamond equipment was the most significant problem that we faced. This was largely overcome through the use of available Cisco and Juniper equipment to perform L3 routing and upgrades in the BlackDiamond 10k firmware. As a result, this problem has largely now been overcome.

The core services, DNS and DCHPv6 are an essential part of the IPv6 deployment process and as such the lack of proper DHCPv6 represents a significant problem. IPv6 enabled DNS deployment is now underway within the University but the lack of widespread DHCPv6 support cannot be overcome at this time. This should again 'fix' itself as more implementations become available and proper support is incorporated into more products over time but at present, this represents perhaps the most significant immediate issue to IPv6 deployment at Lancaster.

Other significant issues include the lack of IPv6 support in other important network services and software. This level of support is mixed but perhaps the most pressing issue is the lack of proper IPv6 support in mainstream Microsoft products such as MS Exchange and Active Directory. In general, while the level of IPv6 support is quite solid in Microsoft Operation Systems, the applications and services that run across them are much less so. Other issues include the lack of file sharing / NFS support and the lack of IPv6 support in web caching software such as Squid among others.

13.4.3 Next Steps

There is still a long way to go until a 'full' IPv6 deployment has been completed at Lancaster, both in terms of supporting the key network services that would be expected in such a network and providing connectivity to the number of users necessary to make IPv6 available at an Enterprise level. As such, this section will outline the major steps that still need to be completed in order to complete the IPv6 deployment process.

This will begin by summarising the current state of IPv6 deployment and highlighting the, as yet, missing pieces of the deployment either due to one of the issues discussed in the previous section or because it has simply yet to be addressed. Thereafter we will focus on discussing our ongoing deployment from the immediate next steps to the ultimate long-term goals.

13.4.3.1 Current Status Summary

The current state of IPv6 the deployment at Lancaster is that native IPv6 has now been enabled all the way down to the Computing Department and is now being used in a number of R&D activities. This is significant not least because it has necessitated upgrading the connectivity all the way from the regional network core, through the University infrastructure down to the Computing Department.

With this now complete, the continued rollout of native IPv6 over the campus is now possible and it is also being used to replace the existing tunnelled infrastructure in the Computing department. Additionally, IPv6 services are expected to come online shortly starting with DNS (and DHCPv6 when possible) and moving out from there.

13.4.3.2 Deployment Goals

With the initial IPv6 deployment now completed, the next steps will be to continue to rollout IPv6 over the rest of the campus and extend its functionality to provide a more complete set of services. This will proceed in three parts, the first of which will complete the deployment of IPv6 in the Computing Department, making it widely available in both the office and research networks. The second will continue to upgrade the University's IPv6 deployment both in terms of the physical deployment over campus to interested groups and departments beyond ourselves and upgrading network services to make them fully IPv6 compatible. Finally, as a long term goal, there must be an effort to offer IPv6 in a ubiquitous manner across the entire campus network and use this to deploy new IPv6 services such as multicast, QoS and mobility.

Immediate Goals

The immediate goals are those related to completing the next stages of IPv6 deployment and include the wider deployment of production IPv6 in the Computing department and the provision of the core IPv6 services such as DNS. With the general deployment of IPv6 in our department, the first use of production IPv6 address space is now occurring and as such represents a significant deployment milestone.

Completing the Campus Rollout

This stage of IPv6 deployment will involve completing the deployment of IPv6 dual stack over the campus backbone by resolving the outstanding issues (particularly with the BlackDiamond 10k) along with the upgrade of essential networking services such as DNS to support the deployment, this has already been largely completed. This provides a basic level of connectivity and will allow production access to the IPv6 Internet. Thereafter, there are will be two parts of the continued deployment, the provision of more IPv6-enabled services and the continued rollout of IPv6 connectivity to other interested groups and departments.

Now that the core IPv6 infrastructure has been deployed, connectivity can be extended on an 'as necessary' basis, initially only to those who request it. There is no obvious limit to the potential rollout of IPv6 to the rest of the campus and so it becomes a matter of policy as to when this actually takes place. The continued provision of IPv6 services will initially include those outlined such as email, www access, file sharing, etc. The goal here will be to continually dual stack enable networking services over time to eventually provide an IPv6 service equivalent to the existing IPv4 infrastructure.

Further IPv6 rollout

With the initial rollout of IPv6 now well underway in the Computing Department, the next logical goal for IPv6 deployment within the University will be to try to improve the IPv6 user-base by increasing the number of IPv6-enabled hosts within the network. There are two logical ways in which this could potentially be pursued in our case: either by enabling dual stack IPv6 on the student network (ResNet) or in the University computer laboratories. Either (or both) of these can be done relatively easily depending on the requirements of ISS for managed IPv6 deployment.

If it is determined that initial IPv6 deployments should be managed then the lab networks are the natural choice as they are heavily managed by ISS whereas the student networks are much less so and so IPv6 can be enabled but left to the students to use IPv6 if they wish. Since the majority of hosts on the both networks will be MS Windows-based, the majority of new IPv6 users here are likely to be Windows XP-based but in the student network case ISS should be prepared for both Linux and Unix support also. Either of these deployments would potentially introduce several hundred new IPv6-enabled hosts to the network (at a conservative estimate) and so would greatly increase the scale of IPv6 deployment within the University campus.

Protocol Selection Policy Definition

With a significant IPv6 deployment in place, an issue that gains relevance at this point is in defining how IPv6 is used within IPv6-enabled hosts. The conventional choice within IPv6 early-adopters is currently not to use IPv6 as the first-choice protocol except in explicit special cases where IPv4 is not supported. This should certainly still be the case in the majority of our deployments where the network is dual stack and IPv6 is not yet able to offer an equivalent service to the existing IPv4 network.

Ultimate Goals

Once this is complete, IPv6 will be available across the entire network and so the 'deployment' will be largely complete. As such, it will then be possible to consider what other services could potentially be deployed across the infrastructure and while it is too early to define these with a great degree of confidence, multicast and mobility are both strong candidates for this as they feature strongly as IPv6-only applications that would showcase the potential of the new protocol.

13.4.3.3 Other Considerations

Beyond the deployment of IPv6 connectivity and services at Lancaster, there are a number of other considerations that must be made alongside it. The prime example of this is the operation and management aspects of the network that are necessary to ensure the safe and secure operation of both the IPv6 and IPv4 networks. In addition to this, another consideration that has yet to be fully addressed are the transitioning requirements of the IPv6 deployment and this will be considered here also.

Network Operations and Management Services

This area of the deployment actually encompasses a wide range of networking applications and technologies that support the management and safe operation of the network. Obviously, the impact of IPv6 deployment will be significant in this area and so it is necessary to consider each aspect of this in turn. This has yet to be fully assessed from the perspective of IPv6 deployment but summary of these areas include:

Firewalling

The addition of IPv6 on the campus backbone will necessitate the provision of IPv6 firewalling in addition to the existing IPv4 firewalls, this is already underway.

Security

This includes both intrusion detection and snooping software and both will need to be upgraded to support IPv6.

Management and Monitoring

A range of management and monitoring services are employed within the University and these will need to be upgraded to support IPv6. This process is also currently in progress.

Secure Remote Access

Remote access to the university is provided via a VPN server that is available to both staff and students. While the campus is still dual stack, this will in all likelihood not be upgraded but an IPv6 VPN service may be provided in the future.

Transitioning Approach

Due to the IPv6 deployment at Lancaster being dual stack, specific transitioning solutions are not necessary at this point in time. Indeed, our existing tunnelled connections will shortly be replaced with native production links thanks to the deployment efforts made to date and since this is going to be deployed from end-to-end, interoperation mechanisms are also largely unnecessary at this stage.

There has however been some discussion of specific scenarios where IPv6-only connections may be needed at some point in the future and as part of our deployment study it would be wise not to rule this out as a possibility. As such, we will briefly outline the mechanisms that may be considered for deployment at Lancaster in the future, either to offer connectivity to isolated IPv6 subnets or to provide IPv4 interoperation to IPv6-only subnets.

To provide IPv6 connectivity, a number of tunnelling mechanisms may be deployed depending on the circumstances. Internal tunnelling will be largely unnecessary since the campus supports dual stack but external connectivity may be supported via 6to4 or perhaps tunnel brokers. Likewise, since IPv6-only networks have not been deployed to date, interoperation mechanisms are not necessary but in the event that they do become deployed, TRT (with a suitable range of ALGs) or DSTM seem the most obvious solutions.

13.5 Other Scenarios

The above scenarios and 'case studies' are reports of ongoing IPv6 deployments at 6NET partner sites. In this section we give brief commentary on other academic-related scenarios, to allow the reader to gain some insight into how we feel solutions will be chosen from the quite large toolbox that is available to a network administrator when faced with these situations.

13.5.1 Early IPv6 Testbed on a Campus

There are two variants of a scenario where a campus wishes to gain early IPv6 experience before a wider adoption. We assume the campus does not have native connectivity to its NREN or regional network (upstream provider).

13.5.1.1 An IPv6 laboratory or single IPv6 subnet

In this case, a single router can be deployed in the testbed subnet and a tunnel used for connectivity from the testbed to an upstream IPv6 provider.

The choice for the site is which tunnel mechanism to use. The options include:

- Manually configured tunnel
- Tunnel broker
- 6to4

While 6to4 is convenient and automatic, it can lack reliability (depending on the 6to4 relays being used). It also means the site does not use production address space, or its own allocated address space. A manual tunnel or tunnel broker would generally be preferred.

If the site is using IPv4 NAT, a tunnel can still be established, but may need specific forwarding of (for example) Protocol 41 on the NAT device, or use of a protocol such as TSP to establish a NAT-friendly tunnel method such as UDP tunnelling.

13.5.1.2 IPv6 hosts scattered around the campus

As per the above case, a router should be deployed with tunnelled uplink/external connectivity.

The decision then is how to connect the sparsely deployed hosts. Where VLANs are available, they could be used to distribute IPv6 by Layer 2 segregation to specific physical ports on the network edge. An alternative is to use ISATAP as an automatic tunnelling solution, or an internal tunnel broker. The tunnel broker and VLAN solutions are more manageable, e.g. the broker can include authentication, and thus may be preferred where a more controlled deployment is desirable.

13.5.1.3 IPv6-only testbed

If the testbed is IPv6-only, then a different approach is required. The reader is referred to the Tromso scenario described earlier in this section.

If there are dual-stack nodes in the IPv6-only testbed, DSTM may be an appropriate solution.

13.5.2 School Deployment of IPv6 to Complement IPv4+NAT

This scenario has been covered in depth by the 6NET report on the IPv6 Deployment in the Greek School Network [D5.14]. Here, IPv6 with global addressing is adding new possibilities to an infrastructure previously focused on IPv4 + NAT.

13.5.3 IPv6 Access for Home Users

Here we consider home user networks (staff, students) wanting connectivity, possibly behind a NAT, possibly with just a single machine, possibly with a dynamic IPv4 address.

The solutions available include

- Teredo
- Tunnel broker
- 6to4

Some tunnel broker implementations, especially with TSP, can support IPv4 NAT traversal and/or dynamic IPv4 addresses. As described above, 6to4 can have reliability issues dependent on the relay location (but is strong when used to connect just to other 6to4 sites, e.g. other home networks using it). Teredo is a method of 'last resort', designed for use behind IPv4 NATs. The broker or 6to4 would generally be preferred to Teredo.

13.6 Summary of Unexpected Results and Unforeseen Difficulties

The case studies above discuss the general scenarios and deployment procedures that were followed in each case. In each case, the challenges in deployment were generally technical but understood, rather than 'exploratory'. Thus very few, if any, unexpected results or difficulties were encountered. Quite the opposite – the deployments described have gone very well and have been very positive.

Here we repeat a small summary of the unforeseen issues captured in the scenarios above:

- A surprising level of fear, uncertainty and doubt (FUD) about the IPv6 technology by certain administrators that we had to interact with.
- The fact that if you want to run a tunnel broker service to your staff or students, a /48 prefix is not big enough for a campus unless the broker users only get a /64 prefix, which is not ideal.
- Lack of VLAN capability where it was desired, preventing the VLAN method being used where desired in all cases.
- Variable performance in software driven VLAN tagging; Southampton's BSD routers hit a forwarding limit with the specific DLINK cards used.
- A desire by network administrators (managers) to use DHCPv6 even when IPv6 supports stateless autoconfiguration. Sites seem used to managing their IP address assets.
- A desire to disable IPv6 Privacy Addresses to make management and monitoring simpler (device identification simpler).
- Unexpected impact on IPv4 security when IPv6 is turned on. This happened in the Lancaster case, but is resolved via a firmware upgrade
- The relative high performance of DSTM versus NAT-PT.

- Various issues with totd at Tromso – interactions with certain DNS implementations, with use of IP literals, and systems with AAAA records that do not offer all services over IPv6 transport.
- Some hardware problems to run IPv6 in old PCs, caused by lack of required multicast support in old Ethernet cards. These can be replaced cheaply.
- Abuse of some transitioning relay services. The spammers will find you.

Although these have been overcome, they may represent generic issues that may resurface in similar situations.

For a discussion of issues and challenges remaining for IPv6 deployment, see [D2.5.3].

13.7 Summary of tradeoffs made in solutions chosen

Many tradeoffs are related to the desirable properties of the mechanisms being chosen from, for example:

- Which IPv4 and IPv6 functionality/connectivity is required?
- The cost of deploying dual-stack, versus IPv6-only with translation to communicate with IPv4 devices
- The cost to 'the Internet architecture' of a certain method, e.g. are relays expected to be deployed by every ISP, or even every site? How do these relays interact?
- Security requirements – is the method open to relay abuse?
- Ease of management – how is the transition mechanism managed?
- Whether dynamic IPv4 addresses on the client need to be handled
- Whether IPv4 NAT traversal is needed from the client
- Whether just hosts or networks need to be connected
- How the solution scales – is there just one point of failure? Is load-sharing or balancing supported?
- Resilience in the solution
- Who owns the transition components (ISP or end site)
- How the service is discovered or configured, if 'plug and play' is desirable
- Whether specific services are enabled, like multicast
- How optimal the routing is (or isn't), e.g. whether there is any route optimisation method
- What performance penalty is suffered from encapsulation/translation methods
- Whether reverse DNS lookups are available for the method
- Accountability – how is usage reported and monitored, or identified?

There is no single, 'best' solution for all scenarios. Factors such as those listed above will determine which is best for which scenario.

Chapter 14

IPv6 on the Move

This chapter describes three case studies of 6NET partners who deployed and trialled Mobile IPv6 testbeds. We first look at the testbed at Fraunhofer Fokus and after that we describe the testbeds at Lancaster University and the University of Oulu.

14.1 Fraunhofer Fokus

The Fokus Mobile IPv6 testbed has undergone several changes throughout the 6NET project. The current environment does not longer distinguish between an internal and an external part as before when there was a local, experimental testbed not constantly connected to the 6NET network and another part with continous provision of native IPv6 connectivity to the outer 6NET world. Furthermore the test environment was completed by several components providing for VoIP and video conferencing capabilities.

The Mobile IPv6 testbed consists of the components illustrated in Figure 14-1.

Connected to the central router "adrahil" there are basically two different networks with prefixes 2001:638:806:2002::/64 and 2001:638:806:2001::/64. Attached to those networks are the corresponding Home Agents for the MIPL- and the KAME-Mobile IP implementation, respectively. A MCU connected to the "2001"-network was used as Corresponding Node for Mobile IPv6 functionality- and interoperability testing: Using a MN with video conferencing equipment, i.e. the GnomeMeeting application with camera and headset, this scenario allowed for establishing a connection to the CN-MCU and subsequently changing the IPv6 network point of attachment while maintaining the connection to the MCU.

Currently the Fokus testbed is made up of the different components:

- End systems with different operating systems

  At the leaves of the network, standard PCs with different operating systems (Windows Server 2003, Windows XP, Linux, FreeBSD) are installed. They are used for testing IPv6 network applications like video conferencing, web surfing, downloading audio and video streams, IP telephony applications etc.

- Home Agents

  Mobile IPv6 Home Agents as offered by the MIPL- and KAME project.

- IP softphone

The original BonePhone application was complemented for performance reasons by the SIP-based KPhone telephony application (also developed in the context of WP5 of the 6NET project) for use as MN.

- FreeBit hardphone for use as MN.
- GnomeMeeting video conference client for use as MN.
- H.323 OpenMCU for use as CN.

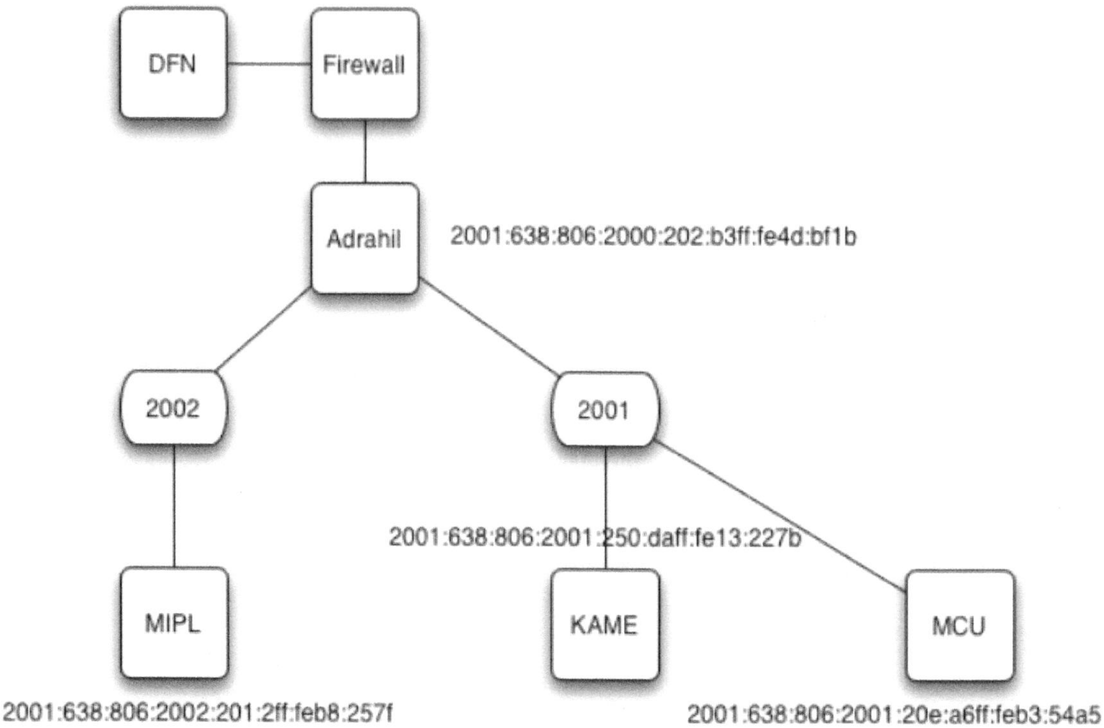

Figure 14-1 Schematic Representation of the Testbed Setup

14.1.1 MIPL-HA

The Linux HA is running version 1.1 of the MIPL implementation. The HA has the address: 2001:638:806:2002:201:2ff:feb8:257f. The home address in the network has the prefix: 2001:638:806:2002::/64.

14.1.2 Kame-HA

The KAME HA is running a snapshot dated 22/03/2004. Due to compatibility reasons you need at least version 1.1 of the MIPL implementation if you want to use the KAME HA in combination with a Linux mobile node. The HA has the address: 2001:638:806:2001:250:daff:fe13:227b.The home address in the network has the prefix: 2001:638:806:2001::/64.

14.1.3 MCU-CN

The MCU is running version 1.1 of the MIPL implementation as well, the address is 2001:638:806:2001:20e:a6ff:feb3:54a5. There are two rooms, the default room is "room101". In order to enable checking of local audio and video settings there is a loopback room simply called "loopback". In case of audio or video problems the MCU room "loopback" can be used to check proper working of audio and video peripherals.

14.1.4 IPSec

IPSec was turned off at the time of MIPv6 testing due to compatibility reasons. Only the KAME implementation supported it at that time.

14.2 Testbed Components

Table 14-1 Fokus MIPv6 Testbed Components

Host	System	OS	Type	IPv6 Address
Trolloc	Cisco 7206VXR[1]	Version 12.2(8)T4	Router	DFN - 6WIN - IPv6 - Network prefix usage for FhG Fokus: 2001:0638:0806::/48
adrahil	PIII/500 MHz	Debian GNU/Linux Rel. 2.4.18, dual stack	Access router IPv6	2001:638:806:2000:202:b3ff:fe4d:bf1b 2001:638:806:2001:202:b3ff:fe4d:c8e0 2001:638:806:2002:250:4ff:fe64:eb78
Mipl.lab6.fokus.fraunhofer.de			HA (MIPL)	2001:638:806:2002:201:2ff:feb8:257f
kame.lab6.fokus.fraunhofer.de			HA (KAME)	2001:638:806:2001:250:daff:fe13:227b
mcu.lab6.fokus.fraunhofer.de (MCU)		GNU/Linux 2.4.26 i686	CN	2001:638:806:2001:20e:a6ff:feb3:54a5

One can think of a scenario in which a Mobile Node is roaming only between foreign networks, never arriving home.

For offering this kind of service one needs a HA connected to the public IPv6 infrastructure. The MN's home address has to have the same prefix as the HA's one.

The Fokus testbed offers this kind of use of MIPv6 Home Agents for functionality and interoperability tests.

The required configuration parameters for the concerning MN are:

In case you want to use the Linux HA: MIPL HA-address: mipl.lab6.fokus.fraunhofer.de (2001:638:806:2002:201:2ff:feb8:257f) Home address in the network: 2001:638:806:2002::/64

In case you want to use the Kame HA: KAME HA-address: kame.lab6.fokus.fraunhofer.de (2001:638:806:2001:250:daff:fe13:227b) Home address in the network: 2001:638:806:2001::/64 (Note: To use the Kame HA with a Linux Mobile Node (MN) you need at least version 1.1 of the MIPL-implementation.)

---

[1] Cisco 7206VXR, 6-slot chassis, 1 AC Supply w/IP Software, 7200VXR NPE-400 (128MB default memory), 256 MB Memory for NPE-400 in 7200 Series, 1-Port Packet/SONET OC3c/STM1 Singlemode (IR) Port Adapter, Cisco 7200 Input/Output Controller with Dual 10/100 Ethernet, Cisco 7200 I/O PCMCIA Flash Disk, 128 MB Option, Cisco 72009 Series IOS IP

In order to support simple MN-CN connectivity/roaming tests an IPv6 H.323-MCU was connected to the "2001"-network: The address of the MCU is: mcu.lab6.fokus.fraunhofer.de (2001:638:806:2001:20e:a6ff:feb3:54a5) There are two conferencing rooms, the default room is "room101". For the convenience of checking local audio settings an audioloopback room called "loopback" was set up. If you encounter any kind of audio problems in "room101", please use the room "loopback" first to check if your local microphone and speaker settings work correctly.

There is no security association or any other restriction whatsoever. Any Mobile Node in the network above should be able to use these HAs.

14.3 Lancaster University

Lancaster University has had a Mobile IPv6 testbed in one form or another since 1997. In those early years we used Lancaster University's own implementation running on Linux. Since then, more extensive research efforts (some with the help of Lancaster University to port their code to different platforms) have spawned other implementations which are much more up to date and robust than the Lancaster University implementation. In our MIPv6 testbed for 6NET we have thus not considered the Lancaster University implementation since it is now not interoperable with more recent implementations.

14.3.1 The Testbed

As simplified diagram of the Lancaster University MIPv6 testbed is shown in Figure 14-2.

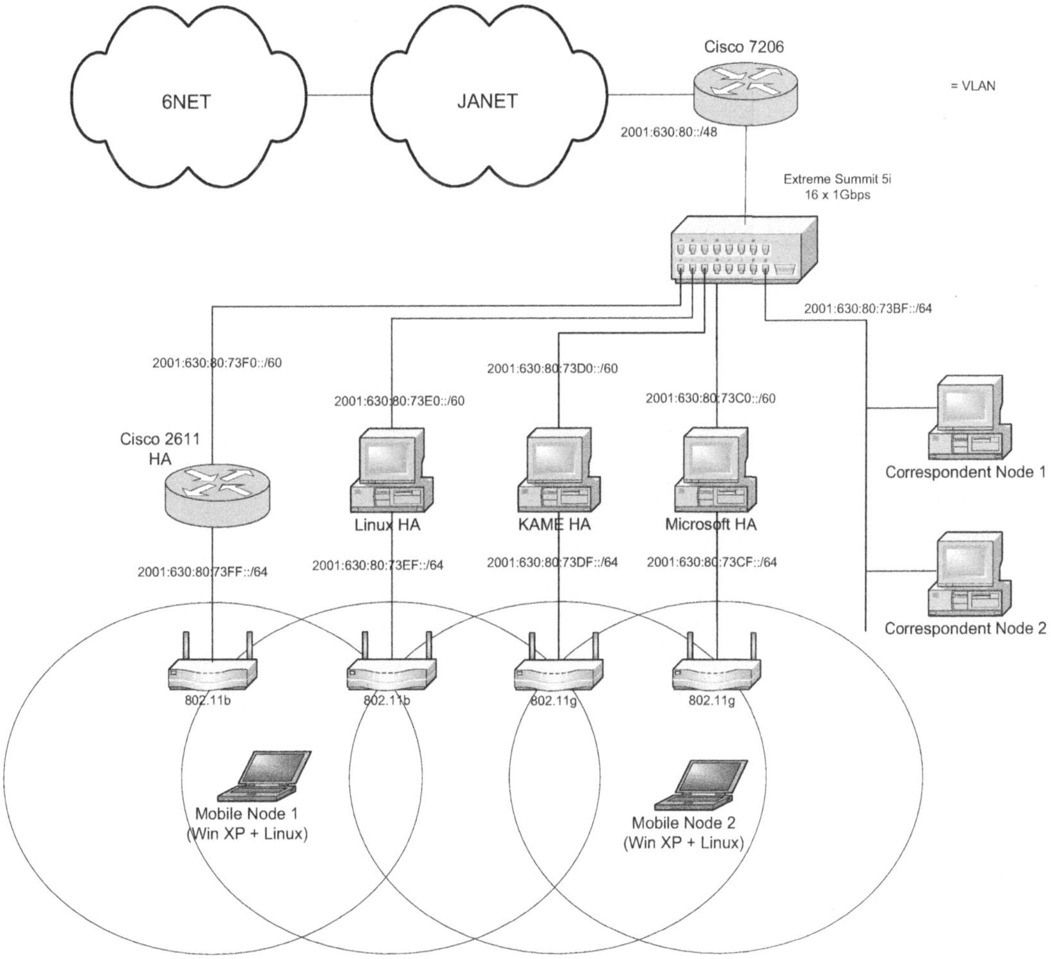

Figure 14-2 Lancaster University MIPv6 Testbed

Connectivity to 6NET (via SuperJANET) is achieved through a Cisco 7206 router. The testbed is then divided into Virtual Local Area Networks (VLANs) with each subnet (generally a ::/60 or a ::/64) comprising its own VLAN. The Extreme Summit Ethernet switch is capable of assigning VLAN tags according to IPv6 prefixes and switching them accordingly (thus, it acts as a virtual IPv6 router). All of the IPv6 VLANs are terminated on the Cisco 7206.

The 802.11 wireless LAN is configured so that each access router (i.e. HA) of the wireless LAN is analogous to one ESSID. Only one Access Point per ESSID is illustrated in the figure, although wireless coverage for each ESSID can be extended with more Access Points. Of course, configuring multiple Mobile IPv6 networks in this manner will eat up the available 802.11b channel space rather quickly. The figure above illustrates how multiple Mobile IPv6 HAs can have their associated Access Points arranged so that a maximum of 3 overlapping channels is seen in one cell footprint. Obviously, this is rather straightforward to accomplish in a lab environment where our main focus is to investigate the interactions between multiple Mobile IPv6 networks. In a real (semi)production environment the close geographical proximity of different distinct Mobile IPv6 networks is much less likely.

14.3.2 Components

The various components in our Mobile IPv6 testbed are as follows.

Home Agents

The testbed employs four different Home Agents. One using the Microsoft MIPv6 technical preview implementation for Windows XP, another using MIPL v1.1, another using the Cisco Ohanami EFT and finally one Home Agent using KAME. The Microsoft, Linux and KAME Home Agents are all PC based routers each comprising AMD Athlon XP 2.6Ghz CPU 512MB RAM. The Cisco Home Agent is a 2611 XM with 128MB on board RAM.

Mobile Nodes

The Mobile Nodes in the testbed are dual-boot (Windows XP and Linux 2.4.26) machines and can therefore use either MIPv6 implementation of the two available operating systems. The Windows XP operating system has Service Pack 1 installed along with Microsoft's Advanced Networking Pack update. The MIPv6 implementation on the Windows XP operating system

Correspondent Nodes

The two PC-based Correspondent Nodes comprise AMD Athlon XP 1.6Ghz CPUs and 256MB RAM. One of the PCs is a dual-boot Windows XP and Redhat Linux system, the other is a FreeBSD system running FreeBSD 4.10-RELEASE. Note that the Mobile Nodes may also perform the role of a Correspondent Node.

The make-up of the various components in our Mobile IPv6 testbed are summarised in Table 14-2.

Table 14-2 Lancaster MIPv6 Testbed Components

	Hardware	System	MIPv6 Implementation
Cisco HA	2611 XM, 128MB RAM	Ohanami IOS EFT	Included in IOS
Microsoft HA	AMD Athlon XP 2.6Ghz, 512MB RAM	Windows XP SP1 + advanced networking update	Draft v24 compliant Technical Preview
KAME HA	AMD Athlon XP	FreeBSD 4.10-RELEASE	SNAP /kame/snap/kame-

	Hardware	System	MIPv6 Implementation
	2.6Ghz, 512MB RAM		20050103-freebsd410-snap.tgz
Linux HA	AMD Athlon XP 2.6Ghz, 512MB RAM	Redhat Linux 2.4.26	MIPL v1.1
Mobile Node 1	Sony Vaio Intel Pentium III Mobile 1Ghz, 256MB	Dual boot Windows XP SP1 with advanced networking update and Redhat Linux 2.4.26	Draft v24 compliant Technical Preview MIPL v1.1
Mobile Node 2	Dell Latitude C610 Pentium III Mobile 1Ghz, 256MB	Dual boot Windows XP SP1 with advanced networking update and Redhat Linux 2.4.26	Draft v24 compliant Technical Preview MIPL v1.1
Correspondent Node 1	AMD Athlon XP 1.6Ghz, 256MB	Free-BSD 4.10 – RELEASE	SNAP /kame/snap/kame-20050103-freebsd410-snap.tgz
Correspondent Node 2	AMD Athlon XP 1.6Ghz, 256MB	Dual boot Windows XP SP1 with advanced networking update and Redhat Linux 2.4.26	MIPL v1.1

14.3.3 Addressing and Subnetting

The rationale behind the addressing and subnet allocations is as follows. The prefix allocated to Lancaster University by JANET is 2001:0630:0080::/48.

Other than some special addresses reserved for e.g. router interface numbering and DNS, Lancaster University IPv6 addresses observe the following format:

<48 UNI> <1 Res> <3 Site> <12 Subnetting> <64 Host>

where:

<48 UNI> - 48 bit University prefix 2001:630:80::/48

<1 Res> - 1 reserved bit for future aggregation

<3 Site> - 3 bit code identifying the site of the network

<12 Subnetting> - 12 bits for site subnetting

<64 Host> - 64 bit host identifier

All of the sites, with the exception of site 7 (Research and Development), use their 12 bits for subnetting as follows:

<8 Building> <4 Network>

where:

<8 Building> - 8 bit code identifying a building within the site

<4 Network> - 4 bits to allocate subnets within each building

However, for our experimental Mobile IPv6 testbed we assigned it to site 7, research and development. We felt it was wise to have production and experimental research networks attributed to different sites and our Mobile IPv6 testbed is very much non-production traffic. The prefix for research and development networks is: 2001:630:80:7000::/52

Site 7, research and development uses its 12 bits for subnetting as follows:

<2 Reserved> <6 Networks> <4 Subnets>

where:

<2 Reserved> - 2 bits reserved for future aggregation

<6 Networks> - 6 bits to allocate to R&D networks

<4 Subnets> - 4 bits to allocate Subnets

Hence the full address format for addresses on the research and development network is:

<48 UNI> <1 Res> <3 Site> <2 Reserved> <6 Networks> <4 Sub-Networks> <64 Host>

There are 6 bits to allocate research and development networks (26 = 64 networks) and they are allocated in a flat manner.

For example:

2001:630:80:700::/60 - Network 0

2001:630:80:701::/60 - Network 1

2001:630:80:702::/60 - Network 2

2001:630:80:703::/60 - Network 3

...

2001:630:80:73F::/60 - Network 63

Further subnets can be defined arbitrarily based on the 4 bits to allocate for subnets.

So each Mobile IPv6 network is assigned a ::/60 prefix as illustrated in Figure 14-2. Currently each Mobile IPv6 network comprises one Home Agent. Each HA will advertise a ::/64 prefix via Router Advertisements to hosts on its link. Currently there is no stateful address configuration (e.g. using DHCPv6) on our MIPv6 networks and all hosts use stateless address autoconfiguration (remember that not every host on the HA's link needs to be a MN). A MN will know that it is on its home network when it sees the RA from its HA. It is possible to have multiple HAs per network but we chose this topology as it facilitates easier debugging during testing.

14.3.4 Testing

We have tested manually configured IPSec security associations between Microsoft MN and KAME HA. This seems to work well in that the Microsoft MN is able to register with the KAME HA and binding updates are performed successfully. When testing a Linux MN or HA we have only used non-IPSec authenticated communication between the MN and HA. The same is true when using a Cisco HA. In general we have found that all the implementations in our testbed are interoperable in a basic form.

For obvious reasons we do not employ any AAA or access control mechanisms when performing handover latency tests. This is especially important when using any streaming applications as the delay incurred when waiting for network access to be granted can result in a considerable number of lost packets. We have found that using IPerf [IPERF] between the CN and MN is a very useful tool for discovering the extent of packet loss during handovers when comparing different network and different tunings of the RA intervals.

Since each Home Agent also acts as the default router on its respective link as shown in Figure 14-2 we configure each Home Agent to announce unsolicited Router Advertisements at more frequent intervals than the default. In general, we use a Router Advertisement interval of 1 second which is sufficient for most adaptable TCP applications such as email, web, ftp etc. However, we have noticed considerable (i.e. unpleasant) disruption when using a 1 second interval when streaming video and/or audio. Reducing the interval to around 300ms seems to be fair benchmark to set for supporting streaming media. Although it is possible to reduce the interval even further, in most tests we did not observe enough improvement in the stream disruption to justify the extra link bandwidth and Home Agent CPU cycles being used.

Initially, the most simple way of testing the operation of the MIPv6 testbed is by testing basic connectivity between the Mobile Node and Correspondent Node with a stream of ping requests from the Correspondent Node to the Mobile Mode while the Mobile Node moves between its home network and a foreign network. In a correctly configured Mobile IPv6 testbed, the ping requests should continue to be answered as the Mobile Node moves. Sometimes we observe one ping timing out as the packet is lost. This can occur if the ping request is sent just as the Mobile Node becomes unreachable in its original location but has not yet completed the binding update procedure to be reachable at its new location. However, on a properly configured testbed we rarely observe more than one ping timeout.

For testing that TCP connections survive movement of the Mobile Node, a simple test is to run telent or similar (using the client and server in either combination of Mobile Node and Correspondent Node) and observe that the session remains active after movement. You should not observe any noticeable effects (save some possible interruption in character echo on the terminal) if all is configured correctly.

Beyond these basic tests some users may want to experiment with the TAHI compliance test suite described at [TAHI].

14.3.4.1 Handover Latency Tests

Figure 14-3 shows the small MIPv6 testbed used for performing the handover tests. A MN running MIPL v1.1 is away from home (the HA also running MIPL v1.1) and can attach to one of two networks represented by the SSIDs 'roam1' and 'roam2'. We decided to conduct handover tests from one foreign network to another (e.g. rather than from home network to foreign network) as the nature of mobility implies that when one is mobile, one is very rarely located at the home network.

Handovers from one network to another were forced by turning off one of the APs so that the MN would immediately associate with the other AP and thus receive different RAs than on the previously connected network.

The handover times were measured from the point at which the AP is switched off (link down notification) to when the Binding Acknowledgement is received from the Correspondent Node with each event being timestamped in the relative logs. Note that the Return Routability protocol was enabled for Route Optimisation.

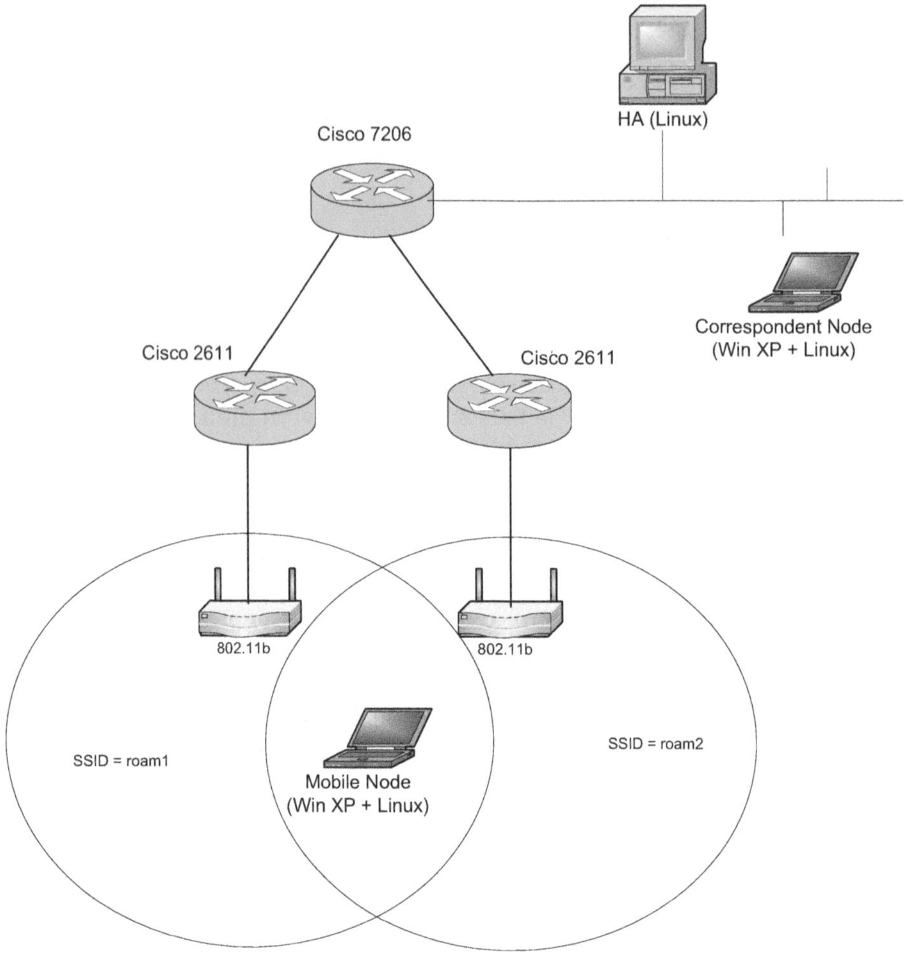

Figure 14-3 Simple MIPv6 Handover Testbed

Reducing the Router Advertisement Intervals

In order to demonstrate the effects of reducing the RA interval we performed handover tests with various configurations of RA intervals on the Cisco 2611 access routers. As described earlier, upon detecting movement, the MN will issue a RS assuming it hasn't received a new RA already. As can be seen from Figure 14-4, the time it takes for the MN to receive a solicited RA is fairly random within a given (configurable) time window.

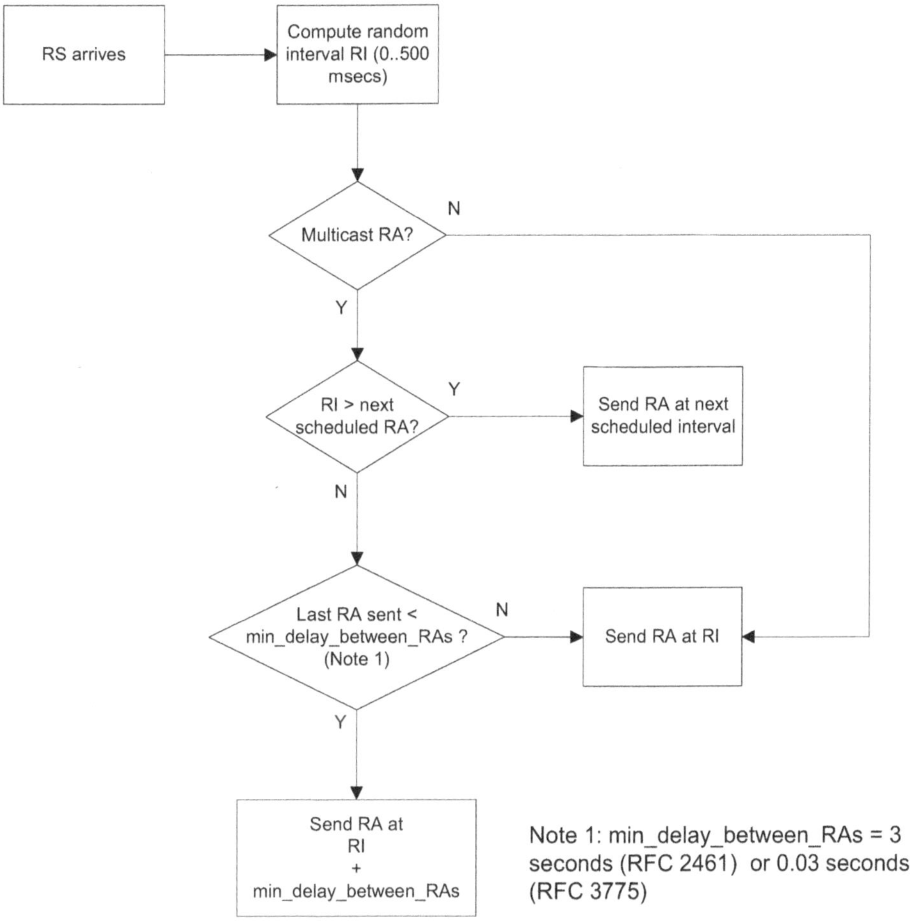

Figure 14-4 Processing Router Solicitations

The test experiment was as follows. The IPv6 capable VoD (Video on Demand) server was located at the Correspondent Node and streamed 1.5Mbps MPEG1 video clip of 30 seconds duration was streamed to the Mobile Node. At 10 seconds into the video clip the AP to which the MN was associated with was switched off, forcing a handover to the other network. At the end of the clip the handover latency and packet loss (reported by the VoD client) were noted. This was repeated 10 times for each value of RA interval configured on the Cisco routers. These RA intervals were 300ms (the RFC 3775 minimum), 1000ms and 3000ms.

Table 14-3 Results of RA Interval Tests

	Avg Latency (seconds)	Avg # Packets Lost
300 ms	1.917	245.376
1000 ms	2.448	313.344
3000 ms	3.013	385.664

It can be seen that changing the RA interval does not have as much effect on reducing the overall latency as we would like. This can be explained in that the rest of the handover procedure after receiving a RA, i.e. CoA configuration, DAD and CoA registration with the HA and CN is completely unaffected by reducing the RA interval. One can also see the number of packets lost in the video stream. On the client playback the stream would recover itself after handover but the break in the video and audio seemed about 1 or 2 seconds longer than the handover latency reported in the logs. It is easy to conclude that even tuning the RA interval to the lowest possible value will not suffice for real-time voice and video applications in a mobile environment.

Unicasting Solicited RAs

Another possible trick is to change the default behaviour of neighbour discovery so that a Router Solicitation is answered with a unicast RAs rather than the default multicast RA. In the standard algorithm depicted in Figure 14-4 it can be seen how a unicast RA only incurs the random delay interval and is not affected by the configured RA interval parameter (since this only applies to multicast RAs). To see what effect this would have on handover latency we had to replace a 2611 router with a linux PC based equivalent (since we were unable to configure the IOS accordingly).

Table 14-4 Using Unicast RAs

	Avg Latency (seconds)	Avg # Packets Lost
Unicast RA	2.072	265.216

From the table we can see that the results are slightly worse than the best we can get from configuring the RA interval. However, since the random interval is between 0 and 500 ms (the MAX_RA_DELAY_TIME constant in [RFC2461], we are unable to reduce this parameter further.

Eliminating DAD / Optimistic DAD

By removing the DAD procedure altogether we can reduce the handover latency even further (potentially by a second or so). However, removing this check altogether is not a realistic option both in terms of ratification by the IETF or by tuning an implementation's configuration. Thus, we are left with the option of fine tuning the DAD procedure in some way that reduces the time it takes for a MN to be able to use its CoA. A procedure called 'Optimistic DAD' which modifies [RFC2461] and [RFC2462] is proposed in [Moo05], which essentially allows a CoA to be used before it has completed DAD. The CoA is marked as 'optimistic' as opposed to 'tentative' before completing DAD and is marked as 'preferred' once DAD is complete.

Unfortunately, we have not been able to source a suitable implementation of Optimistic DAD with which to test. An implementation will soon be made available from Monash University, but this will appear too late for the lifetime of the 6NET project.

Conclusions

Our tests have demonstrated that even with fine tuning the parameters of routers for optimum MIPv6 handover performance, we still do not approach anywhere near good enough handover times for real-time voice/video applications.

We must therefore conclude that MIPv6, in its current form is not by itself sufficient to be the de-facto mobility management model in the mobile IPv6 Internet. Further optimisations relating to handover performance must be made in order to support interactive and real-time IPv6 applications in a mobile context.

We have examined the fast handover protocol for MIPv6, FMIPv6 [RFC4068]. This aims to improve handover latency by eliminating IPv6 configuration latency and also prevents packet loss by the use of a bi-directional tunnel while physical movement and MIPv6 CoA registration are taking place.

To the best of our knowledge no implementation has yet been developed for us to perform handover tests. Yet this does not prevent us from reasoning that FMIPv6 will indeed reduce handover latency in almost all cases. In some cases, e.g. predicted handovers and relatively infrequent movement FMIPv6 promises to be sufficient for the real-time applications, most notably the killer mobile application VoIP. However, without being able to perform real tests it would be rather hasty to take this for granted.

14.4 University of Oulu

The University of Oulu has carried out experiments with Mobile IPv6 for Linux in heterogeneous wireless networks. In particular, the handover performance has been studied.

14.4.1 Testbed

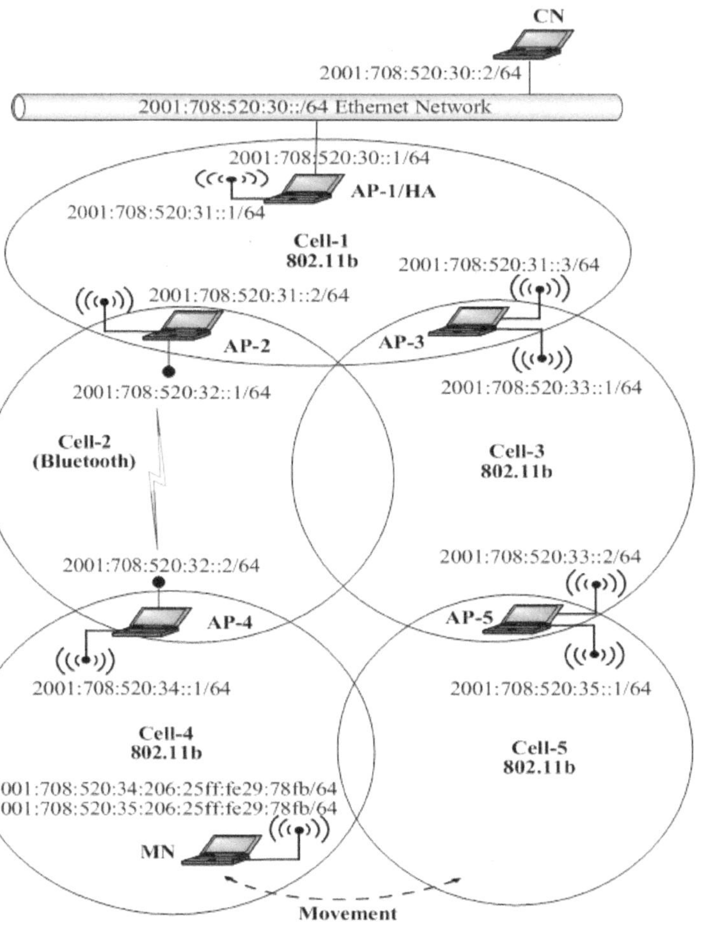

Figure 14-5 University of Oulu Heterogeneous Wireless MIPv6 Testbed

14.4.2 Handover Performance

This series of experiments investigates the effect of handover duration on the TCP disruption time. We will describe handoffs between AP-4 and AP-5 (i.e. between the fast path and the slow path) as shown in Figure 14-5. AP-4 and AP-5 generate one router advertisements every 1.5 seconds. We define the handover time as the amount of time starting from when the mobile node can not get any packets from its old access point until the time when it receive binding acknowledgement from its home agent via the new access point. The first handoff experiment is from AP-5 to AP-4 (i.e. from the fast path to the slow path). The MN starts sending TCP traffic to the CN using AP-5 and moves towards AP-4. Figure 14-6 shows the time sequence number plot of the TCP connection including the handover time. We found that it takes around 4.9 seconds to handoff from AP-5 to AP-4. The TCP disruption time was found to be 10.5 seconds. As illustrated in the figure, the TCP goes through 4 consecutive timeouts and retransmissions. Because of TCP exponential backoff mechanism, TCP doubles the size of its timeout interval each consecutive timeouts. Following the handover, the TCP waits for the last timeout to elapse before starts sending data using the new care-of-address. This result demonstrate that the handover duration contribute approximately 40% of the TCP disruption time. The remaining time delay is due to TCP congestion control mechanism. The average handover duration and TCP disruption time are shown in Table 14-5.

Table 14-5 Handover Duration and TCP Disruption Time

	Average handover duration [seconds]	Average TCP disruption time [seconds]
From fast to slow path	3.94	8.40
From slow to fast path	1.49	3.91

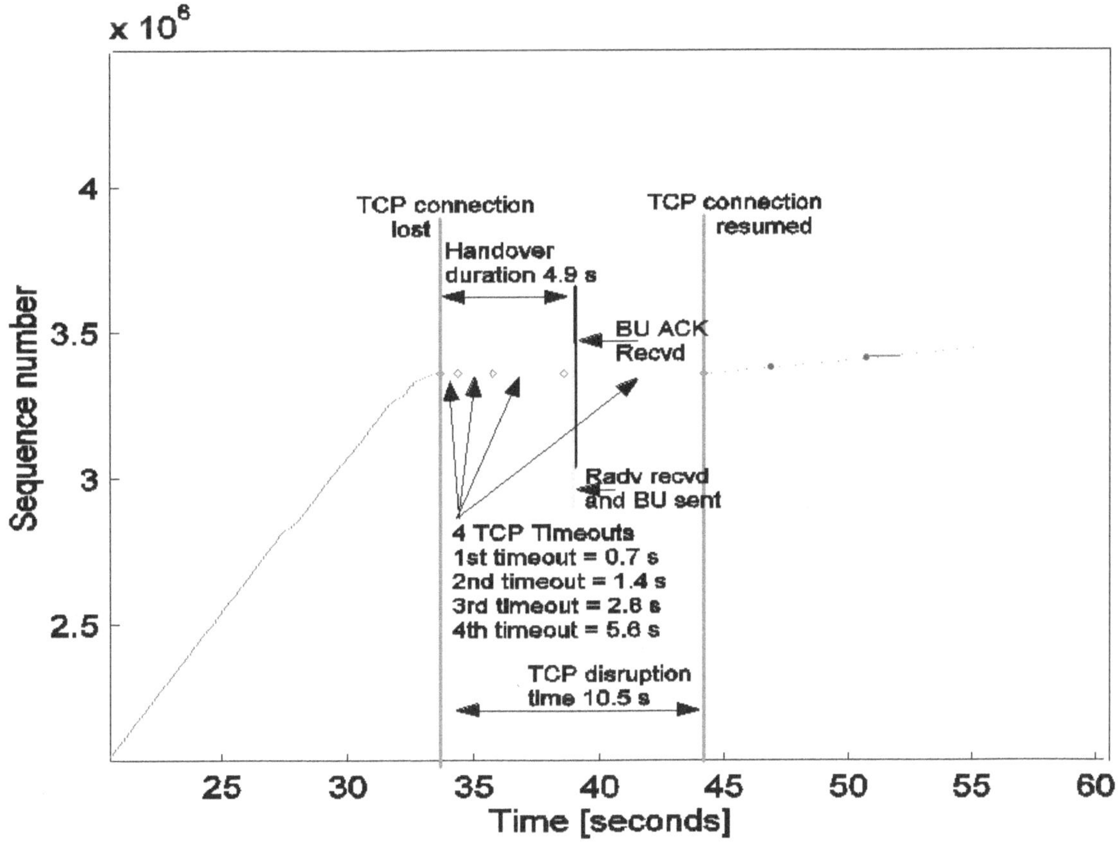

Figure 14-6 TCP Packet Trace During Handover from AP-5 to AP-4

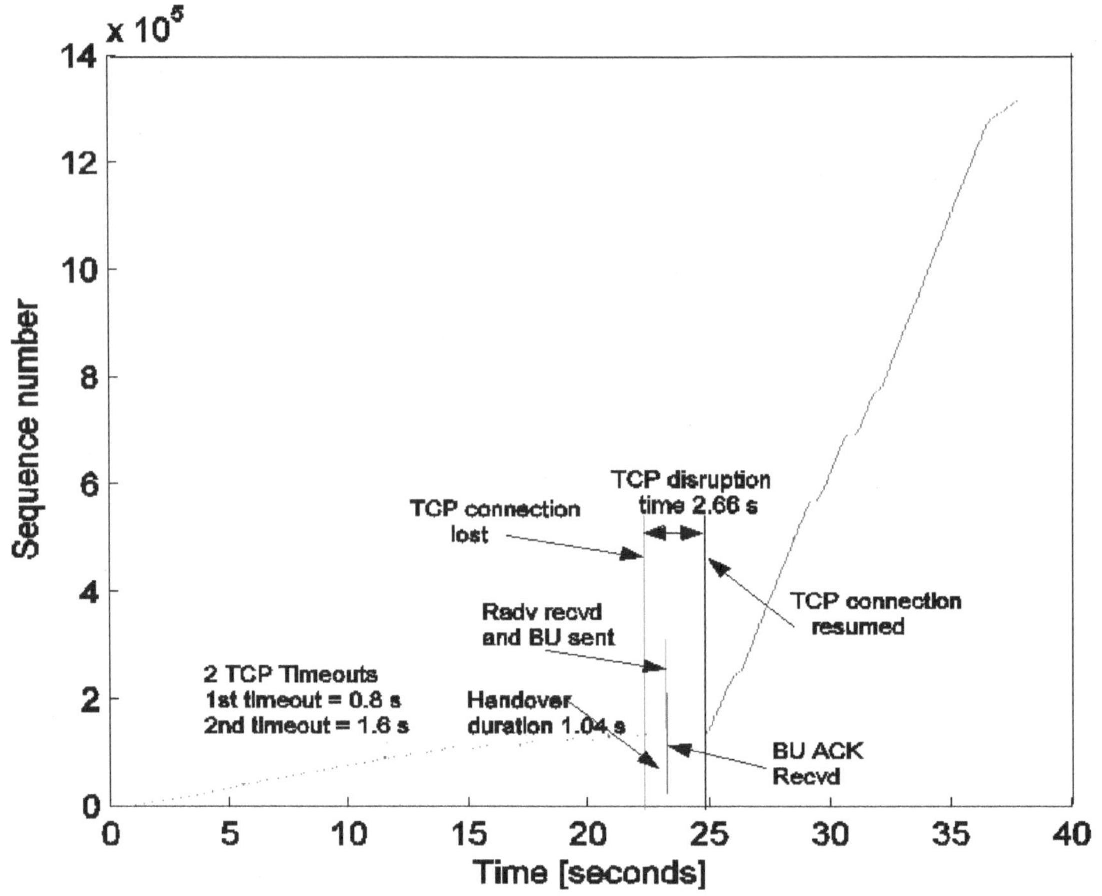

Figure 14-7 TCP Packet Trace During Handover from AP-4 to AP-5

The same behaviour was noticed when the handover was performed from AP-4 to AP-5 (i.e. from the slow path to the fast path). However, handover duration significantly decreased to about 1.04 seconds. The TCP disruption time takes around 2.66 seconds. TCP Packet Trace During Handover from AP-4 to AP-5 shows the TCP behaviour during a handover from AP-4 to AP-5. It can be seen that fewer timeouts and retransmissions have occurred in this experiment. The overall average handover duration and TCP disruption times are shown in Table 14-5.

These results indicate that handover between AP4 to AP5 is faster than from AP5 to AP4. This is because related signalling packets travel faster in the fast path. It also shows that TCP performs well when handover is from a low data rate to a high data rate network. However, due to the TCP slow start mechanism, the recovery is slow when the handover is from the high data rate to the low data rate path. After the handover, the MN starts sending packets at slow rate (sets the congestion window maximum segment size to 1) and increases its sending rate exponentially fast. Several methods have been introduced to optimize the Mobile IPv6 handover process, including hierarchical MIPv6 and fast handover. The fast Handover protocol has been proposed as away to minimize the interruption in service experienced by a Mobile IPv6 node as it changes its point of attachment to the Internet. Using the fast handover mechanism would allow the MN to send and receive packets from the time that it disconnects from one access point to the time it registers a new care-of address from the new access point.

Bibliography

[8021x] LAN MAN Standards Committee of the IEEE Computer Society, "*Port Based Network Access Control*", IEEE Standard 802.1x, June 2001.

[AD05] C. Aoun, E. Davies, "*Reasons to Move NAT-PT to Experimental*", IETF Internet Draft draft-ietf-v6ops-natpt-to-exprmntl-01.txt (work in progress), January 2005.

[BCKR05] T. Bates, R. Chandra, D. Katz, Y, Rekhter, "*Multiprotocol Extensions for BGP-4*", IETF Internet Draft draft-ietf-idr-rfc2858bis-07.txt, August 2005.

[Bel57] R. Bellman, "*Dynamic Programming*", Princeton University Press, 1957.

[BG92] D. Bertsekas, R. Gallagher, "*Data Networks*", Second edition, Prentice Hall, 1992, ISBN 0-13-200916-1.

[BP02] M. Blanchet, O. Medina, F. Parent, "*DSTM Tunnel Setup using TSP*", IETF Internet Draft draft-blanchet-ngtrans-tsp-dstm-profile-01.txt, July 2002.

[BP05] M. Blanchet , F. Parent, "*IPv6 Tunnel Broker with the Tunnel Setup Protocol (TSP)*", IETF Internet Draft draft-blanchet-v6ops-tunnelbroker-tsp-03.txt (work in progress), August 2005.

[Bou05] J. Bound, "*Dual Stack IPv6 Dominant Transition Mechanism (DSTM)*", IETF Internet Draft draft-bound-dstm-exp-03.txt (work in progress), June 2005.

[Cho04a] T. Chown, "*IPv6 Campus Transition Scenario Description and Analysis*", IETF Internet Draft draft-chown-v6ops-campus-transition-01.txt, October 2004.

[Cho04b] T. Chown, "*Use of VLANs for IPv4-IPv6 Coexistence in Enterprise Networks*", IETF Internet Draft, draft-chown-v6ops-vlan-usage-02.txt, October 2004.

[Cla05] B. Claise, "*IPFIX Protocol Specification*", IETF Internet Draft draft-ietf-ipfix-protocol-19.txt, September 2005.

[D1.1] 6NET Deliverable 1.1, "*Design and Implementation of the Testbed Infrastructure*", April 2002.

[D1.2] 6NET Deliverable 1.2, "*Operational Procedures to be Followed by 6NET NOC*", April 2002.

[D2.2.4] 6NET Deliverable 2.2.4, "*Final IPv4 to IPv6 Transition Cookbook for Organisational/ ISP (NREN) and Backbone Networks.*", February 2005.

[D2.3.4] 6NET Deliverable 2.3.4, "*Final IPv4 to IPv6 transition cookbook for end site networks/ universities*", June 2005.

[D2.4.2] 6NET Deliverable 2.4.2, "*Final report on IPv6-specific implications for Wireless LAN/MAN transition to IPv6*", September 2003.

[D2.5.3] 6NET Deliverable 2.5.3, "*Issues for IPv6 deployment (missing pieces for IPv6 deployment and IPv6-only operation)*", June 2005.

[D3.1.1] 6NET Deliverable 3.1.1, "*IPv6 Routing Plan for the 6NET Network*", March 2002.

[D3.1.2] 6NET Deliverable 3.1.2, "*IPv6 cookbook for routing, DNS, intra-domain multicast, inter-domain multicast, security*", November 2004.

[D3.2.1] 6NET Deliverable 3.2.1, "*IPv6 DNS service for the 6NET network*", March 2002.

[D3.2.3] 6NET Deliverable 3.2.3, "*DHCPv6 implementation and test report*", January 2003.

[D3.4.1] 6NET Deliverable 3.4.1, "*IPv6 Intra-domain multicast service*", December 2002.

[D3.4.2] 6NET Deliverable 3.4.2, "*Inter-domain Multicast*", December 2004.

[D3.5.1] 6NET Deliverable 3.5.1, "*Secure IPv6 Operation: Lessons learned from 6NET*", January 2005.

[D3.6.1] 6NET Deliverable 3.6.1, "*Cookbook for IPv6 Renumbering of SOHO and Backbone Networks*", June 2005.

[D3.6.2] 6NET Deliverable 3.6.2, "*Cookbook for IPv6 Renumbering of ISP and Enterprise Networks*", June 2005.

[D4.1.3] 6NET Deliverable 4.1.3, "*Mobile IPv6 Handovers: Performance Analysis and Evaluation*", June 2005.

[D4.1.4] 6NET Deliverable 4.1.4, "*Final Mobile IPv6 Support Guide*", February 2005.

[D4.1.5] 6NET Deliverable 4.1.5, "*Multicast with mobile hosts: analysis and performance evaluation*", January 2005.

[D4.2.1] 6NET Deliverable 4.2.1, "*IPv6 Wireless LAN Access Issues*", July 2002.

[D4.2.2] 6NET Deliverable 4.2.2, "*Framework for the Support of IPv6 Wireless LANs, Version 2*", October 2004.

[D4.3.3] 6NET Deliverable 4.3.3, "*Evaluation report on the advantages demonstrated from use of IPv6 dynamic VPNs over different technologies*", March 2005.

[D4.4.2] 6NET Deliverable 4.4.2, "*Final Report on IPv6 QoS tests*", April 2005.

[D4.5.3] 6NET Deliverable 4.5.3, "*Evaluation of Multihoming Solutions*", February 2005.

[D5.1] 6NET Deliverable 5.1, "*Specification of IPv6 applications to be developed within the project*", May 2002.

[D5.5] 6NET Deliverable 5.5, "*Definition of generic framework for IPv6 applications trials and evaluation*", March 2003.

[D5.14] 6NET Deliverable 5.14: "*IPv6 Deployment in the Greek School Network*", June 2005.

[D5.15] 6NET Deliverable 5.15, "*Final report on applications development and evaluations (including descriptions of the demonstrators of WP5), and PoP deployment*", June 2005.

[D6.1.2] 6NET Deliverable 6.1.2, "*Management Architecture Specifications*", January 2003.

[D6.2.2] 6NET Deliverable 6.2.2, "*Operational procedures for secured management with transition mechanisms*"; February 2003.

[D6.2.4] 6NET Deliverable 6.2.4, "*Final report on IPv6 management tools, developments and tests*", September 2004.

[D6.3.3] 6NET Deliverable 6.3.3, "*Final report on IPv6 management and monitoring architecture design, tools, and operational procedures. Recommendations.*", October 2004.

[DHJNZ04] S. Deering, B. Haberman, T. Jinmei, E. Nordmark, B. Zill, "*IPv6 Scoped Address Architecture*", IETF Internet Draft draft-ietf-ipv6-scoping-arch-02.txt (work in progress), August 2004.

[DKS05] E. Davies, S. Krishnan, P. Savola, "*IPv6 Transition/Co-existence Security Considerations*", IETF Internet Draft draft-ietf-v6ops-security-overview-02.txt (work in progress), July 2005.

[Dro02] R. Droms, "*A Guide to Implementing Stateless DHCPv6 Service*", IETF Internet Draft draft-droms-dhcpv6-stateless-guide-01.txt, October 2002.

[DS04] F. Dupont, P. Savola, "*RFC 3041 Considered Harmful*", IETF Internet Draft draft-dupont-ipv6-rfc3041harmful-05.txt, June 2004.

[Dur03] A. Durand, "*Issues with NAT-PT DNS ALG in RFC2766*", IETF Internet Draft draft-duran-v6ops-natpt-dns-alg-issues-00.txt, September 2003.

[ENST] ENST DSTM web site: http://www.ipv6.rennes.enst-bretagne.fr/dstm/.

[FC05] D. Farinacci, Y. Cai, "*Anycast-RP using PIM*", IETF Internet Draft draft-ietf-pim-anycast-rp-04.txt (work in progress), August 2005.

[FHHK05] B. Fenner, M, Handley, H. Holbrook, I. Kouvelas, "*Protocol Independent Multicast - Sparse Mode (PIM-SM): Protocol Specification (Revised)*", IETF Internet draft draft-ietf-pim-sm-v2-new-11.txt, October 2004.

[FJ94] S. Floyd, V. Jacobson, "*The synchronization of periodic routing messages*", IEEE/ACM Transactions on Networking, vol. 2, no. 2, pp. 122-136, 1994.

[FF62] L. R. Ford, D. R. Fulkerson, "*Flows in Networks*", Princeton University Press, 1962.

[HH05] R. Hinden, B. Haberman, "*Unique Local IPv6 Unicast Addresses*", IETF Internet Draft draft-ietf-ipv6-unique-local-addr-09.txt, January 2005.

[Hop03] C. E. Hopps, "*Routing IPv6 with IS-IS*", IETF Internet Draft draft-ietf-isis-ipv6-05.txt (work in progress), January 2003.

[Hui05] C. Huitema, "*Teredo: Tunneling IPv6 over UDP through NATs*", IETF Internet Draft draft-huitema-v6ops-teredo-05.txt (work in progress), April 2005.

[IPERF] IPerf Homepage, http://dast.nlanr.net/Projects/Iperf/ .

[Kal03] V. Kalusivalingam, "*Timezone Specifier Option for DHCPv6*", IETF Internet Draft draft-ietf-dhc-dhcpv6-opt-tz-00.txt, November 2003.

[Mar01] M. G. Marsh, "*Policy Routing Using Linux*", Sams Publishing 1998, ISBN 0-672-32052-5.

[MFR78] J. M. McQuillan, G. Falk, I. Richer, "*A review of the development and performance of the ARPANET routing algorithm*", IEEE Transactions on Communications, vol. 26, no. 12, pp. 1802-1811, December 1978.

[MHL05] M. Mathis, J. Heffner, K. Lahey, "*Path MTU Discovery*", IETF Internet Draft draft-ietf-pmtud-method-04.txt, February 2005.

[Moh01] J. Mohacsi, "*IPv6 firewalls*", presentation at the 5th TF-NGN meeting, October 2001 available at http:///skye.ki.iif.hu/~mohacsi/athens_tf_ngn_ipv6_firewalls.pdf.

[Moh04] J.Mohacsi, "*Security of IPv6 from firewalls point of view*", presentation at TNC2004 conference, June 2004, available at http://www.terena.nl/conferences/tnc2004/programme/presentations/show.php?pres_id=115.

[Moo05] N. Moore, "*Optimistic Duplicate Address Detection*", IETF Internet Draft draft-ietf-ipv6-optimistic-dad-06.txt, September 2005.

[NDK05] T. Narten, R. Draves, S. Krishnan, "*Privacy Extensions for Stateless Address Autoconfiguration in IPv6*", IETF Internet-Draft draft-ietf-ipv6-privacy-addrs-v2-04.txt, May 24, 2005.

[NG05] E. Nordmark, R. Gilligan, "*Basic Transition Mechanisms for IPv6 Hosts and Routers*", Internet Draft, draft-ietf-v6ops-mech-v2-07.txt (work in progress), March 2005.

[PSS05] T. Przygienda, N. Shen, N. Sheth, "*M-ISIS: Multi Topology (MT) Routing in IS-IS*", IETF Internet Draft draft-ietf-isis-wg-multi-topology-10.txt (work in progress), May 2005.

[Pyth-Lib] Guido van Rossum, Fred L. Drake, "*Python Library Reference*", Release 2.4.1 (http://docs.python.org/lib/lib.html), March 2005.

[RB05] A. Reddy, J. Bound, "*Stack Transition Mechanism (DSTM) Options for DHCPv6*", IETF Internet Draft draft-reddy-dhcpv6-opt-dstm-exp-00.txt (work in progress), April 2005.

[RFC1058] C. Hedrick, "*Routing Information Protocol*", IETF Request for Comments 1058, June 1988.

[RFC1191] J. Mogul, S. Deering, "*Path MTU Discovery*", IETF Request for Comments 1191, November 1990.

[RFC1510] J. Kohl, C. Neuman, "*The Kerberos Network Authentication Service (V5)*", IETF Request for Comments 1510, September 1993.

[RFC1519] V. Fuller, T. Li, J. Yu, K. Varadhan, "*Classless Inter-Domain Routing (CIDR): an Address Assignment and Aggregation Strategy*", IETF Request for Comments 1519, September 1993.

[RFC1631] K. Egevang, P. Francis, "*The IP Network Address Translator (NAT)*", IETF Request for Comments 1631, May 1994.

[RFC1723] G. Malkin, "*RIP Version 2 - Carrying Additional Information*", IETF Request for Comments 1723, November 1994.

[RFC1883] S. Deering, R. Hinden, "*Internet Protocol, Version 6 (IPv6) Specification*", IETF Request for Comments 1883, December 1995.

[RFC1885] A. Conta, S. Deering, "*Internet Control Message Protocol (ICMPv6) for the Internet Protocol Version 6 (IPv6) Specification*", IETF Request for Comments 1885, December 1995.

[RFC1902] J. Case, K. McCloghrie, M. Rose, S. Waldbusser, "*Structure of Management Information for Version 2 of the Simple Network Management Protocol (SNMPv2)*", IETF Request for Comments 1902, January 1996.

[RFC1918] Y. Rekhter, B. Moskowitz, D. Karrenberg, G. J. de Groot, E. Lear, "*Address Allocation for Private Internets*", IETF Request for Comments 1918, February 1996.

[RFC1928] M. Leech, M. Ganis, Y. Lee, R. Kuris, D. Koblas, L. Jones, "*SOCKS Protocol Version 5*", IETF Request for Comments 1928, March 1996.

[RFC2011] K. McCloghrie, "*SNMPv2 Management Information Base for the Internet Protocol using SMIv2*", IETF Request for Comments 2011, November 1996.

[RFC2011bis] S. Routhier, "*Management Information Base for the Internet Protocol (IP)*", IETF Internet Draft draft-ietf-ipv6-rfc2011-update-10.txt, May 2004.

[RFC2012] K. McCloghrie, "*SNMPv2 Management Information Base for the Transmission Control Protocol using SMIv2*", IETF Request for Comments 2012, November 1996.

[RFC2013] K. McCloghrie, "*SNMPv2 Management Information Base for the User Datagram Protocol using SMIv2*", IETF Request for Comments 2013, November 1996.

[RFC2080] G. Malkin and R. Minnear, "*RIPng for IPv6*", IETF Request for Comments 2080, January 1997.

[RFC2096] F. Baker, "*IP Forwarding Table MIB*", IETF Request for Comments 2096, January 1997.

[RFC2096bis] B. Haberman, "*IP Forwarding Table MIB*", IETF Internet Draft draft-ietf-ipv6-rfc2096-update-07.txt, February 2004.

[RFC2131] R. Droms, "*Dynamic Host Configuration Protocol*", IETF Request for Comments 2131, March 1997.

[RFC2132] S. Alexander, R. Droms, "*DHCP Options and BOOTP Vendor Extensions*", IETF Request for Comments 2132, March 1997.

[RFC2283] T. Bates, R. Chandra, D. Katz, Y. Rekhter, "*Multiprotocol Extensions for BGP-4*", IETF Request for Comments 2283, February 1998.

[RFC2292] W. Stevens, M. Thomas, "*Advanced Sockets API for IPv6*", IETF Request for Comments 2292, February 1998.

[RFC2362] D. Estrin, D. Farinacci, A. Helmy, D. Thaler, S. Deering, M. Handley, V. Jacobson, C. Liu, P. Sharma, L. Wei, "*Protocol Independent Multicast-Sparse Mode (PIM-SM): Protocol Specification*", IETF Request for Comments 2362, June 1998.

[RFC2373] R. Hinden, S. Deering, "*IP Version 6 Addressing Architecture*", IETF Request for Comments 2373, July 1998.

RFC2375] R. Hinden, S. Deering, "*IPv6 Multicast Address Assignments*", IETF Request for Comments 2375, July 1998.

[RFC2385] A. Heffernan, "*Protection of BGP Sessions via the TCP MD5 Signature Option*", IETF Request for Comments 2385, August 1998.

[RFC2461] T. Narten, E. Nordmark, W. Simpson, "*Neighbor Discovery for IP Version 6 (IPv6)*", IETF Request for Comments 2461, December 1998.

[RFC2461bis] T. Narten, E. Nordmark, W. Simpson, H. Soliman, "Neighbor *Discovery for IP version 6 (IPv6)*", IETF Internet Draft draft-ietf-ipv6-2461bis-04.txt, July 2005.

[RFC2462] T. Narten, S. Thomson, "*IPv6 Stateless Address Autoconfiguration*", IETF Request for Comments 2462, December 1998.

[RFC2462bis] S. Thomson, T. Narten, T. Jinmei, "*IPv6 Stateless Address Autoconfiguration*", IETF Internet Draft draft-ietf-ipv6-rfc2462bis-08.txt, May 2005.

[RFC2463] A. Conta, S. Deering, "*Internet Control Message Protocol (ICMPv6) for the Internet Protocol Version 6 (IPv6) Specification*", IETF Request for Comments 2463, December 1998.

[RFC2465] D. Haskin, S. Onishi, "*Management Information Base for IP Version 6: Textual Conventions and General Group*", IETF Request for Comments 2465, December 1998.

[RFC2526] D. Johnson, S. Deering, "*Reserved IPv6 Subnet Anycast Addresses*", IETF Request for Comments 2526, March 1999.

[RFC2529] B. Carpenter, C. Jung, "*Transmission of IPv6 over IPv4 Domains without Explicit Tunnels*", IETF Request for Comments 2529, March 1999.

[RFC2535] D. Eastlake, "*Domain Name System Security Extensions*", IETF Request for Comments 2535, March 1999.

[RFC2553] J. Bound, R. Gilligan, S. Thomson, W. Stevens, "*Basic Socket Interface Extensions for IPv6*", IETF Request for Comments 2553, April 1999.

[RFC2710] S. Deering, W. Fenner, B. Haberman, "*Multicast Listener Discovery (MLD) for IPv6*", IETF Request for Comments 2710, October 1999.

[RFC2732] R. Hinden, B. Carpenter, L. Masinter, "*Format for Literal IPv6 Addresses in URL's*", IETF Request for Comments 2732, December 1999.

[RFC2740] R. Coltun, D. Ferguson, J. Moy, "*OSPF for IPv6*", IETF Request for Comments 2740, December 1999.

[RFC2748] D. Durham, J. Boyle, R. Cohen, S. Herzog, R. Rajan, A. Sastry, "*The COPS (Common Open Policy Service) Protocol*", IETF Request for Comments 2748, January 2000.

[RFC2765] E. Nordmark, "*Stateless IP/ICMP Translation Algorithm (SIIT)*", IETF Request for Comments 2765, February 2000.

[RFC2766] G. Tsirtsis, P. Srisuresh, "*Network Address Translation - Protocol Translation (NAT-PT)*", IETF Request for Comments 2766, February 2000.

[RFC2767] K. Tsuchiya, H. Higuchi, Y. Atarashi, "*Dual Stack Hosts Using the 'Bump-in-the-Stack' Technique*", IETF Request for Comments 2767, February 2000.

[RFC2771] R. Finlayson, "*An Abstract API for Multicast Address Allocation*", IETF Request for Comments 2771, February 2000.

[RFC2772] R. Rockell, R. Fink, "*6Bone Backbone Routing Guidelines*", IETF Request for Comments 2772, February 2000.

[RFC2775] B. Carpenter, "*Internet Transparency*", IETF Request for Comments 2775, February 2000.

[RFC2784] D. Farinacci, T. Li, S. Hanks, D. Meyer, P. Traina, "*Generic Encapsulation (GRE)*", IETF Request for Comments, March 2000.

[RFC2827] P. Ferguson, D. Senie, "*Network Ingress Filtering: Defeating Denial of Service Attacks which employ IP Source Address Spoofing*", IETF Request for Comments 2827, May 2000.

[RFC2842] R. Chandra, J. Scudder, "*Capabilities Advertisement with BGP-4*", IETF Request for Comments 2842, May 2000.

[RFC2851] M. Daniele, B. Haberman, S. Routhier, J. Schoenwaelder, "*Textual Conventions for Internet Network Addresses*", IETF Request for Comments 2851, June 2000.

[RFC2858] T. Bates, Y. Rekhter, R. Chandra, D. Katz, "*Multiprotocol Extensions for BGP-4*", IETF Request for Comments 2858, June 2000.

[RFC2893] R. Gilligan, E. Nordmark, "*Transition Mechanisms for IPv6 Hosts and Routers*", IETF Request for Comments 2893, August 2000.

[RFC2974] M. Handley, C. Perkins, E. Whelan, "*Session Announcement Protocol*", IETF Request for Comments 2974, October 2000.

[RFC3041] T. Narten, R. Draves, "*Privacy Extensions for Stateless Address Autoconfiguration in IPv6*", IETF Request for Comments 3041, January 2001.

[RFC3053] A. Durand, P. Fasano, I. Guardini, D. Lento, "*IPv6 Tunnel Broker*", IETF Request for Comments 3053, January 2001.

[RFC3056] B. Carpenter, K. Moore, "*Connection of IPv6 Domains via IPv4 Clouds*", IETF Request for Comments 3056, February 2001.

[RFC3068] C. Huitema, "*Anycast Prefix for 6to4 Relay Routers*", IETF Request for Comments 3068, June 2001.

[RFC3089] H. Kitamura, "*A SOCKS-based IPv6/IPv4 Gateway Mechanism*", IETF Request for Comments 3089, April 2001

[RFC3118] R. Droms, W. Arbaugh, "*Authentication for DHCP Messages*", IETF Request for Comments 3118, June 2001.

[RFC3142] J. Hagino, K. Yamamoto, "*An IPv6-to-IPv4 Transport Relay Translator*", IETF Request for Comments 3142, June 2001

[RFC3162] B. Aboba, G. Zorn, D. Mitton, "*RADIUS and IPv6*", IETF Request for Comments 3162, August 2001.

[RFC3177] Internet Architecture Board, "*IAB/IESG Recommendations on IPv6 Address Allocations to Sites*", IETF Request for Comments 3177, September 2001.

[RFC3291] M. Daniele, B. Haberman, S. Routhier, J. Schoenwaelder, "*Textual Conventions for Internet Network Addresses*", IETF Request for Comments 3291, May 2002.

[RFC3306] B. Haberman, D. Thaler, "*Unicast-Prefix-based IPv6 Multicast Addresses*", IETF Request for Comments 3306, August 2002.

[RFC3307] B. Haberman, "*Allocation Guidelines for IPv6 Multicast Addresses*", IETF Request for Comments 3307, August 2002.

[RFC3315] R. Droms, J. Bound, B. Volz, T. Lemon, C. Perkins, M. Carney, "*Dynamic Host Configuration Protocol for IPv6 (DHCPv6)*", IETF Request for Comments 3315, July 2003.

[RFC3338] S. Lee, M. Shin, Y. Kim, E. Nordmark, A. Durand, "*Dual Stack Hosts Using 'Bump in the API' (BIA)*", IETF Request for Comments 3338, October 2002.

[RFC3416] R. Presuhn, J. Case, K. McCloghrie, M. Rose, S. Waldbusser, "*Version 2 of the Protocol Operations for the Simple Network Management Protocol (SNMP)*", IETF Request for Comments 3416, December 2002.

[RFC3418] R. Presuhn, J. Case, K. McCloghrie, M. Rose, S. Waldbusser, "*Management Information Base (MIB) for the Simple Network Management Protocol (SNMP)*", IETF Request for Comments 3418, December 2002.

[RFC3484] R. Draves, "*Default Address Selection for Internet Protocol version 6 (IPv6)*", IETF Request for Comments 3484, February 2003.

[RFC3490] P. Faltstrom, P.Hoffman, A. Costello, "*Internationalizing Domain Names in Applications (IDNA)*", IETF Request for Comments 3490, March 2003.

[RFC3493] R. Gilligan, S. Thomson, J. Bound, J. McCann, W. Stevens, "*Basic Socket Interface Extensions for IPv6*", IETF Request for Comments 3493, February 2003.

[RFC3513] R. Hinden, S. Deering, "*Internet Protocol Version 6 (IPv6) Addressing Architecture*", IETF Request for Comments 3513, April 2003.

[RFC3531] M. Blanchet, "*A Flexible Method for Managing the Assignment of Bits of an IPv6 Address Block*", IETF Request for Comments 3531, April 2003.

[RFC3539] B. Aboba, J. Wood, "*Authentication, Authorization and Accounting (AAA) Transport Profile*", IETF Request for Comments 3539, June 2003.

[RFC3542] W. Stevens, M. Thomas, E. Nordmark, T. Jinmei, "*Advanced Sockets Application Program Interface (API) for IPv6*", IETF Request for Comments 3542, May 2003.

[RFC3543] W. Stevens, M. Thomas, E. Nordmark, T. Jinmei, "*Advanced Sockets Application Program Interface (API) for IPv6*", IETF Request for Comments 3542, May 2003.

[RFC3569] S. Bhattacharyya, Ed., "*An Overview of Source-Specific Multicast (SSM)*", IETF Request for Comments 3569, July 2003.

[RFC3587] R. Hinden, S.Deering, E. Nordmark, "*IPv6 Global Unicast Address Format*", IETF Request for Comments 3587, August 2003.

[RFC3588] P. Calhoun, J. Loughney, E. Guttman, G. Zorn, J. Arkko, "*Diameter Base Protocol*", IETF Request for Comments 3588, September 2003.

[RFC3618] B. Fenner, D. Meyer, "*Multicast Source Discovery Protocol (MSDP)*", IETF Request for Comments 3618, October 2003.

[RFC3627] P. Savola, "*Use of /127 Prefix Length Between Routers Considered Harmful*" IETF Request for Comments 3627, September 2003.

[RFC3633] O. Troan, R. Droms, "*IPv6 Prefix Options for Dynamic Host Configuration Protocol (DHCP) version 6*", IETF Request for Comments 3633, December 2003.

[RFC3646] R. Droms, "*DNS Configuration options for Dynamic Host Configuration Protocol for IPv6 (DHCPv6)*", IETF Request for Comments, December 2003.

[RFC3701] R. Hink, R. Hinden, "*6bone (IPv6 Testing Address Allocation) Phaseout*", IETF Request for Comments 3701, March 2004.

[RFC3736] R. Droms, "*Stateless Dynamic Host Configuration Protocol (DHCP) Service for IPv6*", IETF Request for Comments 3736, April 2004.

[RFC3756] P. Nikander, J. Kempf, E. Nordmark, "*IPv6 Neighbor Discovery (ND) Trust Models and Threats*", IETF Request for Comments 3756, May 2004.

[RFC3775] D. Johnson, C. Perkins, J. Arkko, "*Mobility Support in IPv6*", IETF Request for Comments 3775, June 2004.

[RFC3776] J. Arkko, V. Devarapalli, F. Dupont, "*Using IPsec to Protect Mobile IPv6 Signaling Between Mobile Nodes and Home Agents*", IETF Request for Comments 3776, June 2004.

[RFC3810] R. Vida, L. Costa, "*Multicast Listener Discovery Version 2 (MLDv2) for IPv6*", IETF Request for Comments 3810, June 2004.

[RFC3849] G. Huston, A. Lord, P. Smith, "*IPv6 Address Prefix Reserved for Documentation*", IETF Request for Comments 3849, July 2004.

[RFC3879] C. Huitema, B. Carpenter, "*Deprecating Site Local Addresses*", IETF Request for Comments 3579, September 2004.

[RFC3898] V. Kalusivalingam, "*Network Information Service (NIS) Configuration Options for Dynamic Host Configuration Protocol for IPv6 (DHCPv6)*", IETF Request for Comments 3898, October 2004.

[RFC3904] C. Huitema, R. Austein, S. Satapati, R. van der Pol, "*Evaluation of IPv6 Transition Mechanisms for Unmanaged Networks*", IETF Request for Comments 3904, September 2004.

[RFC3956] P. Savola, B. Haberman, "*Embedding the Rendezvous Point (RP) Address in an IPv6 Multicast Address*", IETF Request for Comments 3956, November 2004.

[RFC3963] V. Devarapalli, R. Wakikawa, A. Petrescu, P. Thubert "*Network Mobility (NEMO) Basic Support Protocol*", IETF Request for Comments 3963, January 2005.

[RFC3964] P. Savola, C. Patel, "*Security Considerations for 6to4*", IETF Request for Comments 3964, December 2004

[RFC3971] J. Arkko, J. Kempf, B. Zill, P. Nikander, "*SEcure Neighbor Discovery (SEND)*", IETF Request for Comments 3971, March 2005.

[RFC3972] T. Aura, "*Cryptographically Generated Addresses (CGA)*", IETF Request for Comments 3972, March 2005.

[RFC4001] M. Daniele, B. Haberman, S. Routhier, J. Schoenwaelder, "*Textual Conventions for Internet Network Addresses*", IETF Request for Comments 4001, February 2005.

[RFC4007] S. Deering, B. Haberman, T. Jinmei, E. Nordmark, B. Zill, "*IPv6 Scoped Address Architecture*", IETF Request for Comments 4007, March 2005.

[RFC4022] R. Raghunarayan, "*Management Information Base for the Transmission Control Protocol (TCP)*", IETF Request for Comments 4022, March 2005.

[RFC4068] R. Koodli, Ed., "*Fast Handovers for Mobile IPv6*", IETF Request for Comments 4068, July 2005.

[RFC4075] V. Kalusivalingam, "*Simple Network Time Protocol (SNTP) Configuration Option for DHCPv6*", IETF Request for Comments 4075, May 2005.

[RFC4087] D. Thaler, "*IP Tunnel MIB*", IETF Request for Comments 4087, June 2005.

[RFC4113] B. Fenner, J. Flick, "*Management Information Base for the User Datagram Protocol (UDP)*", IETF Request for Comments 4113, June 2005.

[RFC4192] F. Baker, E. Lear, R. Droms, "*Procedures for Renumbering an IPv6 Network without a Flag Day*", IETF Request for Comments 4192, September 2005.

[RMT02] J. Richier, O. Medina, L. Toutain, "*DSTM in a VPN Scenario*", IETF Internet Draft draft-richier-dstm-vpn-00.txt, February 2002.

[SEEREN] SEEREN VNOC, http://admin.seeren.org/ .

[Shi05] M. Shin, "*Ports Option Support in DSTM*", IETF Internet Draft draft-shin-dstm-ports-00.txt (work in progress), June 2005.

[SRC84] J. H. Saltzer, D. P. Reed, D. D. Clark, "*End-to-end arguments in system design*", ACM Transactions on Computer Systems, vol. 2, no. 4, pp. 277-288, November 1984.

[Ste97] W. R. Stevens, "*UNIX Network programming Vol 1: Networking APIs – Sockets and XTI*", Prentice Hall 1997, ISBN 0-13-490012-X.

[TAHI] The TAHI Project Homepage, http://www.tahi.org/

[TGTT05] F. Templin, T. Gleeson, M. Talwar, D. Thaler, "*Intra-Site Automatic Tunnel Addressing Protocol (ISATAP)*", IETF Internet Draft draft-ietf-ngtrans-isatap-24.txt (work in progress), January 2005.

[USAGI] USAGI (UniverSAl playGround for IPv6) Project – Linux IPv6 Development Project, http://www.linux-ipv6.org/.

[Vij03] A.K. Vijayabhaskar, "*Client Preferred Prefix option for DHCPv6*", IETF Internet Draft draft-ietf-dhc-dhcpv6-opt-cliprefprefix-01.txt (work in progress), March 2003.

[Vol02] B. Volz, "*Load Balancing for DHCPv6*", IETF Internet Draft draft-ietf-dhc-dhcpv6-loadb-02.txt (work in progress), August 2002.

[WBEM] Distributed Management Task Force Inc., "*Web-Based Enterprise Management (WBEM)*", http://www.dmtf.org/standards/wbem/ .

[Wil02] A. Williams, "*Requirements for Automatic Configuration of IP Hosts*", IETF Internet Draft draft-ietf-zeroconf-reqts-12.txt, September 2002.

[WUEN05] R. Wakikawa, K. Uehara, T. Ernst, K. Nagami, "*Multiple Care-of Addresses Registration*", IETF Internet Draft draft-wakikawa-mobileip-multiplecoa-04.txt, June 2005.

Glossary of Terms and Acronyms

6PE	IPv6 Provider Edge Router (over MPLS)
ABR	Area Border Router
ACL	Access Control List
AH	Authentication Header
ALG	Application Layer Gateway
AP	Access Point
API	Application Programming Interface
AR	Access Router
ARP	Address Resolution Protocol
AS	Autonomous System
ASM	Any Source Multicast
ASBR	Autonomous System Boundary Router
ASCII	American Standard Code for Information Interchange
ATM	Asynchronous Transfer Mode
BA	Binding Acknowledgement
BDR	Backup Designated Router
BGP	Border Gateway Protocol
BGMP	Border Gateway Multicast Protocol
BIA	Bump in the Stack
BIND	Berkeley Internet Name Daemon
BIS	Bump in the Stack
BOOTP	Bootstrap Protocol
BR	Binding Request
BU	Binding Update
BSD	Berkeley Software Distribution
CIDR	Classless Inter-Domain Routing
CA	Certificate Authority
CCC	Circuit Cross Connect
CEF	Cisco Express Forwarding
CGA	Cryptographically Generated Address
CN	Correspondent Node
CoA	Care-of Address
CoT	Care-of Test
CoTI	Care-of Test Init

CLI	Command Line Interface
COPS	Common Open Policy Service
CPE	Customer Premises Equipment
CPU	Central Processing Unit
CRC	Cyclic Redundancy Check
CVS	Concurrent Versions System
DAD	Duplicate Address Detection
DDos	Distributed Denial of Service
DH	Diffie-Hellman (public key encryption algorithm)
DHAAD	Dynamic Home Agent Address Discovery
DHC	Dynamic Host Configuration
DHCPv4	Dynamic Host Configuration Protocol version 4
DHCPv6	Dynamic Host Configuration Protocol version 6
DMZ	De-Militarised Zone
DNS	Domain Name System
DNS-ALG	Domain Name System Application Layer Gateway
DNSEXT	DNS Extensions
DNSSEC	Secure DNS
DoS	Denial of Service
DR	Designated Router
DSL	Digital Subscriber Line
DSTM	Dual Stack Transition Mechanism
DUID	DHCP Unique Identifier
DWDM	Dense Wavelength Division Multiplexing
EC	European Commission
EGP	Exterior Gateway Protocol
EIGRP	Enhanced Interior Gateway Routing Protocol
ES	End System
ESP	Encapsulating Security Payload
EU	European Union
EUI	Extended Unique Identifier
FDDI	Fibre Distributed Data Interface
FMIPv6	Fast Handovers for Mobile IPv6
FQDN	Fully Qualified Domain Name
FRR	Fast Re-Route
FTP	File Transfer Protocol
GGF	Global Grid Forum

GNU	GNU's Not Unix
GPL	General Public Licence
GRE	Generic Route Encapsulation
GSR	Gigabit Switch Router
GUI	Graphical User Interface
HA	Home Agent
HoA	Home Address
HoT	Home Test
HoTI	Home Test Init
HTTP	Hyper Text Transfer Protocol
HTTPS	Secure Hyper Text Transfer Protocol
iBGP	Interior Border Gateway Protocol
IANA	Internet Assigned Numbers Authority
ICMP	Internet Control Message Protocol
ICMPv6	Internet Control Message Protocol version 6
I-D	Internet Draft
ID	Identifier
IDNA	Internationalizing Domain Names in Applications
IEEE	Institute of Electrical and Electronics Engineers
IESG	Internet Engineering Steering Group
IETF	Internet Engineering Taskforce
IGMP	Internet Group Management Protocol
IGP	Interior Gateway Protocol
IIH	Intermediate System to Intermediate System Hello
IKE	Internet Key Exchange
IMAP	Internet Message Access Protocol
IPFIX	IP Flow Information eXport
IPSec	Internet Protocol Security
IPv4	Internet Protocol version 4
IPv6	Internet Protocol version 6
IRC	Internet Relay Chat
IS-IS	Intermediate System to Intermediate System
ISATAP	Intra-Site Automatic Tunnel Addressing Protocol
ISDN	Integrated Services Digital Network
ISO	International Organisation for Standardisation
ISP	Internet Service Provider
IST	Information Society Technologies

IT	Information Technology
LAN	Local Area Network
LDAP	Lightweight Directory Access Protocol
LIR	Local Internet Registry
LL	Link Layer
LSA	Link State Advertisement
LSP	Link State Packet (IS-IS routing)
LSP	Label Switched Path (MPLS networks)
M-ISIS	Multitopology IS-IS
MAC	Medium Access Control
MAN	Metropolitan Area Network
MBGP	Multiprotocol Border Gateway Protocol
MCU	Multipoint Control Unit
MD5	Message Digest 5
MH	Mobile Header
MIB	Management Information Base
MIPL	MIPv6 for Linux
MIPv6	Mobile IP version 6
MLD	Multicast Listener Discovery
MN	Mobile Node
MPA	Mobile Prefix Advertisement
MPLS	Multi-Protocol Label Switching
MPLS-TE	MPLS Traffic Engineering
MPS	Mobile Prefix Solicitation
MRIB	Multicast Routing Information Base
MRTG	Multi-Router Traffic Grapher
MSDP	Multicast Source Discovery Protocol
MTA	Mail Transfer Application
MTU	Maximum Transmission Unit
MX	Mail eXchange
NA	Neighbour Advertisement
NAT	Network Address Translation
NAT-PT	Network Address Translation - Protocol Translation
NBMA	Non Broadcast Multiple Access
NCC	Network Coordination Centre
NDISC	Neighbour Discovery
NFS	Network File System

NIS	Network Information Service
NLPID	Network Layer Protocol ID
NLRI	Network Layer Reachability Information
NNTP	Network News Transfer Protocol
NOC	Network Operations Centre
NREN	National Research and Education Network
NS	Neighbour Solicitation
NTP	Network Time Protocol
OC	Optical Carrier
OS	Operating System
OSPF	Open Shortest Path First
P2P	Peer to Peer
PEM	Privacy Enhanced Mail (key encryption services for email)
PERL	Practical Extraction and Reporting Language
PIM	Protocol Independent Multicast
PIM-DM	Protocol Independent Multicast – Dense Mode
PIM-SM	Protocol Independent Multicast – Sparse Mode
PKI	Public Key Infrastructure
PoP	Point of Presence
POS	Packet Over SONET
PRC	Partial Route Calculation
PSTN	Public Switched Telephone Network
PTR RR	Pointer Resource Record (DNS)
PVC	Permanent Virtual Circuit
QoS	Quality of Service
RA	Router Advertisement
RADIUS	Remote Authentication Dial-In User Service
RDISC	Router Discovery
RFC	Request For Comment (IETF Document)
RIB	Routing Information Database
RIP	Routing Information Protocol
RIPng	Routing Information Protocol for IPv6
RIPv2	Routing Information Protocol version 2 (IPv4 only)
RIR	Regional Internet Registry
RP	Rendezvous Point
RPC	Remote Procedure Call
RPF	Reverse Path Forwarding

RPM	Red Hat Packet Manager
RPT	Rendezvous Point Tree
RR	Resource Record (DNS)
RS	Router Solicitation
RSVP	Resource reSerVation Protocol
RTCP	RTP Control Protocol
RTE	Route Table Entry
RTP	Real-time Transport Protocol
RTT	Round Trip Time
SAP	Session Announcement Protocol
SEND	Secure Neighbour Discovery
SIIT	Stateless IP/ICMP Translation
SIP	Session Initiation Protocol
SIT	Simple Internet Transition
SLA	Site Level Aggregate
SLAAC	Stateless Auto Address Configuration
SLP	Service Location Protocol
SMTP	Simple Mail Transfer Protocol
SNMP	Simple Network Management Protocol
SNTP	Simple Network Time Protocol
SOA	Start Of Authority
SPF	Shortest Path First
SPT	Shortest Path Tree
SSH	Secure Shell
SSL	Secure Sockets Layer
SSM	Source Specific Multicast
SSMSDP	Source Specific Multicast Source Discovery Protocol
sTLA	subTLA (Top Level Aggregator)
STM	Synchronous Transfer Mode
SVC	Switched Virtual Circuit
TCP	Transmission Control Protocol
TEP	Tunnel End Point
TLA	Top Level Aggregator
TLD	Top Level Domain
TLS	Transport Layer Security
TLV	Type Length Value
TRT	Transport Relay Translator

TSP	Tunnel Setup Protocol
TT	Test Traffic
TTL	Time to Live
TTM	Test Traffic Monitor
uRPF	Unicast Reverse Path Forwarding
UDP	User Datagram Protocol
URL	Uniform Resource Locator
USAGI	UniverSAl playGround for Ipv6 (Linux development project)
VLAN	Virtual Local Area Network
VoIP	Voice over IP
VPN	Virtual Private Network
VTY	Virtual Teletype Terminal
WAN	Wide Area Network
WBEM	Web-Based Enterprise Manager
WLAN	Wireless Local Area Network
WWW	Word-Wide Web
ZSK	Zone Signing Key

Appendices

Appendix A1: List of per-PoP Location Support Domains

Every PoP has its own subdomain within 6net.org. The subdomain name corresponds to the two letter country code of the country where the PoP is located, i.e., <cc>.6net.org. The country codes are the following:

at - Austria

be - Belgium

ch - Switzerland

cz - Czech Republic

de - Germany

es - Spain

fr - France

gr - Greece

hu - Hungary

ie - Ireland

it - Italy

lu - Luxemburg

nl - Netherlands

pl - Poland

pt - Portugal

se - Sweden

si - Slovenia

sk - Slovakia

uk - United Kingdom

Appendix A2: Systems providing DNS service for 6NET

JANET:	uk.6net.org.
Name:	sixpack.ipv6.ja.net.
Platform:	SPARCstation 5 / NetBSD 1.5.2
NS SW Version:	bind 9.2.0
Network:	Ethernet
Addresses:	128.86.66.6
	2001:0630:0000:0005:0a00:20ff:fe77:e773
	3ffe:2100:0000:0000:0a00:20ff:fe77:e773

GRNET:	6net.org
	sixnet.org
	gr.6net.org
Name:	foo.grnet.gr (and foo.grnet6.gr)
Platform:	Sun Ultra 1, UltraSPARC 143MHz, Solaris8
NS SW Version:	BIND 9.2.2
Addresses:	2001:648:0:1000:194:177:210:211
	194.177.210.211
Network:	Fast Ethernet (FullDuplex)

ACONET:	xx.6net.org
Name:	nstest.v6.aco.net
Platform:	IBM RS6000 / AIX 4.3.2
NS SW Version:	bind 9.2.0
Network:	Fast Ethernet
Address:	2001:0628:0402:0001:060:8cff:fe2f:4794
Network:	Fast Ethernet
Address:	193.171.255.78
Name:	sunnysideup.v6.aco.net
Platform:	sparc Ultra-2 / Solaris 8
NS SW Version:	bind 9.2.0

Network:	Fast Ethernet
Address:	2001:0628:0402:0001:0a00:20ff:fe86:9b88
Network:	ATM
Address:	193.171.25.94
Name:	nsipv6.v6.aco.net
Platform:	PC / freeBSD 4.4
NS SW Version:	bind 9.2.0
Network:	Fast Ethernet
Address:	2001:0628:0402:0001:02a0:24ff:fe9d:5094
Network:	Fast Ethernet
Address:	131.130.1.201

SURFNET: 6net.org and sixnet.org

Name:	NS3.surfnet.nl.
Platform:	sparc SUNW,Ultra-5_10 / SunOS 5.8
NS SW Version:	bind 9.2.0 (being upgraded to 9.2.1rc2 to 9.2.1)
Network:	Fast Ethernet
Addresses:	145.41.1.167
	2001:610:100:103:a00:20ff:fe9a:16eb
Name:	zesbot.ipv6.surfnet.nl.
Platform:	Dell PowerEdge server / freeBSD 4.5-STABLE
NS SW Version:	bind 9.2.0 (being upgraded to 9.2.1rc2 to 9.2.1)
Network:	Fast Ethernet
Addresses:	192.87.110.60
	2001:0610:0508:0110:02a0:c9ff:fedd:67e7

SWITCH: {uk,fr,ch,it,de,nl,at,se,gr}.6net.org.
sixnet.org.
0.0.8.9.7.0.1.0.0.2.ip6.{int,arpa}.

Name:	scsnms.switch.ch.
Platform:	SunFire 280R, SPARC/Solaris 9
NS SW Version:	BIND 9.2.3
Network:	fast Ethernet
Addresses	130.59.1.30
	130.59.10.30

		2001:620::1
DANTE:		{uk,fr,ch,it,de,nl,se,at,gr}.6net.org.
	Name:	dns.dante.org.uk
	Platform:	Sun Solaris 6, will be upgraded soon to Solaris 8
	NS SW Version:	bind 8.3.1
	Network:	Fast Ethernet
	Address:	193.63.211.19
	Name:	dns2.dante.org.uk
	Platform:	Sun Solaris 6, will be upgraded soon to Solaris 8
	NS SW Version:	bind 8.2.4
	Network:	Fast Ethernet
	Address:	193.63.211.4
GARR:		it.6net.org.
	Name:	6net.garr.it
	Platform:	PC / freeBSD 4.4
	NS SW Version:	bind 9.2.0
	Network:	Fast Ethernet
	Addresses:	193.206.158.6
		2001:760::202:a5ff:fee3:ad7b
WWU/JOIN:		6net.org
		sixnet.org
	Name:	ns.ipv6.uni-muenster.de (and ns.join.uni-muenster.de)
	Platform:	PC Pentium III (700MHz) with Debian Linux kernel 2.4.24
	NS SW Version:	BIND 9.2.3
	Addresses:	2001:638:500:101::53
		128.176.191.10
	Network:	Fast Ethernet (Full Duplex)

Appendix B: Enabling IPv6

MS Windows XP

Windows XP embeds IPv6 functionality by default, as the TCP/IP protocols suite includes both IPv4 Internet Layer and IPv6 Internet Layer. However, Windows XP contains a separate implemen-tation of TCP and UDP for IPv6.

By typing at the command prompt

```
# ipv6 install
```

it will enable and initialize IPv6 functionality on your host. By default, Windows XP automatically configures the link-local address for each interface that corresponds to installed Ethernet adapters. Link-local addresses have the prefix FE80::/64. The IPv6 address for each Ethernet interfaces de-rives from the FE80::/64 prefix and a 64-bit suffix that derives from the IPv4 plus MAC addresses of the network adapter. For example, a host with IPv4 address 195.225.29.15 and MAC address 00-00-39-3f-7b-90 is assigned the link-local address fe80::200:39ff:fe3f:7b90. The host is now ready to communicate with other hosts in the same Ethernet segment.

Windows XP supports stateless address autoconfiguration mode, with which network site-local addresses, route entries and other configuration parameters are automatically configured based on the router message advertisements. However, Windows XP hosts may manually be configured through the network configuration shell "netsh" and following set of commands:

```
# netsh interface ipv6 {add, set, delete, …} <parameters>
```

The netsh shell allows the configuration of the IPv6 addresses, the manipulation of the route en-tries and many other tuning and showing configuration commands. For example, the following command sets the site local address 2001:648:220::1 to the interface "Local Area Connec-tion":

```
# netsh interface IPv6 add address "Local Area Connection" 2001:648:220::1
```

The complete syntax of the netsh command shell is the following:

```
# netsh interface IPv6 add address InterfaceNameOrIndex \
      IPv6Address [[type=] unicast|anycast] \
      [[validlifetime=]Minutes|infinite] [[preferredlifetime=] \
      Minutes|infinite][[store=]active|persistent]
```

Sun Workstation with Solaris 8+

Solaris 8 and its later versions fully support IPv6 protocols. The IPv6 implementation incorporates all basic services and functionality of the protocol and it supports tunnelled interfaces, such as IPv6 over IPv4. In previous versions of the Solaris operating system, IPv6 is supported only by installing specific protocol patches.

IPv6 is enabled in Solaris 8 during the installation procedure. Otherwise, the following installation steps should be followed:

1. Create an empty file named `/etc/hostname6<interface>`, where `<interface>` is the interface name in which IPv6 will be enabled.
2. Reboot the system
3. Execute the following command to all the IPv6-enabled interfaces:

```
# ifconfig <interface> inet6 plumb up
```

4. Execute the scripts located at `/etc/init.d/inetinit`.

After following the above procedure, the Solaris 8 host automatically start the Network Discovery daemon, which will probe the local router for an IPv6 address and other configuration parameters.

For Solaris 8 and 9, you also need to edit `/etc/nsswitch.conf` to enable DNS resolution for the ipnode entry.

FreeBSD

FreeBSD natively supports IPv6 functionality in its kernel. A FreeBSD host enters to the IPv6 state-less mode by just adding the option `ipv6_enable="YES"` in the `/etc/rc.conf` configuration file. This forces the system to listen for router advertisement in order to set up the IPv6 interfaces and other configuration parameters. In the following output logs, the FreeBSD host picked up two different addresses as there were multiple router advertisements on the same broadcast domain.

```
# ifconfig -a
     fxp0: flags=8843<UP,BROADCAST,RUNNING,SIMPLEX,MULTICAST> mtu 1500
       inet 147.102.220.1 netmask 0xffffff00 broadcast 147.102.220.255
       inet6 fe80::203:47ff:fece:3cee%fxp0 prefixlen 64 scopeid 0x1
       inet6 3ffe:2d00:2:220:203:47ff:fece:3cee prefixlen 64 autoconf
       inet6 2001:648:2:220:203:47ff:fece:3cee prefixlen 64 autoconf
       ether 00:03:47:ce:3c:ee
       media: Ethernet autoselect (100baseTX <full-duplex>)
       status: active
```

In the stateful mode, an IPv6 interface is configured through the options in the `/etc/rc.conf` file. For example, assuming that the IPv6 interface is fxp0 and the IPv6 address is 2001:648:2:220, the configuration file should like as follows:

```
ipv6_enable="YES"
```

```
ipv6_network_interfaces="fxp0"
ipv6_prefix_fxp0="2001:648:2:220"
ipv6_ifconfig_fxp0="2001:648:220::1 prefixlen 64"
ipv6_defaultrouter="2001:648:220::0"
ipv6_prefix_fxp0="3ffe:2d00:2:220"
ipv6_ifconfig_fxp0="3ffe:2d00:220::1 prefixlen 64"
ipv6_default_interface="fxp0"
```

Linux

Enabling IPv6 in the Linux kernel requires to either recompile the kernel with IPv6 support or to compile/load an appropriate module (without recompiling the whole kernel). Most Linux distributions provide such a module with their precompiled kernels.

The IPv6 module is loaded by using the "modprobe" command, e.g. `modprobe ipv6`, or by adding an appropriate line to the module configuration file like `/etc/modules.conf`.

IPv6 stateless address autoconfiguration is the default, so as soon as the module is loaded, IPv6 ad-dresses and appropriate routes should be configured for all interfaces, if router advertisements are present.

Javvin Networking Technology Series

Network Dictionary

Networking, Internet, telecom, wireless, computer, hardware and software - multiple dictionaries in one. A "Must have" reference for IT/Networking professionals and students!

Network Protocols Handbook

Fully explains and reviews all active protocols. Illustrates latest networking technologies.

Information Modeling

Information modeling is a critical process in content management. This book provides basic concepts of information models and explains how to design database based on data analysis and SQL models. It also provides case studies of database design based on information modeling techniques.

Visit www.javvin.com for details about the networking technology series and a complete list of titles.

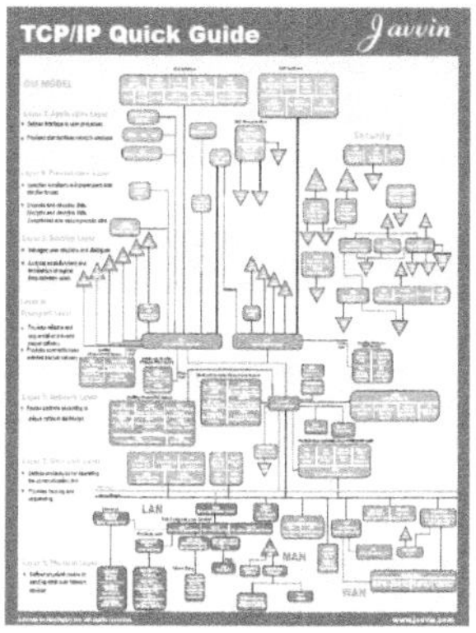

TCP/IP Quick Guide

Practical TCP/IP information extracted from hundreds of pages of TCP/IP books. A comprehensive and clear map of all TCP/IP protocols in OSI 7 layers model. A portable tool for you to carry, insert into a folder or put on your desk.

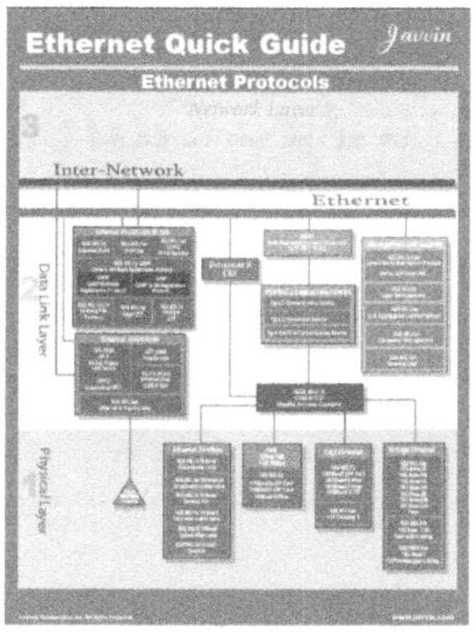

Ethernet Quick Guide

Practical Ethernet information extracted from hundreds of pages of Ethernet books. A comprehensive and clear map of all Ethernet protocols. A portable tool for you to carry, insert into a folder or put on your desk.

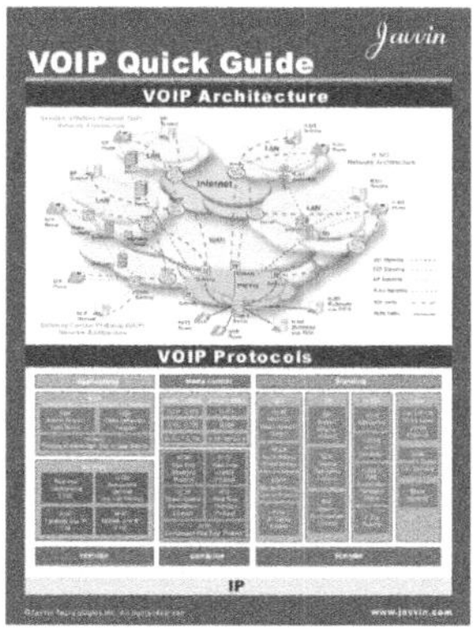

VOIP Quick Guide

All must known VOIP technologies included in this comprehensive yet portable quick reference.

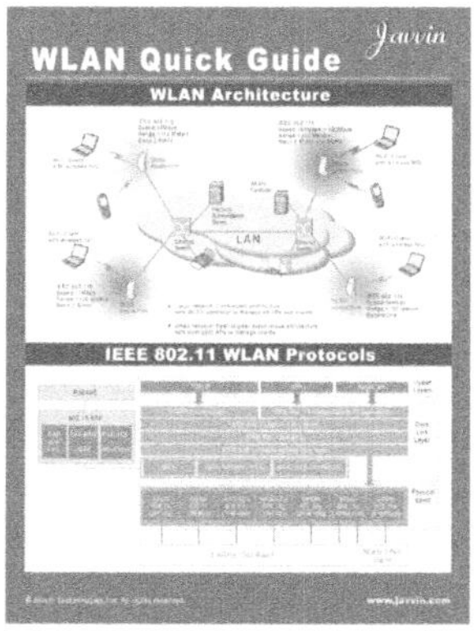

WLAN (WiFi) Quick Guide

A comprehensive quick reference to assist you in WiFi WLAN implementation, learning and operation.

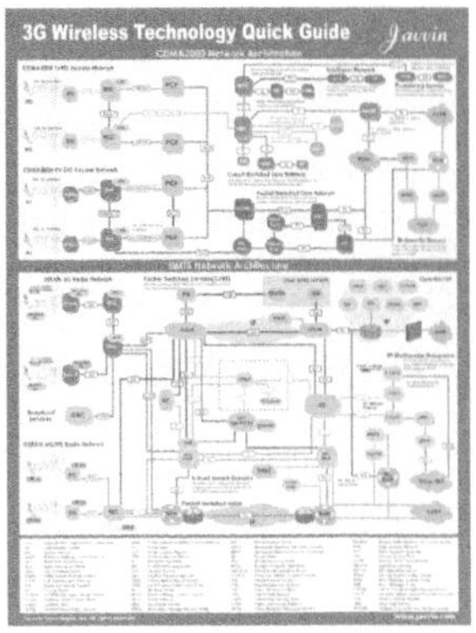

3G Wireless Tech Quick Guide

Highlights the third generation wireless technologies in one portable quick guide.

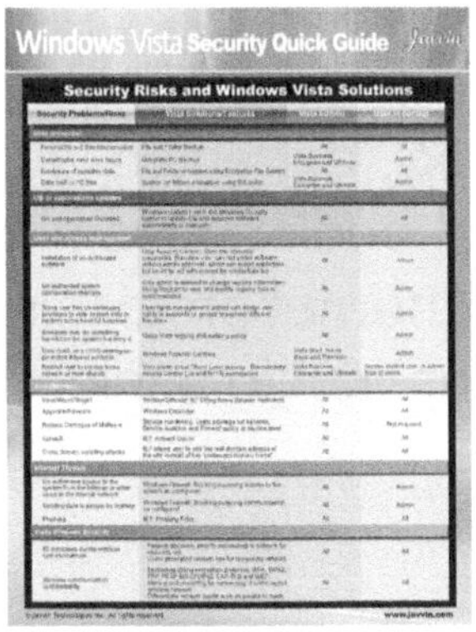

Windows Vista Security Quick Guide

All you must to know about Windows Vista Security on this handy quick guide...useful for all Windows Vista users!

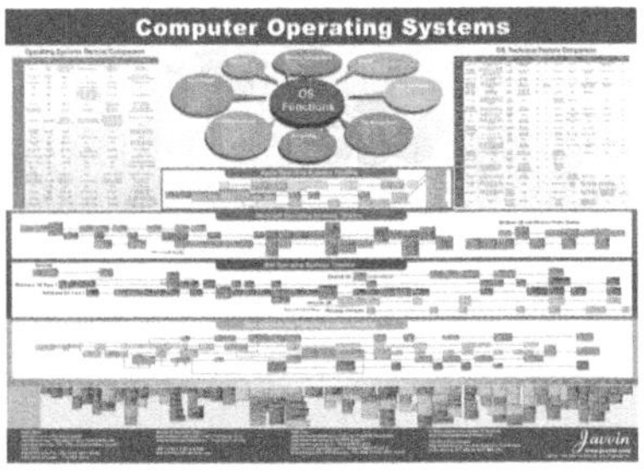

Computer Operating Systems (OS) Poster

Illustrates the computer operating systems now and their evolution path over the past 60 years.

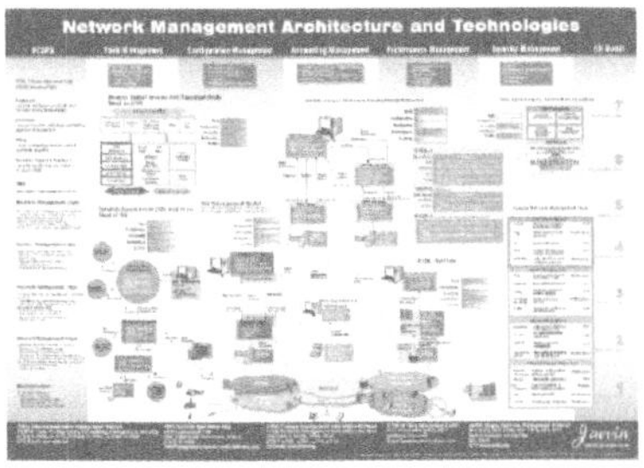

Network Management Architecture and Technology Map

All network management architecture and technologies for both telecom and data communications displayed on one chart.

Made in the USA
Middletown, DE
05 November 2026

36553280R00245